# GOSSIP AND REPUTATION

# THE OXFORD HANDBOOK OF

# GOSSIP AND REPUTATION

*Edited by*
FRANCESCA GIARDINI
RAFAEL WITTEK

OXFORD
UNIVERSITY PRESS

# OXFORD
UNIVERSITY PRESS

Oxford University Press is a department of the University of Oxford. It furthers
the University's objective of excellence in research, scholarship, and education
by publishing worldwide. Oxford is a registered trade mark of Oxford University
Press in the UK and certain other countries.

Published in the United States of America by Oxford University Press
198 Madison Avenue, New York, NY 10016, United States of America.

Library of Congress Cataloging-in-Publication Data
Names: Giardini, Francesca, 1977– editor. | Wittek, Rafael, 1965– editor.
Title: The Oxford handbook of gossip and reputation / [edited by] Francesca
Giardini and Rafael Wittek.
Description: New York, NY : Oxford University Press, [2019]
Identifiers: LCCN 2018053386 | ISBN 9780190494087 (hardcover).
Subjects: LCSH: Gossip. | Reputation.
Classification: LCC BJ1535.G6 O94 2019 | DDC 177/.2—dc23
LC record available at https://lccn.loc.gov/2018053386

1 3 5 7 9 8 6 4 2
Printed by Sheridan Books, Inc., United States of America

# Contents

## PART I  DISCIPLINARY FOUNDATIONS

## PART II  INDIVIDUAL COGNITION AND EMOTION

# PART VI  MARKETS, ORGANIZATIONS, AND NETWORKS

# PART VII  THE WEB, COMPUTERS, AND TECHNOLOGY

# List of Contributors

**Steven Arnocky,** Associate Professor, Department of Psychology, Nipissing University, Canada

**Bianca Beersma,** Department of Organization Sciences, Vrije Universiteit Amsterdam

**Niko Besnier,** Professor of Cultural Anthropology, Faculty of Social and Behavioural Sciences, University of Amsterdam

**Christopher Boehm,** Professor of Biological Sciences and Anthropology, University of Southern California

**Riccardo Boero,** Scientist, Analytics, Intelligence, and Technology, Los Alamos National Laboratory

**Federico Boffa,** Faculty of Economics and Management, Free University of Bozen/Bolzano

**Stefano Castriota,** Faculty of Economics and Management, Free University of Bozen/Bolzano

**Adam Davis,** PhD Candidate, Faculty of Education, University of Ottawa

**Charlotte J. S. De Backer,** Department of Communication Studies, University of Antwerp

**Andreas Diekmann,** Professor of Sociology, ETH Zurich

**Maria T. M. Dijkstra,** Department of Organization Sciences, Vrije Universiteit Amsterdam

**Robert Doyel,** retired U.S. Circuit Court Judge

**Lea Ellwardt,** Institute of Sociology and Social Psychology, University of Cologne

**Nicholas Emler,** Emeritus Professor of Psychology, University of Surrey

**Sally Farley,** Associate Professor of Psychology, University of Baltimore

**Maryanne L. Fisher,** Department of Communication Studies, University of Antwerp

**Stanka A. Fitneva,** Associate Professor, Department of Psychology, Queen's University Canada

**Andreas Flache,** Department of Theoretical Sociology, University of Groningen

**André Grow,** Laboratory of Digital and Computational Demography, Max Planck Institute for Demographic Research, Germany

**Edward H. Hagen,** Department of Anthropology, Washington State University

**Nicole H. Hess,** Department of Anthropology, Washington State University

**Gordon P. D. Ingram,** Department of Psychology, Universidad de los Andes, Colombia

**Onne Janssen,** Department of Human Resource Management and Organizational Behavior, Faculty of Economics and Business, University of Groningen

**Dorottya Kisfalusi,** Hungarian Academy of Sciences, Centre for Social Sciences, Computational Social Science – Research Center for Educational and Network Studies (CSS – RECENS)

**Haykaz Mangardich,** PhD Student, Department of Psychology, Queen's University, Canada

**Elena Martinescu,** King's Business School, King's College London, UK

**Uwe Matzat,** Human-Technology Interaction, Eindhoven University of Technology

**Francis T. McAndrew,** Department of Psychology, Knox College

**Manfred Milinski,** Department of Evolutionary Ecology, Max-Planck-Institute for Evolutionary Biology

**Bernard A. Nijstad,** Department of Human Resource Management and Organizational Behavior, Faculty of Economics and Business, University of Groningen

**Gloria Origgi,** Senior Researcher, CNRS, Institut Nicod-Ecole Normale Supérieure-EHESS

**Gaëlle Ouvrein,** Department of Communication Studies, University of Antwerp

**Judit Pál,** Hungarian Academy of Sciences, Centre for Social Sciences, Computational Social Science – Research Center for Educational and Network Studies (CSS – RECENS)

**Lucio Picci,** Dipartimento di Scienze Economiche, Università di Bologna

**Wojtek Przepiorka,** Department of Sociology / ICS, Utrecht University

**Charles Roddie,** Sidney Sussex College, Cambridge University

**Jordi Sabater-Mir,** Artificial Intelligence Research Institute, CSIC-Spanish National Research Council

**Chris Snijders,** Human-Technology Interaction, Eindhoven University of Technology

**Károly Takács,** Hungarian Academy of Sciences, Centre for Social Sciences, Computational Social Science – Research Center for Educational and Network Studies (CSS – RECENS)

**Tracy Vaillancourt,** Professor, Faculty of Education, University of Ottawa

**Hilde Van den Bulck,** Department of Communication, Drexel University

**Gerben A. van Kleef,** Department of Social Psychology, University of Amsterdam

# CHAPTER 1

# INTRODUCTION

## Gossip and Reputation—A Multidisciplinary Research Program

FRANCESCA GIARDINI AND RAFAEL WITTEK

## INTRODUCTION

GOSSIP and reputation are core processes in all human societies. Consequently, humans invest a great amount of effort to keep track of others' reputation and to effectively manage their own. This is especially true in the contemporary world. New technologies increased the number of potential partners and interactions and changed the way we deal with information about others. Reputation management companies and specialists are no longer employed only by movie stars and firms' CEOs, but these services are required by more and more people. According to Forbes, 82% of executive recruiters report that positive information found online can improve a candidate's job prospects, but also that firms risk losing more than 20% of business when potential customers find a negative review on their first page of search results. In the offline world, positive or negative reputations result from gossip, which is a primary source of information about others, and it is also a very popular activity, widespread across time and culture.

Gossip and reputation are multifaceted social phenomena. As theoretical constructs, they share several characteristics that pose a challenge for attempts to get a grip on them. First and foremost, both are part of a *triadic relation,* in which at least three types of actors "engage" with each other. Gossiping requires somebody (a *sender*) conveying information about a third party (*object*) to somebody else (*receiver*); having a reputation implies that the information we receive about someone's presumed qualities has been generated by somebody else. It involves at least three relational acts: an act of attribution, in which someone attaches an (evaluative) quality to someone else (e.g., Vaidyanathan, Khalsa, & Ecklund, 2016); an act of sharing, in which this attribution is communicated (Hallett, Harger, & Eder, 2009) to others; and an act of perception in which this attribution is recognized and understood as such by a receiver

(Kuttler, Parker, & LaGreca, 2002). In the case of gossip, an additional condition is that it requires the absence of the third party, that is, secrecy at the moment of transmission. Any attempt to systematically observe these phenomena in real-life or in the lab will have to find a way to capture this combination of attribution, communication, and perception in triadic structures. In addition to psychological complexity, the triadic and relational aspects of gossip and reputation also come with structural complexity. For example, for the individuals involved to disclose sensitive or evaluative third-party information, power differences matter (Ellwardt, Wittek, & Wielers, 2012; Jeuken et al., 2015).

Second, in most societies the act of gossiping, but also of strategically "managing" one's own reputation or "damaging" the reputation of others, tends to be normatively regulated and *morally laden* (Alfano & Robinson, 2017; Bertolotti & Magnani, 2014; Fernandes, Kapoor, & Karandikar, 2017; Peters & Kashima, 2015; Radzik, 2016). The discourse on gossip illustrates this nicely, since for each negative view on gossip, there is a positive one. According to the philosopher Henry Lanz: "In gossip we are pleased to discuss other people's faults, seldom their merits. We thus seem to enjoy evil for evil's sake. For we are pleased by faults and errors. We are content to see them endure and grow. We are eager to augment their number and to exaggerate their importance" (Lanz, 1936, p. 494). In contrast, Robin Dunbar, who posited that gossip could have played a major role in the evolution of language, believes that gossip is "the central plank on which human sociality is founded" (2004, p. 109). Similarly, whereas many emphasize effective reputation management as the key to success for individuals and firms, others point to the "dangerous art of impression management."

Third, the moral connotation of both phenomena is related to the fact that they require agency of those involved and therefore allow *strategic behavior*. Individuals may deliberately spread lies about others (Seki & Nakamaru, 2016), or they may attempt to manipulate the image others have about them. Although gossip has been described as "cheap talk" (Coleman, 1990), it is evident that not everybody will share everything about any third party with anyone else: selective disclosure can be of tremendous strategic value for furthering the interests of oneself or one's group (Burt, 1992). Consequently, assessing the veracity of gossip (Hess & Hagen, 2006; Kuttler, Parker, & La Greca, 2002) becomes a challenge of its own.

Fourth, judging from the evidence that has been compiled so far, gossip and reputation are truly *multipurpose* social phenomena. As the chapters in this Handbook also demonstrate, the list of their potential "functions" for individuals and groups is impressive, ranging from their impact on emotions and the fulfilment of basic human needs to the cohesion of groups and human sociality in general.

Fifth, the wide-ranging impact of gossip and reputation may stem from the pivotal role they have played in human evolution (e.g., Massar, Buunk, & Rempt, 2012). Their *evolutionary base* may explain not only the strong emotional and neurophysiological reactions they can trigger (Anderson et al., 2011; Brondino, Fusar-Poli, & Politi, 2017; Peng et al., 2015), but also account for the distinct variations in their behavioral base and impact between the sexes or along social hierarchies.

Finally, whereas recent research provides evidence for cross-cultural measurement invariance for (workplace) gossip (Brady, Brown & Liang, 2017) and for reputation as a "universal currency for human social interactions" (Milinski, 2016), the antecedents, processes, and consequences of gossip and reputation are highly *context dependent*. This holds not only for differences across cultures (Henrich et al., 2006; Marlowe et al., 2008), but also across other kinds of social collectives. For example, the incidence, content, form, and function of gossip and reputation may vary depending on the social-structural environment, such as the kind and degree of (inter)dependence in organizations or communities or the socioeconomic position of those involved.

Despite their importance in social life, academic interest in gossip and reputation has developed relatively recently. In 1993, Bromley wrote, "Reputation is a phenomenon of considerable social and scientific importance, but the interest shown in it by writers and by ordinary people has not been paralleled by an equivalent degree of interest shown by social and behavioural scientists" (Bromley, 1993, p. 8). A similar concern was shared by Goodman (1994), who wrote in the introduction to his edited volume on gossip that "until recently, philosophers and social scientists have paid scant attention to gossip" (p. 1). Still in 2004, Wert and Salovey wrote in their introduction to the Special Issue on Gossip published by the *Review of General Psychology* that "Gossip matters to all things social, yet social scientists have been slow to pursue its secrets" (p. 76).

This Handbook aims at filling the gap. Its main aim is to delineate the contours of the emerging multidisciplinary research agenda on gossip and reputation. As the preceding brief sketch suggests, such a multidisciplinary approach is key to tackling the broad range of problems inherent to the six key dimensions underlying gossip and reputation. The twenty-six chapters of this Handbook present the state-of-the art of academic research on gossip and reputation, but they also lay the foundation for new models and theories by pointing to open questions and missing links to new and unexplored territories. The remainder of this introductory chapter briefly introduces the seven main parts of the book. Each part reflects a set of substantive challenges that current scholarship faces.

Part 1, "Disciplinary Foundations," collects overviews on the state of the art of research on gossip and reputation in the disciplines of sociology, psychology, philosophy, linguistics, and ethnography. Insights from other disciplines, such as biology or economics, are incorporated in other chapters. The diversity of disciplines is featured not only in Part 1, but it is also a common thread running throughout the book.

Part 2, "Individual Cognition and Emotion," focuses on the individual, capturing the dimension of psychological complexity in triadic structures. It explores the neurobiological substrate of gossip and reputation, their development during childhood, and the multiple ways in which they are linked to emotions.

Part 3, "Strategic Interdependencies," analyzes gossip and reputation as part of goal-directed strategic behavior of interdependent individuals. Strategic rationality means that individuals take into consideration the potential moves of other self-interested individuals. The point of departure for the chapters in Part 3 is the assumption of strategically rational individuals who try to maximize their personal benefits in a variety of social dilemmas.

Part 4, "Evolution, Competition, Gender," explores current advances informed by evolutionary approaches, with their emphasis on intra-sexual and in-group competition.

In Part 5, "Power and Status," the focus shifts to the question of how social hierarchies affect and are affected by gossip and reputation. Hierarchies can be rooted in formal and informal power differences, as they are based on dependence resulting from unequal access to resources, but also in differences in social status and prestige.

Variations in the societal context of gossip and reputation take center stage in the final two parts. Part 6, "Markets, Organizations, and Networks," focuses on the role of specific social institutions as settings for gossip and reputation. Part 7, "The Web, Computers, and Technology," shifts the emphasis to the technological environment. It provides more detailed insights into the opportunities and challenges resulting from the introduction of computational systems and the World Wide Web in general.

# Disciplinary Foundations

The first part of this Handbook maps the research questions, findings, and theories coming from behavioral and social scientists. Understanding the impact on individuals and groups of exchanging evaluative information about an absent third party, but also the causes and consequences of these evaluations, is part of the scientific tradition of sociology, psychology, philosophy, linguistics, and anthropology, as well as other disciplines.

This difference between research traditions and the fact that gossip and reputation are multifaceted and complex resulted in a multitude of disciplinary theories and findings. This is especially evident in the case of gossip, as pointed out by Gambetta (1994, p. 199): "It is hard to find a phenomenon which has been attributed as many functions as gossip has, individual and collective, positive and negative, mean and noble alike." Just as an illustration, gossip might have exerted positive selection pressure favoring the evolution of traits associated with altruism (Boehm, 2012) and cooperative behaviors (Feinberg, Willer, Stellar, & Keltner, 2012; Piazza, & Bering, 2008). At the group level, it disciplines minor norm violations in groups, such as among the US cattle ranchers observed by Ellickson (1991) or in rowing teams (Kniffin & Wilson, 2010). Gossip also facilitates bonding with colleagues (Rosnow, 2001), entertainment, and information seeking (Rosnow & Fine, 1976).

Drawing on the experimental literature in behavioral economics and social psychology, on the one hand, and the field and survey traditions in sociology and social anthropology, on the other hand, Giardini and Wittek (this volume) apply an analytical perspective in order to single out and understand the links between gossip, reputation, and cooperation. In their chapter, "Gossip, Reputation, and Sustainable Cooperation: Sociological Foundations," they describe and disentangle four key mechanisms and the conditions under which gossip and reputation sustain or undermine cooperation.

Psychology is another discipline whose scholars have greatly contributed to the study of gossip and reputation, pointing to the individual and group benefits of gossip. For example, gossip can be an inexpensive and indirect way of acquiring information through social comparison (Wert & Salovey, 2004), creating and strengthening social bonds (Dunbar, 1996), and learning group norms and conventions (Barkow, 1992). Gossip provides emotional relief because it helps frustrated individuals vent their negative emotions (Waddington & Fletcher, 2005), even if negative gossip induces painful feelings of being excluded (Martinescu, Janssen, & Beersma, 2017). Gossip is also related to bullying in the workplace (Mikkelsen & Einarsen, 2002). Reviewing a century of psychological research, Emler's chapter, "Human Sociality and Psychological Foundations" (this volume), makes a case for gossip and reputation as serving fundamental needs of adaptation to an uncertain and complex social environment. Social complexity, high-level intellect and language use represent the foundations of his psychological account of gossip. Emler points out that high-quality descriptions of reputation and gossip are still missing, and that too often commonly held beliefs are taken as starting point for research.

According to the philosopher Ronald de Sousa (de Sousa, 1994), gossip gives access to the power of knowledge. The epistemological value of gossip has been advocated by another philosopher, Karen Adkins, who suggests that "the informal and more playful arena that is gossip allows us to consider more casually possibilities that might in more formal settings seem implausible or ridiculous" (Adkins, 2017, p. 60). Origgi (this volume) focuses more on reputation than on gossip. In an encompassing view on the epistemology and ontology of reputation, she analyzes the sociocognitive and motivational side of this theoretical construct. Drawing on the views of several moral philosophers, Origgi's chapter, "Reputation in Moral Philosophy and Epistemology," attributes a very positive role to reputation and puts it at the core of a philosophical theory of human actions and beliefs.

Language is, obviously, an essential part of gossiping. According to Dunbar (1996), language evolved to allow individuals to function more effectively within large social groups. Language is related to gossip and reputation in several ways. It is the means for transmitting and exchanging information about the speaker's or someone else's behavior or relationships (Dunbar, Duncan, & Marriott, 1997), for offering advice on how to handle new social situations (Suls, 1977), and for enacting social control (Enquist & Leimar, 1993). There are many other ways in which language is related to gossip and reputation, as Mangardich and Fitneva (this volume) explain in their chapter, "Gossip, Reputation, and Language," in which they survey the most important aspects of linguistic communication, and the role they play in reputation management, in particular epistemic modals, conversation flow, and speech acts such as apologies. Emphasizing the flexibility and power of linguistic cues, their framework provides a novel perspective on reputation dynamics; for example, on how individuals restore reputation through apologies.

Gossip as a form of power is also well-documented in the ethnographic record, where it is also hotly contested. The debate between Gluckman and Paine exemplifies one of the main tensions in the research on gossip and reputation. Paine defined gossip as a "cultural device used by the individual to forward his own interest" (Paine, 1967, p. 282), whereas Gluckman saw gossip as a form of social control that contributes to the unity of the group. Since then, several other functions have been attributed to gossip, but this tension is still not resolved. Several ethnographic studies suggest that gossip is related to accusations of witchcraft (Stewart & Strathern, 2003). In contrast, "to be talked of in one's absence, in however derogatory terms, is to be conceded a measure of social importance in the gossip set; not to be talked about is the mark of social insignificance, of exclusion from the set" (Epstein, 1969, p. 113).

Anthropologists have considerably enriched our knowledge on the contexts of gossip. It plays a major role in everyday conversations in populations as geographically diverse as the Nukulaelae islanders of Tuvalu in Central Pacific (Besnier, 1995), the Zinacantan of Mexico (Haviland, 1977), and the Hopi of North America (Cox, 1970), among others. Besnier's chapter "Gossip in Ethnographic Perspective" (this volume) provides a thorough description of the main characteristics of ethnography as a methodology for the collection and analysis of gossip data, while also outlining the limitations of this kind of research. He also stresses the importance of embedding gossip "in a larger context of social life" and focusing on local understandings of gossip and reputation.

## INDIVIDUAL COGNITION AND EMOTION

The study of gossip and reputation can be approached from different angles, depending on the level of description chosen. Even if the first and most elementary unit of analysis is the individual, research on the biological, developmental, and emotional aspects of gossip and reputation is surprisingly recent. Are there any specific neural correlates of gossip or reputational decision making? At what age do children start to gossip and how? How do emotions affect the gossiper or the target? These are only few of the questions that are still open, and they deserve further attention, as the chapters in the second section of the Handbook clearly indicate. Experimental evidence shows that cooperative actions are more likely when real observers are present, but they are also prompted by subtle cues of being watched by others (Haley & Fessler, 2005; Bateson, Nettle, & Roberts, 2006). Individuals can maximize their performance of generous acts in situations in which there is an audience present to witness their actions, thus investing in positive reputation building (Piazza & Bering, 2008). This suggests the existence of specialized reputation management abilities in humans. In order to be effective, these abilities need to be flexible and responsive to changing conditions and environments, thus requiring the involvement of several brain areas (Izuma, 2012; Knoch et al., 2009). Looking into the activation of different brain areas improves our understanding of the decision-making processes behind reputation and gossip. Decomposing reputation management into a set of different and separate actions that can be tested by means of functional imaging or transcranic magnetic stimulation is not easy, and this could partially explain the limited number of contributions on the topic, as Boero (this volume) points out. In his chapter "Neuroscientific Methods," Boero reviews the evidence from neuroscientific studies about the role of three main brain networks linked to reputation: the reward system, the mentalizing network, and the self-control system. By highlighting the limited number of findings about the neural substrate of these complex phenomena, Boero points to limitations and suggests open questions about this methodology.

Understanding how the brain processes reputational concerns and the decision to gossip could also explain the late onset of gossip in children. Even if children spontaneously provide information to adults and peers from a young age (Beier, Over, & Carpenter, 2014; Liszkowski, Carpenter, & Tomasello, 2008), few studies have addressed the developmental trajectory of gossip and reputation management. Like other social skills, the ability to actively manage one's reputation develops during ontogeny. The progressive achievement of a complete Theory of Mind (Apperly, 2012; Baron-Cohen, Leslie, & Frith, 1985) and the maturation of the reward system (Panksepp, 2003) may provide the bases for the development of a capacity to track others' reputation and to manage one's own. Five-year-old humans, but not chimpanzees, behave more cooperatively when observed by a peer (Engelmann, Herrmann, & Tomasello, 2012), and they are also consistently more generous when their actions are transparent and visible (Leimgruber, Shaw, Santos, & Olson, 2012). Engelmann and colleagues (2016) investigated prosocial gossip in preschoolers, finding an age effect on the amount of gossip provided: 3-year-old children spontaneously gossip and offer helpful reputational information, but much less than 5-year-old children. Ingram's chapter, "Gossip and Reputation in Childhood" (this volume), brings together the scattered evidence on the developmental aspects of gossip and reputation. It describes the ontogeny of gossip and reputation across five stages through which children and adolescents pass during development: infancy, early childhood, middle childhood, preadolescence and early adolescence, and middle to late adolescence. The changes in cognition and behavior during development show the importance of acquiring an understanding of gossip and reputation in childhood. This understanding not only helps improve children's behaviors, such as the ability to manage conflicts, but also has implications for the study of adult cognition.

Emotions are another fundamental aspect of gossip and reputation. Since both are generally described in the context of rational, strategic decision making, gossip and reputation research has paid little systematic attention so far to the role of emotions. Emotional states can be an intrinsic aspect of gossiping, but they can also arise in response to a gossip message or discovering that you have been gossiped about. Emotions can be linked to gossip in different ways: feeling a particular emotion, like anger or fear, might motivate people to engage in gossip, thereby the emotion operates as an antecedent of gossip, but emotions can also result from gossip. Drawing on theories of human cognition and emotion, the chapter by Martinescu, Janssen, and Nijstad, "Gossip and Emotion" (this volume), explores the interplay between gossip and emotion for all three actors in the gossip triad.

# Strategic Interdependencies

Many social situations are characterized by some form of interdependence. Members of work teams may depend on each other's joint effort to reach production targets. Employees depend on their supervisor's evaluations in order to get promoted. Buyers depend on their suppliers for timely delivery of products. Neighbors in rural communities depend on each other's efforts to prevent and mitigate damages caused by their livestock. In all these cases, gossip and reputation can play a decisive role in successfully managing these interdependencies (e.g., Rooks, Tazelaar, & Snijders, 2010; Ellickson, 1991).

Depending on each other's contribution is not a modern phenomenon, and our ancestors were heavily depending on each other's help for survival. This reliance could explain the importance of gossip as an evolutionary adaptation to interdependence, as posited in the chapter "Gossip as a Social Skill" by McAndrew (this volume). The chapter reviews the main findings in evolutionary psychology and argues that natural selection favored individuals who were more skilled in spreading information about themselves and others, because through this skill they acquired more social bonds and resources. Through gossip, humans could manage their own reputations but also affect those of their allies and competitors.

Social skills become very important in situations characterized by mixed-motive interdependence, the so-called social dilemmas. In a social dilemma, it is individually rational to defect, whereas everybody would be better off through cooperation. Several solutions have been offered to the "puzzle of cooperation" (Rand & Nowak, 2013), and gossip and reputation are among them. Both solutions are reviewed in Milinski's chapter, "Gossip and Reputation in Social Dilemmas" (this volume), which links evolutionary biology and experimental economics. Milinski discusses experimental evidence showing how gossip and reputation have been used in controlled environments and to what extent they can provide low-cost and effective solutions to the problem of cooperation.

The structural aspects of interdependence can be also conceptualized as a "game," a term that was used to identify a branch of mathematics dealing with cooperation and conflict. In his chapter titled "Reputation and Gossip in Game Theory," Roddie (this volume) discusses how game theoretic modeling has helped us understand the process of reputation-formation and the effect of reputations in social and market settings. A key assumption in this literature is that individuals can be classified according to their "behavioral type"; that is, whether they are prosocial cooperators or egoistic defectors, thus suggesting an interplay between the structural aspects of the setting (e.g., interdependence in a work team) and the individual traits.

The same structure of interdependent relationships can have different effects on different people, depending for instance on their status. Maintaining a positive reputation and being insulated from the consequences of gossip depends on one's position on the social ladder (Engle Merry, 1984): in small-scale communities, those in the middle of the status hierarchy are most concerned about their reputations, and therefore most affected by gossip. Unlike high-ranking individuals and those at the bottom of the social ladder, who can ignore gossip for completely different reasons, the individuals in the middle can see their prospects of social success severely hampered by negative gossip about them. Along this line, Grow and Flache's chapter, "Agent-Based Computational Models of Reputation and Status Dynamics" (this volume), argues that reputational processes may be one of the main reasons that most human groups tend to develop status hierarchies, even if there are no objective differences in skills or competences (Gould, 2002). The results of a computational study support their hypotheses. Their contribution also illustrates the added value of agent-based computer models and simulations. This tool has been applied to the study of gossip and reputation (Giardini, Di Tosto, & Conte, 2008; Giardini et al., 2015; Giardini & Vilone, 2016; Sabater, Paolucci, & Conte, 2006; Smith, 2014), and it allows us to get a better grip on the interplay between "micro-motives and macro-behaviors" (Schelling, 1978).

# EVOLUTION, COMPETITION, AND GENDER

Scholars from a variety of disciplines have stressed the important role of gossip and reputation in the evolution of modern humans. They view negative gossip as an informal policing device (Enquist & Leimar, 1993) that is fundamental for gathering information with "fitness-related" value. In this perspective, gossip is a tool for improving control of resources, providing a competitive edge with regard to building alliances, and assessing the reliability of potential partners (Barkow, 1992; De Backer, Nelissen, Vyncke, Braeckman, & McAndrew, 2007; Dunbar, Marriott, & Duncan, 1997; Kniffin & Wilson, 2005; McAndrew & Milenkovic, 2002). Though an evolutionary framework is used for analyzing phenomena in modern society, such as contemporary workplaces (Kniffin & Wilson, 2010), its major testbed is among small-scale hunter gatherer societies. The latter are the focus of Boehm's chapter, "Gossip and Reputation in Small-scale Societies: A View from Evolutionary Anthropology" (this volume). It describes how gossip and reputation help define a social niche characterized by symbols and morality. Based on his reconstruction of a "natural history of gossip and reputation," Boehm argues that gossip and reputation result in an efficient exchange of information that benefits individuals in societies. This claim raises important questions about the link between gossip and inequality. Is this benefit equally distributed among all the members of the society? Are there any categories that can be regarded as more inclined to or more affected by gossip or reputation? In evolutionary terms, how would gossip and reputation benefit societies and their members?

Gossip can also be used as a strategy for conflict, as suggested by Hess and Hagen (this volume) in their chapter "Gossip, Reputation, and Friendship in within-group Competition: An Evolutionary Perspective." They compare gossip with physical aggression as an alternative strategy for deterring competitors. They argue that under conditions of resource competition, gossip—in particular, if supported by allies—is superior to physical aggression as a competitive strategy. Within-group physical aggression is extremely dangerous, because it affects the ability of the group to resist attacks from other groups. In their account of "information warfare," Hess and Hagen (2006) outlined a strategic approach to coalitional indirect aggression, showing that coalitions might be effective in indirect aggression. Having multiple informers means having more opportunities to collect and analyze information and greater effectiveness in disseminating it, especially for retaliatory purposes.

This coalitional approach is often mentioned in studies about the prevalence of gossip in women's circles. In a seminal study on this topic, Levin and Arluke (1987) recorded gossip conversations of male and female students in a US college. Females were found to be more likely than males to socially exclude others—a difference that is visible also in children from the age of six (Benenson, 2013). In fact, gossip has often been portrayed as an instrument of last resort for women, a form of inquiry that remains available when other opportunities are closed to them by circumstance or convention (Ayim, 1994; Collins, 1994). Reviewing major findings in this field, Davis, Vaillancourt, Arnocky, and Doyel (this volume) show in their chapter "Women's Gossip as an Intrasexual Competition Strategy: An Evolutionary Approach to sex and Discrimination" that women prefer to use gossip "as their weapon of choice to derogate same-sex rivals in order to damage their reputation and render them less desirable as mates to the opposite sex." Going beyond the stereotypical representation of women as gossipmongers, these authors analyze how gossip may have evolved as a low-cost form of indirect aggression that is particularly efficient as a strategy for intrasexual competition among women.

## POWER AND STATUS

Gossip and reputation have long been linked to power and status. More specifically, whereas research on reputation mainly explores its interrelationship with status, prestige, or esteem (Brennan & Pettit, 2004), gossip researchers have long been intrigued by the question to what degree talking about third parties can be effective as a power strategy—particularly of the "weak." "Gossip is typically a subversive form of power: an attempt by the weak, and often, though far from exclusively, by women, to use the power of knowledge independently of those who wield more conventional power" (de Sousa, 1994, p. 25; see also Scott, 1986). But whether gossip primarily serves the powerful or the powerless is still a matter of debate.

However, surprisingly little is known about the impact of *positive* gossip on status and power. Celebrity gossip is an exception, as De Backer, Van Der Bulk, Fisher, and Ouvrein (this volume) show in their chapter "Gossip and Reputation in the Media: How Celebrities Emerge and Evolve by Means of Mass-Mediated Gossip." Though targeting individuals who are not among our personal contacts, celebrity gossip can serve two distinct functions. In addition to facilitating the detection of potential allies or threats (reputation gossip), gossip about the achievements of celebrities is a form of vicarious learning of what is considered appropriate or desirable and what is not (strategy learning gossip).

The complexity of the relationship between gossip, reputation, and power is underlined also by Farley in "On the Nature of Gossip, Reputation, and Power Inequality" (this volume), who reviews the psychological literature on the topic. Her chapter disentangles five well-documented psychological key mechanisms affecting power and reputation: group protection, social comparison, status enhancement, negative influence, and social bonding. Her discussion of gossip helps shed light on how gossip serves as both an agent and outcome of power inequality.

There is also growing evidence that gossip and reputation play a key role in the construction of status hierarchies during cognitive development in early childhood (see Ingram, "Gossip and Reputation in Childhood," this volume) and in adolescence (McDonald, 2012). During adolescence, peer groups are extremely influential in developing, internalizing, and putting into practice socially accepted norms and behaviors. In their chapter "Gossip and Reputation in Adolescent Networks," Kisfalusi, Takács, and Pál (this volume) analyze how gossip not only contributes to the development and maintenance of beneficial group norms, coalition formation, and ostracism, but also shapes the reputational hierarchy among adolescents. Drawing on a network study in Hungarian classrooms, they show that being disdained increases the likelihood of becoming the target of negative gossip.

Although power and status are often mentioned in studies on gossip and reputation, the evidence about them as motivations or functions, and the circumstances that might facilitate them, is still limited, as the chapters in this section show.

# MARKETS, ORGANIZATIONS, AND NETWORKS

Sociologists have long stressed the social embeddedness of markets (Polanyi, 1944). Gossip and reputation are key mechanisms through which social embeddedness facilitates economic transactions. One of the main reasons for this is their role in reducing uncertainty about the trustworthiness of potential exchange partners: "If two would-be collaborators are members of a tightly knit community, they are likely to encounter one another in the future—or to hear about one another through the grapevine. Thus, they have reputations at stake that are almost surely worth more than gains from momentary treachery. In that sense, honesty is encouraged by dense social networks" (Putnam, 2000, p. 136). Reputation mechanisms can play a vital role in sustaining the trust that is required to facilitate a wide array of economic transactions inside and outside organizational contexts. Gossip serves to constantly assess, revise, and update the reliability of these reputations.

The effectiveness of formal and informal reputation systems in promoting collective welfare depends on the quality of the information. The chapter "Trust and Reputation in Markets" (Diekmann & Przepiorka, this volume) warns against the risks of a "reputation society" in which individuals, organizations, and communities are assessed through some form of rating system. Quantifying reputations has its merits, as their use by online platforms like TripAdvisor or eBay shows. But there is also increasing awareness about the vulnerabilities and potential downsides of such reputation systems, and their broader implications for the functioning of markets and organizations are still little understood.

In some markets, reputation is a collective good that is created and enforced by a community of individuals who share an interest in having a positive reputation. Drawing on examples from agro-food markets, Boffa and Castriota ("The Economics of Gossip and Collective Reputation," this volume) explain why such collective reputations are harder to preserve than individual or institutional ones. They also discuss the implications that word-of-mouth, gossip, and reputation management have for the design of appropriate incentives and the functioning of markets.

Gossip is pervasive within all kinds of collectives and organizations. It is related to different types of outcomes for work groups, including performance (Loughry & Tosi, 2008), inclusion, and team viability. Reviewing the psychological literature on the topic, Beersma, Van Kleef, and Dijkstra ("Antecedents and Consequences of Gossip in Work Groups," this volume) focus on two questions: "What motivates group members to engage in gossip?" and "What effects does gossip have on members of a work group?" As in other domains, gossip may lead to beneficial or dangerous outcomes for the individuals or the group, but the impact of gossip on organizations can be quite significant, as these authors show.

Social network analysis has emerged as a particularly powerful tool to map variations in social embeddedness. It allows assessment of the complex interplay of gossip and reputation with network structure (Burt, 2005), the quality of ties (Parigi et al., 2013), and the actors' position (Bruggeman, 2008). Advocating a social network perspective, Ellwardt ("Gossip and Reputation in Social Networks," this volume) conceives gossip and reputation as coevolving relational phenomena. For example, since social ties can be both an antecedent and a consequence of gossiping, the informal structure and potential outcomes of work groups need to be considered dynamic.

## THE WEB, COMPUTERS, AND TECHNOLOGY

The creation of the World Wide Web provided a major impulse for the study of reputation. Partner selection supported by reputation is the main principle inspiring web-based "reputation systems." In the online world, evaluations mediate and facilitate the process of assessing reputations within a given community of users (Dellarocas, 2003). Since face-to-face interactions are often not feasible and direct sanctioning not an option in online markets (Dellarocas, 2011), such reputation systems are essential to create and maintain trust (Utz, Matzat, & Snijders, 2009). The resulting "reputational surcharge" (Resnick & Zeckhauser, 2002) is essential for successful business (Przepiorka, 2013). The proliferation of online companies devoted to tracking and polishing the reputation of individuals and firms shows that a good reputation has become a valuable asset on its own.

The three chapters in this section address different aspects of the interplay between web-based technology and gossip and reputation. Sabater-Mir ("Gossip and Reputation in Computational Systems," this volume) describes how Computer Science studies gossip as a solution to engineering problems. The chapter points to a whole range of innovative questions for the study of gossip and reputation. Can we design "virtual gossipers"; that is, artificial agents endowed with the ability to gossip? Can we solve algorithmic problems by looking at the way in which reputations are built, and conversely, can we grasp a better understanding of gossip and reputation through modeling computational systems?

The chapter "Online Reputation Systems" (Snijders & Matzat, this volume) follows this interdisciplinary lead. The authors critically review the current literature on the effects of reputation scores and the (statistical) techniques used to assess the "value of reputation." One of their conclusions is that current approaches grossly underestimate the importance of semantic feedback, and they point to interesting directions for future research.

Finally, Picci's concluding essay ("Gossip, Internet-based Reputation Systems, and Governance," this volume) suggests that notwithstanding their difference, gossip and Internet-based reputation systems are equally valuable. Both generate information with high reputational value that might affect the distribution of resources and thereby also power differences. In a way, internet-based reputation systems have the potential to "democratize" gossip, and this calls for a careful design of these systems, particularly in applications to public governance.

# CONCLUSION

This introductory chapter sketched the contours of an emerging multidisciplinary and interdisciplinary research program on the conceptual foundations, antecedents, dynamics, and consequences of gossip and reputation. This program is rooted in the belief that progress in this field requires a much closer inspection of the interrelation between the two phenomena, which until now often have been studied in isolation. We make three interrelated arguments.

First, both gossip and reputation are *multifaceted theoretical constructs* that share at least six key characteristics. Both are (1) relational and triadic, (2) morally laden, (3) multipurpose (or multifunctional), and (4) context dependent social phenomena that (5) have an evolutionary base and (6) are subject to strategic behavior. Each of the chapters in this Handbook touches upon at least one of these facets.

Second, in order to adequately capture this complexity, a multidisciplinary and eventually interdisciplinary approach is needed. *Intradisciplinary progress* is a precondition for high-quality multidisciplinary and interdisciplinary scholarship. As the contributions to this Handbook demonstrate, many disciplines have made progress over the past two decades or so in their attempt to capture the complexities of gossip and reputation;

unravel their causes; and model their interplay, dynamics, and consequences. These advances within disciplinary boundaries provide an excellent foundation on which to build the next generation of research of gossip and reputation. Disciplines represented in this Handbook cover cognitive neurosciences, linguistics, psychology (in particular its social, experimental, and developmental aspects), cultural anthropology, sociology, philosophy, economics, computer science, organization science, and communication studies. Furthermore, a variety of data collection and analysis methods are addressed, including ethnography, text analysis, conceptual analysis, observations, surveys, lab experiments, statistics, stochastic actor-oriented modeling, agent-based computer simulations, and functional magnetic resonance imaging (fMRI). Each chapter in this Handbook is strongly rooted in at least one discipline, and some make a first deliberate effort toward multidisciplinary synthesis.

Third, besides advances within their respective disciplines, the frontier of much current scholarship crystallizes around a set of six substantive *problem domains*, which also provide the main categories into which the contributions to this Handbook are clustered. These can roughly be ordered along a micro-macro continuum capturing different levels of analysis and their interplay. At the *intraindividual* level, considerable progress is made in the study of the neural, cognitive, and emotional correlates of gossip and reputation. At the *interindividual* level, scholarly interest centers around three issues related to dependence: rational choice approaches to strategic interdependence, evolutionary approaches to (intrasexual and intragroup) competition, and exchange theoretic approaches to status inequalities. At the *level of groups and societies*, a growing body of scholarship acknowledges the importance of three interrelated contexts or environments in which gossip and reputation unfold: the institutional context of markets and organizations, the social context of personal networks, and the technological context of the World Wide Web.

It is these three pillars that define the contours of the multidisciplinary research agenda advocated by this Handbook: the multidimensionality of the gossip and reputation constructs, a problem domain and related level of analysis, and a sound disciplinary base on which to build cross-disciplinary synthesis. The contributions to this volume cover a great deal of ground and provide a unique point of departure for the next generation of scholarship. But they also make clear that what has been covered is only a small fraction of the complex and multidimensional landscape created by gossip and reputation.

## References

Adkins, K. (2017). *Gossip, epistemology, and power: Knowledge underground.* Cham, Switzerland: Palgrave Macmillan.

Alfano, M. & Robinson, B. (2017). Gossip as a burdened virtue. *Ethical Theory and Moral Practice 20,* 473–487.

Anderson, E., Siegel, E. H., Bliss-Moreau, E., & Barrett, L. F. (2011). The visual impact of gossip. *Science 332*(6036), 1446–8.

Ayim, M. (1994). Knowledge through the grapevine: Gossip as inquiry. In R. F. Goodman & A. Ben-Ze'ev (Eds.), *Good gossip* (pp. 85–99). Lawrence: University of Kansas Press.

Barkow, J. H. (1992). Beneath new culture is old psychology: Gossip and social stratification. In J. H. Barkow, L. Cosmides, & J. Tooby (Eds.), *The adapted mind: Evolutionary psychology and the generation of culture* (pp. 627–637). New York: Oxford University Press.

Bateson, M., Nettle, D., & Roberts, G. (2006). Cues of being watched enhance cooperation in a real-world setting. *Biology Letters 2*(3), 412–414.

Beersma, B., Van Kleef, G. A., Dijkstra, M. T. M. (2019). Antecedents and consequences of gossip in work groups. In F. Giardini & R. Wittek (Eds.), *Handbook of gossip and reputation*. New York: Oxford University Press.

Beier, J. S., Over, H., & Carpenter, M. (2014). Young children help others to achieve their social goals. *Developmental Psychology 50*(3), 934–940.

Benenson, J. F. (2013). The development of human female competition: Allies and adversaries. *Philosophical Transactions of the Royal Society: B 368*(1631), 20130079.

Bertolotti, T., & Magnani, L. (2014). An epistemological analysis of gossip and gossip-based knowledge. *Synthese 191*(17), 4037–4067.

Besnier, N. (1995). *Literacy, emotion, and authority: Reading and writing on a Polynesian atoll.* Cambridge, England: Cambridge University Press.

Besnier, N. (2019). Gossip in ethnographic perspective. In F. Giardini & R. Wittek (Eds.), *Handbook of gossip and reputation*. New York: Oxford University Press.

Boehm, C. (2012). *Moral origins: The evolution of virtue, altruism, and shame.* New York: Basic Books.

Boehm, C. (2019). Gossip and reputation in small scale societies: A view from evolutionary anthropology. In F. Giardini & R. Wittek (Eds.), *Handbook of gossip and reputation*. New York: Oxford University Press.

Boero, R. (2019). Neuroscientific methods. In F. Giardini & R. Wittek (Eds.), *Handbook of gossip and reputation*. New York: Oxford University Press.

Boffa, F., & Castriota, S. (2019). The economics of gossip and collective reputation. In F. Giardini & R. Wittek (Eds.). *Handbook of gossip and reputation*. New York: Oxford University Press.

Brady, D. L., Brown, D. J., & Liang, L. H. (2017). Moving beyond assumptions of deviance: The reconceptualization and measurement of workplace gossip. *Journal of Applied Psychology 102*(1), 1–25.

Brennan, H., & Pettit, P. (2004). *The economy of esteem: An essay on civil and political society.* Oxford, England: Oxford University Press.

Bromley, D. (1993). *Reputation, image and impression management.* Chichester, England: Wiley & Sons.

Brondino, N., Fusar-Poli, L., & Politi, P. (2017). Something to talk about: Gossip increases oxytocin levels in a near real-life situation. *Psychoneuroendocrinology 77*(10), 218–224.

Bruggeman, J. (2008). *Social networks: An introduction.* New York: Routledge.

Burt, R. S. (1992). *Structural holes: The social structure of competition.* Cambridge, MA: Harvard University Press.

Burt, R. S. (2005). *Brokerage and closure: An introduction to social capital.* New York: Oxford University Press.

Coleman, J. S. (1990). *Foundations of social theory.* Cambridge, MA: The Belknap Press of Harvard University Press.

Collins, L. (1994). Gossip: A feminist defense. In R. F. Goodman & A. Ben-Ze'ev (Eds.), *Good gossip* (106–114). Lawrence: University Press of Kansas.

Cox, B. (1970). What is Hopi gossip about? Information management and Hopi factions. *Man* 5(1), 88–98.

Davis, A., Vaillancourt, T., Arnocky, S., & Doyel, R. (2019). Women's gossip as an intrasexual competition strategy: An evolutionary approach to sex and discrimination. In F. Giardini & R. Wittek (Eds.), *Handbook of gossip and reputation.* New York: Oxford University Press.

De Backer, C. J. S., Nelissen, M., Vyncke, P., Braeckman, J., & McAndrew, F. (2007). Celebrities: From teachers to friends, *Human Nature 18*, 334–354.

De Backer, C., Van den Bulck, H., Fisher, M. L., & Ouvrein, G. (2019). Gossip and Reputation in the Media: How Celebrities Emerge and Evolve by Means of Mass-Mediated Gossip. In F. Giardini & R. Wittek (Eds.), *Handbook of gossip and reputation*, New York: Oxford University Press.

Dellarocas, C. (2003). The digitization of word of mouth: Promise and challenges of online feedback mechanisms. *Management Science 49*(10), 1407–1424.

Dellarocas, C. (2011). Designing reputation systems for the social web. In M. Masum & H. Tovey (Eds.), *The reputation society* (pp. 3–13). Cambridge, MA: MIT Press.

de Sousa, R. (1994). In praise of gossip: Indiscretion as a saintly virtue. In R. F. Goodman & A. Ben-Ze'ev (Eds.), *Good gossip* (pp. 25–33). Lawrence, KS: University Press of Kansas.

Diekmann, A., & Przepiorka, W. (2019). Trust and reputation in markets. In F. Giardini, R. Wittek (Eds.), *Handbook of gossip and reputation*, New York: Oxford University Press.

Dunbar, R. I. (1996). *Grooming, gossip and the evolution of language.* Harvard: Harvard University Press.

Dunbar, R. I. M., Marriott, A., & Duncan, N. D. C. (1997). Human conversational behavior. *Human Nature 8*(3), 231–246.

Dunbar, R. I. M. (2004). Gossip in evolutionary perspective. *Review of General Psychology 8*(2), 100–110.

Ellickson R., (1991). *Order without law.* Cambridge, MA: Harvard University Press.

Ellwardt, L., Wittek, R., & Wielers, R. (2012). Talking about the boss: Effects of generalized and interpersonal trust on workplace gossip. *Group & Organization Management 37*(4), 521–549.

Ellwardt, L. (2019). Gossip and reputation in social networks. In F. Giardini & R. Wittek (Eds.), *Handbook of gossip and reputation.* New York: Oxford University Press.

Emler, N. (2019). Human sociality and psychological foundations. In F. Giardini & R. Wittek (Eds.), *Handbook of gossip and reputation.* New York: Oxford University Press.

Engelmann, J. M., Herrmann, E., & Tomasello, M. (2012). Five-year olds, but not chimpanzees, attempt to manage their reputations. *PLoS ONE 7*(10), e48433.

Engelmann, J. M., Herrmann, E., & Tomasello, M. (2016). Preschoolers affect others' reputations through prosocial gossip. *British Journal of Developmental Psychology 34*, 447–460.

Engle Merry, S. (1984). Rethinking gossip and scandal. In D. Black (Ed.), *Toward a general theory of social control.* Orlando, FL: Academic Press.

Enquist, M., & Leimar, O. (1993). The evolution of cooperation in mobile organisms. *Animal Behavior 45*, 747–757.

Epstein, A. L. (1969). The network and urban social organization. In J. C. Mitchell (Ed.), *Social networks in urban situations* (pp. 77–116). Manchester: Manchester University Press.

Farley, S. (2019). On the nature of gossip, reputation, and power inequality. In F. Giardini & R. Wittek (Eds.), *Handbook of gossip and reputation*, New York: Oxford University Press.

Feinberg, M., Willer, R., Stellar, J., & Keltner, D. (2012). The virtues of gossip: Reputational information sharing as prosocial behavior. *Journal of Personality and Social Psychology* *102*(5), 1015.

Fernandes, S., Kapoor, H., & Karandikar, S. (2017). Do we gossip for moral reasons? The intersection of moral foundations and gossip. *Basic and Applied Social Psychology 39*(4), 218–230.

Gambetta, D. (1994). Godfather's gossip. *European Journal of Sociology 35*(2), 199–223.

Giardini, F., Di Tosto, G., & Conte, R. (2008). A model for simulating reputation dynamics in industrial districts. *Simulation Modelling Practice and Theory 16*(2), 231–241.

Giardini, F., Paolucci, M., Adamatti, D., & Conte, R. (2015). Group size and gossip strategies: An ABM Tool for investigating reputation-based cooperation. In F. Grimaldo F, & E. Norling (Eds.), *Multi-Agent-Based. Simulation XV. MABS 2014* (pp. 104–120). Lecture Notes in Computer Science, vol. 9002. Cham: Springer.

Giardini, F., & Vilone, D. (2016). Evolution of gossip-based indirect reciprocity on a bipartite network. *Scientific Reports 6*, 37931.

Giardini, F., & Wittek, R. (2019). Gossip, reputation, and sustainable cooperation: Sociological foundations. In F. Giardini & R. Rafael (Eds.), *Handbook of gossip and reputation.* New York: Oxford University Press.

Gluckman, M. (1963). Papers in honor of Melville J. Herskovits: Gossip and scandal. *Current Anthropology 4*(3), 307–316.

Goodman, R. F. (1994). Introduction. In R. F. Goodman & A. Ben-Ze'ev (Eds.), *Good gossip* (1–8). Lawrence, KS: University Press of Kansas.

Gould, R. (2002). The origins of status hierarchies: A formal theory and empirical test. *American Journal of Sociology 107*(5), 1143–1178.

Grow, A., & Flache, A. (2019). Agent-based conmputational models of reputation and status dynamics. In F. Giardini & R. Wittek (Eds.), *Handbook of gossip and reputation.* New York: Oxford University Press.

Haley, T. K. J., & Fessler, D. M. (2005). Nobody's watching? Subtle cues affect generosity in an anonymous economic game. *Evolution and Human Behavior 26*, 245–256.

Hallett, T., Harger, B., & Eder, D. (2009). Gossip at work: Unsanctioned evaluative talk in formal school meetings. *Journal of Contemporary Ethnography 38*(5), 584–618.

Haviland, J. B. (1977). Gossip as competition in Zinacantan. *Journal of Communication 27*, 186–191.

Henrich, J., McElreath, R., Ensminger, J., Barr, A., Barrett, C., Bolyanatz, A., Cardenas, J. C., et al. (2006). Costly punishment across human societies. *Science 312*(5781), 1767–1770.

Hess, N., & Hagen, E. (2006). Psychological adaptations for assessing gossip veracity. *Human Nature 17*, 337–354.

Hess, N., & Hagen, E. (2019). Gossip, reputation and friendship in in-group competition: An evolutionary perspective. In F. Giardini & R. Wittek (Eds.), *Handbook of gossip and reputation.* New York: Oxford University Press.

Ingram, G. P. D. (2019). Gossip and reputation in childhood. In F. Giardini & R. Wittek (Eds.), *Handbook of gossip and reputation.* New York: Oxford University Press.

Izuma, K. (2012). The social neuroscience of reputation. *Neuroscience Research 72*(4), 283–288.

Jeuken, E., Beersma, B., ten Velden, F. S., & Dijkstra, M. (2015). Aggression as a motive for gossip during conflict: The role of power, social value orientation, and counterpart's behavior. *Negotiation and Conflict Management Research 8*(3), 137–152.

Kisfalusi, D., Takács, K., & Pál, J. (2019). Gossip and reputation in adolescent networks. In F. Giardini & R. Wittek (Eds.), *Handbook of gossip and reputation*. New York: Oxford University Press.

Kniffin, K. M., & Wilson, D. S. (2005). Utilities of gossip across organizational levels. *Human Nature 16*(3), 278–292.

Kniffin, K. M., & Wilson, D. S. (2010). Evolutionary perspectives on workplace gossip: Why and how gossip can serve groups. *Group & Organization Management 35*(2), 150–176.

Knoch, D., Schneider, F., Schunk, D., Hohmann, M., & Fehr, E. (2009). Disrupting the prefrontal cortex diminishes the human ability to build a good reputation. *Proceedings of the National Academy of Sciences of the USA 106*, 20895–20899.

Kuttler, A. F., Parker, J. G., & La Greca, A. M. (2002). Developmental and gender differences in preadolescents' judgments of the veracity of gossip. *Merrill-Palmer Quarterly 48*, 105–132.

Lanz, H. (1936). Metaphysics of gossip. *International Journal of Ethics 46*(4), 492–499.

Leimgruber, K. L., Shaw, A., Santos, L. R., & Olson, K. R. (2012). Young children are more generous when others are aware of their actions. *PLoS ONE 7*(10), e48292.

Levin, J., & Arluke, A. (1987). *Gossip: the inside scoop*. New York: Plenum Press.

Liszkowski, U., Carpenter, M., & Tomasello, M. (2008). Twelve-month-olds communicate helpfully and appropriately for knowledgeable and ignorant partners. *Cognition 108*(3), 732–739.

Loughry, M. L., & Tosi, H. L. (2008). Performance implications of peer monitoring. *Organization Science 19*(6), 876–890.

Mangardich, H., & Fitneva, S. A. (2019). Gossip, reputation, and language. In F. Giardini & R. Wittek (Eds.), *Handbook of gossip and reputation*. New York: Oxford University Press.

Marlowe, F. W., Colette Berbesque, J., Barr, A., & Barrett, C. (2008). More 'altruistic' punishment in larger societies. *Proceedings of the Royal Society B: Biological Sciences 275*(1634), 587–90.

Martinescu, E., Janssen, O., & Nijstad, B. A. (2019). Gossip and emotion. In F. Giardini & R. Wittek (Eds.), *Handbook of gossip and reputation*. New York: Oxford University Press.

Massar, K., Buunk, A. B., & Rempt, S. (2012). Age differences in women's tendency to gossip are mediated by their mate value. *Personality and Individual Differences 52*(1), 106–109.

McAndrew, F. T. (2019). Gossip as a social skill. In F. Giardini & R. Wittek (Eds.), *Handbook of gossip and reputation*. New York: Oxford University Press.

McAndrew, F. T., & Milenkovic, M. A. (2002). Of tabloids and family secrets: The evolutionary psychology of gossip. *Journal of Applied Social Psychology 32*, 1064–1082.

McDonald, K. L. (2012). Gossip. In R. J. R. Levesque (Ed.), *Encyclopedia of adolescence* (pp. 1196–1200). New York: Springer.

Mikkelsen, E. G., & Einarsen, S. (2002). Relationships between exposure to bullying at work and psychological and psychosomatic health complaints: The role of state negative affectivity and generalized self-efficacy. *Scandinavian Journal of Psychology 43*, 397–405.

Milinski, M. (2016). Reputation, a universal currency for human social interactions. *Philosophical Transactions of the Royal Society B 371*(1687), 20150100.

Milinski, M. (2019). Gossip and reputation in social dilemmas. In F. Giardini & R. Wittek (Eds.), *Handbook of gossip and reputation*. New York: Oxford University Press.

Origgi, G. (2019). Reputation in moral philosophy and epistemology. In F. Giardini & R. Wittek (Eds.), *Handbook of gossip and reputation*. New York: Oxford University Press.

Paine, R. (1967). What is gossip about? An alternative hypothesis. *Man 2*(2), 278–285.

Panksepp, J. (2003). Feeling the pain of social loss. *Science 302*(5643), 237–239.

Parigi, P., State, B., Dakhlallah, D., Corten, R., & Cook, K. (2013). A community of strangers: The dis-embedding of social ties. *PLoS ONE* 8(7): e67388.

Peng, X., Li, Y., Wang, P., Mo Lei, & Chen, Q. (2015). The ugly truth: Negative gossip about celebrities and positive gossip about self entertain people in different ways. *Social Neuroscience* 10(3), 320–336.

Peters, K., & Kashima, Y. (2015). Bad habit or social good? How perceptions of gossiper morality are related to gossip content. *European Journal of Social Psychology* 45, 784–798.

Piazza, J., & Bering, J. (2008). Concerns about reputation via gossip promote generous allocations in an economic game. *Evolution and Human Behavior* 29, 172–178.

Picci, L. (2019). Gossip, internet-based reputation systems and governance. In F. Giardini & R. Wittek (Eds.), *Handbook of gossip and reputation*. New York: Oxford University Press.

Polanyi, K. (1944). *The great transformation: The political and economic origins of our time.* Boston: Beacon Press.

Przepiorka, W. (2013). Buyers pay for and sellers invest in a good reputation: More evidence from eBay. *Journal of Socio-Economics* 42, 31–42.

Putnam, R. D. (2000). *Bowling alone: The collapse and revival of American community.* New York: Simon & Schuster.

Radzik, L. (2016). Gossip and social punishment. *Res Philosophica* 93(1), 185–204.

Rand, D., & Nowak, M. (2013). Human cooperation. *Trends in Cognitive Sciences* 17(8), 413–425.

Resnick, P., & Zeckhauser, R. (2002). Trust among strangers in internet transactions: Empirical analysis of eBay's reputation system. In M. R. Baye (Ed.), *The economics of the internet and e-commerce*. Greenwich, CT: JAI Press.

Roddie, C. (2019). Reputation and gossip in game theory. In F. Giardini & R. Wittek (Eds.), *Handbook of gossip and reputation*. New York: Oxford University Press.

Rooks, G., Tazelaar, F., & Snijders, C. (2010). Gossip and reputation in business networks. *European Sociological Review* 27(1), 90–106.

Rosnow, R. L. (2001). Rumor and gossip in interpersonal interaction and beyond: A social exchange perspective. In R. M. Kowalski (Ed.), *Behaving badly: Aversive behaviors in interpersonal relationships* (pp. 203–232). Washington, DC: American Psychological Association.

Rosnow, R. L., & Fine, G. A. (1976). *Rumor and gossip: The social psychology of hearsay.* New York: Elsevier.

Sabater-Mir, J. (2019). Gossip and reputation in computational systems. In F. Giardini & R. Wittek (Eds.), *Handbook of gossip and reputation*. New York: Oxford University Press.

Sabater-Mir, J., Paolucci, M., & Conte, R. (2006). Repage: Reputation and image among limited autonomous partners. *Journal of Artificial Societies and Social Simulation* 9(2), 3. http://jasss.soc.surrey.ac.uk/9/2/3.html

Schelling, T. C. (1978). *Micromotives and macrobehavior.* New York: W. W. Norton and Company.

Scott, J. C. (1986). *Weapons of the weak: Everyday forms of peasant resistance.* New Haven: Yale University Press.

Seki, M., & Nakamaru, M. (2016). A model for gossip-mediated evolution of altruism with various types of false information by speakers and assessment by listeners. *Journal of Theoretical Biology* 407, 90–105.

Smith, E. R. (2014). Evil acts and malicious gossip: A multiagent model of the effects of gossip in socially distributed person perception. *Personality and Social Psychology Review* 18(4), 311–325.

Snijders, C., & Matzat, U. (2019). Online Reputation Systems. In F. Giardini & R. Wittek (Eds.), *Handbook of gossip and reputation*. New York: Oxford University Press.

Stewart, P., & Strathern, A. (2003). *Witchcraft, sorcery, rumors, and gossip (New departures in anthropology)*. Cambridge, England: Cambridge University Press.

Suls, J. (1977). Gossip as social comparison. *Journal of Communication 27*(1), 164–168.

Utz, S., Matzat, U., & Snijders, C. (2009). Online reputation systems: The effects of feedback comments and reactions on building and rebuilding trust in online auctions, international. *Journal of Electronic Commerce 13*(3), 95–118.

Vaidyanathan, B., Khalsa, S., & Ecklund, E. H. (2016). Gossip as social control: Informal sanctions on ethical violations in scientific workplaces. *Social Problems 63*(4), 554–572.

Waddington, K., & Fletcher, C. (2005). Gossip and emotion in nursing and health-care organizations. *Journal of Health Organization andMmanagement 19*(4/5), 378–394.

Wert, S. R., & Salovey, P. (2004). A social comparison account of gossip. *Review of General Psychology 8*(2), 122–137.

# PART I

# DISCIPLINARY FOUNDATIONS

CHAPTER 2

..................................................................................

# GOSSIP, REPUTATION, AND SUSTAINABLE COOPERATION

## *Sociological Foundations*

..................................................................................

### FRANCESCA GIARDINI AND RAFAEL WITTEK

## INTRODUCTION

..................................................................................

ONE of sociology's major concerns is to explain why the level of social cohesion differs so strongly within and between social collectivities.[1] Why do some societies, groups, communities, or organizations succeed in eliciting and maintaining high levels of collaboration and contributions to the public good, whereas others fail? How do successful communities enact and foster their participants' sustained compliance with norms and regulations?

Gossip and reputation are key to sustaining or breaking cooperation in human societies. Social and behavioral scientists seem to have taken this claim for granted for more than half a century now (Elias & Scotson, 1965; Simpson & Willer, 2015). This might explain why systematic attempts to scrutinize the interrelation between these phenomena are of a relatively recent date, as the outcomes of a small Web of Science query in the title, abstract, or keyword of indexed publications reveal. Although coarse grained, two noteworthy patterns emerge. First, in the forty years between 1960 and 2000, the search terms "gossip" and "cooperation" were mentioned together only twice. Since then, this figure increased to $n = 80$. For the joint occurrence of "reputation" and "cooperation," the respective figures are 75 publications before, and 1461 after, the year 2000. The terms "reputation" and "gossip" occurred jointly 6 times before the year 2000 and 126 times since then, but before 2000, no single study contained all three search terms.[2] Even if the scholarly interest in the reputation-cooperation link grew dramatically, only few studies pay attention to the interplay between gossip and reputation or their joint link to cooperation.

Most of the studies treat gossip and reputation as different but related phenomena (Ellickson, 1991; Sommerfeld et al., 2007; Feinberg et al., 2012). They show that gossip, reputation, and cooperation are closely intertwined (Sommerfeld et al., 2008; Tennie, Frith, & Frith, 2010; Simpson & Willer, 2015; Wu, Balliet, & Van Lange, 2016): gossip affects reputations (Burt, 2008); reputations can be gained or lost through gossiping (Foster, 2004); and cooperation affects and is affected by both (Milinski, 2016). Hence, although research into the mechanisms through which gossip and reputation sustain or undermine cooperation has made considerable progress, a systematic overview of the links between these three phenomena is still missing. This chapter argues that one of the conditions hampering progress in this field is a major disciplinary divide that resulted in two almost parallel literatures on gossip, reputation, and cooperation. Overcoming this divide requires an integrated analytical framework that is able to accommodate the interplay between two levels of analysis. The first dimension consists in a behavioral micro-foundation that is able to integrate the disparate and seemingly conflicting assumptions about the motives and the effects of gossip. The second dimension refers broadly to *cultural-institutional* context, which represents shared rules, values, and meanings that constrain individuals' actions, defining what is appropriate/ relevant and what is not. It covers, among other things, rule of law and civic norms, gender stereotypes, and culturally legitimate practices. The *social-structural* context consists of the pattern of interdependencies between the involved parties, as well as their position in the broader social structure. It captures variations in the structure of social networks, as well as the degree to which hierarchy and power define a setting.

Sociology, with its emphasis on analyzing the interplay between individual and society, is particularly well equipped for integrating micro-behavioral foundations and macro-level dynamics. Before presenting the four main models (section 2), comparing their relative effectiveness (section 3), and suggesting avenues for future research (section 4), this section concludes by providing a short introduction to this chapter's key concepts.

*Cooperation*, or the joint production of mutual benefits, is needed when individuals cannot achieve specific outcomes on their own. Two dimensions of cooperation are particularly important when studying the mechanisms underlying production of the collective good (Wittek & Bekkers, 2015). First, cooperation can be the result of two types of prosocial behavior: where it results in net benefits for all involved parties, it is also referred to as *mutualism*. It becomes *altruism* in situations in which it benefits others but results in net costs for those engaging in it. Second, whereas first-order cooperation directly benefits another individual or group (e.g., helping someone in need), second-order cooperation refers to sanctioning uncooperative behavior of others, with direct or indirect costs, such as retaliation.

The various attempts to define *reputation* differ in complexity. At the simple end of the continuum, reputation is "one of many signals providing information about the likely behavior of an individual" (Tennie, Frith, & Frith, 2010, p. 482), or a "set of judgements a community makes about the personal qualities of one of its members" (Emler, 1990, p. 171). At the complex end of the continuum, it is a "socially transmitted typically evaluative judgment that is presented as consensual or at least widely shared"

(Conte & Paolucci, 2002, p. 37). This definition emphasizes that reputation is a meta-belief: individuals believe that there are some others who hold an evaluation about someone or something, without any specification about the source of the belief (e.g., "rumor has it/ people say/ I have heard that he is a good doctor"). Here, we define the reputation of an individual person, a social group, or a corporate actor as a *shared evaluation that others hold about these actors with regard to one or more criteria*. This definition emphasizes the collective aspect of reputations and distinguishes them from personal opinions; that is, "private" evaluations that are not known to or shared with others.

*Gossip* is evaluative talk about third parties in their absence (Emler, 1990). Gossip, per definition, takes place in a triad. Although gossip-related encounters in reality are more complex than a simple triadic representation (Besnier, this volume), taking the *gossip triad* as a point of departure is analytically useful for the purposes of this chapter (see Figure 2.1). Distinguishing among a *sender*, a *receiver*, and a *third party* or *target* allows us to spell out the antecedents and the consequences of different mechanisms on reputation and cooperation for each of the actors involved. Often, the information does not stay within the first gossip triad: receivers may pass the information on to somebody else, thereby becoming senders in the next gossip triad (Ellwardt, this volume).

Although it is usually assumed that gossip consists mainly of negative evaluations (Birch Sterling, 1957), the little empirical evidence that is available indicates the incidence of positive and negative evaluations shared in gossip encounters to be equally high, at least in organizational settings (Wittek & Wielers, 1998). Gossip affects a third party's future opportunities for cooperation (Barclay & Willer, 2007) if it evaluates either their competences, their compliance or noncompliance to norms, or both (Giardini, 2012).

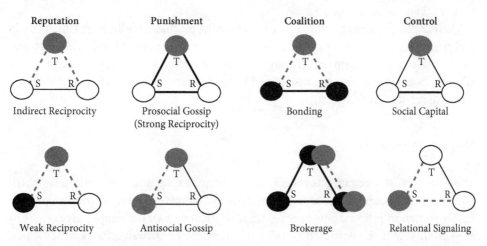

Legend:
- S, R, T: Sender, Receiver, Third Party in the Gossip Triad
- Light grey dot: negative reputation effect of gossip on this actor
- Black dot: positive reputation effect of gossip on this actor
- Dotted grey line: cooperation deteriorates due to gossip and reputation effects
- Continuous black line: cooperation improves due to gossip and reputation effects

FIGURE 2.1.  Summary overview of eight models of cooperation.

Put differently, we can expect gossip to have effects on reputation mainly if it contains judgments about a third party's ability or willingness to cooperate.

# Gossip, Reputation, and Sustainable Cooperation: Four Models

One of the major puzzles in the science of cooperation is to unravel the different social mechanisms behind sustainable cooperation. A social mechanism (Hedstrom & Swedberg, 1998) is a causal explanation that seeks to explicate how variation in collective-level phenomena, such as inter-group differences in the level of sustained contributions to collective goods, can be explained by individual-level processes.

Although previous research has identified a variety of social mechanisms explaining the relationship between gossip, reputation, and cooperation, we lack a systematic overview of their underlying assumptions. This chapter argues that four broad classes of mechanisms need to be distinguished, because they rest on fundamentally different premises concerning (a) their behavioral micro-foundation, in particular the goals and motives of the gossipers; (b) the degree to which gossip affects reputations of senders, receivers, and third parties; (c) the degree to which gossip and reputation affect the sustainability of cooperation in each of the three dyads of the gossip triad (sender–receiver, sender–tertius, and receiver–tertius); and (d) the cultural-institutional or social-structural context, that is, conditions facilitating or hampering the functioning of each mechanism (see Table 2.1).

This chapter presents a comparative review of the mechanisms through which gossip and reputation sustain cooperation. As will become evident in the following sections, the four sets of mechanisms make competing as well as complementary predictions, and all of them are incomplete because they do not explicate the assumptions about all the effects of reputation and gossip.

## Reputation Models

The first class of mechanisms reflects the standard explanation, according to which gossip sustains cooperation because it affects reputations. These *reputation models* are firmly rooted in rational choice reasoning, according to which cooperative relations are sustainable if the expected benefits of an exchange outweigh its expected costs. Since expected benefits and costs are a function of assessing the risk of being cheated, acquiring information about potential exchange partner's cooperative or uncooperative "type" is key to reputation models. The *indirect reciprocity* mechanism focuses mainly on the effects of gossip on the third party, whereas the *weak reciprocity* mechanism is predominantly concerned with the effect of gossip on the gossipmonger and/ or the receiver.

## Indirect Reciprocity

Indirect reciprocity arguments (Nowak & Sigmund, 2005) are at the core of a broad range of reputation models in economics (Kreps & Wilson, 1982; Greif, 1989), sociology (Raub & Weesie, 1990; Burt, 2001), and evolutionary psychology and biology (Alexander, 1987; Molleman, van den Broek & Egas, 2013; Nowak & Sigmund, 1998). Key to these models is that selfish and rational exchange partners base their decision whether to cooperate on information about how the other party behaved toward third parties in the past ("You scratch my back and I'll scratch someone else's" and "I scratch your back and someone else will scratch mine"). Gossip acquired directly from this third party can be one of the sources of this information (Giardini & Vilone, 2016; Ohtsuki, Iwasa, & Nowak, 2015; Sommerfeld et al., 2007).

Indirect reciprocity models do not require assumptions about the effect of gossip on the sender's or the receiver's reputation, nor on the impact of gossip and reputation on the cooperation between gossipmonger and the third party or the receiver. At their core lies the reputation of the target and its effects on cooperation between the receiver and the target. The emphasis is on avoiding the target if he or she has a bad reputation, not on changing the target's behavior through reputational concerns.

The theory of competitive altruism posits a complementary mechanism (Roberts, 1998; Noe & Hammerstein, 1994). It explains cooperation between the receiver and the target as the latter wanting to be selected for profitable relationships. Individuals perform pro-social acts to build up a reputation and to be chosen by cooperative partners. An implicit assumption in this argument is that the target's behavior might be changed by the desire of upholding a positive reputation.

A main limitation of the studies on indirect reciprocity is their lack of attention toward the cultural-institutional context. For example, culture was found to affect the workings of indirect reciprocity (Henrich & Henrich, 2006) in a study comparing the effects of punishment on cooperation between groups of students in Beijing and Boston (Wu et al., 2009). Whereas Beijing students' cooperation decreased, Boston students' cooperation increased when they knew that the other could punish. In their *post hoc* interpretation of the results, the authors attribute the effects to differences in cultural attitudes toward reputation and authority. Since indirect reciprocity was not possible in the experimental setup, direct reciprocity was the basis for reputation formation. This form of reputation is argued to be more important in the individualistic cultures of Western societies, and therefore an important condition sustaining cooperation in the Boston sample, but not in the collectivist culture of the Beijing sample.

## Weak Reciprocity

Another potential indicator of someone's "type" is whether he or she contributed to the production of second-order collective goods, that is, by sanctioning free riders. Several studies indeed suggest that it pays off to build a reputation for being someone who punishes free riders. Engaging in a punitive act against a free-rider signals the punishers' prosocial type to third parties (Barclay, 2006), thus increasing the punisher's perceived trustworthiness (Jordan et al., 2016). Such conspicuous displays of altruism through punishment allow individuals to build and maintain prosocial reputations (Griskevicious, Tybur, & Van den Bergh, 2010), thereby increasing their attractiveness as cooperation partners (Dos Santos, Rankin, & Wedekind, 2013). Furthermore, credible punishment threats warn potential free-riders that their behavior is likely to be sanctioned (Hilbe & Traulsen, 2012).

These arguments are the basis of a growing literature on the emergence and consequences of reputation systems for responsible punishment, in which negative sanctions are allocated only against free-riders. Such responsible sanctions "are a form of weak reciprocity: they are beneficial in the long run, despite being costly in the short run" (Hilbe & Traulsen, 2012, p. 3).

Costly signaling plays a main role in these explanations (Roberts, 1998; Van Vugt, Roberts, & Hardy, 2007), according to which behavior that can easily be faked or mimicked by those who do not have the underlying quality (Grafen, 1990; Zahavi, 1975) has little signaling value. But costly signaling arguments confront gossip researchers with a puzzle, because most scholars emphasize the low cost that gossip has for sender and receiver. More recent accounts cast doubt on the cheap gossip assumption, pointing to two types of potential costs.

First, gossipmongers may incur negative repercussions to their own reputations that can be severe if the gossiper is purposefully lying or misreporting information (Giardini, 2012). As social psychologists Adams and Mullen (2012) point out, gossiping may come with considerable social and psychological costs, because gossipers are less trusted and are more exposed to negative reputations than those who do not gossip.

Second, another potential cost of gossip is the possibility that the receiver will strategically exploit this knowledge for his or her own benefit, because it provides information about the sender's preferences and exchange opportunities. This can be especially true in situations of strategic interdependence and competition, in which gossip may reveal sensitive issues that the receiver may exploit. For example, in a business firm, gossipmongers who disseminate negative gossip about a specific colleague not only provide information about qualities of the object of gossip, but also about themselves and their personal network.

This ongoing debate shows the importance of studying what kind of reputation punishers develop under what conditions, and the consequences that their reputation has for them and the others. Here, too, the field is far from achieving a consensus, both with regard to theory and evidence. For example, Dos Santos and Wedekind (2015), using computer simulations, claim that reputation systems based on punishment would be far more likely to sustain cooperation than reputation systems based on generous actions. In contrast, in a theoretical reflection, Raihani and Bshari (2015) suggest distinguishing between competitive and cooperative reputations of punishers. They propose that punishers will be perceived as cooperative only in settings where it can be ruled out that their punishing behavior is driven by competitive motives. Whether or not a reputation for punishment yields the predicted benefits for the punisher is also a contested question in empirical research. In line with these findings, a recent study assessing how generosity and punishment affect the contributor's perceived trustworthiness in dictator and trust games found that punishers are not considered to be more trustworthy than non-punishers, and are actually trusted less (Przepiorka & Liebe, 2016).

## Coalition Models

The relation between the sender and the receiver is the focus of *coalition models* of gossip in which the underlying motive for cooperation may be the realization of material or affective benefits through social relations. *Social bonding* explanations emphasize that gossip improves the cooperative relationship between the sender and the receiver at the expense of both party's' cooperation with the third party. *Brokerage* explanations, instead, stress that individuals who connect otherwise unconnected persons will strategically gossip with both, with positive effects for the gossipmonger's cooperative relations.

### Social Bonding

Since Dunbar's (1996) influential contribution, gossip as social bonding is probably the most frequently cited mechanism linking gossip to cooperation. It assumes that a sender's motive to initiate a gossip episode is to strengthen the social bond and therefore the cooperation with the receiver. This comes at the expense of the cooperation that both the sender and the receiver have with the target, because gossip damages the reputation of the third party (Shaw, Tsvetkova, & Daneshvar, 2011; Wittek & Wielers, 1998). In a situation in which there are status enhancement opportunities, the sender might use gossip also for signaling his or her access to private information, thus increasing his or her reputation and, as a consequence, becoming a more attractive exchange partner (McAndrew & Milenkovic, 2002).

Strong ties or coalitions can yield important material and psychological benefits, but this mechanism does not address reputation effects for sender and receiver. From a social bonding perspective, gossipers may have multiple self-serving motives to engage in a gossip exchange. They may gossip with those who are potentially important for them, or because it strengthens a relation that is intrinsically emotionally rewarding, providing, as it were, a "warm glow" for the gossiper and the receiver (Gambetta, 1994). Testing the bonding mechanism, a cross-sectional sociometric study carried out in five organizations and five school classes (Wittek & Wielers, 1998) found that an individual's tendency to gossip correlated positively with the number of coalition triads in his or her personal network. A coalition triad is defined by a strong and positive tie between two individuals who both have a "negative" tie to a third party (e.g., through dislike or conflict). Burt (2001) points in the same direction, suggesting that coalition structures favor selective disclosure of negative third-party information, thereby reinforcing predispositions about third parties.

One implicit assumption of bonding models is that for sender and receiver to exchange gossip about a target, they need to trust each other to some degree, which implies a preexisting social relationship between the two. But a study by Ellwardt, Steglich, and

Wittek (2012) reminds us that the causality of this relationship can also be reversed. Investigating the co-evolution of gossip and friendship ties in a network of thirty-six employees of a childcare organization, it found that the likelihood for an employee to initiate a friendship bond with a specific other employee increases after the latter has shared third-party gossip with him or her before (for a review on gossip and social networks, see Ellwardt, this volume).

Although the outcome may be the same (strengthening the tie between sender and receiver), the underlying motives and targets may differ. On closer scrutiny, context conditions play a pivotal role in bonding. Building on research on gender stereotypes and the resulting differences in the functions of strong ties, an empirical study among Canadian undergraduates contextualized the bonding mechanism by introducing gender as a moderator variable (Watson, 2012). This study predicted and found a positive association between the tendency to engage in information and achievement related gossip and the quality of friendship ties for males, but not for females. The finding is in line with earlier research suggesting a stronger status motive in males than in females. However, the literature on sex differences in indirect aggression (for a review see McAndrew, 2014; Davis, Vaillancourt, Arnocky, & Doyel, this volume) also suggests that compared to men, women are much more inclined to use gossip with the intention to socially ostracize rivals, usually other women (Hess & Hagen, this volume). These findings imply that the bonding mechanism may work differently for men and women, with men attempting to impress the receiver, and women attempting to damage female rivals.

Two variations on social bonding explanations of gossip have been proposed. According to the *echo mechanism* (Burt, 2001), gossip does not improve sender's and receiver's reputation in their perception, but reinforces the negative image they already have of each other. Put differently, the receiver double-speaks, echoing the sender's negative accounts and stories about the third party. In a less negative interpretation, the target may simply not be able to change other individuals' opinions about each other. Hence, the echo mechanism draws on a more complex psychological model of human motives and the dynamics of conversations. Individuals are caught in social and cultural conventions proscribing consensus during discussions and the individuals involved prefer to comply with these conventions.

Gossip as a *weapons-of-the-weak* mechanism was first suggested by Scott (1986) in his work on everyday forms of resistance against power and abuse. In his account, gossip allows the unprivileged to ally against those high in power, providing them with a subtle but effective weapon against exploitation. Gossip and other forms of resistance require little coordination or planning, and they are used by both individuals and groups to resist without directly confronting or challenging elite norms (Conte & Paolucci, 2002). Gossip represents a threat for the elite, because it is difficult to identify and to contrast, but it is very effective in highlighting weaknesses and vices of those in power, thus reducing their informal power (for a psychological account of gossip and power see Farley, this volume). At the same time, gossip works as a threat to the high-ranking, who should not forget that they are closely monitored and their public and private life is under constant scrutiny (Brison, 1992; Meyer Spacks, 1985). Boehm (1999) proposed that gossip may serve for neutralizing the dominance tendencies of some individuals who might attempt to compromise the interests of the group. Given this power imbalance, such a mechanism implies that both sender and receiver belong to the same low-status group, whereas the target is part of the elite. No cooperation is possible between the target and the other two actors, whereas sender and receiver might form a coalition. According to Meyer Spacks (1985), "the ferocity of several centuries' attack on derogatory conversation about others probably reflects justifiable anxiety of the dominant about the aggressive impulses of the submissives" (p. 30).

The weapons-of-the-weak mechanism assumes the presence of a hierarchical social structure in which there is a clear distinction between those in power and those who are powerless. Power differences are an important context condition affecting the link between gossip and cooperation, and this leads us to predict that in environments with explicit power differences, the target will always be someone belonging to or connected with the higher-level group (Ellwardt, Wittek, & Wielers, 2012). However, another study found that informal power differences based on asymmetric workflow dependence did not moderate the negative impact of gossip on sustained cooperation (Wittek et al., 2000).

## Brokerage

Tightly connected social structures—in which each individual frequently interacts with and has positive ties with each other individual—are among the most frequently studied social conditions favoring reputation, but also social control effects of gossip. There is some empirical evidence that network closure favors the spread of information about third parties, so that "ego's opinion of alter is correlated with third-party opinion, and networks evolve toward a state of balance in which people bound by a strong relationship have similar opinion of others" (Burt, 2001, p. 41). But overall, the supporting evidence is inconsistent. Based on the results of a sociometric organizational study, Burt (2001 p. 59), concludes that "the broader range of evidence calls into question the common assumption that closed networks improve information flow," that is, strong indirect connections do not enhance disclosure of information about third-party behavior. Similarly, more recent experimental research on the prisoner's dilemma did not find significant differences in cooperation rates between an "embedded" condition, in which subjects were informed about both the outcomes of their own interactions and the outcomes of all other interactions, and the "atomized" condition, in which they only were informed about the outcome of their own interactions (Corten et al., 2016).

The key idea behind Burt's research program on structural holes (Burt, 1992, 2005, 2007, 2008) is that the broker—an individual connecting two otherwise disconnected individuals and their networks—benefits from gossiping either because gossip drives his or her contacts apart (*tertius gaudens*), or it brings them together (*tertius jungens*). Brokerage generates two types of benefits for the broker: information and control benefits. The former includes access, timing, and referrals, with the latter representing reputation benefits as they follow from positive information passed to others about the broker. Control benefits result from the broker's opportunity to strategically move "accurate, ambiguous, or distorted information" (Burt, 2000, p. 355) between the sender and the target. Positive reputation effects and power attributions also derive from others seeing the broker in such a gatekeeper position, passing important and exclusive information. Brokerage in Burt's framework also affects the reputation of both sender and receiver. In situations where brokers play *tertius jungens*, they will convey positive images of each other to both the target and the receiver. And where brokers play *tertius gaudens*, they will convey negative images.

Consequently, gossip through brokerage can have two different effects on cooperation in the gossip triad. In the *tertius gaudens* case, the sender will invest in the maintenance of a cooperative relationship with the receiver but at the same time will attempt to prevent the emergence of a cooperative relationship between the latter and the target. In the *tertius jungens* case, the sender attempts to encourage the emergence of a cooperative relationship between receiver and target. This may weaken or even result in the termination of the cooperative relationship between them. The assumed motivational basis behind brokerage is self-interest: the broker strives for increasing his or her benefits (see also Obstfeld, Borgatti, & Davis, 2014). Thanks to their position as an intermediary, brokers can realize information and control benefits. For example, a broker can selectively pass information from one part of his or her network to another part of the network. To the degree that this information is valuable and scarce, the receiving party may be willing to remunerate the broker.

There are important contextual and institutional elements, however, that could affect the brokerage mechanism. Legitimacy, that is, being fully accepted as a member of the in-group, turned out to be a key moderator in a network study of career patterns of a sample of 284 middle managers in a large American firm. Assessing the returns to gossip for individuals occupying structural holes, Burt (1998) shows that women, but also entry-level men and non-whites, lacked legitimacy. Therefore, they could not benefit from their brokerage position to the same degree as men, seniors, and whites did: their careers progressed significantly more slowly. The reason is negative stereotypes toward them; that is, the widespread belief that members of these categories were less able or qualified for the job than others. The study further shows that this disadvantage disappeared for those who had a "sponsor" in their personal network: powerful representatives of the firm's male, white, senior elite who occupy brokerage positions themselves and could boost the reputation of their mentees.

## Social Control Models

Though gossip has often been portrayed as an instrument of social control, the underlying process is less straightforward than it seems at first sight. Social control explanations emphasize that gossip is inextricably linked to norms: their joint production as well as the prevention and mitigation of norm violations. *Social Capital* explanations focus on the effect of gossip on senders and receivers, in particular their willingness to allocate sanctions against the third party. *Relational signaling* explanations investigate how a reputation of being a gossipmonger impacts on the cooperative relation with the receiver.

## Social Capital

If one follows sociologist James S. Coleman (1990), who reasons from a straightforward rational choice framework, we do not need to invoke emotional reactions to explain under which conditions individuals will be inclined to gossip. Instead, where norms have emerged to manage mutual interdependencies, the beneficiaries of the norm have a regulatory interest to sanction free-riders. However, this does not yet solve the second-order free-rider problem. A solution could be offered by gossip, partly because it "may have little cost for the beneficiary of the norm, the one who passes gossip or the one who receives it, and also brings him potential benefits." But Coleman stresses that the act of sharing information about norm violations by a third party in itself is not the same as enforcing it through allocating a sanction or a punishment (see also Elster, 2003). This will happen only if the receiver indeed holds the norm and there is some degree of consensus among other norm holders concerning the behavior of the third party: "The benefits lie in the facilitation gossip provides, through the consensus it brings about, for sanctions that might not otherwise be possible...It is clear however that gossip itself does not constitute a sanction...the consensus lowers the costs for any holder of the norm to apply a sanction, but does not ensure that a sanction is applied" (Coleman, 1990, pp. 284–285). Coleman's description points to an element often overlooked in most current studies: the role of norms. Although much gossip is most likely triggered by some form of norm violations (Gluckman, 1963; Ellickson, 1991; Kniffin & Wilson, 2005), the link between norm violations, gossip, and cooperation still remains understudied.

In sum, rather than emphasizing the negative reputation effects on the third party and the partner selection effects for the receiver, this mechanism stresses the importance of gossip as a coordination device for the sender and the receiver. Therefore, gossip is the first of two steps in a social control mechanism: it mainly affects the relation between sender and receiver because it leads to some joint deliberation about the kind of norm violation committed by the third party. In order to change the future behavior of the third party, the second step would be to sanction the third party, or to apply some other compliance gaining strategy (Kellerman & Cole, 1994). According to Coleman and other social control theorists, this will be the case only under specific circumstances, in particular in close-knit social structures. In sum, the social control mechanism does not make any specific predictions about the implications that gossip has for the cooperation between *tertius* and the other two members of the gossip triad. In this respect, the social control mechanism differs from explanations based on indirect reciprocity, which stress the decay of cooperation between the target and the receiver as a consequence of gossip.

## Relational Signaling

Relational signals are behavioral cues based on which individuals assess their exchange partners' intention to contribute to a mutually beneficial relationship (Lindenberg, 1997; Wittek, 1999; Wittek et al., 2000). The importance of relational signals increases with mutual interdependence and the strength of the solidarity norms emerging with it. In such cases, gossiping is likely to be seen as a negative relational signal, because it violates a major remedial norm of solidarity relations (Ellickson, 1991), that is, that grievances or problems should be discussed directly with the person in question and not behind the person's back. This is why in work settings with some degree of interdependence, individuals with a reputation for being gossipmongers will be trusted less, making it more difficult for them to sustain cooperative relationships. A longitudinal organizational network study among seventy-four employees of a Dutch Housing corporation (Wittek et al., 2000) showed that dyads in which at least one member has a strong tendency to gossip have an 8%–10% lower likelihood for a sustainable cooperative relationship, compared to pairs without such individuals. This finding suggests that the negative relational signaling effects of reputations as gossipers are not restricted to situations of interdependence, as the theory predicted, but extend to situations of dependence and independence as well. In fact, as a related study found, gossip and other forms of "indirect" social control represent a separate latent cognitive dimension than more "direct" forms of social control (Loughry & Tosi, 2008; Wittek, 1998). In sum, according to relational signaling theory, gossiping has a negative impact on the gossipmonger's reputation and therefore also damages the cooperative relationship with receivers and third parties (see also Noon & Delbridge, 1993).

## Punishment Models

The last class of models we review departs from standard economic reasoning of reputation models. Even if the so-called *strong reciprocity* hypothesis does not explicitly address the role of gossip as a form of sanctioning, this theory can provide useful insights on the relationship between costly punishment and gossip. *Altruistic gossip* explanations focus on the effect of gossip on the third party, whereas *antisocial gossip* explanations are concerned with the motives behind negative gossip about co-operators. Both are rooted in the assumption that emotions drive the behavior of the members of the gossip triad.

### Prosocial Gossip

Research on cooperation received a major and lasting boost from a *Nature* article with the title *Altruistic Punishment in Humans*, written by two behavioral economists and published in the year 2002 (Fehr & Gächter, 2002). Their study was triggered by the puzzle that humans frequently cooperate even in the absence of tangible benefits, including situations "when reputation gains are small or absent." Subjects participated in a public goods experiment with two conditions. In the control condition, they could not punish free riders. As is common in public good experiments, the incidence of cooperative acts (contributions to the collective good) decreased over time. In the treatment condition, subjects had the opportunity to punish free-riders at a cost to themselves. Subjects frequently made use of this opportunity and cooperation increased with each round. The authors concluded that sustained cooperation is possible given there is a sanctioning regime, in which participants are allowed to punish defectors, whereas cooperation is bound to decline in the absence of sanctioning opportunities. Fehr and Gächter's study

**Table 2.1.** Summary overview of stylized social mechanisms linking gossip, reputation, and cooperation. Table 2.1 summarizes the assumptions underlying different mechanisms linking gossip to reputation, on the one hand, and to cooperation, on the other hand. It does not contain mechanisms that do not specify a link to cooperation and reputation, such as social comparison or learning

| | | Explanation | | | Context | | Effect of Gossip on Reputation of… | | | Effect of Gossip and/or Reputation on Cooperation between… | | |
|---|---|---|---|---|---|---|---|---|---|---|---|---|
| **Model** | Label of Mechanism | Behavioral Micro-Foundation | Example studies | | Cultural-Institutional | Social-Structural | Sender | Receiver | Tertius | Sender-Receiver | Sender-Tertius | Receiver-Tertius |
| Reputation | *Indirect Reciprocity* | Receiver: information about previous uncooperative behavior of third party toward sender reveals the third party's uncooperative type, leading the receiver to avoid exchanges with the third party | Nowak & Sigmund, 2005; Wu, Balliet, & Van Lange, 2016 | | | | o | o | − | o | − | − |
| | *Weak Reciprocity* | Sender: gossiping only about defectors signals cooperative type of sender to receiver ("Responsible gossip"), leading to increased cooperation with receiver | Hilbe & Traulsen 2012; Jordan & Rand, 2017 | | Non-competitive culture | Non-anonymity, horizontal, partner selection | + | o | − | + | − | − |
| Punishment | *Prosocial Gossip* | Sender: negative emotional reactions to violation of fairness norms leads to "prosocial gossip" ("altruistic "punishment"). Third party: fear of being ostracized leads to increased contributions to collective good | Feinberg et al., 2012; Feinberg, Willer, & Schultz 2014 | | Fairness norms | Opportunity for partner selection | o | o | − | + | + | + |

(continued)

**Table 2.1. Continued**

| | Explanation | | | | Context | | Effect of Gossip on Reputation of…. | | | Effect of Gossip and/or Reputation on Cooperation between…. | | |
|---|---|---|---|---|---|---|---|---|---|---|---|---|
| Model | Label of Mechanism | Behavioral Micro-Foundation | Example studies | | Cultural-Institutional | Social-Structural | Sender | Receiver | Tertius | Sender-Receiver | Sender-Tertius | Receiver-Tertius |
| | Antisocial Gossip | Sender: having been punished for free-riding leads to emotions of revenge, triggering antisocial gossip against third parties who are cooperators | Herrman, Thoeni, & Gächter 2008; Hauser, Nowak | | Civic norms, rule of law | | – | o | + | – | – | + |
| Coalition | Bonding | Sender: sharing (difficult to verify) information that damages the status of a joint "enemy" enhances status of sender and receiver, leading to more cooperation between them, at the expense of cooperation with the third party | & Hodson, 1993; Dunbar, 1996; Wittek & Wielers, 1998 | | Competitive culture | Negative network closure; strong hierarchy | + | + | – | + | – | – |
| | Brokerage | Sender: sharing information about unrelated third parties yields reputational and other benefits for sender and receiver through encouraging or preventing cooperation between receiver and third party, and sender and receiver | Burt, 1998; | | Legitimacy, (gender) stereotypes, conversational conventions | Structural Holes | + | + | +/– | + | + | +/– |

| Control | | | | Norms | | | | | | | |
|---|---|---|---|---|---|---|---|---|---|---|---|
| | *Social Capital* | Sharing information about norm violation of a third party increases the likelihood that sender and/or receiver sanction the third party, increasing the likelihood that the third party improves cooperation with both | Coleman, 1990 | | Positive network closure; negative externalities | o | o | − | + | + | + |
| | *Relational Signaling* | Third Party: where exchange partners are moderately functionally interdependent, having the reputation of a gossipmonger increases the likelihood that sharing third party information is perceived as a negative relational signal, leading to a decay of cooperation | Wittek & Wielers, 1998; Wittek et al., 2000 | Strong or weak solidarity norms | Functional interdependence (positive and negative externalities), size of personal network, informal power | − | o | o | − | − | o |

The table summarizes the assumptions underlying different mechanisms linking gossip to reputation, on the one hand, and to cooperation, on the other hand. It does not contain mechanisms that do not specify a link to cooperation and reputation, such as social comparison, or learning.

Definitions: The *sender* is the person spreading information about a third party. The *receiver* is the person to whom the sender passes the information about a third party. *Tertius* is the third party about whom the sender discloses information to the receiver.

"+" indicates a positive effect or correlation.

"−" indicates a negative effect or correlation.

"o" indicates the absence of an effect, or that the effect is not mentioned in the original formulation.

contributed to the development of the *strong reciprocity hypothesis.* This notion reflects the two-pronged key mechanisms proposed by their study: humans' willingness to cooperate, and their disposition to punish those who don't. In line with the strong reciprocity argument, a set of recent experimental studies by Feinberg and colleagues (Feinberg, Cheng & Willer, 2011; Feinberg, Willer, & Schultz, 2014) argues that the same negative emotions supporting people's decision to incur costs for punishing free riders also motivate them to gossip (Martinescu, Janssen and Nijstad, this volume). This solves the second order free-rider dilemma because gossiping is virtually costless—some scholars indeed portray gossip as a form of sanctioning at the low-cost end (for the person allocating the sanction) of a continuum of punishment (Boehm, 1999; Ellickson, 1990; Giardini, Conte, 2012; Guala, 2012). A follow up-study (Feinberg, Willer, Schultz, 2014) shows that settings allowing both gossip and the opportunity for partner selection, are better able to sustain cooperation than settings that either only provide the opportunity to gossip, or neither of the two. Gossiping should contribute to the sustainability of the targets' cooperation with both sender and receiver. Feinberg and colleagues' reasoning requires that the third party becomes aware of the threat of being ostracized—an assumption that remains implicit in their study.

## Antisocial Gossip

Research on the strong reciprocity hypothesis soon was enriched by another hypothesis on the link between emotional reactions, punishment, and sustained cooperation. In their study on *antisocial punishment* Herrman, Thöni & Gächter (2008) showed that the opportunity to punish not only enables cooperators to altruistically sanction free-riders, it also allows free-riders to punish cooperators. Computer simulations, lab experiments and field studies suggest that this so-called *antisocial punishment* in fact may undermine cooperation (Hauser, Nowak & Rand, 2014; McCabe & Rand, 2014). The emotional force behind it, so the assumption, is that "people might not accept punishment, and therefore seek revenge" (Herrman, Thöni, & Gächter, 2008, p. 1363). Hence, also gossip may be motivated by revenge, and used as an instrument to punish cooperators. This "antisocial gossip" mechanism would predict a negative effect of gossip on the reputation of those individuals who have previously punished the sender. The consequence would be a decay of the cooperation between the third party and both the sender and the receiver. No specific predictions would follow for the cooperation between or the reputation of the antisocial gossiper and the receiver.

# DISCUSSION

Gossip can affect cooperation through four potentially competing mechanisms. It can be part of a rational logic of indirect reciprocity, making and breaking reputations. It can be a tool for building and reinforcing coalitions or reaping the benefits from brokerage positions. It can be the first step in a two-step process of social control, facilitating coordination between and eventually triggering remedial steps fostering future norm compliance. And it can be prompted by negative emotions, feeding a cycle of punishment and counter-punishment. Gossiping also often comes with considerable costs for those spreading it. It is easily perceived as a violation of remedial norms, and acquiring the reputation of being a gossipmonger undermines one's trustworthiness.

A key question concerns the relative effectiveness of each of the four mechanisms in sustaining cooperation. Attempts to answer this question have created quite some controversy, fueled by the competing behavioral micro-foundations (e.g., altruism vs. selfishness) underlying the four mechanisms. More specifically, it reflects a growing number of studies questioning the standard explanation, according to which third-party reputations—rather than related mechanisms of punishment, coalition, and control—drive the effect of gossip on cooperation.

The potential incompatibility between reputation and coalition models becomes evident when comparing indirect reciprocity with the echo mechanism. The latter draws on a more complex psychological model of human motives and the dynamics of conversations, positing that individuals prefer to comply with social and cultural conventions proscribing consensus during discussions. As a consequence, gossip does not change the reputation of the third party, but simply reinforces the negative image the conversation partners already have of the person. Hence, whereas indirect reciprocity models predict that gossip contributes to sustaining cooperation in the gossip triad, the echo hypothesis implies that no noteworthy changes occur.

Although superficially similar, there are two important ways in which social control differs from indirect reciprocity explanations. First, Coleman's normative consensus model emphasizes the effect of gossip on the expected costs, as perceived by the receiver, of allocating a sanction. These will be lower to the degree that there will be more beneficiaries of the norm being aware of and agreeing about the norm violation. (Indirect) reciprocity theorists stress the effects of gossip on the reputation of the target, which in turn feeds into the receiver's assessment of future exchanges with the target. Whereas in social control gossip will trigger behavioral changes in the receiver only in case the information is about a norm violation, in indirect reciprocity models the crucial feature is the negative reputation of the target, without any specifications about the norm. Second, in case the receiver and others indeed perceive it as a norm violation, avoiding future interaction with the norm violator is a possible reaction, but one that will be used only as a last resort. Instead, the very purpose of social control is to increase future norm compliance of the individual in question.

One criticism against the strong reciprocity argument relates to Fehr and Gächter's (2002) observation that because cooperation was found in a setting that rules out reputation formation and direct reciprocity, reputation mechanisms may be a less powerful explanation for sustainable cooperation than altruistic punishment. But they did not directly compare the relative explanatory power of altruistic punishment and reputational concerns. Several studies set out to do just that. The key issue here is that whereas punishment is costly for the punisher, "reputation mechanisms discipline by withholding action, immediately saving costs for the 'punisher'" (Rockenbach & Millinski, 2006, p. 718).

This option makes punishment less attractive, and it should result in reputation to be the most frequently invoked mechanism to sustain cooperation. Using public good experiments, Rockenbach & Millinski (2006) found only partial support for this prediction: although the use of punishment decreased markedly, it was still used, and cooperation levels remained highest in the scenario in which both punishment and reputation building were possible.

More recent experimental studies using the public goods game argue and find that reputational concerns, whether or not spread through gossip, may be more effective and efficient than punishment in promoting and maintaining cooperation (Wu, Balliet, & Van Lange, 2016; see also Grimalda et al., 2016). Finally, other researchers even consider punishment as maladaptive in the evolutionary sense, and therefore not suited as a strategy to sustain cooperation in the long run.

Since most evidence on strong reciprocity is based almost exclusively on experimental evidence, another line of criticism questions that humans would make widespread use of "costly punishment" also "in the wild" (Guala, 2012). This criticism is based on an examination of results of field studies performed by cultural anthropologists and sociologists. The picture emerging is that costly sanctioning, if it occurs, is carried out by centralized institutions, whereas the bulk of sanctions that can be observed imposes "little or no costs to those who administer them" (Guala, 2012, p. 9). Gossip is considered to be a key low-cost punishment mechanism in what several authors conceived as a continuum of sanctioning (Boehm, 1999; Ellickson, 1991), which ranges, in increasing severity, from ridicule and gossip to direct verbal reproach to social ostracism to homicide (Guala, 2012, p. 8).

Incorporating gossip as a mechanism that can reduce errors in assigning reputations, a simulation study by Ohtsuki, Iwasa, and Nowak (2009) finds that the use of costly punishment tends to reduce the average payoff for the group. It concludes that "the efficient strategy for indirect reciprocity is to withhold help for defectors rather than punishing them" (2009, p. 79). Another agent-based simulation comes to a different conclusion (Giardini, Paolucci, Villatoro, & Conte, 2014; Giardini, Paolucci, Adamatti, & Conte, 2015). Here, too, agents could either incur a cost to reduce the payoff of free-riders, or they could refuse to interact or defect with free-riders based on information about their reputation, distributed through gossip. But the simulations yielded the highest cooperation rates when both punishment and reputation-based partner selection were possible, but also the use of either strategy on its own still resulted in high levels of sustained cooperation. An experimental test of this hypothesis was in line with this prediction (Wu, Balliet, & Van Lange, 2016).

# CONCLUSION

The theories and findings presented in this chapter reveal a rich but fragmented picture, suggesting the existence of two almost parallel literatures on gossip, reputation, and cooperation. On one side there are reputation and punishment models, carried out by behavioral economists, theoretical biologists, and evolutionary psychologists. They lean heavily on highly controlled and therefore almost context-free simulation studies and lab (and more recently also field) experiments, with the relatively short time horizons of a lab session. On the other side there are coalition and control models, carried out by sociologists and anthropologists. They rely strongly on medium and long-term ethnographic fieldwork, longitudinal sociometric studies, or survey research, most of them highly context dependent and not generalizable beyond the specific population under study. Progress in the field might benefit from both literatures taking notice of each other's existence. Such an attempt would need to go beyond the traditional "selfishness versus altruism" divide, as the findings of a recent study with the telling title "Exposure to Superfluous Information Reduces Cooperation and Increases Antisocial Punishment in Reputation-Based Interactions" show (Dos Santos, Braithwaite, & Wedekind, 2014). It found that subjects' working memory in helping games can be easily disrupted by some superfluous words preceding reputation-based interactions, resulting in a decrease of generosity and an increase in anti-social punishment. Hence, behavioral models should not only account for the fact that individuals may sometimes act selfishly and sometimes in the best interest of someone else, but also that their motivation is highly susceptible to subtle changes in the situation. As outlined elsewhere (Wittek, Snijders, & Nee, 2013), theories of social rationality have the potential to do just that. For example, goal-framing theory posits that human behavior is motivated by one of three overarching goals at a time, and that these goals differ in their a priori strength (Keizer, Lindenberg & Steg, 2008), with the strongest being the hedonic goal frame ("improve the way you feel right now"), followed by the gain goal frame ("preserve or improve your resources"), and finally the normative goal frame ("act appropriately"). Being brittle by nature, the normative goal frame needs continuous support from the social and institutional context, for example in the form of group activities emphasizing the importance of joint production (Wittek, Van Duijn, & Snijders, 2003). Where such environmental cues are weak or absent, gain or hedonic motives will push normative motivations into the background. Consequently, goal framing theory's key question would be to what degree and how gossip, reputations, and context foster or undermine norms of cooperation. Norms would need to be center stage in this emerging interdisciplinary research agenda, since they remain the foundation for sustainable cooperation.

## NOTES

1. The authors of this chapter contributed equally.
2. In August 2017, "cooperation," "gossip," and "reputation" occurred together in thirty-two publications.

## REFERENCES

Adams, G. S., & Mullen, E. (2012). The social and psychological costs of punishing. *Behavioral and Brain Sciences* 35(1), 15–16.
Alexander, R. (1987). *The biology of moral systems*. New York: Aldine De Gruyter.

Barclay, P. (2006). Reputational benefits for altruistic punishment. *Evolution and Human Behavior 27*, 325–344.

Barclay, P., & Willer, R. (2007). Partner choice creates competitive altruism in humans. *Proceedings of the Royal Society of London B: Biological Sciences 274*, 749–753.

Birch Stirling R. (1957). Some psychological mechanisms operative in gossip. *Social Forces 34(3)*, 262–267.

Boehm, C. (1999). *Hierarchy in the forest: The evolution of egalitarian behavior*. Cambridge, MA: Harvard University Press.

Brison, K. J. (1992). *Just talk. Gossip, meetings, and power in a Papua New Guinea village*. Berkeley, CA: University of California Press.

Burt, R. S. (1992). *Structural holes: The social structure of competition*. Cambridge, MA: Harvard. University Press.

Burt, R. S. (1998). The gender of social capital. *Rationality and Society 10(1)*, 5–46.

Burt, R. S. (2000). The network structure of social capital. *Research in Organizational Behaviour, 22*, 345–423.

Burt, R. S. (2001). Bandwidth and echo: Trust, information, and gossip in social networks. In A. Casella & J. E. Rauch (Eds.), *Integrating the study of networks and markets*. New York, NY: Russell Sage Foundation.

Burt, R. S. (2005). *Brokerage and closure: An introduction to social capital*. Oxford, England; New York, NY: Oxford University Press.

Burt, R. S. (2007). Secondhand brokerage: Evidence on the importance of local structure for managers, bankers, and analysts. *Academy of Management Journal 50(1)*, 119–148.

Burt, R. S. (2008). Gossip and reputation. In M. Lecoutre & P. Lièvre (Eds.), *Management Et Réseaux Sociaux: Ressource Pour L'action Ou Outil de Gestion?* (pp. 27–42). Paris: Hermès Science Publications Press.

Coleman, J. S. (1990). *Foundations of social theory*. Cambridge, MA: The Belknap Press of Harvard University Press.

Conte, R., & Paolucci, M. (2002). *Reputation in artificial societies. Social beliefs for social order*. Heidelberg, Germany: Springer.

Corten, R., Rosenkranz, S., Buskens, V., & Cook, K. S. (2016). Reputation effects in social networks do not promote cooperation: An experimental test of the Raub & Weesie Model. *PLoS ONE 11(7)*, e0155703. doi:10.1371/journal.pone.0155703

Davis, A., Vaillancourt, T., Arnocky, S., & Doyel, R. (2019). Women's gossip as an intrasexual competition strategy: An evolutionary approach to sex and discrimination. In F. Giardini & R. Wittek (Eds.), *Handbook of gossip and reputation*. New York: Oxford University Press.

Dos Santos, M., & Wedekind, C. (2015). Reputation based on punishment rather than generosity allows for evolution of cooperation in sizable groups. *Evolution and Human Behavior 36(1)*, 59–64.

Dos Santos, M., Braithwaite, V. A., & Wedekind, C. (2014). Exposure to superfluous information reduces cooperation and increases antisocial punishment in reputation-based interactions. *Frontiers in Ecology and Evolution 2*, 41.

Dos Santos, M., Rankin, D. J., & Wedekind, C. (2013). Human cooperation based on punishment reputation. *Evolution 67(8)*, 2446–2450.

Dreber, A., Rand, D. G., Fudenberg, D., & Nowak, M. A. (2008). Winners don't punish. *Nature 452(7185)*, 348.

Dunbar, R. I. (1996). *Grooming, gossip and the evolution of language.* Cambridge, MA: Harvard University Press.

Elias, N., & Scotson, J. L. (1965). *The established and the outsider: A sociological enquiry into community problems.* London, England: *Cass.*

Ellickson, R. (1991). *Order without law.* Cambridge, MA: Harvard University Press.

Ellwardt, L. (2019). Gossip and reputation in social networks. In F. Giardini, R. Wittek (Eds.), *Handbook of gossip and reputation,* New York: Oxford University Press.

Ellwardt, L., Labianca, G. J., & Wittek, R. (2012). Who are the objects of positive and negative gossip at work? A social network perspective on workplace gossip. *Social Networks 34*(2), 193–205.

Ellwardt, L., Steglich, C., & Wittek, R. (2012). The co-evolution of gossip and friendship in workplace social networks. *Social Networks 34*(4), 623–633.

Ellwardt, L., Wittek, R., & Wielers, R. (2012). Talking about the boss: Effects of generalized and interpersonal trust on workplace gossip. *Group & Organization Management 37*(4), 521–549.

Elster, J. (2003). Coleman on social norms. *Revue française de sociologie 44*(2), 297–304.

Emler, N. (1990). A social psychology of reputation. *European Review of Social Psychology 1,* 171–193.

Fehr, E., & Gächter, S. (2002). Altruistic punishment in humans. *Nature 415*(6868), 137–140.

Feinberg, M., Cheng, J. T., & Willer, R. (2011). Gossip as an effective and low cost form of sanctioning. *Brain and Behavioral Sciences.*

Feinberg, M., Willer, R., & Schultz, M. (2014). Gossip and ostracism promote cooperation in groups. *Psychological Science 25*(3), 656–664.

Feinberg, M., Willer, R., Stellar, J., & Keltner, D. (2012). The virtues of gossip: Reputational information sharing as prosocial behavior. *Journal of Personality and Social Psychology 102*(5), 1015.

Foster, E. K. (2004). Research on gossip: Taxonomy, methods, and future directions. *Review of General Psychology 8*(2), 78.

Gambetta, D. (1994). Godfather's gossip. *European Journal of Sociology 35*(2), 199–223.

Giardini, F. (2012). Deterrence and transmission as mechanisms ensuring reliability of gossip. *Cognitive Processing 13*(2), 465–475.

Giardini, F., & Conte, R. (2012). Gossip for social control in natural and artificial societies. *Simulation 88*(1), 18–32.

Giardini, F., Conte, R., & Paolucci, M. (2013). Reputation. In *Simulating social complexity* (pp. 365–399). Berlin, Heidelberg, Germany: Springer.

Giardini, F., Paolucci, M., Villatoro, D., & Conte, R. (2014). Punishment and gossip: Sustaining cooperation in a public goods game. In B. Kamiński, G. Koloch (Eds.), *Advances in Social Simulation* (pp. 107–118). Berlin, Heidelberg, Germany: Springer.

Giardini, F., Paolucci, M., Adamatti, D., & Conte, R. (2015). Group size and gossip. Strategies: An ABM tool for investigating reputation-based cooperation. In F. Grimaldo F. & E. Norling (Eds.), *Multi-agent-based Simulation XV. MABS 2014* (pp. 104–120). Lecture Notes in Computer Science, vol. 9002. Cham: Springer.

Giardini, F., & Vilone, D. (2016). Evolution of gossip-based indirect reciprocity on a bipartite network. *Scientific Reports 6,* 37931.

Gluckman, M. (1963). Papers in honor of Melville J. Herskovits: Gossip and scandal. *Current Anthropology 4*(3), 307–316.

Grafen, A. (1990). Biological signals as handicaps. *Journal of Theoretical Biology. 144*(4), 517–546.

Greif, A. (1989). Reputation and coalitions in medieval trade: Evidence on the Maghribi traders. *The Journal of Economic History 49*(4), 857–882.

Grimalda, G., Pondorfer, A., & Tracer, D. P. (2016). Social image concerns promote cooperation more than altruistic punishment. *Nature Communications 7*, 12288.

Griskevicius, V., Tybur, J. M., & Van den Bergh, B. (2010). Going green to be seen: Status, reputation, and conspicuous conservation. *Journal of Personality and Social Psychology 98*(3), 392–404.

Guala, F. (2012). Strong reciprocity is real, but there is no evidence that uncoordinated costly punishment sustains cooperation in the wild. *Behavioral and Brain Sciences 35*(1), 45–59. doi:10.1017/S0140525X1100166X

Hauser, O. P., Nowak, M. A., & Rand, D. G. (2014). Punishment does not promote cooperation under exploration dynamics when anti-social punishment is possible. *Journal of Theoretical Biology 360*, 163–171.

Hedstrom, P., & Swedeborg, R. (1998). Social mechanisms: An introductory essay. In P. Hedstrom & R. Swedberg (Eds.), *Social mechanisms: An analytical approach to social theory*. Cambridge: Cambridge University Press.

Henrich, J., & Henrich, N. (2006). Culture, evolution and the puzzle of human cooperation. *Cognitive Systems Research 7*(2), 220–245.

Herrmann, B., Thöni, C., & Gächter, S. (2008). Antisocial punishment across societies. *Science 319*(5868), 1362–1367.

Hess, N., & Hagen, E. (2019). Gossip, Reputation, and Friendship in Within-group Competition: An Evolutionary Perspective. In F. Giardini, R. Wittek (Eds.), Handbook of gossip and reputation. New York: Oxford University Press.

Hilbe, C., & Traulsen, A. (2012). Emergence of responsible sanctions without second order free riders, antisocial punishment or spite. *Scientific Reports 2*, 258.

Hodson, R. (1993). Group standards and the organization of work: The effort bargain reconsidered. *Research in the Sociology of Organizations 11*, 55–80.

Jordan, J. J., Hoffman, M., Bloom, P., & Rand, D. G. (2016). Third-party punishment as a costly signal of trustworthiness. *Nature 530*, 473–476.

Jordan, J. J., & Rand, D. G. (2017). Third-party punishment as a costly signal of high continuation probabilities in repeated games. *Journal of Theoretical Biology 421*, 189–202.

Keizer, K., Lindenberg, S., & Steg, L. (2008). The spreading of disorder. *Science 322*(5908), 1681–1685.

Kellerman, K. & Cole, T. (1994). Classifying compliance gaining taxonomies: Taxonomic disorder and strategic confusion. *Communication Theory 4*: 3–60.

Kniffin, K. M., & Wilson, D. S. (2005). Utilities of gossip across organizational levels. *Human Nature 16*(3), 278–292.

Kreps, D. M., & Wilson, R. (1982). Reputation and imperfect information. *Journal of Economic Theory 27*(2), 253–279.

Lindenberg, S. (1997). Grounding groups in theory: Functional, cognitive, and structural interdependencies. *Advances in Group Processes 14*(28), 1–33.

Loughry, M. L., & Tosi, H. L. (2008). Performance implications of peer monitoring. *Organization Science 19*(6), 876–890.

Martinescu, E., Janssen, O., & Nijstad, B. A. (2019). Gossip and emotion. In F. Giardini & R. Wittek (Eds.), *Handbook of gossip and reputation*. New York: Oxford University Press.

McAndrew, F. T. (2014). The "sword of a woman": Gossip and female aggression. *Aggression and Violent Behavior 19*(3), 196–199.

McAndrew, F. T., & Milenkovic, M. A. (2002). Of tabloids and family secrets: The evolutionary psychology of gossip. *Journal of Applied Social Psychology 32*(5), 1064–1082.

McCabe, C. M., & Rand, D. G. (2014). Coordinated punishment does not proliferate when defectors can also punish cooperators. In J. Gallo, & H. Hauppauge (Eds.), *Antisocial behavior: Etiology, genetic and environmental influences and clinical management*, New York: Nova Publishers.

Meyer Spacks, P. (1985). *Gossip*. New York: Knopf.

Milinski, M. (2016). Reputation, a universal currency for human social interactions. *Philosophical Transactions of the Royal Society B 371*(1687), 20150100.

Molleman, L., van den Broek, E., & Egas, M. (April 2013). Personal experience and reputation interact in human decisions to help reciprocally. In *Proceedings of the Royal Society B, 280*(1757), 20123044.

Noë, R., & Hammerstein, P. (1994). Biological markets: supply and demand determine the effect of partner choice in cooperation, mutualism and mating. *Behavioral Ecology and Sociobiology 35*, 1–11.

Noon, M., & Delbridge, R. (1993). News from behind my hand: Gossip in organizations. *Organization Studies 14*(1), 23–36.

Nowak, M. A., & Sigmund, K. (1998). Evolution of indirect reciprocity by image scoring. *Nature 393*(6685), 573–577.

Nowak, M. A., & Sigmund, K. (2005). Evolution of indirect reciprocity. *Nature 437*, 1291–1298.

Obstfeld, D., Borgatti, S. P., & Davis, J. (2014). Brokerage as a process: decoupling third party action from social network structure. *Contemporary Perspectives on Organizational Social Networks 40*, 135–159.

Ohtsuki, H., Iwasa, Y., & Nowak, M. A. (2009). Indirect reciprocity provides a narrow margin of efficiency for costly punishment. *Nature 457*(7225), 79.

Ohtsuki, H., Iwasa, Y., & Nowak, M. A. (2015). Reputation effects in public and private interactions. *PLoS Computational Biology 11*(11), e1004527.

Przepiorka, W., & Liebe, U. (2016). Generosity is a sign of trustworthiness—the punishment of selfishness is not. *Evolution and Human Behavior 37*(4), 255–262.

Raub, W., & Weesie, J. (1990). Reputation and efficiency in social interactions: An example of network effects. *American Journal of Sociology 96*, 626–654. doi: 10.1086/229574

Roberts, G. (1998). Competitive altruism: From reciprocity to the handicap principle. *Proceedings of the Royal Society of London B: Biological Sciences 265*(1394), 427–431.

Rockenbach, B., & Milinski, M. (2006). The efficient interaction of indirect reciprocity and costly punishment. *Nature 444*(7120), 718–723.

Scott, J. C. (1986). *Weapons of the weak: everyday forms of peasant resistance*. New Haven, CT: Yale University Press.

Shaw, A. K., Tsvetkova, M., & Daneshvar, R. (2011). The effect of gossip on social networks. *Complexity 16*(4), 39–47.

Simpson, B., & Willer, R. (2015). Beyond altruism: Sociological foundations of cooperation and prosocial behavior. *Annual Review of Sociology 41*, 43–63.

Sommerfeld, R. D., Krambeck, H. J., & Milinski, M. (2008). Multiple gossip statements and their effect on reputation and trustworthiness. *Proceedings of the Royal Society of London B: Biological Sciences 275*(1650), 2529–2536.

Sommerfeld, R. D., Krambeck, H. J., Semmann, D., & Milinski, M. (2007). Gossip as an alternative for direct observation in games of indirect reciprocity. *Proceedings of the National Academy of Sciences 104*(44), 17435–17440.

Tennie, C., Frith, U., & Frith, C. D. (2010). Reputation management in the age of the world-wide web. *Trends in Cognitive Sciences 14*(11), 482–488.

Van Vugt, M., Roberts, G., & Hardy, C. (2007). Competitive altruism: Development of reputation-based cooperation in groups. In R. Dunbar & L. Barrett, *Handbook of evolutionary psychology*. Oxford: Oxford University Press.

Watson, D. (2012). Gender differences in gossip and friendship. *Sex Roles 67*(9/10), 494–502.

Wittek, R. (1999). *Interdependence and informal control in organizations*. Amsterdam: Thela Thesis.

Wittek, R., & Bekkers, R. (2015). The sociology of altruism and prosocial behavior. In J. Wright (Ed.), *International Encyclopedia of Social and Behavioral Sciences* (2nd rev. ed., vol. 1). (pp. 579–583). Oxford: Elsevier.

Wittek, R., & Wielers, R. (1998). Gossip in organizations. *Computational & Mathematical Organization Theory 4*(2), 189–204.

Wittek, R., Hangyi, H., van Duijn, M., & Carroll, C. (2000). Social capital, third party gossip, and cooperation in organizations." In J. Weesie & W. Raub, *The management of durable relations: theoretical and empirical models for organizations and households* (pp. 1–24). Amsterdam: Thela Thesis.

Wittek, R., Snijders, T., & Nee, V. (2013). Introduction: rational choice social research. In R. Wittek, T. Snijders & V. Nee (Eds.), *The handbook of rational choice social research* (pp. 1–30). Palo Alto: Stanford University Press.

Wittek, R., van Duijn, M. A., & Snijders, T. A. (2003). Frame decay, informal power, and the escalation of social control in a management team: a relational signaling perspective. In *Research in the Sociology of Organizations 20*, 355–380.

Wu, J. J., Zhang, B. Y., Zhou, Z. X., He, Q. Q., Zheng, X. D., Cressman, R., & Tao, Y. (2009). Costly punishment does not always increase cooperation. *Proceedings of the National Academy of Sciences 106*(41), 17448–17451.

Wu, J., Balliet, D., & Van Lange, P. A. (2016). Gossip versus punishment: The efficiency of reputation to promote and maintain cooperation. *Scientific Reports 6*.

Zahavi, A. (1975). Mate selection: a selection for a handicap. *Journal of Theoretical Biology, 53*(1), 205–214.

...........................................................................

# CHAPTER 3

# HUMAN SOCIALITY AND PSYCHOLOGICAL FOUNDATIONS

...........................................................................

## NICHOLAS EMLER

*The purest treasure mortal times afford*
*Is spotless reputation—that away*
*Men are but gilded loam or painted clay*
       William Shakespeare, Richard II

## INTRODUCTION

...........................................................................

THE domain of psychology is the explanation of behavior and individual human behavior in particular. Its distinguishing feature, however, is not this agenda which it shares with other disciplines but the concepts on which it draws. Its explanations refer to human nature and therefore the ways in which all humans are the same but also the ways in which they differ. It considers needs and motives, emotions and judgments, and the processes by which information about the world is acquired, integrated into memory, and subsequently retrieved and deployed in decision making. In the present context it addresses, therefore, the needs and motives that underlie gossip and the judgment processes that surround reputations as products of gossip. This by no means exhausts the ways in which psychology might approach these phenomena, but the "might" in this statement is relevant; psychological theorizing about gossip and reputation is barely developed. It is true that there is a long history of research relating to both phenomena. The relative absence of theorizing, however, is both surprising and unsurprising, surprising given the ubiquity of gossiping in everyday life and the importance of reputations for people's lives and livelihoods, but unsurprising given models of social life and of the person that have been influential within psychology. A task of this chapter therefore must be to assemble the elements of a psychological perspective. Fortunately, there is a reasonable body of material that can be recruited to this task even if its original production has often served other objectives.[1]

Gossip is defined here as informal conversational exchange concerning named third parties not present. Thus, no a priori assumptions are made about content—whether negative, positive or neutral—gossiper characteristics or motivations, or the effects of gossip. These are properly matters to be decided on evidence. Reputation is defined as that set of judgments a community shares about the personal qualities of one of its members, judgments shaped by gossip. The chapter therefore treats gossip and reputation not just as intimately related phenomena but as necessarily interdependent. It makes little sense, psychologically, to consider one without the other.

The chapter is organized as follows. Early psychological research on gossip and reputation is briefly surveyed, and some reasons are identified for the failure of a more comprehensive and integrated treatment of these topics to emerge. Next the central thesis of the chapter is developed, linking gossip and reputation to the distinctive features associated with humans as social animals, namely social complexity, high-level intellect and language use. The following two parts of the chapter are devoted to two roles of the individual in relation to gossip. The first is as gossip provider, a role that underpins reputation as social control mechanism. The second role is as gossip consumer; this role shifts the focus to reputations as predictions. The chapter concludes with some observations on future directions for research.

# EARLY RESEARCH ON GOSSIP AND REPUTATION AND ITS LIMITATIONS

Despite the intimate link being proposed here, long recognized within anthropology (Bailey, 1971), it is nevertheless the case that in the early psychological research on gossip and reputation, with only a very few exceptions (e.g., Janet, 1929), no connection was made between the two. The first studies on gossiping were directed largely at describing its content (Moore, 1922), in particular gender differences in topics (see Bischopping, 1993, for review), and to a lesser extent its personality correlates (Davis & Rulon, 1935). Perhaps the important point, however, was that research did little to test or challenge folklore about gossips and gossiping. In the commonsense or popular view of gossip (Bergmann, 1993; Emler, 2001; Schein, 1994; Spacks, 1985), one that has been widespread across cultures, gossip is spread by people who are either foolish or malicious and who in any event have little regard for the truth. These attributes of gossips, together with the errors introduced into information when it is passed through long communication chains, inevitably render the substance of gossip highly unreliable. Consequently the superficiality and mendaciousness of those who spread gossip is only surpassed by the foolish gullibility of those who give it credence. Throughout history cultural images of gossip have emphasized its malign and damaging consequences and almost universally identified the chief suspects, both the purveyors and consumers, as women.

In the period up to the 1990s there was very little systematic or sustained research attention directed at gossip within psychology. This neglect probably reflects both technical difficulties in studying the phenomenon (Dunbar et al., 1997; Emler, 2001) and a lack of evident connection with other phenomena that were absorbing the attention of researchers. A larger obstacle, however, has been the dominance of the view that social life consists largely of "one shot interactions between anonymous partners" (Nowak & Sigmund, 2005. p. 1291). This view inevitably confined gossip to the periphery of social life as a rather trivial and inconsequential activity, and so long as the popular stereotype of gossips and gossiping went unchallenged, there was little incentive to overcome the technical difficulties inherent in researching the topic.

Across the same period there were initiatives to conceptualize personality in terms of reputation (May, 1932; Vernon, 1933) but these made little progress against prevailing orthodoxy (cf. Allport, 1937; see Craik, 2008, for review).[2] Otherwise reputation appeared in the research literature primarily in the context of methodology; "reputational measures," or observer reports, were regarded as useful supplements to self-reports, as means albeit indirect of assessing personality and character (e.g., Havighurst & Taba, 1949; Winder & Wiggins, 1964). However, there was no implication that multiple observers might share judgments as a consequence of voicing their opinions to one another or that these judgments might draw upon third party reports (i.e., gossip).

Just as prevailing models of society excluded any significant role for gossip in social life so the study of reputation has been hampered by influential models of the person. What became known as the situationist critique of personality psychology (Funder, 1995) was essentially the claim that there is no such entity as personality, coupled with the additional claim that behavior is entirely a function of the situation. From these claims it seemed to follow that people cannot in any meaningful sense have reputations as judgments of their personality or character.

# Human Sociality

The argument to be developed in this section is that the activity of gossiping is a uniquely human solution to needs of predictability and control, needs served by the circulation of reputational information (Enquist & Leimar, 1993; Emler, 1994). Correspondingly, reputations in their basic manifestation can exist only to the extent that the members of human communities do gossip with one another.[3] Gossiping, and the reputational judgments this supports, allows humans to sustain and adapt to the complex social environments they inhabit.

## Social Vertebrates

We now know a great deal about animal societies, including the key insight that these are all only societies to the extent that their members in some manner or degree cooperate (Wilson, 1975). Moreover, we now also understand that evolution can result in cooperating species because natural selection can favor behavioral strategies such as contingent altruism (Trivers, 1971), and specific variants of this such as Tit-for-Tat (Axelrod & Hamilton, 1981), that limit the advantages of non-cooperation. There also appears to be an intimate connection between the complexity of animal societies, such as those of primates, and high-level intelligence (Dunbar, 1993; Humphrey, 1976). One reason for this connection is that for individuals to survive and prosper within such societies they must sustain a detailed knowledge both about one another as individuals and about the ongoing state of social relations within the group.

Another reason arises from the fact that social animals are genetic competitors (Humphrey, 1976). Humphrey argued that that the intellectual challenge for social animals is to sustain a balance between the cooperation from which they benefit, indeed on which they depend utterly, and the pursuit by each individual member of its genetic imperative (to be a successful reproducer). Pushing too hard to realize the genetic imperative would destroy cooperation; being an entirely self-less co-operator would exclude realization of this imperative. Humphrey's insight mirrors psychological arguments for two basic human needs, to get along with others (to be liked and accepted) and to get ahead (to be respected and successful; Abele & Wojciszke, 2014; Bakan, 1966; Baumeister & Leary, 1995; Hogan & Blickle, 2013), but it also highlights the challenges in balancing these.

## Language and Social Knowledge

The capacity for speech communication sets human societies apart from those of all other vertebrate species, and does so in large part because it sidesteps a fundamental constraint on the acquisition of social knowledge, namely dependence on direct observation of the relevant individuals and events. Speech allows humans and no other species to exchange and share social information because language, and no other naturally occurring form of communication, contains the capacity for complex messages referring to the not here and not now (Hockett, 1958).[4] We are thus alone among social animals in our ability to become and remain informed about the significant detail of our societies without having to observe any of it directly.

This capability also transcends a major limitation of Tit-for-Tat reciprocity as a behavioral strategy. The strategy does incur costs to the cooperator; he or she can only avoid the cheats by first being cheated. And the cheat in turn continues to prosper until the supply of one-time victims is exhausted. These costs can of course be reduced if potential victims learn from observation, and not just from direct experience. But they can be reduced much more substantially and rapidly through the use of language to circulate information on others' past behavior (Enquist & Leimar, 1993). So the proposal here is that the basic, original purpose of language, the adaptive advantage it conferred, was cheap acquisition of social knowledge. Talking to each other about each other affords us huge efficiencies in keeping informed as to who among us is powerful, honest, or capable and who is not. But can these benefits of gossiping be sustained under the conditions of contemporary social life? There would appear to be strong arguments to the contrary.

## The Societies of Ancestral and Contemporary Humans

An ancestral environment comprised of small bands of hunter-gatherers is superficially parallel to the societies of the great apes. If we allow that these human societies were nonetheless set apart by language then it is possible to envisage hunter gatherers as communities in which gossip was endemic and reputations mattered. The apparent difficulty in extrapolating to the present day is that modern humans inhabit social worlds in which most of the members are necessarily strangers to one another. This particular feature already seemed incontrovertible to social theorists writing toward the end of the 19th century (e.g., Tonnies, 1887). As they saw it, the industrial revolution had produced a fundamental shift in the nature of social relations. It had resulted not just in the mass displacement of populations from small rural settlements to vast industrial conurbations, but had also replaced the intimacy of the village with the anonymity of the city. In an often repeated phrase, life in the city would be dominated by "impersonal, superficial, transitory, and segmental" encounters (Wirth, 1938, p. 13). This "community lost" (cf. Wellman, 1979) model of social life went on to inform much of 20th century social science. Notably this model appeared to rule out any significant role for gossip or reputation in the contemporary world; in a society of strangers one has no acquaintances in common about whom one can gossip, without gossip reputations cannot even be created, and without continuity of association among acquainted individuals reputation can be of no consequence. The theoretical challenges were to account for orderly and predictable social interactions without any basis in personal acquaintance and to account for good conduct in the absence of effective social control. Sociological role theory answered the first challenge: interactants would only need to recognize the social roles occupied by those involved in the interaction; they would not need to know anything about one another as individuals. Psychological theories of socialization answered the second challenge, positing mechanisms of self-control as entirely sufficient to guarantee good conduct.

The community lost thesis also had a particular if not explicitly acknowledged appeal for social psychology. This appeal lay in the conveniences it allowed to a discipline strongly committed to the experimental method. If one can safely assume that most of the substance of social life is conducted between strangers it greatly simplifies the requirements of experimental control. The alternative of allowing for the complexities of relationships between acquainted individuals for all practical purposes rules out experimentation as a means of studying social behavior.

## The Social Life of Modern Humans Reconsidered

Challenges to the community lost model of social life have come from sociological and anthropological studies of urban communities (Gans, 1962; Young & Wilmott, 1957; see also Besnier, this volume), as well as from studies revealing evidence of primary groups in factories (Roethlisberger & Dickson, 1939), well-developed friendship patterns among city dwellers (Fischer, 1982), and social networks based on personal acquaintance in industrialized societies (Travers & Milgram, 1969; Wellman, 1979). From these, it has become clear that, in Fischer's words, even people who live in very large cities continue "to dwell among friends."

However, these various strands of evidence did not directly confirm the relative significance of exchanges with acquaintances as compared to Nowak and Sigmund's (2005) "one shot interactions between anonymous partners." Efforts to define the behavioral strategies that could sustain cooperation in human societies, including Nowak and Sigmund's (2005) own argument for indirect reciprocity, have continued to emphasize the prevalence of the one shot interaction (Fehr & Gächter, 2002; Leimar & Hammerstein, 2001; Panchanathan & Boyd, 2004; Seabright, 2004; Smith, 2014; Wu et al., 2016). Indeed there is a presumption in these efforts that it is still such incidents of cooperation between strangers that need explanation. Is this presumption justified?

Research drawing on experience recording methods (Csikzentmihalyi et al., 1977; Reis & Gable, 2000; Wheeler & Nezlek, 1977) suggests otherwise. For example, applications of this methodology (Emler, 1990, 2000) indicate that encounters with strangers are in practice very much the exception, perhaps no more than 3–5% of all encounters. Some exchanges are formal and impersonal—purely role-based business or service transactions—but these also make up a tiny proportion of the whole. The great majority of interactions occur between people who know one another. Moreover they will have acquaintances in common and thus it seems highly likely that conduct, both good and bad, is chronically visible, that actors are routinely identifiable as the authors of their actions. If this is the case then conduct is accessible to social control.

# GOSSIP, REPUTATION, AND SOCIAL CONTROL

The idea that gossip has a role in the social control of behavior is not new (Gluckman, 1963; Lumley, 1925; Ross, 1901; see also Giardini and Wittek, this volume) but how exactly is this role performed? There is an emerging consensus in disciplines as diverse as biology and economics that gossip encourages cooperation through its impact on reputation; if a consequence of gossip is rapid and wide dissemination of one's conduct record then one might be expected to take care that one's conduct is consistently above reproach. What psychology is able to bring to this analysis is clarification of the underpinning dynamics.

The basic requirement is that actors should be sensitive to the reputational consequences of their actions. Studies of young children confirm that this awareness is present early in life, at least by eight years and possibly earlier (Hill & Pillow, 2006; Tomasello & Vaish, 2013). Correspondingly, various experimental studies with adults indicate that when future partners can access gossip about an actor this encourages the actor to be more cooperative or pro-social (Feinberg et al., 2014; Piazza & Bering, 2008; Wu et al., 2016), while potential future partners' decisions are indeed influenced by information about actors' past conduct (Stiff & Van Vugt, 2008). Insofar as gossip plays a role in social control this also requires a credible capacity on the part of gossip providers to injure the interests of norm violators. Notably Wu et al. (2016) find evidence that credibility in this respect is greater when the provider is well connected, which is to say occupying a network position that allows them to reach a wide audience.

## Gossiping: Risks and Motivations

Less straightforward is what motivates an individual to be gossip provider given the risks this role carries. Gossiping may not be a punishable offence in the 21st century[5] but it can still carry a stigma (Farley et al., 2010; Gawronski & Walter, 2008; Turner et al., 2003). Farley (2011) found the risk was greatest to those seen to engage in frequent negative observations about others. But, in the light of experimental evidence indicating that people who witness anti-social behavior do seem compelled to pass their observations on to others (Feinberg et al., 2012),[6] this creates a puzzle.

The following are plausible motives of gossip providers. First, the role of critic is not necessarily disparaged when the focus is others' evident delinquencies. Vaish et al. (2016) found that even young children prefer others who enforce norms and criticize those who violate them. Consistent with this, studies of adults confirm an inclination to moralistic gossip, a desire to see cheats exposed, albeit while indicating this inclination may be unevenly distributed through human populations (e.g., Fehr & Gätcher, 2002). Second, the motivation can be more personal; if one is the victim of another's bad behavior then reporting on that bad behavior to third parties offers indirect pay-back or retaliation; desire for retribution is a powerful motivator (Hogan & Emler, 1981). Third, sharing information about others, including negative information, could arise from obligations of reciprocity and mutual support between friends; if you have told me of your bad experiences with a mutual acquaintance you might expect me to be similarly candid about other acquaintances we share. This is consistent with Feinberg et al.'s (2012) finding that negative critical gossip can be intended to protect others from victimization and also allows providers to feel good about themselves. Finally, Peters and Kashima (2015) show that gossip providers are perceived more positively when they share gossip that helps its consumers regulate their relations with others.

Pinning down in greater detail where the risks in gossiping lie may require more differentiated treatment both of the substance of what is disclosed and the provenance of the information or opinion disclosed. What little we still know about the substance of conversational exchanges between acquaintances indicates that while much of it meets a minimal definition of gossip—it refers to third parties not present—very little is actually negative (Dunbar et al., 1997). This does raise questions as to the purpose of such gossip if it is not to sanction delinquencies.

But consider first another source of potential risk to the provider, not that the gossip is critical of others but that the provider is guilty of bad faith. Bergman (1993) talked of gossip as discreet indiscretion, the implication being that the provider betrays confidences. The risk to providers is that they are identified as untrustworthy. Giardini (2012) notes one strategy that may mitigate this risk is to attribute the disclosure to other unnamed sources. The risk may also be managed by careful choice of audience and close monitoring of audience reaction. As matters stand, however, there is insufficient evidence to indicate how often this risk arises or how it is managed when it does.

To return briefly to the manner in which gossip is employed to achieve control, the basic aim is to persuade an audience of a particular view of the target. However, there are likely to be motives additional to encouraging the good behavior of targets. Consistent with needs both to get along with others and to promote one's own interests there is evidence that gossip can be deployed to support friends and denigrate rivals (Barkow, 1992; Buss & Dedden, 1990; McAndrew, et al., 2007).

## Imperfections and Limitations of Social Control

If gossip is intended to encourage cooperative or otherwise decent behavior, then manifestly it is an imperfect remedy because delinquencies are common-place. The significant thing about the chronically delinquent is not that they are the minority who have slipped temporarily or more permanently through the net of informal social surveillance; they are as likely as any other member of their community to be identifiable as the authors of their actions (Emler, 1984; Emler & Reicher, 1995). Neither are they individuals unaware of the reputational consequences of their actions or lacking in the skills to construct and sustain a "good" reputation. Rather, they appear to have quite different reputational priorities. This should encourage us to recognize that more generally gossip will be an imperfect guarantee of good conduct because not everyone cares to the same degree about having a "good" reputation and gossip can equally well be valued for its capacity to disseminate quite different kinds of reputation. The attractions of a delinquent reputation may reflect considerations particularly salient in adolescence (Emler, 2009), but pursuit of "darker" reputations—for ruthlessness, vengefulness, and so on—will be found among the adult members of any human community.

Because social control is imperfect, because the motivational balance, as between getting along and getting ahead together with their distinct reputational goals, can vary from one individual to another, and because people differ in numerous other ways, successful adaptation to an environment populated by one's fellow human beings requires prediction as well as control.

# Gossip, Reputation, and Prediction

The role of gossip in social control relates primarily to the motives and interests of social actors as gossip providers. When we turn to role of gossip in prediction[7] our attention necessarily shifts to the interests of the same actors as gossip consumers. There are two broad sets of reasons why prediction matters. The first, alluded to earlier, is that people differ, the second relates to circumstances surrounding rather than qualities intrinsic to individuals, but circumstances that have a bearing on how they behave. Three categories of such circumstance can be distinguished. The first reflects a sociological truism: role and status in the social structure matter. People's actions are conditioned by the roles they occupy and the duties and obligations associated with these roles. The level at which an individual sits in an organization constrains the opportunities that individual has for action, their capacity to exercise discretion, the power they can wield over the fate of others. The second set of circumstances concern the ways in which an individual is connected to others at any time; these include both the existence of ties—who do they know, who do they talk to—and the content or quality of current ties—who are their friends and intimates, to whom do they owe loyalty, who are their rivals and enemies, against whom do they have grievances. The third set concerns changes of fortune. Things happen to people that alter their capacities for action; they inherit property, suffer bereavements, marry and divorce, sustain injuries and so forth.

What matters to the gossip consumer with respect to these details about others is timeliness. If gossip is news then kudos is earned by being first (Levin & Arluke, 1987). But competition for kudos also protects consumers from blatant misrepresentation; multiple sources will be seeking to be first with the same news.

## Gossip as Evidence of Actor Characteristics

In making predictions with respect to differences between people what should matter to us is the reliability of the evidence on which these can draw. The important differences fall into three categories, (1) differences of personality, character and temperament, (2) differences in values, tastes and interests, and (3) differences in abilities, skills, and expertise. Of these three, the cluster relating to abilities has behind it the longest history of psychological research. At the other end of the scale work on values, tastes and interests is much more limited, though the relevance of these to the way people live their lives, for example, with respect to career choices and political commitments, is well established. However, neither category of characteristic has figured to any significant degree in psychological research on gossip and reputation (for exceptions, Denissen et al., 2011, Emler et al., 2007). Most of what we know relates to personality or character.

One potential challenge to the value of gossip as a source of information about others' personalities is that there is no truth about personality to be had, whether by this route or any other. It may be common sense that the personalities of people differ in various ways but psychology has a history of dissenting from this common sense. Indeed, a major reason historically for the absence of a well-established psychology of reputation has been a model of the person quite at odds with common beliefs. In the 1920s, psychological research was casting in doubt the very existence of moral character as a meaningful, enduring and generalized quality of individuals (Hartshorne & May, 1928) and for the next 50 years researcher sought to show first that conduct is a function of the situation not the person and second that various information processing flaws endemic in human perceivers lead them to see consistency in others' behavior where none actually exists. So if people are perceived to have reputations, whether for honesty or generosity, emotional stability or reliability, these may be compelling illusions but they are illusions nonetheless.

## Rediscovering the Reality of Character and Personality

Matters have changed but slowly. One source of change has been appreciation that the experimental methods providing evidence of error in perception have their own limitations. In particular, they often fail to engage the motivations and effort of perceivers who will then choose to use low-cost methods to process presented information (Fiske & Neuberg, 1990), choices that produce error or inaccuracy often enough to sustain the hypothesis of the human as incorrigibly flawed perceiver. Other sources have included reassertion of the value of basic psychometric principles underlying accurate measurement of differences between people, and more robust methods for studying interpersonal perception (Funder, 1995; Kenny, 1994).

With respect to this latter point, and with parallel implications for reputational judgments, deserving of particular mention is the emergence of research designs that properly resolved the methodological weaknesses of early person perception research (Cronbach, 1955). One valuable innovation in research design has involved a round-robin procedure (Kenny, 1994); in the basic version, groups of people make judgments about their own personalities and those of all other members of the group. A crucial asset of this design is that different sources of influence on perceptions of personality can be precisely quantified. So perception of the degree to which an individual is perceived as, for example, cooperative may in part reflect the tendency of perceivers to see others as more or less cooperative (a perceiver effect). On the other hand, to the extent that observers agree as to who is more or less cooperative, this points to real differences between people in their cooperativeness. Kenny (1994) labelled this a target effect. Third, perceptions of cooperativeness could reflect something specific to the relationship between perceiver and target. A particular target may have a cooperative relation with one perceiver but not with others. To the extent that perceptions reflect this possibility they can be described as products of a relationship effect (Kenny, 1994).

Research inspired by Kenny's design recommendations has delivered a number of important outcomes. Perhaps the most important is that, with respect to many qualities of the person that may be judged and under a variety of conditions, of the relative contributions of the different sources of influence—perceiver, target, relationship—target effects are often the largest. In other words, it seems that there are real differences between people and these can be accurately identified by others.

## Personality as Reputation

Psychometrically inspired research on personality has produced a consensus about the principal ways in which personality varies. This consensus is sometimes described as the Big Five model of personality: the principal differences between people can be captured by five broad sets of characteristics, often labelled respectively as neuroticism, extraversion, conscientiousness, agreeableness and openness to experience. Significantly, however, this model did not initially arise out of conventional psychometric work on personality measurement but from studies of the terms that exist in natural languages to describe people. Given the argument advanced in this chapter, that language uniquely equips humans to exchange social information, we therefore might expect natural languages to be rich in their capacity to code for such information. This turns out to be the case. Allport and Odbert (1934) identified over four and a half thousand terms in the English language that are person descriptive.[8] But it also turns out that this extensive lexicon can be clustered into groups of terms, five in number, that convey similar meanings (Norman, 1963; Peabody & Goldberg, 1989). This "lexical hypothesis" as to the structure of personality then inspired a variety of personality measures employing self-reports. Individuals' descriptions of themselves on the five broad dimensions satisfy the basic psychometric requirement of high reliability. Does the big five also provide a map for reputations, an indication of the main ways in which reputations as judgments of character vary?

In this respect there has been a significant cross fertilization of the psychometric tradition of personality assessment employing self-reports and the new wave of person perception research. In probing the accuracy of observer impressions of personality, efforts initially defined accuracy as convergence with self-reports (the conventional psychometric evidence). But it became increasingly apparent that this had matters the wrong way about. Research had already shown that aggregating or combining the judgments of knowledgeable informants generates reliable assessments of personality (Cheek, 1982; Moskowitz & Schwarz, 1982). Recent work indicates that these assessments can also be more accurate than self-reports (Vazire, 2010; Oh, Wang, & Mount, 2011). Evidence of this kind has led Hogan (1996; Hogan & Blickle, 2013) to argue that personality traits should be regarded not as qualities inherent in individuals but as predictions about their behavior made by others who know them. In other words personality should properly be understood as reputation. And the five factors perhaps reflect not the main ways in which people differ from one another but what it is most important for people to know about the character of their fellow human beings. We are now in a better position to consider the utility of gossip with respect to reputation as a predictive tool.

# Gossip Utility in Person Perception

Funder (1995) argued that the accuracy of perceiver's impressions of others' personality will be a function of the quality and quantity of evidence available to the perceiver. He linked this to the proposition that evidence is more plentiful the better acquainted the perceiver is with the target. However, his discussion of accuracy implies that the evidence available to the perceiver derives from his or her relationship with the target and the accumulated interactions between them represented by this relationship. But consider what psychometrics tells us: larger samples of behavior or performance are more representative of a person's behavior in general and yield more reliable assessments. And, in the absence of systematic error, more reliable assessments are also more accurate. However, large samples are also costly, and what is true of self-report measures is also true of observer assessments. I have argued that language confers on humans a huge adaptive advantage in enabling low cost information sharing; socially transmitted information gives access to very large samples of others' behavior much more efficiently and cheaply than any single observer could achieve by personal observation alone. Nonetheless, this is only an advantage to the extent that observers are also disposed and equipped to make good use of this information. But what does "good use" of socially transmitted information mean, and how might human observers accomplish this?

Smith (2014) has shown, using "agent based modelling" (see also Grow & Flache, this volume), that observers who rely exclusively on their own direct observation are less likely to detect character flaws in others than those who additionally make use of third party reports. He makes the point that evil may be manifested in rare behaviors; by definition these are more likely to occur in large samples. So it makes sense for observers to supplement their own direct impressions with those of others. In passing there is an additional important point in Smith's analysis: if reputations are the aggregate of a set of individual impressions, each of these latter is some synthesis of direct personal experiences of the target and evidence provided by third parties. There are nonetheless numerous challenges to the value of third party reports, from benign distortion to the possibility of deliberate misrepresentation.

## Benign Distortions

A, as observer, might make the default assumption that B can be an honest and reliable witness to the conduct of C. Recall, however, that evidence using Kenny's recommended research design consistently indicates a relationship effect. Part of what B can report about C will be particular to their relationship (Kenny et al., 2001); honest witnesses will therefore unavoidably provide partial reports. This being so, it makes sense for the observer to proceed in a manner akin to Kenny's research design: integrate the reports of multiple observers. Evidence as to this happening naturally is still scarce. Note, however, Kenny et al. (2001) also find that target effects are larger relative to relationship effects when data are aggregated across several partners (people who interact with the target). As to the number of third party reports likely to optimize efficiency, a further prediction can be derived from the principles underlying Kenny's round robin design. For statistical reasons the minimum number of perceivers required to allow partitioning of variance is three. It would be interesting to know whether naïve observers naturally apply the same rule. A study by Hess and Hagen (2006) of perceptions of gossip veracity is at the very least consistent with this possibility. They found that, presented with a hypothetical scenario, gossip was perceived as believable when the same observations were repeated by at least three witnesses.

Other possible sources of benign distortions in gossip arise from the dynamics of opinion sharing. It has long been known that opinions and judgments tend to converge when they are shared (cf. Sherif, 1936).[9] In addition, it has been shown that people will tend to adjust their expressed views to match those their audience is believed to hold (Higgins & Rholes, 1978; Higgins, 1992) while decision making groups are poor at exposing information that is not already widely shared within the group (Stasser & Titus, 1985). Burt (2005) argued that for these kinds of reasons gossip is likely to be of little value as a source of truth about others. Respect for etiquette, he proposed, means we do not tell others all we know or believe about third parties. We select and, in the interests of politeness, we select those things we believe a particular other wishes to hear, namely things consistent with what the other already believes or thinks. Burt goes on to endorse Gambetta's (1994) view that gossip is not primarily about truth; it is about sociability (cf. also arguments for the role of gossip in social bonding and friendship formation, Dunbar, 1993; Foster, 2004). One possible way out of this difficulty is to accept that gossip has multiple functions but that these are not all operative in the same settings or the same relationships. Thus politeness may be a salient consideration for interactions in relatively public settings and pressures to opinion convergence may be strong in group settings. But a majority of conversational exchanges involve just two parties and many of these involve close friends or intimates between whom candor may be more valued than politeness (Emler, 2001; cf. also Lyons et al., 2008).

## Information Loss in Communication Chains

A different kind of objection to the reliability of gossip carries echoes of its image in the popular imagination: the message is necessarily distorted as it passes from one person to another, and the longer the chain of communication the greater the distortion. There are some different but related possibilities here. The first is noise; communicated information is always degraded to some degree by noise and successive repetitions along a chain of communication magnify noise effects. Second, information tends to become both simplified and exaggerated as it moves along a communication chain (Baron et al., 1997; Thompson et al., 2000). Third, the source of the information becomes progressively difficult to identify with each successive link and correspondingly easier to misrepresent (Giardini, 2012).

In a study of the accuracy with which information is transmitted along extended chains, Mesoudi et al. (2006) found that gossip about third party relationships was successfully transmitted with little information loss, in marked contrast to non-social information.[10] In contrast, Gilovich (1987) found that information transmitted through just one intermediary lost mitigating detail; the originating disclosure contained revelations potentially damaging to the source while the intermediary's account painted a more unambiguously negative picture of the source. However, a problem exists here with the plausibility of the scenario the experiment created. In the normal course of events, which is to say outside of the unnatural worlds one can create in experiments, people do not naturally entrust their own accounts of their failings to anyone; they will tend to choose close friends, audiences likely to speak supportively on their behalf to third parties (Emler, 1990). The intermediaries in Gilovich's experiment had no motive to be careful with the accounts they were given; they had no personal connection to the source and subject of the account.

As regards the unreliability introduced by long communication chains Wilson et al. (2000) found that people expect to give less weight to information about another that has been mediated by more than one link. Moreover there is little evidence that gossip normally involves long chains and good reasons to expect the reverse; both Boissevain (1974) and Granovetter (1973) argue that the effective reach of a person's influence seldom reaches beyond the friends of their friends (for a contrary view, see Fowler & Christakis, 2009).

## Motivated Data Corruption

A more serious challenge to gossip's utility is motivated data corruption. We have already seen that providers can have mixed motives; they will exaggerate the virtues of those close to them and correspondingly overplay the shortcomings of their rivals (McAndrew et al., 2007). If the gossip consumer is to make effective use of third party reports we should expect some degree of discounting when motivated distortion on the part of providers is a possibility. Hess and Hagen (2006) found just such discounting to occur when the gossip provider's report concerned either a friend or a competitor. Smith (2014), again using agent based modelling, demonstrates the value of an alternative, content-based strategy, which is for observers to discount third party reports that are clearly discrepant with their own existing impression of a target. Smith's argument for the value of this strategy is that it circumvents uncertainty about the origins of third party reports. However, where communication chain are very short, filtering evaluations of gossip through knowledge about the relationship between provider and target becomes viable. This of course presupposes good knowledge about the state of the relevant relationships. In this respect, note that gossip may inform people about the state of relationships among others (cf. Dunbar et al., 1997). In addition, it turns out people are highly and accurately attuned to these matters (Kenny et al., 1996). In other words, we are in a position to be good at the necessary discounting.

A final potential corrupter of data is the target of gossip. Should we not expect actors to seek reputations better than they deserve and so manage the information that is available to others? The directly related, and more extensively researched, case is that of self-presentation. In an influential analysis, Jones (1990) argued that actors routinely seek to persuade audiences of a view of themselves that it is not in the interests of the audience to believe, that they the actors are more worthy, powerful, likeable, successful, or devout than is in fact the case. In other words, the goals of self-presentation are essentially manipulative, and thus audiences in the role of gossip providers, however honest and accurate they seek to be, can only offer evidence that is corrupted at source.

Goffman (1959) took a different view of impression management, captured in his concept of "dramatic realization." For Goffman the actor's problem is not to create a fake persona to mislead the audience but to explain or dramatize the actual persona. The problem arises because, whatever talents or virtues people possess, these are not automatically evident to others and may actually remain obscured without active dramatization by the actor. If Goffman is correct, and I think there is merit in his argument, then reputation management will have more to do with clarification than manipulation.

As to the principal tools of reputation management we have already encountered these from other directions. Reputations are constructed, sustained and dissected in conversations from which the actor is absent. What matters therefore to the objects of reputational judgments is the involvement of intimates, allies, and admirers when these conversations take place. Therefore, to manage their reputations with some measure of success, individuals must invest in relationships that will provide this kind of social support, reciprocate in kind and, because scope for reputation management lies substantially with resolution of ambiguities in conduct and performance, keep potential supporters updated with disambiguating accounts (Emler, 1990).

The preceding discussion points to a further reason for variations in the accuracy of reputations: people differ in social visibility (Granovetter, 1985). People will attract greater social attention to the extent that they are perceived to be powerful, but will also have higher visibility to the extent that they sustain more frequent contacts with a wider circle of acquaintances. Under these circumstances the volume of gossip about them will be greater and thus also will be the pool of data on which their reputations will be based. Correspondingly, those who by temperament or choice have more limited social contacts will have less precisely calibrated reputations (Anderson & Shakro, 2008).

# Conclusions and Future Directions

It has been the thesis of this chapter that gossip and reputation serve fundamental needs of adaptation to the social environment, needs realized through achievement of prediction and control. The latter can be seen as the aggregate effect of individuals acting as gossip providers and acting through a mix of motives, including defense of friends and denigration of adversaries. Prediction shifts the focus to the consumer role, one that involves a complex exercise in evaluating and integrating the social information provided through gossip. Evidence is consistent with this role being exercised in the manner of an intuitive but sophisticated psychometrician. That is to say, it involves drawing on large samples, maximizing data quality (avoiding long chains), filtering for data corruption, discarding outliers (rejecting extreme values), and partitioning variance across reports to distinguish target effects from relationship effects. Finally, if all individuals participate in social life simultaneously in three guises their objective in the third guise, as the focus of others' gossip, is successfully to dramatize the reputations they seek.

As to future challenges for research, one such relates to social functions of the intellect (Humphrey, 1976). If these functions include making judgments about others then there is much still to be understood about the information processing requirements of assimilating, weighing and integrating information from multiple sources for this cognitive activity to serve an adaptive purpose. Among related questions still to be researched in detail are the strategies people use, both as providers and consumers of gossip, to distribute social attention, and as targets of gossip the strategies they use to manage their own reputations. And beyond these are questions about differences between people in both areas of strategy, including differences in objectives and skills (see also McAndrew, "Gossip as a Social Skill," this volume).

A final requirement for the future, but one that deserves priority treatment because it underlies our ability to answer the other questions already set out, is a more thorough and accurate description of the phenomena we seeks to explain. In the case of reputation but particularly gossip, the hypotheses we have tested in research have too often taken commonly held beliefs as their starting point. Our science would be better served by building on a foundation of high quality description. To this end, and notwithstanding the technical difficulties involved, we need to know much more about the natural rhythms of social life, who talks to whom, how frequently and extensively, under what circumstances, and about what.

## Notes

1. For earlier reviews covering the psychology of gossip, see Emler (2001), Foster (2004), and of reputation, see Bromley (1993), Craik (2008), Emler (1990).
2. Ironically, Allport criticized this approach on the grounds that reputations might reflect gossip.
3. Many kinds of entity have reputations in contemporary society—football teams, financial institutions, wines, etc. The focus of the chapter is the reputations of individual people.
4. Crucial features of language would appear to be (a) names to identify those to whom information refers, and (b) grammar to construct complex messages relating actors to actions in numerous ways.
5. In medieval England, gossip, at least when women were its practitioners, was outlawed (Oakley, 1972) and the punishments were often fatal. Much more recently, researchers have documented the extreme lengths women continue to go to in some cultures to avoid the suspicion they are gossiping (Hutson, 1971; Naish, 1978).

6. An inclination to share gossip about others has been found in children as early as five (Englemann, Hermann & Tomasello, 2016).

7. Properly speaking, *prediction* can have two meanings with respect to behavior, first in the sense of predicting how people in general will behave given a particular set of circumstances, and second in the sense of predicting the behavior of a specific named individual where this might differ from the behavior of others. The term is used here in this second sense.

8. Norman (1967) later identified around 18,000 such terms. To give this some context, estimates for the typical vocabulary size of native English speakers range from 15,000 to 25,000.

9. This is in fact an adaptive response when there is known to be a truth but it is difficult to determine, for instance, how many beans are contained in a jar.

10. A potential limitation of the study as representative of gossiping is that the information was passed on in writing and with no interaction between source and recipient.

## REFERENCES

Abele, A. E., & Wojciszke, B. (2014). Communal and agentic content in social cognition: A dual perspective model. *Advances in Experimental Social Psychology 50*, 198–255.

Allport, G. W. (1937). Personality: A psychological interpretation. New York: Holt.

Allport, G. W., & Odbert, H. (1934). Trait names: A psycho-lexical study. *Psychological Monographs 47*(211).

Anderson, C., & Shakro, A. (2008). Do people's reputations correspond to their records of behavior? *Journal of Personality and Social Psychology 94*, 320–333.

Axelrod, G., & Hamilton, W. (1981). The evolution of cooperation. *Science 211*, 1390–1396.

Bailey, F. G. (1971). *Gifts and poison: The politics of reputation*. Oxford: Blackwell.

Bakan, D. (1966). *The duality of human experience*. Boston: Beacon.

Barkow, J. H. (1992). Beneath new culture is old psychology: Gossip and social stratification. In J. H. Barkow, L. Cosmides, & J. Tooby, (Eds.). *The adapted mind; Evolutionary psychology and the generation of culture* (pp. 627–637). New York: Oxford University Press.

Baron, R. S., David, J. P., Brunsman, B. M., & Inman, M. (1997). Why listeners hear less than they are told: Attentional load and the teller–listener extremity effect. *Journal of Personality and Social Psychology 72*(4), 826–838.

Baumeister, R. F., & Leary, M. R. (1995). The need to belong: Desire for interpersonal attachments as a fundamental human motivation. *Psychological Bulletin 117*(3), 497–529.

Bergmann, J. R. (1993). *Discreet indiscretions: The social organization of gossip*. New York: deGruyter.

Besnier, N. (2018). Gossip in ethnographic perspective. In F. Giardini & R. Wittek (Eds.), *Handbook of gossip and reputation*. New York: Oxford University Press.

Bischoping, K. (1993). Gender differences in conversation topics 1922–1990. *Sex Roles 28*(1–2), 1–18.

Boissevain, J. (1974). *Friends of friends: Networks, manipulators and coalitions*. Oxford: Blackwell.

Bromley, D. B. (1993). *Reputation, image and impression management*. New York: John Wiley & Sons.

Burt, R. S. (2005). *Brokerage and closure: An introduction to social capital*. Oxford: Oxford University Press.

Buss, D. M., & Dedden, L. A. (1990). Derogation of competitors. *Journal of Social and Personal Relationships* 7(3), 395–422.

Cheek, J. M. (1982). Aggregation, moderator variables, and the validity of personality tests: A peer-rating study. *Journal of Personality and Social Psychology* 43(6), 1254–1269.

Craik, K. H. (2008). *Reputation: A network interpretation.* Oxford: Oxford University Press.

Cronbach, L. (1955). Processes affecting scores on understanding of others and assumed similarity. *Psychological Bulletin* 52(3), 177–193.

Csikszentmihalyi, M., Larson, R., & Prescott, S. (1977). The ecology of adolescent activity and experience. *Journal of Youth and Adolescence* 6(3), 281–294.

Davis, F. B., & Rulon, P J. (1935). Gossip and the introvert. *Journal of Abnormal and Social Psychology* 30(1), 17–21.

Denissen, J. A., Schönbrodt, F. D., van Zalk, M., Meeus, W. H. J., & van Aken, M. A. G. (2011). Antecedents and consequences of peer-rated intelligence. *European Journal of Personality* 25(2), 108–119.

Dunbar, R. I. M. (1993). Coevolution of neocortical size, group size and language in humans. *Behavioral and Brain Sciences* 16(4), 681–735.

Dunbar, R. I. M., Marriott, M., & Duncan, N. D. C. (1997). Human conversational behavior. *Human Nature* 8(3), 231–246.

Emler, N. (1984). Differential involvement in delinquency: Toward an interpretation in terms of reputation management. In B. A. Maher & W. B. Maher, *Progress in experimental personality research* (pp. 173–239). New York: Academic Press.

Emler, N. (1990). A social psychology of reputation. *European Review of Social Psychology* 1(1), 171–193.

Emler, N. (1994). Gossip, reputation and social adaptation. In R. Goodman & A. Ben Ze'ev (Eds.), *Good gossip* (pp. 117–133). Kansas: Kansas University Press.

Emler, N. (2000). Social structures and individual lives: Effects of participation in the social institutions of family, education, and work. In J. Bynner & R. K. Silbereisen (Eds.), *Adversity and challenge in the life course in England and the new Germany* (pp. 62–84). London: Macmillan.

Emler, N. (2001). Gossiping. In H. Giles & W. P. Robinson (Eds.), *The new handbook of language and social psychology* (pp. 317–338). Chichester: Wiley.

Emler, N. (2009). Delinquents as a minority group: Accidental tourists in forbidden territory or voluntary émigrés? In F. Butera & J. Levine (Eds.). *Coping with minority group status: Responses to exclusion and inclusion.* (pp. 127–154). Cambridge: Cambridge University Press.

Emler, N., & Reicher, S. (1995). *Adolescence and delinquency: The collective management of reputation.* Oxford: Blackwell Publishing.

Emler, N., Tarry, H., & St. James, A. (2007). Post-conventional moral reasoning and reputation. *Journal of Research in Personality* 41(1), 76–89.

Engelmann, J. M., Herrmann, E., & Tomasello, M. (2016). Preschoolers affect others' reputations through prosocial gossip. *British Journal of Developmental Psychology* 34(3), 447–460.

Enquist, M., & Leimar, O. (1993). The evolution of cooperation in mobile organisms. *Animal Behaviour* 45(4), 747–757.

Farley, S. D. (2011). Is gossip power? The inverse relationships between gossip, power, and likability. *European Journal of Social Psychology* 41(5), 574–579.

Farley, S. D., Timme, D. R., & Hart, J. W. (2010). On coffee talk and break-room chatter: Perceptions of women who gossip in the workplace. *The Journal of Social Psychology* 150(4), 361–368.

Fehr, E., & Gächter, S. (2002). Altruistic punishment in humans. *Nature* 415(6868), 137–140.

Feinberg, M., Willer, R., & Schultz, M. (2014). Gossip and ostracism promote cooperation in groups. *Psychological Science* 25(3), 656–664.

Feinberg, M., Willer, R., Stellar, J., & Keltner, D. (2012). The virtues of gossip: Reputational information sharing as prosocial behavior. *Journal of Personality and Social Psychology* 102(5), 115–130.

Fischer, C. S. (1982). *To dwell among friends: Personal networks in town and city.* Chicago: University of Chicago Press.

Fiske, S. T., & Neuberg, S. L. (1990). A continuum of impression formation, from category-based to individuating processes: Influences of information and motivation on attention and interpretation. *Advances in Experimental Social Psychology* 23, 1–74.

Foster, E. K. (2004). Research on gossip: Taxonomy, methods, and future directions. *Review of General Psychology* 8(2), 78–99.

Fowler, J. H., & Christakis, N. A. (2009). Dynamic spread of happiness in a large social network: Longitudinal analysis over 20 years in the Framingham heart study. *British Medical Journal* 338, 1–13.

Funder, D. C. (1995). On the accuracy of personality judgment: A realistic approach. *Psychological Review* 102(4), 652–670.

Gambetta, D. (1994). Godfather's gossip. *European Journal of Sociology/Archives Européennes De Sociologie* 35(2), 199–223.

Gans, H. J. (1962). *The urban village.* New York: Free Press.

Gawronski, B., & Walther, E. (2008). The TAR effect: When the ones who dislike become the ones who are disliked. *Personality and Social Psychology Bulletin* 34(9), 1276–1289.

Giardini, F. (2012). Deterrence and transmission as mechanisms ensuring reliability of gossip. *Cognitive Processing* 13(2), 465–475.

Giardini, F., & Wittek, R. (2018). Gossip, Reputation, and Sustainable Cooperation: Sociological Foundations. In F. Giardini & R. Wittek (Eds.), *Handbook of gossip and reputation.* New York: Oxford University Press.

Gilovich, T. (1987). Secondhand information and social judgment. *Journal of Experimental Social Psychology* 23(1), 59–74.

Gluckman, M. (1963). Gossip and scandal. *Current Anthropology* 6, 281–293.

Goffman, E. (1959). *The presentation of self in everyday life.* New York: Doubleday.

Granovetter, M. (1973). The strength of weak ties. *American Journal of Sociology* 78, 1360–1380.

Granovetter, M. (1985). Economic action and social structure: The problem of embeddedness. *American Journal of Sociology* 91(3), 481–510.

Grow, A., & Flache, A. (2018). Agent-based models of reputation and status. In Giardini, F., & Wittek, R. (Eds.), *Handbook of gossip and reputation.* New York: Oxford University Press.

Hartshorne, H., & May, M. (1928). *Studies in nature of character,* vol. 1. *Studies in deceit:* New York: Macmillan

Havighurst, R. J., & Taba, H. (1949). *Adolescent character and personality.* New York: Wiley.

Hess, N. H., & Hagen, E. H. (2006). Psychological adaptations for assessing gossip veracity. *Human Nature: An Interdisciplinary Biosocial Perspective* 17(3), 337–354.

Higgins, E. T. (1992). Achieving 'shared reality' in the communication game: A social action that creates meaning. *Journal of Language and Social Psychology* 11(3), 107–131.

Higgins, E. T., & Rholes, W. S. (1978). "Saying is believing": Effects of message modification on memory and liking for the person described. *Journal of Experimental Social Psychology* 14(4), 363–378.

Hill, V., & Pillow, B. H. (2006). Children's understanding of reputations. *Journal of Genetic Psychology 167*(2), 137–157.

Hockett, C. F. (1958). *A course in modern linguistics*. New York: Wiley.

Hogan, R. (1996). A socioanalytic perspective on the five-factor model. In J. Wiggins (Ed.). *The five-factor model of personality* (pp. 163–179). New York: Guilford Press.

Hogan, R., & Blickle, G. (2013). Socioanalytic theory. In N. D. Christiansen & R. P. Tett (Eds.). Handbook of personality at work (pp. 53–70). New York: Routledge.

Hogan, R., & Emler, N. P. (1981). Retributive justice. In M. Lerner & S. Lerner (Eds.). *The justice motive in social behavior: Adapting to times of scarcity and change* (pp. 125–143). New York: Springer.

Humphrey, N. K. (1976). The social function of intellect. In P. P. G. Bateson & R. Hinde (Eds.). *Growing points in ethology* (pp. 303–317). Cambridge: Cambridge University Press.

Hutson, S. (1971). Social ranking in a French alpine community. In F. G. Bailey (Ed.). *Gifts and Poisons: The Politics of Reputation* (pp. 41–68). Oxford: Blackwell.

Janet, P. (1929). *L'évolution psychologique de la personalité* Paris: Chahine.

Jones, E. E. (1990). *Interpersonal perception*. New York: W. H. Freeman/Times Books/Henry Holt & Co.

Kenny, D. A. (1994). *Interpersonal perception: A social relations analysis.* New York: Guilford Press.

Kenny, D. A., Bond, C. F. Jr., Mohr, C. D., & Horn, E. M. (1996). Do we know how much people like one another? *Journal of Personality and Social Psychology 71*(5), 928–936.

Kenny, D. A., Mohr, C. D., & Levesque, M. J. (2001). A social relations variance partitioning of dyadic behavior. *Psychological Bulletin 127*(1), 128–141.

Leimar, O., & Hammerstein, P. (2001). Evolution of cooperation through indirect reciprocity. *Proceedings of the Royal Society B: Biological Sciences 268*(1468), 745–753.

Levin, J., & Arluke, A. (1987). *Gossip: The inside scoop*. New York: Springer.

Lumley, F. E. (1925). *Means of social control*. Ann Arbor, MI and New York: The Century Co.

Lyons, A., Clark, A., Kashima, Y., & Kurz, T. (2008). Cultural dynamics of stereotypes: Social network processes and the perpetuation of stereotypes. In Y. Yashima, K. Fiedler, & P. Freitag (Eds.) *Stereotype Dynamics: Language-Based Approaches to the Formation, Maintenance, and Transformation of Stereotypes* (pp. 59–92.). New York: Erlbaum.

McAndrew, F. T. (2018). Gossip as a social skill. In F. Giardini & R. Wittek (Eds.), *Handbook of gossip and reputation*. New York: Oxford University Press.

McAndrew, F. T., Bell, E. K. and Garcia C. M. (2007). Who do we tell and whom do we tell on? Gossip as a strategy for status enhancement. *Journal of Applied Social Psychology 37*(7), 1562–1577.

Mesoudi, A., Whiten, A., & Dunbar, R. (2006). A bias for social information in human cultural transmission. *British Journal of Psychology 97*(3), 405–423.

Moore, H. T. (1922). Further data concerning sex differences. *Journal of Abnormal Psychology and Social Psychology 4*, 81–89.

Moskowitz, D. S., & Schwarz, J. C. (1982). Validity comparison of behavior counts and ratings by knowledgeable informants. *Journal of Personality and Social Psychology 42*(3), 518–528.

Naish, J. (1978). Desirade: A negative case. In P. Caplan & J. M. Burja (Eds.), *Women united women divided. Cross cultural perspectives on female solidarity.* (pp. 38–258). London: Tavistock.

Norman, W. T. (1963). Toward an adequate taxonomy of personality attributes: Replicated factor structure in peer nomination personality ratings. *Journal of Abnormal and Social Psychology 66*(6), 574–583.

Norman, W. T. (1967). *2,800 personality trait descriptors: Normative operating characteristics for a university population.* Michigan: Department of Psychology, University of Michigan.

Nowak, M., & Sigmund, K. (2005). Evolution of indirect reciprocity. *Nature 437,* 1291–1298.

Oakley, A. (1972). *Sex, gender and society.* London: Temple Smith.

Oh, I.-S., Wang, G., & Mount, M. K. (2011). Validity of observer ratings of the five-factor model of personality traits: A meta-analysis. *Journal of Applied Psychology 94,* 762–773.

Panchanathan, K., & Boyd, R. (2004). Indirect reciprocity can stabilize cooperation without the second-order free rider problem. *Nature 432,* 499–502.

Peabody, D., & Goldberg, L. R. (1989). Some determinants of factor structures from personality-trait descriptors. *Journal of Personality and Social Psychology 57*(3), 552–567.

Peters, K., & Kashima, Y. (2015). Bad habit or social good? How perceptions of gossiper morality are related to gossip content. *European Journal of Social Psychology 45*(6), 784–798.

Piazza, J., & Bering, J. M. (2008). Concerns about reputation via gossip promote generous allocations in an economic game. *Evolution and Human Behavior 29*(3), 172–178.

Reis, H. T., & Gable, S. L. (2000). Event-sampling and other methods for studying everyday experience. In H. T. Reis & C. M. Judd (Eds.). *Handbook of Research Methods in Social and Personality Psychology* (pp. 190–222). Cambridge: Cambridge University Press.

Roethlisberger, Jules, F., & Dickson, W. J. (1939). *Management and the worker: Technical vs. social organization in an industrial plant.* Cambridge, MA: Harvard University Press.

Ross, E. A. (1901). *Social control: A survey of the foundations of order.* New York: The Macmillan Company.

Seabright, P. (2004). *The company of strangers: A natural history of economic life.* Princeton, NJ: Princeton University Press.

Schein, S. (1994). Used and abused: Gossip in medieval society. In R. F. Goodman & A. Ben Ze'ev (Eds.), *Good gossip* (pp. 139–153). Lawrence, KS: University of Kansas Press.

Sherif, M. (1936). *The psychology of social norms.* New York: Harper.

Smith, E. R. (2014). Evil acts and malicious gossip: A multiagent model of the effects of gossip in socially distributed person perception. *Personality and Social Psychology Review 18*(4), 311–325.

Spacks, P. M. (1985). *Gossip.* New York: Knopf.

Stasser, G., & Titus, W. (1985). Pooling of unshared information in group decision making: Biased information sampling during discussion. *Journal of Personality and Social Psychology 48*(6), 1467–1478.

Stiff, C., & Van Vugt, M. (2008). The power of reputations: The role of third party information in the admission of new group members. *Group Dynamics: Theory, Research, and Practice 12*(2), 155–166.

Thompson, M. S., Judd, C. M., & Park, B. (2000). The consequences of communicating social stereotypes. *Journal of Experimental Social Psychology 36*(6), 567–599.

Tomasello, M., & Vaish, A. (2013). Origins of human cooperation and morality. *Annual Review of Psychology 64,* 231–255.

Tonnies, F. (1887). *Community and society.* New York: Harper.

Travers, J., & Milgram, S. (1969). An experimental study of the small world problem. *Sociometry 32*(4), 425–443.

Trivers, R. L. (1971). The evolution of reciprocal altruism. *Quarterly Review of Biology 46*(1), 35–57.

Turner, M. M., Mazur, M. A., Wendel, N., & Winslow, R. (2003). Relational ruin or social glue? The joint effect of relationship type and gossip valence on liking, trust, and expertise. *Communication Monographs 70*(2), 129–141.

Vaish, A., Herrmann, E., Markmann, C., & Tomasello, M. (2016). Preschoolers value those who sanction non-cooperators. *Cognition 153*, 43–51.

Vazire, S. (2010). Who knows what about a person? The self–other knowledge asymmetry (SOKA) model. *Journal of Personality and Social Psychology 98* (2), 281–300.

Vernon, P. E. (1933). The biosocial nature of the personality trait. *Psychological Review 40*(6), 533–548.

Wellman, B. (1979). The community question: The intimate networks of East Yorkers. *American Journal of Sociology 84*(5), 1201–1231.

Wheeler, L., & Nezlek, J. (1977). Sex differences in social participation. *Journal of Personality and Social Psychology 35*(10), 742–754.

Wilson, D., Wilczynski, C., Wells, A., & Weiser, L. (2000). Gossip and other aspects of language as group-level adaptations. In C. Heyes (Ed.), *The Evolution of Cognition* (pp. 347–365). Cambridge, MA: MIT Press.

Wilson, E. O. (1975). *Sociobiology: The new synthesis.* Cambridge, MA: Harvard University Press.

Winder, C. L., & Wiggins, J. S. (1964). Social reputation and social behavior: A further validation of the peer nomination inventory. *Journal of Abnormal and Social Psychology 68*(6), 681–684.

Wirth, L. (1938). Urbanism as a way of life. *American Journal of Sociology 44*(1), 1–24.

Wu, J., Balliet, D., & Van Lange, P. A. M. (2016). Reputation management: Why and how gossip enhances generosity. *Evolution and Human Behavior 37*(3), 193–201.

Young, M., & Wilmott, P. (1957). *Family and kinship in East London.* Harmondsworth: Penguin.

..................................................................................................

# CHAPTER 4

# REPUTATION IN MORAL PHILOSOPHY AND EPISTEMOLOGY

..................................................................................................

GLORIA ORIGGI

## INTRODUCTION
..................................................................................................

WE monitor the informational environment and catch reputational cues, gather signals from our informants, and develop our trustful attitudes in context. We monitor also our own behavior to send signals that contribute to build our reputation in the eyes of other people. Reputation is a way of acquiring knowledge and a way of managing our image. This central feature of our cognitive and social life is emerging in informationally dense, hyperconnected societies as a fundamental social commodity that orientates our social interactions and our epistemic practices, such as evaluating information or choosing a doctor. Yet the very nature of this commodity needs to be defined more precisely. Although reputation is a concept already in use in many branches of social science, as this Handbook shows, it still lacks a sound philosophical definition and an appropriate conceptual analysis. What is "reputation"? Is it a social value that motivates our action, a measurable quantity that indicates the value of other people and things, a collective cognitive state, a cloud of opinions that influences how social information circulates? Reputation seems shrouded in a mystery: the reasons it waxes or wanes and the criteria that define it as good or bad often appear fortuitous and arbitrary. Yet reputation is also ubiquitous. On the one hand, we care intensely about the opinion of others, sometimes to the point of committing irrational acts in a bootless effort to determine how others see us. On the other hand, we rely on reputation to guide our choice of doctors, newspapers, websites, and even ideas. It seems to insinuate itself into the most intimate recesses of our existence. Yet reputation has been inexplicably neglected by philosophy: no entries until recently in philosophical dictionaries, few scholarly monographs devoted to the concept (Origgi, 2018). Apart from some rare mentions of the concept in the literature on classical moralists, contemporary philosophy seems to dismiss the notion as a vestige of pre-modern and anti-individualist societies where "fama", honor, and the effort to win and maintain prestige in a social hierarchy played a pivotal role that modernity has allegedly demolished. Reputation nevertheless remains critically important to the many challenges of contemporary society. The way in which it is created, managed, earned, and lost; the biases that influence our ways of reading reputations, its reliability, and influence will be the subject of this chapter on the philosophical foundations of reputation.

In this chapter, I tackle reputation both as a sociocognitive and a motivational attitude. Reputation is a special kind of social information: it is social information about the value of people, systems, and processes that release information. Reputation is also the informational trace of our actions: it is the credibility that an agent or an item earns through repeated interactions. This social track of ourselves is a constant feedback of the social effects of our actions that motivates us in acting in certain ways. If interactions are repeated, reputation may conventionalize in "seals of approval" or disapproval or social stigmas.

Reputation is thus an epistemological resource to navigate the social world by extracting social information from other people's behavior and gossip (who says what to whom) and also a motivational resource for individual and collective behavior: if I am aware that my actions leave a reputational track that can be read by others and influences my credibility, I will be motivated in developing strategies of management of my "image" in order to control my reputation in the eyes of others.

This chapter aims at (1) providing a conceptual analysis of the notion that can unify its different uses in different areas of social science; (2) connecting the philosophical tradition on "symbolic motivations" (honor, vanity, sympathy) to the contemporary reflection on reputation; (3) critically assessing other theories of "symbolic motivation," such the quest of esteem and honor, in contemporary moral philosophy; and (4) presenting some rudiments of an *epistemology of reputation*, that is, the possible uses of reputation to extract information from the social world.

My philosophical inquiry on what reputation is can be framed by these two main questions: (1) Is reputation a rational motivation for action? (2) Is reputation a rational justification for coming to believe new information? My answer to both questions is positive: reputation *can* be a rational motivation for action and a rational justification of belief, if we come to understand the social dimension of our actions and beliefs as essentially constitutive of our moral and epistemic life.

But let me start with a brief review of the concept in the history of philosophy.

# REPUTATION IN THE HISTORY
# OF PHILOSOPHY

The few reflections in the history of philosophy about reputation are to be found in the domain of *moral philosophy*. Between the fifteenth and the seventeenth century in Europe, a rich tradition of *moralist writings* develops, especially in Italy and France. These writings explore the human passions and vices, give up to the idea of constructing an ideal image of the human being, and favor a realistic portrait of our deepest motivations. *The Prince* of Machiavelli, published in 1532, is one of the first texts in which *reputation* is considered as an instrument of power for the prince: he must care about his reputation and conceive his strategies to earn a good reputation even through mean actions. Machiavelli insists on the importance of concentrating the evil in just one action (e.g., a big massacre of opponents to the regime) while slowly distributing good actions, because what is important is what people will remember, and they will forget a single bad action quickly and will attach a positive reputation to the government who continues to distribute good things.

Many other authors, among whom Montagne, La Bruyère, La Rochefoucauld, Pascal, wrote about one of the most dangerous human passions: *l'amour-propre* (vanity), that is, when esteem depends on the opinion of others, a concept that is very close to that of reputation. Jean-Jacques Rousseau contrasts *amour-propre,* that is, a form of love for oneself that depends on others, and *amour-de-soi* (self-love), a more primitive and natural form of love for oneself that our survival and happiness depend on. In his *Discourse upon the Origin and the Foundation of Inequality among Mankind,* Rousseau explains the origins of inequality among men as in the emergence of a distinction between what men are and how they are perceived by others and in the need to be esteemed:

> Men no sooner began to set a value upon each other, and know *what esteem was,* than each laid claim to it, and it was no longer safe for any man to refuse it to another. Hence the first duties of civility and politeness, even among savages; and hence every voluntary injury became an affront, as besides the mischief, which resulted from it as an injury [....] It was requisite for men to be *thought what they really were not.* To be and to appear became two very different things, and from this distinction sprang pomp and knavery, and all the vices which form their train.    (Rousseau, 1754)

Thus, according to Rousseau (even if he doesn't use the word), the quest for esteem and the distinction between our self and our social existence are the two aspects that make reputation a crucial ingredient to grow a society, even if he sees them as vicious passions that corrupt the good nature of human being.

In his *Elements of Law and Natural Politics,* Thomas Hobbes defines "honor" as a fundamental *comparative passion,* that is, something that has value only insofar it is acknowledged by others:

> The signs of honour are those by which we perceive that one man acknowledges the power and worth of another. Such as these: To praise; to magnify; to bless, or call happy; to pray or supplicate to; to thank; to offer unto or present; to obey; to hearken to with attention; to speak to with consideration; to approach unto in decent manner, to keep distance from; to give the way to, and the like; which are the honour the inferior gives to the superior.    (Hobbes, 1640)

The fundamental feature of reputation, that is, being the part of ourselves that depends on the judgments of the others, and its role in the maintenance of social relations was thus already acknowledged by these classical authors.

But it is Adam Smith, moral philosopher and founder of modern economics, who first recognizes the central role of reputation in coordinating social interactions. In Adam Smith's liberal social theory, reputation is considered as a way of coordinating activities in a decentralized social space of transactions. According to Smith, in a free society, markets coordinate diffused knowledge in an asymmetrical way: people have a partial view of what other people know and how they will act. Also, given that most transactions occur over a lapse of time, parties have to trust each other that they will satisfy their reciprocal interest. These informational and temporal asymmetries call for efficient means of storing and retrieving information about possible partners in interactions. Reputation is more than pure information: it is evaluated information—a shortcut of the many judgements and interpretations that people have cumulated about an actor. That is why people are interested in keeping a "good" reputation by signaling to potential business partners their trustworthiness. In his *Theory of Moral Sentiments*, Smith famously states:

> The success of most people almost always depends upon the favor and the good opinion of their neighbors and equals; and without a tolerably regular conduct these can very seldom be obtained. The good old proverb, therefore, that honesty is the best policy, holds, in such situations, almost perfectly true.   (Smith, 1759)

For Smith, a good reputation pays in the marketplace. If you are a reliable player, your business will thrive because your potential clients will form positive expectations about your actions in the future based on your records. Reputation is thus, in this tradition, a cognitive notion: it is the expectation about your future actions that agents form, given your past behavior. Your past records are a signal of your future intentions, a signal on which people can rely if they decide to interact with you. Yet Although Smith endorses a vision of reputation as advantageous cooperation, in other passages of the *Theory of Moral Sentiments*, he puts forward another view of reputation, one based on the human passion for sympathy and more related to the Hobbesian concept of honor or Rousseau's idea of self-love as a basic need for recognition:

> Nature, when she formed man for society, endowed him with an original desire to please, and an original aversion to offend his brethren. She taught him to feel pleasure in their favorable and pain in their unfavorable regard. She rendered their approbation most flattering and most agreeable to him for its own sake; and their disapprobation most mortifying and most offensive.   (Smith, 1759)

And again: "It is the vanity, not the ease or the pleasure, that interests us." In this second sense, Adam Smith puts reputation into the family of social passions, such as honor, glory, esteem, and recognition, as in the classical moral tradition we have seen earlier.

The development of contemporary social sciences such as economic, social, and behavioral sciences made Smith's first interpretation of reputation—that is, the idea that *reputation pays*—triumph. Reputation is thus treated in the contemporary literature in game theory, market theory, and rational choice theory as a form of indirect *interest* instead of a social passion. We care about our reputation because we have an interest in doing this. The moralist tradition has been basically forgotten as a vestige of pre-modern philosophy where passions had not been already submitted to interest (Hirschman, 1977). Until recently, reputation has been considered mainly within the paradigm of strategic rationality, as an interested strategy to cumulate social and economic advantages. We will come back in the next section to some recent treatments of reputation in moral philosophy that consider it as an ultimate aim, in line with the classical moralists, not reducible to any strategic quest for gains.

# REPUTATION AS A MOTIVATION FOR ACTION

This section explores a different paradigm than that of strategic rationality that can account for our care of reputation without reducing it to a form of indirect interest. But let me first introduce briefly the mainstream paradigm that considers reputation as interest.

## Altruism and Reputation

One of the conundrums of the theories of human action based on rational self-interest is that of explaining altruistic actions (Wittek, Snijders, and Nee, 2013). Why should selfish individuals invest time and energy to helping others, even people they won't interact with again? Is altruism rationally possible?

In his celebrated 1971 article, "The Evolution of Reciprocal Altruism," the sociobiologist Robert Trivers showed that natural selection can explain altruism in a way compatible with the selfish rationality of agents. An altruistic gesture, such as saving someone from drowning, allows the agent to accumulate a positive *reputation* and thereby creates in the beneficiary of the altruistic act a moral-emotional pressure to reciprocate in the future. In other words, altruists expose themselves to momentary risks contrary to their short-term interests because they are anticipating future gains. The pervasiveness of this hope to obtain future benefits from acts of seemingly self-denying generosity has been amply confirmed by experimental economics, which conducts laboratory studies on the behavior of agents asked to follow simple rules of interaction and transaction. In the *dictator game*, for instance, one experimental subject receives a sum of money that he can divide however he wishes with a second participant (see Engel, 2011, for a meta-review of the literature on Dictator Game; see also Roddie, this volume; and Milinski, this volume). The two subjects do not know each other. Yet the dictator, that is, the individual who can unilaterally decide how to distribute the money, seldom acts in a wholly self-interested way. On average, he or she gives at least 20 percent of the original sum to the other participant. This shows, according to behavioral economists, that human beings expect to be able to draw some benefit from behaving at least "somewhat" generously (Henrich et al. 2004).

The principal benefit they anticipate receiving is *a good reputation*. This approach thus reduces reputation to a sort of *indirect interest*: it is the strategic anticipation of the benefits related to having a good reputation that motivates the agent. What I would like to explore here is a different approach: Is it ever possible to be motivated *only* by reputation as an ultimate end and not as a mean to get an interested result? When people care, for example, for their reputation after their death, and act in order to maximize their reputation afterlife (such as by making donations), are they to be considered as acting in a sort of indirectly interested way or can we try to explain their acts by appealing to their care of reputation? Let us see if it possible to frame a theory of reputation as an ultimate end instead of one of means.

In what sense can our care for reputation be an ultimate motivation for action? To answer this question, we need a theory of action that treats reputation as an independent variable; in other words, as a factor that, when varied, causes subsequent actions to vary accordingly. Examples include moral theories arguing that individuals act morally not from a love of justice but with an eye to how others will judge them. Among economic theories, the most relevant are those that interpret reputation as a scarce resource and that see demand for this scarce resource as a constraint on behavior.

From a philosophical perspective, we need a slightly different ontology of the agents and their motivations. For this purpose, let me introduce some elements of an ontology of *homo comparativus*, the human animal whose decisions and actions hinge on relations with others and whose choices and actions are driven by a crying need for recognition and approval by others.

Not only are human beings competitive and cooperative (Baumard, André, and Sperber, 2013), but they are also "comparative," that is to say, born and bred to draw comparisons and contrasts between themselves and others. Their actions and achievements mean nothing unless and until they are compared with the achievements and actions of others and are assessed according to some generally applicable scale of values. Value—be it moral, economic, or epistemic—is created through contextually specified differentiations. It exists by virtue of a normative contrast made manifest through comparison. Value is not inherent in things or persons themselves. Rather, like images reflected ad infinitum in two facing mirrors, value is wholly relational. It originates in the relationship between things or persons. It is the autonomous product of comparative exchange; and it has no other purpose or significance. We create value to create value. Value cannot be reduced to other pre-existent factors, such as utility, scarcity, or labor as understood in economics. It is the cognitive footprint and the matrix of opinions that all human interaction engenders and that structures the perceptions we have of ourselves and others. We can grasp reality only on the basis of a scale of values that presupposes a hierarchically organized world. But this unavoidable perspective on the world is not solely sociocultural. It is also rooted in our physiology of perception. Our perceptual faculties are structured to detect variations in the environment (Kahneman and Tversky, 1981). The way our organs of perception process information depends on discrepancies between qualities or attributes within any given context. Our perceptual apparatus is designed to register differences, focusing on variations, disparities, and incongruities to identify the salient characteristics of what we perceive. This essentially comparative nature can be found at all levels of our psychology: perceptual, cognitive, and social (Festinger, 1954; Suls and Wheeler, 2013; Gibbons and Buunk, 1999).

A hard-wired *comparative consciousness* is one of the most distinctive characteristics of human nature. It influences our perception of the world, our cognition, our emotions, and our decisions. We read the world through an evaluative prism. Our very sense of *objectivity* presupposes a hierarchy of values. This does not mean that the world around us does not exist or that it is completely relative to our point of view. Evaluative distinctions are inscribed in the relational dimension of our world, in the plethora of social networks that knit together our reality and that permit us to extract information from the world. These networks are constitutive of the world. In that sense, there is no humanly accessible ultimate reality lying beyond or behind the experienced interconnection of events. It is thanks to these relations that we perceive the world and that information acquires salience, meaning, and value. It is on this essential comparative dimension of our judgment that contemporary theories of reputation as a motivation for action are based.

## Reputation and Esteem

In developing the rudiments of an *economy of esteem* (or *kudonomia*, from the Greek for "glory" or "acclaim"), the philosopher Philip Pettit and the economist Geoffrey Brennan have identified two sides of esteem: the *comparative* and the *directive* (Brennan and Pettit, 2004). Esteem is comparative because, most of the time, the intensity of esteem depends not on an absolute ranking but on a ranking relative to others: "x does better than y along this dimension." But esteem is also "directive" because expressing esteem for others encourages them, in numerous situations, to behave in a way that will earn our further esteem. The evaluative nature of esteem is therefore double. On the one hand, esteem is evaluative because it implies a ranking of better and worse. On the other hand, it is normative because it involves a value-judgment, distinguishing actions that merit esteem from those that merit contempt or disapproval and thereby implicitly encouraging action that will predictably earn esteem rather than scorn. The quest for esteem can thus for them be an essential motivation, not a further reducible form of interest. Although Brennan and Pettit apply standard micro-economic theory to model the implications of this assumption, arguing for example, that individuals will engage in actions that improve their reputation and avoid those that reduce it, they do not reduce the quest for esteem to any form of indirect interest. People look for esteem because they like to be esteemed by others, not because their interests will be best served if they have a good reputation.

Although this approach is one of the few that considers the quest for esteem and reputation as an ultimate aim that motivates action, their theory doesn't consider an important dimension of reputation; that is, its *communicative* dimension. Our reputations are clouds of social representations of ourselves that circulate through gossip and the various forms of "formal" and "informal" communication. In Pettit and Brennan's model, esteem is a *linear* quantity; that is, the esteem we receive is directly proportional to the estimability of our act. Yet reputation and esteem are essentially *nonlinear*. We launch a signal of our good intentions to earn esteem by others but we are never sure of the result: the signal doesn't reach the target linearly, it breaks out into many bits of information that circulate because they depend on communication: they are propagated by networks and depend on the differing levels of prestige of the authorities who accord their esteem. Standard linear situations, in fact, where the action of the agent is taken at its face value, and thus the agent can expect to be estimated as he would like to be just from behaving in a way that carries esteem from his social environment, are the exception rather than the rule. The mechanisms through which esteem circulates in a society are more complex. Also, we never accord esteem autonomously, without regard to the way others may morally praise or condemn any particular decision to grant esteem. Indeed, most of my allocations of esteem echo authorities whom I believe to be "competent" at evaluating the esteem-worthiness of an action or person.

Thus, Brennan and Pettit's theory, although is one of the most advanced attempts in contemporary philosophy to provide a theory of reputation as a motivation for action, doesn't fully capture the complexities of the phenomenon. We are motivated by reputation and esteem because we defer to the authority and the prestige of other people in conforming to a certain behavioral norm. Our quest for reputation is thus indissociable to the prestige we attribute to our judges and the way their prestige is earned depends on a complex socio-communicative network.

## Reputation and Honor

We care about our reputation and invest time and energy to defend our "honor," that is, the image of ourselves that we think other people owe us to respect. As we have seen, honor is a possible candidate for a theory of moral action that takes into account our reputational concerns. Although honor is usually considered as a pre-modern motivation for action, typical of the values of chivalry and heroism of the aristocratic world, a number of philosophers claim today that honor can still be a motivation in a contemporary, disenchanted world.

In moral philosophy, Stephen Darwall and Antony Appiah (Appiah, 2010, Darwall, 2013) have "rehabilitated" honor in contemporary moral theories, again, by considering it as an ultimate motivation that is not reducible to interested strategies.

Although honor is often dismissed as a premodern norm, Appiah argues that it remains an important motivation for moral action. To make his case, he focuses on three historical episodes of moral revolution: the discontinuation of dueling in Great Britain, the abandonment of foot-binding in China, and the end of the trans-Atlantic slave trade. In all three cases, traditional moral practices were upended in a remarkably short span of time even though the rupture was neither enforced by explicit new legal prohibitions nor accompanied by a genuine shift in moral sentiments. Although every one of these practices had been criticized earlier on moral grounds, they nevertheless had survived in social habits and personal conduct. At a certain moment, however, they suddenly and completely collapsed. What these three examples of moral revolution have in common, according to Appiah, is that each was motivated by *honor*. Moral revolutions occur, according to Appiah, when an implicit honor code emerges with the following dual purpose: to give honor or respect to the victims of the moral practice being overturned and to gain honor or respectability for those who boldly acknowledge the (previously besmirched) honor of these victims. As he says: "So, honor is no decaying vestige of a premodern order; it is, for us, what it has always been, an engine, fueled by the dialogue between our self-conceptions and the regard of others, that can drive us to take seriously our responsibilities in a world we share"(Appiah, 2010).

Yet our need to have our esteem for others reciprocated is not only a desire to be loved and recognized by others. It is also a strategy of social cognition. It represents a search for external feedback to strengthen our confidence in our evaluative choices. If those I esteem also esteem me—at least to some extent—then I am presumably on the right track when making value judgments about the social world around me. Admittedly, this self-reinforcing exchange of esteem for esteem can lead to vicious circles. Like La Fontaine's fox who convinces himself that the plump red grapes before his eyes are not yet ripe simply because he cannot reach them, we sometimes withhold or withdraw our esteem from those who fail to reciprocate. With all due respect to Groucho Marx, who didn't care to join any club that would have him as a member, we routinely seek to integrate ourselves into social groups that we admire and that, at the same time, treat us respectfully. As for Pettit and Brennan's analysis of esteem, Appiah's notion of honor as a motivation doesn't consider a fundamental component of this symbolic resource: its circulation. We want to be honored by those whom we honor in a circle of mutual recognition that allows social norms to stabilize and thrive.

These recent approaches based on "symbolic commodities" such as esteem and honor go toward the direction of a theory of reputation as a rational motivation for action. Yet the struggle for prestige and recognition is therefore always two-sided. When we act in a way that displays our esteem for others we are establishing social hierarchies; but, in doing so, we are also changing our own social position. Can reputation, esteem, and honor function as motivations for actions? The answer is "Yes," to the extent that granting and being granted a reputation are two faces of the same dynamic. It is the process by which we all seek and find our relative place in the shifting social worlds we inhabit.

# Reputation as a Rational Justification for Belief

Let us turn now to the second main question of this chapter, that is, if reputation can be a rational mean to extract information from the environment. Although this may seem highly counterintuitive for philosophers who think that *cognitive autonomy* is one of the key features of knowledge, that is, you know only those facts which you have either directly experienced or you have inferred from other experiences in a rational way, the cognitive overload of information in which we all live now requires an extension of our traditional epistemological means, thus including reputation as social information about the judgements of others as a rational means of acquiring knowledge.

Quality uncertainty and informational asymmetries have become crucial epistemological issues in contemporary information-dense societies. The vast amount of information available on the Internet and in the media makes the problem of reliability and credibility of information a central issue in the management of knowledge. Items that do not come with some label, or seal of approval from the appropriate communities, are lost in the data deluge of the information age.

From the evaluator's perspective—the agent who has to filter information—reputation has thus an informational value. Reputation is a relation between an agent or an item and the set of social and cultural representations of the agent or the item. It may be useful here to distinguish between *cultural representations* and social representations. A cultural representation is a cognitive artefact that is typically stored in a community. It represents the *shared knowledge* of that community. In this sense it is a "metarepresentational" phenomenon; that is, a representation of a representation that is socially distributed. Each one in that particular community is supposed to share a certain number of representations that are considered *common knowledge* (Sperber, 1996; 2000). Thus, I judge your reputation through a social representation that is not only generated by our ongoing interaction, but also by cultural representations that have previously been attached to you, that have circulated about you, and that are held by people I trust or to whom I defer. Having a reputation is thus being attached to an evaluative representation of ourselves that is socially and culturally generated and stabilized (Sperber et al. 2010). A reputation is the shortcut of the many strategies, heuristics, and evaluations that have positioned a person or an item in a certain hierarchical configuration. As we have seen, reputation is not only a cognitive notion, but also a social and cultural notion that has to do with the way in which the social environment is organized: it spreads through networks, cumulates through ratings, and manifests various effects that are independent of our cognition.

Reputation serves the cognitive purpose of making us navigate among things and people whose value is opaque for us because we do not know enough about them. We use seals, scales, grades, indexes, and classifications not only to evaluate them, but also to create valuable categories that allow us to classify reality. The very act of classifying entities orders them according to the reputational rankings that sometimes are already available in our culture and sometimes are ad hoc artefacts that organize a space of discrimination. Let us start with the timeline of "classification" and "evaluation." When we think about categorization, we commonly view taxonomies as cognitive tools that describe objective relations and properties between classes and objects. Taxonomies, then, provide an ontological structure for a domain. Evaluative tools come afterward to impose a ranking on these items. Contrasting this classical picture of knowledge organization, I would like to argue that reputation is prior to classification. In many epistemic practices, we use rating systems to categorize and classify items. Our capacity of organizing our thoughts about how the world is structured and conceiving appropriate institution would be much more limited without the contribution of the preferences already aggregated in the past by others. In this sense, cultural representations help reduce cognitive complexity. Another important aspect of reputational and rating systems is that they combine two types of information for the sake of knowledge organization and evaluation: (1) information about the *fact* of the matter (for example, perceptual information about the taste of wine, factual information about the wine region), and (2) *social* information about people and past interactions; that is, what people have said about a particular product and how the cultural representations of that product are conveyed in a series of labels, signs, and received discourses (as, for example, the cultural representations of a particular wine that we may infer from its label on the bottle). One of the examples I have analyzed elsewhere of the interplay between reputation and classification is the system of *classification of wines* (Origgi, 2007).

The presence of these "reputational devices," that is the complex sociocultural mechanisms that organize social information, is a necessary condition for any acquisition of information: the unbiased interaction with the external world, an image so dear to the traditional epistemology, is an unrealistic limit-case of a subject in contact with a reality not filtered by others. Without the presence of filters, of already existing evaluations that shape a corpus of knowledge, we would face the impossible task of *Bouvard et Pécuchet*, the two heroes of Flaubert who decided to retire and to go through every known discipline without, in the end, being able to learn anything.

Preferences, conventions, and values that others have expressed thus play a central epistemic role in the making of knowledge: they shape the reputational landscape that we use to organize our own heuristics to extract information and provide a sometimes reliable and sometimes too biased shortcut to what is worth keeping, remembering, and preserving as knowledge. The epistemological enquiry I am advocating here implies that reputation and rating systems are an *essential ingredient* of knowledge. Reputation *is* a rational criterion of information extraction, a fundamental shortcut for cumulating knowledge in processes of collective wisdom, and an ineludible filter to access facts. In an environment where sources are in constant competition to get attention and the option of the direct verification of the information is simply not available at reasonable costs, evaluation and rankings are epistemic tools and cognitive practices that provide an inevitable shortcut to information. This is especially striking in contemporary, informationally overloaded societies, but I think it is a permanent feature of any extraction of information from a corpus of knowledge. There is no ideal knowledge that we can adjudicate without the access to previous evaluations and adjudications of others. No Robinson Crusoe's minds that investigate and manipulate the world in a perfect solitude. The higher the uncertainty is on the content of information, the stronger the weight of the opinions of others is to establish the quality of this content.

# CONCLUSION

In this chapter on the philosophical foundations of reputation, I have advanced a definition of the concept of "reputation" suitable for philosophical purposes, that is, as *social
information* that spreads from our actions to a myriad of representations that circulate
about us. I have argued for this definition by trying to answer to two main questions
that a philosophy of reputation puts forward: (1) Is reputation a rational motivation for
action? (2) Is reputation a rational justification for belief? I positively answer both questions, thus putting reputation at the core of a plausible theory of our actions and beliefs.

Although the systematic study of reputation in philosophy is at its beginnings, a
relevant literature already exists that I have reviewed here about its role as a rational
motivation for action and its epistemological role as an information filter. Further
research in philosophy and social science could benefit from a clearer perspective on
what it means to "count" or have significance in the minds of others. The cognitive order
in which the world is given is not separable from its social order; that is, from the judgment of others and the way they influence our perception of ourselves and of the world.

# REFERENCES

Appiah, Anthony. 2010. *The Honor Code: How Moral Revolutions Happen.* 1st ed. New York: W. W. Norton.
Baumard Nicolas, André Jean Baptiste, and Sperber Dan. 2013. "A Mutualistic Approach to Morality: The Evolution of Fairness by Partner Choice." *The Behavioral and Brain Sciences* 36 (1): 59–78.
Brennan, H. Geoffrey, and Phillip Pettit. 2004. *The Economy of Esteem: An Essay on Civil and Political Society.* Oxford: Oxford University Press.
Darwall, Stephen L. 2013. *Honor, History, and Relationship: Essays in Second-Personal Ethics II.* Oxford: Oxford University Press.
Engel, Christoph. 2011. "Dictator Games: A Meta Study." *Experimental Economics: A Journal of the Economic Science Association* 14 (4): 583–610.
Festinger, Leon. 2016. "A Theory of Social Comparison Processes." *Human Relations* 7 (2): 117–140.
Gibbons, Frederick X., and Bram P. Buunk. 1999. "Individual Differences in Social Comparison: Development of a Scale of Social Comparison Orientation." *Journal of Personality and Social Psychology* 76 (1): 129–142.
Henrich, Joseph, Boyd, Robert, Samuel Bowles, Colin Camerer, Ernst Fehr, and Herbert Gintis. 2004. *Foundations of Human Sociality: Economic Experiments and Ethnographic Evidence from Fifteen Small-Scale Societies.* Oxford: Oxford University Press.
Hirschman, Albert O. 1977. *The Passions and the Interests: Political Arguments for Capitalism before Its Triumph.* Princeton, NJ: Princeton University Press.
Hobbes, Thomas, and J. C. A. Gaskin. 1640/1994. *The Elements of Law, Natural and Politic: Part I, Human Nature, Part II, De Corpore Politico; with Three Lives.* World's Classics. Oxford; Oxford University Press.

Milinski, Manfred. 2019. "Gossip and Reputation in Social Dilemmas." In Francesca Giardini and Rafael Wittek (Eds.), *Handbook of Gossip and Reputation*. New York: Oxford University Press.

Origgi, Gloria. 2007. "Wine Epistemology: The Role of Reputational and Ranking Systems in the World of Wine." In Barry C. Smith (Ed.), Questions of Taste. The Philosophy of Wine, 183–197. Oxford: Signal Books.

Origgi, Gloria. 2012. "A Social Epistemology of Reputation." *Social Epistemology* 26 (3–4): 399–418.

Origgi, Gloria. 2018. *Reputation. What it is and why it matters*, Princeton, NJ: Princeton University Press.

Rousseau, Jean Jacques. 1754. *Discourse on the Origins of Inequality*, Second Part, in *The Major Political Writings of Jean-Jacques Rousseau.: The Two "Discourses" and the "Social Contract"*, 95–96. Chicago: University of Chicago Press, 2012.

Smith, Adam, and Knud Haakonssen. 1759/2002. *The Theory of Moral Sentiments*. 1 online resource (xxxi, 411 pp.). Cambridge Texts in the History of Philosophy. Cambridge: Cambridge University Press. Cambridge Books Online http://dx.doi.org/10.1017/CBO9780511800153.

Sperber, Dan. 1996. *Explaining Culture: A Naturalistic Approach*. Oxford: Blackwell.

Sperber, Dan. 2000. *Metarepresentations: A Multidisciplinary Perspective*. 1 online resource (448 pp.). Vancouver Studies in Cognitive Science, vol. 10. Oxford: Oxford University Press.

Sperber, Dan, Fabrice Clément, Christophe Heintz, Olivier Mascaro, Hugo Mercier, Gloria Origgi, and Deirdre Wilson. 2010. "Epistemic Vigilance." *Mind & Language* 25 (4): 359–393.

Suls, Jerry, and Ladd Wheeler, Eds. 2000. *Handbook of Social Comparison: Theory and Research*. The Plenum Series in Social/Clinical Psychology, 1. New York: Kluwer.

Trivers, Robert L. 1971. "The Evolution of Reciprocal Altruism." *The Quarterly Review of Biology* 46 (1): 35–57.

Tversky, Amos, and Kahneman, Daniel. 1981. "The Framing of Decisions and the Psychology of Choice." *Science* 211 (4481): 453–458.

Wittek, Rafael, Tom A. B. Snijders, and Victor Nee. 2013. *The Handbook of Rational Choice Social Research*. 1 online resource (xiii, 610 pp.) Stanford, California: Stanford Social Sciences, an imprint of Stanford University Press.

...................................................................................................

# CHAPTER 5

# GOSSIP, REPUTATION, AND LANGUAGE

...................................................................................................

HAYKAZ MANGARDICH
AND STANKA A. FITNEVA

## INTRODUCTION

In G. B. Shaw's *Pygmalion*, the protagonist Eliza Doolittle, a poor flower girl, is willing to pay the phonetician Professor Higgins two-fifths of her daily income for speech lessons. She articulates her motivation clearly: "I want to be a lady in a flower shop stead of selling at the corner of Tottenham Court Road. But they won't take me unless I can talk more genteel." One hundred years after *Pygmalion* premiered, the demand for accent modification, public speaking, and voice coaching services confirms the point: language can have a dramatic effect on one's relations and place in society.

Our social relations affect every aspect of our lives. We depend on others to learn the skills and knowledge required to survive and accomplish tasks outside our individual reach. We also depend on them for companionship and entertainment as well as indispensable goods and services. Yet human group living often puts an individual's interests in conflict with the group's interests and people vary in the likelihood of acting in ways that benefit the group (Ostrom, 1998). It is in this context that *reputation* serves as an important marker revealing an individual's personal qualities, intentions, and past actions within the group (Emler, 1990). Reputation is a "universal currency" (Milinski, 2016), providing members of a community with insight about whether an individual will behave cooperatively and in ways that align with the group norms.

Our goal in this chapter is to provide evidence that illustrates the complex and nuanced ways humans use language to construct and manipulate their own and others' relations and reputations. Understanding the links between language and reputation is important for at least two reasons. First, the unfolding of language and conversational exchanges in time helps explain the probabilistic nature of different acts on reputation. Second, this understanding helps to illuminate the task that children face in becoming competent participants in their communities, which consists of, in part, mastering the linguistic devices required for reputation management. Although the ability to share evaluative information appears to be present at the preschool age (Engelmann, Herrmann, and Tomasello, 2016; for a review on gossip and reputation in childhood development see Ingram, this volume), we know very little about how it develops and what strategies children use to enhance the impact of their gossip on reputation.

In the remainder of the Introduction, we set up the rest of our discussion by briefly defining reputation and gossip and considering the question of how language may be affected by its evolutionary links with the human reputation system. In the following three sections of the chapter, we first situate the study of gossip and reputation with respect to different approaches to the study of language. Then we shift our focus to reputation-related features of language. Finally, we highlight some aspects of the structure of gossip episodes.

## The Concepts of Reputation and Gossip

An individual's reputation encompasses the opinions and beliefs others hold about the individual's behavior, personality, and physical characteristics. Reputation is important because it affects the individual's relationships and place in the group's social network. Whether a person is strong, tough, loyal, shy, cheery, trustworthy, unscrupulous, and competent determines whether and why others seek or avoid that person. Being liked and included is related to the need to belong, and we experience the various forms of exclusion (from ostracism at work to the occasional perception of social isolation) as extreme punishment (Fiske, 2004). As reputation in one domain may affect reputation in other domains (the so-called 'halo' effect), a single event can have cumulative effects. haykaz' suggestion.

Gossip can be seen as a subset of reputation-related verbal behaviors, as it concerns the provision of evaluative information about absent third parties (Fine and Rosnow, 1978; Foster, 2004; Hallett, Harger and Eder, 2009). Defining gossip in this way contrasts it with other forms of social communication. First, gossip is not a purely narrative form of communication: it contains a decidedly evaluative component (Bergmann, 1993; Eder and Enke, 1991; Foster, 2004). Although the evaluation can be positive, most studies of gossip note that it has a negative, derogatory, or slanderous tone (Georgoudi and Rosnow, 1985). Second, gossip differs from other forms of evaluative talk such as insulting, ridicule, and teasing in that the target of the evaluation is not present (Eder and Enke, 1991). Not all third party talk is gossip though. For instance, discussing a student's performance at a parent–teacher conference is generally not considered gossip. In formal settings, the definition of gossip needs to be restricted to the *unsanctioned* discussion of others (Hallett et al., 2009). This preliminary sketch of the construct of gossip represents a number of investigative approaches and is sufficient to ground our discussion. As we will also show, gossip is not a phenomenon that can be easily restricted to a single assertion by a single individual. To explain how gossip influences the reputation of its target and conversation participants, a better unit of analysis is gossip *episodes*, which are segments of conversation.

## Evolutionary Links

A number of theories relate the evolution of language and the evolution of the human reputation system (e.g., Dunbar, 1997; Tomasello et al., 2012). For instance, Dunbar (1997, 2004) suggests that language may have evolved to support the reputation system needed by large human communities. Directly observing others' actions and behaviors provides valuable reputational information. However, as human social groups became larger, it became difficult for group members to keep track of other individuals through direct observation. Language may have evolved to overcome this difficulty, allowing individuals to keep track of what is going on within larger social networks. A more general position is that language evolved under pressure to support coordination between relative strangers in complex problem solving situations (Tomasello et al., 2012).

These theories raise a number of important questions. For example, are there features of language that are dedicated to reputation management? Unfortunately, questions such as this one are currently difficult, if not impossible, to answer. Thus, we do not address them here. The research we draw from focuses on the observable relations between language and the reputation system.

Regardless of how and why language evolved, symbolic communication enables in humans a much richer and qualitatively different reputation system from that in animals. It is qualitatively different in (1) its reach (speed and distance), (2) its impact on those involved, and (3) its flexibility—the options it provides to its experienced users in the construction of their own and other's qualities and behaviors. Animal signaling concerns an individual's properties and thus has reputational value (Zahavi, 1977). Some animals even engage in tactical deception (Byrne and Whiten, 1991). However, animal signals do not appear to afford the inferential richness that language affords, nor do they appear to afford gossip—the transmitting of reputational information about others.

## Gossip, Reputation, and the Study of Language

Gossip and reputation are inherently relational concepts. Not all approaches to studying language use align with such concepts. For instance, some theories of language and language processing consider meaning as contained in the linguistic expression itself and conversation as involving the encoding and decoding of messages. In this section, we leave these theories aside and introduce the three major theoretical approaches that have contributed to framing the linguistic study of gossip and reputation.

First, Grice (1975, 1957) proposed that speakers derive the meaning of each other's utterances based on a set of assumptions collectively termed the "Cooperative Principle." The set consists of four assumptions about conversational contributions, namely about their quality (they are truthful), quantity (they are informative given the context), relation to context (they are relevant), and the manner in which they are provided (clear, brief, and orderly). Grice argued that apparent violations of these assumptions trigger inferences to the nonliteral meaning of utterances. In other words, conversation participants aim to preserve the belief that speakers are cooperative with regard to information exchange. Grice's model (see also Sperber and Wilson, 1986) explains the richness of linguistic meaning. Crucially, by introducing the concept of "cooperation," even though at the level of computation of meaning, Grice paved the way to considering how speakers' relations are affected by the conversational exchange.

Second, the speech act theory developed by Austin (1962) and elaborated by Searle (1969) and others introduced the idea that in saying something, speakers *do* something (besides saying). For example, they promise, command, greet, protest, and apologize. Furthermore, speech affects addressees, for example, by influencing, scaring or inspiring them. Austin argued that speech acts are at the core of language and this theory contributed to the movement to equate the meaning of an expression with its use. Of particular importance to the topic of reputation is that speech acts highlight the relational and interactional aspects of communication. Doing things with words is associated with interpersonal relations and thus, ultimately, with reputation.

Finally, several approaches to language, including Goffman's dramaturgic approach and ethnography (Goffman, 1959), conversation analysis (Sacks, Schegloff and Jefferson, 1974), and more recently Herb Clark's joint-action theory of language use (Clark, 1996, see also Kashima, Klein, and Clark, 2007), take meaning as emerging from the joint communicative actions of the interactants who have to coordinate the goals, content, and process of communication. Meaning here is not "individual," that is, in the heads of individuals, as in the other approaches, but constructed through the interaction. Speakers try to establish a mutual understanding through their collaborative efforts. Communication is construed as a collaborative speech activity that is situated within the context of a social network and shaped by the specific context in which it occurs. The methodological toolkits developed by ethnographic and conversation analysis approaches have been widely used in research on the language of gossip and reputation. Applying them to naturalistic data, researchers have helped elucidate how gossip emerges through talk, and how individuals can actively shape both the interpretation and the course of a gossip episode through linguistic, prosodic, and nonverbal means (e.g., Bergmann, 1993; Coates, 1988; Eder and Enke, 1991).

In the next section, we draw extensively on ethnographic studies to illustrate how language factors in reputation management. We also draw on experimental research from psychology which has proven successful in isolating and clarifying several proposals. The section shows that social relations are a key focus of conversational interactions. Speakers are concerned with group solidarity and belonging and they make linguistic choices that protect their reputations and do not infringe on the addressees.

# Reputation Management

In this section, we discuss three ways in which language factors in the human reputation management system. First, the form and content of speech serve as a reputation signal *about the speaker*. Second, we review several relatively subtle devices implicated in the management of reputations in conversation. This management concerns both the conversation participants' reputations and third party reputations. Third, language provides devices that are explicitly dedicated to reputation management. We focus on apology, which is an example of a reputation repair tool.

## Language as a Reputation Signal

Both the form and content of speech are relevant to speakers' reputations. Animal communicative signals provide valuable fitness information about the individuals emitting them (Zahavi, 1977). Similarly, speech is a powerful social marker influencing individuals' places in the group's social network. Perhaps most directly, language indexes the linguistic community to which a speaker belongs. It is thus a major determinant of partner choice. Even preverbal infants show preference for speakers of their language (Kinzler, Dupoux, and Spelke, 2007). Additionally, the physical form of speech is associated with characteristics of the individual. For instance, the credibility of Western English speakers is higher when their speech is faster and does not contain hedges and pauses (Giles and Street, 1994). The significance of these features, however, is often contextually bound as it relates to normative expectations (Burgoon, 1990). Hedges may convey lower credibility in a lecture setting but relational closeness in an intimate one. They are also more likely to undermine a man's than a woman's reputation as they are expected to be used by women but not men.

The propositional content of speech—what we say—also matters. Participants in any interaction have to build a reputation for having desirable qualities. Of these qualities, reliability is key when information is being sought. Even though lying is ubiquitous and some (white) lies appear to be culturally sanctioned, all cultures punish some forms of truth distortion. This clearly speaks to the existence of reputational incentives to be truthful. At an interpersonal level, sensitivity to speaker reliability is evident early on. By age four, if not earlier, children prefer to learn from and interact with speakers who have been accurate in the past than speakers who have been inaccurate or have shown ignorance (Harris, 2012; Robinson and Einav, 2014). Even a single utterance can sway their subsequent choice of an informant (Fitneva and Dunfield, 2010).

Thus, both the form and content of speech contribute to a speaker's reputation. They differ in the amount of control speakers have over them, with content more likely to be under intentional control. Correspondingly, the response of the audience is more likely to be conscious for speech content than form. This raises interesting questions about what interventions would most effectively facilitate a change in a person's place in the social network. Speech lessons or expertise development? But what others say about us can have an enormous impact on our reputations as well. We turn to this issue next.

## Language and the Management of Relations in the Group

In this section we illustrate how language contributes to the management of social relations. These relations include those among the speakers, who are involved in a conversation, and the relations between the speakers and third parties, the latter not in the conversation. By managing these relations, speakers influence their own and others' place in the social network and thus their own and others' reputations. We will consider two linguistic tools. First, all languages provide speakers with means to qualify their relation with, or attitude to, the information they provide. For example, English speakers use expressions such as "I think" and "I guess" to signal their confidence. These so-called epistemic markers belong to the large set of politeness devices and show how speakers can manage relationships in exchanging information. Second, we will consider the conversation's structure, in particular speakers' use of silences. Speakers develop expectations about the turn-taking structure of conversation (Levinson, 2016). Deviation from this expected structure impacts the speaker's place in the group and consequently his or her reputation.

### Politeness

Politeness is an important concept for understanding how language is involved in reputation management. Communication often involves risks for public images that speakers claim for themselves, or their "face" (Brown and Levinson, 1987; Goffman, 1959). For example, as people try to persuade others or make them do things, they encroach on others' autonomy. Gossiping is also risky; the gossipers' knowledge and evaluation of the target may not align. Communication participants must act in ways that minimize the risk toward their own and others' personal and social identities. Brown and Levinson (1987) defined politeness as actions taken to counteract the disruptive effect of face-threatening acts. Positive politeness refers to acts such as assuming agreement, hedging and avoiding disagreement, and explicitly attending to the needs of partners that affirm their desired face and demonstrate respect. Negative politeness refers to acts that, in addition to those mentioned for positive politeness, recognize that in some way the speaker is imposing on the partner (e.g., through a request). Negative politeness acts include indirectness, asking for forgiveness or minimizing imposition in making requests.

One way speakers can express politeness is through the use of epistemic modal forms. Epistemic modality concerns the speaker's confidence or commitment to the truth of the proposition (Lyons, 1977; Palmer, 2001) and involves a wide variety of forms, from the restricted class of modal auxiliaries such as *must* and *might*, to open class lexical expressions such as *I think,* and hedges such as *like* and *sort of.* Epistemic modal forms serve a complex and rich set of epistemic and affective functions (Coates, 1987; 1988; Holmes, 1985; 1990). Both are relevant to reputation. Epistemically, these forms express the speaker's degree of confidence in the truth of the main proposition in the utterance. The greater the speaker's confidence, the more the speaker's reputation is at stake (Hill and Irvine, 1993). Affectively, epistemic modal forms convey deference to and solidarity with the addressee. As they contribute to positive relationships, they also contribute to stronger reputations.

We focus on *sort of* and *I think* to illustrate the epistemic and affective functions of epistemic modal forms. The epistemic function of *sort of* is to signal that the referential content of the utterance is in some way imprecise. Speakers acknowledge that the modified element, either lexical item or an entire proposition, should be interpreted approximately (Holmes, 1988). Speakers may also directly signal that they are in the process of searching for a word or phrase that better serves to express their intention (Coates, 1987). In contrast, *I think* can convey certainty or uncertainty (Holmes, 1985). The distinction relates to the position of *I think* in the sentence and its prosodic features. Coates (1987) shows that when used to express confidence and certainty, *I think* was associated with falling rather than with rising or fall-rise intonation, and was normally in clause-initial position. Further, utterances where *I* was stressed expressed greater confidence than utterances where *think* is stressed.

In conversation, speakers do not just communicate ideas and their attitudes toward these ideas but also affective meaning, that is, an attitude toward the addressee. Conveying affective meaning toward the addressee is particularly important in informal interactions and communications that have an evaluative component because in these instances the maintenance of social relationships takes priority over the exchange of information (Holmes, 1988; Stubbe and Holmes, 1995). Both *sort of* and *I think* serve to ensure that speakers do not impose on the addressee by softening the effect of the utterance and suggesting interest in establishing shared understanding (Coates, 1987; Holmes, 1993).

To get a better sense of how *sort of* and *I think* can be used for reputation management, it is helpful to consider their use in different contexts. In (1), the speaker is about to utter an unflattering description of a person. In (2), the speaker offers an opinion on a funeral.

1.  She looks very **sort of** um kind of matronly **really**.
    [Speaker describes old friend she had recently bumped into]

    (Coates, 2003, p. 335)

2.  **I mean I think** it **really** depends on the attitude of the survivors who are there.
    [Speaker discusses funeral]

    (Coates, 2003, p. 334)

What these examples have in common is the sensitive nature of the information. Evaluative conversations on topics such as the speaker's attitudes and feelings toward other people and conversations where speakers recount personal or embarrassing experiences tend to contain a greater number of epistemic modal forms compared to narratives from which the speaker is more removed (Coates, 1987, 1988; Holmes, 1988). These conversations are potentially face-threatening or damaging to the speaker's and others' reputation. *Sort of* and *I think* signal that speakers do not want to be firmly committed to their evaluative statements. Importantly, their use is independent of whether speakers think the proposition was true (Coates, 1987).

Another way to conceptualize the contribution of epistemic modal forms is as signaling the speaker's desire to reduce social distance to the addressee. For example, by suggesting a degree of imprecision, *sort of* indicates desire for a relaxed relationship with the addressee (Coates, 1987). Stubbe and Holmes (1995) note that when speakers felt that there was a gap in their shared knowledge, *I think* was used to diminish this interpersonal distance. By reducing the social distance and emphasizing the shared experiences of the participants, epistemic modal forms facilitate the creation of a shared common ground among the conversation participants.

In sum, fine-grained analyses of conversational data that consider the interactional context provide evidence on how speakers use epistemic modal forms to mitigate the force of what they say, thereby showing deference to each other's face and preserving each other's reputation. In these analyses, speakers are aware of the effect their propositions might have on the addressee and are concerned with their social identity. Epistemic modals allow speakers to express politeness by clouding the potentially face-threatening precision and force of their propositions. Thus, epistemic modals fulfill important interpersonal functions.

## Conversational Flow

An emerging body of evidence points to the impact that the *form* of communication has on interpersonal processes. In particular, this body of work examines how the flow of conversation—the extent to which a conversation is subjectively experienced as "smooth", efficient, and mutually engaging—affects speakers' sense of group solidarity, and conformity to group social norms (Collins, 2005; Koudenburg, Postmes, Gordijn, 2016). For instance, a smoothly flowing conversation is likely to reflect a high degree of agreement among speakers. In contrast, breaks in the conversation flow may negatively influence speakers' perceptions of the quality of their relationship, mutual trust, and perceived mutual understanding. These correlates of conversation flow are clearly relevant to reputation. As they affect the speakers' relationship, they also affect each speaker's future partner opportunities.

Conversation analysis reveals extensive usage of silences that are evaluative and indicative of a norm violation. Coates (1987) cites examples in which speakers precede or follow *sort of* with a pause. Similarly to the disfluency filler *um* that follows *sort of* in (1), where the speaker is about to describe an old friend in an unflattering way, silences may signal that the proposition to follow might be a threat to group solidarity. Furthermore, the length of pauses between speaking turns correlates with conversationalists' interest in the topic. Pilkington (1998) found that when gossipers were interested in the conversation, there was little pausing in between speaking turns. Short turns with minimal pauses were used as an indication of involvement. When participants were not interested in the topic, the silences between turns were longer.

Experimental investigations confirm that people are sensitive to disruptions in conversational form and that these disruptions impact one's sense of belonging.

Koudenburg et al. (2011) presented undergraduate participants with a 6-minute video of three female students having a conversation about relationships. Participants were asked to imagine being one of the conversation partners in the videotaped conversation in which either a silent moment did or did not occur. They found that participants who imagined being in the conversation with the 4-second silence reported feeling more rejection than participants who did not experience a silence in conversational flow. In addition, the perceived consensus within the group had also significantly decreased and communicators felt less socially validated. Silence can in fact influence opinions. Speakers, especially ones with a high motivation to belong, whose opinions are met with a brief silence shift their attitudes according to the group norm (Koudenburg et al., 2013).

The findings reviewed here suggest that control over the conversation flow may effectively regulate or influence attitudes within groups. Pauses, disfluencies, and backtracking all interfere with the flow of conversation. Their usage does not exclusively pertain to reputation management. For example, speakers may use a pause to signal that they are re-thinking what they have said and that change is impending. Nevertheless, speakers appear to use and perceive silences as signals that a group norm may be violated. This leads to redressive actions by the affected party aiming to preserve his/her reputation and place in the group.

## Reputation Repair

Offenses and transgressions of social norms are frequently punished. Apology is a verbal act that can be used to express attention to the victim's and transgressor's face needs in the context of an offense (Brown and Levinson, 1987). The offense could be behavioral such as stealing, hurting or some other way of damaging culturally recognized rights (e.g., to personal property and physical safety). It could also be verbal aspersion toward another's character, conduct, skills, and motives. For the victims, an apology provides recognition of their rights and potentially compensates for the suffered losses. For the transgressors, an apology provides a chance to repair both their self-image and their public image and potentially avoid punishment.

Apologies convey little referential content but express a message high in affect and solidarity. They have several elements (Blum-Kulka, House, and Kasper, 1989). First, a mandatory element is the expression of regret. The acceptance of blame and admission of responsibility involved in the expression of regret convey to the victim (and other listeners) that the speaker is aware of the violation of social norms (Scher and Darley, 1997; Schlenker and Darby, 1981). Second, optionally, apologies may contain an offer for repair ("What can I do to make it up?") and the promise that the offense will not re-occur. Third, also optionally, apologies may contain an explanation. These three elements can be found in the apologies of speakers of different languages (Blum-Kulka et al., 1989). Together, they signal that the transgression is not representative of what the transgressors are "really like" (Schlenker, 1980).

What elements are included in an apology depends on the seriousness of the offense. A light offense such as bumping into someone is likely to be followed by a simple explicit apology, for example, *sorry*. In contrast, for heavier violations such as making someone miss an important engagement, people tend to issue an explicit apology accompanied by acknowledgements of responsibility and offers of restitution. For instance, undergraduate students issued a perfunctory form of an apology such as *pardon me* when the consequences of the social predicament were minimal but when the consequences heightened, they also expressed remorse about the situation and offered to help the victim (Schlenker and Darby, 1981).

Apologies draw on a narrow range of syntactic patterns and lexical items. In informal English conversation, speakers use some form of *sorry* approximately 75% of the time to apologize (e.g., Holmes, 1990; Kampf and Blum-Kulka, 2007; Owen, 1983). Holmes (1990) identified that approximately another 10% of the apologies in her study involved a small number of linguistic strategies such as *excuse me/us, pardon me/I beg your pardon, forgive me,* and *we regret that.*

Acts of apology are recognized in both institutional and interpersonal settings. Apologies play a significant role in the restorative justice system where the offender is provided with an opportunity to apologize to the victim and the victim is then given the opportunity to accept the offender's apology and reach a mutual settlement (Poulson, 2003). In interpersonal relations, experimental research demonstrates that an apology can inhibit retaliation and thus the spread of aggressive behaviors (Ohbuchi, Kameda, and Agarie, 1989). Furthermore, relative to no apology, an apology following an injustice helps reduce, if not eliminate, negative feelings toward the transgressor (De Cremer and Schouten, 2008; Smith, Chen, and Harris, 2010; Takaku, 2001). Not all apologies succeed in repairing the victim's and transgressor's reputations but language uniquely equips our species with the means to do that.

To conclude this section, we note that the data we surveyed are almost exclusively from English speakers. There is enormous variability in how speakers of different languages achieve the goals of managing their own and others' reputations through communication. This is due both to the cross-cultural variation in social norms and individual rights and to the multifunctional nature of linguistic devices. For example, explicit shaming—another reputation management tool—is a common practice for the Samoan while middle class Americans prefer offering indirect criticisms (Schieffelin and Ochs, 1986). Furthermore, a linguistic device may play one role in one linguistic community and a different role in another. Pilkington (1998) found much longer pauses between speaking turns in male than female gossip, even when a speaker had invited a response by using tags or questioning intonation. This cultural and linguistic variability suggests that the skill of managing social identities and reputations through language has to be learned.

# GOSSIP EPISODES

Gossip is intuitively recognized across cultures. It is a genre of conversation that involves judgments of others and has repercussions for the reputation not only of the gossip's targets but also the gossipers. The extent to which gossip influences reputation depends on the information being transmitted and the context of interpretation gossipers create. Speakers use various linguistic strategies, including those discussed in the previous section, to reveal the intended effect of their utterance (Bergmann, 1993). In this section, we focus on two features of gossip episodes: their ordered components and the inclusion of minimal responses. These features underscore the temporal dynamics of gossip. As mentioned in the introduction, gossip definitions often refer to single utterances (e.g., evaluative statement about an absent person, Fine and Rosnow, 1978). In comparison to these approaches, recognizing the temporal dynamics of gossip helps better understand its relation with the reputation of the target and of the gossipers.

The term "gossip episode" highlights the unfolding of gossip in time. A common finding across ethnographic studies of gossip is that it contains a set of ordered acts (Bergmann, 1993; Besnier, this volume; Eder and Enke, 1991; Eggins and Slade, 1997). At the beginning, interactants establish initial common ground, which involves an understanding of the topic and target of the conversation. Through the subsequent response acts, the group modifies this common ground and finds a new point of shared understanding and solidarity. The new shared understanding impacts the target's reputation, while the solidarity of opinion impacts the sense of belonging and the reputations of speakers.

This structure of gossip episodes is characteristic of the exchanges of people of various ages and in various settings, for example, adolescent gossip during informal lunch breaks (Eder and Enke, 1991) and adult gossip in a German housing project (Bergmann, 1993). Setting up the common ground, the beginning of gossip involves the identification of the target, which could be expanded or clarified, and the target's initial evaluation. Bergmann observed that after establishing an absent third person as the target of gossip, gossipers used evaluative accentuation and appropriate descriptive terms to dictate how they wanted the information they presented to be interpreted. For instance, they emphasized and dramatized aspects of an individual's actions that they wanted to be viewed as characteristic of the individual's personal qualities.

The central role of the target's reputation is easy to see in the beginnings of gossip episodes but the reputations of gossipers are also at stake because, at its core, gossip concerns group norms. The emphasis on group norms is apparent in the labels applied to the target. For instance, adolescent initiators labeled targets as "a snob" or "a flirt," challenging their reputation as individuals who adhere to the guidelines for behavior set forth by the group (Eder and Enke, 1991). Implicitly, this sets up a contrast between the target and the gossipers. The contrast can be even made explicitly. Bergmann (1993) observed that gossip initiators sometimes highlighted the gossip target's transgressions by proclaiming that they would have acted differently had they been in the same situation.

The reputation of the initiators of gossip is particularly vulnerable because both their targets and their conversation partners can challenge them. Consequently, initiators employ numerous authentication strategies to prove the credibility of their information and the truthfulness of their presentations. For instance, they may emphasize that the information is first-hand by mentioning different situational details or using quotations (Bergmann, 1993). Both devices support the accuracy of the introduced claims.

The response acts following the target's identification and initial evaluation can vary substantially. These acts serve to modify the initial evaluation in some way. For example, some initiators may use explanations and exaggerated affect to strengthen their initial identification and evaluation of the target, while other participants in the conversation may provide support for the initial evaluation (Eder and Enke, 1991).

Not all gossip episodes result in agreement within the group about the evaluation of a target. Eder and Enke (1991) showed that in some gossip episodes, interactants did not share the expressed viewpoint. In these cases, individuals issued challenges, explicitly suggesting that they differed in their opinions about the target. Interestingly, challenges always occurred immediately following the initial evaluation, before the group could reach an agreement regarding the expressed evaluation of the target. Eder and Enke suggest that this timing is not accidental: it is easier to challenge an idea immediately after it is introduced than after it becomes shared within the group. The latter could risk tarnishing the challenger's reputation because it might be perceived as a threat to the solidarity of the group.

As gossip emerges as a collaborative action situated in the context of shared knowledge of the conversation partners, the actions of the non-initiators are just as important for the course of gossip. Minimal responses such as *mm* and *yeah* are one type of verbal indicator that a listener can use to signal his or her active participation and involvement in the conversation (Reid, 1995; Stubbe, 1998). Coates (1988) provides evidence that women who engaged in interaction-focused conversations used minimal responses such as *mm* and *yeah* to lend support to the speaker and to indicate that they were actively participating in the conversation and that the interaction was jointly produced. In the narrative or more information-focused sections of conversation, participants seemed to use minimal responses to acknowledge the shift of conversation from one stage to another. For instance, they used *mm* to indicate that they had accepted the point of an utterance as a topic of conversation. Pilkington (1998) similarly reports usage of minimal responses by listeners to indicate agreement with the topic of gossip. By making a positive minimal response, listeners effectively signaled that they have nothing to say at that juncture of the gossip episode and that the story can continue.

Minimal responses mostly occur at the end of an utterance and do not disrupt the speaker's flow (Coates, 1988). As described earlier, the flow of conversation is an important indicator marking that the speakers agree and flow-disrupting behavior may reflect poorly on speakers by threatening the solidary of the group. Indeed, Zimmerman and West (1975) and Fishman (1983) both note that male speakers delayed minimal responses to indicate a lack of interest or attention.

Speakers need to learn the culturally appropriate ways to use minimal responses. Stubbe (1998) analyzed the number of verbal feedback and minimal responses in two cultural groups in New Zealand: Maori and Pakeha. She found that the type and placement of feedback varied according to the norms of the group to which the participants belonged. For instance, the Maori listeners provided lower levels of explicit verbal feedback than the Pakeha listeners and were more likely to indicate attention and interest by means of facilitative silence. Whereas the Pakeha speakers were active and enthusiastic contributors throughout the discussion signaling involvement overtly and immediately, the Maori made greater use of implicit signals for collaborative feedback. Thus, the pragmatic strategies required to participate in gossip episodes vary across languages and cultures, and the same interactional goals can be achieved by different means in different cultural groups.

In sum, ethnographic studies have facilitated the unpacking of the natural of dynamics of gossip episodes and have clarified how gossip relates to reputation. Although risky, the collaborative nature of gossiping is particularly well suited to building common ground and the creation and affirmation of relationships. The structure of gossiping allows participants to develop and institute cultural norms. The solidarity of opinion that emerges does not only concern the target's reputation. It also contributes to gossipers' reputation by suggesting acceptance and belonging to the group. Importantly, not all evaluative statements lead to full-blown gossip episodes and timely challenges may protect the reputation of the target.

# CONCLUSION

Language contributes substantially to how individuals construct and manage their own and others' reputation. We dedicate as much as 70% of our time in conversation to the discussion of personal matters and other people (Dunbar, 1997). But how this content is presented, received, and transformed during the conversation also impacts the relations among speakers and others' standing in the group.

We have reviewed a small number of language features that relate to reputation management, including epistemic modals, conversation flow, and speech acts such as apologies. These features confer simultaneously enormous flexibility and power to the human reputation system. Its flexibility is apparent in the opportunity afforded by language to restore reputation through the speech act of apology. Its power is apparent in the speed with which reputational information spreads.

One implication of the research we have discussed is that reputation is not the result of a single act, contrary to the operationalization of reputation creation and transmission in experimental studies and computational models. In the human language-mediated reputational system, interactants continuously construct and reconstruct reputation. This change in perspective on reputation has a significance consequence. As reputation is not an inevitable result of specific acts, it suggests the existence of opportunities for the interactants to change the outcome for themselves and others. Being able to intervene is particularly important when reputations might be tarnished because negative information is especially memorable for both children and adults (Barclay and LaLumiere, 2006; Kinzler and Shutts, 2008).

A second implication is that learning to yield language in the service of reputation management could be an extended process. Indeed, children appear to attempt nonverbal reputation management by age five, suggesting the existence of sensitivity to reputational payoffs to behavior (Engelmann, Over, Herrmann, and Tomasello, 2013), but their tattling behavior at the same age suggests that they may not be quite aware of the costs associated with spreading damaging information about others (Ingram and Bering, 2010). Certain reputational signals (including forms of address such as *tu—vous*) and politeness routines (from saying *thank you* to complex forms of indirect requests) take years of explicit tutoring (Snow, Perlmann, Gleason, and Hooshyar, 1990). Learning how to transmit information about oneself and others to achieve desired reputational outcomes is part of learning to speak.

Finally, progress in understanding the role of language in human reputation management likely rests on interdisciplinary insight and methodological innovations. One source of evidence we used was studies employing the ethnographic method and conversation analysis. In this tradition, researchers are interested in how speakers use language to accomplish social acts and interact. They focus on the abstract, structural properties of the discourse (the clauses, words, and sentences) and how their organization allows speakers to convey meaning in diverse social and cultural contexts. Future research can better integrate experimental techniques to investigate the cognitive and social correlates of these properties. As suggested by the experimental evidence we discussed (e.g., on the impact of conversation flow on reputation), such an endeavor could contribute to uncovering the mental processes and representations involved in linguistic behavior and thus deepen our understanding of the phenomenon of reputation.

## REFERENCES

Austin, John L. 1962. *How to Do Things with Words.* London: Oxford University Press.

Barclay, Pat, and Martin L. Lalumiere. 2006. "Do People Differentially Remember Cheaters?" *Human Nature* 17 (1): 98–113. doi:10.1007/s12110-006-1022-y.

Bergmann, Jorg R. 1993. *Discreet Indiscretions: The Social Organization of Gossip.* New York: Aldine.

Besnier, Nico. 2019. Gossip in Ethnographic Perspective. In *Handbook of Gossip and Reputation*, edited by Francesca Giardini and Rafael Wittek, New York: Oxford University Press.

Blum-Kulka, Shoshana. 2000. "Gossipy Events at Family Dinners: Negotiating Sociability, Presence and the Moral Order." In *Small Talk,* edited by Justine Coupland, 213–240. London: Longman.

Blum-Kulka, Shoshana, Juliane House, and Gabriele Kasper. 1989. "Investigating Cross-Cultural Pragmatics: An Introductory Overview." In *Cross-Cultural Pragmatics: Requests and Apologies,* edited by Shoshana Blum-Kulka, Juliane House, and Gabriele Kasper, 1–34. Norwood, NJ: Ablex.

Brown, Penelope, and Stephen C. Levinson. 1987. *Politeness: Some Universals in Language Usage.* 4th ed. Cambridge: Cambridge University Press.

Burgoon, Michael. 1990. "Language and Social Influence." In *Handbook of Language and Social Psychology,* edited by William P. Robinson and Howard Giles, 51–72. Chichester: John Wiley and Sons.

Byrne, Richard, and Andrew Whiten. 1991. "Computation and Mindreading in Primate Tactical Deception." In *Natural Theories of Mind: Evolution, Development and Simulation of Everyday Mindreading,* edited by Whiten, A., 127–141. Cambridge: Basil Blackwell.

Clark, Herbert H. 1996. *Using Language.* Cambridge: Cambridge University Press.

Coates, Jennifer. 1987. "Epistemic Modality and Spoken Discourse." *Transactions of the Philological Society* 85 (1): 110–131. doi:10.1111/j.1467-968X.1987.tb00714.x.

Coates, Jennifer. 1988. "Gossip Revisited: Language in All-Female Groups." In *Women in Their Speech Communities*, edited by Jennifer Coates and Deborah Cameron, 94–122. London: Longman.

Coates, Jennifer. 2003. "The Role of Epistemic Modality in Women's Talk." In *Modality in Contemporary English*, edited by Roberta Facchinetti, Manfred Krug and Frank Robert, 331–348. Berlin: Walter de Gruyter.

Collins, Randall. 2005. *Interaction Ritual Chains*. Princeton, NJ: Princeton University Press.

De Cremer, David, and Barbara C. Schouten. 2008. "When Apologies for Injustice Matter: The Role of Respect." *European Psychologist* 13 (4): 239–247. doi:10.1027/1016-9040.13.4.239.

Dunbar, Robin I. M. 1997. *Grooming, Gossip, and the Evolution of Language*. Cambridge, MA: Harvard University Press.

Dunbar, Robin I. M. 2004. "Gossip in Evolutionary Perspective." *Review of General Psychology* 8 (2): 100–110. doi:10.1037/1089-2680.8.2.100.

Eder, Donna, and Janet Lynne Enke. 1991. "The Structure of Gossip: Opportunities and Constraints on Collective Expression among Adolescents." *American Sociological Review* 56 (4): 494–508.

Eggins, Suzanne and Diana Slade. 1997. *Analysing Casual Conversation*. London: Cassell.

Emler, Nicholas. 1990. "A Social Psychology of Reputation." *European Review of Social Psychology* 1 (1): 171–193. doi:10.1080/14792779108401861.

Engelmann, Jan M., Esther Herrmann, and Michael Tomasello. 2016. "Preschoolers Affect Others' Reputations Through Prosocial Gossip." *British Journal of Developmental Psychology* 34 (3): 447–460. doi:10.1111/bjdp.12143.

Engelmann, Jan M., Harriet Over, Esther Herrmann, and Michael Tomasello. 2013. "Young Children Care More About Their Reputation with Ingroup Members and Potential Reciprocators." *Developmental Science* 16 (6): 952–958. doi:10.1111/desc.12086.

Fine, Gary Alan, and Ralph L. Rosnow. 1978. "Gossip, Gossipers, Gossiping." *Personality and Social Psychology Bulletin* 4 (1): 161–168. doi:10.1177/014616727800400135.

Fishman, Pamela. 1983. "Interaction: The Work Women Do." In *Language, Gender and Society*, edited by Barrie Thorne, Cheris Kramarae and Nancy Henley, 89–101. Rowley, MA: Newbury House.

Fiske, Susan T. 2004. *Social Beings: A Core Motives Approach to Social Psychology*. New York: John Wiley & Sons.

Fitneva, Stanka A., and Kristen A. Dunfield. 2010. "Selective Information Seeking After a Single Encounter." *Developmental Psychology* 46 (5): 1380–1384. doi:10.1037/a0019818.

Foster, Eric K. 2004. "Research on Gossip: Taxonomy, Methods, and Future Directions." *Review of General Psychology* 8 (2): 78–99. doi:10.1037/1089-2680.8.2.78.

Georgoudi, Marianthi, and Ralph L. Rosnow. 1985. "Notes Toward a Contextualist Understanding of Social Psychology." *Personality and Social Psychology Bulletin* 11 (1): 5–22. doi:10.1177/0146167285111001.

Giles, Howard, & Richard L. J. Street. 1994. "Communicator Characteristics and Behavior." In *Handbook of Interpersonal Communication*, edited by Mark L. Knapp and Gerald R. Miller, 103–161. Thousand Oaks, CA: Sage.

Goffman, Erving. 1959. *The Presentation of Self in Everyday Life*. Garden City: NY: Doubleday Anchor Books. Doubleday & Co., Inc.

Grice, Herbert P. 1957. "Meaning." *Philosophical Review* 66, pp. 377–388.

Grice, Herbert P. 1975. "Logic and Conversation." In *Syntax and Semantics*, edited by Peter Cole and Jerry L. Morgan, 41–58. New York: Academic Press.

Hallett, Tim, Brent Harger, and Donna Eder. 2009. "Gossip at Work: Unsanctioned Evaluative Talk in Formal School Meetings." *Journal of Contemporary Ethnography* 38 (5): pp. 584–618. doi:10.1177/0891241609342117.

Harris, Paul L. 2012. *Trusting What You're Told: How Children Learn from Others*. Cambridge, MA: Belknap Press/Harvard University Press.

Hill, J. H., and Irvine, J. T. 1993. *Responsibility and Evidence in Oral Discourse*. Cambridge: Cambridge University Press.

Holmes, Janet. 1985. "Sex Differences and Miscommunication: Some Data from New Zealand." In *Cross-Cultural Encounters: Communication and Miscommunication*, edited by J. Pride, 24–43. Melbourne, Australia: River Seine.

Holmes, Janet. 1988. "Sort of in New Zealand Women's and Men's Speech." *Studia Linguistica* 42 (2): 85–121. doi:10.1111/j.1467-9582.1988.tb00788.x.

Holmes, Janet. 1990. "Hedges and Boosters in Women's and Men's Speech." *Language and Communication* 10 (3): 185–205. doi:10.1016/0271-5309(90)90002-S.

Holmes, Janet. 1993. "New Zealand Women Are Good to Talk to: An Analysis of Politeness Strategies in Interaction." *Journal of Pragmatics* 20 (2): 91–116. doi:10.1016/0378-2166 (93)90078-4.

Ingram, Gordon P. D. 2019. "Gossip and Reputation in Childhood Development." In *Handbook of Gossip and Reputation*, edited by Francesca Giardini and Rafael Wittek, New York: Oxford University Press.

Ingram, Gordon P. D., and Jesse M. Bering. 2010. "Children's Tattling: The Reporting of Everyday Norm Violations in Preschool Settings." *Child Development* 81 (3): 945–957. doi:10.1111/j.1467-8624.2010.01444.x.

Kampf, Zohar, and Shoshana Blum-Kulka. 2007. "Do Children Apologize to Each Other? Apology Events in Young Israeli Peer Discourse." *Journal of Politeness Research. Language, Behaviour, Culture* 1 (1): 11–37. doi:10.1515/PR.2007.002.

Kashima, Yoshihisa, Olivier Klein, and Anne E. Clark. 2007. "Grounding: Sharing Information in Social Interaction." In *Social Communication*, edited by Klaus Fiedler, 30–77. New York: Psychology Press.

Kinzler, Katherine D., Emmanuel Dupoux and Elizabeth S. Spelke. 2007. "The native language of social cognition." *Proceedings of the National Academy of Sciences* 104 (30): 12577–12580. doi:10.1073/pnas.0705345104.

Kinzler, Katherine D., and Kristin Shutts. 2008. "Memory for 'Mean' Over 'Nice': The Influence of Threat on Children's Face Memory." *Cognition* 107 (2): 775–783. doi:10.1016/j.cognition.2007.09.005.

Koudenburg, Namkje, Tom Postmes, and Ernestine H. Gordijn. 2011. "Disrupting the Flow: How Brief Silences in Group Conversations Affect Social Needs." *Journal of Experimental Social Psychology* 47 (2): 512–515. doi:10.1016/j.jesp.2010.12.006.

Koudenburg, Namkje, Tom Postmes, & Ernestine H. Gordijn. 2013. "Resounding Silences: Subtle Norm Regulation in Everyday Interactions." *Social Psychology Quarterly* 76 (3): 224–241. doi:10.1177/0190272513496794.

Koudenburg, Namkje, Tom Postmes, & Ernestine H. Gordijn. 2016. "Beyond Content of Conversation the Role of Conversational Form in the Emergence and Regulation of Social Structure." *Personality and Social Psychology Review* 21: 50–71. doi:10.1177/1088868315626022.

Levinson, Stephen. C. 2016. Turn-taking in Human Communication–Origins and Implications for Language Processing.' *Trends in Cognitive Sciences* 20 (1): 6–14. doi:10.1016/j.tics.2015.10.010.

Lyons, John. 1977. *Semantics*. Cambridge: Cambridge University Press.

Milinski, Manfred. 2016. "Reputation, a Universal Currency for Human Social Interactions." *Philosophical Transactions of the Royal Society B: Biological Sciences* 371 (1687): 20150100. doi:10.1098/rstb.2015.0100.

Ohbuchi, Ken-ichi, Masuyo Kameda, and Nariyuki Agarie. 1989. "Apology as Aggression Control: Its Role in Mediating Appraisal of and Response to Harm." *Journal of Personality and Social Psychology* 56 (2): 219–227. doi:10.1037/0022-3514.56.2.219.

Ostrom, Elinor. 1998. "A Behavioral Approach to the Rational Choice Theory of Collective Action: Presidential Address, American Political Science Association, 1997." *American Political Science Review* 92 (1): 1–22.

Owen, Marion. 1983. *Apologies and Remedial Interchanges: A Study of Language Use in Social Interaction*. Berlin: Mouton De Gruyter.

Palmer, Frank R. 2001. *Mood and Modality*. Cambridge: Cambridge University Press.

Pilkington, Jane. 1998. "'Don't Try and Make Out That I'm Nice!' The Different Strategies Women and Men use When Gossiping." In *Language and Gender: A Reader*, edited by Jennifer Coates, 254–269. Oxford, UK: Blackwell.

Poulson, Barton. 2003. "Third Voice: A Review of Empirical Research on the Psychological Outcomes of Restorative Justice, A." *Utah Law Review* 15(9): 167–203.

Reid, Julie. 1995. "A Study of Gender Differences in Minimal Responses." *Journal of Pragmatics* 24 (5): 489–512. doi:10.1016/0378-2166(94)00066-N.

Robinson, Elizabeth, J., & Shiri Einav. 2014. *Trust and Skepticism: Children's Selective Learning from Testimony*. New York, NY: Psychology Press.

Sacks, Harvey, Emanuel A. Schegloff, and Gail Jefferson. 1974. "A Simplest systematics for the Organization of Turn-Taking for Conversation." *Language 50*: 696–735. doi:10.2307/412243.

Scher, Steven J., and John M. Darley. 1997. "How Effective Are the Things People Say to Apologize? Effects of the Realization of the Apology Speech Act." *Journal of Psycholinguistic Research* 26 (1): 127–140. doi:10.1023/A:1025068306386.

Schieffelin, B. and Ochs, E. 1986. *Language Socialization across Cultures*. Cambridge: Cambridge University Press.

Schlenker, Barry R. 1980. *Impression Management: The Self-Concept, Social Identity, and Interpersonal Relations*. Monterey, CA: Brooks/Cole.

Schlenker, Barry R., and Bruce W. Darby. 1981. "The Use of Apologies in Social Predicaments." *Social Psychology Quarterly* 44 (3): 271–278.

Searle, John R. 1969. *Speech Acts: An Essay in the Philosophy of Language*. Cambridge: Cambridge University Press.

Smith, Craig E., Diyu Chen, and Paul L. Harris. 2010. "When the Happy Victimizer Says Sorry: Children's Understanding of Apology and Emotion." *British Journal of Developmental Psychology* 28 (4): 727–746. doi:10.1348/026151009X475343.

Snow, Catherine E., Rivka Y. Perlmann, Jean Berko Gleason, and Nahid Hooshyar. 1990. "Developmental Perspectives on Politeness: Sources of Children's Knowledge." *Journal of Pragmatics* 14 (2): 289–305. doi:10.1016/0378-2166(90)90084-Q.

Sperber, Dan, and Dierdre Wilson. 1986. *Relevance: Communication and Cognition* (2nd ed.). Cambridge, MA: Blackwell, Oxford.

Stubbe, Maria. 1998. "Are You Listening? Cultural Influences on the Use of Supportive Verbal Feedback in Conversation." *Journal of Pragmatics* 29 (3): 257–289. doi:10.1016/S0378-2166(97)00042-8.

Stubbe, Maria, and Janet Holmes. 1995. "You know, Eh and Other 'Exasperating Expressions': An Analysis of Social and Stylistic Variation in the Use of Pragmatic Devices in a Sample of New Zealand English." *Language and Communication* 15 (1): 63–88. doi:10.1016/0271-5309(94)00016-6.

Takaku, Seiji. 2001. "The Effects of Apology and Perspective Taking on Interpersonal Forgiveness: A Dissonance-Attribution Model of Interpersonal Forgiveness." *The Journal of Social Psychology* 141 (4): 494–508. doi:10.1080/00224540109600567.

Tomasello, Michael, Alicia P. Melis, Claudio Tennie, Emily Wyman, and Esther Herrmann. 2012. "Two Key Steps in the Evolution of Human Cooperation." *Current Anthropology* 53 (6): 673–692. doi:10.1086/668207.

Tyler, Tom R., & Heather J. Smith. 1999. "Justice, Social Identity, and Group Processes." In *The Psychology of Social Self*, edited by Tom R. Tyler, Roderick M. Kramer, and Oliver P. John, 223–264. Mahwah: Lawrence Erlbaum Associates, Inc.

Zahavi, Amotz D. 1977. "Reliability in Communication Systems and the Evolution of Altruism." In *Evolutionary Ecology*, edited by Bernard Stonehouse and Christopher M. Perrins, pp. 253–259. London: Macmillan Education.

Zimmerman, Don, & Candace West. 1975. "Sex Roles, Interruptions and Silences in Conversation." In *Language and Sex: Difference and Dominance*, edited by Barrie Thorne and Nancy Henley, 105–129. Rowley, MA: Newbury House.

# CHAPTER 6

........................................................................................

# GOSSIP IN
# ETHNOGRAPHIC
# PERSPECTIVE

........................................................................................

## NIKO BESNIER

GOSSIP can be approached from a variety of perspectives, which can fruitfully inform and complement each another. One of these approaches is ethnography. Ethnographic methods of the kind that endure as the mainstay of data collecting and analysis in socio-cultural anthropology and a number of other disciplines can shed a particular light on gossip and provide insights that other approaches to the topic may not be equipped to provide. At the same time, ethnographic methods present limitations in comparison to other research methods. Ethnographic approaches to gossip emphasize the importance of analyzing gossip as it occurs naturally in social life; investigating how it relates to other social and cultural practices; understanding it from the perspective of the local context rather than assuming its universality; and embedding it in a range of other communicative and social practices that occur in the same society or across societies, which complement and articulate with gossip. This chapter outlines the main characteristics of ethnography as a research method for the collection and analysis of gossip data. In particular, it will show that an ethnographic approach embeds gossip in a larger context of social life, in contrast to other methodological approaches that might seek to control the factors that come into play in the analysis of particular human activities; focuses on local understandings of what gossip (and reputation) consists of and what it is not, in contrast to approaches that begin with an a priori parsimonious definition based on alleged minimal structural features (e.g., an interactional triad) and the characteristics of the speech act (e.g., negative information about an absent party); engages with conflicting understandings and evaluations of gossip (and reputation) that may coexist in a particular group (e.g., "women gossip but men exchange information"), rather than seeking a consensual definition; and is sensitive to effects of scale (e.g., interactions in microscopic contexts articulate with large-scale dynamics), in contrast to approaches that limit observation to single contexts.

# Ethnography as a Data-Collecting and Analytic Method

Ethnography emerged as an analytic method at the beginning of the twentieth century on both sides of the Atlantic. In the United States, the emergence of ethnography is associated with the efforts by Franz Boas and his numerous students to establish anthropology as a legitimate endeavor, which was originally focused in particular on conducting "salvage ethnography" among American Indians, in the belief that their societies, social practices, cultural systems, and languages were on the brink of disappearing under pressure from settler colonialism and had to be documented for posterity.

In Britain, early efforts by researchers such as the members of the 1898 Cambridge Anthropological Expedition to the Torres Straits, a vast project conducted under the leadership of zoologist A. C. Haddon, established ethnography as a method designed to collect information about every aspect of a people's society and culture, yielding at the time a vast catalogue of concepts and practices. But it was not until a couple of decades later that ethnography was systematized in the foundational work of Bronisław Malinowski, who conducted fieldwork in the Trobriand Islands off the coast of New Guinea in 1915–1918. Malinowski was arguably the first anthropologist to lay out the cornerstones of a classic ethnographic method. In the introduction to the classic *Argonauts of the Western Pacific* (Malinowski, 1922), he argued that ethnography had to be based on a long-term intimate engagement with the people whose lives are recorded, presupposed language learning, and had to involve both the observation of human activities under investigation and the analyst's participation in these activities (thus departing radically from methods that are contingent on a strict separation between observer and observed). It is from this latter injunction that we have inherited the term "participant observation."

Ethnographers aim to collect as much information about the context of all human activities they are interested in understanding, the assumption being that the fuller the context the researcher brings to a particular strip of activity, the richer the analysis. This is the principle that US anthropologist Clifford Geertz (1973) would popularize as "thick description" (a term he borrowed from ordinary language philosopher Gilbert Ryle), which aims for an understanding of an ethnographic situation that derives from exploring it under multiple guises and acknowledging that human action is subject to a multiplicity of interpretations and perspectives.

As the founding fathers of anthropology saw it, ethnography as data collection is fundamentally naturalistic, in that the ethnographer makes no effort to control the situation or otherwise interfere with the normal course of events, and thus rarely involves experimentation. Much later, however, anthropologists of the "reflexive turn" (Clifford and Marcus, 1986; Marcus and Fisher, 1986) criticized earlier anthropologists for the contradiction inherent in the injunction that ethnographer conduct participant observation, and thus be fully involved in the social relations under study, and the fact that, in their writings, they present the materials they analyze as if they had observed them through a one-way mirror. Furthermore, the ethnographer's very presence has an impact on how people act, and thus the belief that one can observe human activities without having an impact on these activities is a fallacious fantasy. Since then, ethnography have tended to problematize the context of data gathering as an inherent aspect of the data themselves and anthropologists often give sustained analytic consideration to their own role in shaping the dynamics they seek to understand.

Gossip and, to a lesser extent, reputation are primarily interactional categories of human activity, and thus the ethnographic methods that are relevant to their analysis present specific issues that are not shared with the study of other aspects of society and culture, such as kinship, ritual, or exchange. In the history of anthropology (particularly in North America), these specific issues gradually became the bailiwick of the emerging subdiscipline of linguistic anthropology, which Franz Boas in the early part of the twentieth century had declared to be one of the four subdisciplines of his "four field" endeavor to document disappearing North American lifeways (in addition to cultural anthropology, archeology, and physical anthropology).

However, during the first half of the twentieth century, North American anthropologists had viewed the description of a language as merely consisting of a grammar, a dictionary, and a collection of texts elicited from bilingual consultants, assuming that these representations of language were also representations of culture. It was not until the 1960s that a much more focused and sophisticated research program was laid out, particularly by linguistic anthropologists John Gumperz and Dell Hymes, which they referred to as the "ethnography of communication" (Gumperz and Hymes, 1972; Hymes, 1974: see Mangarditch and Fitneva, this volume). For this new way of researching human interactions ethnographically, data consisted of speech as it occurred naturally in face-to-face interactions that were part of people's ongoing lives. This was a different project from previous efforts that sought to collect information through elicitation or that analyzed verbal interactions as a social phenomenon without referring to the actual text of these interactions. This new focus was made possible in large part by improvements in recording technologies, particularly the development of the portable tape recorder. It brought about an important methodological and theoretical shift, with researchers now able to make audio (and later video) recordings of interactions in different kinds of social activities and listen to them (and later watch them) to try to make sense of them. Gumperz and Hymes conceptualized language as a set of resources drawn upon selectively to accomplish various social actions, or what Hymes referred to as different "functions" of language. The "speech genre," or "form of talk," became an important unit of analysis. Interactional units have continued to the present to be treated as units of analysis in linguistic ethnography (Philips, 2013).

Parallel developments in linguistics further contributed important insights into the relationship between language and its social context, particularly the emergence, spurred on by William Labov (1966), of sociolinguistics as a subfield of linguistics. Its impetus was a reaction to mentalist theories of language that were emerging at the same time, which sought to investigate the grammatical structures of the language or an idealized speaker/hearer of a language, assumed that all languages share a universal and innate core, and sidelined all social factors in language as unworthy of serious attention and not conducive to any useful hypothesis testing (Chomsky, 1957). In contrast, socio-linguistics documented and went some ways toward theorizing how social inequalities are reflected and reproduced in language practices. While not ethnographic in the strict sense of the term, in that its main focus was on language and not on the social context of interaction, it highlighted the fact that interactional practices were deeply intertwined with social stratifications in particular societies, an insight that later researchers would combine with the ethnographic analysis of these social stratifications to view language as a commodity enmeshed in the political economic structure of society (e.g., Gal, 1989; Irvine, 1989). As we shall see presently, this approach is particularly relevant to the ethnographic study of gossip.

The problems associated with studying gossip ethnographically is that, cross-culturally, gossip (restricted here to its face-to-face manifestations) tends to be hidden from public view and in particular from the prying eyes and ears of outsiders, including ethnographers. It also tends to be socially devalued across different societies, and people may be anxious to deflect researchers' attention away from gossip so that their society not be represented through devalued activities. Gossip is often incidental, and thus its occurrence is difficult to predict and its distinctiveness from other forms of interaction difficult to determine. For fieldworkers who conduct research in societies to which they are not native, understanding gossip is particularly challenging as it requires an intimate acquaintance with the complexities of language and a subtle understanding of the social dynamics and cultural norms that background gossip and that gossip brings to the fore.

One additional constraint placed on the naturalistic observation and recording of gossip is the increased institutionalization, in many countries, of research ethics since the end of the last millennium. Being based on the long-term interpersonal involvement of the researcher, the development and maintenance of trust, and the researcher's personal commitment to research participants, ethnography engages with the complexities of ethics more than any other social scientific method, for example, with the fact that ethical responsibilities cannot be expediently spirited away by asking research participants to sign informed consent forms (Lederman, 2006). While institutional regulations in many countries today require the use of such documents of all social science research, procedures that were developed primarily for medical research in the aftermaths of historical scandals (e.g., the US Public Health Service's Tuskegee syphilis experiments of 1932–1972), they often hinder ethnographic research, as when ethnographers are required to abide by them when simply observing daily life as it unfolds. This renders the task of obtaining from ethical review boards approval for ethnographic research on such topics as gossip particularly difficult (Besnier and Philips, 2014). New international developments in the bureaucratic regulation of ethical practices may in future alleviate some of these constraints.

Despite all the factors that make it difficult to access it, gossip can offer an extraordinarily rich entry point into the sociocultural dynamics that inform people's everyday practices. As John Haviland demonstrated in the first substantial ethnography of gossip ever published, "there is an intimate relation between the native's knowledge of his own society and his ability to gossip (and to understand gossip)" (1977, p. 3), and thus understanding gossip amounts to understanding society and culture.

# Gossip through an Ethnographic Lens

The ethnographic analysis of gossip can be classified into two methodological approaches that are roughly contingent on the period when the work was conducted and the discipline in which it is based. Early ethnographic works approached gossip macroscopically as a social activity that could be analyzed interpretively on the basis of what people said about it, the ethnographer's participant observation in gossip contexts, and the analyst's understanding of how gossip articulates with other spheres of activity in the society in which it takes place. In such works, one does not read transcripts of actual verbal interactions; rather, one learns about what the researcher found out from local research participants. A macroscopic ethnographic approach to gossip is particularly useful in shedding light into the social, cultural, and ideological context in which gossip takes place and the way in which gossip both affects and is informed by this context. This approach addresses general questions in the social sciences about how societies and communities are held together (or not), how conflict is exacerbated or deflected, and how social inequalities are created, maintained, or challenged.

The second approach, which is less common but nevertheless potentially very rich, consists in recording naturally occurring gossip, transcribing the texts, and analyzing their conversational organization and discourse structure. For obvious reasons, all works in this vein postdate the emergence of portable recording devices. Many are grounded in the analysis of naturalistic, spontaneous texts that emerged in the 1970s and 1980s in sociolinguistics, discourse analysis, and conversation analysis. This approach, which we may characterize as microscopic, treats gossip as a text, with a particular structure (grammatical, prosodic, interactional) that may be specific to it or that may share commonalities with other interactional genres (Bergmann, 1993; Goodwin, 1990). The analyst takes seriously the fact that meaning is not only embedded in the literal (referential) aspects of the language, but also, and perhaps more importantly in the case of gossip, in its non-referential aspects, particularly in what C. S. Peirce, and many scholars of language in its social context after him, call the "indexical" value of language; that is, aspects of language that contextually evoke ideas and events (Parmentier, 1994). This means that the meaning of gossip cannot be simply "read" in what people say, it must be interpreted in terms of what they do not say but evoke through non-segmental aspects of interaction like prosody, omission, deictics, choice of referential expressions, turn-taking structure, and so on.

The most fruitful ethnographic approach to gossip is one that focuses equally on the its microscopic aspects as interaction and on macroscopic aspects of the sociocultural context in which it takes place, and seeks to understand how they are related (Besnier, 2009). For example, the moral evaluation of gossip in a particular society may encourage people engaging in a gossip session to give to their interaction a particular structural configuration that helps them manage the morally tainted nature of what they are doing, as I will illustrate presently. Thus the textual characteristics of the gossip interaction are indexical of the cultural and social context in which its takes place: the structure of gossip both defines this context and is determined by it. To date, however, few scholars have managed to mobilize the analytic resources necessary to articulate microscopic and macroscopic analyses; this goal is one of the open challenges for the ethnographic analysis of gossip.

# Defining Gossip Ethnographically

One of the first questions that concerned ethnographers with an interest in gossip is the extent this category of interaction is recognizable as a distinct form of social activity (i.e., a "speech genre") across the world's societies. The question of the cross-cultural recognition of a gossip speech genre, which remains largely unresolved to date, is contingent on how one defines gossip, itself a thorny question to answer in the abstract. A general working definition identifies gossip as an exchange of information of a negative nature about an absent third party among a bounded group of people gathered in a private setting (in anthropology, the term "person" is preferred over the term "individual" as the former highlights the social nature of the category). It is often denigrated as a morally reprehensible and social devalued activity from which people often wish to distance themselves, no matter how much they actually engage in it.

Immediately, this working definition is confronted with exceptions and presents problems of definitional circularity. For example, one can exchange negative information about someone who is within earshot, for example by creating collusion involving a subset of participants that excludes the target of the gossip (Goodwin, 1991). "Gossip columns" about celebrities in print media and in cyberspace are public forms of communication (see De Backer et al., this volume), in that anyone can read them including the target of the gossip, although they are often framed so as to create the illusion of confidentiality between the writer and the reader (Gamson, 1994). Furthermore, people sometimes tell stories about themselves that resemble storytelling about others that would in other contexts be termed gossip (Besnier, 2016). In addition, the extent to which gossip is a morally tainted activity with potentially damaging effects for the reputation of the target depends on many factors; in some societies or for some people, gossip of is little consequence and does not arouse particular moral disapproval (Merry, 1984). A recurrent problem is that, as a genre of talk that people consider to be of little value in probably all societies of the world, gossip generally lacks clear markers that isolate it from what comes before or after, in the way that a public lecture in academic circles or formal speeches in many societies are bounded, temporally and otherwise, by an introduction, a conclusion, a particular way of interacting, and so on. To use Goffman's (1974) terminology, gossip often lacks a clear socially sanctioned frame, but rather its frame emerges from the interaction itself (Besnier, 1989).

An alternative route to identifying what counts as gossip is to ask whether it is a recognized category within local theories of social action. Ethnographers favor this approach in that it privileges local concepts in preference to the imposition of predetermined categories onto the contexts they study. For example, in Rijsburg, a small community in the Netherlands that specializes in growing and selling flowers, villagers clearly identify a type of verbal activity, *roddel*, that corresponds closely to what English speakers term "gossip," which has characteristics that are familiar from other ethnographic contexts: it is socially marginal yet an important way of maintaining social control, it defines the moral order, and provides a context to distinguish locals from others (Strating, 1998). But here again problems can arise. In Zinacantan, Southern Mexico, for example, people engage in talk about each other with great enthusiasm, gather information about one another to form cultural knowledge that construct reputations, and "are aware of a domain of behavior similar to what we call 'gossip,'" but they do not identify the activity with a specific term (Haviland, 1977, p. 46). Thus while the local typology of communicative activities can be helpful in identifying a locally recognized speech genre that has roughly the same characteristics as gossip in other societies, it is not always a reliable criterion.

In many societies, furthermore, what counts as gossip is subject to different interpretations among social groups. Gender is one dimension of social difference and inequality that is a particularly common parameter of disagreement about what counts as gossip. For example, in the village of southern France where anthropologist F. G. Bailey conducted fieldwork in the 1960s, men's gossip is called "*bavarder*: a friendly, sociable, light-hearted, good-natured, altruistic exchange of news, information and opinion. But if women are seen talking together, then something quite different is happening: very likely they are indulging in *mauvaise langue*—gossip, malice, 'character assassination'" (Bailey, 1971, p. 1; Bailey evidently took as default men's evaluations of who gossips and who does not, since he did not tell us what women think). These patterns are very common cross-culturally and are intertwined with the workings of gender hierarchies: men's assessment of women's interactional activities as gossip become the group's default assessment; gossip is unimportant, morally problematic, and potentially dangerous; and because women gossip, they are not to be trusted with important matters.

Yet in other contexts, such logical reasoning does not go unchallenged. For example, on Nukulaelae Atoll, in the Central Pacific, where gossip occupies considerable social space in daily life (Besnier, 2009), but where both women and men associate it primarily with women, some women retort that men's interminable political meetings are just as time wasteful, morally problematic, and reputation damaging as women's gossip. This illustrates the fact that the denigration of some people's activities as "mere gossip" can become the object of resistance. These remarks demonstrate that the question, "Do women gossip more than men?" which is frequently asked in both academic and popular writings (e.g., Coates, 1989; Levin and Arluke, 1985; among many others), is problematic, since it assumes that what counts as gossip can be evaluated independently of whose perspective one takes.

An important aspect of the relationship between gossip and its social context is the contrast between the public and the private: people define the context of gossip as private by definition, but gossip also helps define and circumscribe a context as private. The mutual constitution of gossip and the private demonstrates that the private, as well as its counterpart the public, is not a place, a sphere of activity, or a kind of relationship. Rather, it is a discursive phenomenon that operates like a Peircean index: it means nothing independently of a context, but once this context has been established, it serves to help people classify, characterize, and understand human activity (Gal, 2002). It is this semiotic complexity that bestows on it its slippery quality, which gossip conducted through new communicative technologies like social media showcases even more dramatically than ever before.

What these ethnographic vignettes and the caveats they suggest is that the distinction between what counts as morally problematic, reputation damaging, and privately bounded gossip and other forms of interaction lies in the eyes of the beholder. It is itself a politically, morally, and culturally laden judgment that is open to different interpretations, as well as contestation. What constitutes gossip in contrast to other forms of interaction is thus an ideological construct, whose dynamics are related to other aspects of social life and culture, such as morality, social inequality, and identity.

## GOSSIP IN ITS SOCIAL AND CULTURAL CONTEXT

A question that hovers over ethnographic works on gossip since anthropologists began to pay attention to it is what gossip does to people, how, and why. Early works framed this question in terms of the "function" of gossip, the assumption being that people's actions are designed to reinforce the cohesion of the group and its reproduction over time (see Boehm, this volume). This assumption prevailed in the school of structural functionalism, which dominated anthropology in the first part of the twentieth century, particularly in Britain. The first anthropologist to write explicitly about gossip was South African anthropologist Max Gluckman, had been trained in that tradition; but he had also turned his attention, under the (considered at the time problematic) influence of Marxism, to problems of conflict and ethnic mixing in urban contexts, thus departing from the traditional insistence on the cohesion and modularity of society. His foundational article on the topic, "Gossip and Scandal" (Gluckman, 1963), argued that the function of gossip was to maintain the social cohesion of the group and to distinguish the group from other groups: as "the hallmark of membership" (1963, p. 313), it helps define the boundary between socially accepted and deviant behavior, thus contributing to solidifying consensus among group members and control dissent without resorting to open conflict. In this view, gossip has both integrative and differentiating "functions."

The publication of Gluckman's article was soon followed by a long series of exchanges among anthropologists of diverse theoretical persuasions. In particular, anthropologists inspired by forms of methodological individualism that were then emerging in anthropology on both sides of the Atlantic, namely transactionalism and the symbolic interactionism of Erving Goffman, argued that, far from reinforcing the cohesion of society, gossip was a tool that particular individuals utilized to manipulate information, further their own political designs, and undermine the interests of others (Gilmore, 1978; Hannerz, 1967; Paine, 1967; and many others). In this view, the information about others that people transmit through gossip is a commodity that they accumulate and exchange in calculated fashion, in the same way that they manipulate material commodities in systems of exchange, indebtedness, and reciprocity. Here we see a shift from an understanding of human action as having a singular "function" with a specific end to a perspective on human action as process, which may have multiple intents, effects, and meanings. This shift enables us to see that social cohesion and strategic manipulation are in fact not mutually incompatible aspects of gossip, but can coexist variously as intent, effect, or both.

Early ethnographic works on gossip in its social context tended to neglect one important aspect of gossip, namely the participant structure of gossip events themselves, particularly the relationship between people who are speaking and who are listening (Giardini and Wittek, this volume). In certain contexts, such as the Indo-Fijian village where linguistic anthropologist Donald Brenneis (1984, 1987) conducted fieldwork, it is very difficult to distinguish between a gossiper and his or her audience because everyone participates in gossip sessions, interrupting each other, engaging in word play, and repeating, overlapping, or finishing each other's utterances, all in a collaborative effort in which the pleasure derived from the form of the conversation counts as much as the information being circulated. This work is an excellent illustration of the kind of light that ethnographic methods can shed: rather than assuming that gossip is necessarily based on a triadic relationship between speaker, listener, and topic of the gossip, the ethnographer observes and records people gossiping in naturalistic settings and realizes that the participant structure is considerably more complex. Here, gossip is an aesthetic production with a collaborative poetic structure that is an iconic representation of the egalitarianism and collectivism that this society values. In a similar vein, on Nukulaelae Atoll, storytellers in gossip sessions tend to let their interlocutors fill in some of the details of their stories, such as the actual names of people (sometimes leaving audience members guessing over several turns at speaking) and the dénouement of stories that explicitly articulate the moral precepts that the target of gossip is alleged to have violated (Besnier, 1989, 2009). These interactional devises draw audiences into the conversation so that they become "coauthors" (Brenneis and Duranti, 1986) of the gossip, and by the same token assume moral responsibility for engaging in what is potentially a morally reprehensible activity.

While early ethnographers of gossip more or less agreed that gossip provides a way of asserting the boundary between morally acceptable action and deviant behavior, and thus helps to solidify consensus about morality, developments in the discipline since then have demonstrated that, far from forming a coherent whole that is the subject of consensus, culture in general (and morality in particular) is a site of contestation and disagreement (e.g., Abu-Lughod, 1991; and many others). Local morality may be superposed with other forms of morality associated with such entities as the state, development, modernity, or transnational mobility. For example, agents of development (e.g., state agents, NGO workers, religious figures) may urge people to save their resources, and thus demonstrate their moral worth as modern strategic thinkers, while local moral codes may insist that people meet traditional expectations of reciprocity and resource redistribution, and thus demonstrate their moral worth as generous and tradition-abiding people. Those who opt for the first of these conflicting moral injunctions may become prime targets of gossip (Besnier, 2009, pp. 120–142; Van Vleet, 2003). Alternatively, people may gossip about each other and about themselves to find comfort in retreating in a well-defined local morality that excludes their participation in a wider world where they feel lost and no longer have a well-defined moral compass to live by (Besnier, 2016). Here we see the methodological importance of contextualizing what people say about others during gossip in a broader context in which moral precepts may be heterogeneous and contested.

In other cases, people may be anxious to maintain their reputation as morally worthy individuals in different societies at once. The stories of success and wealth that migrants from impoverished areas of the world tell about themselves on social media and through other forms of transnational communication often contrast sharply with a reality of struggles in inhospitable societies of the global North (e.g., Mains, 2012; Newell, 2012). Migrants run the serious risk of being exposed by fellow migrants' long-distance gossip about their real predicaments, and must carefully manage their social relations in various locations at once (e.g., Cole, 2014). Moral codes, in Krista Van Vleet's words (2003), always constitute "partial theories," and gossip is one site where members of a society negotiate the frictions created by the coexistence of different partial theories. And this is also precisely why studying gossip can be a methodological stepping stone to questions of broader scope, such as what keeps society running despite its heterogeneity.

In spite of its stigmatized triviality in many social contexts, gossip can have serious political consequences. This dimension of gossip has received considerable attention in the work of sociocultural anthropologists, who are traditionally interested in how gossip articulates with a larger context of hierarchy, inequality, power, belonging, and the state. In particular, they have recognized that, despite its appearance of inconsequentiality, gossip can have seriously damaging effects on the reputation, social standing, and even life of the person being gossiped about. In other words, gossip can be a powerful tool for enacting political action, and this recognition argues for an understanding of politics as not confinement to the juridical-political spheres of social life.

Recognizing the power of gossip as political action, however, does not allow one to draw generalizations about *how* gossip operates as politics. Indeed, in some contexts, gossip can be a useful counter-hegemonic or resistant device in the hands of the oppressed against the power of the oppressor. Here, a rich corpus of materials emerged in the 1980s and 1990s in anthropology on "everyday forms of resistance," the subaltern's quotidian struggle to undermine power structures and their agents (e.g., in addition to gossip, theft, sabotage, foot dragging), which often appear to be designed for purposes other than political action but which, when anonymous and away from the eyes of power, have a cumulative effect of hampering power. This line of thinking was spurred on by the influential writings of James Scott (1985, 1990), which argued against a view of power as totalizing and of oppressed groups as complicit in their own oppression for believing that structures of inequality are inevitable and just (Giardini and Wittek, this volume).

This approach gave rise at the time to a rich corpus of ethnographic and historical case studies that documented the power of gossip as resistance across different societies and communities (e.g., Briggs, 1992; Feldman and Stall, 2003; Harding, 1975; Wickham, 1998). For example, witchcraft accusation through gossip in many societies can have serious effects on those who enrich themselves excessively or too quickly and bring about their downfall (e.g., Ashforth, 2005; Geschiere, 2013; Niehaus, 2013; White, 2000). However, critics of resistance theory have argued that its valorization of the subaltern's actions as counterhegemonic is grounded in a romantic celebration of the resilience and resourcefulness of the human spirit even under conditions of oppression; that resistant action often gives rise to renewed forms of repression; and that researchers often "read" resistance in actions that may completely different intents and consequences (e.g., Abu-Lughod, 1990; Brown, 1996; Ortner, 1995). Badmouthing people who make one's life miserable may make one feel temporarily better but does not necessarily have any lasting impact on the situation.

In other contexts, however, the political effects of gossip may have exactly the opposite configuration: it can potentially supplement dynamics of power and coercion and thus exacerbate structures of inequality and oppression, weaken the weak, strengthen the powerful, and marginalize the marginalized, as those in power can deploy it to control others or to control material and symbolic resources. For example, Karen Brison's (1992) exemplary ethnography of gossip and power among the Kwanga, in the East Sepik province of Papua New Guinea, demonstrates how leaders in this society encourage gossip about their own ability to perform maleficent sorcery to enhance their own prestige and intimidate potential rivals and dissidents.

To date, ethnographers have mostly documented how gossip escalates conflict, or at least maintains situations that are fundamentally conflictual, in that the best interests of some are upheld at the expense of those of others. But in some circumstance gossip may have no effect at all on the target of gossip: people who are already socially marginalized or whose reputation is either irrelevant or already tainted may be largely immune to gossip. Such is the case of the poor and the abject (unless they have designs to move up in the world) and of the very rich. Alternatively, the target of the gossip can sometimes benefit from it. Besnier (2009, pp. 143–165) recounts the different effects that gossip has on two women on Nukulaelae Atoll, who are somewhat on the margins of society because they are widows, and who have been accused of engaging in sorcery. In the case of one woman, who was anxious to maintain a reputation as an upstanding and peace-loving Christian, the gossip had devastating psychological and social effects; in contrast, the other woman, who was both valued and feared because of her skills as a bush doctor and midwife (skills that always arouse suspicions of sorcery in that society), never tried to deny the gossip and basked in the resulting ambiguity that only increased her prestige and her desirability as a medical practitioner.

Gossip can also act as a leveling mechanism between not only those who engage in it but also between the gossipers and the target of the gossip. Marjorie Goodwin's (1990) now classic linguistic anthropological study of African American children's interactions in working-class Philadelphia is a case in point: the children tattle on one another about each other, accusing each other of gossiping about one another (see Ingram, this volume). Their narratives are structured as complex recursively embedded structures of reported speech (e.g., A says to B, "C said to me that you [B] said to C something disparaging about me [A]"). Because these narratives implicate several individuals, they obscure responsibility and easily lead to denials of wrongdoings, thereby avoiding more serious physical confrontation, allowing protagonists to save face, and reestablishing compromised friendships.

Gossip is clearly involved in the workings of interpersonal and group-level politics, but the uses to which social actors put it depend not only on the social structure but also on other political, social, and cultural dynamics at play. Thus, if beliefs in witchcraft are such that people see it as a potentially serious way of harming others, gossiping about witchcraft (or openly accusing someone of it) can lead to very serious harm for the target of the gossip. Whether gossip acts as a way to maintain power structures or to undermine them depends on a multitude of other factors, including the extent to which power rests of reputation. One generally expects that, where power is achieved (i.e., earned through one's personal qualities and one's ability to persuade others), gossip may be more serious than where power is ascribed (i.e., earned as part of one's birthright). But many other factors come into play, and no simple model of causality can account for the wide variety of effects. The sociopolitical makeup of the group determines who benefits and who suffers from gossip, but the reverse is also true: gossip creates particular sociopolitical configurations. What may appear at first glance to be a tautology actually captures the constitutive relationship between gossip and politics, to which one should add all other forms of talk and political action: agency, whether it manifests itself in talk or nonverbal action, creates social structures just as structures give rise to agency. The multiplicity of potential configurations and outcomes gives gossip its unpredictability, power, and productivity as an object of inquiry for the social and behavioral sciences.

## AREAS FOR FUTURE RESEARCH

In contrast to other approaches to gossip, ethnographic works on the topic do not generally showcase the relationship between gossip and reputation as an analytic category, even though reputation in its various guises (e.g., fame, prestige, honor) does have a long genealogy in the discipline. In anthropology, "reputation" is particularly strongly associated with one specific ethnographic area, namely the Anglophone Caribbean. The category was first used as an analytic category in the 1960s by Peter Wilson (1969), who argued that the moral and cultural structure extant in Caribbean societies was subsumed by a dialectic tension between "respectability," namely norms of conduct that emphasize conformity, dignity, and participation in a social order inherited from the agents of colonialism (through church attendance, schooling, officially sanctioned marriage, etc.), and "reputation," defined as "a kind of improvisational adaptability—or flexibility—associated primarily with a lower-class and masculine public sphere of performance and sociality encompassing such venues as street corners, the political platform, the rum shop, the market, and the musical stage and with such attributes as sexual prowess, verbal wit, musical flair, and economic guile" (Freeman, 2007, 254). Perhaps as a result of this very specific definition, which is widely recognized in anthropology, the category "reputation" does not figure in ethnographic works on gossip. (The term "reputation" is part of the title of John Haviland's pioneering 1977 monograph on gossip in Zinacantan, but the author does not define it and uses it in a way that anthropologists would subsequently use the category "personhood.") It may also be the case that ethnographers' greater emphasis on social relations than on individuals deflects their attention away from reputation as an analytic category.

One aspect to which little research has been devoted is the role of emotions in gossip, such as shame, envy, anger, and pleasure. This lack of attention is surprising given the importance that anthropologists have historically bestowed on trying to understand emotions, the cross-cultural variability, and their articulation with other aspects of social life, such as inequality, ritual, and kinship (e.g., Lutz and White, 1986), an area of inquiry that is currently the object of renewed interest under the different guise of "affect," whose relationship to emotion remains to be fully explored (McElhinny, 2010; Wilce, 2009; Rutherford, 2016). Shame can emerge in a number of ways, including the shame of being gossiped about or of suspecting that one is the target of gossip, or the shame of being caught gossiping in societies that deem the activity reprehensible. Envy and anger can also motivate people to gossip in the first place or they can be emotions that gossiping about someone else arouses in either the listener or the storyteller (Martinescu, Janssen, and Nijstad, this volume; Van Vleet, 2003); alternatively, anger can be a reaction to being gossiped about if word of the gossip reaches its target. But pleasure can also figure prominently. In addition to the aesthetic and sociable enjoyment that Indo-Fijian gossipers experience (Brenneis, 1984, 1987), there is the pleasure of one-upmanship that skillful gossipers experience when they have a juicy story to tell to an attentive audience. Such vignettes suggest that emotions play an important role in gossip worldwide and that the topic deserves more attention than it has been given to date.

Gossip, of course, does not "do things" on its own; rather, like other forms of interactions, it achieves whatever it achieves because it stands in relation to other forms of talk (or writing, singing, signing, etc.) and social action. When people gossip, they are intensely aware of the fact that their words and actions articulate with (i.e., repeat, elaborate, comment on, contradict, ridicule) words and actions that take place in other contexts. So, rather than focusing exclusively on gossip, one needs to embed it in a broad context of alternative forms of interaction and seek to understand how the various channels of communication feed into one another in various ways: the same information circulates across genres, but also absorbs different aspects of context in each situation; and gossip that circulates across different contexts of communication can create powerful webs of entanglement with potentially serious effects on people's lives (e.g., when the target of gossip is prevented from confronting it in public). Gossip circulating across communicative genres is not anyone's property, it is never localized anywhere, but it remains ever present in the social domain and in the social relations in which it is embedded. How information circulates in and out of genres of communication, how it is transformed in the process of this circulation, and how the information in different contexts can be associated with different forms of credibility and deniability (e.g., which kind of information is acceptable in a court of law) are topics that remains largely unexplored ethnographically (Besnier, 2009, pp. 166–188).

In a related fashion, gossip can travel over large distances and across different moral worlds, particularly in the age of social media and other forms of instant communication. Here traditional accounts of gossip as enforcing and regulating the moral consensus of a society no longer work well, as the participants are no longer encompassed in anything that one can call a "group" of any kind; attempts to talk about people connected via the internet as "cyber communities" stretch the meaning of "community" to its logical extreme. The mediating role of gossip in a world in which local lives are deeply connected to global dynamics is one area of research that awaits further scrutiny.

## ACKNOWLEDGMENTS

I thank Francesca Giardini and Rafael Wittek for having invited me to the "Gossip and the Management of Reputation" Workshop at the Lorentz Center in Leiden in September 2013, where I presented an early version of this chapter. Some passages of this chapter are rewritten, expanded, and updated versions of text that appears in chapter 1 of Besnier (2009).

## REFERENCES

Abu-Lughod, Lila. 1990. "The Romance of Resistance: Tracing Transformations of Power through Bedouin Women." *American Ethnologist* 17: 41–55.

Abu-Lughod, Lila. 1991. "Writing Against Culture." In *Recapturing Anthropology: Working in the Present*, edited by Richard G. Fox. Santa Fe, N. M.: School of American Research Press.

Ashforth, Adam. 2005. *Witchcraft, Violence, and Democracy in South Africa*. Chicago: University of Chicago Press.

Bailey, F. G. 1971. "Gifts and Poison." In *Gifts and Poison: The Politics of Reputation*, edited by F. G. Bailey. Oxford, England: Basil Blackwell.

Bergmann, Jorg R. 1993. *Discreet Indiscretions: The Social Organization of Gossip*, translated by John Bednarz, Jr. New York: Aldine De Gruyter.

Besnier, Niko. 1989. "Information Withholding as a Manipulative and Collusive Strategy in Nukulaelae Gossip." *Language in Society* 18: 315–341.

Besnier, Niko. 2009. *Gossip and the Everyday Production of Politics*. Honolulu: University of Hawai'i Press.

Besnier, Niko. 2016. "Humour and Humility: Narratives of Modernity on Nukulaelae Atoll." *Etnofoor* 28 (1): 75–95.

Besnier, Niko, and Susan U. Philips. 2014. "Ethnographic Methods for Language and Gender Research." In *The Handbook of Language, Gender, and Sexuality*, 2nd ed., edited by Janet Holmes, Miriam Meyerhoff, and Susan Ehrlich. Chichester, England: Wiley-Blackwell.

Boehm, Christopher. 2019. "Gossip and Reputation in Small Scale Societies: A View from Evolutionary Anthropology." In *Handbook of Gossip and Reputation*, edited by Francesca Giardini and Rafael Wittek. New York: Oxford University Press.

Brenneis, Donald L. 1984. "Grog and Gossip in Bhatgaon: Style and Substance in Fiji Indian Conversation." *American Ethnologist* 11: 487–506.

Brenneis, Donald L. 1987. "Talk and Transformation." *Man* [n.s.] 22: 499–510.

Brenneis, Donald L., and Alessandro Duranti, eds. 1986. *The Audience as Co-Author*. Special issue of *Text* 6 (3).

Briggs, Charles L. 1992. "'Since I Am a Woman, I Will Chastise My Relatives': Gender, Reported Speech, and the (Re)construction of Social Relations in Warao Ritual Wailing." *American Ethnologist* 19: 337–361.

Brison, Karen J. 1992. *Just Talk: Gossip, Meetings, and Power in a Papua New Guinea Village*. Berkeley: University of California Press.

Brown, Michael F. 1996. "On Resisting Resistance." *American Anthropologist* 98: 729–735.

Chomsky, Noam. 1957. *Syntactic Structures*. The Hague: Mouton.

Clifford, James, and George Marcus, eds. 1986. *Writing Culture: The Poetics and Politics of Ethnography*. Berkeley: University of California Press.

Coates, Jennifer. 1989. "Gossip Revisited: An Analysis of All Female Discourse." In *Women in Their Speech Communities*, edited by Jennifer Coates and Deborah Cameron. London: Longman.

Cole, Jennifer. 2014. "The Téléphone Malgache: Transnational Gossip and Social Transformation among Malagasy Marriage Migrants in France." *American Ethnologist* 41: 276–289.

De Backer, Charlotte J. S., Hilde Van den Bulck, Maryanne L. Fisher, and Gaëlle Ouvrein. 2019. "How Celebrities Emerge and Evolve by Means of Mass Mediated Gossip." In *Handbook of Gossip and Reputation*, edited by Francesca Giardini and Rafael Wittek. New York: Oxford University Press.

Feldman, Roberta M., and Susan Stall. 2003. *The Dignity of Resistance: Women Residents' Activism in Chicago Public Housing*. Cambridge: Cambridge University Press.

Freeman, Carla. 2007. "The 'Reputation' of Neoliberalism." *American Ethnologist* 34: 252–267.

Gal, Susan. 1989. "Language and Political Economy." *Annual Review of Anthropology* 18: 345–367.

Gal, Susan. 2002. "A Semiotics of the Public/Private Distinction." *differences* 13 (1): 77–95.

Gamson, Josh. 1994. *Claims to Fame: Celebrity in Contemporary America*. Berkeley: University of California Press.

Geertz, Clifford. 1973. "Thick Description: Toward an Interpretive Theory of Culture." In *The Interpretation of Cultures: Selected Essays*. New York, NY: Basic Books.

Geschiere, Peter. 2013. *Witchcraft, Intimacy, and Trust: Africa in Comparison*. Chicago: University of Chicago Press.

Giardini, Francesca, and Rafael Wittek. 2019. "Gossip, Reputation, and Sustainable Cooperation: Sociological Foundations." In *Handbook of Gossip and Reputation*, edited by Francesca Giardini and Rafael Wittek. New York: Oxford University Press.

Gilmore, David. 1978. "Varieties of Gossip in a Spanish Rural Community." *Ethnology* 17: 89–99.

Gluckman, Max. 1963. "Gossip and Scandal." *Current Anthropology* 4: 307–315.

Goffman, Erving. 1974. *Frame Analysis: An Essay on the Organization of Experience*. New York: Harper & Row.

Goodwin, Marjorie H. 1990. *He-Said-She-Said: Talk as Social Organization among Black Children*. Bloomington, IN: Indiana University Press.

Goodwin, Marjorie H. 1991. "Byplay: Participant Structure and the Framing of Collaborative Collusion." In *Les formes de la conversation*, vol. 2, edited by Bernard Conein, Michel de Fornel, and Louis Quéré. Paris: CNET.

Gumperz, John J., and Dell Hymes, eds. 1972. *Directions in Sociolinguistics: The Ethnography of Communication*. New York: Holt, Rinehart & Winston.

Hannerz, Ulf. 1967. "Gossip, Networks and Culture in a Black American Ghetto." *Ethnos* 32: 35–60.

Harding, Susan. 1975. "Women and Words in a Spanish Village." In *Toward an Anthropology of Women*, edited by Rayna R. Rapp. New York: Monthly Review Press.

Haviland, John B. 1977. *Gossip, Reputation, and Knowledge in Zinacantan*. Chicago: University of Chicago Press.

Hymes, D. 1974. *Foundations in Sociolinguistics: An Ethnographic Approach*. Philadelphia: University of Pennsylvania Press.

Ingram, Gordon P. D. 2019. "Gossip and Reputation in Childhood." In *Handbook of Gossip and Reputation*, edited by Francesca Giardini and Rafael Wittek. New York: Oxford University Press.

Irvine, Judith T. 1989. "When Talk Isn't Cheap: Language and Political Economy." *American Ethnologist* 16: 248–267.

Labov, William. 1966. *The Social Stratification of English in New York City*. Washington, DC: Center for Applied Linguistics.

Lederman, Rena. 2006. "Introduction: Anxious Borders between Work and Life in a Time of Bureaucratic Ethics Regulation." *American Ethnologist* 33: 477–481.

Levin, Jack, and Arnold Arluke. 1985. "An Exploratory Analysis of Sex Differences in Gossip." *Sex Roles* 12: 281–286.

Lutz, Catherine, and Geoffrey M. White. 1986. "The Anthropology of Emotions." *Annual Review of Anthropology* 15: 405–436.

Mains, Daniel. 2012. *Hope Is Cut: Youth, Unemployment, and the Future in Urban Ethiopia*. Philadelphia: Temple University Press.

Malinowski, Bronislaw. 1922. *Argonauts of the Western Pacific: An Account of Native Enterprise and Adventure in the Archipelagoes of Melanesian New Guinea*. London: Routledge & Kegan Paul.

Mangardich, Haykaz, and Stanka A. Fitneva. 2019. "Gossip, Reputation, and Language." In *Handbook of Gossip and Reputation*, edited by Francesca Giardini and Rafael Wittek. New York: Oxford University Press.

Marcus, George E., and Michael M. J. Fisher, eds. 1986. *Anthropology as Cultural Critique: An Experimental Moment in the Human Sciences*. Chicago: University of Chicago Press.

Martinescu, Elena, Onne Janssen, and Nijstad Bernard A. 2018. "Gossip and Emotions." In *Handbook of Gossip and Reputation*, edited by Francesca Giardini and Rafael Wittek. New York: Oxford University Press.

McElhinny, Bonnie. 2010. "The Audacity of Affect: Gender, Race, and History in Linguistic Accounts of Legitimacy and Belonging." *Annual Review of Anthropology* 39: 309–328.

Merry, Sally Engle. 1984. "Rethinking Gossip and Scandal." In *Toward a General Theory of Social Control*, edited by Donald Black. Orlando, FL: Academic Press.

Newell, Sasha. 2012. *The Modernity Bluff: Crime, Consumption, and Citizenship in Côte d'Ivoire*. Chicago: University of Chicago Press.

Niehaus, Isak. 2013. *Witchcraft and a Life in the New South Africa*. Cambridge: Cambridge University Press.

Ortner, Sherry. 1995. "Resistance and the Problem of Ethnographic Refusal." *Comparative Studies in Society and History* 37: 173–193.

Paine, Robert. 1967. "What Is Gossip About? An Alternative Hypothesis." *Man* [n.s.] 2: 278–285.

Parmentier, Richard. 1994. *Signs in Society: Studies in Semiotic Anthropology*. Bloomington: Indiana University Press.

Philips, Susan U. 2013. "Method in Anthropological Discourse Analysis: The Comparison of Units of Discourse." *Journal of Linguistic Anthropology* 23: 83–96.

Rutherford, Danilyn. 2016. "Affect Theory and the Empirical." *Annual Review of Anthropology* 45: 285–300.

Scott, James C. 1985. *Weapons of the Weak: Everyday Forms of Peasant Resistance*. New Haven, CT: Yale University Press.

Scott, James C. 1990. *Domination and the Arts of Resistance: Hidden Transcripts*. New Haven, CT: Yale University Press.

Strating, Alex. 1998. "Roddelen en de verbale constructie van gemeenschap." *Etnofoor* 11 (2): 25–40.

Van Vleet, Krista. 2003. "Partial Theories: On Gossip, Envy, and Ethnography in the Andes." *Ethnography* 4: 491–519.

White, Luise. 2000. *Speaking with Vampires: Rumor and History in Colonial Africa*. Berkeley: University of California Press.

Wickham, Chris. 1998. "Gossip and Resistance among the Medieval Peasantry." *Past & Present* 160: 3–24.

Wilce, James. 2009. *Language and Emotion*. Cambridge: Cambridge University Press.

Wilson, Peter J. 1969. "Reputation and Respectability: A Suggestion for Caribbean Ethnology." *Man* [n.s.] 4 (1): 70–84.

# PART II

## INDIVIDUAL COGNITION AND EMOTION

# CHAPTER 7

# NEUROSCIENTIFIC METHODS

RICCARDO BOERO

## INTRODUCTION

NEUROSCIENTIFIC methods are aimed at investigating the structure and function of the brain. The application of these tools to social phenomena significantly extends social researchers' toolbox. For instance, they can be used to test the existence of "unique" social cognitive processes, they can map social behavior on social brain and attribute it to psychological processes, they allow us to differentiate social and cultural influences and individual differences, and ultimately they are crucial to explain social behavior (Adolphs, 2010).

Social neuroscience and the interdisciplinary approaches merging social sciences with neuroscientific methods have only recently started the investigation of the neurobiological foundations of gossip and reputation.

Being very recent research fields and approaches, scientific knowledge about the neurobiological foundations of gossip and reputation is still incomplete. Nevertheless, some initial interesting results shed light on the complex causal network underlying most common human behavior associated with gossip and reputation.

The aim of this chapter is to support research by providing a critical presentation of approaches and results in the investigation of the neurobiological foundations of human behavior associated with reputation and gossip. Despite the relative scarcity and incompleteness, the richness and potential impact of neuroscientific investigations and their capability of being fruitfully interconnected with other approaches make this approach extremely interesting for all researchers interested on gossip and reputation.

The neuroscientific approach in fact supports research on these fields by providing a rigorous and empirical way to test hypotheses about the two phenomena. For instance, it is possible to investigate whether motivations, such as bond attachment, play a specific role in gossip, or whether reputation-based cooperative behavior is mostly explained by internal means of social control (e.g., internalized moral codes) or by careful assessments of alternatives decisions and of their future consequences. Neuroscientific methods allow answering these kinds of questions and many more, such as those mentioned in the concluding part of this chapter. They obviously require a rigorous methodological approach, and their use is obviously not straightforward for the inexperienced researcher. Despite their complexity and the "cost" associated with their use (e.g., the extensive research activities required to get to a robust experimental protocol), they provide the possibility to test hypotheses, and as such they provide a unique and significant contribution to the research fields of interest here.

This chapter is organized as follows. The *Neuroscientific Methods* section presents the tools and approaches adopted in neuroscientific studies. That section has not the ambition of completeness, and it is not a substitute for the many good manuals presenting methodologies and tools typically used in neuroscience. In contrast, the section is aimed at providing the reader with the information that is essential to understand the power and the limits of the methods and thus to better comprehend the validity of presented results. This section also discusses why so much attention has been spent so far on the behavioral side of these phenomena.

The *A Four-Step Approach to the Neurobiology of Gossip and Reputation* section is then focused on recent results, and it outlines a map of the existing state of the art in the neurobiological foundations of behavior associated with gossip and reputation.

Finally, *The Intersection between Reputation and Gossip and the Many Open Issues* section identifies the mechanisms concurrently influencing both gossip and reputation, and it integrates such knowledge with behavioral and theoretical evidence linking gossip to reputation and vice versa. This section concludes by outlining the neurobiological mechanisms that influence the intersection between gossip and reputation and the many issues that remain open in this field.

# NEUROSCIENTIFIC METHODS

Methods adopted in social neuroscience have the principal aim of identifying the neural correlates of behavioral tasks framed in social settings. The environment in which the behavioral tasks are administered and observed is typically a laboratory where most nuisance factors can be controlled and tasks replicated. The focus on neural correlates does not prescribe a priori the kind of answer looked for, such as a single area in the brain or a network of areas and systems. At the same time, the initial focus on correlation does not exclude ambitiously peering into the realm of causation too.

The behavioral tasks that are most often adopted in neuroscientific experiments are social because they require multiple subjects interacting, and they usually are derived from cooperation dilemmas developed in game theory and experimental economics. These games, in fact, present a dilemma to subjects in which essentially they have to choose between two alternatives, one in which they cooperate with others, aiming at uncertain future gains, and one in which non-cooperation leads to an immediate "small" gain (see Milinski, this volume; see Roddie, this volume). Any kind of task centered on a cooperative dilemma can be the base for neuroscientific experiments of reputation and gossip. In fact, adding to the simple decision scheme that has been just outlined, the possibility of being observed and communicated is the only step necessary. Once behavior can be observed, reputation can emerge. Once behavior and reputation can be communicated, gossip can be modeled.

Because of the reasons just outlined, economic games such as the trust game (also known as the investment game; Berg et al., 1995) and the prisoner's dilemma are often used in these experiments. Other approaches, however, are also possible, in particular if the hypothesis to be tested is limited to a specific step of decision making. In fact, any task capable of providing individual and social metrics to assess subjects' behavior and evaluations can be used. For instance, in experiments on gossip the task may be developed with the aim of measuring how gossip shapes subjects' attention (see details in contributions presented in *A Four-Step Approach to the Neurobiology of Gossip and Reputation* section).

The tool mostly used in this kind of studies is the functional magnetic resonance imaging (fMRI), which is used to observe blood oxygenation level-dependent responses to stimuli (for an introduction to fMRI see Huettel et al., 2008).

In layman's terms, an fMRI machine is a big item that occupies half a room, it is usually located in hospitals, it is quite noisy when running, and it has been designed to let a person introduce any body part inside a big magnet. For the kinds of applications of interest here, the part of the body that is introduced is the head, and claustrophobic reactions are quite common. The magnet is an essential part of this machine, and not only for its noticeable size. Scientist would prefer directly observing the activation of neurons inside the brain, but that is very invasive. Instead, they observe blood cells passing oxygen to neurons when they are fired or immediately after that. In scientific terms, scientists look for hemodynamic responses, and they measure them through blood-level changes of magnetic orientation, observable thanks to the strong artificial magnetic field.

Another tool used in social neuroscience is the repetitive transcranial magnetic stimulation (rTMS), which is used to selectively and temporarily impair neurons in the brain (for an introduction to rTMS see Wassermann et al., 2008; and Rotenberg et al., 2014).

In layman's terms, rTMS is a small helmet connected to a computer. Its working mechanism is based on a pulsed current produced by a coil that creates a magnetic field, which in turn depolarizes neurons located in superficial areas of the brain. By using rTMS aimed at specific, well-known brain areas, scientists are capable of precisely interrupting cognitive functions to test whether they actually interfere with the ability to perform tasks.

Besides the intrinsic limitations and the specific features and biases in data collection through both methods (e.g., Hayasaka, 2013; and Sliwinska et al., 2014), rTMS is usually not the preferred choice because of the temporary impairment of subjects. Nevertheless, rTMS provides the possibility to directly test causality, which is impossible through fMRI.

Designing an experiment with fMRI thus presents some specific challenges that should be understood to better comprehend the often very complicated designs of the experiments reported in this kind of literature. In fact, besides controlling for the usual nuisance and environmental factors that should be accounted for in experiments regarding social behavior, social neuroscientific experiments must deal with the fact that brain area activation are not fully controllable. It is thus a matter of designing tasks that, because of their sharp differences, will show the activation of various areas in evident contrast. This issue is even more complex if considering that while observing the brain in a resting state is not an easy task per se, observing a resting state for a specific brain area and cognitive function is even more difficult.

In contrast, fMRI can easily be related to other measurement techniques that support social neuroscience investigations. For instance, it is possible to integrate fMRI with other measures of brain activity such as electroencephalograms or with rTMS (e.g., Binney & Ralph, 2015). It is also possible to integrate observations collected through these tools with completely different measurements, such as the measures of personality traits considered in the contributions of Meshi, Garbarini, and coworkers (Meshi et al., 2013; Garbarini et al., 2014) discussed in the following section.

The integration of neuroscientific tools with those developed in fields such as social psychology seems to be a particularly fruitful way to overcome the limitations of using of neuroscientific tools alone to account for group and individual differences.

# A Four-Step Approach to the Neurobiology of Gossip and Reputation

The search for the neurobiological foundations of reputation and gossip is far from complete. Recent literature in this field has so far reached only one main objective in its research agenda; namely, the identification of the neural systems usually involved in dealing with reputation and gossip. It remains largely unclear what specific brain areas are activated within the systems and how they interact. Similarly, these scientific investigations have several limitations, such as the number of subjects involved, and it is often impossible to extend their validity beyond the specific behavior observed.

In other words, existing knowledge is incomplete and not very precise, and its external validity is still very limited. Nevertheless, the first interesting results available today provide several important insights into the neural mechanisms behind gossip and reputation and set the foundation for further research.

Both reputation and gossip involve mainly three neural systems, and other systems can be activated for the recognition of stimuli and the implementation of decisions (Izuma, 2012). The three main networks are the reward system, the mentalizing network, and the self-control system (for details on their location, composition, and significance see "Steps 1–4"). Their role in reputation and gossip dynamics is straightforward.

For instance, a person trying to establish a good reputation has to value it through the reward system. At the same time, that person must form an opinion of what others think of him or her through some meta-representation of others' thoughts. Finally the implementation of the pro-social behavior that supports a good reputation often happens at the cost of some other alternatives that can provide immediate benefits (i.e., social defection), and thus there is the need for executive functions associated with planning and for self-control. From the perspective of gossip and from that of using others' reputations for decision making, there is a need for selective attention toward these kinds of information and for the capability of evaluating them, which are activities supported by the reward system.

In general terms, reputation and gossip seem to follow a broadly defined sequence of steps of complex decision making (Izuma, 2012). The procedure should not necessarily be considered as a straight line connecting one step after another and directly leading from social stimuli (i.e., the input) to decisions (i.e., the output). In contrast, between the input and the output there is a complex network of activations that can also be simultaneous and with feedbacks and loops.

Nevertheless, the procedure starts with the perception of external stimuli (step 1). This step allows inputs to be observed in the external (social) environment and transformed in a way useful for decision making. The first step, however, is particularly relevant because both reputation and gossip are based on particular kinds of stimuli, which must be focused on, detected, and which may trigger affective unique responses with consequences for following steps.

In step 2, individuals develop a meta-representation of others, which is crucial to evaluate the reputational impacts of possible courses of action. In fact, without a theory of the mind it would be impossible to evaluate whether an action is socially acceptable and consistent with social norms and expectations, and consequently whether actions improve or damage personal reputation and if they may fuel the gossip.

Then, in step 3, possible courses of actions are evaluated in terms of a sort of cost-benefit analysis that uses the same measurement unit for rewards and costs that are intrinsically different and uncertain. In this phase, possible courses of action are evaluated and ranked according to assessments capable of both aggregating different units, such monetary rewards and reputational cost, and accounting for uncertainty about the future and the others.

Step 4 involves the execution of actions that have been selected. This step is not trivial, and it requires further cognitive and neural processes. For instance, because execution may take some time, this step often requires a certain degree of attention and effort, self-control may be crucial.

## Step 1: Perception of Stimuli

Going into details about both neural processes and applications to reputation and gossip, the first neural processes that are of interest for reputation and gossip are the ones that allow the perception of social stimuli (step 1, as defined above). They are areas that allow understanding the social context, the possibility of social cooperation and thus the relevance of reputation and gossip signals.

The main brain area with these functions is the amygdala, which receives inputs from senses (Zald, 2003) and, often with the contribution of affective processes, interconnects with prefrontal and temporal cortices and with the striatum (see "Steps 2–4" for details about the roles of these areas in this context). Further, given the vast behavioral evidence of the impact of the mere fact of "being observed" in order to establish social perception (e.g., Bateson et al., 2006), the amygdala seems crucial for reputation and gossip because of its role in the recognition of eye and gaze direction (Kennedy & Adolphs, 2010).

Concerning gossip and the importance of stimuli recognition, Anderson et al. (2011) have used a binocular rivalry experiment to show that human faces previously associated with a negative gossip are dominant, while those associated with positive or neutral gossip are not. In fact, in a binocular rivalry experiment, an image is presented to one eye and a very different image is presented to the other eye. As well known for centuries (Wade, 1996), images presented as such are not composed or superimposed and only one image is seen. In the case of gossip, in other words, there is proof of a process of selective visual attention that, probably for aims of learning, focuses on negative gossip.

Going back to the eventual role of affective processes, the recent contribution of Zheng and colleagues (Zheng et al., 2016) focuses on empathy as a driver of social behavior and investigates whether reputation influences empathic neural responses to pain. In this context, reputation is measured by the level of cooperation in repeated prisoner's dilemma games (i.e., reputation is indirectly observed through partners' reactive behavior that rewards good reputation with cooperation), and results confirm the link between reputation and emotions by showing more activation in the bilateral anterior insula (AI) and dorsal anterior cingulate cortex (dACC) when observing pain in other subjects with good reputation.

## Step 2: Development of Meta-representations

Regarding mentalizing and the formation of meta-representations of others (Izuma, 2012), the main research points out a predominant role of the prefrontal cortex, which has been recognized also as a key area for maintaining goals (Miller & Cohen, 2001). In particular, the medial prefrontal cortex (MPFC) is activated when others are forming opinions about the subject, and that is independent from the possible rewards derived from meta-representations (Izuma et al., 2008).

The MPFC has been noted also in Garbarini et al. (2014) along other areas associated with theory of the mind (e.g., the left precuneus). This study also points out a gender difference. Females activate these areas significantly more and in conjunction with the left fusiform and the parahippocampal gyrus, a finding that, consistently with observed differences in personality traits, suggests a mechanism whereby females care more about self-identity and others' opinion and react upon these traits with more cooperative behavior.

## Step 3: Evaluation of Choices

In the case of the reward system (step 3), almost all the areas usually associated with this function have been found to be significantly activated by reputation. Among them, a predominant role is played by the striatum (Izuma et al., 2008), which serves as a sort of unique evaluator of rewards, transforming various reward (e.g., monetary and food vs. reputation and social) into a common currency (Izuma, 2012). In this context, the striatum allows the possibility of comparing possible courses of action (e.g., whether investing in reputation or not) and thus supports decision making.

In reputation building, Garbarini et al. (2014) show that all areas usually associated with reward evaluation (i.e., anterior cingulate cortex, striatum, insula, and ventral tegmental area) are significantly activated by reputation, and the activation is larger in males than in females.

Concerning reputation information that may be derived not from direct experience, Stanley et al. (2012) investigate whether social group membership carries on reputational information and the underlying neural networks. The authors investigate non-repeated interactions between subjects of varying races and found two important activations, amygdala and striatum. Amygdala is probably associated only with the process of group membership identification (as noted above), while the striatum is involved in representing the reputation that individuals attach to different races.

Concerning the reward associated with the mere fact of establishing a cooperative environment, Phan et al. (2010) confirm that cooperative outcomes activate reward centers such as the ventral striatum and the orbitofrontal cortex. The authors show also that successful cooperation with partners who have a positive reputation modulates with activation in the striatum only, enriching results presented by Delgado et al. (2005) that observe similar patterns but that are based on description of moral character and not on directly experienced reputation.

Reward evaluation in reputation settings also requires accounting for trust dynamics and dynamics of reciprocity. In this context, other areas such as the caudate are particularly important.

For instance, Watanabe et al. (2014) focused on the areas that may be behind mechanisms of indirect reciprocation. They separate two kinds of cooperation associated with indirect reciprocity. The first is reputation-based cooperation in which individuals cooperate with other individuals with good reputation to gain a good reputation themselves. The second, which the authors define as pay-it-forward cooperation, occurs when a person only reciprocates because of being helped by someone else. They found that in cooperative behavior associated with reputation-based reciprocity there is a conjoint activation of precuneus and caudate, and in pay-it-forward reciprocity there is the conjoint activation of the anterior insula and the caudate.

At the intersection between reputation building and reputation gains, Meshi et al. (2013) focus on the bilateral nucleus accumbens, which has been recognized as another area processing rewards (Airely & Berns, 2010). The authors use a self-reported measure of Facebook use as behavioral proxy for reputation building (i.e., assuming that active engagement on the social media platform is a good approximation of the personal investment in reputation) and find that, when observing another person's reputation in comparison with the self, activation of the nucleus accumbens is explained by Facebook use. At the same time, self-relevant gains in reputation and monetary gains both correlate with the ventral striatum, confirming previously mentioned research identifying this area as a common evaluator for different kinds of rewards.

King-Casas et al. (2005) use multiround trust games to investigate trust dynamics and reputation building. Although in these settings, reciprocity is a strong predictor of behavioral patterns, results also point out the role of the dorsal striatum (and in particular of the caudate), which is involved in evaluating the fairness of a partner's decisions in terms of reward and thus contributes to the intention to trust the partner. When subjects deviate from neutral reciprocity (e.g., when individuals reciprocate to changes of a partner's cooperation with larger or smaller variations of their own cooperation level than the triggering ones by their partner), partners activate neural areas consistent with a surprise signal, suggesting that neutral reciprocity is the social norm expected in these settings.

In repeated interactions where reputation evolves, the timing of activations in the dorsal striatum anticipates in the game. Activations shift from evaluation to prediction of rewards. In fact, at the behavioral level investors' changes in reciprocity predict trustees changes in repayment (in trust games "investors" split an endowment with partnering "trustees," who in turn decide whether to repay anything to investors). Cross-brain analysis (King-Casas et al., 2005, p. 80) confirms the behavioral evidence, and it shows correlations between the cingulate cortices of partners (i.e., between the middle cingulate cortex of investors and the anterior cingulate cortex of trustees). The timing of activations across partners over repeated interactions show a shift in time toward an anticipatory signal of the intention to trust, which testifies to the building of a model of the partner.

A further behavioral experiment reported in King-Casas et al. (2005) confirmed the learning over game repetitions of investors' reputation through accurate guesses of investors' decisions. The experiment supports further the interpretation of caudate activations in the trustee's brain as reputation development. With the accumulation of experience, rewards anticipate, activating progressively more quickly, until they become expectations of others' behavior that can be interpreted as reputation.

Finally, taking the perspective of gossip, Peng et al. (2015) point out the activation of different areas of the prefrontal cortex belonging to the reward system in the case of stimuli of two kinds, positive gossip about the self and negative gossip about celebrities. Similar results have been previously found in Ochsner et al. (2004), where distinct areas of the prefrontal cortex have been recognized as fundamental for the evaluation of judgments about the self and others.

## Step 4: Execution of Actions

Finally, about the execution of selected actions, in the case of the self-control system the main area activated in reputation settings is the dorsolateral prefrontal cortex (DLPFC), which allows exchanging a short-term, immediate benefit for future larger benefits. Knoch et al. (2009) present a rTMS study where the inhibition of that area does not allow offsetting immediate benefits with future rewards, thus impeding the development of a good reputation. This result is confirmed by Garbarini et al. (2014): the authors show that the right DLPFC is significantly activated by both sexes and the left DLPFC is activated by males only, probably resulting in a more risk-prone behavior by males. The same authors also find that reputation significantly activates the rostral prefrontal cortex, which is another area usually associated with the capability to carry on long-term mental plans.

In conclusion, evidence on brain area activations in settings of reputation and gossip is very much limited, but it seems to outline a complete (and complex) decision making process. Further, identified areas and the cognitive processes associated with them are consistent with other neuroscientific contributions and in particular with those focusing on social cooperation issues. For instance, rewards evaluation areas are similar to the ones found in investigations about social exclusion (Eisenberger et al., 2003; Will et al., 2015) and punishment (Knutson et al., 2000; Delgado et al., 2000; O'Doherty et al., 2001).

# The Intersection between Reputation and Gossip and the Many Open Issues

Although incomplete, the recent literature about the neurobiological foundations of gossip and reputation suggests some similar mechanisms behind the two phenomena. From a behavioral perspective, information at the core of both mechanisms has a two-fold value, deterring anti-social behavior and supporting social cooperation. As such, it is plausible to assume that gossip and reputation at the neural level require functions similar to those provided by the systems listed previously. Reputation and gossip in fact require perceiving social stimuli, evaluating the outcomes of possible courses of action, and selecting one of them. From this perspective, research findings available today do not point out significant differences between directly experienced or observed reputation and indirect information received as gossip.

However, results are incomplete and limited, and it is not even possible to make hypotheses about similarities and differences between gossip and reputation concerning many several important aspects, such as for instance reputation building. The rest of this section is thus devoted to discussing the many issues that remain open about gossip, reputation, and their intersection relative to the neural systems identified above, but first there are some open issues to talk about that regard all systems.

In fact, our knowledge is, first, very much limited with respect to explaining heterogeneity in behavior. Behavioral results, in particular in reputation settings just because gossip has been less studied from this perspective, point out a high degree of individual heterogeneity. It is unclear whether this behavioral heterogeneity can be explained in terms of heterogeneity at the level of neural foundations and what could be its cause.

In this context, enriching neuroscientific tools with other approaches seems to be the only option, as confirmed by the use of personality traits analysis in Garbarini et al. (2014) that significantly supports the explanation of heterogeneity across genders.

Second, there is still much confusion about the existence of differences due to the kind of information at the basis of reputation and gossip. Behavioral evidence suggests different behavioral reactions to different kinds of information, which has been explained under a unique neurobiological framework in the case of reputation. However, many studies on reputation do not effectively separate behavioral effects of reputation building from those lead by the information provided by others' reputation, and research in gossip suggests selective attention to only specific kinds of stimuli, such as negative gossip about others and positive gossip about the self. Today it remains unclear whether various kinds of information are treated differently in reputation and gossip.

Related to this last point, there is still much to investigate about proactive behavior in gossip. In other words, is there anything comparable to reputation building in gossip? And if so, what are the foundations? Research suggests that a significant reward is associated to positive gossip about the self, but it doesn't say anything yet on this implying the promise of future benefits, similarly to reputation.

Fourth, the evidence reported above has been analyzed for a very limited set of decision settings. In fact, reputation analyses have been mostly based on economic cooperation and gossip analyses have focused on celebrities. Although the evidence at disposal does not suggest any impact, it is important to check the external validity of the neurobiological foundations of gossip and reputation in order to extend results to most common and daily activities based on social interaction.

Fifth, inquiries into the neurobiological foundations of gossip have so far completely ignored the potential role of the source of gossip. It is in fact conceivable that the reliability and significance of gossipers may be perceived differently, and that this features of the source of gossip may influence gossip-influenced decision making both at the level of stimuli perception and reward evaluation. In case of "gossip building" gossiper features may impact the same neural systems for mentalizing and self-control, and gossips by unreliable sources may affect, either positively or negatively, the self-control system.

Sixth, we ignore the foundations of some specific events, in particular at the intersection of gossip and reputation. For instance, we do not know why a person decides to pass his own personal evaluation of another person's reputation to third parties, initiating the diffusion of gossip. It may be hypothesized that this process is a sort of cheap punishment aimed at supporting cooperation (Egas & Riedl, 2008), and as such it could activate all neural systems mentioned so far. In contrast, it may also be possible that completely different reward areas may be involved by the social nature of gossip diffusion.

Finally, the state of the art does not capture dramatic changes and failures concerning all activated systems. For instance, it is unclear what happens when a person discovers that the information diffused by gossip is unreliable. Would this impact the stimuli perception system only (e.g., starting to ignore that source of information) or would this impact the reward system too? For both reputation and gossip there may be a learning process to select trustworthy signals and information sources when direct social interaction does not happen. Further, it seems very likely that learning processes drive meta-representation formation and maybe also self-control.

Concerning stimuli perception, it is unclear whether the areas activated by reputation are different depending on the fact that partner actions are known because of direct interaction (i.e., social interaction with a partner) or just because of observation (i.e., observing the partner interacting with a third party). Knowledge about this issue should then be extended to gossip and to the many degrees of separation that gossipers may have from direct experience or observation.

Regarding the mentalizing system, we know that gossip sometime does not originate from an individual's own opinion but instead from the individual's opinion of what others think. In other words, gossip may be already the outcome of meta-representations and a social meta-product if it changes while diffusing. In this context, when people deal with gossips about the self, do they activate different meta-representations to account for these peculiarities of gossip?

Regarding issues specific to the reward system, the most important knowledge gap concerns the interaction of the areas activated in this system with affective processes. For instance, assuming that different gossipers may influence reward evaluation because of reliability and trustworthiness, could something similar be true also about affective impacts of such social relationships?

Finally, there are many open issues concerning if and how gossip affects self-control. For instance, it is plausible to hypothesize that negative gossip that is perceived unfair may push the balance towards short-term benefits. Similarly, it may be worth investigating whether processes of reputation and gossip building interact. From this perspective, gossip may be interpreted as enhancing the reward of a good reputation and thus enhancing self-control.

In conclusion, many of these open issues will also benefit from future innovations of neuroscientific methods and tools. Reductions in size and cost of tools and the development of less invasive approaches will support external validity and more effective and immediate analyses. Gossip and reputation are in fact complex social phenomena where social relationships and the multiple decisions and actions involved may not always be reduced to the simplified representations adopted in the experimental protocols feasible today.

## REFERENCES

Adolphs, R. (2010). Conceptual challenges and directions for social neuroscience. *Neuron* 65(6), 752–767.

Anderson E., Siegel, E. H., Bliss-Moreau, E., & Feldman Barrett, L. (2011). The visual impact of gossip, *Science* 332(6036), 1446–1448.

Ariely, D., & Berns, G. S. (2010). Neuromarketing: The hope and hype of neuroimaging in business. *Nature Reviews Neuroscience* 11(4), 284–292.

Bateson, M., Nettle, D., & Roberts, G. (2006). Cues of being watched enhance cooperation in a real-world setting. *Biology Letters* 2(3), 412–414.

Berg, J., Dickhaut, J., & McCabe, K. (1995). Trust, reciprocity, and social history. *Games and Economic Behavior 10*(1), 122–142.

Binney, R. J., & Ralph, M. A. L. (2015). Using a combination of fMRI and anterior temporal lobe rTMS to measure intrinsic and induced activation changes across the semantic cognition network. *Neuropsychologia 76*, 170–181.

Delgado, M. R., Frank, R. H., & Phelps, E. A. (2005). Perceptions of moral character modulate the neural systems of reward during the trust game. *Nature Neuroscience 8*(11), 1611–1618.

Delgado, M. R., Nystrom, L. E., Fissell, C., Noll, D. C., & Fiez, J. A. (2000). Tracking the hemodynamic responses to reward and punishment in the striatum. *Journal of Neurophysiology 84*(6), 3072–3077.

Egas, M., & Riedl, A. (2008). The economics of altruistic punishment and the maintenance of cooperation. *Proceedings of the Royal Society of London B: Biological Sciences 275*, 871–878.

Eisenberger, N. I., Lieberman, M. D., & Williams, K. D. (2003). Does rejection hurt? An fMRI study of social exclusion. *Science, 302*(5643), 290–292.

Garbarini, F., Boero, R., D'Agata, F., Bravo, G., Mosso, C., Cauda, F.,...Sacco, K. (2014). Neural correlates of gender differences in reputation building. *PLoS One 9*(9), e106285.

Hayasaka, S. (2013). Functional connectivity networks with and without global signal correction. *Frontiers in Human Neuroscience 7*, 880.

Huettel, S. A., Song, A. W., & McCarthy, G. (2008). *Functional magnetic resonance imaging,* 2nd ed. Sunderland: Sinauer Associates.

Izuma, K. (2012). The social neuroscience of reputation. *Neuroscience Research 72*(4), 283–288.

Izuma, K., Saito, D. N., & Sadato, N. (2008). Processing of social and monetary rewards in the human striatum. *Neuron 58*(2), 284–294.

Kennedy, D. P., & Adolphs, R. (2010). Impaired fixation to eyes following amygdala damage arises from abnormal bottom-up attention. *Neuropsychologia 48*(12), 3392–3398.

King-Casas, B., Tomlin, D., Anen, C., Camerer, C. F., Quartz, S. R., & Montague, P. R. (2005). Getting to know you: Reputation and trust in a two-person economic exchange. *Science 308*(5718), 78–83.

Knoch, D., Schneider, F., Schunk, D., Hohmann, M., & Fehr, E. (2009). Disrupting the prefrontal cortex diminishes the human ability to build a good reputation. *Proceedings of the National Academy of Sciences USA 106*(49), 20895–20899.

Knutson, B., Westdorp, A., Kaiser, E., & Hommer, D., (2000). FMRI visualization of brain activity during a monetary incentive delay task. *Neuroimage 12*(1), 20–27.

Milinski, M. (2019). "Gossip and reputation in social dilemmas." In F. Giardini & R. P. M. Wittek (Eds.), *Handbook of gossip and reputation.* New York: Oxford University Press.

Meshi, D., Morawetz, C., & Heekeren, H. R. (2013). Nucleus accumbens response to gains in reputation for the self relative to gains for others predicts social media use. *Frontiers in Human Neuroscience 7*, 439.

Miller, E. K., & Cohen, J. D. (2001). An integrative theory of prefrontal cortex function. *Annual Review of Neuroscience 24*(1), 167–202.

Ochsner, K. N., Knierim, K., Ludlow, D. H., Hanelin, J., Ramachandran, T., Glover, G., & Mackey, S. C. (2004). Reflecting upon feelings: An fMRI study of neural systems supporting the attribution of emotion to self and other. *Journal of Cognitive Neuroscience 16*(10), 1746–1772.

O'Doherty, J., Kringelbach, M. L., Rolls, E. T., Hornak, J., & Andrews, C. (2001). Abstract reward and punishment representations in the human orbitofrontal cortex. *Nature Neuroscience 4*(1), 95–102.

Peng X., Li, Y., Wang, P., Mo, L., & & Chen, Q. (2015). The ugly truth: Negative gossip about celebrities and positive gossip about self entertain people in different ways. *Social Neuroscience* 10(3), 320–336.

Phan, K. L., Sripada, C. S., Angstadt, M., & McCabe, K. (2010). Reputation for reciprocity engages the brain reward center. *Proceedings of the National Academy of Sciences USA 107*(29), 13099–13104.

Roddie, C. (2019). Reputation and Gossip in Game Theory. In F. Giardini, R. P. M. Wittek (Eds.), *Handbook of Gossip and Reputation*. New York: Oxford University Press.

Rotenberg, A., Horvath, J. C., & Pascual-Leone, A. (Eds.). (2014). *Transcranial magnetic stimulation*. New York: Springer.

Sliwinska, M. W., Vitello, S., & Devlin, J. T. (2014). Transcranial magnetic stimulation for investigating causal brain-behavioral relationships and their time course. *Journal of Visualized Experiments: JoVE, 89*, 51735.

Stanley, D. A., Sokol-Hessner, P., Fareri, D. S., Perino, M. T., Delgado, M. R., Banaji, M. R., & Phelps, E. A. (2012). Race and reputation: Perceived racial group trustworthiness influences the neural correlates of trust decisions. *Philosophical Transactions of the Royal Society of London B: Biological Sciences 367*(1589), 744–753.

Wade, N. J. (1996). Descriptions of visual phenomena from Aristotle to Wheatstone. *Perception* 25(10), 1137–1175.

Wassermann, E., Epstein, C., & Ziemann, U. (2008). *Oxford handbook of transcranial stimulation*. New York: Oxford University Press.

Watanabe, T., Takezawa, M., Nakawake, Y., Kunimatsu, A., Yamasue, H., Nakamura, M.,… Masuda, N. (2014). Two distinct neural mechanisms underlying indirect reciprocity. *Proceedings of the National Academy of Sciences USA 111*(11), 3990–3995.

Will, G. J., Crone, E. A., & Güroğlu, B. (2015). Acting on social exclusion: Neural correlates of punishment and forgiveness of excluders. *Social Cognitive and Affective Neuroscience, 10*(2), 209–218.

Zald, D. H. (2003). The human amygdala and the emotional evaluation of sensory stimuli. *Brain Research Reviews 41*(1), 88–123.

Zheng, L., Wang, Q., Cheng, X., Li, L., Yang, G., Sun, L.,… Guo, X. (2016). Perceived reputation of others modulates empathic neural responses. *Experimental Brain Research 234*(1), 125–132.

# CHAPTER 8

# GOSSIP AND REPUTATION IN CHILDHOOD

### GORDON P. D. INGRAM

## INTRODUCTION

THIS chapter attempts to show how an understanding of gossip and reputation in adults can be informed by an analysis of the growth of simpler forms of behavioral reporting and character evaluation in children. There are two key assumptions behind this approach: first, that children are not simply little adults with access to less information and a quantitatively smaller brain capacity, but beings who think in qualitatively different ways; and second, that adult ways of thinking and behaving do not simply replace children's ways, but are in some sense constructed on top of the latter via an increase in information-processing complexity. In common with much of modern developmental psychology—and while acknowledging more recent research that has resulted in significant modifications to Piaget's ideas—this approach is broadly Piagetian in focus, Piaget's conception of stages being effectively levels of complexity of information-processing that serve as "building blocks" for fully adult ways of thinking.

While not all developmental psychologists share Piaget's belief in the utility of a stage-based analysis such as this one, it should be noted that stage theory does not rest on the authority of a single theorist but also makes scientific sense from an evolutionary developmental perspective (Bjorklund and Pellegrini, 2000; Tomasello and Gonzalez-Cabrera, 2017). As has recently been argued (Burman, 2013; Ingram, 2013), Piaget's stages represent the psychological effects of underlying biological changes in the developing individual. It is thus possible to accept the utility of dividing children's development into stages, without accepting all the details of Piaget's theory, or regarding either the stages, or the ages at which stage transitions take place, as strictly invariant (cf. Lourenço, 2016). Unlike Piaget, evolutionary developmental stage theory posits the existence of early hard-wired biases (e.g., toward social stimuli and therefore social information) that persist throughout later stages of development. And from an evolutionary point of view, the main reason for the existence of stages in the development of gossip and reputation may be a progressive lack of dependence on adult caregivers to meet one's fitness needs and an increased interdependence with peers (paralleling the classic theory of Piaget [1932] on the transition from heteronomous to autonomous morality). Reflecting this focus on children's needs, a more indirect aim of the chapter is to show how gossip, reputation and their developmental precursors pervade many different aspects of children's social lives, and can therefore be useful for understanding and improving their lives.

This review of the ontogeny of gossip and reputational understanding is divided into five sections, based on five ontogenetic stages through which children and adolescents pass during development: infancy, early childhood, middle childhood, preadolescence and early adolescence, and middle to late adolescence. For each stage, I outline the characteristics of gossip production and reputational understanding in that age group. The overall intent is to provide a description of the cognitive building blocks that need to be in place for the very socially sophisticated adult behavior of gossip to be constructed. Finally, in the conclusion, I offer a tentative synthesis of the relationship between gossip and reputation through development. I argue that the ontogenies of these two phenomena are closely intertwined: changes in reputational understanding affect children's linguistic accounts of third parties, including gossip; while their experiences of producing and consuming gossip enable the development of a more sophisticated understanding of reputation.

# INFANCY (0–2 YEARS)

The stage of infancy is broadly defined, as with Piaget's sensorimotor stage, by the absence or only rudimentary presence of language. As such, infants cannot really gossip. However, their early social interactions with others do show several interesting features that hint at a future capacity for gossip. First, from the age of 9 months, and probably earlier, children exhibit an interest in triadic communication with caregivers: that is, in referring to an entity outside of the communication partnership that is the object of their "joint attention" (Carpenter et al., 1998), rather than just to something in themselves or their audience. Tomasello's early work showed that children had longer, more complex conversations with their mothers in this type of interaction than when they were only focused on each other (Tomasello and Farrar, 1986), leading to his postulation of joint attention as a key factor in the evolution of human language and cooperation (Tomasello, 1999; 2008). Second, even very young children are sensitive to their audience's knowledge state. Thirteen-month-old infants understand that seeing leads to knowing and that someone who has not had perceptual access to that information will not act based on that information (Surian et al., 2007), and they can even modify their communicative behavior to take account of an interaction partner's lack of knowledge when playing a hiding game (Bourdais et al., 2013). Third, even the youngest infants are interested in the social world. They will, for example, selectively orient to human faces

(Frank et al., 2014; Jakobsen et al., 2016; Johnson et al., 1991), and prefer to pay attention to a strange peer than to their mother (Lewis et al., 1975). Many of an infant's first words also refer to agents—that is, to potentially social beings (Dromi, 1999).

Thus, although gossip per se does not exist in infancy, putting these early characteristics of infant communication together we can see that humans are prepared for three crucial aspects of gossip right from the start of their communicative careers. Infants attempt to communicate about third-party entities of mutual interest to them and their audience; they attempt to communicate novel information; and they attempt to communicate social information. A fourth characteristic of gossip in adults is the communication of *reputationally relevant* information. Apparently no study has attempted to examine whether infants preferentially communicate such information. However, it certainly seems to be the case that infants are aware of what might be called the moral valence of an action, and react to it accordingly. Studies of selective association have shown that young children and infants as young as 5 months (Hamlin et al., 2011) prefer to interact with toys or puppets that they have witnessed exhibiting prosocial rather than antisocial behavior, and expect other characters to do the same (see also Hamlin et al., 2007; Kenward and Dahl, 2011; Meristo and Surian, 2014; Vaish et al., 2010; Vaish et al., 2016).

Some authors (e.g., Meristo and Surian, 2013) have interpreted these findings as reflecting an understanding of indirect reciprocity, which is often taken to be a foundation of reputation-based cooperation in humans (Alexander, 1987; Nowak and Sigmund, 1998; 2005). However, this seems like an over-interpretation of the data, given that similar patterns of selective association are also found in dogs (if strange humans are used instead of toys/puppets; Chijiiwa et al., 2015). This suggests that the infant results may reflect a general adaptive tendency in social animals to avoid individuals who are likely to do them harm, and approach individuals who are likely to help them (sometimes known as "social selection"; Baumard et al., 2013; Kuhlmeier et al., 2014), rather than a human-specific tendency to explicitly reward or punish other individuals, in line with Alexander's (1987) theoretical conception of indirect reciprocity. More empirical work is needed in order to carefully test for differences in what might be called "implicit" indirect reciprocity at early ages, based on selective association, and "explicit" indirect reciprocity at older ages, based on attempts to punish or reward certain behaviors in other people.

# EARLY CHILDHOOD (2–4 YEARS)

Moving on to the development of verbal behavior, what is clear is that almost as soon as young children can speak in full sentences, they are using them to report the behavior of other people, especially siblings (den Bak and Ross, 1996) or peers (Ingram and Bering, 2010). Children's third-party reporting meets a broad definition of gossip in terms of the description of other individual's behavior to a third party, although unlike prototypical adult gossip it is often overt in that it takes place in front of the person whose behavior is being reported (Ingram, 2014). This definitional ambiguity may explain why some authors have claimed that young children gossip frequently, but in front of the target (Fine, 1977), while others have claimed, from observations of young children in a daycare center, that "It was surprisingly difficult to catch the children gossiping" (Engel and Li, 2004, 160).

The overt reporting of negative (and especially counter-normative) behavior by other individuals is known as *tattling*. In children, it has been recorded observationally in homes between siblings (den Bak and Ross, 1996; Ross and Den Bak-Lammers, 1998), in preschools between peers (Ingram and Bering, 2010), and under controlled experimental conditions (Hardecker et al., 2016; Rakoczy et al., 2008; Schmidt et al., 2011; Vaish et al. 2011), even when these involve transgressions committed by an unfamiliar adult (Heyman et al. 2016). The prevalence of negative over positive or neutral reporting was demonstrated by Ross and Den Bak-Lammers (1998) and by Ingram and Bering (2010). Ingram (2014) argued that this was due to a social pressure on young children to express aggressive impulses in more and more indirect ways, since physical violence between siblings or peers is not usually tolerated by supervising adults.

There is some disagreement over exactly when tattling starts. Tomasello and Vaish (2013) claimed, based mainly on the experimental results of their own research group, that "normative protest" does not become common until children reach 3 years of age. However, in naturalistic environments regular tattling of 2-year-old children on their 4-year-old siblings was observed by den Bak and Ross (1996), while in audio-recordings made by Wells (1981), available in the CHILDES online corpus (MacWhinney, 2000) and re-analyzed by Ingram (2009), there were also several examples of tattling by 2-year-olds. The question of whether 2-year-olds are fully aware of the existence and importance of social norms is critical to analyzing the extent of their awareness of their own and others' reputation. This is because norm psychology is another building block of reputational understanding: the concept of reputation only really makes sense if it is placed in front of a background of social norms against which it can be measured, whether it is a bad reputation from failing to comply with norms or a good reputation from fully complying with, or even exceeding, normative expectations (Fu et al., 2016).

For reputation to be useful to others it has to be not only shared (e.g., via gossip) but an evaluation against shared standards: it is not very informative to tell someone about behavior you don't like, unless you assume that they also wouldn't like it. In a way, therefore, social norms represent an abstraction of shared intentionality extended to the judgment of action against (explicitly or implicitly) agreed standards (Schmidt and Rakoczy, forthcoming), rather than being simply joint attention paid to objects or actions that are immediately present. Tomasello and Vaish (2013) argued that this process develops in 3-year-olds based on theory-of-mind (and particularly false-belief) understanding. This does not make much sense because while often described as first appearing in 3-year-olds, explicit false-belief understanding in fact does not arrive in the majority of children until closer to 4 years (on average; see the meta-analysis of false-belief studies by Wellman et al., 2001); while other forms of explicit theory of mind, such as the understanding that individuals can have different desires, appear months earlier, and implicit theory of mind may develop as early as 15 months (Doherty, 2008). A scenario that may better fit the empirical evidence is that children gradually and intuitively learn to follow social norms between 2 and 3 years of age (about the same time that they learn grammatical rules, which after all are just a form of social norms). After 3 years of age they develop more of a metacognitive, representational awareness of social norms (cf. Perner, 1991), which includes the possibility of breaking them, and leads to more sophisticated forms of tattling and representational awareness. This is a related ability to false-belief understanding and develops in parallel with it, but there does not seem to be currently any direct empirical evidence that one is dependent on the other.

On the subject of normative understanding, young 3-year-olds, and indeed 2-year-olds, can also show a sophisticated understanding of the difference between "moral" norms that are universally applicable, and "conventional" norms that are restricted to a specific social context (Nucci and Turiel, 1978; Smetana, 1981; but see Hardecker et al. [2016] for evidence that in actual behavioral responses such as tattling, 3-year-olds may be less sensitive than 5-year-olds to the difference between moral and conventional norms). As we have seen, this is in line with the propensity of 2-year-olds (den Bak and Ross, 1996) and 3-year-olds (Ingram and Bering, 2010) to make contextually sensitive kinds of protests about siblings' or peers' norm violations. So, are 2-year-olds' protests against others' behavior truly norm-oriented, or simply advertising behavior that they don't like (a kind of negativity bias in line with the results of work on selective association, and with work that shows a bias toward descriptions of negative events in the stories that young children tell to parents about the past; Miller and Sperry, 1988)? This is a question that remains to be answered by future experimental research. If such research does show that children's early protests are truly oriented toward violation of social norms, and that their normative awareness develops between the ages of 2 and 3 rather than afterward, then it is possible that improvements in norm-understanding actually lead to key developments in theory of mind, and particularly in false-belief understanding, rather than vice versa.

# MIDDLE CHILDHOOD (4–8 YEARS)

Whatever the cause of the advance in theory-of-mind understanding between 3 and 4 years, it is clear that it precedes extensive changes in children's social cognition, social relations and cooperative behavior during middle childhood (Caputi et al., 2012; House et al., 2013; Slaughter et al., 2015), a once-neglected period of child development that is beginning to attract increased theoretical interest (Bosmans and Kerns, 2015; Del Giudice, 2014; Ingram, 2014). These changes naturally have effects on children's communication about others' social behavior. One such change is a drop in the relative importance of tattling: Ross and Den Bak-Lammers (1998) compared 4-year-old children's tattling on their 2-year-old siblings with the same children's levels of tattling when the former were 6 years old and their siblings 4 years old, and found that while overall rates of tattling increased (presumably reflecting an enhanced facility with narrative forms of language), it decreased as a proportion of children's total speech during the observational period. Indeed, Engelmann et al. (2016) showed that in an experimental situation involving a choice of potential collaborative partners, 5-year-olds but not 3-year-olds were capable of spontaneously providing positive reputational information about others. It is noteworthy however that just because children even at the start of middle childhood are capable of talking positively about others, this does not mean that they will necessarily do so very often in their everyday lives: in Ross and Den Bak-Lammers's (1998) data, 6-year-olds still spent more time tattling on their young siblings than they did describing their positive and neutral actions combined. Nevertheless, attitudes toward tattling change during middle childhood. In line with a classic experiment by Piaget (1932), a study by Chiu Loke et al. (2011) found that while 6-year-olds believed that tattling on both major and minor transgressions was acceptable, older children found it appropriate only for serious transgressions such as cases of physical violence (see also Chiu Loke et al. [2014] for a replication with both American and Japanese children).

Perhaps not coincidentally, it is during middle childhood and its accompanying decline in tattling that children first begin to gossip extensively, in the normal sense of the word (i.e., covert reporting of other people's behavior, in place of the overt reporting involved in tattling). After coding and analyzing the natural conversations of dyads of girls aged 6–7, 11–12, and 16–17 years, Mettetal (1983) found that the frequency of gossip increased dramatically between the youngest and middle age groups, remaining at about the same level in the oldest group. A similar longitudinal pattern, for younger children, was found by Engel and Li (2004), who asked three groups of participants—aged 4, 7, and 10 years—to tell stories about their friends in semi-structured interviews. The length, descriptiveness, and evaluative content of the stories increased significantly with age, implying that younger children's stories were much less informative than older children's.

If changes in children's social communication, including gossip, are just beginning in middle childhood, there are more dramatic changes taking place simultaneously in their reputational understanding. While the capacity to comprehend social norms may have developed in early childhood, it is in middle childhood—a relatively stable period of ontogeny—that children really spend significant amounts of time learning and internalizing normative behavior. This leads to more pronounced individual differences, as well as advancement across the board, in various culturally specific technical skills (Del Giudice, 2014; Locke and Bogin, 2006) and also in general levels of prosocial behavior (Caputi et al., 2012; House et al., 2013). Increased internalization of social norms coincides with a well-known development in moral psychology known as the outcome-to-intention shift (Cushman et al., 2013). In this developmental change, first outlined by Piaget (1932), children between the ages of 4 and 8 years who are morally evaluating an action come to assign more weight to the good or bad intention behind it, rather than focusing solely on the good or bad outcome as younger children do. (It is worth noting here that at age 4, even though they can typically pass false-belief tests and realize that other people have different preferences, many children still find it difficult to accept verbally that people can have wicked intentions [Cushman et al., 2013], which might seem to be another prerequisite for assigning someone a permanently bad reputation.)

Also at around this age, between about 6 and 8 years, children become aware that people can hold different but equally valid evaluations of the same stimulus, a development that has been called the beginning of the interpretive mind (Carpendale and Chandler, 1996) and has consequences for children's understanding of reputation as it may lead to the realization that an actor's actions can be interpreted differently by witnesses (and gossip recipients) than by the actor themselves (Ross et al., 2005). The complex social cognition involved in considering the various possible interpretations in such situations may depend on the development of more complex forms of theory of mind: Fu et al. (2014) found that second-order theory of mind (the ability to consider what another person thinks a third person is thinking) made unique contributions, on top of first-order theory of mind, to performance by 4- to 7-year-old children on moral judgement tasks.

In line with the developments that are taking place in theory of mind and related areas, children in middle childhood start to show greater sensitivity to the presence of an observer, suggesting further building blocks toward a fully developed concept of reputation. For example, Engelmann et al. (2012; see also Engelmann et al., 2013) found that 5-year-old humans, but not chimpanzees, behaved more cooperatively when observed by a peer. Meanwhile, Piazza et al. (2011) showed that 5- to 6-year-old children were less likely to cheat not only in the presence of a human observer but even in the presence of an imaginary invisible princess, invented by the experimenter. These studies are more suggestive than the evidence presented in the first section of a possible sensitivity in young children to generalized, linguistically mediated indirect reciprocity: since young children are not typically punished directly by peers or invisible princesses, the implication is that they might tell someone who could punish the participant. Interestingly, children's sensitivity to monitoring at this age may be a function of explicit (strategic) rather than implicit cognition (Leimgruber et al., 2012): an experimental study by Fujii et al. (2015) found that 5-year-olds' generosity increased when they were monitored by an experimenter, but not when they were "monitored" by a picture of staring eyes on a computer (but see Manesi et al. 2016); while in Piazza et al.'s (2011) results, the level of cheating was mediated by explicitly stated belief in the invisible agent.

Even these results, however, are compatible with a picture of development in which 5-year-olds are sensitive to how they are evaluated by direct witnesses (which we might call image-scoring; cf., e.g., Wedekind and Milinski, 2000), but not to the effects of gossip on linguistically mediated reputation. This last development probably has to wait until later in middle childhood: in a pivotal study for the purposes of the current chapter, Hill and Pillow (2006) showed that kindergarten children (aged 5–6 years) did not typically understand that an individual would have a lower opinion of a peer after learning about his or her antisocial activity indirectly, via gossip, though they did understand that direct observation of antisocial behavior would affect the witness's opinion. Seven- to eight-year-old children, on the other hand, did have both kinds of awareness. A recent study by Haux et al. (2016) supported this finding by showing that while 5-year-old children trusted gossip and direct observation equally, 7-year-olds gave more weight to their own observations. It remains to be investigated how this new understanding of the effects of language on reputation—and the potential of linguistic reports about others to be untrustworthy—rests upon and interacts with developments in the areas of theory of mind and morality that have also been discussed in this section.

# Preadolescence and Early Adolescence (8–13 years)

The studies of Mettetal (1983) and Engel and Li (2004) discussed in the previous section indicate that gossip becomes more common between middle childhood and pre-adolescence. This has not gone unnoticed by researchers, so that in contrast to the paucity of studies on gossip-like behavior in young children, more research has focused directly on pre-adolescent gossip. In a vignette study, for example, Kuttler et al. (2002) showed that 8- to 12-year-old children already understood what gossip meant, considered it generally inappropriate, treated it with skepticism (surprisingly, less so in older children), and judged false gossip harshly. Despite this apparent evaluation of gossip as inappropriate, preadolescents seem to have a drive to spread social information: in an experimental "transmission chain" study in a fifth-grade classroom (10- to 11-year-olds), McGuigan and Cubillo (2013) found that social information was transmitted more readily than non-social information, and (in contrast to stereotypes about gossip) that boys transmitted more social information than girls.

As well as sex differences, there may be interesting individual differences and age-related changes in gossiping within the preadolescent age range. The complex effects of gossip on personal relationships for this age group was shown by Menzer et al. (2012), who found that frequent gossip in 10- to 12-year-old girls' friendship dyads could lead to higher or lower levels of perceived friendship quality or friendship quality, depending on the levels of anxious withdrawal of the individuals concerned. The specific content of gossip is likely to be important for how well it is received. When McDonald et al. (2007) analyzed videos of female friends' (aged 9–10 years) conversations, they found that gossip was frequent and primarily neutral in content; popular girls however gossiped even more frequently, and more evaluatively (see Aikins et al. [2015] for a similar relationship between popularity and gossip frequency in 13- to 15-year-old girls). In contrast, working observationally with a sample of 10- to 14-year-olds, Eder and Enke (1991) found that negative evaluations of others in response to hearing gossip about them were more common than positive or neutral reactions, and that the first reaction from an individual within a group was important in influencing the reactions of other group members. Putting these two studies together, and assuming that popular children would be more likely both to react first and to influence other group members' opinions, provides a potential mechanism by which gossip might evolve from a more neutral to a more evaluative and critical form of conversation.

Another possible mechanism behind this process is that at this age gossip may take on some of the negative characteristics of tattling in younger children, since at younger ages negative tattling greatly outweighs positive or neutral comments about others, but overt tattling tends to become frowned upon as children reach adolescence. Goodwin (1990), one of the few people to have studied the transition between gossip and earlier forms of discourse about others' behavior, showed observationally that 10- to 11-year-old black urban American girls went through a kind of transitional phase that she labelled the "he-said-she-said" confrontation. This behavior consisted of aggressively confronting a peer who had been heard, through a third party, to have said something unpleasant about the confronter. The initial part of this activity was therefore covert, like adult gossip, but was then made overt through the tattling of the gossip recipient and the confrontational actions of the gossip target. Emphasizing, perhaps, the implicit nature of the negative evaluation involved, Goodwin (2007) even found that evaluations of absent peers were reflected in patterns of body language as well as in speech. Unfortunately there has been little or no research on similar kinds of transitional verbal behavior in other contexts, even within North America (though see Burdelski and Morita [2017] for some related data from Japan), so it is hard to say how common they are.

Also worth mentioning in the context of preadolescents and adolescents is the large volume of data collected by aggression researchers on gossip in this age group. As Archer and Coyne (2005) have shown, negative gossip is one of the primary ways of operationalizing all three of the related constructs of indirect aggression (Lagerspetz et al., 1988), relational aggression (Crick and Grotpeter, 1995), and social aggression (Cairns et al., 1989). It is noticeable that in Archer and Coyne's tabulation of the different yet similar ways in which these three forms of aggression are operationalized (Archer and Coyne, 2005, table 2), gossip is placed first in the list of type behaviors for all three forms during middle childhood and preadolescence, yet does not appear in the type behaviors for early childhood or adult forms. Since all these forms of aggression are typically defined in terms of an intent to damage someone's reputation (for instance, Galen and Underwood [1997, 589] define social aggression as "directed toward damaging another's self-esteem, social status, or both"), there is a clear conceptual link in the literature between gossiping in preadolescence and reputational conflicts at the same age. The underlying evolutionary reason for this link may be a reorganization of social relationships at the start of adolescence, as mating opportunities become adaptively salient (Ingram, 2014; Krebs, 2005), leading to a new concern for teenagers about their reputation in their peers' eyes.

# Middle to Late Adolescence and Adulthood (13 to 19+ years)

As children pass through adolescence, norms against overt tattling become more explicit (Friman et al., 2004). Gossip concomitantly becomes subtler and more covert: negative evaluations often become cloaked in ambiguity, allowing what is sometimes known as "plausible deniability" if the gossiper is accused of making a negative evaluation in a "he-said-she-said" type of confrontation. (At the same time, the pragmatic intent may be made quite clear to the audience, through nuances such as context or tone of voice.) This change in the nature of gossip can be seen in the changing operationalization of indirect, relational and social aggression in aggression studies with adolescents and adults. In Archer and Coyne's tabulation of the various type behaviors of these constructs at different ages (2005, table 2), the simple terms of "Gossip," "Spread rumors," and "Backbite" in pre-adolescent forms of aggression are replaced by more nuanced phrasings such as "Say something hurtful that appears rational when questioned," and "Judge others' work in an unjust manner" in the adult forms.

This change is likely to reflect a growing understanding of the negative reputational consequences (to the gossiper) of spreading explicitly negative gossip about others. While little work exists that directly tackles the full development of an adult understanding of reputation in the teenage years, this development may be associated with several concomitant developments that have been better studied: the growth of a sense of personal identity, linked to a clearer idea of the social role that the developing adolescent is likely to play in her/his community (Nurmi, 2004); the formal-operational understanding of hypothetical possibilities (Inhelder and Piaget, 1958), which would help in modelling the likely perceptions of one's actions by different types of onlookers (cross-sex as well as same-sex, for example); and an increased sophistication in moral reasoning, based on the idea of indirectly reciprocal rights and obligations within a community (Kohlberg, 1976; Krebs, 2005). Added to these developments is a considerable expansion in what counts as counter-normative behavior that might affect an adolescent's reputation (Steinberg, 2008), as they are granted more freedom to take risks by adults and start to experience new desires—leading to reputational effects of licentious sexual behavior (especially for girls; Bamberg, 2004), drinking and smoking (Engels et al., 2006), drug-taking (Carroll et al., 2003), and joyriding and other delinquent behavior (Carroll et al., 2009).

# SUMMARY OF THE STAGE MODEL OF GOSSIP AND REPUTATION

It is clear from this examination of the ontogeny of gossip and reputation that children come into the world prepared to participate in both processes, but that the maturation of both is dependent on their experience of social (and in particular verbal) interactions with other individuals. Even before they can talk, infants are sensitive to social stimuli, show a tendency to approach or avoid social agents who act positively or negatively to others, and are also inclined to point their interaction partners toward relevant information. Between about 2 and 4 years, as young children become capable of grammatically structured verbal reports, these early tendencies are articulated into pragmatic phenomena such as normative protest and tattling (responses to social norm violations by others that are differentiated according to whether they are addressed to the perpetrator or to a third party, usually an authority figure who can be expected to punish the perpetrator). These linguistic practices do not seem to reflect a sophisticated concept of linguistically mediated reputation, so much as a kind of image score which is attached to individuals who behave in unwelcome ways and a drive to draw attention to their negative behavior.

A more abstract concept of reputation, as something which is understood differently by different people depending on their level of knowledge about another individual's actions, has to wait until middle childhood, after the development of theory of mind and false-belief understanding. Even after this development, tattling continues (though it makes up a lower proportion of talk about others), but children start to understand something of the nature of gossip. Moving into preadolescence, between about 8 and 10 years, children begin to accuse each other of making negative reports to third parties—presumably influenced by their newfound awareness of the power of language to affect reputation. However, this does not seem to lead to substantial amounts of deliberately covert gossip until after 10 years of age. Finally, during adolescence—in line with a general reduction in all types of aggression—gossip becomes not only more covert but also more marked by ambiguity and thus less openly negative.

The model here proposed to account for this developmental picture is one in which there is a reciprocal interaction between gossip (and more generally, social interactions with peers that are mediated by language) and reputation awareness (more generally, a child's socio-cognitive understanding of how their actions are perceived by others). These two processes feed back into each other as the child grows, and lead to the development of different stages of reputation at various ages. The proposed stages, and what leads to the developmental shifts between them, are outlined in Table 8.1.

In addition to the rough correspondences between the different stages of gossip/reputation and Piaget's classic stages of child development, the developmental progression described here has two other features in common with a Piagetian analysis: first, later stages of development are seen as constructed out of earlier stages—more complex ways of thinking are built on top of simpler ways; and second, the agent of change between successive stages is seen to be the dynamic between children's increasingly sophisticated social cognition, and their increasingly complicated social interactions with others. More specifically, the covert, indirect behavior of adolescent and adult gossip is built on top of more direct forms of overt normative protest and tattling that are found in young children. Progression between the two types of linguistic behavior is influenced first by early interactions with peers in the preschool years, which leads to a developing understanding of the contents of other minds, which is then generalized into higher-order theory of mind and an abstract knowledge of how information is transmitted by language (as the child enters the concrete-operational stage). This complex social cognition is then reflected in a new propensity to accuse others of damaging one's reputation, creating an inhibitory pressure against overt gossip and tattling (and eventually, for many people, even against negative gossip to some extent, except in carefully controlled circumstances).

Table 8.1. Proposed stages in children's development of gossip- and reputation-related behavior

| Age in Years (and Piagetian Stage) | Summary of Gossip/Reputation-related Behavior | What Causes This Behavior? |
|---|---|---|
| 0–2 (sensorimotor) | Sensitivity to social stimuli; differentiation of positive/negative behavior; attraction of audience to joint attention | Largely instinctual; perhaps reinforced by reciprocal interactions with caregivers |
| 2–4 (pre-operational: pre-conceptual) | Protesting (either to perpetrator or to third party) about social norm violations | Development of language; learning of social rules from adults |
| 4–6 (pre-operational: intuitive) | Peak age for tattling; development of representative theory of mind (including false-belief understanding) | Exposure to more social contact with peers, including peers with different beliefs and normative behaviors |
| 6–8 (early concrete-operational) | First understanding of nature of gossip and its effect on reputation | Development of second-order theory of mind (essential for understanding how information flows between minds); experience with how tattling affects audience's behavior? |
| 8–10 (mid concrete-operational) | "He-said-she-said" confrontations; continued development in awareness of gossip and reputation | Knowledge of how gossip affects reputation means children become more concerned about what other people are saying about them |
| 10–12 (late concrete-operational) | Increase in covert gossip; tattling starts to become derogated, except in cases of serious harm | He-said-she-said confrontations inhibit tendency to gossip openly; affiliation starts to shift toward peer group instead of adult authority figures |
| 12–14 (concrete-operational to formal-operational transition) | Peak age for negative gossip; tattling becomes almost universally proscribed, even in cases of quite serious harm | Hormonal and brain changes and reorganization of social relationships leads to spike in conflict (including indirect aggression) and also drive to affiliate with peer social networks |
| 14+ (formal-operational) | Negative gossip becomes increasingly covert and cloaked in ambiguity; positive gossip may also become more common | Increased sophistication in thinking about hypothetical effects on reputation (formal-operational reasoning) leads to more care about what is said about others; understanding that benefits to social partners also benefit the self |

As stated in the introduction, the underlying logic behind the existence of stages in the development of gossip and reputation may be a progressive lack of dependence on adult caregivers to meet one's fitness needs and an increased interdependence with peers. This helps explain why one of the biggest transitions in the development of gossip and reputation—from overt tattling to covert gossip, and from identifying with an authority figure's interests to identifying with a peer's interests—takes place in preadolescence, as a child becomes physically capable of meeting all their own basic survival needs without adult support, and prepares for the new fitness challenges of achieving an advantageous position in a social network and finding a beneficent mate.

## CONCLUSION AND FUTURE DIRECTIONS

This account of the ontogeny of gossip and reputation is a necessarily sketchy one, especially given that little attention has been paid in the literature to the development of children's explicit awareness of how reputation works. Therefore, several important potential research questions are raised that would help fill the gaps in our knowledge. First, despite the vast literature on theory of mind, there is a lack of a knowledge base on how theory of mind plays out in everyday social interactions. This is especially the case with higher-order theory of mind. Theoretically, children who understand better the contents of other minds, and that information can be passed between minds using language, should be able to model their own reputation better in other people's minds, and thus behave better in order to reap the benefits of positive indirect reciprocity and avoid the consequences of negative indirect reciprocity. While the ages (between about 3 and 7 years) at which developments in first- and second-order belief understanding take place are certainly associated with general improvements in behavior, and various studies have shown negative cross-sectional associations between theory of mind and aggression, there is still little known about whether social cognitive breakthroughs at an individual level are associated longitudinally with an increase in cooperative behavior and a reduction in direct aggression, and nothing at all known about whether such an association might be mediated by an improved understanding of reputation and indirect reciprocity. Second, there is also very little known about the transitions from overt tattling to covert gossip and thence to cloaked, ambiguous gossip, during preadolescence and later adolescence. How do children come to realize that their words, not just their actions, can affect their reputations—and thus become more careful about to whom they spread gossip and how they phrase it? Why do audiences to negative gossip start to inhibit who they spread the information to—is it simply in order to avoid "he-said-she-said" types of confrontations? Or does this require an advanced level of moral reasoning based on the explicit upholding of communal norms (Kohlberg, 1976), which function to reduce intra-group conflict?

Finally, a number of important connections are suggested with other novel areas of research on gossip and reputation. A key question concerns the biological basis of the developmental changes highlighted in this chapter. It is tempting to link the timing of the shift to peer-network identification (and covert gossip) in pre-adolescence with the adrenarche—the change in hormonal balance that prepares children for adolescence—at roughly the same age. It remains to be demonstrated that hormonal changes cause the changes in behavior described here, but it is worth noting that one of the last brain areas to develop in young people, the prefrontal cortex, both starts to develop during preadolescence (apparently in response to the adrenarche; Blakemore et al., 2010) and is highly activated, relative to other areas, during gossip processing (Peng et al., 2015; Boero, this volume). It would certainly be worth investigating the brain areas that are activated in children of various ages as they think about their own and others' reputation.

A second question concerns the effects of online social networks on children's gossip and reputational awareness. This is likely to have two possibly contradictory effects: at first, young children are potentially exposed to many more interaction partners (via online games) than they would have been in the past, leading to an early pressure to develop theory-of-mind processing in order to understand the varying normative behaviors and reactions of all these different partners (for gossip and reputation in offline networks of adolescents, see Kisfalusi, Takács, and Pál, this volume). However, later on during preadolescence, when older children have normally had to learn to accommodate very different points of view in their own nascent social networks, the ability to join communities of like-minded individuals online might inhibit the pressure to engage in perspective-taking toward people with very different views and interests. With the growing popularity of online games and social networks among children and young people, both these possibilities are clearly worth investigating and have important potential applications in combating cyberbullying (see Ingram, 2016), which is in many cases a technologically mediated form of negative gossip.

Finally, there is the question of how the ontogeny of gossip and reputation is reflected in our adult lives. According to both Piagetian theory and dual-process theories (Stanovich et al., 2011), earlier stages of cognitive development are not completely replaced by later ones, but instead remain in some sense submerged under later ones and can still be activated in particular situations—for example, if an individual feels stressed, powerless, or highly emotional—due to the processing that they involve being cognitively "cheaper" to perform. Knowledge of how this works might be particularly useful to researchers on gossip and reputation formation in professional settings, allowing them to identify the conditions in which normal adult injunctions against explicitly negative gossip and even overt tattling can break down, poisoning social relations in the workplace (see Beersma, van Kleef, and M. Dijkstra, this volume, and also Ellwardt, this volume, on organizational networks). One hypothesis worth investigating is that if bosses treat employees more like collegial adults and less like dependent children, they may be less likely to spread negative information about each other or compete on reputational terms in the manner of preadolescents, which could well result in more harmonious working relationships. An understanding of gossip and reputation in childhood might thus be of importance not only for improving children's lives, for example by reducing or defusing their conflicts, but also for understanding adult cognition and improving adults' lives.

## References

Aikins, Julie Wargo, Charlene Collibee, and Jessica Cunningham. 2015. "Gossiping to the Top: Observed Differences in Popular Adolescents' Gossip." *Journal of Early Adolescence* 37 (5): 1–20.

Alexander, Richard. 1987. *The Biology of Moral Systems*. New York: Aldine de Gruyter.

Archer, John, and Coyne, Sarah. 2005. "An Integrated Review of Indirect, Relational, and Social Aggression." *Personality and Social Psychology Review* 9 (3): 212–230.

Bamberg, Michael. 2004. "Form and Functions of 'Slut Bashing' in Male Identity Constructions in 15-year-olds: 'I Know It May Sound Mean to Say This, but We Couldn't Really Care Less About Her Anyway.'" *Human Development* 47 (6): 331–353.

Baumard, Nicolas, Jean-Baptiste André, and Dan Sperber. 2013. "A Mutualistic Approach to Morality: The Evolution of Fairness by Partner Choice." *Behavioral and Brain Sciences* 36 (1): 59–78.

Beersma, Bianca, van Kleef Gerben A., Dijkstra, Maria T. M. 2019. Antecedents and Consequences of Gossip in Work Groups. In *Handbook of Gossip and Reputation*, edited by Francesca Giardini and Rafael Wittek. New York: Oxford University Press.

Bjorklund, David, and Anthony Pellegrini. 2000. "Child Development and Evolutionary Psychology." *Child Development* 71 (6): 1687–1708.

Blakemore, Sarah-Jayne, Stephanie Burnett, and Ronald Dahl. 2010. "The Role of Puberty in the Developing Adolescent Brain." *Human Brain Mapping* 31 (6): 926–933.

Boero, Riccardo. 2019. "Neuroscientific Methods". In *Handbook of Gossip and Reputation*, edited by Francesca Giardini and Rafael Wittek. New York: Oxford University Press.

Bosmans, Guy, and Kathryn Kerns. 2015. "Attachment in Middle Childhood: Progress and Prospects." *New Directions for Child and Adolescent Development* 148: 1–14.

Bourdais, Cécile, Agnès Danis, Camille Bacle, Amaud Santolini, and Charles Tijus. 2013. "Do 10- and 13-month-old Infants Provide Informative Gestures for Their Mothers in a Hiding Game?" *Infant Behavior and Development* 36 (1): 94–101.

Burdelski, Matthew, and Emi Morita. 2017. "Young Children's Initial Assessments in Japanese." In *Children's Knowledge-in-Interaction: Studies in Conversation Analysis*, edited by Amanda Bateman and Amelia Church, 231–255. Singapore: Springer.

Burman, Jeremy. 2013. "Updating the Baldwin Effect: The Biological Levels behind Piaget's New Theory." *New Ideas in Psychology* 31 (3): 363–373.

Cairns, Robert, Beverley Cairns, Holly Neckerman, Lynda Ferguson, and Jean-Louis Gariépy. 1989. "Growth and Aggression: 1. Childhood to Early Adolescence." *Developmental Psychology* 25 (2): 320–330.

Caputi, Marcella, Serena Lecce, Adriano Pagnin, and Robin Banerjee. 2012. "Longitudinal Effects of Theory of Mind on Later Peer Relations: The Role of Prosocial Behavior." *Developmental Psychology* 48 (1): 257–270.

Carpendale, Jeremy, and Michael Chandler. 1996. "On the Distinction between False Belief Understanding and Subscribing to an Interpretive Theory of Mind." *Child Development* 67 (4): 1686–1706.

Carpenter, Malinda, Katherine Nagell, and Michael Tomasello. 1998. "Social Cognition, Joint Attention, and Communicative Competence from 9 to 15 Months of Age." *Monographs of the Society for Research in Child Development* 63 (4): 1–143.

Carroll, Annemaree, Shauna Green, Stephen Houghton, and Robert Wood. 2003. "Reputation Enhancement and Involvement in Delinquency among High School Students." *International Journal of Disability, Development and Education* 50 (3): 253–273.

Carroll, Annemaree, Stephen Houghton, Kevin Durkin, and John Hattie. 2009. *Adolescent Reputations and Risk: Developmental Trajectories to Delinquency*. Berlin: Springer Science+Business Media.

Chijiiwa, Hitomi, Hika Kuroshima, Yusuke Hori, James Anderson, and Kazuo Fujita. 2015. "Dogs Avoid People Who Behave Negatively to Their Owner: Third-party Affective Evaluation." *Animal Behaviour* 106: 123–127.

Chiu Loke, Ivy, Gail Heyman, Julia Forgie, Anjanie McCarthy, and Kang Lee. 2011. "Children's Moral Evaluations of Reporting the Transgressions of Peers: Age Differences in Evaluations of Tattling." *Developmental Psychology* 47 (6): 1757–1762.

Chiu Loke, Ivy, Gail Heyman, Shoji Itakura, Rie Toriyama, and Kang Lee. 2014. "Japanese and American Children's Moral Evaluations of Reporting on Transgressions." *Developmental Psychology* 50 (5): 1520–1531.

Crick, Nicki, and Jennifer Grotpeter. 1995. "Relational Aggression, Gender, and Social-psychological Adjustment." *Child Development* 66 (3): 710–722.

Cushman, Fiery, Rachel Sheketoff, Sophie Wharton, and Susan Carey. 2013. "The Development of Intent-based Moral Judgment." *Cognition* 127 (1): 6–21.

Del Giudice, Marco. 2014. "Middle Childhood: An Evolutionary-developmental Synthesis." *Child Development Perspectives* 8 (4): 193–200.

den Bak, Irene, and Hildy Ross. 1996. "'I'm telling!' The Content, Context, and Consequences of Children's Tattling on Their Siblings." *Social Development* 5 (3): 292–309.

Doherty, Martin. 2008. *Theory of Mind: How Children Understand Others' Thoughts and Feelings.* Hove, England: Psychology Press.

Dromi, E Esther. 1999. Early lexical development. In *The Development of Language*, edited by Martyn Barrett, 99–132. Hove: Psychology Press.

Eder, Donna, and Janet Enke. 1991. "The Structure of Gossip: Opportunities and Constraints on Collective Expression among Adolescents." *American Sociological Review* 56 (4): 494–508.

Ellwardt, Lea. 2019. "Gossip and Reputation in Social Networks." In *Handbook of Gossip and Reputation*, edited by Francesca Giardini and Rafael Wittek. New York: Oxford University Press.

Engel, S., and Li, A Engel, Susan and Li, Alice. 2004. "Narratives, Gossip, and Shared Experience: How and What Young Children Know about the Lives of Others." In *The Development of the Mediated Mind*, edited by Joan Lucariello, Judith Hudson, Robyn Fivush, and Patricia Bauer, 151–174. Mahwah, NJ: Lawrence Erlbaum.

Engelmann, Jan, Esther Herrmann, and Michael Tomasello. 2012. "Five-year-olds, but Not Chimpanzees, Attempt to Manage Their Reputations." *PLoS One.* doi:10.1371/journal.pone.0048433.

Engelmann, Jan, Esther Herrmann, and Michael Tomasello. 2016. "Preschoolers Affect Others' Reputations through Prosocial Gossip." *British Journal of Developmental Psychology* 34: 447–460.

Engelmann, Jan, Harriet Over, Esther Herrmann, and Michael Tomasello. 2013. "Young Children Care More about Their Reputation with Ingroup Members and Potential Reciprocators." *Developmental Science* 16 (6): 952–958.

Engels, Rutger, Ron Scholte, Cornelis van Lieshout, Raymond de Kemp, and Geertjan Overbeek. 2006. "Peer Group Reputation and Smoking and Alcohol Consumption in Early Adolescence." *Addictive Behaviors* 31 (3): 440–449.

Fine, Gary. 1977. "Social Components of Children's Gossip." *Journal of Communication* 27 (1): 181–185.

Frank, Michael, Dima Amso, and Scott Johnson. 2014. "Visual Search and Attention to Faces during Early Infancy." *Journal of Experimental Child Psychology* 118: 13–26.

Friman, Patrick, Douglas Woods, Kurt Freeman, Rich Gilman, Mary Short, Ann McGrath, and Michael Handwerk. 2004. "Relationships between Tattling, Likeability, and Social Classification: A Preliminary Investigation of Adolescents in Residential Care." *Behavior Modification* 28 (3): 331–348.

Fu, Genyue, Wen Xiao, Melanie Killen, and Kang Lee. 2014. "Moral Judgment and Its Relation to Second-order Theory of Mind." *Developmental Psychology* 50 (8): 2085–2092.

Fu, Genyue, Gail Heyman, Miao Qian, Tengfei Guo, and Kang Lee. 2016. "Young Children with a Positive Reputation to Maintain Are Less Likely to Cheat." *Developmental Science* 19 (2): 275–283.

Fujii, Takayuki, Haruto Takagishi, Michiko Koizumi, and Hiroyuki Okada. 2015. "The Effect of Direct and Indirect Monitoring on Generosity among Preschoolers." *Scientific Reports* 5: 9025. doi:10.1038/srep09025.

Galen, Britt, and Marion Underwood. 1997. "A Developmental Investigation of Social Aggression among Children." *Developmental Psychology* 33 (4): 589–600.

Goodwin, Marjorie Harness. 1990. *He-said-she-said: Talk as Social Organization among Black Children*. Bloomington: Indiana University Press.

Goodwin, Marjorie Harness. 2007. "Participation and Embodied Action in Preadolescent Girls' Assessment Activity." *Research on Language and Social Interaction* 40 (4): 353–375.

Hamlin, Kiley, Karen Wynn, and Paul Bloom. 2007. "Social Evaluation by Preverbal Infants." *Nature* 450: 557–559.

Hamlin, Kiley, Karen Wynn, Paul Bloom, and Neha Mahajan. 2011. "How Infants and Toddlers React to Antisocial Others." *Proceedings of the National Academy of Sciences* 108 (50): 19931–19936.

Hardecker, Susanne, Marco Schmidt, Meike Roden, and Michael Tomasello. 2016. "Young Children's Behavioral and Emotional Responses to Different Social Norm Violations." *Journal of Experimental Child Psychology* 150: 364–379.

Haux, Lou, Jan Engelmann, Esther Herrmann, and Michael Tomasello. 2016. "Do Young Children Preferentially Trust Gossip or Firsthand Observation in Choosing a Collaborative Partner?" *Social Development*, October 24, 2016. doi:10.1111/sode.12225.

Heyman, Gail, Ivy Chiu Loke, and Kang Lee. 2016. "Children Spontaneously Police Adults' Transgressions." *Journal of Experimental Child Psychology* 150: 155–164.

Hill, Valerie, and Bradley Pillow. 2006. "Children's Understanding of Reputations." *Journal of Genetic Psychology* 167 (2): 137–157.

House, Bailey, Joan Silk, Joseph Henrich, H. Clark Barrett, Brooke Scelza, Adam Boyette, et al. 2013. "Ontogeny of Prosocial Behavior across Diverse Societies." *Proceedings of the National Academy of Sciences of the United States of America* 110 (36): 14586–14591.

Ingram, Gordon. 2009. *Young Children's Reporting of Peers' Behaviour*. Unpublished PhD dissertation, Queen's University Belfast.

Ingram, Gordon. 2013. "Piaget on Moral Judgement: Towards a Reconciliation with Nativist and Socio-cultural Approaches." In *Mental Culture: Towards a Cognitive Science of Religion*, edited by Dimitris Xygalatas and William McCorkle, Jr., 128–144. Sheffield: Equinox.

Ingram, Gordon. 2014. "From Hitting to Tattling to Gossip: An Evolutionary Rationale for the Development of Indirect Aggression." *Evolutionary Psychology* 12 (2): 343–363.

Ingram, Gordon. 2016. "Gossip, Cooperation and Cyberbullying in Children's Online Communication: Designing an Intervention Based on Original Empirical Research." *Proceedings of the 15th International Conference on Interaction Design and Children*, Manchester, United Kingdom, June 21–24, 2016, 535–540. New York: ACM.

Ingram, Gordon, and Jesse Bering. 2010. "Children's Tattling: The Reporting of Everyday Norm Violations in Preschool Settings." *Child Development* 81 (3): 945–957.

Inhelder, Bärbel, and Jean Piaget. 1958. *The Growth of Logical Thinking from Childhood to Adolescence: An Essay on the Construction of Formal Operational Structures.* Abingdon, England: Routledge.

Jakobsen, Krisztina, Lindsay Umstead, and Elizabeth Simpson. 2016. "Efficient Human Face Detection in Infancy." *Developmental Psychobiology* 58 (1): 129–136.

Johnson, Mark, Suzanne Dziurawiec, Hadyn Ellis, and John Morton. 1991. "Newborns' Preferential Tracking of Face-like Stimuli and Its Subsequent Decline." *Cognition* 40 (1–2): 1–19.

Kenward, Ben, and Matilda Dahl. 2011. "Preschoolers Distribute Scarce Resources According to the Moral Valence of Recipients' Previous Actions." *Developmental Psychology* 47 (4): 1054–1064.

Kisfalusi, Dorottya, Takács, Károly, Pál, Judit. 2019. Gossip and Reputation in Adolescence Networks. In *Handbook of Gossip and Reputation*, edited by Francesca Giardini and Rafael Wittek, New York: Oxford University Press.

Kohlberg, Lawrence. (1976). "Moral Stages and Moralization." In *Moral Development and Behavior: Theory, Research and Social Issues*, edited by Thomas Lickona, 31–53. New York: Holt, Rinehart, and Winston.

Krebs, Dennis. 2005. "An Evolutionary Reconceptualization of Kohlberg's Model of Moral Development." In *Evolutionary Perspectives on Human Development*, edited by Robert Burgess and Kevin MacDonald (2nd ed., pp. 243–274). Thousand Oaks, CA: Sage.

Kuhlmeier, Valerie, Kristen Dunfield, and Amy O'Neill. 2014. "Selectivity in Early Prosocial Behavior." *Frontiers in Psychology*, June 29, 2014. doi:10.3389/fpsyg.2014.00836.

Kuttler, Ami Flam, Jeffrey Parker, and Annette La Greca. 2002. "Developmental and Gender Differences in Preadolescents' Judgments of the Veracity of Gossip." *Merrill-Palmer Quarterly* 48 (2): 105–132.

Lagerspetz, Kirsti, Kaj Björkqvist, and Tarja Peltonen. 1988. "Is Indirect Aggression Typical of Females? Gender Differences in Aggressiveness in 11- to 12-year-old Children." *Aggressive Behavior* 14 (6): 403–414.

Leimgruber, Kristin, Alex Shaw, Laurie Santos, and Kristina Olson. 2012. "Young Children Are More Generous When Others Are Aware of Their Actions." *PLoS One* 7 (10): e48292. doi:10.1371/journal.pone.0048292.

Lewis, Michael, G. Young, J. Brooks, and L. Michalson. 1975. "The Beginning of Friendship." In *Friendship and Peer Relations*, edited by Michael Lewis and Leonard Rosenblum, 27–66. Chichester: Wiley.

Locke, John, and Barry Bogin. 2006. "Language and Life History: A New Perspective on the Development and Evolution of Human Language." *Behavioral and Brain Sciences* 29 (3): 259–280.

Lourenço, Orlando. 2016. "Developmental Stages, Piagetian Stages in Particular: A Critical Review." *New Ideas in Psychology* 40 (B): 123–137.

MacWhinney, Brian. 2000. *The CHILDES Project: Tools for Analyzing Talk.* Mahwah, NJ: Lawrence Erlbaum.

Manesi, Zoi, Paul Van Lange, and Thomas Pollet. 2016. "Eyes Wide Open: Only Eyes That Pay Attention Promote Prosocial Behavior." *Evolutionary Psychology* 14 (2). doi:10.1177/1474704916640780.

McDonald, Kristina, Martha Putallaz, Christina Grimes, Janis Kupersmidt, and John Coie. 2007. "Girl Talk: Gossip, Friendship, and Sociometric Status." *Merrill-Palmer Quarterly* 53 (3): 381–411.

McGuigan, Nicola, and Marcus Cubillo. 2013. "Information Transmission in Young Children: When Social Information is More Important than Nonsocial Information." *Journal of Genetic Psychology* 174 (6), 605–619.

Menzer, Melissa, Kristina McDonald, Kenneth Rubin, Linda Rose-Krasnor, Cathryn Booth-LaForce, and Annie Schulz. 2012. "Observed Gossip Moderates the Link between Anxious Withdrawal and Friendship Quality in Early Adolescence." *International Journal of Developmental Science* 6 (3–4): 191–202.

Meristo, Marek, and Luca Surian. 2013. "Do Infants Detect Indirect Reciprocity?" *Cognition* 129 (1): 102–113.

Meristo, Marek, and Luca Surian. 2014. "Infants Distinguish Antisocial Actions Directed towards Fair and Unfair Agents." *PLoS One* 9: e110553. doi:10.1371/journal.pone.0110553.

Mettetal, Gwendolyn. 1983. "Fantasy, Gossip, and Self-Disclosure: Children's Conversations with Friends." *Annals of the International Communication Association* 7 (1): 717–735. doi:10.1080/23808985.1983.11678561.

Miller, Peggy, and Linda Sperry. 1988. "Early Talk about the Past: The Origins of Conversational Stories of Personal Experience." *Journal of Child Language* 15 (2): 293–315.

Nowak, Martin, and Karl Sigmund. 1998. "Evolution of Indirect Reciprocity by Image Scoring." *Nature* 393: 573–577.

Nowak, Martin, and Karl Sigmund. 2005. "Evolution of Indirect Reciprocity." *Nature* 437: 1291–1298.

Nucci, Larry, and Elliot Turiel. 1978. "Social Interactions and the Development of Social Concepts in Preschool Children." *Child Development* 49 (2): 400–407.

Nurmi, Jari-Erik. 2004. "Socialization and Self-Development." In *Handbook of Adolescent Psychology*, edited by Richard Lerner and Laurence Steinberg, 85–124. Hoboken, NJ: Wiley.

Peng, Xiaozhe, You Li, Pengfei Wang, Lei Mo, and Qi Chen. 2015. "The Ugly Truth: Negative Gossip about Celebrities and Positive Gossip about Self Entertain People in Different Ways." *Social Neuroscience* 10 (3): 320–336.

Perner, Josef. 1991. *Understanding the Representational Mind*. Cambridge, MA: MIT Press.

Piaget, Jean. 1932. *The Moral Judgment of the Child*, translated by M. Gabain. London: Paul, Trench, and Trubner.

Piazza, Jared, Jesse Bering, and Gordon Ingram. (2011). "'Princess Alice Is Watching You': Children's Belief in an Invisible Person Inhibits Cheating." *Journal of Experimental Child Psychology* 109 (3), 311–320.

Rakoczy, Hannes, Felix Warneken, and Michael Tomasello. 2008. "The Sources of Normativity: Young Children's Awareness of the Normative Structure of Games." *Developmental Psychology* 44 (3): 875–881.

Ross, Hildy, and Irene Den Bak-Lammers. 1998. "Consistency and Change in Children's Tattling on Their Siblings: Children's Perspectives on the Moral Rules and Procedures of Family Life." *Social Development* 7 (3): 275–300.

Ross, Hildy, Holly Recchia, and Jeremy Carpendale. 2005. "Making Sense of Divergent Interpretations of Conflict and Developing an Interpretive Understanding of Mind." *Journal of Cognition and Development* 6 (4): 571–592.

Schmidt, Marco, and Hannes Rakoczy. 2019. "On the Uniqueness of Human Normative Attitudes." In *The Normative Animal? On the Anthropological Significance of Social, Moral and Linguistic Norms*, edited by K. Bayertz and N. Roughley. Oxford: Oxford University Press. https://philpapers.org/rec/SCHOTU-8.

Schmidt, Marco, Hannes Rakoczy, and Michael Tomasello. 2011. "Young Children Attribute Normativity to Novel Actions without Pedagogy or Normative Language." *Developmental Science* 14 (3): 530–539.

Slaughter, Virginia, Kana Imuta, Candida Peterson, and Julie Henry. 2015. "Meta-analysis of Theory of Mind and Peer Popularity in the Preschool and Early School Years." *Child Development* 86 (4): 1159–1174.

Smetana, Judith. 1981. "Preschool Children's Conceptions of Moral and Social Rules." *Child Development* 52 (4): 1333–1336.

Stanovich, Keith, Richard West, and Maggie Toplak. 2011. "The Complexity of Developmental Predictions from Dual Process Models." *Developmental Review* 31 (2–3): 103–118.

Steinberg, Laurence. 2008. "A Social Neuroscience Perspective on Adolescent Risktaking." *Developmental Review* 28 (1): 78–106.

Surian, Luca, Stefania Caldi, and Dan Sperber. 2007. "Attribution of Beliefs by 13-month-old Infants." *Psychological Science* 18 (7): 580–586.

Tomasello, Michael. 1999. *The Cultural Origins of Human Cognition*. Cambridge, MA: Harvard University Press.

Tomasello, Michael. 2008. *Origins of Human Communication*. Cambridge, MA: MIT Press.

Tomasello, Michael, and Michael Farrar. 1986. "Joint Attention and Early Language." *Child Development* 57 (6): 1454–1463.

Tomasello, Michael, and Ivan Gonzalez-Cabrera. 2017. "The Role of Ontogeny in the Evolution of Human Cooperation." *Human Nature* 28 (3): 274–288.

Tomasello, Michael, and Amrisha Vaish. 2013. "Origins of Human Cooperation and Morality." *Annual Review of Psychology* 64: 231–255.

Vaish, Amrisha, Malinda Carpenter, and Michael Tomasello. 2010. "Young Children Selectively Avoid Helping People with Harmful Intentions." *Child Development* 81 (6): 1661–1669.

Vaish, Amrisha, Esther Herrmann, Christiane Markmann, and Michael Tomasello. 2016. "Preschoolers Value Those Who Sanction Non-cooperators." *Cognition* 153: 43–51. doi:10.1016/j.cognition.2016.04.011.

Vaish, Amrisha, Manuela Missana, and Michael Tomasello. 2011. "Three-Year-Old Children Intervene in Third-Party Moral Transgressions." *British Journal of Developmental Psychology* 29 (1): 124–130.

Wedekind, Claus, and Manfred Milinski. 2000. "Cooperation through Image Scoring in Humans." *Science* 288 (5467): 850–852.

Wellman, Henry, David Cross, and Julanne Watson. 2001. "Meta-analysis of Theory-of-Mind Development: The Truth about False Belief." *Child Development* 72 (3): 655–684.

Wells, Gordon. 1981. *Learning through Interaction: The Study of Language Development*. Cambridge: Cambridge University Press.

CHAPTER 9

........................................................................

# GOSSIP AND EMOTION

........................................................................

## ELENA MARTINESCU, ONNE JANSSEN, AND BERNARD A. NIJSTAD

## INTRODUCTION

An overlooked, but crucially important, aspect of gossip is emotion. Not only is the spread of gossip often driven by emotions of the gossiper (Feinberg, Willer, Stellar, & Keltner, 2012; Foster, 2004; Stirling, 1956; Waddington & Fletcher, 2005), but it also generates emotional reactions for the receiver of the gossip (Baumeister, Zhang, & Vohs, 2004; Martinescu, Janssen, & Nijstad, 2014) and for the target who becomes aware of the gossip (Martinescu, Janssen, & Nijstad, 2019). Consider, for example, the following gossip episode from George R. R. Martin's epic fantasy series *A Song of Ice and Fire*, Book Two: *A Clash of Kings* (Martin, 2011, pp. 45–46). In this episode, Tyrion Lannister (the dwarf), and his nephew (king Joffrey) are talking in the presence of Joffrey's wife to be, Sansa Stark, in the context of a war between the Lannisters and the Starks.

> Tyrion replied, "[ . . . ] Joffrey, where might I find your mother?"
> "She's with my council," the king answered. "Your brother Jaime keeps losing battles." He gave Sansa an angry look, as if it were her fault. "He's been taken by the Starks and we've lost Riverrun and now her [i.e., Sansa's] stupid brother is calling himself a king."
> The dwarf smiled crookedly. "All sorts of people are calling themselves kings these days."
> [ . . . ][Sansa] glanced about nervously, but there was no one close enough to hear [ . . . ].Once she had loved Prince Joffrey with all her heart, and admired and trusted his mother, the queen. They had repaid that love and trust with her father's head. Sansa would never make that mistake again.

In this scene, Joffrey (gossiper) is angry because his uncle Jaime is losing battles to Sansa's brother, and he expresses his rage in a brief evaluative statement about her brother (gossip target). Tyrion (gossip receiver) seems to agree with Joffrey, thus offering him support and comfort. Furthermore, upon hearing how much Joffrey despises her brother, Sansa (passive gossip receiver) becomes nervous and feels afraid about how Joffrey may treat her in the future. If he becomes aware of the gossip about him, Sansa's brother is likely to feel extremely angry toward his enemies Joffrey and Tyrion, who minimize his accomplishments on the battlefield and his legitimacy as a king. This example illustrates that all members of the gossip triad (senders, receivers, and targets) are likely to experience emotions during the transmission of gossip. But not only in fantasy novels is it recognized that gossip is intimately associated with emotion. For example, according to the Bible, "As surely as a north wind brings rain, so a gossiping tongue causes anger" (*Holy Bible*, Proverbs, 25: 23, New Living Translation, 1996).

Broadly defined, gossip is *evaluative talk exchanged informally about an absent third party* (e.g., Dunbar, 2004; Foster, 2004). Gossip communicates reputational information, which may influence whether individuals are accepted in groups, and therefore whether they can optimally fulfill their needs or goals (Burt, 2008; Emler, 1994). People rely on gossip for coping with interpersonal issues that arise from living in social groups, such as keeping track of other's behaviors (information function); influencing perceptions about group members (influence function); warning others about selfish, exploitative group members (group protection function); creating stable alliances that provide support (social bonding); or evaluating their own strengths and weaknesses (self-evaluation function; e.g., Beersma & Van Kleef, 2012; Fine & Rosnow, 1978; Rosnow, 2001; Stirling, 1956).

The functioning of gossip as a regulation mechanism of interpersonal behavior may rely heavily on emotion processes. Because gossip is fundamentally related to the well-being and adaptive success of all the individuals who are involved in gossip (i.e., senders, receivers, and targets), emotions are likely to both shape and result from the transmission of gossip. First, emotions can motivate people to engage in gossip behavior, thereby operating as *antecedents* of gossip. Second, emotions can be experienced by gossipers and receivers as an intrinsic aspect of the gossiping activity, and therefore emotions are *endogenous* to gossip. Third, emotions can be generated as reactions to a gossip message and may function to prepare behavioral responses for gossip receivers and targets; thus, emotions are important *consequences* of gossip.

Therefore, we propose that emotions are inherently related to the gossip process. A deeper understanding of the emotional nature of gossip's antecedents, intrinsic mechanisms, and consequences may complement previous work focusing on the functional role of gossip for individuals and groups. Emotions seem to be related to every step of the gossip process, and therefore may be key mechanisms that activate, regulate, and accompany different functions of gossip. Furthermore, an emotional account of gossip may help solve apparent dilemmas in the gossip literature, which portrays negative gossip as functional but socially undesirable (Baumeister et al., 2004; Beersma & Van Kleef, 2012; Dunbar, 2004; Fine & Rosnow, 1978; Foster, 2004). This paradox may be explained, for example, by considering the different roles negative emotions play in the gossip mechanism. On the one hand, negative emotions stimulate prosocial gossip behavior (i.e., gossip aimed at protecting the group), but on the other hand, people are discouraged from gossiping because they can infer that gossip feels unpleasant for targets, or may even anticipate that they are likely to become targets themselves in an environment where gossip is abundant.

Some of gossip's functions are clearly enabled by emotional processes, whereas other functions seem more indirectly related to emotion. For example, social bonding is facilitated between people who express their negative emotions regarding a social target, and the gossip exchange is directly related to feelings of comfort (Bosson, Johnson, Niederhoffer, & Swann, 2006; Peters & Kashima, 2007). Furthermore, uncertainty and anxiety may trigger a need for more information about a specific (social) situation, and gossip may function to fulfill this need.

With a few exceptions (e.g., Baumeister et al., 2004; Feinberg et al., 2012; Georganta Panagopoulou, & Montgomery, 2014; Waddington & Fletcher, 2005), however, empirical research has largely overlooked the role of emotions in how gossip functions. Instead, recent studies have mostly investigated gossip using a cognitive-rational perspective, in which members of the gossip triad are (implicitly) assumed to be emotionally neutral social actors, who can rely fully on logical reasoning in their judgments and decisions surrounding engagement in gossiping. For example, a popular experimental setup is an economic game theory paradigm (e.g., public goods games, dictator games), in which participants circulate gossip in a computer mediated interaction to serve pro-social or selfish interests in a more or less rational way (e.g., Milinski, this volume; Sommerfeld, Krambeck, Semmann, & Milinski, 2007; Sommerfeld, Krambeck, & Milinski, 2008; Wu, Balliet, & Van Lange, 2015; 2016). Other studies asked participants to rationally estimate the extent to which different motives, such as gaining information or influencing the receiver, were important in spreading or interpreting gossip (e.g., Beersma & Van Kleef, 2012; Martinescu, Janssen, & Nijstad, 2017a).

Although these research paradigms are valuable in clarifying the functions of gossip, they omit the emotional processes and mechanisms involved in gossip. Because gossip spreading and reactions to gossip are not always driven and regulated by rational, cognitively mediated processes, but may occur more automatically through affective mechanisms, we propose that emotions are important in understanding gossip. More specifically, we propose that emotions can motivate gossip (emotions as antecedents), can be experienced as intrinsic aspects of gossiping acts (emotions as endogenous to gossip), or can be felt as reactions to gossip messages (emotions as consequences).

In this chapter we aim to clarify the complex role of emotion in the gossip process for senders, receivers and targets of gossip. In what follows, we first define emotions and describe their relationship to gossip, after which we delineate the distinct roles of emotions as motivators of gossip behavior, as intrinsic rewards of the act of gossiping itself, and as regulators of behavioral responses to gossip messages, respectively. We close with suggestions and directions for future research on the role of emotion in gossip.

# EMOTIONS, GOSSIP, AND THEIR RELATIONSHIP

There is no unanimously accepted definition of emotions among researchers, but it is commonly recognized that emotions are short-lived conscious affective states, highly differentiated (e.g., anger, fear, joy), which have high intensity and high hedonic content (pleasure/displeasure, Cabanac, 2002), and clear behavioral implications (Lazarus, 1991). Emotions are reactions to a person or event, and they depend on appraising and interpreting events in relation to a particular concern or goal (Frijda, 1986; Lazarus, 1991). Therefore, emotions have a definite cause and a clear cognitive content, helping individuals make judgments and behave adaptively (Forgas, 1995).

Damasio (1994) distinguishes between primary and secondary emotions, which interact to create conscious emotional experiences. Primary emotions are biologically determined affective reactions to basic perceptual stimuli, based on the success or failure of an outcome, such as happy, sad, or frustrated. Secondary emotions are learned reactions, based on associations between categories of past events and their affective meanings in one's social and cultural context, and therefore are characterized by higher cognitive involvement. Secondary emotions, such as pride, guilt, or anger, are based on attributions of causality, indicating, for example, if the self or someone else is responsible for the success or failure of an outcome. Attributions shape the nature of the emotion, and generate more differentiated emotional experience, which make it possible for individuals to adopt a wide range of situationally appropriate coping responses (Roseman, 1984; Smith & Ellsworth, 1985; Weiner, 1985).

Thus, specific emotions can be related to appraisal dimensions, which determine how individuals interpret and react in specific situations. For example, anger occurs in response to important goal strivings being blocked, and prepares for action to remove these obstacles; fear and anxiety occur when there are threats, and prepare us for a fight or flight response; and happiness occurs when goal progress is made, and signals that the situation may offer further possibilities to achieve our goals (e.g., Frijda, 1986). Guilt and shame are moral emotions, which signal that a social norm or a moral principle has been violated. However, guilt occurs in relation to negative outcomes that are under one's control (e.g., lack of effort) and prepares us to repair our mistakes, whereas shame occurs when we have no control over the outcome (e.g., lack of ability), and is associated with withdrawal from the situation (Weiner, 1985).

Emotions have a wide range of functions. As outlined earlier, their primary role is to alert us to opportunities and threats and prepare situationally appropriate behavioral responses, enabling us to survive and thrive in daily life (Lazarus, 1991). Furthermore, emotions are social, as they help us understand other people (e.g., their goal strivings and motivations) and allow other people to understand us, which is essential for establishing and coordinating interpersonal relationships (Ekman, 1992). Emotions also facilitate adaptation to life in a cultural society, helping people analyze the meaning of current events and draw useful lessons from them (Baumeister et al., 2004). Thus, emotions are affective mechanisms relevant in helping people navigate and interact with the physical, social, and cultural world (Keltner & Haidt, 1999).

Because humans are social beings, who need to rely on each other in order to survive and thrive, gossip is considered fundamental to human functioning or even hard-wired into human nature (Emler, 1994; Nicholson, 2001; Rosnow, 2001). Gossip is an essential form of social communication and social regulation, helping individuals identify and respond adaptively to the opportunities or threats present in their social environment. Individuals engage in gossip to discuss other people's pro-self and pro-social behavior, thereby evaluating whether these individuals are worthy group members (e.g., Beersma & Van Kleef, 2012; Emler, 1994; Kniffin & Wilson, 2010). By creating an informal reputational system, gossip can regulate the social inclusion or exclusion of individuals from groups (Burt, 2008), which may have strong consequences for the success of the group in fulfilling the needs of its members.

When people rely on each other to fulfill needs and goals, conflicts between parties may occur frequently. Even though gossip may seem trivial and purposeless, people gossip about topics that are of high importance to their needs and goals in their specific social context (e.g., Ben-Ze'ev, 1994; Emler, 1994). Human interactions, such as the ones that precede gossip, are addressed or emerge during gossip, or follow gossip, are accompanied by emotions, because emotions are associated with any events that are related to goal fulfillment (Frijda, 1988). Emotions allow people to cope with interpersonal problems, set priorities, and work toward fulfilling their needs, without full knowledge of implications; they help appraise social events quickly and are functional in choosing the best course of action (Oatley, 1992). As such, emotions may be fundamentally related to gossip, because emotions are dynamic processes that mediate individuals' relation to a continually changing social environment, and represent a basic system of interpersonal regulation (Keltner & Haidt, 1999).

Furthermore, due to its characteristics, gossip is likely to be an emotion-laden process. First, gossip is concealed from its targets and from the general public. It is exchanged privately, usually between senders and receivers of gossip who have gradually built a trusting relationship (Ellwardt, Steglich, & Wittek, 2012). Under the protective cover of privacy, the gossip discourse may contain sincere expressions of socially undesirable emotions related to the target: anger, hubristic pride, envy, or contempt. Because the target or other individuals are not included during the gossip exchange, people are likely to express their felt emotions and genuine opinions more bluntly. Although gossip can be aimed at manipulating the receiver or harming the target, malicious gossip is rather exceptional (Ben-Ze'ev, 1994). Most gossip is a sincere but subjective evaluation of targets' qualities or behaviors. As such, gossip is likely to reveal one's "true" evaluation and emotions concerning a target.

Second, gossip contains subjective evaluations of others, which do not reflect facts as much as the opinion of the speaker about the target, in the context of a speaker's needs, motives, or goals. As such, gossip is based on moral judgments, beliefs and attitudes resulting from interpretation of social cues, or perceived attributes and behaviors of targets (Michelson, Van Iterson, & Waddington, 2010; Rosnow, 2001). Because gossip is influenced by one's own needs or interests in a social situation, it is likely to be shaped by the associated emotions gossipers experience toward targets.

# EMOTIONS AS ANTECEDENTS OF GOSSIP

Gossip represents an attractive way to express and regulate emotions generated by observing or interacting with social targets. People are likely to exchange gossip in situations that are emotionally charged, because gossip can provide cathartic expressions of emotions like anger, guilt, anxiety, contempt, and pride, and helps gossipers return to a state of emotional balance (e.g., Foster, 2004; Stirling, 1956; Feinberg et al., 2012). Therefore, in line with theories portraying emotions as adaptive regulatory mechanisms which generate situationally appropriate coping responses (e.g., Frijda, 1986; Izard, 1977), we propose that emotions can operate as primary motivators of gossip. We illustrate this proposition by delineating why and how the distinct emotions of anger and fear can motivate people to engage in the spreading of gossip.

Gossip has been frequently portrayed as a social control mechanism, providing a relatively risk-free means of pressuring people to behave in line with standards, expectations, and group norms (see Giardini & Wittek, this volume). People who observe transgressions are likely to experience anger or outrage, energizing them to take action against the perpetrator of a transgression (Izard & Ackerman, 2000; Lazarus, 1991). Gossiping is a way in which anger can be expressed with low risks for the gossiper, because it helps avoid a direct confrontation with the target, but still influences the reputation of the target (e.g., Burt, 2008). Because gossip can be as efficient as direct punishment (Wu et al., 2016), but less risky, people who are angry at social targets may gossip in order to punish them indirectly, by revealing their flaws or shortcomings. Furthermore, gossip can communicate to receivers that group norms have been broken, and that this is considered unacceptable, which might lead to a shared perspective about the transgression and a coordinated action toward the gossip target (Peters & Kashima, 2007). Thus, anger resulting from observing antisocial behavior triggers gossip aimed at protecting potential victims of the antisocial actors (Feinberg et al., 2012).

Moreover, gossip offers catharsis from anger, helping people "let off steam" (Stirling, 1956). For example, research found that employees who experience abusive supervision or violations of the psychological contract (i.e., employees' beliefs and expectations regarding what they owe to their employer and what the employer owes them) tend to engage in gossip to express their negative attitude toward their organization regarding their unmet expectations (i.e., cynicism, Kuo, Chang, Quinton, Lu, & Lee, 2015). As such, gossip is likely to be driven by anger or outrage whenever people perceive that others threaten their well-being directly, or the functioning of their groups (Beersma & van Kleef, 2012).

Another prominent trigger of gossip is a state of stress or anxiety. Both trait anxiety (Jaeger, Anthony, & Rosnow, 1980) and situational anxiety, brought about by features of the social environment such as role conflicts, unpredictable work outcomes, and emotional demands, can operate as antecedents of gossip. Anxious individuals need to protect their self-system, and gossip may represent an attempt to cope with the unpleasant anxious state and regain some control over one's social environment (e.g., Georganta et al., 2014). Gossip might relieve anxiety in several ways: it might provide information that reduces uncertainty or feelings of threat, for example during organizational change (Mills, 2010), it might help individuals find comfort and support in social relations with others who are experiencing similar threats (Ellwardt et al., 2012), or it may offer a way to vent stress generated by an emotionally demanding job (Waddington & Fletcher, 2005, Georganta et al., 2014).

To summarize, interpersonal events or other social stimuli that people encounter create emotional experiences, which may be expressed or regulated through gossip. Emotions can motivate gossip, depending on individuals' needs and goals and on the situational layout. Expressing emotions through gossip might be a way to cope with the events that triggered them without a direct confrontation with others. Because gossip provides an outlet for emotions in a private and safe environment, it may help stabilize and control hierarchies or conflicts between individuals (Foster, 2004).

# EMOTIONS AS INTRINSIC REWARDS OF GOSSIP: ENJOYMENT AND INTEREST

Gossip is often seen as a leisure activity, driven by individuals' wish to escape the monotony they encounter in their work and have a good time with others (Beersma & Van Kleef, 2012; Noon & Delbridge, 1993). People enjoy gossiping because the social interactions in which they can share important concerns with others are intrinsically rewarding. People experience gossip as intrinsically rewarding because it satisfies needs, for example a need for affiliation, competence, or autonomy (cf. self-determination theory, Deci & Ryan, 2002).

First, people may enjoy gossiping because it produces a sense of bonding and fulfills the need for affiliation. Gossipers create an enjoyable interpersonal experience by selectively gossiping with those who are likely to understand and support their point of view—often their peers, who may be experiencing similar threats or opportunities. Talking about social targets often involves sharing an emotional reaction between the sender and the receiver of the message (Peters & Kashima, 2007; Van Kleef, 2009). Over time, gossip interactions create trust, mutual liking, and strong social bonds between gossipers (Bosson et al., 2006; Ellwardt et al., 2012, Wittek & Wielers, 1998).

Furthermore, gossip may be intrinsically rewarding because it creates a sense of superiority (competence) or agency (autonomy). Gossip is an excellent opportunity to covertly promote one's own qualities and accomplishments in comparison to those of the gossip target (Wert & Salovey, 2004). Fulfilling the underlying goal of punishing a perpetrator of transgressions through gossip may be satisfying, because one has implemented social justice: gossipers feel good about their sharp social skills and pro-social behavior. Thus, gossip is associated with high emotional rewards derived from indirectly or symbolically achieving goals or desired states: finding allies, feeling good about oneself, and punishing others.

# EMOTIONS AS CONSEQUENCES OF GOSSIP

The gossip triad contains two members who may be more passive than the message sender in the transmission of gossip, but whom are likely to be affected by the gossip. Both the receiver and the target are likely to react emotionally to the gossip they hear, because the gossip is important in shaping how these individuals relate to others in their social environment. However, the positions of receiver and target are fundamentally different. Gossip affects the well-being of the receiver, but only indirectly, because the message is about someone else. As such, receivers must first determine the implications of gossip for themselves and their relationships. However, gossip concerns targets directly, either promoting or blocking their needs, which has clear implications for targets' relationships with others. Thus, for targets, gossip may be more directly related to emotions and action tendencies. The distinct ways in which receivers and targets react emotionally to gossip are important, because their emotions influence their behavior and well-being differently.

# EMOTIONS OF GOSSIP RECEIVERS

Gossip contains social information that is likely to be relevant for a receiver's goals or interests, in the context of his or her relationships with other people. People are interested in receiving gossip information about potential allies or rivals, because such information may give the self an advantage in cooperation or competition (Hess & Hagen, this volume; McAndrew, this volume; McAndrew & Milenkovic, 2002; McAndrew, Bell, & Garcia, 2007). Because gossip about others is relevant for one's own outcomes, hearing gossip can trigger specific emotions, such as surprise, admiration, anger, and fear related to the target, the gossiper, or the self. Indeed, research showed that the majority of people who were asked to recall gossip they received, reported that they had an emotional reaction to the gossip, which the authors interpret as an indication of gossip's motivational significance (Baumeister et al., 2004). Participants reported experiencing a broad spectrum of emotions, suggesting that gossip has important implications for the receivers and their relations with gossipers (as illustrated in the previous sections) and targets.

Gossip can generate emotional reactions of the gossip receiver toward the target, and these emotions fulfill the social function of shaping the receivers' relation with the target: affiliation or distancing (Fischer & Manstead, 2008). Because gossip contains evaluations of the target, it is likely to trigger emotions that are consistent with the evaluative message. Positive gossip about high performers might generate happiness, admiration and respect, signaling that the target has accomplished desired outcomes, and the self would gain from affiliation with this person. However, emotions triggered by gossip may also create social distancing of receivers from targets. For example, people who hear about someone's transgressions from an angry gossiper may become angry with the target as well (Peters & Kashima, 2007; van Kleef, 2009). Receivers' emotions may drive them to take action against the target, especially when the transgression affects the receivers or someone in their group (Frijda, 1986; Lazarus, 1991). Thus, receivers' emotional reaction to the gossip may generate a behavioral response directed at determining one's position relative to the target, commensurate to the transgression and their available means of action (Fischer & Manstead, 2008).

People who receive gossip about others are likely to engage in social comparison with the target in order to evaluate themselves as better or worse than the target on specific dimensions (Wert & Salovey, 2004). According to the Self Enhancing Tactician Model (SCENT; Sedikides & Strube, 1997), a positive evaluation of the self is a fundamental human need, which allows us to cope with threats and problems in an adaptive way. As such, people use the social information available to them, obtained for example by making social comparisons, in order to find evidence that allows them to maintain or promote a positive image of themselves. A recent study using the SCENT model (Martinescu et al., 2014) showed that gossip helped receivers evaluate themselves because it triggered social comparison processes of receivers who compared themselves with targets. These social comparisons, in turn, generated self-conscious emotions for the receivers of gossip. Specifically, compared to positive gossip, receiving negative gossip had self-promotion value for receivers: receivers drew favorable conclusions about themselves and were more inclined to think that they are better than targets after receiving negative (vs. positive) gossip. Consequently, gossip receivers experienced elevated feelings of pride. However, negative gossip compared to positive gossip also had self-protection value: receivers felt that they may be exposed to the same threats and share the target's fate, which made them experience fear (Martinescu et al., 2014). These different emotional outcomes (and their associated behavioral patterns) point to the complexity of reactions triggered by gossip, in the sense that receivers may draw different implications for themselves from one gossip story. Thus, gossip can activate different emotional reactions and further associated behavioral responses, which help receivers interact adaptively with their social environment.

## EMOTIONS OF GOSSIP TARGETS

For its targets, gossip is an evaluation of their flaws or qualities, which may affect important outcomes like one's self-esteem, reputation or acceptance in a group of reference. Gossip is therefore likely to generate strong emotions, because it directly concerns the self (Frijda, 1986; Lazarus, 1991). The target's emotions contain useful cues and help them make sense of the gossip event and take appropriate action. Targets are evaluated positively or negatively by gossipers, usually in line with their subjective perceptions of the target's attributes or behavior. For example, targets who make substantial contributions to the group will be seen as high performers, and are likely to be praised in acts of gossiping. Targets who use group resources more than they contribute to the group, in contrast, will be seen as low performers or social loafers, and are likely to be criticized (Burt, 2008; Kniffin & Wilson, 2010). Such negative gossip entails pressure to conform to social norms, and signals that targets might face social exclusion.

Overhearing others' gossip about the self causes an intense emotional experience, because targets are confronted with (often genuine) evaluations of themselves. Therefore the gossip message concerns targets directly and affects their well-being, because it describes how the person has met or failed expectations and internalized social standards. Because maintaining a positive self-image is crucial for the functioning of the self (e.g., Sedikides & Strube, 1997), candid evaluations of the self may affect the functioning and integrity of the self-system, and are likely to generate strong self-directed emotions and associated adaptive behavioral patterns (Arkin & Appelman, 1983; Frijda, 1986). A study investigating targets' reactions to gossip (Martinescu et al., 2019) showed that people felt proud when they overheard positive compared to negative gossip, suggesting that people are likely to take other's positive evaluations as an indicator of their performance and reinforce their positive self-views. Furthermore, negative gossip (compared to positive gossip) generated shame and guilt, indicating that targets feel responsible for the shortcomings revealed by gossip. As postulated by emotion theories (Lazarus, 1991; Smith & Ellsworth, 1985), self-directed blame (shame and guilt) predicted participants' intention to repair their mistakes. Furthermore, guilt and repair intentions were higher when targets had low core self-evaluations—that is, people felt higher guilt when they had less confidence in their coping abilities and a less positive self-image. Thus, gossip helps targets adopt behaviors that are in line with the social norms, through self-conscious emotions.

Gossip does not only affect targets' self-image, but also shapes their social reputation: people can be depicted as valued group members or as pariah (e.g., Burt, 2008). Through its reputational effects, gossip has consequences for targets' social acceptance and access to group resources (see Giardini & Wittek, this volume). Therefore, people strive to maintain a positive reputation, and because negative gossip may harm their reputation and well-being, targets are likely to react emotionally to gossip. Reputation is socially constructed, and does not require direct input from the target. Targets are quite powerless when others gossip about them, because evaluations about the target are spread informally, in their absence (Foster, 2004). Thus, gossipers make targets vulnerable because they shape the way others see and interact with them. As such, people are likely to experience strong emotions directed at people who gossip about them. Because negative gossip includes threats of social exclusion, targets often become angry at gossipers. Moreover, when gossipers are subjective and self-interested, they may not represent the target very accurately, which may add to targets' rage.

An empirical study showed that negative gossip angered targets, and increased their intention to retaliate against the gossiper (Martinescu et al., 2019). Furthermore, especially participants who were highly concerned for their reputation were more likely to be angry and to intend to harm the gossiper, because the gossip felt more harmful and destructive to these people. Anger reactions help targets dispute that they have deviated from a social norm and construe the gossiper as a perpetrator (e.g., malicious gossip, inaccurate gossip). Moreover, results also showed that gossip made targets feel angrier with their evaluators in comparison to feedback obtained from formal organizational feedback systems, suggesting that the way evaluations about the self are circulated affect the emotional response of the target: gossip is more angering perhaps because the target has no control over it. Thus, by eliciting other-directed emotions and behaviors that seem appropriate in particular gossip situations, emotions help targets cope with gossipers in an adaptive manner.

People avoid committing blatant social transgressions, to avoid being socially excluded. People are aware that negative gossip can damage their reputation and may result in their exclusion from valued groups (an important condition for living an adaptive life). A recent study (Martinescu, Jansen, & Beersma, 2017b) showed that negative gossip made targets feel socially excluded; the negative emotions generated by the gossip helped targets understand that they are not valued members of their group. Furthermore, feeling that one's group does not understand or appreciate the self was related to low well-being, low satisfaction and reduced intentions to contribute to the group and behave proactively. Over time, people are likely to withdraw from groups where they are frequently the target of negative gossip, and strive to become members of groups where they may be appreciated. Thus, emotions generated by gossip episodes help people choose groups in which they have functional and adaptive relations with others.

Although some of the emotions experienced by gossip targets may seem disruptive (anger with the gossiper, anxiety, fear of social exclusion), their role is to signal to the individual what the most appropriate response is in the current situation: repair one's mistake, retaliate against the gossiper, or perhaps withdraw from the group. Gossip has complex social implications for targets, and their emotions may guide people to choose the most adaptive response given their circumstances and predispositions.

# GENERAL DISCUSSION

Gossip is a ubiquitous social regulation process (Dunbar, Duncan, & Marriott, 1997), and inherently an emotional event. Gossip can help individuals behave adaptively, by finding a balance between the urge to be *selfish*—using resources for one's own well-being, and more generally engaging in self-promoting behaviors, and the pressure to be *altruistic*—sharing resources, cooperating, and building positive relationships with group members (Axelrod & Hamilton, 1981; Dawkins, 1989; Williams, 1966). Gossip may be omnipresent in daily life, across contexts, because it helps individuals solve problems of adaptation in an efficient and organic manner, through emotion. The primary function of emotions is to mobilize organisms to cope with threats or opportunities; they enable people to interpret signals from the social environment and react quickly, and to communicate their true motives, judgments, and intentions to others (Owren & Bachorowski, 2001).

As we have discussed, gossip can be triggered by emotions, gossip is intrinsically emotionally rewarding, and gossip is likely to cause strong emotional reactions in receivers and targets (if targets become aware of the gossip). We believe that these emotions are highly functional for people to adapt to their social environment. For example, gossip may be used to relieve anxiety and to fulfill individual and group needs, such as one's needs for relatedness, competence, and autonomy, and the need to regulate group life. Because emotions prepare for and facilitate action, emotions may trigger behavioral responses to gossip, both for gossip receivers and gossip targets. Receiving positive gossip about a target may lead receivers to affiliate with the gossip target, whereas receiving negative gossip may lead to behaviors that distance the receiver from the target. Targets of negative gossip may feel guilt and shame, which will drive them to restoration activities (e.g., work harder for the group), or anger toward the gossiper, which may further lead to retaliatory behavior aimed at discrediting or harming the gossiper.

Previous research on gossip has, unfortunately, largely ignored emotions (but see Baumeister et al., 2004; Feinberg et al., 2012; Georganta et al., 2014; Waddington & Fletcher, 2005). Therefore our knowledge about the role of emotions in gossip behavior and responses to it is still relatively limited. This may partly be a consequence of the implicit assumption in much research that gossip is (to some extent) rational behavior that people consciously use to achieve certain goals. For example, gossip has been studied in the context of (rational) economic games (e.g., Sommerfeld et al., 2007; Wu et al., 2015), or people have been asked to explicitly reflect on the functions of gossip (Beersma & van Kleef, 2012; Martinescu et al., 2017a). However, it seems possible that gossip is mostly driven by emotions, rather than by cognitive and deliberate decision processes.

Therefore, the functions that gossip fulfills may not always be subject to introspection, but other than rational considerations (i.e., emotions) may be more important in naturalistically occurring gossip episodes. Rational economic game paradigms emphasize gossip's functions in enhancing decision making and group outcomes that are based merely on gossip's capacity to convey reputational information. However, in naturalistic settings, conveying reputational information is accompanied and nuanced by the emotions of the sender, receiver, and target of gossip. Given the importance of emotions in generating adaptive responses in any situation or interaction that is relevant for individuals' goals or well-being, emotions are an essential aspect of gossip as an adaptive behavior.

# FUTURE RESEARCH DIRECTIONS

As outlined in this chapter, gossip is likely to be fundamentally related to emotion, because emotion offers quick and intuitive ways of solving adaptive problems that arise from social interactions. However, some gossip seems to be driven by cognitive-rational processes. Humans have a limited information processing capacity (cognitive miser model, Taylor, 1981) and rely heavily on heuristics, which represent quick and imperfect ways to solve problems, by decreasing the cognitive load. To make judgments more efficiently, people may rely on stereotypes, rules of thumb, affective cues, or other heuristics (see Tversky & Kahneman, 1974). Kahneman (2011) describes System 1 as the default thinking mode that humans use for interpreting the meaning of social events and interactions with others as a fast and automatic type of cognitive processing, relying on heuristics, stereotypes, and emotions. System 2 is characterized by slow, effortful, logical, and fully conscious cognitive processing.

In Kahneman's terms (2011), System 1 may be activated most of the time people spread or react to gossip. Prototypical gossip is spontaneous, intrinsically motivated, based on heuristic processes and saturated with emotion. Furthermore, as an organic interaction, typical gossip may be humorous, unstructured, and spontaneously reactive to gossip partners' input (Goodman & Ben-Ze'ev, 1994; Bergmann, 1993). However, some gossip, which is purposeful and premeditated, may be related to the System 2. This type of gossip is driven by motives which become conscious goals (e.g., to seek information; to punish a transgressor), and may be extrinsically motivated, entailing lower emotional involvement. As such, malicious gossip, used for purposefully harming others is likely to be disconnected from emotion, and driven by rational cognitive processes characteristic of System 2.

It remains for future research to better integrate theories of gossip, emotion and cognition, by investigating when and how gossip spreading and reactions to gossip are related to emotional and rational cognitive processes. It would be interesting to study whether gossip can prompt people to switch flexibly between the two cognitive systems, in accordance with situational demands, as the dual thinking system theory would predict (Kahneman, 2011). Gossip helps people extract reputational information about others in their network, without becoming overloaded with information. As a screening mechanism for the social world, gossip may rely mostly on automatic and intuitive processing strategies. It is plausible that people who are involved in prototypical gossip, will switch to a more logical or rational approach when they encounter information that is of high relevance for their goals; in addition, it is likely that gossip related to one's well-being will also activate distinct high arousal emotions which prepare for action. Furthermore, future studies should investigate whether gossip is associated with emotional or rational thinking styles depending on the context and on individuals' characteristics and predispositions.

As part of complex social networks, individuals depend on others for fulfilling their goals and needs. Gossip has an important normative role, because it helps regulate social actors' behavior, by pressuring them to behave in line with group norms, and by threatening uncooperative targets with social exclusion (Burt, 2008; Sommerfeld et al., 2007). Although gossip is highly functional for groups and individuals, occupying up to 60–70% of the time spent in conversation (Dunbar et al., 1997; Emler, 1994), most people agree that gossip is not a socially desirable behavior, because gossip violates privacy norms and is out of targets' control. Thus, it seems that people dedicate a considerable amount of time to an activity they view in very negative terms.

An important question that arises is why do people have such conflicting views on gossip and how do they cope with the dissonance generated by their "unacceptable" behavior. Gossipers may be moral hypocrites, who need to use self-deception strategies such as misperceiving one's behavior as moral, or avoiding to compare one's behavior with moral standards (Batson, Thompson, Seuferling, Whitney, & Strongman, 1999). Another possibility is that the emotions which stimulate engagement in gossip offer justifications or blur people's moral concerns about gossip. Furthermore, when the welfare of group members can be secured by gossiping, negative views of gossip change, and those who fail to gossip about a misbehaving target are seen more negatively (Baumeister et al., 2004; Beersma & Van Kleef, 2012). Thus, gossip may be seen as moral or immoral, depending on who is making this judgment, and on individuals' interests and emotions in a particular situation (Rozin, Lowery, Imada, & Haidt, 1999). As such, future research should investigate in more detail how moral evaluations of gossip are constructed and how they shape the gossip process.

In the case of targets, the link between emotion and gossip's (anti)normative function is most evident: due to its implications for targets' subjective well-being and reputation, gossip has a strong emotional impact and associated normative or antinormative behavioral implications. Research suggests that angry targets are likely to retaliate, whereas guilty gossip targets are likely to engage in reparative behaviors (Martinescu et al., 2019). Future research could investigate whether specific emotions of targets and their following behaviors are related to the moral framing of gossip (benign gossip vs. malicious gossip). It is however possible that targets unequivocally feel harmed by gossip, because any gossip represents a reputational threat, regardless of whether the gossip is justified by their behavior or not. Furthermore, it would be interesting to explore how the moral identities of gossipers, receivers and targets may shape the way they view and react to gossip.

Even though we have emphasized the adaptive function of gossip and emotion, it should be recognized that gossip can in fact be malicious and may have severe negative consequences for the functioning of individuals and groups. Unjustified negative gossip and strategic lying about others may, of course, seriously harm reputations and well-being of targets. Furthermore, negative gossip may sometimes lead to harmful vicious cycles, in which different people or factions try to destroy each other's reputation through malicious gossip. This may undermine cooperation and cohesion of groups, can potentially lead to a toxic group or organizational climate, and to high levels of distrust. Yet because gossip is rarely meant to be truly malicious (e.g., Baumeister et al., 2004, Ben-Ze'ev, 1994, Dunbar et al., 1997), it seems more likely that such vicious cycles will only occur in situations in which distrust is high and cohesion and cooperation are low to start with. Future research should clarify the circumstances in which malicious gossip is likely to occur, its emotional impact, and potential strategies to manage it.

As a social control mechanism, gossip promises to protect groups against members who may threaten the welfare of the group. However, because gossip is deeply connected with emotions, gossip may have unintended consequences on other group processes or outcomes through affective channels. It may be interesting for future research to investigate the effect of gossip frequency, valence and affective tone on outcomes such as group performance in terms of productivity, creativity, or decision making.

Emotional intelligence (EI), which indicates an individual's ability to use emotion to enhance thought and decision making (Mayer, Roberts, & Barsade, 2008) should also be included in future research on gossip and emotion, because EI is a factor that is likely to shape the way individuals use and react to gossip. For example, individuals with high-EI may be better at interpreting social cues, or may be able to better regulate their emotional responses to gossip they receive.

The core thesis of this chapter is that gossip has a functional role for the individuals involved in it, and these functions are operationalized through emotions. For example, the influence function of gossip is observable when an angry individual gossips in order to control a target's behavior, or when a gossip target is afraid of social exclusion and engages in reparative actions. Furthermore, it seems plausible that anxiety fuels gossip aimed at searching for information, whereas anger fuels gossip aimed at punishing a transgression. As such, future research may investigate more systematically whether certain emotions accompany specific gossip functions. Emotions may activate and regulate stable behavioral paths that outline how gossip can be used for fulfilling needs or goals.

# References

Arkin, R. M., & Appelman, A. J. (1983). Social anxiety and receptivity to interpersonal evaluation. *Motivation and Emotion 7*, 11–18.

Axelrod, R. & Hamilton, W. D. (1981). The evolution of cooperation. *Science 211*, 1390–1396.

Batson, C., E., Thompson, G. Seuferling, H. Whitney, & J. Strongman (1999). Moral hypocrisy: Appearing moral to oneself without being so. *Journal of Personality and Social Psychology 77*, 525–537.

Baumeister, R. F., Zhang, L., & Vohs, K. D. (2004). Gossip as cultural learning. *Review of General Psychology 8*, 111–121.

Beersma, B., & Van Kleef, G. A. (2012). Why people gossip: An empirical analysis of social motives, antecedents, and consequences. *Journal of Applied Social Psychology 42*, 2640–2670.

Ben-Ze'ev, A. (1994). The vindication of gossip. In R. F. Goodman & A. Ben-Ze'ev (Eds.), *Good gossip* (pp. 11–24). Lawrence, KS: Kansas University Press.

Bergmann, J. R. (1993). *Discreet indiscretions: The social organization of gossip*. New York: Aldine de Gruyter.

Bosson, J. K., Johnson, A. B., Niederhoffer, K., & Swann, W. B., Jr. (2006). Interpersonal chemistry through negativity: Bonding by sharing negative attitudes about others. *Personal relationships 13*, 135–150.

Burt, R. S. (2008). Gossip and Reputation. In M. Lecoutre & P. Lièvre (Eds.), *Management Et Réseaux Sociaux: Ressource Pour L'action Ou Outil de Gestion?* (pp. 27–42). Paris: Hermès Science Publications Press.

Cabanac, M. (2002). What is emotion? *Behavioural Processes 60*, 69–83.

Damasio, A. (1994). *Descartes' error: Emotions, reason, and the human brain*. New York: Avon Books.

Dawkins, R. (1989). The selfish gene (2nd ed.). Oxford, UK: Oxford University Press.

Deci, E. L., & Ryan, R. M. (2002). *Handbook of self-determination research*. Rochester, NY: University of Rochester Press.

Dunbar, R. I. M. (2004). Gossip in an evolutionary perspective. *Review of General Psychology 8*, 100–110.

Dunbar, R. I. M., Duncan, N. D. C. & Marriott, A. (1997). Human conversational behaviour. *Human Nature 8*, 231–246.

Ekman, P. (1992). An argument for basic emotions. *Cognition and Emotion 6*, 169–200.

Ellwardt, L., Steglich, C., & Wittek, R. (2012). The co-evolution of gossip and friendship in workplace social networks. *Social Networks 34*, 623–633.

Emler, N. (1994). Gossip, reputation and social adaptation. In R. Goodman and A. Ben Ze'ev (Eds.), *Good gossip* (pp. 117–133). Kansas: Kansas University Press.

Feinberg, M., Willer, R., Stellar, J., & Keltner, D. (2012). The virtues of gossip: Reputational information sharing as prosocial behavior. *Journal of Personality and Social Psychology 102*, 1015–1030.

Fine, G. A., & Rosnow, R. L. (1978). Gossip, gossipers, gossiping. *Personality and Social Psychology Bulletin 4*, 161–168.

Fischer, A. H., & Manstead, A. S. R. (2008). Social functions of emotion. In M. Lewis, J. Haviland, & L. Feldman Barrett (Eds.), *Handbook of emotion* (3rd ed.). New York: Guilford.

Forgas, J. P. (1995). Mood and judgement: The affect infusion model (AIM). *Psychological Bulletin 117*, 39–66.

Foster, E. K. (2004). Research on gossip: Taxonomy, methods, and future directions. *Review of General Psychology 8*, 78–99.

Frijda, N. H. (1986). *The emotions*. Cambridge: Cambridge University Press.

Frijda, N. (1988). The laws of emotion. *American Psychologist 43*, 349–358.

Georganta, K., Panagopoulou, E., & Montgomery, A. (2014). Talking behind their backs: negative gossip and burnout in hospitals. *Burnout Research 1*, 76–81.

Giardini, F., Wittek, R. (2019). Gossip, Reputation, and Sustainable Cooperation: Sociological Foundations. In F. Giardini & R. Wittek (Eds.), *Handbook of gossip and reputation*. New York: Oxford University Press.

Goodman, R. F., & Ben-Ze'ev, A. (1994). *Good gossip*. Lawrence, KS: University Press of Kansas.

Hess, N., Hagen, E. (2019). Gossip, reputation, and friendship in in-group competition. In F. Giardini, R. Wittek (Eds.), *Handbook of gossip and reputation*. New York: Oxford University Press.

*Holy Bible*, NLT. (1996). Wheaton Il: Tyndale House Publishers, Inc.

Izard, C. E. (1977). *Human emotions*. New York: Plenum.

Izard, C. E., & Ackerman, B. P. (2000). Motivational, organizational, and regulatory functions of discrete emotions. In M. Lewis & J. Haviland-Jones (Eds.), Handbook of emotions (2nd ed., pp. 253–322). New York: Guilford Press.

Jaeger, M. E., Anthony, S., & Rosnow, R. L. (1980). Who hears what from whom and with what effect: A study of rumor. *Personality and Social Psychology Bulletin 6*, 473–478.

Kahneman, D. (2011). *Thinking, fast and slow*. New York: Farrar, Straus and Giroux.

Keltner, D., & Haidt, J. (1999). Social functions of emotions at four levels of analysis. *Cognition and Emotion 13*, 505–521.

Kniffin, K. M., & Wilson, D. S. (2010). Evolutionary perspectives on workplace gossip: Why and how gossip can serve groups. *Group & Organization Management 35*, 150–176.

Kuo, C., Chang, K., Quinton, S., Lu, C., & Lee, I. (2015). Gossip in the workplace and the implications for HR management: A study of gossip and its relationship to employee cynicism. *International Journal of Human Resource Management 26*, 2288–2307.

Lazarus, R. S. (1991). *Emotion and adaptation*. Oxford, UK: Oxford University Press.

Martin, G. G. R. (2011). *A clash of kings*. Book Two of *A song of ice and fire*. London: Harper Voyager.

Martinescu, E., Janssen, O., & Nijstad, B. A. (2014). Tell me the gossip: The self- evaluative function of receiving gossip about others. *Personality and Social Psychology Bulletin 40*, 1668–1680.

Martinescu, E., Janssen, O., & Nijstad, B. A. (2017a). Gossip is the weapon of the weak: How power differences shape gossip behavior. (Doctoral dissertation, pp. 23–59). Groningen: University of Groningen.

Martinescu, E., Jansen, W., & Beersma, B. (2017b). Does gossip make targets prosocial or antisocial? The role of social inclusion. Manuscript in preparation.

Martinescu, E., Janssen, O., & Nijstad, B. A. (2019). Emotional and behavioral responses to gossip about the self. *Frontiers in Psychology, 9, 2603*. doi: 10.3389/fpsyg.2018.02603.

Mayer, J. D., Roberts, R. D., & Barsade, S. G. (2008). Human abilities: Emotional intelligence. *Annual Review of Psychology 59*, 507–536.

McAndrew, F. T. (2019). Gossip as a social skill. In F. Giardini & R. Wittek (Eds.), *Handbook of gossip and reputation*. New York: Oxford University Press.

McAndrew, F. T., Bell, E. K., & Garcia, C. M. (2007). Who do we tell, and whom do we tell on? Gossip as a strategy for status enhancement. *Journal of Applied Social Psychology 37*, 1562–1577.

McAndrew, F. T., & Milenkovic, M. A. (2002). Of tabloids and family secrets: The evolutionary psychology of gossip. *Journal of Applied Social Psychology 32*, 1064–1082.

Michelson, G., Van Iterson, A., & Waddington, K. (2010). Gossip in organizations: Contexts, consequences and controversies. *Group and Organization Management 3*, 371–390.

Milinski, M. (2019). Gossip and reputation in social dilemmas. In F. Giardini & R. Wittek (Eds.), *Handbook of gossip and reputation*. New York: Oxford University Press

Mills, C. (2010). Experiencing gossip: The foundations for a theory of embedded organizational gossip. *Group & Organization Management 35*, 213–240.

Nicholson, N. (2001). The new word on gossip. *Psychology Today, June*, 41–45.

Noon, M., & R. Delbridge (1993). News from behind my hand: Gossip in organizations. *Organization Studies 14*, 23–36.

Oatley, K. 1992. *Best laid schemes: The psychology of emotions*. Cambridge, England: Cambridge University Press.

Owren, M. J., & Bachorowski, J.-A. (2001). The evolution of emotional expression: A "selfish-gene" account of smiling and laughter in early hominids and humans. In T. J. Mayne & G. A. Bonnanno (Eds.), *Emotions: Current issues and future directions* (pp. 152–191). New York: Guilford.

Peters, K., & Kashima, Y. (2007). From social talk to social action: Shaping the social triad with emotion sharing. *Journal of Personality and Social Psychology 93*, 780–797.

Roseman, I. J. (1984). Cognitive determinants of emotion. *Review of Personality and Social Psychology 5*, 11–36.

Rosnow, R. L. (2001). Rumor and gossip in interpersonal interaction and beyond: A social exchange perspective. In R. M. Kowalski (Ed.), *Behaving badly: Aversive behaviors in interpersonal relationships* (pp. 203–232). Washington, DC: American Psychological Association.

Rozin, P., Lowery, L., Imada, S., & Haidt, J. (1999). The CAD triad hypothesis: A mapping between three moral emotions (contempt, anger, disgust) and three moral codes (community, autonomy, divinity). *Journal of Personality and Social Psychology 76*, 574–586.

Sedikides, C., & Strube, M. J. (1997). Self-evaluation: To thine own self be good, to thine own self be sure, to thine own self be true, and to thine own self be better. In M. P. Zanna (Ed.), *Advances in experimental social psychology* (Vol. 29, pp. 209–269). New York: Academic Press.

Smith, C. A., & Ellsworth, P. C. (1985). Patterns of cognitive appraisal in emotion. *Journal of Personality and Social Psychology 48*, 813–838.

Sommerfeld, R. D., Krambeck, H. J., & Milinski, M. (2008). Multiple gossip statements and their effect on reputation and trustworthiness. *Proceedings of the Royal Society of London B: Biological Sciences 275*, 2529–2536.

Sommerfeld, R. D., Krambeck, H., Semmann, D., & Milinski, M. (2007). Gossip as an alternative for direct observation in games of indirect reciprocity. *Proceedings of the National Academy of Sciences USA 104*, 17435–17440. doi:10.1073/pnas.0704598104.

Stirling, R. B. (1956). Some psychological mechanisms operative in gossip. *Social Forces 34*, 262–267.

Taylor, S. E. (1981). The interface of cognitive and social psychology. In J. H. Harvey (Ed.), *Cognition, social behavior, and the environment* (pp. 189–211). Hillsdale: Erlbaum.

Tversky, A., & Kahneman, D. (1974). Judgment under uncertainty: Heuristics and biases. *Science 185*, 1124–1131.

Van Kleef, G. A. (2009). How emotions regulate social life: The emotions as social information (EASI) model. *Current Directions in Psychological Science 18*, 184–188.

Waddington, K., & Fletcher, C. (2005). Gossip and emotion in nursing and health-care organizations. *Journal of Health Organization and Management 19*, 378–394.

Wert, S. R., & Salovey, P. (2004). A social comparison account of gossip. *Review of General Psychology 8*, 122–137.

Weiner, B. (1985). An attributional theory of achievement motivation and emotion. *Psychological Bulletin 92*, 548–573.

Williams, G. C. (1966). *Adaptation and natural selection: A critique of some current evolutionary thought*. Princeton, NJ: Princeton University Press.

Wittek, R., & Wielers, R. (1998). Gossip in organizations. *Computational & Mathematical Organization Theory 4*, 189–204.

Wu, J., Balliet, D., & Van Lange, P. A. M. (2015). When does gossip promote generosity? Indirect reciprocity under the shadow of the future. *Social Psychological and Personality Science 6*, 923–930.

Wu, J., Balliet, D., & Van Lange, P. A. M. (2016). Reputation management: Why and how gossip enhances generosity. *Evolution and Human Behavior 37*, 193–201.

# PART III

## STRATEGIC INTERDEPENDENCIES

# CHAPTER 10

# GOSSIP AS A SOCIAL SKILL

FRANCIS T. McANDREW

## INTRODUCTION

In spite of its generally negative reputation, studies indicate that most gossip is not malicious in its intent (Ben-Ze'ev, 1994; Dunbar, Duncan, & Marriott, 1997; Goodman & Ben-Ze'ev, 1994; Spacks, 1985). Levin & Arluke (1987), among others, have proposed that gossip is universal because it is psychologically and socially useful. Anthropologists have frequently identified gossip as a cultural device that can be used not only by individuals to advance their own interests, but also as a means by which groups can enforce conformity to group norms (Abrahams, 1970; Cox, 1970; Lee, 1990). It is this dual nature of gossip that creates so much ambivalence toward it. The recognition of its importance in maintaining group life makes acceptance of it a necessity, but its potential for advancing the interests of one individual at the expense of another poses a threat that must be contained if the group is to function effectively. Thus, paradoxically, gossip can serve as both a form of antisocial behavior *and* as a means of controlling antisocial behavior (Wilson, Wilczynski, Wells, & Weiser, 2000). In his book *Grooming, Gossip, and the Evolution of Language* (1996), British psychologist Robin Dunbar also suggested that gossip is a mechanism for bonding social groups together, analogous to the grooming that is found in primate groups, and other researchers have proposed that gossip is one of the best tools that we have for comparing ourselves socially with others (Suls, 1977; Wert & Salovey, 2004).

The distinction between "gossip" and "rumor." The terms "gossip" and "rumor" are often used interchangeably, and the average person on the street may see little difference between the two words. Researchers, however, need to be a bit more precise about such distinctions. In a sense, gossip can be thought of as a subset of rumor. Rumors are unsubstantiated bits of information that may involve future events, people, or some other topic of collective interest. Gossip is defined more specifically as talk about people. Whether the information being discussed is true or false is irrelevant to labeling it as a gossip or rumor. In work organizations, common topics of rumor are personnel shakeups and anything related to job security, pay, and benefits (DiFonzo & Bordia, 2006), and they are a pervasive part of day-to-day life in all organizations (Houmanfar & Johnson, 2003). Bordia & DiFonzo (2005) have proposed that rumors can serve a range of different functions, including the uncovering of new information, the management of relationships with co-workers, and satisfying self-serving motives such as wish fulfillment, revenge, and the maintenance of self-esteem.

**How did gossip develop such a bad reputation?** The word "gossip" is derived from the Old English phrase *God Sib*, which literally translates as "god parent." The term originally referred to companions who were not relatives, but who were intimate enough to be named as godparents to one's child. These companions were almost always females and they were usually present during labor and the birth of a child. Apparently, medieval European births were very social affairs restricted entirely to women. The hours were passed in conversation and moral support, and it undoubtedly was a strong bonding experience among those who were present (Rysman, 1977). Thus, the original word was a noun specifically referring to the female companions of a woman during childbirth, and it was entirely benign in its usage. However, by the 1500s, the word had taken on a decidedly negative connotation. The first known literary use of the word in this negative context occurred in Shakespeare's *Midsummer Night's Dream*, and the Oxford English Dictionary defines the 16th century use of the word as describing a woman "of light and trifling character" who delights in "idle talk" and was a "newsmonger" or a "tattler" (www.OED.com, retrieved on February 16, 2016). Rysman suggested (perhaps facetiously) that the word acquired negative connotations over time because one of the side effects of women coming together in solidarity was an increase in hassles for men! It was not until the 1800s that the word was applied to a type of conversation rather than to the person engaging in the conversation.

The recognition of gossip's potential for social disruption has historically been reflected in a wide variety of laws, punishments, and moral codes designed to control it going as far back as the Old Testament (Emler, 1994; Goodman & Ben-Ze'ev, 1994).

There has long been legal and religious sanctions that could be brought to bear upon gossipers who crossed a line and gossiped about the wrong people at the wrong time. Most nations still have laws against slander on the books, and until relatively recently dueling to the death was considered an honorable way of dealing with those who had transgressed against one's reputation and good name. Curiously, an examination of historical European tactics for handling gossips reveals an especially persistent concern with clamping down on the gossip of women (McAndrew, 2014).

The strong negative reaction to the word "gossip" persists into the 21st century. I have written numerous popular press articles on gossip, and such pieces reliably attract a barrage of scathing comments from individuals, often writing from a religious point of view, who are completely unreceptive to the possibility that gossip can serve any redeeming social function whatsoever.

# How Might Gossip be an Evolutionary Adaptation?

The prominent role played by gossip in the conversation of everyday people has been documented in populations as geographically diverse as Medieval Europeans (Schein, 1994), the !Kung Bushmen of West Africa (Lee, 1990), the Hopi of North America (Cox, 1970), and the Kabana people of Papua New Guinea (McPherson, 1991). When evolutionary psychologists stumble upon something that is shared by people of all ages, times, and cultures, they usually suspect that they have identified a vital aspect of human nature—something that became a part of who we are in our long-forgotten prehistoric past. Examples of such evolutionary adaptations include our appreciation of landscapes containing fresh water and vegetation, our never-ending battle with our sweet tooth, and our infatuation with people who look a certain way. These adaptations enabled us to not only survive, but to thrive in our prehistoric ancestral environments. Our preoccupation with gossip may very well be another of these evolutionary adaptations.

It will be obvious to most readers that being drawn to environments that provide resources, food that provides energy, and romantic partners who appear able to help you bear and raise healthy children might very well be psychological adaptations that evolved because of their indisputable advantages. However, it may not be so clear at first glance how an interest in gossip could possibly be in the same league as these other human characteristics. If one thinks in terms of what it would have taken to be successful in our ancestral social environment, however, the idea may no longer seem quite so far-fetched.

Our ancestors lived their lives as members of small cooperative groups that were in competition with other relatively small groups (Dunbar, 1996; Lewin, 1993; Tooby & DeVore, 1987). To make matters more complicated, it was necessary to cooperate with in-group members so that the group as a whole could be successful, but competition between members of the same group was also unavoidable insofar as there is only a limited amount of food, mates, and other resources to go around (Krebs & Denton, 1997). Living in such groups, our ancestors faced a number of consistent adaptive problems that were social in nature: obtaining a reproductively valuable mate and successfully managing friendships, alliances, and family relationships (for an evolutionary anthropology account of this see Boehm, this volume; Shackelford, 1997). The social intelligence needed for success in this environment required an ability to predict and influence the behavior of others, and an intense interest in the private dealings of other people would have been handy indeed and it would have been strongly favored by natural selection. In short, people who were fascinated with the lives of others were simply more successful than those who were not, and it is the genes of those individuals that have come down to us through the ages (Alexander, 1979; Barkow, 1989, 1992; Davis & McLeod, 2003; Humphrey, 1983; McAndrew, 2008).

A related social skill that would have had a big payoff is the ability to remember details about the temperament, predictability and past behavior of individuals who were personally known to you. We need to be on guard against individuals who have taken advantage of us in the past so that it does not happen again (hence, our often regrettable tendency to hold grudges), and also to have clear recollections of those who are helpful and could be counted on in future times of need. In our prehistoric past, there would have been little use for a mind that was designed to engage in abstract statistical thinking about large numbers of unknown outsiders. In today's world, it is advantageous to be able to think in terms of probabilities and percentages when it comes to people, because predicting the behavior of the strangers whom we deal with in everyday life requires that we do so. This task is difficult for many of us because the early wiring of the brain was guided by different needs. Thus, natural selection shaped a thirst for, and a memory to store information about, specific people. This information that we store and then transmit to others constitutes the building blocks of *reputation*.

It is well established that we have a brain area specifically dedicated to the identification of human faces (de Haan, Pascalis, & Johnson, 2002; Nelson, 2001), and that we perceive and remember faces best when they have been paired with negative reputational information about individuals who are described as cheaters or as socially undesirable in other ways (Anderson, Siegel, Bliss-Moreau, & Barrett, 2011; Mealey, Daood, & Krage, 1996). For better or worse, this is the mental equipment that we must rely on to navigate our way through a modern world filled with technology and strangers.

If gossip evolved in response to both competition among in-group members and pressure to cooperate within one's group in order to successfully compete against rival groups, the evolution of gossip as we now see it (or hear it?) would have been a delicate balancing act. Competition among members of a social group would only remain adaptive to the individuals involved so long as these competitive forces did not completely undermine the ability of the group to function as a cooperative unit. Similarly, a highly cooperative group that thwarted the reproductive fitness of too many of its members would not survive for long. Theoretically then, the gossip we see in modern humans is really a finely balanced double-bladed weapon, with one blade (a broadsword?) wielded on behalf of the group to deter free-riders and other disruptive individuals, while the other blade (a dagger?) is used more selectively and quietly by one group member against another in a quest to climb the social ladder. So, even though gossip has a bad reputation, it also serves essential positive social functions and human society could not exist without it (Emler, 2001). Furthermore, natural selection would have favored the socially skilled individual who managed to skillfully balance these different aspects of gossip.

# The Multi-Dimensional Nature
# of Gossip-Related Social Skills

*"Good Gossip:" Skillful gossipers help groups thrive.* Gossip probably evolved as a social control mechanism that served the interests of the group as well as the interests of individuals. Boehm (1999) proposes that gossip can serve as a "leveling mechanism" for neutralizing the dominance tendencies of others, making it a "...stealthy activity by which other people's moral dossiers are constantly reviewed" (p. 73). Boehm believes that small-scale foraging societies such as those typical during human prehistory emphasized an egalitarianism that suppressed internal competition and promoted consensus seeking in a way that made the success of one's group extremely important to one's own fitness. These social pressures discouraged free riders and cheaters and encouraged altruists (Boehm, 1997). He also believes that such egalitarian societies were necessary because of the relatively equal and unstable balance of power among individuals with access to weapons and shifting coalitions. In these societies, the manipulation of personal reputations through gossip, ridicule, and ostracism became a key way of keeping potentially dominant group members in check (Boehm, 1993).

There is in fact ample evidence that gossip can indeed be a positive force in the life of a group. Gossip can be a way of learning the unwritten rules of social groups and cultures by resolving ambiguity about group norms and an avenue for socializing newcomers into the ways of the group (Ayim, 1994; Baumeister, Zhang, & Vohs, 2004; Laing, 1993; Noon & Delbridge, 1993; Suls, 1977). Gossip is also an efficient way of reminding group members about the importance of the group's norms and values, and it can be an effective deterrent to deviance and a low-cost form of punishment useful for enforcing cooperation in groups (Barkow, 1992; Feinberg, Cheng, & Willer, 2012; Levin & Arluke, 1987; Merry, 1984). Evolutionary biologist Robert Trivers (1971, 1985) has discussed the evolutionary importance of detecting "gross cheaters" (those who fail to reciprocate altruistic acts) and "subtle cheaters" (those who reciprocate but give much less than they get). Gossip can be an effective means of uncovering such information about others and an especially useful way of controlling these "free-riders" who may be tempted to violate group norms of reciprocity by taking more from the group than they give in return (Dunbar, 1996; Feinberg, Cheng, & Willer, 2012).

Barclay (2016), among others, has commented on the importance of gossip as a tool for monitoring the reputations of others. Studies in real-life groups such as California cattle ranchers (Ellickson, 1991), Maine lobster fishermen (Acheson, 1988), and college rowing teams (Kniffin & Wilson, 1998; Wilson & Kniffin, 1999) confirm that gossip is used in these quite different settings to maintain boundaries between the in-group and out-group, and to enforce group norms when individuals fail to live up to the group's expectations. In all these groups, individuals who violated expectations about sharing resources and meeting responsibilities became frequent targets of gossip and ostracism, which put pressure on them to become better citizens. Anthropological studies of hunter-gatherer groups have typically revealed a similar social control function for gossip in these societies (Lee, 1990; McPherson, 1991). There is also experimental evidence that the protecting one's reputation from sanctions wrought by the grapevine causes individuals to modify their behavior for the good. Beersma & Van Kleef (2011) used a laboratory "dictator game" to study this problem. In their experimental game, people could contribute lottery tickets for a large monetary prize to a group pool (which would be spilt evenly among the group if there was a winning ticket), or they could keep the tickets for themselves instead. People who believed that other people in the group might gossip about them reduced their free-riding and increased the level of their contributions compared to people who did not believe that gossip about them would be possible or likely. Similarly, Wu, Balliet, & Van Lange (2015; 2016) discovered (in a series of laboratory experiments) that individuals behaved more generously to gossip partners with whom they expected to have future interactions, and that this effect was primarily driven by concerns about one's reputation. Finally, another study has demonstrated that people will use gossip pro-socially to rat out selfish, exploitative individuals in experimental game situations even when they have to spend money to do so (Feinberg, Willer, Stellar, & Keltner, 2012). In other words, prosocial gossip is so rewarding that people will even incur a cost for the opportunity to engage in it. In keeping with all of the findings described earlier, it has been documented that gossip that occurs in response to the violation of a social norm is met with approval and is often perceived as the "moral" thing to do (Beersma & Van Kleef, 2012; Wilson et al., 2000).

*"Bad Gossip": Selfish Gossip intended only for self-promotion.* The average person's reaction to the word "gossip" is reflexively negative, probably because we most easily think of the negative, selfish use of gossip. It is true that when gossip is examined in the light of competition between people in the same social group, it is very much about enhancing one's own social success (Barkow, 1989; Hess and Hagen, this volume). Gossip offers a means of manipulating others' reputations by passing on negative information about competitors or enemies as well as a means of detecting betrayal by others in our important relationships (Shackelford, 1997; Spacks, 1985). According to one of the pioneers of gossip research, anthropologist Jerry Barkow (1992), we should be especially interested in information about people who matter most in our lives: rivals, mates, relatives, partners in social exchange, and high-ranking figures whose behavior can affect us. Given the proposition that our interest in gossip evolved as a way of acquiring fitness-enhancing information, Barkow also suggested that the type of knowledge that we seek should be information that can affect our social standing relative to others. Hence, we would expect to find higher interest in negative news (such as misfortunes and scandals) about high-status people and potential rivals because we could exploit it. Negative information about those lower than us in status would not be as useful. There should also be less interest in passing along negative information about our friends and relatives than about people who are not allies. Conversely, positive information (good fortune and sudden elevation of status, for example) about allies should be likely to be spread around, whereas positive information about rivals or non-allies should be less enticing because it is not useful in advancing one's own interests.

For a variety of reasons, our interest in the doings of same-sex others ought to be especially strong. Wilson & Daly (1996), among others, have identified same-sex members of one's own species as our principal evolutionary competitors, and Shackelford (1997) has verified the cross-culturally universal importance of same-sex friendships and coalitional relationships. According to Shackelford, managing alliances and friendships posed important adaptive problems throughout human history because it was important to evaluate the quality and intentions of one's allies and rivals if one was to be successful. Given how critical such relationships are in all areas of life, and also given that such relationships would be most likely to exist between members of same-aged cohorts, we should be most interested in gossip about other people of the same sex who are close to us in age. Hence, the 18-year-old male caveman would have done much better by attending to the business of other 18-year-old males rather than to the business of 50-year-old males or females of any age. Interest about members of the other sex should be strong only when their age and situational circumstances would make them appropriate as mates.

The gossip studies that my students and I have worked on at Knox College over the past 15 years have focused on uncovering what we are most interested in finding out about other people and what we are most likely to spread around. We have had people of all ages rank their interest in tabloid stories about celebrities (McAndrew & Milenkovic, 2002), and we have asked college students to read gossip scenarios about unidentified individuals and tell us which types of people they would most like to hear such information about, whom they would gossip about, and with whom they would share gossip (McAndrew & Milenkovic, 2002; McAndrew, Bell, & Garcia, 2007). In keeping with the evolutionary hypotheses suggested earlier, we have consistently found that people are most interested in gossip about individuals of the same sex as themselves who also happen to be around their own age. We have also found that information that is socially useful is always of greatest interest to us: we like to know about the scandals and misfortunes of our rivals and of high-status people because this information might be valuable in social competition. Positive information about such people tends to be uninteresting to us. Finding out that someone who is already higher in status than ourselves has just acquired something that puts him even further ahead of us does not supply us with ammunition that we can use to gain ground on him. Conversely, positive information about our friends and relatives is highly prized and likely to be used to our advantage whenever possible. For example, we consistently found that college students were not much interested in hearing about academic awards or a large inheritance if it involved one of their professors, and that they were also not very interested in passing that news along to others. Yet the same information about their friends or romantic partners was rated as being quite interesting and likely to be spread around.

*Gossip is a mechanism for creating bonds between individuals.* Another important function of gossip is that it serves as a bonding mechanism among individuals who must interact with each other on a daily basis. Sharing gossip with another person is a sign of deep trust because the gossiper is clearly signaling that he or she believes that the person receiving the gossip will not use this sensitive information in a way that will have negative consequences for the gossiper, and shared secrets have a way of bonding people together. Field studies in work organizations indicate that harmless gossiping with one's colleagues builds friendship, group cohesiveness, and morale, and all of this leads to greater job satisfaction (Ellwardt, Steglich, & Wittek, 2012; Grosser, Lopez-Kidwell, & Labianca, 2010). Ellwardt et al. (2012) also discovered in their research that gossip between two individuals increases the bonds of friendship between them, rather than the reverse of this (i.e., people becoming friends first and then gossiping more). Similarly, Waddington (2012) draws upon her experiences of researching gossip in health care and higher educational institutions to challenge the assumption that workplace gossip is always problematic. In fact, she describes gossip as a way of organizing people in the workplace rather than as an impediment to organizing people in the workplace. Consequently, an individual who is not included in the office gossip network is obviously an outsider who is not trusted or accepted by the group. Surprisingly, our interest in gossip about celebrities may also be part of our social bonding mechanisms, as celebrities may provide a common interest and topic of conversation between people who otherwise might not have much to say to one another.

*Strategy-Learning Gossip: Paying attention to other people can help us learn strategies for being successful.* We love stories. As I indicated in an earlier section of this chapter, our brains have evolved a thirst for, and a facility for storing information about, specific people and episodes. This proclivity exists for a reason. Stories about how other people deal with life-threatening experiences and social challenges fascinate us and stick with us, imparting lessons through social learning that might be very costly to acquire through trial-and-error learning. Cognitive psychologist and novelist Keith Oatley (1999) describes stories as "simulations that run on minds" and suggests that stories may act as "flight simulators for real life." Evolutionary psychologist Steven Pinker (2007) believes that storytelling may have evolved for similar reasons. According to Pinker, the mental rehearsal that occurs through storytelling equips us to deal with real life situations that may come along later, and people who were drawn to stories had an evolutionary advantage over those who weren't.

A quick glance at stories aimed at children reveals a historical preoccupation with imparting lessons that may have life or death implications. The often gruesome *Grimm's Fairy Tales* in particular are full of stories about what happens to children who wander off into the forest on their own despite the warnings of their parents. This may also explain why humans regularly spend time and money to terrorize themselves by going to horror movies and visiting commercial haunted houses. Horror movies and haunted houses trigger feelings of dread because they push buttons that warn us of potential danger. However, we like being scared by these things and it is fun precisely because we know that it is not real and that we are safe. Scary movies allow for mental practice and provide a template for dealing with real-life threatening situations. Just pick up the newspaper any day and you will see stories about people getting their houses broken into and undergoing frightening experiences; watching people deal with this in movies prepares for action in our own lives if it should become necessary.

# Individual Differences in Skillfulness at Gossip and Reputation Management

*Gossip: Is it quantity or quality that matters?* In a well-written popular book on the importance of managing social reputation, John Whitfield (2012) identified gossip as the premier tool by which people monitor the reputation of others while simultaneously managing their own reputations. Given that being in possession of gossip gives an individual a position of power relative to others in the group, it might be expected that gossipers would be better liked, more influential, and good at reputation management. Therefore, social success should depend to a great extent on being a good gossiper. But what exactly makes an individual "good" at gossip? Until now, research on individual differences in gossip behavior has focused entirely on the *quantity* of an individual's gossip rather than on the average *quality* of his or her gossip. In other words, the few studies on individual differences in gossip that have been conducted have simply looked at *how often* an individual does or does not participate in gossip, but no attempt has been made to study gossipers based upon the quality of the gossip they provide or the skill with which they conduct themselves in gossip situations. I believe that using the mere frequency of gossiping as a research variable is something of a red herring, and that it is quality, not quantity, that counts. It is probably the case that skillful gossipers are indeed well liked and wield a great deal of social power in groups (Farley, 2011; Farley, this volume), but we are not yet in a position to know this for sure.

Successful gossiping should be about being a good team player and sharing key information with others in a way that will not be perceived as self-serving and about understanding when to keep your mouth shut. Becoming that person who indiscriminately blabs everything you hear to anyone who will listen will quickly get you a reputation as an untrustworthy busybody. Future studies need to work on developing a valid and reliable way of assessing skill as a gossiper.

*What do we know about individual differences in gossip behavior?* As with most psychological traits, the tendency to gossip and the need to compare one's self to others appear to be stable and measurable individual differences. Nevo, Nevo, & Derech-Zehavi (1993) have constructed a measure called the "Tendency to Gossip Questionnaire (TGQ)" which appears to have acceptable validity and reliability. A subsequent study using the TGQ found that individuals employed in people-oriented professions such as counselors and psychotherapists score especially high on this scale (Nevo, Nevo, & Zehavi, 1993). A high need to exert social power seems to be one factor that distinguishes heavy gossipers from the rest of us (Farley, Timme, & Hart, 2010), and the amount of power that an individual holds strongly influences the motivations and triggers of his or her gossiping behavior (Jeuken, Beersma, ten Velden, & Dijkstra, 2015). Not surprisingly, the "Dark Triad" personality traits of narcissism, psychopathy, and Machiavellianism are good predictors of one's motivation for gossip as well as how likely an individual will be to use gossip as a way of manipulating others (Lyons & Hughes, 2015).

The jury is still out on how gossipers are perceived by others. Jaeger, Skleder, Rind, & Rosnow (1994) looked at gossip in a college sorority. They found that "low gossipers" scored higher in the need for social approval than "high gossipers." They also found that the high gossipers tended to have more close friends than low gossipers, but paradoxically were perceived as less likeable than the low gossipers. Similarly, Farley (2011) discovered that high-frequency gossipers were liked significantly less than low-frequency gossipers, and "negative" gossipers were liked less than "positive" gossipers. At least among 4th through 6th grade girls, however, gossipers are liked *more* than the targets of their gossip (Maloney, 1999).

*Is Gossip an equally important social skill for males and females?* It is a mundanely obvious fact that both men and women engage in gossip. Men may refer to gossiping as "bull sessions" or "shop talk" as a way of avoiding the stigma attached to engaging in a stereotypically female activity, but such male talk clearly meets the criteria for gossip laid out in the beginning of this chapter. However, it is still an open question as to whether or not there is more than just a kernel of truth to the long-standing stereotype of gossip as "women's talk."

Women spend more time gossiping overall than do men, and they are more likely to gossip about close friends and relatives (Levin & Arluke, 1987). Men, on the other hand, are more likely to talk about themselves, their work, their own relationships, and generally engage in more self-promotion and personal reputation management than do women (Dunbar, et.al., 1997). The amount of gossiping that occurs between two people is a good predictor of friendship quality in men, especially if the gossip concerns achievement-related information, but the amount of gossip between two women does not predict the quality of their friendship in such a straightforward fashion (Watson, 2012). When pairs of friends gossip, it is rare for listeners to respond negatively to gossipy information, and such information usually evokes agreement and supportive responses rather than disapproval (Eder & Enke, 1991). Females in particular tend to demonstrate highly encouraging responses to gossip that they hear from their friends (Leaper & Holliday, 1995).

So, both men and women gossip. I will now turn to the question of whether *negative* gossip is more prevalent in relationships among women, and whether it is more essential for women to master the social skills associated with gossiping. The universality of the perceived link between women and malicious gossip is reflected in an ancient Chinese proverb stating that "the tongue is the sword of a woman—and she never lets it go rusty." Is there any evidence to suggest that women are in fact more prone to gossip than are men or that women are more likely to use gossip in an aggressive or socially destructive manner? The data suggest that the answer to these questions is *yes.*

There is evidence that it is specifically the gossip that occurs between women that is most likely to be aggressive and competitive (see the chapter by Davis, Vaillancourt, Arnock, & Doyel, this volume). The nature of the topics that are discussed between women is qualitatively different from those that are featured in gossip between men or between a man and a woman, and the frequency of negative gossip is highest of all in gossip between female friends (Leaper & Holliday, 1995). The way that female-to-female gossip plays out is also consistent with what would be expected if gossip developed as a response to evolutionary pressures. Younger women are more likely to gossip about rivals than are older women, possibly because the competition for mates is more intense during the earlier, reproductive part of a woman's life (Massar, Buunk, & Rempt, 2012). Furthermore, the characteristics of rivals that are most likely to be attacked through malicious gossip are precisely those characteristics that have traditionally been most vital to a woman's reputation in the mating market: her physical appearance and sexual reputation (Buss & Dedden, 1990; Vaillancourt, 2013; Watson, 2012). A recent study fuels the perception that physical appearance is a primary arena of competition among women in that a woman with a "hypercompetitive personality" is significantly more likely to undergo cosmetic surgery than is a less competitive woman (Thornton, Ryckman, & Gold, 2013).

In general, an interest in the affairs of same-sex others is especially strong among females, and women have somewhat different patterns of sharing gossip than men do. Studies I have conducted with my students (e.g., McAndrew & Milenkovic, 2002; McAndrew et al., 2007) reveal that males report being far more likely to share gossip with their romantic partners than with anyone else, but females report that they would be just as likely to share gossip with their same-sex friends as with their romantic partners. And although males are usually more interested in news about other males, females are virtually obsessed with news about other females. This fact can be demonstrated by looking at the actual frequency with which males and females selected a same-sex person as the most interesting subject of the gossip scenarios presented to them in a study by McAndrew & Milenkovic (2002). On hearing about someone having a date with a famous person, 43 out of 44 women selected a female as the most interesting person to know this about, as compared with 24 out of 36 males who selected a male as most interesting. Similarly, 40 out of 42 females (versus 22 out of 37 males) were most interested in same-sex academic cheaters, and 39 out of 43 were most interested in a same-sex leukemia sufferer (as opposed to only 18 out of 37 males). In fact, the only two scenarios among the 13 studied in which males expressed more same-sex interest than females involved hearing about an individual heavily in debt because of gambling or an individual who was having difficulty performing sexually.

A female preoccupation with the lives of other women has been noted by other researchers as well. For example, De Backer, Nelissen, & Fisher (2007) presented college students with gossip-like stories containing male or female characters in which the nature of the gossip presented in the stories was an important variable. After reading the stories, the participants were given a surprise recall test for the information they had been exposed to. Women remembered more about other women than men did about other men. Also, the attractiveness of female characters and the wealth of male characters were most easily recalled.

The fascination that women have with the doings of other women is not always benign. It has been well established that men are more physically aggressive than women (McAndrew, 2009). However, women are much more likely to engage in indirect "relational" aggression (Vaillancourt, 2013), and gossip (with the goal of socially ostracizing rivals) is the weapon of choice in the female arsenal (Campbell, 2012; Hess & Hagen, 2006; Hines & Fry, 1994; Owens, Shute, & Slee, 2000a). Females are more likely than males to socially exclude others, a sex difference that appears as early as the age of six (Benensen, 2013). The motivation for this relational aggression can be as trivial as simple boredom, but it more often transpires in retaliation for perceived slights or envy over physical appearance or males (Owens, Shute, & Slee, 2000b). The fact that highly attractive adolescent girls (who may be threatening because of their high mate value) are at greater risk for victimization by indirect aggression is consistent with the notion that mate competition is a motive for such aggression (Vaillancourt, 2013). Whatever the reason for it, the goal is usually to exclude competitors from one's social group and to damage their ability to maintain a reliable social network of their own (Geary & Flinn, 2002). As it turns out, this is a highly effective way of hurting other women. When a workplace bully is a woman, indirect relational aggression is the usual *modus operandi* and her victim is almost always another woman. The levels of stress reported by the victims in these situations are extreme (Crothers, Lipinski, & Minutolo, 2009), and other studies have confirmed that females are more sensitive than males to indirect aggression and report being more devastated by it (Galen & Underwood, 1997). These findings may be connected to other research results which show that a majority of women who suffer from persecutory delusions identified familiar people such as friends and relatives as their persecutors and what they specifically feared was that they were being "talked about" or excluded from the in-group. Men suffering from persecutory delusions were much more likely to fear physical attacks by other men who were strangers (Walston, David, & Charlton, 1998).

## GOSSIP AND SOCIAL MEDIA

Understanding the nature of reputation management and the role played by gossip in this important social activity can lead to an understanding of other seemingly unrelated phenomena. After all, the gossip behaviors that developed to manage the social lives of our prehistoric ancestors provide the skeleton for the global social world of the Internet that we now inhabit. Theoretically, the same selection pressures that produced good gossipers should now translate into the savvy use of social media.

For example, understanding the dynamics of reputation and gossip can generate hypotheses about how people will pursue social information and present themselves on the Internet through social media such as Facebook. The Internet provides unprecedented opportunities to spread and track gossip, and never before has it been possible to manage one's public reputation on the scale that is available in the 21st century. Given that gossip and ostracism are primarily female tactics of aggression, might we not also find that female aggression can be amplified by the Internet more than male aggression would be? Troubling media stories about cyberbullying on Facebook, sometimes even resulting in the suicide of the victim, usually involve female aggressors and almost always involve female victims. Studying Internet behavior in light of what we know about gossip shows great promise for helping us deal with this important problem.

Gossip studies by McAndrew et al. (2007), McAndrew & Milenkovic (2002), and De Backer, Nelisson, & Fisher (2007) discovered that most people have a greater interest in gossip about same-sex and same-age individuals, with women being especially interested in gossip about other women. The researchers concluded that this was rooted in the evolutionary necessity of keeping tabs on our competitors for status and mates, and traditionally our chief competitors are those in our own age and sex cohorts. Similarly, it is well replicated that men and women have very different mating strategies and preferences, with men seeking attractiveness, youth, and fertility in mates while advertising their own status, achievement, and access to resources; women show the opposite pattern (Buss, 1989a, 1989b; Buss & Schmitt, 1993; Geary, 2010). These findings suggest the following predictions about how people might use Facebook.

It might be expected that everyone should spend more time looking at the Facebook pages of people about the same age as themselves. However, to the extent that this interest is driven by the social competition needs described earlier, older people should be under less pressure to do so and will exhibit less interest in same-sex peers and more interest in family. There should also be more interest in looking at the pages of same sex others vs. opposite sex others, and this tendency will be even stronger in females than in males. Because of the greater emphasis placed on the physical appearance of women, females, compared to males, will spend more time on activities related to impression management with their profile pictures, and females will also spend more time looking at the photos of other people. Finally, males, compared to females, will spend more time looking at items on the pages of others' that reflect an individual's status or prestige: Educational background, work/career information, and number of Facebook friends.

In an Internet survey utilizing an international sample of 1,026 Facebook users (284 males, 735 females; mean age = 30.24) I conducted with one of my students, Hye Sun Jeong (McAndrew & Jeong, 2012), we discovered that overall, females engaged in far more Facebook activity than did males. They spent more time on Facebook and they had more Facebook friends, and, consistent with previous research on gossip seeking behavior, females were more interested than males in the relationship status of others and they were more interested in keeping tabs on the activity of other women than men were in keeping tabs on the activity of other men. They also expended more energy than men in using profile photographs as a tool for impression management and in studying the photographs of other people. On the other hand, males, aside from the fact that they were more interested in how many friends their Facebook friends had, were not more likely than women to attend to the educational and career accomplishments of others.

There is evidence that time on Facebook is positively correlated with more frequent episodes of jealousy-related feelings and behaviors, especially among women (Elphinston & Noller, 2011; Morris et al., 2009; Muise, et al., 2009; Utz & Beukeboom, 2011). In one recent episode, a woman actually stabbed her boyfriend simply because he received a Facebook friend request from another woman! (Timesleader.com, 2012). Overall, research indicates that men and women do not differ in the frequency or magnitude of episodes of experienced jealousy, but different factors serve as the triggers for jealousy for men than for women (Buss, 2012). Given its emphasis on relationships and physical appearance, Facebook seems to be more likely to pull the triggers relevant to female jealousy. The inherent ambiguity of many Facebook comments, photos, and other activities offers ample opportunity for flirting (or at least perceptions of flirting), creating new avenues for eliciting jealousy, intentional and otherwise. Sahil Shah (another one of my students) and I explored this issue in a study of sex differences in jealousy over Facebook activities. We confirmed that females are in fact more prone to Facebook-evoked jealousy than males, and perhaps surprisingly, we also found that males are more sensitive to this sex difference than are females. This suggests that misunderstandings between romantic partners over Facebook use will more likely be due to females misunderstanding their partners' reactions to Facebook activity than the other way around (McAndrew & Shah, 2013).

If the predisposition to gossip has evolved to facilitate an interest in those who are socially important to us and an interest in information that would be essential for success in social competition, learning about how it all works could even help us to understand the sex differences in what entertains us. Soap operas and similar entertainment venues press the buttons that pique women's interests in relationships, appearance, and competition for mates. These programs always feature deception, backstabbing, and yes, gossip. The intrigue surrounding questions such as "when will he catch her cheating on him?" or "when will everyone find out whose baby that *really* is?" plays directly into the competitive interests and tactics utilized by women. In contrast, male entertainment interests in movies and TV shows featuring physical violence, warfare, and athletic competition is more reflective of male competitive interests, and hence they become intrinsically entertaining to men. The otherwise inexplicable popularity of some American reality television program such as *Survivor, Fear Factor*, and *the Amazing Race* may be due at least in part to the skill with which they tap into the competitive interests of men and women alike.

## SUMMARY AND CONCLUSION

This impressive volume about gossip and reputation has in some ways set an impossible goal for itself. It not only tries to organize research on behaviors that permeate the entire human social world, but it has also tried to track the antecedents, processes, and outcomes of these behaviors at each level ranging from small intimate groups to large scale societies. Furthermore, the editors have had to corral the diversity of approaches taken by researchers in disciplines as different as literature and evolutionary biology. This particular chapter had a much more modest mission: to make the argument that gossiping well is an important social skill rather than a tragic character flaw.

I have attempted to establish the fact that gossip is not always bad and that research has definitively shown that it serves an important role in controlling the behavior of cheaters and keeping dominant individuals in check (Boehm, 1993, 1997, 1999a; Emler, 2001). I have also made the case that being an effective gossiper is not simply about the *quantity* of one's gossiping, but more about its *quality*. Becoming skilled in the use of gossip helps you bond with other people (Ellwardt et al., 2012) and manage your social reputation and the reputations of others in a way that is not unfair or mean spirited (Barkow, 1992; McAndrew et al., 2007). Attending to gossip can also make you a quick and astute learner of the rules of new social groups and provide you with strategies for becoming socially successful by learning from the experience of others (De Backer, Nelissen, Vyncke, Braeckman, & McAndrew, 2007). Natural selection would have favored the socially skilled individual who managed to skillfully balance these different aspects of gossip.

The evidence at this time also suggests that there may be more pressure on women to hone the social skills associated with gossip, if for no other reason than to manage and minimize the reputational damage that may come their way at the hands (tongues?) of other women (McAndrew, 2014). Gossip is not irrelevant in competition between men, but it does not seem to play as essential a role and it may be easier for men to compensate for deficits in gossiping skill with other talents.

As essential as managing one's reputation and tapping into the gossip grapevine was for our ancestors in small hunter gatherer groups, having such skills may be even more important today. In our ancestral groups, you probably knew each individual's reputation through first-hand experience or at the very least through the first-hand experience of someone you knew well (Dunbar, 1996). We now live in a world of strangers and social media where gossip can be broadcast and reputations can built and destroyed on a scale that would have been unimaginable a mere 20 years ago. Tracking how our gossiping caveman minds respond in this unfolding era of technology tailor-made for reputation management will be an exciting and challenging task to say the least.

## References

Abrahams, R. D. (1970). A performance-centered approach to gossip. *Man* 5, 290–301.

Acheson, J. M. (1988). *The lobster gangs of Maine*. Hanover & London: University Press of New England.

Alexander, R. D. (1979). *Darwinism and human affairs*. Seattle: University of Washington Press.

Anderson, E., Siegel, E. H., Bliss-Moreau, E., & Barrett, L. F. (2011). The visual impact of gossip. *Science* 332, 1446–1448.

Ayim, M. (1994). Knowledge through the grapevine: Gossip as inquiry. In R. F. Goodman & A. Ben-Ze'ev (Eds.), *Good gossip* (pp. 85–99). Lawrence, KS: University of Kansas Press.

Barclay, P. (2016). Reputation. In D. M. Buss (Ed.), *The Handbook of Evolutionary Psychology* (2nd ed. Vol. 2, pp. 810–28). Hoboken, NJ: John Wiley & Son.

Barkow, J. H. (1989). *Darwin and status: Biological perspectives on mind and culture*. Toronto: University of Toronto Press.

Barkow, J. H. (1992). Beneath new culture is old psychology: Gossip and social stratification. In J. H. Barkow, L. Cosmides, & J. Tooby (Eds.), *The adapted mind: Evolutionary psychology and the generation of culture* (pp. 627–637). New York: Oxford University Press.

Baumeister, R. F., Zhang, L., & Vohs, K. D. (2004). Gossip as cultural learning. *Review of General Psychology 8*, 111–21.

Beersma, B., & Van Kleef, G. A. (2011). How the grapevine keeps you in line: Gossip increases contributions to the group. *Social Psychological and Personality Science 2*, 642–649.

Beersma, B., & Van Kleef, G. A. (2012). Why people gossip: An empirical analysis of social motives, antecedents, and consequences. *Journal of Applied Social Psychology 42*, 2640–2670.

Benenson, J. F. (2013). The development of human female competition: Allies and adversaries. *Philosophical Transactions of the Royal Society B 368*, 20130079.

Ben-Ze'ev, A. (1994). The vindication of gossip. In R.F. Goodman & A. Ben-Ze'ev (Eds.), *Good gossip* (pp. 11–24). Lawrence, KS: University of Kansas Press.

Boehm, C. (1993). Egalitarian behavior and reverse dominance hierarchy. *Current Anthropology 34*, 227–254.

Boehm, C. (1997). Impact of the human egalitarian syndrome on Darwinian selection mechanics. *The American Naturalist 150*, S100–S121.

Boehm, C. (1999). *Hierarchy in the forest: The evolution of egalitarian behavior.* Cambridge, MA: Harvard University Press.

Boehm, C. (2019). Gossip and reputation in small scale societies: A view from evolutionary anthropology. In F. Giardini, R. P. M. Wittek (Eds.), *Handbook of Gossip and Reputation.* New York: Oxford University Press.

Bordia, P., & DiFonzo, N. (2005). Psychological motivations in rumor spread. In G. A. Fine, C. Heath, & V. Campion-Vincent (Eds.), *Rumor mills: The social impact of rumor and legend* (pp. 87–101). New York: Aldine.

Buss, D. M. (1989a). Conflict between the sexes: Strategic interference and the evocation of anger and upset. *Journal of Personality and Social Psychology 56*, 735–747.

Buss, D. M. (1989b). Sex differences in human mate preferences: Evolutionary hypotheses tested in 37 cultures. *Behavioral and Brain Sciences 12*, 1–49.

Buss, D. M. (2012). *Evolutionary psychology: The new science of the mind* (4th ed.). Boston: Allyn & Bacon.

Buss, D. M., & Dedden, L. (1990). Derogation of competitors. *Journal of Social and Personal Relationships 7*, 395–422.

Buss, D. M., & Schmitt, D. P. (1993). Sexual strategies theory: An evolutionary perspective on human mating. *Psychological Review 100*, 204–232.

Campbell, A. (2012). Women and aggression. In T. K. Shackelford & V. A. Weekes-Shackelford (Eds.), *The Oxford Handbook of evolutionary perspectives on violence, homicide, and war* (pp. 197–217). New York: Oxford University Press.

Cox, B.A. (1970). What is Hopi gossip about? Information management and Hopi factions. *Man 5*, 88–98.

Crothers, L. M., Lipinski, J., & Minutolo, M. C. (2009). Cliques, rumors, and gossip by the watercooler: Female bullying in the workplace. *Psychologist-Manager Journal 12*, 97–110.

Davis, A., Vaillancourt, T., Arnocky, S., & Doyel, R. (2019). Women's Gossip as an intrasexual competition strategy: An evolutionary approach to sex and discrimination. In F. Giardini & R. P. M. Wittek (Eds.), *Handbook of gossip and reputation.* New York: Oxford University Press.

Davis, H., & McLeod, S. L. (2003). Why humans value sensational news: An evolutionary perspective. *Evolution and Human Behavior 24*, 208–216.

De Backer, C. J. S., Nelissen, M., & Fisher, M. L. (2007). Let's talk about sex: A study on the recall of gossip about potential mates and sexual rivals. *Sex Roles 56*, 781–791.

De Backer, C. J. S., Nelissen, M., Vyncke, P., Braeckman, J., & McAndrew, F. T. (2007). Celebrities: From teachers to friends. A test of two hypotheses on the adaptiveness of celebrity gossip. *Human Nature* 18, 334–354.

de Haan, M., Pascalis, O., & Johnson, M. H. (2002). Specialization of neural mechanisms underlying face recognition in human infants. *Journal of Cognitive Neuroscience 14*, 199–209.

DiFonzo, N., & Bordia, P. (2006). Rumor in organizational contexts. In R. L. Rosnow & D. A. Hantula (Eds.), *Advances in social and organizational psychology*, pp. 249–274. Hillsdale, NJ: Lawrence Erlbaum.

Dunbar, R. I. M. (1996). *Grooming, gossip, and the evolution of language.* Cambridge, MA: Harvard University Press.

Dunbar, R. I. M., Duncan, N. D. C., & Marriott, A. (1997). Human conversational behavior. *Human Nature 8*, 231–246.

Eder, D., & Enke, J. L. (1991). The structure of gossip: Opportunities and constraints on collective expression among adolescents. *American Sociological Review 56*, 494–508.

Ellickson, R. C. (1991). *Order without law: How neighbors settle disputes.* Cambridge, MA: Harvard University Press.

Ellwardt, L., Steglich, C., & Wittek, R. (2012). The co-evolution of gossip and friendship in workplace social networks. *Social Networks 34*, 623–633.

Elphinston, R. A., & Noller, P. (2011). Time to face it! Facebook intrusion and the implications for romantic jealousy and relationship satisfaction. *Cyberpsychology, Behavior, and Social Networking 14*, 631–635.

Emler, N. (1994). Gossip, reputation, and social adaptation. In R. F. Goodman & A. Ben-Ze'ev (Eds.), *Good Gossip* (pp. 117–138). Lawrence, KS: University of Kansas Press.

Emler, N. (2001). Gossiping. In W. P. Robinson & H. Giles (Eds.), *The new handbook of language and social psychology* (pp. 317–338). New York: John Wiley & Sons.

Farley, S. D. (2011). Is gossip power? The inverse relationships between gossip, power, and likability. *European Journal of Social Psychology 41*, 574–579.

Farley, S. D. (2019). On the nature of gossip, reputation, and power inequality. In F. Giardini & R. P. M. Wittek (Eds.), *Handbook of gossip and reputation.* New York: Oxford University Press.

Farley, S. D., Timme, D. R., & Hart, J. W. (2010). On coffee talk and break-room chatter: Perceptions of women who gossip in the workplace. *Journal of Social Psychology 150*, 361–368.

Feinberg, M., Cheng, J. T., & Willer, R. (2012). Gossip as an effective and low-cost form of punishment. *Behavioral and Brain Sciences 35*, 25.

Feinberg, M., Willer, R., Stellar, J., & Keltner, D. (2012). The virtues of gossip: Reputational information sharing as prosocial behavior. *Journal of Personality and Social Psychology 102*, 1015–1030.

Galen, B. R., & Underwood, M. K. (1997). A developmental investigation of social aggression among children. *Developmental Psychology 33*, 589–600.

Geary, D. C. (2010). Male, female: The evolution of human sex differences (2nd ed.). Washington, DC: American Psychological Association.

Geary, D. C., & Flinn, M. V. (2002). Sex differences in behavioral and hormonal response to social threat: Commentary on Taylor et al. (2000). *Psychological Review 109*, 745–750.

Goodman, R. F., & Ben-Ze'ev, A. (1994). *Good gossip.* Lawrence, KS: University of Kansas Press.

Grosser, T. J., Lopez-Kidwell, V., & Giuseppe Labianca, G. A. (2010). Social network analysis of positive and negative gossip in organizational life. *Group and Organization Management 35*, 177–212.

Hess, N. H., & Hagen, E. H. (2006). Sex differences in indirect aggression: Psychological evidence from young adults. *Evolution and Human Behavior 27*, 231–245.

Hess, N. H., & Hagen, E. H. (2019). Gossip, Reputation, and Friendship in Within-group Competition: An Evolutionary Perspective. In Giardini, F., Wittek, R. P. M. (Eds.), *Handbook of gossip and reputation*. New York: Oxford University Press.

Hines, N. J., & Fry, D. P. (1994). Indirect modes of aggression among women of Buenos Aires, Argentina. Special Issue: On aggression in women and girls: Cross-Cultural perspectives. *Sex Roles 30*, 213–236.

Houmanfar, R., & Johnson, R. (2003). Organizational implications of gossip and rumor. *Journal of Organizational Management 23*, 117–138.

Humphrey, N. K. (1983). *Consciousness regained: Chapters in the development of mind*. Oxford: Oxford University Press.

Jaeger, M. E., Skleder, A. A., Rind, B., & Rosnow, R. L. (1994). Gossip, gossipers, gossipees. In R. F. Goodman & A. Ben-Ze'ev (Eds.), *Good gossip* (pp. 154–168). Lawrence, KS: University of Kansas Press.

Jeuken, E., Beersma, B., ten Velden, F. S., & Dijkstra, M. T. M. (2015). Aggression as a motive for gossip during conflict: The role of power, social value orientation, and counterpart's behavior. *Negotiation and Conflict Management Research 8*, 137–152.

Kniffin, K. M., & Wilson, D. S. (1998, July). *Gossiping for the good of the group*. Paper presented at the annual meeting of the Human Behavior and Evolution Society, Davis, California.

Krebs, D. L., & Denton, K. (1997). Social illusions and self-deception. In J. A. Simpson & D. T. Kenrick (Eds.), *Evolutionary Social Psychology* (pp. 21–48). Mahwah, NJ: Lawrence Erlbaum Associates.

Laing, M. (1993). Gossip: Does it play a role in the socialization of nurses? *Journal of Nursing Scholarship 25*, 37–43.

Leaper, C., & Holliday, H. (1995). Gossip in same-gender and cross-gender friends' conversations. *Personal Relationships 2*, 237–246.

Lee, R. B. (1990). Eating Christmas in the Kalahari. In J. B. Spradley & D. W. McCurdy (Eds.), *Conformity and conflict: Readings in cultural anthropology*. (7th ed., pp. 30–37). Glenview, IL: Scott, Foresman & Company.

Levin, J., & Arluke, A. (1987). *Gossip: The inside scoop*. New York: Plenum Press.

Lewin, R. (1993). *Human evolution: An illustrated introduction*. Cambridge, MA: Blackwell.

Lyons, M. T., & Hughes, S. (2015). Malicious mouths? The Dark Triad and motivations for gossip. *Personality and Individual Differences 78*, 1–4.

Maloney, T. M. (1999). Social status, peer liking, and functions of gossip among girls in middle childhood. *Dissertation Abstracts International: Section B: The Sciences and Engineering 59*, 6094.

Massar, K., Buunk, A. P., & Rempt, S. (2012). Age differences in women's tendency to gossip are mediated by their mate value. *Personality and Individual Differences 52*, 106–109.

McAndrew, F. T. (2008). Can gossip be good? *Scientific American Mind Magazine 19*, 26–33.

McAndrew, F. T. (2009). The interacting roles of testosterone and challenges to status in human male aggression. *Aggression and Violent Behavior 14*, 330–335.

McAndrew, F. T. (2014). The "Sword of a Woman:" Gossip and female aggression. *Aggression and Violent Behavior 19*, 196–199.

McAndrew, F. T., Bell, E. K., & Garcia, C. M. (2007). Who do we tell, and whom do we tell on? Gossip as a strategy for status enhancement. *Journal of Applied Social Psychology 37*, 1562–1577.

McAndrew, F. T., & Jeong, H. S. (2012). Who does what on Facebook? Age, sex, and relationship status as predictors of Facebook use. *Computers in Human Behavior 28*, 2359–2365.

McAndrew, F. T., & Milenkovic, M. A. (2002). Of tabloids and family secrets: The evolutionary psychology of gossip. *Journal of Applied Social Psychology 32*, 1064–1082.

McAndrew, F. T., & Shah, S. S. (2013). Sex differences in jealousy over Facebook activity. *Computers in Human Behavior 29*, 2603–2606.

McPherson, N. M. (1991). A question of morality: Sorcery and concepts of deviance among the Kabana, West New Britain. *Anthropologica 33*, 127–143.

Mealey, L., Daood, C., & Krage, M. (1996). Enhanced memory for faces of cheaters. *Ethology and Sociobiology 17*, 119–128.

Merry, S. E. (1984). Rethinking gossip and scandal. In D. Black (Ed.), *Toward a general theory of social control, Volume 1: Fundamentals* (pp. 271–302). Orlando: Academic Press.

Morris, J., Reese, J., Beck, R., & Mattis, C. (2009). Facebook usage as a measure of retention at a private 4-year institution. *Journal of College Student Retention: Research, Theory, and Practice 11*, 311–322.

Muise, A., Christofides, E., & Desmarais, S. (2009). More information than you ever wanted: Does Facebook bring out the green-eyed monster of jealousy? *CyberPsychology & Behavior 12*, 441–444.

Nelson, C. A. (2001). The development and neural bases of face recognition. *Infant and Child Development 10*, 3–18.

Nevo, O., Nevo, B., & Derech-Zehavi, A. (1993). The development of the Tendency to Gossip Questionnaire: Construct and concurrent validation for a sample of Israeli college students. *Educational and Psychological Measurement 53*, 973–981.

Nevo, O., Nevo, B., & Zehavi, A. D. (1993). Gossip and counseling: The tendency to gossip and its relation to vocational interests. *Counseling Psychology Quarterly 6*, 229–238.

Noon, M., & Delbridge, R. (1993). News from behind my hand: Gossip in organizations. *Organization Studies 14*, 23–36.

Oatley, K. (1999). Why fiction may be twice as true as fact. *Review of General Psychology 3*, 101–117.

Owens, L., Shute, R., & Slee, P. (2000a). "Guess what I just heard!" Indirect aggression among teenage girls in Australia. *Aggressive Behavior 26*, 67–83.

Owens, L., Shute, R., & Slee, P. (2000b). "I'm in and you're out…": Explanations for teenage girls' indirect aggression. *Psychology, Evolution, and Gender 2*, 19–46.

Pinker, S. (2007). Toward a consilient study of literature. *Philosophy and Literature 31*, 161–77.

Rysman, A. (1977). How the "gossip" became a woman. *Journal of Communication 27*, 176–180.

Schein, S. (1994). Used and abused: Gossip in medieval society. In R. F. Goodman & A. Ben-Ze'ev (Eds.), *Good gossip* (pp. 139–53). Lawrence, KS: University of Kansas Press.

Shackelford, T. K. (1997). Perceptions of betrayal and the design of the mind. In J. A. Simpson & D. T. Kenrick (Eds.), *Evolutionary social psychology* (pp. 73–107). Mahwah, NJ: Lawrence Erlbaum Associates.

Spacks, P. M. (1985). *Gossip*. New York: Alfred A. Knopf.

Suls, J. M. (1977). Gossip as social comparison. *Journal of Communication 27*, 164–168.

Thornton, B., Ryckman, R. M., & Gold, J. A. (2013). Competitive orientations and women's acceptance of cosmetic surgery. *Psychology 4*, 67–72.

Timesleader.com (July 23, 2012). Man stabbed after receiving Facebook friend request. Timesleader.com, Wilkes-Barre, Pennsylvania. http://www.timesleader.com/stories/Police-Man-stabbed-after-receiving-Facebook-friend-request-,180035 (accessed July 24, 2012)

Tooby, J., & DeVore, I. (1987). The reconstruction of hominid behavioral evolution using strategic modeling. In W. G. Kinzey (Ed.), *Primate models for the origin of human behavior.* (pp. 183–237). New York: SUNY Press.

Trivers, R. L. (1971). The evolution of reciprocal altruism. *Quarterly Review of Biology 46,* 35–57.

Trivers, R. L. (1985). *Social evolution.* Menlo Park, CA: Benjamin Cummings.

Utz, S., & Beukeboom, C. J. (2011). The role of social network sites in romantic relationships: Effects on jealousy and relationship happiness. *Journal of Computer-Mediated Communication 16,* 511–527.

Vaillancourt, T. (2013). Do human females use indirect aggression as an intrasexual competition strategy? *Philosophical Transactions of the Royal Society of London B 368,* 20130080.

Waddington, K. (2012). *Gossip and organizations.* New York: Routledge.

Walston, F., David, A. S., & Charlton, B. G. (1998). Sex differences in the content of persecutory delusions: A reflection of hostile threats in the ancestral environment? *Evolution and Human Behavior 19,* 257–260.

Watson, D. C. (2012). Gender differences in gossip and friendship. *Sex Roles 67,* 494–502.

Wert, S. R., & Salovey, P. (2004). A social comparison account of gossip. *Review of General Psychology 8,* 122–137.

Whitfield, J. (2102). *People will talk: The surprising science of reputation.* New York: John Wiley & Sons.

Wilson, D. S., & Kniffin, K. M. (1999). Multilevel selection and the social transmission of behavior. *Human Nature 10,* 291–310.

Wilson, D. S., Wilczynski, C., Wells, A., & Weiser, L. (2000). Gossip and other aspects of language as group-level adaptations. In C. Heyes & L. Huber (Eds.), *Evolution and cognition.* Cambridge, MA: MIT Press.

Wilson, M. I., & Daly, M. (1996). Male sexual proprietariness and violence against wives. *Current Directions in Psychological Science 5,* 2–7.

Wu, J., Balliet, D., & Van Lange, P. A. M. (2015). When does gossip promote generosity? Indirect reciprocity under the shadow of the future. *Social Psychological and Personality Science 6,* 923–930.

Wu, J., Balliet, D., and Van Lange, P. A. M. (2016). Reputation management: Why and how gossip enhances generosity. *Evolution and Human Behavior 37,* 193–201.

# CHAPTER 11

# GOSSIP AND REPUTATION IN SOCIAL DILEMMAS

## MANFRED MILINSKI

## INTRODUCTION

OUR species is regarded to be social, we are called even champions of cooperation (Fehr and Fischbacher, 2003). Until recently, evolutionary theorists predicted the evolution of only nice and cooperative social strategies (Axelrod, 1984; Nowak and Sigmund, 1992; 1993). However, both the daily news and Charles Darwin tell us otherwise. Darwin's basic rule of evolution is the following: Heritable programs of individuals that transform resources into offspring better will dominate the next generations. The product of evolution, from micro-organisms to our ancestors, are individuals that maximally exploit resources with no respect for anything: ruthless exploiters. With increasing population size, competition became inevitable. Individuals that maximally exploit resources under competition produced most offspring, resulting in ruthless competitors with no motivation to sustain resources. Garrett Hardin (1968, 1998) coined the term "tragedy of the commons," an apocalyptic vision as follows: Whenever people have free access to a public resource, the resource will be overused and collapse. Many examples proved Hardin right, from over-fishing fish stock to destroying the global climate because of voracious use of fossil energy.

Our research problem is clearly laid out: People need to be social to achieve personal gain that cannot be achieved alone. In a social interaction, all strategies are favored by evolution that maximize their gain even at the expense of social partners. Because each social player has been selected to maximize her or his gain, there is tension, a continuous conflict of interest between the individual and the group, which defines a social dilemma. A social dilemma is a situation in which an individual profits from selfishness as long as there are others who are altruistic. When all are selfish, nobody gains anything. "Free riders" need "producers." In a social dilemma, each player needs to trust co-players and needs to be trusted herself to allow for mutual cooperation. If there are cooperative and uncooperative "types," the safest way to learn about other players' trustworthiness is to observe their actions. Often direct observation is not possible but others might have this information and are willing to talk. Gossip can fill the information gap. Gossip is usually orally transmitted information about another person's social behavior that the gossiper has observed herself or has heard about from yet another person. The receiver of the gossip has usually no possibility to check the veracity of the gossip. Thus, we have the next research problems: Is gossip reliable? Is the gossiper trustworthy? What do you know about the gossiper: direct observation of his actions, or again only gossip? When you gossip, what do you tell other people about their interaction partners in a social dilemma? Do you tell the truth? Or do you profit from not telling the truth? Would people trust you if they know that you would profit from lying? If people are able to gossip about their own actions hoping others will not recognize its origin, do you trust a detected self-gossip in the same way as you would trust gossip produced by others about the same person? Some of these questions have been studied experimentally; most need to be investigated in the future.

Social dilemmas come in various variants, for example, with many people involved or only two (for a game-theoretic account, see Roddie, this volume). In the following, I will introduce different types of social dilemmas for which experimental paradigms have been developed to study them with human volunteers. The benefit of this approach is by simulating the essential properties of a complex real situation we can test "in a nutshell" whether there are solutions for the simulated problem. Of course these solutions can only be a proof of principle leaving out all complexities of the natural situation. These experimental paradigms are called games, that is, the prisoner's dilemma game, the Public Goods game, and the Trust game. We will see that the need for gaining a good reputation can solve these social dilemmas to some extent. The experimental paradigm for gaining and using reputation is the Indirect Reciprocity game. In direct reciprocity I help you and you help me later (Trivers, 1971). In indirect reciprocity you help those who have helped others, not necessarily you. For deciding whether to help a person, you need to know whether and how often this person has helped or refused to help others, that is, his reputation for helping. As a necessary next step I introduce gossip as a means for spreading information about a person's reputation. Since people see only a few of a person's interactions with other people, gossip needs to fill this information gap at the risk of being manipulated. I will discuss experiments by which the role of positive or negative gossip has been investigated.

## REPUTATION IN SOCIAL DILEMMAS

A person's reputation is a score that members of a social group update whenever they see the person interacting with others. Reputation is the current standing the person has gained from previous investments or refusal of investments in helping others. A good reputation pays off by attracting help from others, even from strangers or members from another group, if the recipient's reputation is known. Any costly investment in others, i.e. direct help, donations to charity, investment in averting climate change, etc., increases a person's reputation. A person's known reputation functions like money that can be used whenever the person needs help.

## The Prisoner's Dilemma

The simplest form of cooperation is direct reciprocity (Trivers, 1971), I help you now and you help me later, if helping costs €2 and receiving help provides a gain of €5, we both have a net gain of €3 each (Figure 11.1a); however, if you refuse to help me later, you have a gain of €5 and I have a net deficit (Figure 11.1b). The pending risk of refused reciprocation turns this simple potential exchange into a social dilemma. Economists, as well as sociologists, have invented experimental paradigms to study social dilemmas. In the simplest social dilemma when two persons interact with each other, each can either cooperate or not ("defect"). It is a dilemma if they together earn most when both cooperate (e.g., €3 each, earn less if both defect (€1 each), but if one cooperates and the other defects, the cooperator earns €0 and the defector earns the maximum payoff of €5 (Axelrod, 1984; see Table 11.1). Irrespective of what your co-player does, defection has the higher profit (€5 or €1) than cooperation (€3 or €0); since this holds for both players, both will defect, if they are gain maximizers, and end up with €1 each instead of €3 had they both cooperated. This game is called the "Prisoner's Dilemma" (Rapoport and Chammah, 1970; Pounstone, 1992).

Thus, if the game is played only once, mutual defection is the predicted outcome. However, if the game is played repeatedly with the same players, numerous strategies of

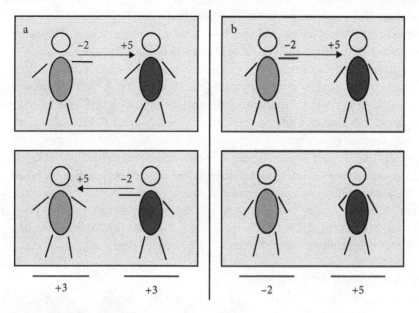

FIGURE 11.1. Direct reciprocity pays off for both players after mutual help (a). If one player refuses to reciprocate, the defector has the highest gain (b).

**Table 11.1. The prisoner's dilemma game; two players can either cooperate of defect. (From Axelrod 1984)**

| | | The Prisoner's Dilemma | |
| --- | --- | --- | --- |
| | | Decision of your co-player | |
| | | Cooperate | Defect |
| Your decision | Cooperate | R = 3, R = 3<br>Reward for mutual cooperation | S = 0, T = 5<br>Sucker's payoff, and temptation to defect |
| | Defect | T = 5, S = 0<br>Temptation to defect and sucker's payoff | P = 1, P = 1<br>Punishment for mutual defection |

*Note:* The payoffs to the row chooser are listed first.

alternating Cooperate (C) and Defect (D) are possible in response to the other player's previous decisions: for example, DD, CC, DC, CD, DD, DD, CD, CC, CC, DD. Therefore the best strategy for the iterated prisoner's dilemma cannot be calculated analytically. A computer tournament performed by Robert Axelrod (1984) with strategies provided by leading specialists depicted Tit for Tat as the clear winner of simulated evolution. Tit for Tat starts cooperatively and then repeats the co-player's previous move. It is a nice, retaliatory and forgiving strategy. Later champions were Generous Tit for Tat (Nowak and Sigmund, 1992) and win–stay–loose shift (Nowak and Sigmund, 1993; Milinski, 1993), also nice strategies that cooperate with other cooperators. All the bright specialists might have missed the real champion beating any previous strategy. Recently, a new champion has been predicted to evolve: Extortion (Press and Dyson, 2012). All known adaptive strategies are exploited by extortion, which enforces cooperation of the co-player just the proportion of C with which it reacts to the co-player's C and D. Against such a player, an evolutionary player's best response is to accede to the extortion (Press and Dyson, 2012). Extortion appears as nice, because it responds in about 60 percent of the co-player's C with C. Therefore the co-player can gain only by being 100 percent cooperative, meaning that after 40 percent of the co-player's C Extortion plays D and collects the highest gain, whereas the co-player earns nothing. With increasing cooperation of the co-player its own payoff increases, because he needs to harvest the C—C payoff from the extortioner's 60 percent C, whereas the extortioner's payoff increases much more (Figure 11.2). A great number of theoretical papers extended Press and Dyson's analysis. However, only four empirical studies were published up to now (Hilbe et al. 2014; Milinski et al. 2016; Hilbe et al. 2016; Xu et al. 2016) confirming extortion's superiority. The studies showed that about 40 percent of the human subjects are potential extortioners, who readily exploit their peers when the opportunity shows up (Milinski et al. 2016; Hilbe et al. 2016).

As long as we expected that only nice strategies have evolved, it was not important to know one's potential co-player's strategy in a prisoner's dilemma. But now we expect to

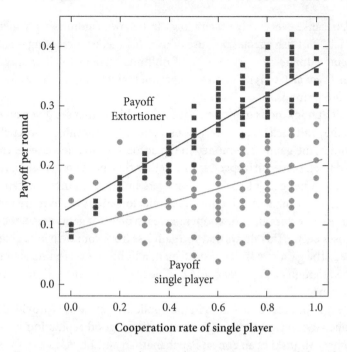

**FIGURE 11.2.** Extortioners incentivize their co-players to cooperate, and they obtain an excessive share of the resulting payoffs. (After Hilbe et al., 2016.)

meet either a nice co-player or an extortioner with almost equal probability. Both appear nice, which is the extortioner's disguise. The discovery of the extortion strategy is too recent that experience exists whether and how fast the news about someone being an extortioner spreads in the community. Are people willing to gossip about their disappointing experience or prefer to keep silent? Is such gossip trustworthy? It might be tempting to get rid of a competitor by calling him an extortioner. Extortioners might spread positive self-gossip to avoid being detected. Press and Dyson's discovery might change our understanding of social behavior because we now expect to be exploited with high probability by apparently nice social partners. Research on the role of gossip in unmasking extortioners and spreading the news about them is badly needed in the near future. Because using extortion strategies is not new, even the culture of talking about extortioners is probably well developed. It needs to be uncovered.

# THE TRAGEDY OF THE COMMONS
# OR PUBLIC GOODS GAME

A Prisoner's Dilemma game that is played with more than two players is a "Public Goods" game, that is, the experimental paradigm to study "the tragedy of the commons" (Hardin, 1968). There are numerous examples for natural Public Goods games such as traffic jams, because everybody prefers to go in his own car, missing hygiene in public toilets, extinction of fish species because of over fishing, or increasing global temperature producing climate change because of unlimited use of fossil energy. The Public Goods game (Ledyard, 1995) is used to experimentally test hypotheses for solving the tragedy of the commons.

In a typical Public Goods game you have four subjects that are given an endowment from which they can each invest anonymously either €1 or nothing into a public account in each round of the game. The money in the account is doubled after each round and redistributed to all players irrespective of whether they have contributed. If all subjects invest, each has a net gain of €1. If three players invest, each investor gains €0.50, the defector gains, however, €1.50 (Figure 11.3). Defectors always gain more than cooperators. With three defectors and one cooperator, each defector gains €0.50, the cooperator, however, looses €0.50. This shows that you gain less from your own investment than you have invested. The gain maximizing strategy in a Public Goods game is to never invest anything even though each player could double his investment each round if all invest, thus the dilemma.

A cheap way to induce cooperation in the Public Goods game is provided by combining the Public Goods game with a game, in which a good reputation is necessary for gaining money (Milinski et al. 2002a; Panchanathan and Boyd, 2004), for example, an Indirect Reciprocity game (Alexander, 1987; Boyd and Richerson, 1989; Nowak and Sigmund, 1998). In indirect reciprocity a prediction from the bible is verified—"help and you shall receive." Indirect reciprocity has two steps: (1) A observes that B helps C. (2) A helps B.

Nowak and Sigmund (1998) showed by both computer simulations and an analytical model that cooperation through indirect reciprocity can evolve if everybody has an "image score" that is increased by one point after each act of helping and is decreased by one point after each act of refused help. A helps B only if she has a positive image score, that is, reputation. If a person has helped more often than he has refused help, he can expect help from others. An experimental test with Swiss students showed that subjects helped others who had a positive image score, or reputation, even though they knew that direct reciprocity was excluded (Wedekind and Milinski, 2000). Other experimental studies found similar results (Bolton et al. 2005; Milinski et al. 2002b; Seinen and

| | | | | |
|---|---|---|---|---|
| give € : | 1.00 | 1.00 | 0 | 1.00 |
| receive € : | 1.50 | 1.50 | 1.50 | 1.50 |
| net gain € : | 0.50 | 0.50 | 1.50 | 0.50 |

FIGURE 11.3. In a public goods game, you gain more by not contributing.

Shram, 2006; Semmann et al. 2004). A person's reputation is a score that members of a social group update whenever they see the person interacting or hear gossip about the person's social interactions. Reputation is the current standing the person has gained from previous investments or refusal of investments in helping others. Is he a good guy, can I trust him, or better avoid him as a social partner? A good reputation pays off by attracting help from others, even from strangers, members from another group, if the recipient's reputation is known (Semmann et al. 2005).

If rounds of the Public Goods game are alternated with rounds of the Indirect Reciprocity game and players have the same pseudonym in both games, the public good is maintained at the high starting level (Milinski et al. 2002a; Figure 11.4). Players who did not contribute to the public good in one round were less often rewarded in the next indirect reciprocity round than those that had contributed. Thus a good reputation gained in the Public Goods game is rewarded in the Indirect Reciprocity game and defectors do not risk losing their reputation. When this risk is removed by telling players after round 16 that only rounds of the Public Goods game will follow, contributions to the public good collapsed (Figure 11.4). Thus, the pending risk of rounds where reputation

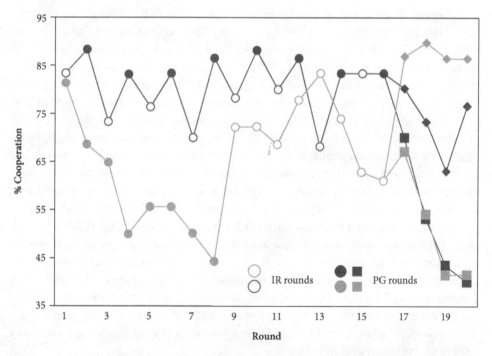

FIGURE 11.4. Percentage of cooperation ('yes') per group of six subjects in each round of the public goods game (filled symbols) and in each round of the indirect reciprocity game (open symbols). In one treatment, the groups alternated between rounds of indirect reciprocity and rounds of public goods game until round 16; in the other treatment, groups started with eight consecutive rounds of the public goods game and continued with eight rounds of the indirect reciprocity game; in rounds 17–20, groups of both treatments played the public goods game, which was either announced (squares) or not announced (diamonds). (After Milinski et al. 2002a.)

matters had enforced cooperation. A theoretical analysis later showed that the reputation effect is predicted to be stable (Panchanathan and Boyd, 2004). Similarly, Barclay (2004) found that when players knew that they would play a Trust game, that is, another game in which reputation matters (see next section), contributions to the public good stayed at a high level. Obviously people manage their reputation by taking into account whether their present behavior can have reputational consequences or not, and behave in a cooperative or selfish manor, respectively (see Semmann et al. 2004 for a specific test of this hypothesis). There are also potential psychological adaptations for reputation management (Wu et al. 2016a).

# THE TRUST GAME

Cooperation between two partners implies costs and benefits for either partner. If investments do not pay off immediately, because the partner invests later, there is the risk of being exploited (Figure 11.1). No guarantee exists that the partner will reciprocate. The investor takes the risk to trust his partner. The experimental paradigm to study this scenario is the "Trust" game (e.g., Berg et al. 1995). There are two players, the sender and the receiver. The sender is given, for example, €10 that he can either retain or send to the receiver who receives it tripled: €30. The receiver can retain the money or send any amount back to the sender. The fair share would be to send back €15. Should the sender risk losing his €10 hoping to receive 15? Any information about the receiver's trustworthiness would reduce the risk of deceit. He may observe the receiver's potential smile. A "Duchene smile" is costly to produce (Duchenne, 1862) and thus assumed to be an honest signal of trustworthiness. It has been predicted (Centorino et al. 2015a) and shown that receivers produce it with high probability when they have decided to send money back, but only if the stakes are high in the Trust game. When only little money can be gained they do not smile "Duchenne" (Centorrino et al. 2015b). Another way to learn whether a partner can be trusted is observing, "eavesdropping" (Earley, 2010) a potential partner's interactions with somebody else. The best way to judge the trustworthiness of a partner would be to know the proportion of all his previous social interactions in which he reciprocated help or invested in others, that is, his reputation. Reputation can be gained by any kind of altruistic investment, for example, helping group mates or donating money to charity (Milinski et al. 2002b). All add up in a single currency—reputation. Therefore I call it a universal currency that can be used in any other social interaction (Milinski, 2016).

## Gossip in Social Dilemmas

Gossiping, that is, the exchange of social information about an absent third party (Giardini, 2012), is the core of human social relationships, indeed of society itself;

without gossip, there would be no society, as Dunbar (2004) argues. Conversation group sizes typically contain up to four individuals—invariably one speaker and up to three listeners (Figure 11.5) (Dunbar et al. 1995). Gossiping is likely to affect the emergence, stability and decay of strong social ties in organizations (Beersma, Van Kleef, Dijkstra, this volume; Ellwardt et al. 2012; Ellwardt, this volume). A key function of gossip may be related explicitly to controlling free riders. The exchange of information on free riders has undoubtedly been important in the large dispersed societies of modern humans (Dunbar, 2004). Free-riders are the major cause of social dilemmas for being dilemmas. Free-riders only take but do not give. Gossip can be a policing mechanism that helps individuals track those who have exploited other group members, even when such exploitation was not directly observed (Dunbar, 2004; Wu et al. 2015). In this way gossip can play an important and ubiquitous role in helping solve social dilemmas (Dunbar, 2004; Sommerfeld et al. 2008; Willer et al. 2010; Feinberg et al. 2012; Wu et al. 2015). Even gossip alone likely promotes cooperation because gossiping and knowing that others could gossip about you makes reputation salient (Piazza and Bering, 2008; Willer et al. 2010; Beersma and Van Kleef, 2011). Compared with using punishment (Yamagishi, 1986; Fehr and Gächter, 2002; Rockenbach and Milinski, 2006) gossip reduces the cost of social control without lowering its efficacy (Giardini and Conte, 2012). From the age of 5 onward children not only manage their own reputation,

FIGURE 11.5. "Drei Schwätzer" (Three Gossipers) by Karl-Henning Seemann, photo by C. Störmer.

but also attempt to influence others' reputation via prosocial gossip (Engelmann et al. 2016). Even 3- to 4-year-olds tend to report others' norm violations to third parties in social interactions (Ingram and Beering, 2010; Ingram, this volume). The tendencies to monitor, spread, and manage each other's reputation help explain the abundance of human cooperation with strangers (Wu et al. 2016b).

# THE GOSSIPER'S DILEMMA

To fulfil its function gossip must be true, otherwise it would even hinder solving a social dilemma. Being influenced by potentially false gossip has been called the gossiper's dilemma (Smith, 2014). Especially, to discriminate lying defectors is a problem (Nakamura and Kawata, 2004). Hess and Hagen (2006) describe psychological adaptations for assessing gossip veracity, for example, using multiple (see also Sommerfeld et al. 2008) and independent sources of gossip increases veracity. Competition between gossiper and her target rather decreases veracity. Some theoretical studies of the evolution of cooperation assume that a person's reputation is public knowledge (e.g., Ohtsuki et al. 2009), known either from direct observation of social interactions or from gossip. If gossip cannot fill up the public information gap to 100 percent, some theoretical predictions do not hold. There is the risk that cheating signaling strategies undermine the coherence of reputational scores maintained by gossip, which in turn may result in the collapse of cooperation (Számadó et al. 2016). However, despite the temptation to manipulate gossip, people who spread biased gossip affecting reputation are vulnerable to punishment by both the targets and the recipients of the gossip (Giardini, 2012).

The mere fact that gossip is used a lot suggests that both senders and receivers of gossip have a net benefit, otherwise nobody would pay attention to gossip, in which case it would not pay sending it. There might be even more sophisticated ways to assess veracity than the ones suggested by Hess and Hagen as there might also be more sophisticated ways to lie convincingly. We search each other's faces and expressions for cues of honesty and dishonesty (Dunbar, 2004). In a meta-analysis, Sparks et al. (2016) confirm that humans can predict, using facial and vocal traits, each other's Prisoner's Dilemma decisions after a brief interaction with people who have an incentive to defect. In economic exchanges between strangers, negative information is more salient for withholding trust than positive information is for placing trust. However, a friend's gossip has a strong effect on trusting, whereas positive information from a stranger does not matter for the truster (Bozoyan and Vogt, 2016).

The unique brain growth trajectory of modern humans has made a significant contribution to our species' cognitive and linguistic abilities (Sherwood et al. 2008), as the use of deception within the primates is well predicted by the neocortical volume (Byrne and Corp, 2004; for a detailed account of the neurobiology of gossip and reputation, see Boero, this volume). The possibilities for games of manipulation have provided the selective challenge driving the cerebral expansion in human evolution (Nowak and

Sigmund, 2005). Or as Dunbar (2004) put it: "The cognitive demands of gossip are the very reason why such large brains evolved in the human lineage." A never-ending arms race of manipulating and avoiding being manipulated may drive our language to become increasingly elaborate to serve the cognitive demands generated by the gossiper's dilemma—a rich and fruitful area for future research.

# Gossip Helps Indirect Reciprocity

To which extent gossip can replace direct observation was tested experimentally (Sommerfeld et al. 2008). In groups of twelve students, each subject acted as a potential donor in six indirect reciprocity rounds for a receiver; they could give ("yes") or refuse ("no"). In rounds two to six donors were informed about all previous decisions of their receivers, for example, yes, no, yes,...In the following gossip rounds each subject was provided with all previous decisions of another subject and was asked to write a short (≤50 characters) comment about that person. Subjects played again indirect reciprocity rounds with the following information about their receiver: either (1) all six previous YES/NO decisions of their receiver, or (2) a single gossip statement about this player on his YES/NO list written by another subject, or (3) a set of three gossip statements about this player written by three different subjects on his YES/NO list. At the end, subjects were asked to rate the valence of each gossip they had encountered during the game on a scale from 1 (very negative) to 7 (very positive).

The more YES decisions the subjects saw, the more positive was the gossip they wrote according to the rating at the end. Thus, gossip can replace direct observation to some extend. Would subjects also cooperate more when they see only the gossip about more YES decisions among the six?

Yes, but three gossips from three different gossipers on the same observed behavior transports the information better and transforms into respective cooperation levels than when it comes from only one gossiper (Figure 11.6). What does happen if gossips disagree, for example, two negative and one positive written on the same list of YES/NO?

In unbalanced situations (nnp, npp), people were more likely to cooperate if the majority of statements were positive, and were more likely to defect if the majority of statements were negative (Figure 11.7.). This indicates that a single deviating gossip statement does not have a strong impact on the donor's decision. Thus, if the valence of most of the gathered gossip is in line with a person's real behavior, the power of single inaccurate statements is very limited. In this way, cooperators seem to be able to detect defectors reliably by the use of gossip. Three negative gossips were, however, treated as less extreme than they were.

What, if people see the sequence of YES/NO decisions together with a gossip that pretendedly was written about exactly that sequence? In indirect reciprocity rounds the donor was always shown the previous YES/NO decisions of the receiver, together with (1) no gossip, (2) a positive gossip, or (3) a negative gossip. It was explicitly stated that the

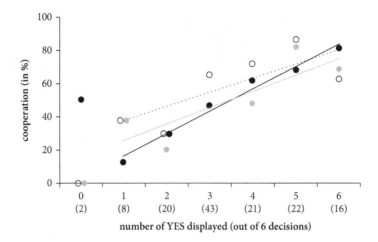

FIGURE 11.6. Elicited cooperation based on observed cooperation or gossip information. Open circles show the percentage of participants cooperating dependent on observed cooperation (as the number of YES decisions out of six decisions) of their game partner. Grey circles represent the resulting cooperation after the original information (x-axis) was transmitted via a single gossip statement. Black circles represent the resulting cooperation after transmission via three gossip statements. Numbers in brackets indicate sample size for each group. (Sommerfeld et al., 2008)

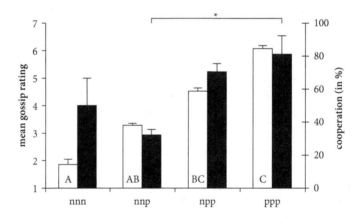

FIGURE 11.7. Mean gossip rating and resulting cooperation in rounds in which three gossip statements were encountered. The graph shows the mean (+SE) gossip rating (white bars, left y-axis) and the cooperation level (black bars, right y-axis) according to the number and valence (positive, p, and negative, n) of gossip statements encountered. Note that the extreme groups (nnn and ppp) refer to the gossip written by participants, whereas the intermediate groups (nnp and npp) refer to preset gossip. Different letters show significant differences (each $p < 0.001$) for gossip ratings (white bars) (Sommerfeld et al., 2008).

gossip was exactly about the information they saw. Since the original YES/NO decisions were shown, no influence of the gossip was expected.

Gossip has a strong influence on the resulting behavior even when participants have access to the original information (i.e., direct observation) as well as gossip about the same information (Figure 11.8). People believe more in what they are told than what they

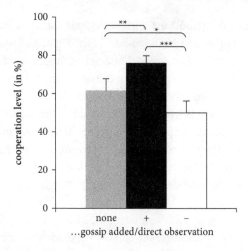

**FIGURE 11.8.** Cooperation levels of rounds with added preset gossip. Bars represent mean cooperation levels (+SE) of rounds in which players were provided with six former decisions (direct observation) of another player without (none, gray bar) or with preset positive (+, dark bar) or negative (–, light bar) gossip that was pretended to be about the same decisions, $*P < 0.05$; $**P < 0.01$; $***$, $P < 0.001$ (Sommerfeld et al., 2007).

directly see. Thus, it is evident that gossip has a strong manipulative potential. The advantage of this apparently irrational behavior could be that gossip may supposedly originate from several observations averaged over a longer period and may thus be a better predictor of trustworthiness than a single set of direct observations.

Players cooperate less, when they know that the gossip stems from the target about himself, compared to when they do not know the origin of the gossip (Sommerfeld et al. manuscript). Thus, people compensate for their receivers' presumed overrating their own behavior in a self-gossip, with the consequence that honest self-gossip would be underrated.

## Gossip in Public Goods Games

If rounds of the Public Goods game are alternated with a game in which a good reputation is necessary for being rewarded, the public good is maintained at a high level, because people are concerned about their reputation. Having contributed to the public good may be transmitted also through gossip. Two studies (Feinberg et al. 2014; Wu et al. 2016c) had Public Goods games played by four subjects over several rounds, however, with subjects exchanged such that no two subjects met again. After each round subjects learned how much each co-player had contributed. Among their treatments both studies included a pure Public Goods game (control) and a Public Goods game after which participants could write gossip about one (Feinberg et al. 2014) or up to three (Wu et al. 2016c) individual co-players that was presented to those others' new group members. Participants readily communicated reputational information about their recent co-players. Both contributions and individual earnings increased significantly when playing the gossip game in both studies. Feinberg et al. (2014) had an additional treatment where they combined gossip with ostracism: one subject could be excluded by an anonymous majority vote from playing in the upcoming round after all present subjects had received gossip from subjects from the previous round. The more negatively previous interaction partners portrayed an individual, the more likely his or her new interaction partners would subsequently ostracize that individual. When participants returned from exclusion, they increased their contributions substantially. So gossip can also foster cooperation by facilitating partner selection.

Participants chose to exclude defectors known through gossip. Contributions were highest when both gossip and ostracism were available in a Public Goods game (Figure 11.9). A previous study (Rockenbach and Milinski, 2011) found similar results, when before joining a group an observer chose to exclude one group member after she had directly observed the group in several public goods rounds; the ostracized player was the one who had contributed least. Gossip can substitute this kind of direct observation (Feinberg et al. 2014; Wu et al. 2016c).

When either a punishment or gossip-and-punishment option was added to the Public Goods game (Wu et al. 2016c), the mere option to gossip about each other was relatively more effective than punishment itself in promoting cooperation. The extra option to gossip combined with punishment significantly increased the cooperative efficiency of punishment. The authors conclude that gossip may be more effective and efficient than punishment to promote and maintain cooperation (Wu et al. 2016c). Finally, they found

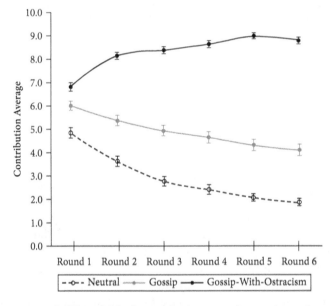

FIGURE 11.9. Average (+SE) individual contribution in each round as a function of type of game. The opportunity to gossip increases contributions to the public good, especially when combined with ostracism (Feinberg et al., 2014).

that gossip makes people more likely to trust others and be trustworthy during future interactions. Beersma and Van Kleef (2011) present evidence that gossip constitutes a social sanction.

Thus, in Public Goods games cooperation is increased when information about the previous reputation of joining participants can be transported by and learned from gossip. Gossip makes people more likely to trust others and be trustworthy during future interactions. Partner selection and ostracism are facilitated by gossip that is readily provided by previous group mates.

# GOSSIP IN TRUST GAMES

After the sender has committed to send money to the receiver in a Trust game, his or her fate of receiving anything back is completely "in the hands" of the receiver, who received the money tripled and is trusted to send a fair amount back to the sender. Any information about the trustworthiness of the receiver helps the sender's decision to give money away. Reputation gained in a preceding game helps in the Trust game; the senders' decisions were strongly influenced by the gossip that was based on reciprocating behavior in a preceding Indirect Reciprocity game (Sommerfeld et al. 2008). This shows the strong relationship between reciprocity, trust and reputation as described by Ostrom (1998).

Also senders in the Trust game take gossip about contributions in a preceding Public Goods game into account. The main effect of gossip on trust and trustworthiness was significant with greater percentage of money returned when participants were initially able to gossip (Wu et al. 2016c). When two sequential Trust games were played with the same receiver but different senders, the first sender was offered the opportunity to send gossip on the receiver to the subsequent sender after having experienced no money being sent back by the receiver. Participants overwhelmingly chose to engage in pro-social gossip, sharing evaluative information about the receiver that would protect the second sender from being exploited, even when no apparent social or material incentives were present. Sharing such information reduced negative affects created by observing the first sender's anti-social behavior. Individuals possessing more pro-social motivations were the most motivated to engage in such gossip. The authors highlight the roles of pro-social motivation and negative affective reactions to injustice in reputational information sharing through gossip (Feinberg et al. 2012).

When senders in two sequential games know that the receiver from the first game would send evaluative gossip to the receiver in the second game, would the sender be more generous in the first game compared to a control where the gossip was send to a person participating in another unrelated game (Wu et al. 2015)? The first game was a dictator game (Forsythe et al. 1994; Hoffman et al. 1996), in which the sender just splits a sum of money between himself and the receiver with the latter having no say on the dictator's decision. In a Trust game, the receiver has the last word on the sender's payoff by sending some amount (triplet) back or nothing. The second game was a Trust game with the former dictator being the sender and another person the receiver. The dictator was more generous in the dictator game only in the gossip-to-future-partner condition where he was at risk that his present receiver would send gossip to his future receiver in the subsequent Trust game with the potential consequence that the latter won't send any money back (Wu et al. 2015). Thus, gossip only yields enhanced generosity when transmitted to a future interaction partner (rather than to someone one would never interact with; see also Wu et al. 2016a); reputational concern serves as the primary mediator of this effect.

Piazza and Bering (2008) studied another kind of combination of a dictator game with the risk that future interaction partners could know about the dictator's allocation decision. A third party was involved, a confederate person, who left alone with the dictator for a short while started small talk according to a prescribed script to find out the participant's name, University, his subject of study and place of living—personal information from the participant that would allow this other person to identify and locate the participant in the future. After the confederate left the room the participant was instructed on the allocation task. They were also told that their receiver would have the opportunity to discuss the outcome with a third party, either the previously met person or a stranger (control). The threat of gossip to a stranger did not increase participants' offers. However, participants who disclosed personally identifying information to the future gossiper were more generous. Again, the threat of gossip served to promote generous behavior only when people have the opportunity to enhance their reputation.

# Conclusion

In a social dilemma, there is a conflict of interest between the individual and the group. As a rule individuals are maximizing their gain at the expense of their group (Hardin, 1968; 1996). Strategies that act for the good of the group can evolve through "group selection," however, only under very restrictive conditions that are unlikely to be met under natural conditions: the population needs to be subdivided into small demes of ten– to fifteen subjects each, has at least 50 percent extinction probability of pure egoist demes per generation, and almost no migration among demes (Levin and Kilmer, 1974; Traulsen and Nowak, 2006). So group selection, sometimes called "multi-level selection" (Traulsen and Nowak, 2006), is not an option to support cooperative behavior. Apart from kin-selected cooperation, for example, in eusocial insect societies (Hamilton, 1964; Hölldobler and Wilson, 2009), we expect that individuals behave for the good of their group only if they have a personal net benefit later on: they can gain reputation, a currency that is of value in almost any other social interaction (Milinski, 2016). To achieve this effect, altruistic actions need to be observed by others. If players are anonymous in some rounds of a Public Goods game, they stop cooperation in those rounds (Milinski et al. 2006, Semmann et al. 2005). This is similar when people know that observers may gossip to their future interaction partners (Piazza and Beering, 2008; Beersma and

Van Kleef, 2011; Wu et al. 2015, Wu et al. 2016a) or to an anonymous stranger, they save the effort for cooperation in the latter case. In this way gossip is by itself a powerful tool to promote trust and cooperation. The cooperative reaction of a person, when she is observed by potential gossipers, seems to be unconscious because if players are alone, when paying their tea to an honesty box, but there are stylized eyes on pictures "watching" them (e.g., Bateson et al. 2006; Haley and Fessler, 2005), they pay more. Gossip involves reputational consequences that extent over time, are enduring, and in many ways escape from one's own control (Wu et al. 2015). This should make people especially vigilant of gossip and its effect on their reputation. Concerns about being identified and gossiped about play an important role in promoting social behavior. The threat of gossip may have encouraged the evolution of altruistic behavior or even society (Dunbar, 2004) by activating reputational concerns (Piazza and Bering, 2008).

Gossip is not only a surrogate for direct observation of cooperative or uncooperative behavior, but it also combines observations from different people rendering this information more representative for the person gossiped about. Surprisingly, human subjects decide less according to their own observations than according to the gossip by others about that observed behavior (Sommerfeld et al. 2007); the gossip may be assembled from different sources and thus more reliable. Not only Ebay presents multiple positive and negative gossips about their selling clients but also "gossiping" newspapers such as The Sun, Bildzeitung, Blick or Neue Kronenzeitung make their profit because people want to hear assembled gossip about others that they unconsciously assume to meet in a future social dilemma. The latter examples suggest that people are eager to hear especially negative gossips, that is, what other people got wrong. Negative information is more salient for withholding trust than positive information is for placing trust (Bozoyan and Vogt, 2016), or as Warren Buffett put it: "It takes 20 years to build a reputation and five minutes to ruin it. If you think about that, you'll do things differently" (cited from Wu et al. 2016b). People's social connectedness in social networks may also increase their social visibility (Wu et al. 2016b). Our bright new world's information and communication systems, "social media" and the "internet of things," might, however, soon sabotage the previously net positive function of gossip of promoting cooperation in social dilemmas. Our well-founded desire for collecting multiple gossips about future interaction partners makes some people addicted to the internet that provides unlimited gossip. We could unintentionally create a digital nightmare, a "global time bomb" as Helbing (2015) fears. This development not only prevents gossip from being used as a surrogate for deducing a person's reputation from directly observing her interactions with other people but also turns it into a dangerous vehicle for any kind of manipulation. Either we pay attention only to gossip from reliable sources or gossip will lose its function of enhancing cooperation in social dilemmas.

Open questions that would need attention by future research: To what extent can gossip be used to manipulate future interaction partners? The consequences would be most severe in a one-shot social dilemma, that is, played for only one round. If you believe from gossip that your partner(s) is (are) cooperative, you will invest and lose. This effect will soon disappear in an iterated game when you learn after some rounds that the gossip was wrong. Is self-gossip, if known as such, trusted to some extent or just ignored? It would be very interesting to know whether people believe or disbelieve in gossip that the sender has propagated about himself. Is the reputation of the sender of gossip decisive whether to trust it? My guess is, yes it is. But we need to know. Does gossip about extortioners limit their success? Nobody will like to be exploited by an extortioner. I can imagine that gossip from those that have been exploited might prevent extortioners to be chosen as partners in a Prisoner's Dilemma game. Gossip might be the strongest force to prevent extortion to spread.

# References

Alexander R. D. 1987. *The biology of moral systems.* New York: De Gruyter.

Axelrod R. 1984. *The evolution of cooperation.* New York: Basic Books.

Barclay P. 2004. Trustworthiness and competitive altruism can also solve the "tragedy of the commons." *Evolution and Human Behavior* 25: 209–220.

Bateson M., Nettle D., and Roberts G. 2006. Cues of being watched enhance cooperation in a real-world setting. *Biology Letters* 2: 412–414.

Beersma B., Van Kleef G. A., and Dijkstra M. T. M. 2018. Antecedents and Consequences of Gossip in Work Groups. In *Handbook of gossip and reputation*, edited by Giardini F. and Wittek R. P. M. New York: Oxford University Press.

Beersma B., and Van Kleef G. A. 2011. How the grapevine keeps you in line: Gossip increases contributions to the group. *Social Psychological and Personality Science* 2: 642–649.

Berg J., Dickhaut J., and McCabe K. 1995. Trust, reciprocity, and social-history. *Games and Economic Behavior* 10: 122–142.

Boero R. 2018. Neuroscientific Methods. In *Handbook of gossip and reputation, edited by* Giardini F. and Wittek R. P. M. New York: Oxford University Press.

Bolton G. E., Katok E., and Ockenfels A. 2005. Cooperation among strangers with limited information about reputation. *Journal of Public Economics* 89: 1457–68.

Boyd R., and Richerson P. J. 1989. The evolution of indirect reciprocity. *Social Networks* 11: 213–36.

Bozoyan C., and Vogt S. 2016. The impact of third-party information on trust: valence, source and reliability. *PLoS One* 11: e0149542. doi:10.1371.

Byrne R. W. and Corp N. 2004. Neocortex size predicts deception rate in primates. *Proceedings of the Royal Society of London B* 271: 1693–9.

Centorrino S., Djemai E., Hopfensitz A., Milinski M., and Seabright P. 2015a. A model of smiling as costly signal of cooperation opportunities. *Adaptive Human Behavior and Physiology* 1: 2–18.

Centorrino S., Djemai E., Hopfensitz A., Milinski M., and Seabright P. 2015b. Honest signaling in trust interactions: smiles rated as genuine induce trust and signal higher earning opportunities. *Evolution and Human Behavior* 36: 8–16.

Duchenne de Boulogne G. 1862. *The mechanism of human face expression.* Paris: Jules Renard.

Dunbar R. I. M. 2004. Gossip in evolutionary perspective. *Review of General Psychology* 8: 100–10.

Dunbar R. I. M., Duncan N. D. C., Nettle D. 1995. Size and structure of freely forming conversational groups. *Human Nature* 6: 67–78.

Earley R. L. 2010. Social eavesdropping and the evolution of conditional cooperation and cheating strategies. *Philosophical Transactions of the Royal Society of London B* 365: 2675–2686.

Ellwardt L. 2018. Gossip and Reputation in Social Networks. In *Handbook of gossip and reputation, edited by* Giardini F. and Wittek R. P. M. New York: Oxford University Press.

Ellwardt L., Steglich C., and Wittek R. 2012. The co-evolution of gossip and friendship in workplace social networks. *Social Networks* 34: 623–633.

Engelmann J. M., Herrmann E., and Tomasello M. 2016. Preschoolers affect others' reputation through prosocial gossip. *British Journal of Developmental Psychology* 34: 447–460.

Fehr E. and Gächter S. 2002. Altruistic punishment in humans. *Nature* 415: 137–140.

Fehr E. and Fischbacher U. 2003. The nature of human altruism. *Nature* 425: 785–791.

Feinberg M., Willer R., Stellar J., and Keltner D. 2012. The virtues of gossip: Reputational information sharing as prosocial behavior. *Journal of Personality and Social Psychology* 102: 1015–1030.

Feinberg M., Willer R., and Schultz M. 2014. Gossip and ostracism promote cooperation in groups. *Psychological Science* 25: 656–664.

Forsythe R., Horowitz J. L., Savin N. E., and Sefton M. 1994. Fairness in simple bargaining experiments. *Games and Economic Behavior* 6: 347–369.

Giardini F. 2012. Deterrence and transmission as mechanisms ensuring reliability of gossip. *Cognitive Processing* 13 (Suppl. 2): S465–S475.

Giardini F. and Conte R. 2012. Gossip for social control in natural and artificial societies. Simulation: *Transactions of the Society for Modeling and Simulation International* 88: 18–32.

Haley K. J. and Fessler D. M. T. 2005. Nobody's watching? Subtle cues affect generosity in an anonymous economic game. *Evolution and Human Behavior* 26: 245–256.

Hamilton W. D. 1964. The genetical evolution of social behaviour. *Journal of Theoretical Biology* 7: 1–52.

Hardin G. 1968. The tragedy of the commons. *Science* 162: 1243–1248.

Hardin G. 1998. Extensions of "the tragedy of the commons." *Science* 280: 682–683.

Helbing D. 2015. The automation of society is next. How to survive the digital revolution.

Hess N. H. and Hagen E. H. 2006. Psychological adaptations for assessing gossip veracity. *Human Nature* 17: 337–54.

Hilbe C., Roehl T., and Milinski M. 2014. Extortion subdues human players but is finally punished in the prisoner's dilemma. *Nature Communications* 5: 3976.

Hilbe C., Hagel K., and Milinski M. 2016. Asymmetric power boosts extortion in an economic experiment. *PLoS One* 11 (10): e0163867.doi:10.1371/journal.pone.0163867

Hoffmann E., McCabe K., and Smith V. 1996. Social distance and other-regarding behavior in dictator games. *The American Economic Review* 86: 653–660.

Hölldobler B. and Wilson E. O. 2009. *The superorganism. The beauty, elegance, and strangeness of insect societies.* New York, London: W. W. Norton & Company.

Ingram G. P. D. 2019. Gossip and reputation in childhood. In *Handbook of gossip and reputation,* edited by Giardini F. and Wittek R. P. M. New York: Oxford University Press.

Ingram G. P. D. and Bering J. M. 2010. Children's tattling: The reporting of everyday norm violations in preschool settings. *Child Development* 81: 945–957.

Ledyard J. O. 1995. In Kagel J. H., Roth A. E. (eds.). *Handbook of experimental economics,* 111–194. Princeton, NJ: Princeton University Press.

Levin B. R. and Kilmer W. L. 1974. Interdemic selection and evolution of altruism: computer-simulation study. *Evolution* 28: 527–545.

Milinski M. 1993. Cooperation wins and stays. *Nature* 364: 12–13.

Milinski M., Semmann D., and Krambeck H. J. 2002a. Reputation helps solve the "tragedy of the commons." *Nature* 415: 424–426.

Milinski M., Semmann D., and Krambeck H. J. 2002b. Donors to charity gain in both indirect reciprocity and political reputation. *Proceedings of the Royal Society of London B* 269: 881–883.

Milinski M., Semmann D., Krambeck H. J., and Marotzke J. 2006. Stabilizing the Earth's climate is not a losing game: Supporting evidence from public goods experiments. *Proceedings of the National Academy of Sciences of the United States of America* 103: 3994–8.

Milinski M., Hilbe C., Semmann D., Sommerfeld R. D., and Marotzke J. 2016. Humans choose representatives who enforce cooperation in social dilemmas through extortion. *Nature Communications* 7:10915.

Milinski M. 2016. Reputation, a universal currency for human social interactions. *Philosophical Transactions of the Royal Society B* 371:20150100.

Nakamuru M. and Kawata M. 2004. Evolution of rumours that discriminate lying defectors. *Evolutionary Ecology Research* 6: 261–283.

Nowak M. and Sigmund K. 1992. Tit for tat in heterogeneous populations. *Nature* 355: 250–253.

Nowak M. and Sigmund K. 1993. A strategy of win-stay, lose-shift that outperforms tit-for-tat in the Prisoner's Dilemma game. *Nature* 364: 56–8.

Nowak M. A. and Sigmund K. 1998. Evolution of indirect reciprocity by image scoring. Nature 393: 573–577.

Nowak M. A. and Sigmund K. 2005. Evolution of indirect reciprocity. *Nature* 437: 1291–1298.

Ohtsuki H., Iwasa Y., and Nowak M. A. 2009. Indirect reciprocity provides only a narrow margin of efficiency for costly punishment. *Nature* 457: 79–82.

Ostrom E. 1998. A behavioural approach to the rational choice theory of collective action. *American Political Science Review* 92: 1–22.

Panchanathan K. and Boyd R. 2004. Indirect reciprocity can stabilize cooperation without the second-order free rider problem. *Nature* 432: 499–502.

Piazza J.and Bering J. M. 2008. Concerns about reputation via gossip promote generous allocations in an economic game. *Evolution and Human Behavior* 29: 172–178.

Pounstone W. 1992. *Prisoner's dilemma*. New York: Oxford University Press.

Press W. H. and Dyson F. J. 2012. Iterated prisoner's dilemma contains strategies that dominate any evolutionary opponent. *Proceedings of the National Academy of Sciences of the United States of America* 109: 10409–10413.

Rapoport A. and Chammah A. M. 1970. *Prisoner's dilemma: A study in conflict and cooperation*. Ann Arbor: University of Michigan Press, p. 261.

Rockenbach B. and Milinski M. 2006. The efficient interaction of indirect reciprocity and costly punishment. *Nature* 444: 718–723.

Rockenbach B. and Milinski M. 2011. To qualify as a social partner, humans hide severe punishment, although their observed cooperativeness is decisive. *Proceedings of the National Academy of Sciences of the United States of America* 108: 18307–18312.

Roddie C. 2018. Reputation and Gossip in Game Theory. In *Handbook of gossip and reputation*, edited by Giardini F. and Wittek R. P. M. New York: Oxford University Press.

Seinen I., Schram A. 2006. Social status and group norms: Indirect reciprocity in a repeated helping experiment. *European Economic Review* 50: 581–602.

Semmann D., Krambeck H. J., and Milinski M. 2004. Strategic investment in reputation. *Behavioral Ecology and Sociobiology* 56: 248–252.

Semmann D., Krambeck H. J., and Milinski M. 2005. Reputation is valuable within and outside one's own social group. *Behavioral Ecology and Sociobiology* 57: 611–616.

Sherwood C. C., Subiaul F., and Zawidtki T. W. 2008. A natural history of the human mind: Tracing evolutionary changes in brain and cognition. *Journal of Anatomy* 212: 426–454.

Smith E. R. 2014. Evil acts and malicious gossip: A multiagent model of the effects of gossip in socially distributed person perception. *Personality and Social Psychology Review* 18: 311–325.

Sommerfeld R. D., Krambeck H. J., Semmann D., and Milinski M. 2007. Gossip as an alternative for direct observation in games of indirect reciprocity. *Proceedings of the National Academy of Sciences of the United States of America* 104: 17435–17440.

Sommerfeld R. D., Krambeck H. J., Milinski M. 2008. Multiple gossip statements and their effect on reputation and trustworthiness. *Proceedings of the Royal Society of London B* 275: 2529–2536.

Sparks A., Burleigh T., and Barclay P. 2016. We can see inside: Accurate prediction of prisoner's dilemma decisions in announced games following a face-to-face interaction. *Evolution and Human Behavior* 37: 210–216.

Számadó S., Szalai F., and Scheuring I. 2016. Deception undermines the stability of cooperation in games of indirect reciprocity. *PLoS One* 11: e0147623. doi:10.1371

Traulsen A., Nowak M. A. 2006. Evolution of cooperation by multi-level selection. *Proceedings of the National Academy of Sciences of the United States of America* 103: 10952–10953.

Trivers R. L. 1971. The evolution of reciprocal altruism. *The Quarterly Review of Biology* 46: 35–57.

Wedekind C. and Milinski M. 2000. Cooperation through image scoring in humans. *Science* 288: 850–852.

Willer R., Feinberg, Irwin K., Schultz M., and Simpson B. 2010. The trouble with invisible men. How reputational concerns motivate generosity. In *Handbook of the sociology of morality, handbooks of sociology and social research*, edited by Hiltin S. and Vaisey S. New York: Springer Science + Business Media, LLC.

Wu J., Balliet D., and Van Lange P. A. M. 2015. When does gossip promote generosity? Indirect reciprocity under the shadow of the future. *Social Psychological and Personality Science* 6: 923–930.

Wu J., Balliet D., and Van Lange P. A. M. 2016a. Reputation management: why and how gossip enhances generosity. *Evolution and Human Behavior* 37: 193–201.

Wu J., Balliet D., and Van Lange P. A. M. 2016b. Reputation, gossip, and human cooperation. *Social and Personality Psychology Compass* 10: 350–364.

Wu J., Balliet D., Van Lange P. A. M. 2016c. Gossip versus punishment: The efficiency of reputation to promote and maintain cooperation. *Scientific Reports* 6: 23919.

Yamagishi T. 1986. The provision of a sanctioning system as a public good. *Journal of Personality and Social Psychology* 51: 110–116.

Xu B., Zhou Y., Lien J. W., Zheng J., and Wang Z. 2016. Extortion outperforms generosity in iterated prisoner's dilemma. *Nature Communications* 7: 11125.

## CHAPTER 12

...................................................................................................

# REPUTATION AND GOSSIP
# IN GAME THEORY

...................................................................................................

### CHARLES RODDIE

## INTRODUCTION

...................................................................................................

REPUTATION refers to the opinions held about an agent by others, and a good reputation is one which is advantageous to its holder. An agent's reputation is based on his past behavior, and so there is an incentive to act in ways that are likely to build a good rather than a bad reputation. Reputation involves interactions between the choices of two or more agents: a reputation-builder's choices generate a reputation which other agents respond to; in the other direction, the reputation-builder's choices are affected by how those others will respond.

Game theory studies how agents form beliefs and make choices to achieve varying objectives when interacting with other agents, and it has been applied productively to the study of reputation. Its method is to use models—simplified mathematical descriptions of situations—to clarify strategic logic.

This article explores how game theoretic modelling has helped to understand the process of reputation-formation and the effect of reputations in social and market settings. How do others form opinions and expectations about a reputation-builder? How do incentives to acquire or maintain a reputation affect choices over time? Whom is reputation good for? How do information channels and agents' degrees of concern for the future affect the ability to acquire a reputation?

Within the broad meaning of reputation, there exist two main forms. In one form, reputation is about managing future expectations. This is the most common use of the word "reputation" in game theory. Since others use the past to predict the future, what you are seen to have done in the past affects what people expect you to do in future. You have a good reputation if others have favorable expectations of what you will do, based on what they have seen you do in the past. For example, a government that has defaulted on past debt may be considered more likely to default on future borrowing. Defaulting results in future lenders not lending because they consider future default likely: a bad reputation has generated unfavorable expectations. This form of reputation is considered in section "Reputation, Form 1: Influencing Others' Expectations".

A second form of reputation refers to whether an agent is seen to have complied with his community's expectations. Non-compliance may lead to some sort of punishment from the group in future. For example, lenders may make a convention to avoid lending to a government that has defaulted, as a deterrent. Here a government that defaults has a bad reputation which triggers a punishment response from lenders. This type of reputation is considered in section "Reputation, Form 2: Conformity to Norms". Theoretical and experimental work on this topic is discussed, which largely focuses on how cooperative behavior is sustained.

As can be seen from the example, the two forms of reputation can overlap: both may be important in the same setting. Nevertheless, they are different mechanisms, and there are settings where only one of the two applies, or where both apply but tend in opposite directions.

In both forms of reputation, it is important that information about previous behavior is available to allow a reputation to be formed. In many contexts there is no hard information, but instead, information about others' behavior is passed by word of mouth: "gossip." This is most commonly studied in contexts where the second form of reputation applies, and where gossip can enable group norms, particularly cooperative norms, to be enforced. This is studied in section "Gossip and Reputation Games." There is little in the way of formal models here, perhaps owing to the difficulty of simultaneously studying incentives to maintain reputations and incentives to transmit gossip. Much of the literature studies how people play cooperation games in experiments. But theoretical models of reputation can still cast light on the mechanisms at work and suggest questions for experimental testing.

# REPUTATION, FORM 1: INFLUENCING OTHERS' EXPECTATIONS

Consider a firm that manufactures a product and has to decide how much to invest in quality. High-quality products are more expensive to make but are less likely to break down in future. We can model this as a *game* by describing the agents, the moves that they can make, and their *payoffs*, which are numerical representations of their objectives.

The firm and consumers (treated as single entity) are the two agents. The firm chooses whether its product will be low quality (LQ) or high quality (HQ). Simultaneously, consumers choose whether to have low demand (LD) or high demand (HD) for the product. Simultaneous moves implies that consumers cannot observe the firm's choice before deciding how much to demand, and vice versa. Payoffs are given in Figure 12.1: each cell gives payoffs of the firm and consumers respectively, where higher payoffs indicate preferred outcomes for the firm (higher profits) and consumers.

| | | Consumers | |
|---|---|---|---|
| | | Low Demand | High Demand |
| Firm | Low Quality | 2, 1 | 6, −1 |
| | High Quality | 0, 3 | 4, 5 |

FIGURE 12.1. payoffs in a product quality game

Game theory devotes most attention to *Nash Equilibria* of games. A *Nash Equilibrium* is a specification of the choices of all agents, such that each agent is making his preferred choice given the choices of the other agents. Here, regardless of the consumers' choice, the firm prefers LQ (since 2 > 0 and 6 > 4), so the firm must choose LQ in a Nash Equilibrium. Consumers' preferred choice given that the firm is choosing LQ is LD (since 1 > −1). So the unique Nash equilibrium is (LQ, LD).

Suppose on the other hand that the firm had the ability to move first and commit to a quality level, which the customer responds to. This game is shown in Figure 12.2. For non-simultaneous games like this one, game theory usually studies *subgame perfect Nash equilibria*. In such an equilibrium, each agent makes a payoff-maximizing choice at each point in the game, given the strategies used by other players. Here if the firm chooses LQ, consumers will choose LD (since 1 > −1), and if the firm chooses HQ, consumers will choose HD (since 5 > 3). The firm, anticipating this, will choose HQ (since 4 > 2), resulting in a payoff of 4 for the firm, higher than the simultaneous game payoff of 2.

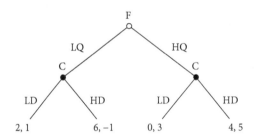

FIGURE 12.2. The firm (F) moves first, then consumers (C)

The firm's low payoff in the simultaneous game stems from an inability to commit credibly to HQ: consumers know that it will be in the firm's interest to underinvest in quality. This outcome would describe the situation of a firm which is anonymous, whose customers have no past or future dealings with it. Consumers then cannot make use of past information, and the firm will have little incentive to choose HQ. Normally, however, consumers will have some information about a firm's past performance: they may have purchased before; the firm may be a well-known brand or reviews from other customers may be available. Then the firm will have an incentive to choose HQ, so that future consumers expect HQ. Now it has a reputation to build, which affects its future sales. If consumers also understand that the firm has this incentive, then the (HQ, HD) outcome should result.

In order to understand this phenomenon fully, the mechanism by which the past is used to predict the future needs to be understood. Customers may not always assume that the future will be exactly the same as the past; this will not be the case if the market changes or the firm's incentives change over time.

A complete model needs to specify how consumers receive information and how they use this information to form beliefs about the firm, which form the firm's reputation. It also needs to study how consumers make buying decisions based on the firm's reputation, thereby determining the firm's incentives to achieve a good reputation, and finally how the reputation builder will act given these incentives.

The degree to which reputational considerations affect current behavior depends on the quality of information that customers have. It also depends on the degree of long-term thinking by the firm: the length of time the firm expects to be in business, and its "patience"—how much it cares about current profits relative to future profits.

The firm has the ability and incentive to exploit current customers with low quality services. Aware of this, consumers buy fewer products, and the firm is overall worse off as a result of having this ability. The firm would rather have the ability to *commit*, binding itself to a chosen higher level of quality.

Reputational models suggest that even without the ability to commit, concerns for reputation generate incentives for higher quality and can benefit the firm, moving it away from its short-term interests in the direction of the choices that it would wish to commit to. It is a broad conclusion of the literature, sometimes obscured by technical details, that the ability to acquire a reputation makes the reputation-builder better off, preventing him from being undermined by his own short term incentives. Whether other players are better off depends on the setting.

## Information, Signaling, and Reputation

Early game theory assumed that each player has complete information about other players' preferences. Under this assumption, there is generally no clear way for your current actions to affect what you are expected to do in future. Suppose that the firm in our example deals with one customer at a time, repeating the same type of interaction with a finite sequence of different customers. This is a *finitely repeated game*. Under the standard methods of such games (subgame perfect equilibrium), the outcome of the final interaction is usually determined by the two players' payoffs in that stage, and is independent of what has happened before. Therefore previous choices do not influence the outcome in the final period. This logic can be continued to previous periods to show that past choices have no impact on the future in this game. So we are left with the same equilibrium (LQ, LD) as we had with a single interaction.[1]

In reality, agents often have incomplete information, about others and about their environment. To act in such a setting, they have to process information. Incomplete information has become central to modern game theory since its introduction in the 1960s.

Incomplete information allows consumers to learn about the firm from its previous choices, and gives a mechanism for the firm to establish a reputation. Most models assume that consumers do not know what *type* of firm they are dealing with. *Type* refers to the characteristics of a player, which he is aware of but which other players may not be aware of. This sort of incomplete information is *asymmetric*, since the firm knows its type, but consumers do not. Consumers would like to know the firm's type to determine what quality they can expect. While they cannot observe the firm's type directly, they can learn something about it from the past behavior of the firm, which is a *signal* of (i.e. informative about) the firm's type.

The initial customer starts with an initial belief about the type of the firm, and does not have access to any other information. Future customers see the quality of the service provided to previous customers, and they use this to adjust their beliefs about the type of the firm. This is generally modelled as a rational process where customers update probabilities associated with each type of firm as they see its choices. Based on their current probabilistic assessment of the firm's type, they form an expectation about the quality they will receive from the firm.

The firm can then use its quality choices to *signal* good information about itself, creating a better reputation. Producing at a higher quality is costly in the present, but may generate future profits by signaling to consumers that the firm is a better type, so that future customers will expect higher quality and be more likely to buy. Games where the type of an agent is unknown, but where this agent may take costly actions to *signal* that he is a better type to others, are known as signaling games. See Kreps and Sobel (1994) for an overview.

Within the general framework of asymmetric information, there are two main approaches. In a behavioral type model, consumers do not know if the firm is *strategic*, adjusting quality flexibly to maximize profits, or *behavioral*, with a fixed production process and quality level. A strategic type will often mimic the choices of a good behavioral type to establish a reputation. In a model with strategic types, consumers know that the firm is profit maximizing but do not know the firm's level of technology, which affects how costly it is to produce high-quality products. Here, a good firm will choose higher quality in order to distinguish itself from worse firms.

## Behavioral Type Models: Mimicking Good Types

Consider an alteration of the model described in Figure 12.1. Suppose the firm is very likely to be a Normal type (N), which has the payoffs of Figure 12.1, but also has a small probability of being a Conscientious type (C), which always gives high quality services regardless of cost. Type C is called a *behavioral* type because its behavior is simple and non-strategic. If the firm choose LQ, then consumers observing this will know that the firm is type N rather than C, since C never chooses LQ. If the firm chooses HQ, then consumers observing this will infer that the firm is more likely to be type C, and will therefore believe they are more likely to receive HQ.

Although somewhat contrived, the model is designed to allow a clean and plausible argument to be made: if a firm always chooses HQ for a long period of time, consumers will learn to expect HQ.[2] So by always choosing HQ, the firm will eventually convince consumers to expect HQ, and so this strategy will result in a high payoff of 4 in the long run.

This does not necessarily mean that this is the firm's preferred strategy. Call the payoff stream from playing HQ "Long Run High Payoffs (LRHP)." The firm may make different choices and get a different payoff stream, but this must be at least as good to the firm as LRHP, or else it would always choose HQ instead. This conclusion is stronger if the firm is patient. An impatient firm puts more weight on present payoffs and little weight on future payoffs. LRHP may be unattractive to this firm, since it cares about the short run costs incurred in establishing a reputation. The fact that the firm does at least as well as LRHP therefore says little. On the other hand, if the firm is very patient, LRHP is very attractive. The fact that the firm does at least as well as this is then a strong result, which must involve choosing HQ and receiving HD very often.[3]

Fudenberg and Levine (1989) made this argument in a general model where a reputation builder interacts sequentially with many other players. If the reputation builder is sufficiently patient, he effectively gains the ability to commit to a course of action. The model gives a clear conclusion but requires strong assumptions, including that there is a chance of the reputation builder being a behavioral type who always chooses the ideal long-run quality level. This chance is allowed to be small but the smaller it is, the more patient the reputation-builder has to be to generate long-run profits close to the commitment profit.

Milgrom and Roberts (1982b) gave this type of model in a setting of entry deterrence. A monopolist is present in multiple markets over a long period of time and faces a finite number of potential competitors sequentially. If a competitor decides to enter, the monopolist has to decide whether to fight (expel the competitor with a price war), which is costly to both firms, or to accommodate (compete normally). From a short-term perspective accommodation is best for the monopolist if the competitor has decided to enter, and if the competitor knows the monopolist will accommodate, then it will want to enter. However the monopolist would prefer to fight if it can thereby persuade future competitors that they can expect to be fought, and deter them from entering. Here the behavioral type is a belligerent type, which always fights competitors regardless of the costs. This is the "good" type here, "good" not because it is good for the market but because it is good for the monopolist to have a belligerent reputation. The conclusion is that apart from near the end of the game (when the number of possible future entrants is running low), the monopolist, even if it is strategic and not belligerent, will want to mimic the belligerent type. Competitors know that the monopolist, even if strategic, will be mimicking the belligerent type, and so do not enter the market. Here the monopolist's ability to acquire a reputation reduces competition in the market, and makes other firms and also consumers worse off.

In Backus and Driffill (1985), a central bank has a short-term incentive to increase inflation for the sake of lowering unemployment. Without reputational incentives it would run a "loose" policy with high inflation. But the short-term incentive for high inflation only works if the market does not expect it, and in the long run leads to an expected and suboptimally high level of inflation. However if the bank can mimic a "good" type which is tough on inflation, it then has reputational incentives to pursue a lower rate of inflation.

Firms have the property that they can be bought and sold, and their reputation may attach to the name of the firm. Tadelis (2002) considers a product quality model with normal and behavioral types, when firms change hands and may outlive their owners. The buying and selling of firms gives a reason to invest in the reputation of a firm, which increases the market value of its name. Firms with a sufficiently poor record are abandoned in favor of setting up new firms.

## Strategic Type Models: Distinguishing Yourself from Worse Types

A second approach involves strategic rather than behavioral types. In our example, imagine that there are two types of firm, one of which has a higher level of technology that makes it less costly to deliver higher-quality services. The high-tech type of firm has an incentive to produce at a higher level of quality than would satisfy its short-term interests, because by doing so it can persuade the market that it is high tech. This type of model is a classic costly signaling game, where in a *separating equilibrium*, low- and high-tech firms make different quality choices. If low-tech firms chose the high quality chosen by high-tech firms, they would gain a reputation as being high tech, but high-tech firms choose a level of quality high enough that it is not worth it for low-tech firms to imitate them.

Milgrom and Roberts (1982a) gave a "limit-pricing" model of quantity competition in which a monopolist wants a reputation for producing more, to discourage a potential competitor from entering the market. In the separating equilibrium, a low-cost monopolist has to produce more to demonstrate its low costs to the competitor. If the competitor believes the monopolist has high costs, it will enter the market, anticipating higher prices. The signaling the monopolist has to do in the first period is costly, and the signaling mechanism does not lead to an unambiguously lower probability of entry.

In games with more than two stages, how much of a player's history of behavior will others use to work out what he is likely to do now? If only very recent information is used, then there is always an incentive to act to maintain a reputation: your current behavior affects how others will respond to you in the near future. In some tractable models, such as Vincent (1998), the signaller's current behavior is highly informative about his current type, and so only the most recent information is used. Investment in reputation is important because it influences the other player's choice in the next period. In these models, if the signaller's type is relatively stable, reputation can be maintained at a stable level. In a long game and with a patient reputation-builder, Roddie (2016) shows that the ideal level of reputation, from the point of view of the reputation builder, can be maintained, similarly to the behavioral type models.

If one's current actions are an imperfect signal of one's type, then others will need to use your history of behavior, not just your most recent behavior. Mailath and Samuelson

(2001) consider such a model of product quality. There can be times at which it is important to build reputation and times when it is optimal to invest less and spend one's good reputation.

Reputation can also affect what we say as well as do. Morris (2001) studies a model where an adviser provides information which is acted on by a decision-maker. Some bad advisers are biased; for example a racist advisor may always report that a minority candidate is inadequate. An unbiased adviser wants the decision maker to have accurate information. But he also has a reputational incentive to avoid being perceived to be racist, so that his future advice gets taken. This can lead to a politically correct bias in the opposite direction. While a rational decision-maker will try to factor this out, concerns for reputation lead to less information being conveyed.

# Reputation, Form 2: Conformity to Norms

Another form of reputation concerns whether players are viewed well or badly by others. Individuals who have previously acted against the interests of the group—or who are believed to have—are liable to be punished. Game theorists have studied this topic extensively in theoretical and experimental work to understand how cooperation can be maintained in groups and societies.

The theoretical work has to do with repeated games and when cooperation can be an equilibrium strategy. A cooperative action is often assumed to be one which is undesirable ("costly") for an individual in the short term but which benefits others in the group, in such a way that the group as a whole prefers more cooperation. The prisoners' dilemma game (Figure 12.3) is the simplest example of this.

|  |  | Player 2 | |
|---|---|---|---|
|  |  | Defect | Cooperate |
| Player 1 | Defect | 1, 1 | 3, 0 |
|  | Cooperate | 0, 3 | 2, 2 |

FIGURE 12.3. payoffs in the prisoners' dilemma game

In this game cooperation is costly to the individual, giving a payoff of 0 instead of 1 if the other player defects, and 2 instead of 3 if the other player cooperates. If the game is played once, there is a unique equilibrium (defect, defect). Similarly to the product quality game of section "Reputation, Form 1: Influencing Others' Expectations," there is an incentive problem resulting from an inability to commit; here it is the inability to mutually commit to the mutually beneficial outcome (cooperate, cooperate).

If the game is played repeatedly, then incentives to cooperate could come from a future reward from cooperation or cost from not cooperating. In a finitely repeated game, backwards induction usually implies no cooperation: no cooperation in the final period, so no incentives to cooperate in the previous period, and so on. To support cooperation, infinite horizons are usually necessary.

Unfortunately infinitely repeated games have many possible equilibria, and so it is hard to give theoretical predictions about how people will play these games. Results that describe this large range of equilibria, including Abreu, Pearce, and Stacchetti (1990), are called "folk theorems." The most that can be said for cooperation games is to what extent cooperation is possible in equilibrium.

This makes empirical and experimental work even more important for understanding the reputation and punishment strategies that people use. Experimental work looks at these questions in laboratory settings, attempting to find when and how groups will punish individuals for failing to cooperate and how cooperation and punishment strategies can be maintained.

The theoretical study of repeated games doesn't only produce results on the range of equilibria but also casts light on more basic strategic considerations. What can give a player the incentive to cooperate? What can give a player the incentive to reward or punish another? These considerations are very helpful for understanding the results of experimental games, and they also suggest questions for future experimental work to answer.

First, cooperation needs to be incentivized by future benefits from cooperating or costs from not cooperating. After taking an action which you are not supposed to, the subsequent equilibrium needs to be worse for you than if you had taken a better action. The simplest form of this is where players revert to an equilibrium of the single-stage game. This is called a *Nash reversion* or *grim trigger* equilibrium. For example, in the prisoner's dilemma game above, a Nash reversion strategy is: Cooperate, unless one of the players has Defected in the past, in which case Defect (the single-stage Nash equilibrium choice).

Second, sometimes Nash reversion is not a large enough penalty to maintain a social norm. Then give Player A the incentive to maintain the norm, norm-violation may need to be punished by a costly action by player B, which is itself supported by threats of punishment of player B if he does not carry out the punishment on player A.

Third, if there are many players, a third player C may need to punish player B for something he has done to player A: indirect reciprocity.

For example Sugden (1986) considers a cooperation game where each turn you play with a randomly chosen other player. Since any particular pair does not play together often enough, cooperation cannot be sustained by the threat of future non-cooperation by the same partner. In an equilibrium with *standing*, you are supposed to cooperate if your current partner is in good standing: otherwise you lose your standing. You may fail to cooperate with players in bad standing with no penalty. Together standing rules give a reward for being in good standing and enforce the social mechanism. Standing is not lost permanently and can be regained by cooperating later, so that punishment is of finite duration.

## Imperfect Monitoring and Reputation

In order to reward or punish a player for past behavior, others need to be informed about what he has done. The simplest situation is one of *perfect monitoring*, where players observe what the other players have done in earlier stages of the game. Much of the modern literature considers *imperfect monitoring*, where players are only imperfectly informed about the previous choices of other players. The role of imperfect information here is different from that of section "Reputation, Form 1: Influencing Others' Expectations". There, asymmetric information played a key role in generating reputational incentives: others' lack of knowledge about who you really are allows you to act in ways that alter their opinion. Here, on the other hand, imperfect information is a realistic feature that may make it harder to maintain a social norm.

Since maintaining social norms requires a degree of coordination among members of a society, there is an important distinction between whether this imperfect information is public or private. In *imperfect public monitoring*, all players observe the same information about previous play. Alternatively players may observe different information about previous play: *imperfect private monitoring*.

Suppose a man and woman are seen together. This is a weak suggestion that they may be having an affair, and is therefore imperfect information. If others do not communicate, some people have seen them together, and some people have not seen anything; this is imperfect private monitoring. If people gossip extensively and honestly, then everyone will know they have been in the same place together, and have the same imperfect information. This is imperfect public monitoring.

Under imperfect public monitoring, we have the "folk theorem" of Abreu, Pearce, and Stacchetti (1990) showing that an extensive range of equilibria are possible if players are patient. At any point in the game, the public information allows players to coordinate on a subsequent equilibrium which rewards and punishes players appropriately. Similar results have been less forthcoming under imperfect private monitoring, and typically require high quality private information (Piccione, 2002). And strategies supporting cooperation may also become more complex.

Communication and gossip may therefore make cooperation easier by increasing information. You receive information not only from your own observations but also from others' observations. Also, information is more common, allowing coordination of strategies and use of simpler strategies.

A concern for a good or bad reputation may derive from the future responses of others, or from a direct concern about one's image. A motivation for charitable giving and good social behavior, beyond any direct interest in the good results of one's actions, is to project a good image. Benabou and Tirole (2006) study a setting where agents wish both to appear pro-social and also disinterested in money, which can lead to "crowding out" where monetary incentives can reduce pro-social behavior.

## Evolutionary Models

Classical game theory studies equilibrium behavior of agents. Evolutionary game theory considers out of equilibrium play and how this evolves over time. Players have limited strategic ability and respond to others' play via well-defined rules. They may use fixed "genetic" strategies, and more successful strategies may become dominant through selection. Or they may observe others' play, either imitating the successful strategies, or using others' past play to predict their current play. In the study of cooperation, evolutionary games often restrict attention to strategies that are simple and plausible from the study of human and animal life.

Brandt, Hauert, and Sigmund (2003) study a public good game in a spatial evolutionary setting. Strategies that are more successful than neighbors' strategies tend to get copied. Defecting does not necessarily dominate: if you defect and your neighbors cooperate then you are more successful and your neighbors copy your uncooperative strategy, but then you end up with some uncooperative neighbors, which hurts you and can put you at a disadvantage against other neighbors. The ability to punish neighbors who defect results in the existence of cooperative equilibria under a wider set of parameters. If players have a chance to detect that the people they are playing with are not the sort to punish defectors, and are assumed to defect when this happens, this gives more of an incentive to take the burden of punishing defectors, and results in cooperative equilibria under a still wider set of parameters.

See Nowak and Sigmund (2005) for a review of evolutionary work on the maintenance of cooperative behavior, in particular through "indirect reciprocity", where cooperative behavior is rewarded by other members of society than its direct beneficiaries.

# Gossip and Reputation Games

This section considers reputation games with gossip, i.e. where information is transmitted by potentially unreliable personal communication.

## Theory

If gossip is truthful, and the decision to gossip or not is not strategic, then it functions like generic information and does not add any additional difficulties to game theoretic analysis. On the other hand if gossip statements are made to serve the interests of the gossiper, then there are additional strategic considerations: whether to gossip and whether to tell the truth. These will affect the quantity or quality of information available. The complexity involved has resulted in a lack of study of gossip in theoretical work. Bowles and Gintis (2008) express skepticism that communication can be truthful and similar to public information, "because in any practical setting individuals may benefit by reporting dishonestly on what they have observed."

To understand the quantity of gossip, we need to understand the direct and reputational benefits that individuals receive by gossiping. For example it may be time consuming or costly for you to communicate information to others, but could lead to a good reputation as a source of information, which may be rewarded if others give good information to you in return.[4]

To understand the quality of gossip, we need to understand how agents can benefit by lying. Malicious gossip is designed to punish the object of the gossip. Biases in the other direction may result from loyalty to friends or a desire to avoid a conflict state where cooperation breaks down. One may also be trying to achieve a reputation as a source of information, without a concern for its truthfulness. If untrue gossip may be subsequently discovered to be untrue, then there is danger of a bad reputation from lying, which may lead to losing credibility or being punished by others.

Gossip may be private, passed from one agent to another (perhaps on a network), or public, disclosed to all. The theoretical literature is more optimistic about public gossip than private gossip as a means of enforcing social norms, for two reasons: (1) Public gossip results in more people being informed as it is disclosed to everyone. Moreover if each person's behavior is observed by at least two others, requiring consistency between statements can be used as a check on honesty (Ben-Porath and Kahneman, 1996). (2) Public gossip allows for coordination in how society reacts to the information, even if this information is not perfect (Compte, 1998; see section "Imperfect Monitoring and Reputation" on imperfect public monitoring). This can allow for a "folk theorem" result with many equilibria, including cooperative ones.

## Experiments

Experimental games provide another way to learn about the workings of reputation. These replace the perfectly rational agents of pure game theory with the choices made by real people in artificial settings. Generally an experiment mimics a formal game, specifying: the available choices, the information available, the order of moves, and how rewards are determined, which are usually small and monetary.

The most common type of game used to test cooperation and social norms is the public good game. Here individuals contribute to a common pool of resources and may make a financial contribution, which is multiplied by a factor when it goes into the pool. Assuming this factor is greater than one, contributing increases the total wealth of the group, and if everyone contributes one additional unit, everyone ends up richer. The prisoners' dilemma is an example of a public goods game with two players. Often to test the use of punishments, a separate stage is added after the main contribution stage, in which individuals may pay a cost to punish other players individually (reducing their payouts).

Ostrom, Walker, and Gardner (1992) and Fehr and Gaechter (1999) study group cooperation games where previous choices within a group are observed. This gives a benchmark for understanding the role of gossip. In both experiments the availability of punishments greatly increased the level of cooperation. The availability of punishments did not always increase total wealth as punishments were sometimes "overused," but in Fehr and Gaechter (1999), this was not the case once subjects had gained enough experience of the game. The ability to communicate in Ostrom, Walker, and Gardner (1992) increased the level of cooperation. In Fehr and Gaechter (1999) punishments are used and generate more cooperation even in a game with a single cooperation stage, implying psychological motivations for punishment beyond future deterrence. However the highest level of cooperation was observed when each group played together repeatedly and punishments were available.

Sommerfeld et al. (2007) study a prisoners' dilemma game played by pairs of players within a group. They tested the effects of observing partners' past play, receiving gossip (comments about partners from their previous partners), and receiving ratings of the gossip. As expected, gossip is less acted on than hard information, although it is still acted on to some extent even when full information is available. This suggests that gossip may have a role beyond providing information on past behavior: coordinating social rewards and punishments.

It would be useful to have more experimental tests of motivations for punishment and the treatment of players who punish others. For example, suppose Player A has not cooperated in the past and has a bad reputation. Player B does not cooperate with A as a result. If B's uncooperative play is then reported, do future players punish B (because B seems less generous) or reward B (because B is upholding the social norm by punishing A)? Strategic considerations about incentivizing punishments in general, and the standing model in particular (Sugden, 1986), would suggest the latter.

Feinberg et al. (2014) and Wu et al. (2016) consider games in which there is more than one type of punishment for uncooperative behavior. Feinberg et al. (2014) study a public good game, where a player may make a financial contribution to the group, which is multiplied by a factor. Uncooperative behavior can now be punished by exclusion or by less cooperation in future. Groups change over time, and players may have the chance to give gossip about a participant to his subsequent group, allowing for punishment strategies and consequent incentives to cooperate. When groups do not have the ability to exclude members, gossip increases contributions a little. The possibility of exclusion leads to a much larger effect of gossip. So exclusion seems to be a more effective punishment mechanism than lower contributions. Exclusion targets the excluded party, while lower contributions punishes everyone in a diluted way; moreover exclusion may be carried out not only to maintain a social norm (form 2 of reputation) but because it is in the interest of players to avoid playing with uncooperative individuals (form 1 of reputation).

Wu et al. (2016) study the effectiveness of both gossip and punishments. Gossip here means comments about an agent made by former partners to subsequent partners. Introducing the ability to gossip had a positive effect on contributions. While the use of punishments was effective in encouraging contributions, there was "overuse" which resulted in lower overall earnings. The availability of gossip provided an alternative means of encouraging cooperation and reduced the amount of active punishment by participants. Gossip also increased cooperation in a subsequent trust game, perhaps because communication itself had a direct positive effect on cooperation. Further experimental work may cast light on the ability of groups and societies to select efficient punishment mechanisms and calibrate them.

Piazza and Bering (2007) study incentives for generous behavior motivated by intrinsic concerns for reputation. The experiment centered on a dictator game, where in each round a dictator gets a chance to propose a division of new resources. A dictator's partner would sometimes get the chance to communicate after the game with a third party, who may know the identity of the dictator. Dictators who can be identified are more generous than dictators who are discussed but cannot be identified (offering 1 extra unit out of 10 to the other), and these in turn are more generous than dictators whose play is not discussed. There is no opportunity for punishment of ungenerous offers within the experiment, so the experiment should be seen as studying intrinsic concern for others' opinions about oneself.

# CONCLUSION

Reputations play a critical role in many social and economic settings. Game theory studies the mechanism of reputation by analyzing three connected issues: the information mechanism that connects an agent's choices and the resulting reputation, the incentives of agents to act in a way that builds a good reputation, and the incentives of other agents in responding to this reputation.

Two forms of reputation have been studied extensively in game theory. In the first form, reputation creates expectations about the future behavior of the reputation-builder. These models often conclude that a patient reputation-builder effectively gains the ability to commit, as if moving first. The case of multiple agents simultaneously building reputations is an unsolved problem. In the second form, reputation measures past compliance with social norms, including cooperative norms. A number of "folk theorem" results show that in repeated games a wide range of equilibria of repeated games are possible, including equilibria in which norms are enforced by social rewards for compliance or punishments for non-compliance.

The first form of reputation represents an open area for experimental research. Experimental studies and evolutionary models have largely studied the second form of reputation, and cooperation games in particular. In theory, whether agents punish norm-violators is determined by present benefits and costs (sense of justice and cost of punishment), and future results of punishment. Experimental analysis of whether players who fail to punish violators are themselves punished would cast light on the incentives for punishment, and could suggest which of the many equilibria of these games are more plausible.

Game theory give insights into the role of information in maintaining reputation systems. But adding gossip decisions formally to reputation models is challenging. Agents may decide whether to gossip truthfully, gossip falsely, or not gossip at all. This decision affects the information available about the object of the gossip, and affects the reputational incentive to act in ways that avoid negative gossip about oneself. Incorporating this decision can easily lead to an intractable model. We need to describe the motivation for giving true or false gossip. Various motivations suggest themselves: to promote a social norm, to help or hurt the person gossiped about, or to pass on useful information. Each of these motivations could, with simplifications, lead to tractable models that give insights into the role of gossip and communication in reputation. And future experimental work could clarify the relative importance of these motivations.

## NOTES

1. Infinitely repeated games with complete information do not have this logic, but instead have a large range of equilibria. A simple example is a norm which specifies a certain quality level such that if it has always been maintained before, it is expected to continue, but if it is ever broken by the firm, everyone reverts to the low-quality equilibrium in future. Assuming the firm cares sufficiently about the future, this is an equilibrium because the present gains from switching to LQ are outweighed by the future losses resulting from the bad (LQ, LD) outcome. Unfortunately this model doesn't predict which norm is likely to emerge, and this type of equilibrium is only one possibility.
2. The argument from this involves conditional probabilities, assuming that agents update probabilities using Bayes' rule. Type N sometimes chooses HQ, sometimes LQ. Given an unknown strategy of N, we can divide N into two cases: N1, a normal type which decides to always choose HQ, and N2, which doesn't always choose HQ. Suppose you observe a large number of HQ observations and none of LQ. If the firm is N2, those observations were very unlikely because N2 sometimes chooses LQ. But if the firm is N1 or C, the observations were completely expected. So after observing such a sequence, a Bayesian update will give a high probability of the firm being N1 or C, and so you will expect HQ in future, since both N1 and C always play HQ.
3. Patience is modelled as *discounted utility*. If a player with *discount factor* $\delta \in [0, 1)$ receives payoffs of $u_0, u_1, u_2, \ldots$, his *average discounted utility* is $\frac{1}{1-\delta}(u_0 + \delta u_1 + \delta^2 u_2 + \ldots)$. A very patient firm has $\delta \approx 1$, and the fact that LRHP is close to 4 implies that its average discounted utility is close to 4. In this terminology, the result is that the firm must receive an average discounted utility close to 4.
4. Similar arguments apply to information disclosure where the information is not about the choices of other agents. For example, it can be a cooperative act to reveal market information which will benefit other participants, instead of profiting from a monopoly on this information.

## REFERENCES

Abreu D., Pearce D., and Stacchetti E. 1990. "Toward a Theory of Discounted Repeated Games with Imperfect Monitoring." *Econometrica* 58: 251–269.

Backus D. and Driffill J. 1985. "Inflation and Reputation." *American Economic Review* 75: 530–38.

Bénabou R. and Tirole J. 2006. "Incentives and Prosocial Behavior." *American Economic Review* 96: 1652–1678.

Ben-Porath E. and Kahneman M. 1996. "Communication in Repeated Games with Private Monitoring." *Journal of Economic Theory* 70: 281–297.

Bowles S. and Gintis H. 2008. "Cooperation." *The New Palgrave Dictionary of Economics*, 2nd ed., edited by Durlauf and Blume. New York: Palgrave Macmillan.

Brandt H., Hauert C., and Sigmund K. 2003. "Punishment and reputation in spatial public goods games." *Proceedings of the Royal Society* 270: 1099–1104.

Compte O. 1998. "Communication in Repeated Games with Imperfect Private Monitoring." *Econometrica* 66: 597–626.

Fehr E. and Gaechter S. 1999. "Cooperation and Punishment in Public Goods Experiments." *The American Economic Review* 90: 980–994.

Feinberg M., Willer R., and Schultz M. 2014. "Gossip and Ostracism Promote Cooperation in Groups." *Psychological Science* 25: 656–664.

Fudenberg D. and Levine D. 1989. "Reputation and Equilibrium Selection in Games with a Patient Player." *Econometrica* 57: 759–778.

Kreps D. and Sobel J. 1994. "Signalling." *Handbook of Game Theory with Economic Applications* 2: 849–867.

Mailath G. J. and Samuelson L. 2001. "Who Wants a Good Reputation?." *Review of Economic Studies* 68: 415–441.

Milgrom P. and Roberts J. 1982a. "Limit Pricing and Entry under Incomplete Information: An Equilibrium Analysis." *Econometrica* 50: 443–459.

Milgrom P. and Roberts J. 1982b. "Predation, Reputation, and Entry Deterrence." *Journal of Economic Theory* 27: 280–312.

Morris S. 2001. "Political Correctness." *Journal of Political Economy* 109: 231–265.

Nowak M. and Sigmund K. 2005. "Evolution of Indirect Reciprocity." *Nature* 437: 1291–1298.

Ostrom E., Walker J., and Gardner R. 1992. "Covenants with and without a Sword: Self-Governance Is Possible." *American Political Science Review* 86: 404–417.

Piazza J. and Bering J. 2007. "Concerns about Reputation via Gossip Promote Generous Allocations in an Economic Game." *Evolution and Human Behavior* 29: 172–178.

Piccione M. 2002. "The Repeated Prisoner's Dilemma with Imperfect Private Monitoring." *Journal of Economic Theory* 102: 70–83.

Roddie C. 2016: "Reputational Signaling and Discounted Commitment", mimeo.

Sommerfeld R., Krambeck H.-J., Semmann D., and Milinski M. 2007. "Gossip as an Alternative for Direct Observation in Games of Indirect Reciprocity." *Proceedings of the National Academy of Sciences* 104: 17435–17440.

Sugden R. 1986. *The Economics of Rights, Co-operation and Welfare.* Oxford: Basil Blackwell.

Tadelis S. 2002. "The Market for Reputations as an Incentive Mechanism." *Journal of Political Economy* 110: 854–882.

Vincent D. 1998. "Repeated Signalling Games and Dynamic Trading Relationships." *International Economic Review* 39: 275–294.

Wu J., Balliet D., and Van Lange P. 2016. "Gossip Versus Punishment: The Efficiency of Reputation to Promote and Maintain Cooperation." *Scientific Reports* 6, 23919.

CHAPTER 13

........................................................................................

# AGENT-BASED COMPUTATIONAL MODELS OF REPUTATION AND STATUS DYNAMICS

........................................................................................

## ANDRÉ GROW AND ANDREAS FLACHE

## INTRODUCTION

........................................................................................

SOCIAL evaluations in the form of reputation and status play a fundamental role in shaping social order (Giardini, Conte, and Paolucci, 2013; Ridgeway, 2014). Whenever actors need to decide with whom they want to interact or collaborate, they have to form expectations about the qualities and future behavior of their potential interaction partners. For example, when a firm wants to form an R&D alliance with other members of its industry, its managerial board needs to determine which of the candidates have sufficient know-how to make valuable contributions and can be relied upon not to take unfair advantage of the knowledge that will be exchanged. Similarly, when researchers are looking for collaborators for a new study or research proposal, they need to determine which of their colleagues have the required expertise and are motivated to invest the effort necessary to make the project a success. Finally, when human resource managers want to fill a vacant position, they need to judge the capabilities and reliability of the members of a potentially large pool of applicants. Reputation and status can shape the decisions that are made in each of these examples. High-status actors with good reputations—be it individuals or organizations—are usually expected to be reliable and of high quality and they are therefore more likely to be selected (Hardy and van Vugt, 2006). This is especially the case when first-hand information about the quality and (past) behavior of the candidates is not available (Stewart, 2005).

The words "reputation" and "status" have often been used interchangeably in the existing research literature (Rhee and Haunschild, 2006). However, as Sorenson (2014) highlighted, reputation and status are distinct social evaluations, even though they are empirically connected. According to Sorenson (2014), reputation is an evaluation of the traits of actors, such as their reliability, aggressiveness, or quality, that often derives from the actors' prior actions. Information about past actions can be acquired through first-hand experience or can be obtained from others. Status, by contrast, refers to the rank that actors hold in a hierarchy of respect and deference in the wider social system (e.g., the respect that a given researcher enjoys in his/her research field or the respect that a given firm is accorded in its industry). Status can accrue directly to individual actors because of the respect and deference they have managed to obtain during past interactions with others, but it can also derive from belonging to certain organizations (e.g., working at a prestigious university) or social groups (e.g., being a member of a "professional" occupation). Despite this distinction, reputation and status are closely linked. A positive reputation (in particular a reputation for high quality) can lead to respect and esteem, whereas high-status actors are often assumed to be of high quality, especially if their quality cannot be assessed directly. Hence, differences in the reputations that actors hold can lead to status differentiation and status differentiation can engender a reputation for quality (Sorenson, 2014, p. 66).

The social processes by which reputations form and lead to status differentiation are often complex. The reason is that reputations and the resulting hierarchies derive from decentralized interactions and the exchange of information among an often large number of people. The behavioral and cognitive principles that underlie these interactions and exchanges have the potential to generate self-reinforcing dynamics that are difficult to predict. Even more, processes of reputation formation and status differentiation can have unintended consequences that might be undesirable both for individuals and society as a whole. For example, reputation dynamics may bias the allocation of resources and the distribution of life chances in society in a way that is socially inefficient and that many might consider as unfair. One prominent example is the persistent disadvantage that women face in their competence and ability reputations compared to men (cf. Schmader, 2002; Moss-Racusin et al,. 2012). This disadvantage is one possible reason for women's underrepresentation in the most prestigious occupations and ranks in organizations and it prevails even though women have caught up with men in their average educational attainment and often outperform them educationally. Some have argued that this persistence is the consequence of self-reinforcing reputation and status dynamics, that occur even in the light of the economic and social inefficiencies that they create (cf. Ridgeway, 2011; Correll, 2001).

In this chapter, we highlight the potential that the method of agent-based computational modeling (ABCM) has for studying reputation and status dynamics. ABCM represents the behavior and characteristics of actors explicitly and formally in computer code and construes the artificial actors (called agents) as both autonomous and interdependent in their actions. As such, computational methods can be used to assess how reputations and status differences emerge from the interactions of multiple actors, and how such emergence can depend on the assumptions modelers make about actors' actions and behavior, as well as about the social structures (e.g., networks, distributions of resources in society) within which they interact.

In what follows, we first provide a brief introduction to ABCM. Subsequently, we discuss earlier ABCM research, with a particular focus on research that studied the ways in which reputation formation processes can create and reinforce inequality between individuals (e.g., between individual researchers) and status differences between social groups (e.g., between professionals/non-professionals, whites/non-whites). After this, we further illustrate the method by developing an agent-based model that we use to explore one possible reason why women as a social group are still often reputed to be less worthy of respect and of lower competence than men. We close the chapter with a discussion of future research directions. In this discussion, we focus in particular on the role that gossip might play in future models of hierarchical differentiation, given that earlier modeling work in this area has largely neglected gossip.

The reader should be aware that our discussion of earlier ABCM work is not intended to provide an exhaustive review of all the questions that *have* been addressed with this method in reputation and status research. Instead, our discussion is intended to illustrate the type of questions that *can* be addressed with ABCM. Other questions that were tackled with ABCM relate to, for example, the role that reputation might play in the evolution of cooperation (e.g., Traag, Van Dooren, and De Leenheer, 2013) and the effect that it might have on the performance of firms in industrial districts (e.g., Giardini, Di Tosto, and Conte, 2008; Di Tosto, Giardini, and Conte, 2010).

## AGENT-BASED COMPUTATIONAL MODELING

ABCM originated in computer science and artificial intelligence to study complex adaptive systems composed of large numbers of autonomous but interdependent actors. Agent-based models of self-organized behavior have been applied in a variety of scientific disciplines. Social scientists are increasingly using this methodology to better understand the mechanisms by which the actions and interactions of human individuals bring about social phenomena. In some applications, collective actors–such as firms and states–have been in the analytical focus, but even in these cases the individuals that make up these collective actors are usually assumed to be the driving force of behavior, if only implicitly.

ABCM can be seen as a specific elaboration of the social-mechanism approach to social theory (Coleman, 1986; Coleman, 1990; Hedström and Swedberg, 1998; Hedström, 2005). Both ABCM and the social mechanism approach put the analytical primacy in the study of social phenomena on the actors that make up a social system. The approaches have their roots in the tradition of methodological individualism. In methodological individualism, associations between macro-level societal properties (e.g., the negative association between the level of modernization and the fertility rate across countries that has been observed in the past) are viewed as the result of the actions of the individuals that make up society at the micro-level. Proponents of the social-mechanism approach argue that explanations of such associations should refer to these individuals and the causes and consequences of their actions (Hedström and Swedberg, 1998, p. 12). From this view, an explanation usually contains three steps (Coleman, 1990), sometimes referred to as a macro-micro-macro scheme of explanation (see also Raub, Buskens, and van Assen, 2011). The first step is the specification of *situational mechanisms* by which characteristics of the macro level affect the conditions and constraints that individuals face. The second step comprises the formulation of an *action-formation mechanism* by which these constraints and conditions affect the actions and interactions of individuals. Finally, the third step elaborates *transformational mechanisms* by which the actions and interactions of a large number of individuals bring about the macro-level outcomes to be explained.

The last step, modeling transformational mechanisms, is the most difficult to address with standard methods in the social science toolkit (cf. Billari, 2015). For example, in multiple regression models, the basic goal is to determine associations between variables (Coleman, 1986, p. 1328), such as the relation between the political system of different countries and their economic performance at the macro level. But this does not explicate the processes by which individual actions and interactions generate these associations. With multilevel regression models (see Snijders and Bosker, 1999 for an introduction) it is possible to separate effects of macro-level variables on individual outcomes from influences of individual-level variables. But even with such models we cannot study the ways in which individual outcomes are brought about by interactions between individuals nor how these generate macro-level properties of a social system (cf. Courgeau et al., 2016; Macy and Flache, 2009).

ABC models make it possible to study macro-micro-macro links because they take individual actors as the theoretical starting point and represent them as "agents" that can perform their own computations and can have their own local knowledge. Agents can also exchange information with, and react to, input from others. By implementing rules for behavior in computer code and conducting computational experiments, the dynamics and outcomes that these rules generate can be derived from the underlying assumption with a formal method (i.e., the execution of the computational algorithm that these assumptions constitute), even under assumptions that make it difficult to derive mathematically general statements about model behavior (e.g., heterogeneous network structures or non-linear decision rules of individuals). Scholars in a range of disciplines are therefore increasingly interested in ABCM as a tool to elaborate macro-micro-macro explanations of social phenomena, in particular when large heterogeneous populations are considered (cf. Van Bavel and Grow, 2016).

A model of agents in an ABCM comprises both assumptions about actors' decision making and assumptions about social interdependence. In modeling decision making, ABC modelers often impose low demands on the cognitive ability of agents, motivated by critique of the descriptive inaccuracies of the decision-making model of rational choice (Macy and Flache, 2009). One elaboration is heuristic decision making in which agents follow simple behavioral rules that model social habits, rituals, routines, or norms (Simon, 1982). Another prominent approach is adaptive decision making, as opposed to decision making based on "forward-looking" anticipation of the possible consequences of an action. Adaptive agents respond to – possibly unintended – consequences of their actions in their environment, so that learning and evolution can entail behavioral change (Macy and Flache, 2002).

Following early accounts of ABCM in artificial intelligence (Wooldridge and Jennings, 1995), social agents are construed simultaneously as *autonomous, interdependent, heterogeneous*, and *embedded*. While autonomous agents control their own internal states, their autonomy is constrained by interdependence. Each agent's actions and possibilities for future actions depend on what happens in the agent's local environment, and these actions in turn have consequences that alter the agent's own environment and that of others. Heterogeneity relaxes the assumption common to many game theoretic and system dynamics models that populations are composed of representative agents. Important for many applications in the social sciences, agents are embedded in networks that link them with only a (typically small) subset of the overall population, such that macro-level outcomes are an emergent property of local interaction. While in some special cases the designer of a model might assume that all members of a population can interact with each other, local interaction is often seen as a key ingredient to a realistic description of social dynamics in large populations (e.g., Axelrod, 1997). In addition, ABC models increasingly include assumptions about how agents change their position in geographical space or break off relations and establish new ones with other agents (Centola et al., 2007).

ABC models have been applied to study the emergence and dynamics of a wide range of social phenomena, including residential segregation (Schelling, 1971; Clark and Fossett, 2008), cultural differentiation (Axelrod, 1997; Flache and Macy, 2011), cooperation (Axelrod, 1984; Traag, Van Dooren, and De Leenheer, 2013), and assortative mating (Kalick and Hamilton, 1986; Grow and Van Bavel, 2015). For a broader coverage of examples, we refer the reader to recent overviews (e.g., Macy and Flache, 2009; Squazzoni, 2012; Bianchi and Squazzoni, 2015) and to leading journals in the field, in particular *The Journal of Artificial Societies and Social Simulation* and *Computational and Mathematical Organization Theory*.

# Models of Reputation and Status Dynamics

In this section, we illustrate how ABCM has been used in two areas of reputation and status research. The first area is the emergence of social inequality in the scientific system. In particular, an increasing number of scholars seek to understand the processes by which initially small differences in the reputations that individual researchers hold can increase over time and lead to large differences in the recognition and resources they receive. The second area is the emergence of status differences between social groups—such as between men and women, blacks and whites, the young and the elderly—that take the form of reputations for social worth and competence.

## Reputation and Cumulative Advantage in Science

Merton was among the first to describe what he called the "Matthew Effect" in science, "the accruing of greater increments of recognition for particular scientific contributions to scientists of considerable repute and the withholding of such recognition from scientists who have not made their mark" (Merton, 1968, p. 58). According to Merton, a form of self-fulfilling prophecy is at the heart of this effect (Merton, 1968, p. 61). Given the uncertain quality of new ideas and contributions, researchers often rely on the reputation of the person who puts forward a new idea. Ideas put forward by eminent figures are therefore received more widely and are evaluated better than they would have if they were put forward by somebody less known. Over time, this can lead to inequality between researchers who initially were not so different in the number and quality of their ideas. Those who have been able to gain some recognition early on (even if only coincidentally) will find it easier to increase their standing and to acquire resources for making additional contributions (e.g., grants, collaborators). Much theoretical and empirical follow-up research has been conducted to explore causes and consequences of Merton's Matthew Effect and an increasing number of those studies rely on ABCM (e.g., Börner, Maru, and Goldstone, 2004; Roebber and Schultz, 2011; Watts and Gilbert, 2011; Milojević, 2014; Thorngate and Chowdburry, 2014).

One important question addressed with ABCM is why, despite the self-reinforcing nature of reputation and recognition, the distribution of prestige is often skewed, but usually does not show extreme "winner-takes-all" characteristics. Börner et al. (2004) addressed this issue in the context of citation networks, given that the number of citations that the works of individual researchers receive is one central indicator of their reputation. To model the distribution of citations, Börner et al. (2004) suggested that the common preference among researchers to cite recent work over citing older work might counterbalance extreme winner-takes-all dynamics. They developed a model in which authors write papers together with some co-authors. Whenever a paper is generated, its reference list is compiled from known papers on the topic and/or from the papers cited in these works. In this process, authors are assumed to have a preference for citing more recent works. To study effects of this preference, a recency parameter was included in the model that scales the strength of this preference. Börner et al. (2004) showed that the practice of citing papers because they have been cited before can lead to skewed citation distributions, but that this effect is offset if authors prefer recent citations. Unexpectedly, Börner et al. (2004) also found that increasing the number of research topics reduces the skew in the citation distribution. As an explanation, they offered that "dividing science into separate fields [implies that] the global rich-get-richer effect is broken down into many local rich-get-richer effects" (Börner et al., 2004, p. 5272).

Watts and Gilbert (2011) also modeled citation networks, but asked what impact the Matthew Effect might have on the advancement of knowledge. They conceptualized science as a collective problem-solving task. In their model, each author is characterized by a number of scientific opinions that are partially represented by the solutions they propose in their papers. In addition, each paper can contain a number of the opinions that are expressed in the papers the authors have read, and a number of randomly created (i.e., new) opinions. The combinations of opinions in a given paper locate it in some pre-defined fitness landscape that determines the quality of the proposed solution. Watts and Gilbert (2011) suggested that the Matthew Effect comes due to preferred citing of highly reputed (i.e., often cited) work. Yet they also highlighted that this practice might be based on two bodies of work, namely papers that have been published after undergoing quality assessment through peer review versus all papers that have been written, regardless of having been peer reviewed or not. Arguably, the practice of mostly relying on work cited by others might limit the area of the fitness landscape that is searched and thereby might reduce the quality of the solutions that are found, but relying mostly on work that has passed peer review might avoid that researchers search parts of the fitness landscape that have low fitness value. The simulation experiments by Watts and Gilbert (2011) showed that when artificial authors rely only on the body of peer reviewed work, the best proposed solutions are usually of higher quality than when they also consider unpublished work, and for this it matters little whether or not the authors prefer to rely on works cited by others.

The ABC work we discussed here highlights how common citation practices might lead to considerable inequality among individual researchers, but our review of ABCM models of emergent reputation effects in science is far from exhaustive. Examples of further important work include the study of self-reinforcing effects of author reputation on editors' publication decisions by Thorngate and Chowdhury (2014), as well as a line of modeling studies addressing reputation effects in peer review (e.g., Squazzoni and Takács, 2011).

## Reputation and Status Differentiation Between Social Groups

A large body of sociological and social psychological research has explored two related questions: (1) "Why do small groups with a collective task focus often develop patterns of differential influence and task participation among their members?" (2) "Why is it that members of high-status social categories (e.g., men and whites) often are more active and influential than members of low-status categories (e.g., women and non-whites)?" Agent-based models have been developed to address these questions, frequently drawing on the expectation states framework (ESF; Berger, Wagner, and Webster Jr., 2014).

The ESF assumes that small groups with a collective task focus develop differentiated structures of influence and task participation (also called *interactional hierarchies*) because individuals perceive the situation as if it is one of their sub-tasks to determine who is highly skilled at the task at hand, so that their collective work can be guided by the contributions and inputs of highly skilled group members. By that, groups strive to structure their work effectively and efficiently (Driskell Jr., 1982). Assumptions about relative abilities are *performance expectations* that group members hold for each other (Berger et al., 1977). When objective information about relative abilities is lacking, the performance expectations that group members have for each other can be affected by resource differences among them. The reason is that the acquisition of superior resources is often assumed to require superior qualities, which might enable resource holders to also perform well on the task at hand (cf. Cook, 1975). A second source of performance expectations are salient social distinctions, such as gender and race, if they have status value in the larger society (i.e., if they are *status characteristics*). A distinction becomes a status characteristic when members of one group (say men) are believed to be worthier of respect and generally more competent than members of another social group (women). Such *status beliefs* are a "social reputation [that entails] beliefs about what "most people" do or would think about the status worthiness and competence of one categorical group compared to another" (Ridgeway and Correll, 2006, p. 433). Individuals apply such beliefs to the local interaction context, expecting specific members of status advantaged groups to be worthier of respect and more competent than members of status disadvantaged groups. This *status generalization* is most likely to occur when interacting individuals are previously unacquainted with each other, lack objective information about each other's competence, and when the salient status characteristic has not been explicitly disassociated from the task at hand (Webster Jr. and Driskell Jr., 1985). Thus, differences in the reputations that social groups have at the societal level tend to affect the status of their individual members in small group interaction. Skvoretz, Fararo, and Faust (Skvoretz, Faust, and Fararo, 1996; Skvoretz and Fararo, 1996) were among the first to use ABCM to explore how status characteristics might affect the formation of interactional hierarchies in small groups. Their simulation model focuses on task groups of size six and assumes that agents engage in dyadic interactions (e.g., directing a suggestion for solving the task at somebody else) that can lead one of them to appear more respected and competent than the other, even if they are objectively similar in these aspects. The model implements several mechanisms by which such perceptions might form. Most, importantly, one mechanism is based on a status characteristic that classifies group members into one of two categories: one of high status, whose members are reputed to be more respected and competent, and one of low status, whose members are reputed to be less respected and competent. Exploring the interplay of the different mechanisms, Skvoretz and Fararo (1996) found that the reputations linked to the status characteristic have the consequence that members of status advantaged categories are typically more likely to attain high ranks in the groups' interactional hierarchies.

The status that social groups hold in society does not only affect the interactional inequalities that develop in small group interaction. In addition, the ESF suggests that systematic resource differences and interactional inequalities can also lead to the formation of reputations and thereby to status differences between social groups (Ridgeway, 1991;

Ridgeway, 2000; Webster Jr. and Hysom, 1998; Ridgeway et al., 1998). A systematic resource difference between the members of two social groups (i.e., members of one group tend to be resource rich, whereas the members of the other group tend to be resource poor) can turn a social distinction into a status characteristic. The reason is that such resource differences consistently juxtapose seeming ability and competence differences (as implied by differences in resource possession) with differences in the social distinction (Ridgeway et al., 1998). Yet social distinctions can attain status value even in the absence of systematic resource differences between the members of the different groups (Mark, Smith-Lovin, and Ridgeway, 2009; Ridgeway, 2000; Ridgeway and Correll, 2006). For example, when members of two social groups interact and the members of one group appear coincidentally more respected and competent than members of the other group, observers and interactants can come to believe that members of the former group are generally more respectable and competent than members of the latter group. Once individuals have formed such a belief, they are likely to carry it into subsequent interactions and treat members of the different groups accordingly. By that, they teach their belief to others, leading it to diffuse throughout society (Ridgeway, 2000; Mark, Smith-Lovin, and Ridgeway, 2009).

Early formal models (e.g., Markov models) of belief emergence focused on the diffusion of status beliefs in large populations, and abstracted from some of the interactional processes that can lead to the formation of interactional hierarchies in small groups (Ridgeway and Balkwell, 1997; Mark, Smith-Lovin, and Ridgeway, 2009). Grow, Flache, and Wittek (2015) used ABCM to explore how these processes might affect belief emergence in small group contexts. In particular, given that small-group interaction is the context in which status beliefs need to emerge before they can diffuse throughout society, Grow et al. (2015) sought to explore how likely it is that the processes that the ESF describes spontaneously create status beliefs. Their model considers groups of size two to ten (in steps of size two) whose members are equally split into two social categories. It assumes that all group members are initially equally respected and perceived as equally competent. However, during the dyadic interactions that take place between them, it can coincidentally happen that one group member appears more respected and competent than his/her interaction partner. This perception can affect subsequent interactions so that agents who appeared more respected and competent before will be seen as more respected and competent again. This generates a self-reinforcing process in which small random differences between group members tend to generate larger systematic differences over time. Grow et al. (2015) showed that if group members are distinguished by a salient social distinction, this self-reinforcing dynamic has a strong tendency to align perceived differences in respect and competence with differences in category membership, thereby leading to the generalized belief that the members of one category are more respectable and competent than members of the other category.

The insights derived from the ABC models that we have discussed in this section suggest that the strong tendency of human groups to develop interactional hierarchies might partly be the result of reputational processes. When individuals rely on the reputations of social groups for guiding their own behavior towards the members of these groups, hierarchies can quickly emerge, even when there are no objective competence differences between group members. At the same time, it seems likely that basic principles of small group interaction have a strong tendency to generate systematic reputation differences between social groups.

# AN ILLUSTRATIVE MODEL OF THE EMERGENCE OF STATUS DIFFERENTIATION

To illustrate the ABCM approach in more detail, we present in this section an agent-based model of the emergence of status beliefs based on the ESF. The model addresses the question of why status differences between men and women continue to persist in modern societies, even though objective differences in resources from which these status differences could emerge have decreased in recent years (Ridgeway, 2011).

In traditional male-breadwinner societies, such as the United States of the 1950s, women were on average less educated than men, were less attached to the labor market, and often worked in less prestigious occupations. In recent decades, however, women's participation in the workforce has increased and has almost reached parity with that of men. Women are also making increasingly important contributions to family incomes and enter prestigious occupations that were previously dominated by men (e.g., Esping-Andersen, 2009; England, 2010; Ridgeway, 2011). If resource differences matter for the formation of status beliefs, why has the increase in women's access to symbolic and tangible resources compared to men's not led to a disappearance of the female status disadvantage (Ridgeway, 2011, p. 4)? According to Ridgeway, one factor that might contribute to this is that existing status beliefs can affect the interactional hierarchies that emerge between members of different social groups in face-to-face interactions (as described earlier), and thereby can contribute to their own reinforcement, even in the absence of resource differences. This has the effect "that changes in cultural beliefs about gender *lag* changes in material arrangements based on gender" (Ridgeway, 2011, p. 159, italics as in original).

Ridgeway's (2011) argument is compelling, but it rests on assumptions about a dynamic interplay between changes in macro-structural conditions and micro-level interactions that are difficult to assess (cf. Ridgeway and Balkwell, 1997). In particular, if resource differences vanish over time or even are reversed, there are two counteracting forces: the possible disconfirmation of existing (false) beliefs in interactions between men and women, but also self-reinforcing interaction dynamics that result from existing beliefs. The question of which one will prevail under what conditions cannot be answered by verbal reasoning alone. Our agent-based model enables us to explore the consistency of Ridgeway's reasoning and address these questions.

Here, we provide an intuitive account of the model. Interested readers can obtain a more technical and detailed description from the CoMSES Net Computational Model

Library (https://www.comses.net/codebases/5422), together with the model code and the input files. We have implemented the model in NetLogo (Wilensky, 1999), a modeling platform that is freely available from https://ccl.northwestern.edu/netlogo/ and allows readers to experiment themselves with the model.

## Model Structure

Our model is inspired by earlier models that have explored the formation of status beliefs within the ESF (Ridgeway and Balkwell, 1997; Mark, Smith-Lovin, and Ridgeway, 2009; Grow, Flache, and Wittek, 2015). The model focuses on the emergence of status beliefs from dyadic interactions between men (*M*) and women (*W*). It assumes that individuals encounter each other to collaborate to reach important goals. During these interactions, hierarchies can emerge spontaneously and the observation of hierarchical differentiation between men and women can lead to the formation of status beliefs.

Gender is associated with systematic resource differences and this association changes over successive agent cohorts. As a proxy of the resources that individuals possess, we employ historical data about the educational attainment of men and women, given that education is one of the most important determinants of occupational success and economic resources (Blossfeld, 2009). For simplicity, we only distinguish two educational levels. Tertiary degrees indicate a high level of resources, and individuals with less than tertiary education are resource poor. Figure 13.1 illustrates for the United States the dramatic changes that have taken place in educational attainment since the mid of the 20th century. Until the 1970s, the share of men with tertiary degrees among those aged 25–79 years was almost twice as high as the share of women with tertiary degrees. Since then, women have caught up and today are almost on par with men (cf. Schofer and Meyer, 2005). If this trend continues, women are anticipated to be considerably more likely to hold a tertiary degree than men by 2050.

We initialize agents' resource levels based on the data that we used to create Figure 13.1 for the cohorts born between 1936–2050. The simulation proceeds in discrete time steps and each step represents one year. In each step, agents can meet, interact, and acquire status beliefs. At the end of each step, agents can reproduce and die. Every time a given agent reproduces, a new agent with the same sex is added to the population. The resources that the new agents possess are determined probabilistically at birth, based on distributions derived from the data that underlie Figure 13.1.

During a given time step, adult agents (i.e., agents who are at least 16 years old) are randomly selected one at a time (with replacement) to interact with a randomly selected adult member of the opposite sex. During each interaction, a hierarchy forms between the interaction partners *i* and *j*, depending on the resources and the status beliefs they hold. This is implemented in a simple two-step algorithm. In step one, the model counts for *i* and *j* the pieces of information that might make agents inclined to think that one of them might be more competent on the task at hand than the other. For example, when *j* is resource richer than *i*, agents perceive this as a signal that *j* might perform better

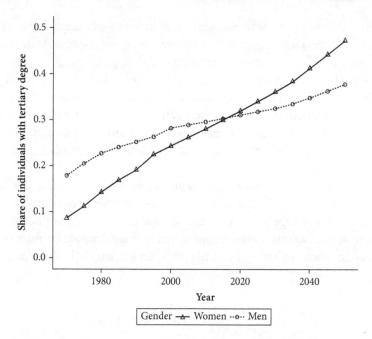

**FIGURE 13.1.** Share of men and women age 25–79 years with a tertiary degree in the United States.

> *Note:* calculations are based on the global educational trend scenario in the reconstructions and projections of educational attainment by country, year, gender, and five-year birth cohort provided by the International Institute for Applied Systems Analysis/Vienna Institute of Demography (Lutz et al. 2007; KC et al., 2010). Tertiary education is operationalized as categories 5 and 6 of the International Standard Classification of Education (ISCED-97 version).

than $i$. If $j$ is additionally female and the agents already believe that women are more competent than men, this is another piece of information in favor of $j$. In step two, the model determines for both agents the number of pieces of information that suggest that he/she is more (less) competent than the other and assigns the agent supported by more pieces of information the higher hierarchical rank in their interaction. If these numbers are the same for both agents, the model assigns these ranks randomly. This implies that in every encounter a clear hierarchy is established, even when two agents have the same resource level.

Agents use the hierarchies that they have been part of to infer general differences in the respectability and competence between men and women. For example, when agent $i$ is male and was in the status advantaged position in his interaction with a female $j$, both will perceive this as indicating that men are more respectable and competent than women. Agents remember the outcome of up to $E$ recent interactions. Once the number of experiences in their memory has reached $E$, new experiences are added and older ones are "forgotten." For example, if $E = 4$, each agent remembers information from up to four of their most recent interactions. If a new experience is added after this, the oldest experience is removed. The exact content an agent's memory determines the status beliefs she will acquire after each interaction. For example, if the memory of agent $i$ consists of the experiences $\{M,M,F,M\}$, the evidence favors the belief that men are more respectable and competent than women and $i$ therefore will acquire this belief. This happens even if $i$ previously believed that women were more respectable and competent. If the evidence is balanced between opposing beliefs (e.g., {$M,F,F,M$}), agents lose any belief they might currently hold and thus do not use gender as a cue to infer competence differences between themselves and their interaction partners. Hence, personal experiences of hierarchical differentiation can lead to the formation of reputations regarding the respectability and competence of the different genders in agents' minds. They carry these reputations into subsequent encounters and are influenced by them in their future behavior.

Over the course of a simulation run, agents age by one year at the end of each year, until they are 80 years old. At this moment, they are removed from the population and replaced by a new-born agent with the same sex that does not hold any belief. The likelihood that new-born agents will be resource rich or poor depends on their sex and the simulation year in which they are born, in correspondence with the input data.

## Results of Simulation Experiments

For illustration, we focused on populations of 1,000 agents that were equally split into men and women. Each simulation run continued for 115 simulation years, representing the period 1936–2050. Each run started with initializing a starting population. For this population, there was no empirical input data available. We therefore assigned the agents their resource levels based on the share of people with low/high educational attainment who were born in 1936. We also randomly assigned them an age in the range 0–80. None of the initial agents held a status belief.

The outcome of interest was the share of adult agents that believed that men or women are more competent than members of the respective other sex at the end of each simulation year. Given the stochastic nature of the model, all results are based on averages of 50 independent simulation runs. To assess whether status beliefs can contribute to their own maintenance even in the light of changing resource inequality, we compared the outcomes of our *full model* (as described previously) to a *reduced model* in which status beliefs do not affect the hierarchies that form during agents' interactions. That is, in the reduced model, the status hierarchies that emerge can lead to the formation of status beliefs, but the hierarchies themselves are only affected by resource differences between members of the two sexes and by random chance (in case two agents with equal resource levels interact). In addition, we assessed a key reason that Ridgeway (2011) proposed for the resilience of status beliefs, which is that individuals draw on past experiences and do not change longstanding beliefs simply because of a single disconfirming experience. To test the consistency of this intuition, we varied the length of agents' memory ($E$) in the steps 1, 5, 10, and 20.

Figure 13.2 shows the results of our simulation experiments separately for the full model and the reduced model and for the different lengths of agents' memory ($E$). As a baseline for comparison, consider the scenario in which memory is maximally short

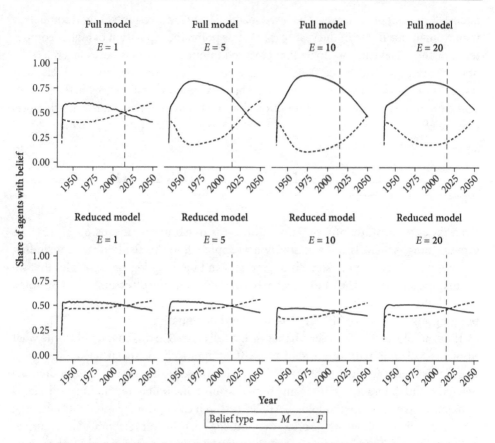

**FIGURE 13.2.** Results of simulation experiments with two model versions.

*Note:* The vertical dashed line indicates the year from which there were on average across runs at least as many resource-rich female adult agents as there were resource-rich male adult agents.

($E = 1$). In this case, a single (disconfirming) experience is sufficient for agents to acquire (lose) a status belief. Our results demonstrate that the full model nevertheless generates self-reinforcing dynamics that lead to a distribution of beliefs that is more biased in favor of men than the distribution of resources among men and women. Yet these beliefs are not very persistent and change quickly as the resource difference between men and women changes. Thus, in the simulations, men initially became quickly reputed to be worthier of respect and more competent than women, but this reputation faded as women began to outperform them in terms of resource possession. In the reduced model, the development of status beliefs was less pronounced and more aligned with what we would expect based on the likelihood that resource rich/poor men and women interact with each other, given the objective resource difference shown in Figure 13.1. The results displayed in Figure 13.2 show how status beliefs become more persistent if memory length increases. Increasing the number of past interactions that agents remember in the full model drastically increases the diffusion and persistence of the belief that women are less worthy and competent than men. At its peak, a maximum of almost 88 percent of adult agents believed that males are more respectable and competent than women (for $E = 10$ in the year 1972). At this point, the reputation of higher competence of the social category male that emerged in our simulations far exaggerated the objective resource differences between male and female based on empirical data and lasted for a considerable time even after objective resource differences had inverted. This supports Ridgeway's (2011) intuition that the behavioral and cognitive principles that the ESF describes can lead change in cultural beliefs to lag structural change.

# DISCUSSION AND OUTLOOK

Even though the study of reputation and status dynamics by means of ABCM is a growing area, ABCM is still a relatively new approach in this field. In this concluding section, we briefly point to some best practices and methodological principles that we deem important in ABCM, and we want to outline promising directions–but also some of the challenges–that lie ahead. In particular, we discuss the importance of better incorporating gossip in future ABC models of status differentiation.

The examples of ABCM research that we have discussed in this chapter illustrate what in our view is the main promise of the ABCM approach for social science research, namely its ability to shed light on the social complexity that ensues from individual behavior and interactions in many social realms, including reputation and status dynamics. Like every methodology, ABCM research can optimally unfold its potential when researchers follow a range of key methodological principles elaborated in a number of overview and introductory contributions to the field (e.g., Macy and Flache, 2009; Squazzoni, 2012; Bianchi and Squazzoni, 2015). Most importantly, we think that researchers should resist the temptation to try to capture all the details of a given social phenomenon to design the model as close to reality as possible, especially in early stages of model development. More detail typically implies an increase in the number of assumptions that need to be made and in the number of parameters that need to be specified. This reduces researchers' ability to fully understand the behavior of the model and to identify the most important causal mechanisms that link model assumptions to model outcomes.

This call for simplicity notwithstanding, we argue that future models of hierarchy formation would benefit from integrating gossip as an additional source of status differentiation that so far has largely been neglected. In existing models, the conferral of respect and prestige usually depends on the availability of information that makes it possible to gauge the qualities and contributions of others. In reality, this information is often difficult to obtain and this makes reputation management by strategic information diffusion possible. To illustrate this, consider the example of co-authorship among the members of a larger science department at some university. As Merton (1968) pointed out, the credit that authors receive for their work on co-authored papers not only depends on the quality of the paper, but also on the perception of which of the authors made the most important contributions. For outsiders, such information is often obscure, and this creates the possibility to self-enhancement and social control through gossip. A department member who is in direct competition for status with some of the authors of a given paper might try to undermine their recognition by spreading (possibly incorrect) information about their contributions to the paper. Conversely, co-authors might counterbalance undeserved claims to credit by spreading information about their actual contributions in the department. Indeed, Gluckman (1963, p. 309) suggested that "[g]ossip [...] is one of the chief weapons which those who consider themselves higher in status use to put those whom they consider lower in their proper place," whereas Paine (1967) suggested that individuals might also try to employ gossip for status enhancement. Gossip might thus aid or undermine the effectiveness of status hierarchies as a device for meritocratic advancement, depending on who employs gossip for what purpose (for the relationship between gossip and power see Farley, this volume).

Loch, Huberman, and Stout (2000) have made first steps in modeling such conflicting outcomes of status competition, by developing a model in which work group members might attain status either by contributing to the collective task, or by unproductive politicking. The latter strategy might involve gossip, but the model is too unspecific on this point to allow inferences about how gossip might affect the formation of status hierarchies and group reputations. A particularly difficult step in integrating more detailed representations of gossip into ABC models of hierarchy formation will be their integration with existing cognitive models of deference and respect. For example, in standard formalizations of the ESF, individuals weigh the information obtained from status beliefs and personal interactional experiences similarly. For the evaluation of information obtained from others, by contrast, it often matters from whom the information was obtained (cf. Kurland and Pelled, 2000). Information that comes from people who are considered credible might be weighted stronger than information that comes from less credible sources. Integrating these processes into cognitive representations of agents will be a challenging but crucial aspect of future simulation work. For this, researchers might be able to draw upon another prominent area in which ABC modeling of gossip dynamics has already a longer tradition, namely research on the role of gossip in the emergence and stabilization of norms through social control (Giardini and Conte, 2012).

Next to incorporating gossip into models of status differentiation, the improving availability of detailed behavioral data is likely to make it possible to study reputation and status dynamics with ABCM in areas that have hitherto not been explored. One reason why agent-based modeling has been so popular in the study of processes of cumulative advantage in science arguably is the wealth of easily accessible data for calibrating and validating the presented simulation models (cf. Watts and Gilbert, 2011). It is easy to obtain information about co-authorship patterns and citations over a long period of time and virtually all of the studies in this area that we have cited in this chapter have used empirical data. Recent technical developments in the areas of big data and web science will very likely make it possible to use similarly extensive empirical data for studying reputation and status dynamics in others areas. For example, Stewart (2005) has employed peer certificates available from online panels for studying reputation and status dynamics in an open-source software community. In this context, peer certificates rate the contributions that fellow developers have made to the software and "can be used as evidence that a status evaluation has been given" (Stewart, 2005, p. 829). This is but one of numerous examples of how online platforms and social media generate a wealth of longitudinal behavioral data that can be used both to fine-tune and calibrate agent-based models in the future, as well as to validate their outcomes against indicators obtained from such data. The increasing availability, richness, and magnitude of online data sources will undoubtedly turn out to be one of the most important developments that bring theoretical ABCM studies together with empirical research in the social sciences.

## Acknowledgments

The work of the first author received funding from the European Research Council under the European Union's Seventh Framework Programme (FP/2007–2013)/ERC Grant Agreement no. 312290 for the GENDERBALL project. The authors wish to thank the editors for their inspiring and helpful comments on earlier versions of this chapter.

## References

Axelrod, Robert. 1984. *The Evolution of Cooperation*. New York: Basic Books.

Axelrod, Robert. 1997. "The Dissemination of Culture: A Model with Local Convergence and Global Polarization." *Journal of Conflict Resolution* 41 (2): 203–226.

Berger, Joseph, M. Hamit Fisek, Robert Z. Norman, and Morris Zelditch Jr. 1977. *Status Characteristics and Social Interaction: An Expectation-States Approach*. New York: Elsevier.

Berger, Joseph, David G. Wagner, and Murray Webster Jr. 2014. "Expectation States Theory: Growth, Opportunities, and Challenges." In *Advances in Group Processes*, edited by Shane R. Thye and Edward J. Lawler, 19–55. Bingley: Emerald Publishing.

Bianchi, Federico, and Flaminio Squazzoni. 2015. "Agent-Based Models in Sociology." *WIREs Computational Statistics* 7 (4): 284–306.

Billari, Francesco C. 2015. "Integrating Macro- and Micro-Level Approaches in the Explanation of Population Change." *Population Studies* 69 (S1): S11–20.

Blossfeld, Hans-Peter. 2009. "Educational Assortative Marriage in Comparative Perspective." *Annual Review of Sociology* 35: 513–30.

Börner, Katy, Jeegar T. Maru, and Robert L. Goldstone. 2004. "The Simultaneous Evolution of Author and Paper Networks." *Proceedings of the National Academy of Sciences of the United States of America* 101 (suppl. 1): 5266–5273.

Centola, Damon, Juan C. González-Avella, Victor M. Eguíluz, and Maxi S. Miguel. 2007. "Homophily, Cultural Drift, and the Co-Evolution of Cultural Groups." *The Journal of Conflict Resolution* 51 (6): 905–929.

Clark, William A. V., and Mark Fossett. 2008. "Understanding the Social Context of the Schelling Segregation Model." *Proceedings of the National Academy of Sciences of the United States of America* 105 (11): 4109–4114.

Coleman, James S. 1986. "Social Theory, Social Research, and a Theory of Action." *American Journal of Sociology* 91 (6): 1309–1335.

Coleman, James S. 1990. *Foundations of Social Theory*. Cambridge: Harvard University Press.

Cook, Karen S. 1975. "Expectations, Evaluations and Equity." *American Sociological Review* 40 (3): 372–388.

Correll, Shelley J. 2001. "Gender and the Career Choice Process: The Role of Biased Self-Assessments." *American Journal of Sociology* 106 (6): 1691–1730.

Courgeau, Daniel, Jakub Bijak, Robert Franck, and Eric Silverman. 2016. "Model-Based Demography: Towards a Research Agenda." In *Agent-Based Modelling in Population Studies: Concepts, Methods, and Applications*, edited by André Grow and Jan Van Bavel, 29–51. Cham: Springer International Publishing.

Di Tosto, Gennaro, Francesca Giardini, and Rosaria Conte. 2010. "Reputation and Economic Performance in Industrial Districts: Modelling Social Complexity through Multi-Agent Systems." In *Simulating Interacting Agents and Social Phenomena: The Second World Congress*, edited by K. Takadama, C.-R. Claudio, and G. Deffuant, 165–176. Tokyo: Springer.

Driskell Jr., James E. 1982. "Personal Characteristics and Performance Expectations." *Social Psychology Quarterly* 45 (4): 229–37.

England, Paula. 2010. "The Gender Revolution: Uneven and Stalled." *Gender & Society* 24 (2): 149–166.

Esping-Andersen, Gøsta. 2009. *The Incomplete Revolution: Adapting to Women's New Roles*. Cambridge: Polity Press.

Farley, Sally. 2019. On the Nature of Gossip, Reputation, and Power Inequality. In *Handbook of Gossip and Reputation*, edited by Francesca Giardini and Rafael Wittek. New York: Oxford University Press.

Flache, Andreas, and Michael W. Macy. 2011. "Small Worlds and Cultural Polarization." *The Journal of Mathematical Sociology* 35 (1–3): 146–176.

Giardini, Francesca, and Rosaria Conte. 2012. "Gossip for Social Control in Natural and Artificial Societies." *Simulation: Transactions of the Society for Modeling and Simulation International* 88 (1): 18–32.

Giardini, Francesca, Rosaria Conte, and Mario Paolucci. 2013. "Reputation." In *Simulating Social Complexity: A Handbook*, edited by Bruce Edmonds and Ruth Meyer, 365–399. Berlin, Heidelberg: Springer.

Giardini, Francesca, Gennaro Di Tosto, and Rosaria Conte. 2008. "A Model for Simulating Reputation Dynamics in Industrial Districts." *Simulation Modelling Practice and Theory* 16 (2): 231–241.

Gluckman, Max. 1963. "Gossip and Scandal." *Current Anthropology* 4 (3): 307–316.

Grow, André, Andreas Flache, and Rafael P. M. Wittek. 2015. "An Agent-Based Model of Status Construction in Task Focused Groups." *Journal of Artificial Societies and Social Simulation* 18 (2): 4.

Grow, André, and Jan Van Bavel. 2015. "Assortative Mating and the Reversal of Gender Inequality in Education in Europe: An Agent-Based Model." *PLoS ONE* 10 (6): e0127806.

Hardy, Charlie L., and Mark van Vugt. 2006. "Nice Guys Finish First: The Competitive Altruism Hypothesis." *Personality and Social Psychology Bulletin* 32 (10): 1402–1413.

Hedström, Peter. 2005. *Dissecting the Social: On the Principles of Analytical Sociology*. Cambridge: Cambridge University Press.

Hedström, Peter, and Richard Swedberg. 1998. "Social Mechanisms: An Introductory Essay." In *Social Mechanisms: An Analytical Approach to Social Theory*, edited by Peter Hedström and Richard Swedberg, 1–31. Cambridge: Cambridge University Press.

Kalick, S. Michael, and Thomas E. Hamilton. 1986. "The Matching Hypothesis Reexamined." *Journal of Personality and Social Psychology* 51 (4): 673–682.

KC, Samir, Bilal Barakat, Anne Goujon, Vegard Skirbekk, Warren C. Sanderson, and Wolfgang Lutz. 2010. "Projection of Populations by Level of Educational Attainment, Age, and Sex for 120 Countries for 2005–2050." *Demographic Research* 22 (March): 383–472.

Kurland, Nancy B., and Lisa H. Pelled. 2000. "Passing the Word: Toward a Model of Gossip and Power in the Workplace." *The Academy of Management Review* 25 (2): 428–438.

Loch, Christoph H., Bernardo A. Huberman, and Suzanne Stout. 2000. "Status Competition and Performance in Work Groups." *Journal of Economic Behavior & Organization* 43 (1): 35–55.

Lutz, Wolfgang, Anne Goujon, Samir KC, and Warren C. Sanderson. 2007. "Reconstruction of Populations by Age, Sex and Level of Educational Attainment for 120 Countries for 1970–2000." *Vienna Yearbook of Population Research* 5: 193–235.

Macy, Michael W., and Andreas Flache. 2002. "Learning Dynamics in Social Dilemmas." *Proceedings of the National Academy of Sciences of the United States of America* 99 (suppl. 3): 7229–7236.

Macy, Michael W., and Andreas Flache. 2009. "Social Dynamics from the Bottom up: Agent-Based Models of Social Interaction." In *The Oxford Handbook of Analytical Sociology*, edited by Peter Hedström and Peter Bearman, 245–268. Oxford: Oxford University Press.

Mark, Noah P., Lynn Smith-Lovin, and Cecilia L. Ridgeway. 2009. "Why Do Nominal Characteristics Acquire Status Value? A Minimal Explanation for Status Construction." *American Journal of Sociology* 115 (3): 832–862.

Merton, Robert K. 1968. "The Matthew Effect in Science." *Science* 159 (3810): 56–63.

Milojević, Staša. 2014. "Principles of Scientific Research Team Formation and Evolution." *Proceedings of the National Academy of Sciences of the United States of America* 111 (11): 3984–3989.

Moss-Racusin, Corinne A., John F. Dovidio, Victoria L. Brescoll, Mark J. Graham, and Jo Handelsman. 2012. "Science Faculty's Subtle Gender Biases Favor Male Students." *Proceedings of the National Academy of Sciences of the United States of America* 109 (41): 16474–16479.

Paine, Robert. 1967. "What Is Gossip About? An Alternative Hypothesis." *Man* 2 (2): 278–285.

Raub, Werner, Vincent Buskens, and Marcel A. L. M. van Assen. 2011. "Micro-Macro Links and Microfoundations in Sociology." *The Journal of Mathematical Sociology* 35 (1–3): 1–25.

Rhee, Mooweon, and Pamela R. Haunschild. 2006. "The Liability of Good Reputation: A Study of Product Recalls in the U.S. Automobile Industry." *Organization Science* 17 (1): 101–117.

Ridgeway, Cecilia L. 1991. "The Social Construction of Status Value: Gender and Other Nominal Characteristics." *Social Forces* 70 (2): 367–386.

Ridgeway, Cecilia L. 2000. "The Formation of Status Beliefs: Improving Status Construction Theory." In *Advances in Group Processes*, edited by Shane R. Thye and Edward J. Lawler, 17:77–102. Bingley, West Yorkshire, England: Emerald Publishing.

Ridgeway, Cecilia L. 2011. *Framed by Gender: How Gender Inequality Persists in the Modern World*. Oxford, England: Oxford University Press.

Ridgeway, Cecilia L. 2014. "Why Status Matters for Inequality." *American Sociological Review* 79 (1): 1–16.

Ridgeway, Cecilia L., and James W. Balkwell. 1997. "Group Processes and the Diffusion of Status Beliefs." *Social Psychology Quarterly* 60 (1): 14–31.

Ridgeway, Cecilia L., Elizabeth H. Boyle, Kathy J. Kuipers, and Dawn T. Robinson. 1998. "How Do Status Beliefs Develop? The Role of Resources and Interactional Experience." *American Sociological Review* 63 (3): 331–350.

Ridgeway, Cecilia L., and Shelley J. Correll. 2006. "Consensus and the Creation of Status Beliefs." *Social Forces* 85 (1): 431–453.

Roebber, Paul J., and David M. Schultz. 2011. "Peer Review, Program Officers and Science Funding." *PLoS ONE* 6 (4): e18680.

Schelling, Thomas C. 1971. "Dynamic Models of Segregation." *The Journal of Mathematical Sociology* 1 (2): 143–186.

Schmader, Toni. 2002. "Gender Identification Moderates Stereotype Threat Effects on Women's Math Performance." *Journal of Experimental Social Psychology* 38 (2): 194–201.

Schofer, Evan, and John W. Meyer. 2005. "The Worldwide Expansion of Higher Education in the Twentieth Century." *American Sociological Review* 70 (6): 898–920.

Simon, Herbert A. 1982. *Models of Bounded Rationality*. Cambridge: MIT Press.

Skvoretz, John, and Thomas J. Fararo. 1996. "Status and Participation in Task Groups: A Dynamic Network Model." *American Journal of Sociology* 101 (5): 1366–1414.

Skvoretz, John, Katherine Faust, and Thomas J. Fararo. 1996. "Social Structure, Networks, and E-State Structuralism Models." *The Journal of Mathematical Sociology* 21 (1–2): 57–76.

Snijders, Tom A. B., and Roel J. Bosker. 1999. *Multilevel Analysis: An Introduction to Basic and Advanced Multilevel Modeling*. London: Sage.

Sorenson, Olav. 2014. "Status and Reputation: Synonyms or Separate Concepts?" *Strategic Organization* 12 (1): 62–69.

Squazzoni, Flaminio. 2012. *Agent-Based Computational Sociology*. Chichester: Wiley & Sons.

Squazzoni, Flaminio, and Károly Takács. 2011. "Social Simulation That 'Peers into Peer Review.'" *Journal of Artificial Societies and Social Simulation* 14 (4): 3.

Stewart, Daniel. 2005. "Social Status in an Open-Source Community." *American Sociological Review* 70 (5): 823–842.

Thorngate, Warren, and Wahida Chowdburry. 2014. "By the Numbers: Track Record, Flawed Reviews, Journal Space, and the Fate of Talented Authors." In *Advances in Social Simulation*, edited by Bogumil Kaminski and Grzegorz Koloch, 177–188. Berlin: Springer.

Traag, Vincent A., Paul Van Dooren, and Patrick De Leenheer. 2013. "Dynamical Models Explaining Social Balance and Evolution of Cooperation." *PLoS ONE* 8 (4): e60063.

Van Bavel, Jan, and André Grow. 2016. "Introduction: Agent-Based Modelling as a Tool to Advance Evolutionary Population Theory." In *Agent-Based Modelling in Population Studies: Concepts, Methods, and Applications*, edited by André Grow and Jan Van Bavel, 3–27. Cham: Springer International Publishing.

Watts, Christopher, and Nigel Gilbert. 2011. "Does Cumulative Advantage Affect Collective Learning in Science? An Agent-Based Simulation." *Scientometrics* 89 (1): 437–463.

Webster Jr., Murray, and Stuart J. Hysom. 1998. "Creating Status Characteristics." *American Sociological Review* 63 (3): 351–378.

Webster Jr., Murray, and James E. Driskell Jr. 1985. "Status Generalization." In *Status, Rewards, and Influence: How Expectations Organize Behavior*, edited by Joseph Berger and M. Zelditch Jr., 108–41. The Jossey-Bass Social and Behavioral Science Series. San Francisco: Jossey Bass.

Wilensky, Uri. 1999. *NetLogo*. Evanston, IL: Center for Connected Learning and Computer-Based Modeling, Northwestern University. http://ccl.northwestern.edu/netlogo/.

Wooldridge, Michael, and Nicholas R. Jennings. 1995. "Intelligent Agents: Theory and Practice." *Knowledge Engineering Review* 2: 115–132.

PART IV

# EVOLUTION, COMPETITION, AND GENDER

CHAPTER 14

# GOSSIP AND REPUTATION IN SMALL-SCALE SOCIETIES

## *A View from Evolutionary Anthropology*

### CHRISTOPHER BOEHM

## INTRODUCTION

HUMANS and humans alone are morally judgmental, and we are the only species equipped with symbolic language. As a result, it is no surprise that when people gossip about others who break rules, this is a human universal. In our natural history, gossip has always served as a social antidote to behaviors such as thievery, bullying, and sexual deviance, even as it has been positively associated with social bonding, social networks, and acquiring information.

Everyday gossiping is pleasurable in and of itself. Because we are a curious and sometimes prurient species, we enjoy forming partnerships to ferret out behaviors that others try to hide, and we also are a species that simply enjoys exchanging information on an intimate basis. Gossip is part of bonding, and it satisfies curiosity.

We also gossip because we share feelings like moral disapproval or disgust, or fear, or anger. We readily trust our kin, our friends, and our allies, and these are precisely the people we gossip with. When we talk with them about other people, it is social reputations that interest us, and it is through such private talk that public reputations are made and lost.

In this chapter I discuss gossiping in a variety of social and evolutionary contexts, including hunter-gatherers, tribesmen, peasants, and people living in modern societies, and especially including anthropologists, who use gossip as a tool necessary to their field work. The contexts range from an instance of murder in the community to public displays of gossip.

The idea that gossip serves as an indirect form of social control because people fear its sting is standard in sociology (e.g., Black, 1984; Giardini, Wittek, this volume), but here, in taking an evolutionary perspective, this perspective will be expanded upon as we examine gossip's equally important functions as a basis for moral consensus, a consensus that is critical for groups that have to deal with dangerous deviants.

Robin Dunbar's (1996) theory that gossip was preadapted in the form of great apes' grooming behavior will be considered, but the main evolutionary theory to be applied to gossip is from Richard D. Alexander, (1987), whose "selection by reputation" theory will link gossiping and its positive reputational effects with the evolution of human altruism.

## Defining Gossip and Reputation

As an anthropological linguist, John Haviland (1977b, 1998) has defined gossip simply as stories about others who are absent (see also Gilmore, 1978). This parsimonious descriptive definition will help focus this anthropological treatment of gossiping behavior on a core feature of gossiping, which is aimed at privately exchanging insightful social information. This can be enjoyable, or socially useful, or both.

The usefulness of gossiping to individuals is that it helps our everyday life (and also our Darwinian fitness) by telling us whom to trust and cooperate with, and which free-riders to avoid. The usefulness to groups is that it informs the identification of deviants and the application of moral sanctions, which in terms of multilevel selection (Wilson and Wilson, 2007) may profoundly affect our biological evolution (Kniffin and Wilson, 2010).

Without such a lean definition, "gossiping" comprises an unwieldy and sprawling domain. Some scholars, including those who study modern organizations, look mainly to the information content of gossiping, and see it as a network for the general exchange of social knowledge about the workplace (Handleman, 1973; Kniffin and Wilson, 2005; see also Beersma, Van Kleef, and Dijkstra, this volume). Others (e.g., Gluckman, 1963) associate it with scandal and rumor-mongering (for a modern discussion, see de Backer, Van den Bulck, Fisher, and Ouvrein, this volume), yet see it as functioning to enhance small-group cohesion and cooperation. Still others (e.g., Paine, 1967) look to individual self-advancement as people try to enhance their interests by manipulating information (e.g., Besnier, 1989; McAndrew et al. 2007) that impinges on their reputation.

The uses of gossip in everyday life are many, and so are the emphases of those who study it. However, Haviland's precise definition captures the essence of gossiping privately and its relation to public reputation. To expand a little, gossiping is a careful means of talking judgmentally about absent others, including information that might upset or anger or embarrass them. Because this private activity involves a relationship of trusting confidentiality (Burt and Knez, 1995), people can build rather complete social and moral dossiers on others in the group.

It is largely through this surreptitious practice that people in primary, face-to-face groups are quietly sorted out by their reputations. At the same time some anthropologists link gossiping to public events in which private gossip information surfaces for group consumption as personal disputes are aired and hopefully are resolved (e.g., Arno, 1980), and as people go after deviants verbally in public (e.g., Wiessner, 2005, 2014).

Reputation is nicely defined by Barrow (1976, p. 107) in her anthropological discussion of a small community she lived in in Barbados, and her definition extends beyond morality:

> The fund of knowledge concerning a particular individual, which is shared by others and evaluated according to their moral code, is his reputation. It is not an innate personal quality, but rather the opinion of him shared by others. Reputations are derived from all aspects of an individual that are known about, including his appearance, wealth, occupation, behaviour in social relations, manner, accent, deportment, family background and so on.

Here, it will be chiefly the moral dimensions ("behavior in social relations," and "deportment") that will concern us, for gossiping is intimately connected with moral regulation. In fact, it is viewed by sociologists (e.g., Black, 1984; Feinberg et al. 2012) as an indirect mechanism of social control: people behave themselves partly because they have consciences, partly because they fear punishment, and partly because they simply don't want others talking about them (Boehm, 2012). In addition, people everywhere try to present themselves to others in a favorable light (Goffman, 1959), morally and in other ways, and for many this may be a corrective against gossip as an insidious activity that can destroy moral reputations.

Gossip can be about nonmoral as well as moral traits, and it can involve moral praise as well as criticism. However, as an anthropologist who has collected gossip for years on end, I can tell you that much of the time gossip and reputation are heavily involved with issues of right and wrong, and that everywhere it is deviant behavior that occupies center stage.

# A COMPETITIVE SPECIES

Haviland (1977a) has linked gossiping to competition. Whether we live in cities or in hunting bands, the immediate social matrix in which gossiping takes place is always competitive. This is because humans are innately given to dominance, submission, and the formation of hierarchies (Boehm, 1999), and this includes rivalry over reputations.

Curiously, we often are geared to be selfishly envious of others who reduce our wealth or power or well-being by competing with us—even when such competition exists only in our imaginations. This is very much the case with peasant societies (Foster, 1972) like the Mayan speakers studied by Haviland, where envy is endemic even with respect to goods that objectively are not in short supply. It is for a wide variety of reasons that we need to understand our rivals, and especially our active enemies and their potential to hurt us (Hess and Hagen, this volume). And it is by gossiping about social reputations that this is accomplished. Moral deviants, who are mostly opportunistic free-riders, are a major focus.

As members of a cunning species, we must be on the lookout for those who would trick us. Further, in the small, unpoliced egalitarian communities in which we humans evolved, people also had to keep abreast of the doings of bullies who wanted more than their fair share of food, mating partners, or power. In facing these opportunistic and sometimes dangerous moral deviants, the potential victims needed to actively arrive at a consensus. This was accomplished privately, in stages, as people shared all the relevant information they knew about with a succession of gossip partners, and gradually built an accurate and shared picture of what they were up against. If this led to a group consensus, then they could act collectively to curb the malefactor.

All of this required communication, first in doing the necessary "police work" to get at the facts, and then to arrive at a consensus as to what should be done about a thief, a bully, or a committer of incest. Especially when the deviant in question was dangerous, it was a major advantage to be able to gather the information and make a decision on the sly, without the deviant's having any idea about this. For this reason and many others, gossiping has had to be surreptitious, and it still is, in today's bands.

As a result of this continuous evaluative talking, group members everywhere develop social reputations that are good, bad, or mixed. People are aware that they have reputations, even though they may not know exactly what others are thinking, and from personal experience they know that gossip between trusted friends can readily become uncharitable. Because there is no way to testify on one's own behalf in this secretive court of public opinion, most try hard to present themselves publically in a favorable light. However, A psychopathic bully simply may not care, and as a result his group may surprise him by engaging in capital punishment.

# An Unusual Anthropological Case History

Fortunately, very few readers will have been close to a murder. However, when I was a graduate student in the late 1960s I was right in the middle of a homicide situation, sharing the experience with dozens of other graduate students. This killing took place in Cambridge, Massachusetts, in 1969, the night before the annual winter qualifying examination in Harvard's Anthropology Department.

A female archaeology graduate student named Jane Britton was murdered that night in her apartment near Harvard Square. She was bludgeoned cruelly with a heavy cutting object, and we were told that her half-covered naked body was placed on the bed in her apartment precisely in the manner of a Persian ritual burial. She had just come back from doing field work in Iran, and a book left open on a table showed a page that depicted just such a burial. Typically of archaic Persian burials, a substance like red ochre was sprinkled all around the bedroom. The police were mystified, while Harvard's small anthropological community was in shock.

It is worth noting that this community was about the same size as a very large hunting band. For the next several months, all we anthropology graduate students did was talk about the likely suspects, in an atmosphere of real fear. We were all but certain there was a murderer in our midst, for obviously the killer was sophisticated archaeologically. Our curiosity was almost as strong as our fear, and unfortunately the Cambridge police were never able to solve the case, or even line up a prime suspect although there were some lie-detector tests. The killer remained in circulation, and as the nonstop gossiping proceeded, people kept adding in new information. In the newspapers a series of police interrogations indicated that Ms. Brinton had had several recent boyfriends, and with multiple logical murder candidates our sense of general paranoia was intensified.

The likely suspects occupied center stage in our private discussions, which had to be very cautious because we knew better than to engage in such speculation in the presence of someone who might tell the target—possibly a murderer—about our suspicions. The safest gossip sessions were dyadic, with trusted friends, but sometimes they took place in groups of three or four people who knew one another well enough to form an intimate clique; in larger groups people were extremely guarded in what they said, or they spoke not at all.

Fear compelled us to talk, but the same fear constrained our talking because we were dealing with a murderer. Much of the gossiping had to do with who had been called in for police interviews: that person's life, and whatever was known of the person's relationship with Jane Brinton, would then be dissected endlessly. New information would be added as each of us talked with a nervous succession of close friends, and we all became amateur detectives, desperately weighing the various possibilities.

It would be unseemly for me to go into any of the specifics, naming police suspects who are still living or other possible suspects we speculated about, but our gossip networks alerted us each time a new person became of interest to the police, or whenever someone came up with a new fact. For instance, Jane was struck with a heavy sharp object, and missing from her apartment was an archaeological stone object that might have been used. It turned out that this "clue" led nowhere.

Our paranoia was not helped when exactly a month later, to the day, a 50-year-old widow living in Cambridge was also killed by bludgeoning and had covers draped over her like an Iranian burial. In both cases the murderer seemed to have easy access to the apartments. Eventually, the fact that the new victim was not an anthropologist led us to believe that perhaps the original serial killer was not of our community, but we also had to consider copycats.

New information was the straw we grasped at. Half a century later I can say that we were desperately frightened of the potential deviant in our midst and that living with all the suspicions, and endlessly gossiping about them, seriously damaged the fabric of our community. Several people otherwise in good social standing were suspected of a horrible crime, and I am sure they still bear the scars.

Had we all lived in a small, self-contained community like a hunting band, the large-city anonymity that shielded Jane Britton's killer might have made it possible to at least arrive at a very small short list, for in hunting bands people usually know who a killer is or can easily guess. As it was, we found ourselves in a desperate informational limbo, which of course intensified our gossiping.

At the end of several months we were left with several competing hypotheses. One was that both murders were by a crazy archaeologist or perhaps a cultural anthropologist. Another was that the second time it was a copycat. The third was that one or both murders were by a non-anthropologist who cleverly used information learned from his victim about Persian burials to throw the police off of his trail. Half a century later I am inclined to believe the latter, which helps explain the police failure. But this will never eradicate the damage done to the reputations of the several known police suspects.

## GOSSIP'S NATURAL HISTORY

I have told of this long-ago event because it so beautifully exemplifies gossip at work in one of its most important and necessarily private phases. From time to time earlier humans in their groups had to deal with serious immoral acts, and some culprits were obvious while others (mainly thieves) were able to carefully conceal themselves. In small indigenous bands, single homicides were quite frequent statistically (Knauft, 1991), and they were dealt with by close relatives taking revenge. Serial killers were rarer, and they galvanized entire groups to bring on capital punishment (Boehm, 2014).

In a band of thirty people, usually such a killer was readily identified, so gossiping was not often needed as detective work. However, it was vitally important as a means of quietly arriving at a decision in favor of killing such a menace (Boehm, 2016), which could be done only by ambush after a group consensus was reached. In the case of thieves, the band also would have to engage in extensive discreet gossiping, with the hope of identifying them to ostracize or eliminate them.

To summarize, gossip is necessary to social control, and social control has been practiced by humans for at least tens of thousands of years (Boehm, 2012). Gossip provides the culpability information on which group actions like shaming, ostracism, and capital punishment are based, and it also enables a group to quietly and safely arrive at a consensus about taking such action.

## HOW GOSSIPING ORIGINATED

Several decades ago, evolutionary psychologist Robin Dunbar (1996, 2004) took a new tack in explaining the origins of language. He suggested that grooming partnerships, common in most primates, provided a special, intimate means for ancestral social bonding that was strongly innate. As language began to evolve in our species, this intimate, prosocial type of relationship evolved from a mutually pleasurable and trusting physical relationship to a similar relationship of trust and social bonding that was based on the symbolic exchange of social information.

This theory not only helps explain the origin of language, but it also provides an hypothesis for the origin of gossiping. Implicit in Dunbar's theory and that of other evolutionists (e.g., Barkow, 1992; Ingrahm, 2014; Shermer, 2004; Wilson et al. 2000) is the position that gossiping is well-prepared by genes. This jibes nicely with the fact that all humans appear to engage in gossip, and that we learn to do it so easily.

To help us place gossiping in a natural history context, there are also some general cultural or evolutionary studies by anthropologists and others (e.g., Abraham, 1971; Foster, 2004; Handelman, 1973; Machin and Lancaster, 1974; Merry, 1984; Pinker et al. 2008; Spacks, 1985; Wilson, 1974; Wilson et al. 1975). In addition, gossip information available from ethnography includes a wide variety of nonliterate cultures and specific research foci (see Besnier, this volume). Relevant nonliterate field sites cover the Arctic (Briggs, 1970); the Americas (Barrow, 1976; Bricker, 1980; Brison, 1992; Geertz, 2011; Haviland, 1977a,b; Martinez, 2005; McCall, 1979; Van Vleet, 2003); Oceania and Melanesia (Besnier, 1993; Brenneis, 1984; Brison, 1992; McCall, 1979; Nachman, 1986); and Africa (Amster, 2004; Gluckman, 1968; Rasmussen, 1991; Wiessner, 2005, 2014). In addition, anthropologists focusing on gossip have studied small literate societies in Europe (Gilmore, 1978; Zinovieff, 1987) and also the Mafia (Chattoe and Hamill, 2005; Gambetta, 1994), where serious errors in gossip information have cost important people their lives.

# A UNIVERSAL TOOL FOR CULTURAL ANTHROPOLOGY

As a graduate student I first engaged in gossip professionally when I went out into the field on the Navajo Reservation to work for a large research project collecting case histories of mental illness. Later, when I did my own field work on ethical values in a Serbian mountain tribe in Montenegro, I realized that cultural anthropologists literally make their living by being "professional gossips." (My third field work site was at Gombe National Park in Tanzania, where the apes I studied gossiped not a whit and a wholly different approach to field work was necessary.)

During the Cold War I lived for two years in an isolated Serbian mountain tribe in Montenegro, and as language proficiency advanced and indigenous familiarity with the American outsider grew in this Socialist Republic, what began as a highly constrained experience of hearing just a little about what others were up to became intimate, with people who were becoming good friends confiding in me more and more. Previously unanswered questions finally were being answered, and anthropological insights were growing accordingly.

Anthropologists sometimes contend that there are no secrets at all in these small, watchful communities, but in my experience there were. In spite of the way that intimate secrets so often managed to become public, there were instances in which this "leakage" simply did not take place. In one case, I heard of a man's catching his wife *in flagrante*, something he confided only to one person, an old woman who, after knowing me for well over a year and seeing that I was discreet in keeping confidences, confided this to me, abjuring me to tell no one. (Today, the parties are no longer alive.)

# GOSSIP CHAINS

My reputation for discretion also led a young man to confide in me about sleeping with his patrilateral cousin, a very serious business in the tribe; he wanted my advice on how to cope with the situation, and, knowing the likely tribal reaction to what was considered a serious degree of incest, I suggested that the two of them emigrate, get married, and lose themselves in a faraway city. I also reassured him that first cousins marry all the time without genetic defects.

I promised to tell no one, but then as a careful gossip I told the 77-year-old woman who was my best informant about this, the one who had confided similarly in me. I assumed she would tell no one, and I am all but certain she did not. However, on considering my own behavior I realized something about gossip, and why so many people's darkest secrets do become known. This insight can be diachronically modeled as a gossip chain:

1. A man A confides something highly controversial about a third party to female relative B, abjuring B to tell no one. B, having learned in this case that the person has had an illegal abortion, agrees.
2. However, B implicitly trusts her best friend, C, so she passes on the tidbit, abjuring her strongly to tell no one. C agrees.
3. C promptly tells her boyfriend D, and naturally D promises not to tell. But several months later they break up.
4. Later D tells his best friend, E, and because D doesn't know the woman being gossiped about very well, he doesn't even insist on E's silence even though it is tacitly assumed.
5. E similarly passes along the information to F, a well-connected gossip who has no tie to the woman being gossiped about, and within a few days the entire village knows that she has had an abortion. In a patrifocal Montenegrin tribe, such information can be profoundly damaging to a woman's reputation.

What is fascinating about this type of communication chain is that especially early on in the gossiping chain, the parties imparting this damaging information thought they were properly guarding both the woman's reputation, and the confidentiality of a close gossiping relationship. Thus, the leakage is unintentional.

# REPUTATIONS

The patrifocal Montenegro I studied was like the Middle East (see Awwad, 2001), for women's behavior was placed under a special microscope and the reputational conse-quences of gossip could become seriously damaging. Among these Serbs there were basically two kinds of reputation. One was ascribed by birth and it had to do with how good or bad your clan's name was. The other was earned, and some prime criteria were honesty, being hardworking, sexual virtue if you were a woman, and hospitality and courageousness if you were a man. Because much of the gossiping had a nosy, prying air to it, people intensely resented such talk because virtually everybody had at least something small to hide.

In talking with one young man who hadn't married, he told me that "the village" was ever watchful and that if anyone saw you in an illicit act, this would go right into the grapevine to hurt your reputation. The man in question confided that he was having an affair with an unmarried woman whose reputation was very much at stake, and they had to be extremely careful in such a watchful community. Their houses were widely separated, and when things were right for a visit she would lean a rake to one side of the barn door as a signal to the boyfriend, faraway down the mountainside. I never heard any gossip about the two of them, so I assumed the rake-deception was working.

People who had much less to hide were still wary and resentful of gossip. In a former warrior culture in which personal social standing and honor were still a major focus, they disliked the nosy intention of others to intrude against their privacy and damage their reputations. This animus against village gossips became especially apparent in the case of a man who gossiped weirdly by local standards. Growing up he obviously had learned about the value of gossip to others, but then, in trying to ingratiate himself with others, he took a wrong turn. In social meetings with up to a dozen people present, he would launch into gossip that a normal person would reserve for highly confidential exchanges. This man was called a *prepricalica*, or a hyper-gossip, and he was detested for making things normally talked only in private utterly public. What he was doing to people's reputations was monstrous by local standards, and everyone hated him. But he was unaware of this.

As anthropological investigators who depended on gossip, my wife and I had friends in common, and we also had friends of our own, our special informants. We watched with interest as our originally cautious friends and neighbors gradually opened up. Building trust takes time, and had my field stay lasted just one year instead of two, there was a great deal of information I would never have known about.

Two things were immediately apparent as I put gossip to work as a tool for gaining cultural information. One was that people enjoyed gossiping and engaged in it unself-consciously. The other, obviously, was that they feared gossip when it focused on them personally. Gossip was a continual threat, and they referred to the *selo* (the scattered local settlement) as though it were a single thinking organism, an inimical community intent on ferreting out their deepest secrets.

During my two years of fieldwork, there was one incident that was somewhat reminiscent of the Jane Britton murder. In the tribe, most of the houses stood alone with no close neighbors, and a schoolteacher's wife left her house for an hour, having looked at their stash of money just before she left. When she returned, it was gone. Two obvious suspects lived nearby, one with a less upright moral reputation and one with a very good one; both issued denials. It was also possible that someone else had simply come to the door, and found it unlocked.

As with the Britton murder the result was a perfect mystery. For the next several weeks people talked about nothing else, to no avail. The intensity with which these informal inquiries were carried out was striking, but easy to understand because people living in isolated houses feel especially vulnerable to thievery. As in the case of Jane Britton, no culprit was ever settled upon, but this wasn't from lack of trying.

Afterward, there were lingering doubts about the reputations of these two closest neighbors, even though there were major differences of reputation, and even though at least one of them had to be innocent. Similar reputational damage was done to the Britton suspects, for gossip systems have no built-in protections for the innocent.

## REPUTATION AND ENVY

There has been one great (and rather predictable) debate on gossip and its social uses in nonliterate societies. Max Gluckman, a British sociological functionalist who did his field work in Africa, made the case that gossiping served to unite and integrate societies by backing up mores that made for cooperative cohesion (Gluckman, 1963). That is the type of argument that functionalists always make, and it is an important contribution. However, Robert Paine (1967), who did his fieldwork in the Arctic, focused on the individual, not on the group, to argue that gossiping behavior was a way for individuals to advance their own personal interests. That, too, is apparent from the findings of ethnographers in the field.

What these divergent opinions represent is an ancient type of academic game in which a divide is created, in this case one between methodological individualism and methodological collectivism, and then, in my cynical view, a prominent, unresolvable debate proceeds to enhance the reputations of the debaters. As with most of these tussles, it turns out that neither side is right or wrong; they are picking favorite abstractions to represent different aspects of the whole cloth of life—and then are arguing about them as though something like "the truth" were at stake. Fortunately many anthropologists have remained untouched by this polarizing argument, and here we cover some of their efforts in the realm of reputation and gossip.

As a linguist particularly adept at learning native languages, Haviland (1977a) published a highly descriptive book four decades ago on gossip and reputation in Zinacantan. This is the most detailed and theoretically sophisticated linguistic treatment of private gossip undertaken in a nonliterate society, and the focus was colorfully obscene stories about absent others, which damaged their reputations.

Not surprisingly, Haviland tells us that

> ...Zinacantecos have a morbid sense of privacy. While being fascinated with events across the fence, they strive to keep other prying eyes and ears away from their own affairs.    (Haviland, 1977b, p. 186)

Competition figures prominently in this analysis, and such peasant societies seem to be especially prone to think competitively.

Anthropologist George Foster (1972) speaks of the image of the limited good, meaning that people in peasant communities are especially prone to look at desirable goods as being scarce, even when that is not the case. Thus, in patrifocal Montenegro if a neighbor has a son born this is resented competitively—even though one's neighbor's having a son does not affect one's own chances of lucking out. When gossip informs a Montenegrin about how others are doing, one dimension of this talk is envy. The same is true in Zinacantan, while generally an enviously zero-sum view of human affairs seems less prominent with hunter-gatherers (e.g., Wiessner, 2005).

## GOSSIP AND WITCHCRAFT

Often empty witchcraft accusations are based on envy (e.g., Kluckhohn, 1962), but in many nonliterate societies individuals actually try to kill others using sorcery and others believe this is possible. Sorcerers are basically shamanistic healers (socially defined as altruists) who go wrong, very wrong. Good shamans may be able to diagnose such acts, but gossiping also serves as an agency of discovery because sorcerers and "witches" operate stealthily. In small societies they can be difficult to identify, and the same is true always of thieves and sorcerers, and occasionally of a multiple killer who is unusually elusive.

Studies on the North American Hopi Indians by Cox (1970) and Geertz (2011), along with Bleek (1976) with the Kiwahu of Ghana and Besnier (1993) on the Nukulaelae in Oceania, all deal with these dynamics of identifying sneaky, supernaturally connected deviants. Just as with an unknown murderer like the killer of Jane Britton, a self-concealing sorcerer or witch poses a formidable threat in people's minds. Once the local group becomes convinced of a sorcerer's identity and potency, capital punishment may be next (Boehm, 2014).

## PERSONAL USES OF GOSSIP

Gossip often becomes self-serving (Paine, 1967), and because people choose what to divulge or ask about in gossip sessions, they may become inventive as they try to help their own reputation or hurt someone else's. An example is the Makah, hierarchical foragers on the Northwest Coast who were assimilating and competing for land claims when Colson (1953) interviewed them. They manipulated the facts they gave her accordingly.

Such manipulation is little investigated, but there are a few studies (e.g., Besnier, 1989; McAndrew et al. 2007; Rosnow, 2001; Rosnow and Fine, 1976; Semman et al. 2004). Anecdotally, from my own experience in American culture, I remember once "planting" a piece of information useful to me, by imparting it to an individual I knew to be a compulsive gossip who was lax in protecting his sources. I actually abjured him to tell nobody, knowing this would increase the value of the information in his eyes and ensure its transmission. This was a trick I learned in Montenegro.

# When Gossip Becomes Public

A great deal of a small community's dirty laundry will be known but remain unspoken publicly, but in some cases gossip information may be used openly as people engage in verbal disputes using real slings and arrows in going after each other's reputations. Again, this fits with Paine's (1967) methodologically individualist approach. On the positive side, funeral eulogies often make public the noncontroversial, positive information that people gossip about, and prosocial aspects of gossiping have received some attention (e.g., Ben-Ze'ev, 1994). Negative private knowledge may also be exposed deliberately through customs that provide a channel for conflict to be expressed openly in ways that help the community.

Among the Mayans studied by Haviland, Bricker (1980) points out that elements of colorfully derogatory private gossip may be employed unabashedly in ridiculing someone privately, but in public disputes the degree of ridicule at least is toned down. In a Spanish town, Gilmore (1982) tells how during the Fiesta of Gossip, people wearing costumes openly make slanderous accusations based on private gossip that they would rarely make otherwise.

In Montenegro, where because of a warrior background there persisted a robust tradition of singing heroic epics, I recorded the antisocial custom of surreptitiously writing a mock epic, rife with slanderous ridicule, about an enemy. Copies were placed at crossroads, where they would be found and carefully passed around and read privately to small audiences. Montenegrin gossip often included delightful ridiculing of subjects in private, and these antisocial public mock epics actually caricatured this. They were aimed at destroying social reputations, and surely they had some effect. There were always guesses about the authors, but that was all. These rare mock epics made public the ridicule that normally took place in private.

On the positive side, when conflicts in Fiji were openly adjudicated, information normally reserved for private gossiping was made public in a prosocial attempt to resolve interpersonal conflicts (Arno, 1979). Airing such disputes amounts to an informal legal procedure, and the prosocial aim is to clear the air and resolve the conflict.

# Reputations and Evolution

We know for certain that humans were "behaviorally modern" (Shea, 2007) by 45,000 years ago, and this figure might easily be increased to 80,000. To see what people were doing socially back then, we can carefully select contemporary hunter-gatherers who would fit with that Late-Pleistocene epoch, see what they are doing today, and project this into the past. We know that earlier humans were keen on social reputations, and that these reputations were shaped by gossiping, for this can be established simply by working backwards from today's ethnography. Like all other humans, egalitarian hunter-gatherers all gossip and attend to one another's reputations, and their Late-Pleistocene forebears surely did the same.

Evolutionary biologist Richard D. Alexander put this basic human capacity to gossip to an interesting theoretical use when he developed a new theory to resolve the evolutionary paradox of altruism. We know from studies of nonliterate people that humans everywhere are given not only to selfish behavior but also to giving away some of their resources to nonrelatives at a cost to themselves and that, genetically, such loser-traits should be selected out. But, in fact, they aren't.

Alexander (1979, 1987) created *indirect reciprocity* theory, based on selection by reputation. The idea is that if someone in a small band is unusually generous, gossiping ensures an exceptionally good reputation, which, in turn, will result in these altruists being chosen by others as partners in marriage or economic cooperation. This aids their fitness so substantially that the costs of being altruistic are more than defrayed. This explains how altruists can afford to help unrelated others even if there is no prospect of their being paid back directly for their services.

Alexander's hypothesis has been tested in the laboratory (e.g., Sommerfeld et al. 2007), and it was found to work in the case of Aché foragers in South America (Gurven, 2004): individuals who on a daily basis were productive and also unusually generous were given significantly more help when they fell on hard times than people who normally were stingy. Thus, being known as unusually generous has many payoffs, but it all depends on gossip and reputation. There are other studies of reputation and its evolution that connect it directly with social norms (e.g., Dos Santos et al. 2011; Engert, 2006).

# Gossip in Organizations

It would appear that gossip and reputation are so natural to human life that they remain important not only in small, face-to-face communities like bands or modern neighborhoods, but also in workplaces and, more broadly, in business organizations—a topic covered by Beersma, Van Kleef and Dijkstra in this volume. James March (1988), a founder of the study of organization behavior, led this movement, and as evolutionary theory became increasingly popular, a number of studies followed (e.g., Wittek and Wielers, 1998), including a study of the trust component in gossiping (Ellwardt et al. 2012c).

The more empirical studies have focused on the articulation of gossiping behavior with social networks (Ellwardt et al. 2012 a,b; Grosser et al. 2012; Kurland and Hope, 2000; Michelson et al. 2010; Noon and Delbridge, 1993; Shaw et al. 2011; Tasgin and Haluk, 2012), while theoretical studies mostly have an evolutionary emphasis (e.g., Kniffen and Wilson, 2005; Nicholson, 2001; Semman et al. 2005; Suzuki and Eizo, 2005). One finding is that gossip transmits a great deal of information over networks that can become quite extended, and that this is vital to staying informed in business settings, while personal reputations also are shaped by gossiping.

# Media Gossip

The capacity for gossiping evolved in small hunting bands, in which men were away from camp for days at a time in pursuit of large game and women were out gathering much of the time. As a result, people often were absent when significant events took place in their bands, and the only way to accurately keep abreast of group affairs was to learn about them through constant gossiping.

Be it in a hunting band or in a modern workplace such as a general hospital, gossip always has a similar feel to it. Information is transmitted or exchanged privately in an atmosphere of trust and confidentiality, and it is oriented to understanding reputations as an aid to navigating socially. In modern large-scale societies, one-on-one gossiping is less important to society's everyday functioning, for we can leave the serious detective work and law enforcement to the police. However, the pleasure principle involved in exchanging candid information continues, and gossip information still helps us navigate our immediate social milieus. The internet provides a new avenue for this (see Picci, this volume; Snijders, Matzat, this volume; Solove, 2007).

As our gossiping behavior has enabled us to adapt to modern life (Barkow, 1992), this has led to a new and major art form. Not only do we engage in traditional gossip at work or over the backyard fence, but we also watch soap operas of various types. Originally the soaps were created for a generation of traditional female home-makers who were socially isolated, and they provided fantasy communities with diverse characters that viewers could become involved with and keep track of, just as male and female foragers do with their real peers within the band.

Eventually, the prime-time soap evolved and brought men solidly into the picture (see also De Backer, Van den Bulck, Fisher, Ouvrein, this volume). There may be stereo-types of gossip being the province of women (see Levin and Amluke, 1985), but males gossip everywhere, perhaps equaling or surpassing women in this respect, and lavishly produced prime-time serials like *Dallas* and *Dynasty* led the way in bringing the soap medium not only to all of America, including both males and females, but also to much of the world (see Davis, Vaillancourt, Arnocky, Doyel, this volume).

The tradition continues as new serials are created, for instance the artistically excellent six-year *Justified* series, produced by Elmore Leonard, which provides an intriguingly intimate view of the ordinary (often criminal) folk in Harlan County, Kentucky. It is no accident that there have been such a variety of these serialized shows, for each can answer the same needs that gossiping does in a different situational context, like in a hospital or a crime lab. They offer a series of fascinating communities to keep track of, combined with an in-depth knowledge of each of the main characters.

What all of these "soaps" share in common is that the social life of a forager-sized community is traced over time. Count the number of characters in a typical serial, and this will jibe with the number of people in a small to medium-sized hunting band. For instance, a cast picture for *The Young and the Restless* included twenty-four actors, which matches the number of people in a typical, smallish nomadic band (Hill et al. 2011).

In watching these shows, one reaps the benefits of gossiping without actually engaging in it or being vulnerable to it. People in soaps exchange intimate information privately all the time, and in effect this allows the viewer to eavesdrop on other people's gossip. The audience's birds-eye view of the community in question is paralleled, in a hunting band, by people who stay abreast of everyone else's doings by gossiping. In talking constantly about people's doings and reputations and exchanging such intimate information, they can remain almost equally well-informed.

As one engages vicariously with one of these soap-opera communities, one comes to know reputations: there are bad guys and altruists, there are individuals driven by ambition and passive doormats, and there are a variety of other personality types, including individuals who are haplessly naïve and generous, who contrast with unbelievably ruthless scheming villains. The chief focus always seems to be on moral issues of character and behavior, not on a story line.

A friend of mine who had a long career in soap opera began as a nice little Italian girl who served as a doormat for an over-aggressive architect, not the most challenging role for an actress. She left soap opera, but then returned to a different show when she was offered a more interesting role, playing an arch-bitch. In visiting her set in Brooklyn, I learned from the director that soap operas are written only two weeks in advance, and that viewer mail is carefully vetted to see where the writers should go next. In short, like gossiping, these daytime soap operas are keyed closely to the ongoing interests of the participants.

As societies became larger, and literate, some of our yearning for gossiping information was satisfied by written gossip columns in newspapers (Walter Winchell and Hedda Hopper were pioneering classics), which eventually were transformed into tawdry newspapers and television shows that made public any dirt they could dig up on movie stars or other highly recognizable people. It is digging up such dirt that gives gossip a bad name, and this goes back long before the appearance of the tabloids.

Newspapers like the *National Inquirer* appeal to the intrusive, prurient interests of people as nosy gossips, but they also move the information out of the private domain to make everything painfully public (McAndrew and Milenkovic, 2002). Traditional, discreet gossip determines reputations and also protects them. Tabloid gossip willfully damages them, under the protection of modern legal norms.

Nonliterate people know the pain and stress and conflict that would result from carrying on intimate, probing gossip in public and, as has been seen, if they do bring things out into the open, they usually have a reason. The fact that malicious gossips who gratuitously stir up trouble in their bands can be socially sanctioned explains why hunter-gatherers may be more "civilized" than literate people, with their tabloids and the untold emotional suffering they bring about.

## Gossiping and Norm Enforcement

In closing we will briefly examine an ethnographic snapshot of moralistic public talking in a band society, a hunter-gatherer group that increasingly is acculturating and engaging with alcohol consumption. This will help flesh out the points made earlier about gossiping, deviant behavior, and reputation. Polly Wiessner (2005) has worked with Kalahari foragers (!Kung-speakers) for upwards of 30 years, and she has published in detail about their conversations as they take place publicly in sizable groups. This isn't gossip by our definition, but it definitely relates to people's reputations, and we may assume that the publicly exposed information is arrived at by means of private gossiping.

The average number of persons participating was 7.2, and these public conversations often had to do with deviant actions that were detrimental to the personal reputations of deviants. There were more than 300 conversations recorded in all, and the criticism of deviants could move from mocking put-downs and mild, face-to-face verbal criticism, to harsh criticism that could lead to serious action, including ostracism.

I have already indicated some of the antisocial behaviors that stir gossiping, and elsewhere I have provided some statistics for Pleistocene-type contemporary foragers and the major types of behavior they punish (Boehm, 2012). My survey included bullying, thieving, sexual crimes, and taboo violations. For her Bushman groups, Wiessner quantifies the behaviors that receive open verbal rebukes (taken as a relatively mild kind of social punishment) or more serious punitive action, and we would expect *private* gossiping to follow similar channels, in terms of which deviants have been discussed.

Based on fourteen weeks of recording, she identifies failure in kin obligations, patterns of being stingy or lazy, and big-shot behavior as statistically prominent offenses, along with trouble-making, reclusive behavior, and inappropriate sexual behavior. Jealousy reared its head, but envy over possessions was a less-frequent cause for censure. Big-shot types were criticized for bullying, not individually but by entire groups who dared to do so, and Wiessner also counts repeated stinginess, greed, or laziness as publicly disapproved free-riding behaviors.

These less-aggressive "cheating" free-riders comprised only 14 percent of the punishments, but if we count big-shot behavior also as a means of taking free rides (Boehm, 2012), the overall percentage of punishments directed at opportunistic free-riders rises to 26 percent. All of this punishment begins at the verbal level, and often it persists over time so the implications for reputation are obvious. They can become quite serious, as when highly resented antisocial behaviors like not sharing meat are concerned.

Wiessner found, importantly, that punishment, per se, did not further damage a person's reputation. However, the more morally unacceptable the deed, the greater the reputation loss. Wiessner also lists malicious gossip as a cause for group aggression, and this jibes with the preceding analysis in that not only do people fear being gossiped about personally, but also the malicious gossips that stir up trouble for everyone. In one faraway case, a town in Colombia actually tried to formally outlaw gossiping for this reason (Martinez, 2005).

# CONCLUSIONS

If talking about people privately is God's gift to ethnography, gossip and reputation are natural selection's gift to humanity. Gossip and reputation go together, and they place humans in a social niche that is extraordinary in its being involved with symbols and morality. While gossiping can be compared with grooming as a physical activity, no other species recognizes symbolically elaborated reputations or gossips about them. The result is an efficient exchange of information that aids individuals socially. It also enables groups to detect deviance when this is necessary—and to quietly arrive at decisions to ostracize or sometimes kill intractable or dangerous deviants.

People have egos so they care about their reputations, and they also reckon the reputations of others. They gossip accordingly but refrain from making all of their insights public—unless they work for the tabloids, or temporarily if they have a Festival of Gossip. It is because gossiping is essentially private that it cumulatively provides people with social information that is usually accurate and hence useful, as well as always pleasurable in the exchange.

Gossiping should be included on any list of behaviors that make us human, and I have tried to make clear the individual benefits that stem from gossiping even as I have emphasized gossip's benefit to group processes involved in cooperation. An important manifestation of this is the universal practice of moralistic group social control, which gossip informs.

The natural history of gossip and reputation is open to future research, and Alexander's theory of indirect reciprocity is one area in which empirical research should be able to enhance the theorizing, for this important evolutionary theory is keyed to reputations, which are formed in the crucible of gossiping. With respect to Dunbar's "grooming" approach, further study could clarify the relations between gossiping behavior and later stages of language evolution, while in the case of moral origins the functions of gossiping in today's small human foraging groups merit further study because Late-Pleistocene humans were very likely to have had similar behaviors. Only half of the evolutionary story has been told so far, and the story is fascinating.

## References

Abraham, Roger D. 1971. "A Performance-Centered Approach to Gossip." *Man* 5: 290–301.

Alexander, Richard D. 1979. *Darwinism and Human Affairs.* Seattle: University of Washington Press.

Alexander, Richard D. 1987. *The Biology of Moral Systems.* New York: Aldine de Gruyter.

Amster, Matthew H. 2004. "The 'Many Mouths' of Community: Gossip and Social Interaction among the Kelabit of Borneo." *Asian Anthropology* 3: 97–127.

Arno, Andrew. 1979. "Conflict, Ritual, and Social Structure on Yanuyanu Island", *Fiji. Bijdragen* 135: 1–17.

"Fijian Gossip as Adjudication: A Communication Model of Informal Social Control." *Journal of Anthropological Research* 36: 343–360.

Awwad, Amani M. 2001. "Gossip, Scandal, Shame and Honor Killing: A Case for Social Constructionism and Hegemonic Discourse." *Social Thought and Research,* 24: 39–52.

Barkow, Jerome. 1992. "Beneath New Culture Is Old Psychology: Gossip and Social Stratification." In *The Adapted Mind,* edited by Jerome Barkow, Leda Cosmides, and John Tooby, 627–638. New York: Oxford University Press.

Barrow, Christine. 1976. "Reputation and Ranking in a Barbadian Locality." *Social and Economic Studies* 25: 106–121.

Beersma, Bianca, Van Kleef, Gerben A., and Dijkstra, Maria T. M. 2019. "Antecedents and Consequences of Gossip in Work Groups." In *Handbook of Gossip and Reputation,* edited by Francesca Giardini and Rafael Wittek. New York: Oxford University Press.

Ben-Ze'ev, Aaron 1994. "The Vindication of Gossip." In *Good Gossip,* edited by Robert F. Goodman, 11–24. Lawrence, KS: University Press of Kansas.

Besnier, Niko. 1989. "Information Withholding as a Manipulative and Collusive Strategy in Nukulaelae Gossip." *Language in Society* 18: 315–341.

Besnier, Niko. 1993. "The Demise of the Man Who Would Be King: Sorcery and Ambition on Nukulaelae Atoll." *Journal of Anthropological Research* 49: 185–215.

Besnier, Niko. 2019. "Gossip in Ethnographic Perspective. In *Handbook of Gossip and Reputation,* edited by Francesca Giardini and Rafael Wittek, New York: Oxford University Press.

Black, Donald. 1984. *Toward a General Theory of Social Control.* Orlando: Academic Press.

Bleek, Wolf. 1976. "Witchcraft, Gossip and Death: A Social Drama." *Man* 11: 526–541.

Boehm, Christopher. 1999. *Hierarchy in the Forest: The Evolution of Egalitarian Behavior.* Cambridge: Harvard University Press.

Boehm, Christopher. 2012. *Moral Origins: The Evolution of Altruism, Virtue, and Shame.* New York: Basic Books.

Boehm, Christopher. 2014. "The Moral Consequences of Social Selection." *Behaviour* 151: 168–183.

Brenneis, David. 1984. "Grog and Gossip in Bhatgaon: Style and Substance in Fiji Indian conversation. *American Ethnologist* 11: 487–506.

Bricker, Victoria Reifler. 1980. "The Function of Humor in Zinacantan." *Journal of Anthropological Research* 36: 411–418.

Briggs, Jean L. 1970. *Never in Anger: Portrait of an Eskimo Family.* Cambridge: Harvard University Press.

Brison, Karen J. 1992. *Just Talk: Gossip, Meetings, and Power in a Papua New Guinea Village.* Berkeley: University of California Press.

Burt, Ronald S., and Knez, Marc. 1995. "Trust and Third Party Gossip." In *Trust in Organizations: Frontiers of Theory and Research*, edited by Roderick M. Kramer and Tom R. Tyler, 58–89. New York: Sage.

Chattoe, Edmund, and Heather, Hamill. 2005. "It's Not Who You Know, It's What You Know about People You Don't Know that Counts: Extending the Analysis of Crime Groups as Social Networks." *The British Journal of Criminology* 45: 860–876.

Colson, Elizabeth E. 1953. *The Makah Indians: A Study of an Indian Tribe in modern American Society*. Manchester: Manchester University Press.

Cox, Bruce A. 1970. "What Is Hopi Gossip About? Information Management and Hopi Factions." *Man* 5: 88–98.

Davis, Adam, Vaillancourt, Tracy, Arnocky, Steven, and Doyel, Robert. 2019. "Women's Gossip as an Intrasexual Competition Strategy: An Evolutionary Approach to sex and Discrimination." In *Handbook of Gossip and Reputation*, edited by Francesca Giardini and Rafael Wittek. New York: Oxford University Press.

De Backer, Charlotte, Van den Bulck, Hilde, Fisher, Maryanne L., and Ouvrein, Gaëlle. 2019. "Gossip and Reputation in the Media: How Celebrities Emerge and Evolve by Means of Mass-Mediated Gossip." In *Handbook of Gossip and Reputation*, edited by Francesca Giardini and Rafael Wittek. New York: Oxford University Press.

Dos Santos, Miguel, J., Rankin Daniel, and Claus, Wedekind 2011. The Evolution of Punishment through Reputation." *Biological Sciences* 278: 371–377.

Dunbar, Robin. 1996. *Grooming, Gossip and the Evolution of Language*. London: Faber and Faber.

Dunbar, Robin. 2004. "Gossip in Evolutionary Perspective." *Review of General Psychology* 8: 100–110.

Ellwardt, Lea, Labianca, Joe and Wittek, Rafael. 2012. "Who Are the Objects of Positive and Negative Gossip at Work?" A Social Network Perspective on Workplace Gossip." *Social Networks* 34: 193–205.

Ellwardt, Lea Steglich, Christian, and Wittek, Rafael. 2012. "The Co-evolution of Gossip and Friendship in Workplace Social Networks." *Social Networks* 34: 623–633.

Ellwardt, Lea., Wittek, Rafael, and Wielers, Rudi. 2012. "Talking about the Boss: Effects of Generalized and Interpersonal Trust on Workplace Gossip." *Group & Organization Management* 37: 521–549.

Engert, Andreas. 2006. "Norms, Rationality, and Communication: A Reputation Theory of Social Norms." *Archives for Philosophy of Law and Social Philosophy* 92: 335–362.

Feinberg, Matthew, et al. 2012. "The Virtues of Gossip: Reputational Information Sharing as Prosocial Behavior." *Journal of Personality and Social Psychology* 102: 1015–1030.

Foster, E. K. 2004. "Research on Gossip: Taxonomy, Methods, and Future Directions." *Review of General Psychology* 8: 78–99.

Foster, George M. 1972. "The Anatomy of Envy: A Study in Symbolic Behavior." *Current Anthropology* 13: 165–202.

Gambetta, Diego. 1994. "Godfather's Gossip." *European Journal of Sociology* 35: 199–223.

Giardini, Francesca, Wittek, Rafael. 2019. "Gossip, Reputation, and Sustainable Cooperation: Sociological Foundations." In *Handbook of Gossip and Reputation*, edited by Francesca Giardini and Rafael Wittek. New York: Oxford University Press.

Gilmore, David. 1978. "Varieties of Gossip in a Spanish Rural Community." *Ethnology* 17: 89–99.

Gilmore, David D. 1982. "Some Notes on Community Nicknaming in Spain." *Man* 17: 686–700.

Geertz, Armin W. 2011. "Hopi Indian Witchcraft and Healing: On Good, Evil, and Gossip." *American Indian Quarterly* 35: 372–393.

Gluckman, Max. 1963. "Papers in Honor of Melville J. Herskovits: Gossip and Scandal." *Current Anthropology* 4: 307–316.

Gluckman, Max. 1968. "Psychological, Sociological and Anthropological Explanations of Witchcraft and Gossip: A Clarification." *Man* 3: 20–34.

Goffman, Erving. 1959. *The Presentation of Self in Everyday Life.* New York: Anchor Books.

Grosser, Travis J., Lopez-Kidwell, Virginie, and Labianca, Giuseppe. 2012. "A Social Network Analysis of Positive and Negative Gossip in Organizational Life." *Group and Organization Management* 35: 177–212.

Gurven, Michael. 2004. "To Give and to Give Not: The Behavioral Ecology of Human Food Transfers." *Behavioral and Brain Sciences* 27: 543–583.

Handleman, Don. 1973. "Gossip in Encounters: The Transmission of Information in a Bounded Social Setting." *Man* 8: 210–227.

Harrington, C. Lee and Bielby, Denise. 1995. "Where Did You Hear That? Technology and the Social Organization of Gossip." *The Sociological Quarterly* 36: 607–628.

Haviland, John B. 1977b. *Gossip, Reputation, and Knowledge in Zinacantan.* Chicago: University of Chicago Press.

Haviland, John Beard. 1977a. "Gossip as Competition in Zinacantan." *Journal of Communication* 27: 186–191.

Haviland, John B. 1998. "Mu'nuk Jbankil To, Mu'nuk Kajvaltik: 'He Is Not My Older Brother, He Is Not Our Lord': Thirty Years of Gossip in a Chiapas Village." *Etnofoor* 2: 57–82.

Hess, Nicole, Hagen, Edward. 2018. In "Gossip, Reputation, and Friendship in Within-group Competition: An Evolutionary Perspective" edited by Francesca Giardini and Rafael Wittek. New York: Oxford University Press.

Hill, Kim R., et al. 2011. "Co-Residence Patterns in Hunter-Gatherer Societies Show Unique Human Social Structure." *Science* 331: 1286–1289.

Ingram, Gordon P. D. 2014. "From Hitting to Tattling to Gossip: An Evolutionary Rationale for the Development of Indirect Aggression." *Evolutionary Psychology* 12: 343–363.

Kluckhohn, Clyde. 1962. *Navajo Witchcraft.* Boston: Beacon Press.

Knauft, Bruce M. 1991. "Violence and Sociality in Human Evolution." *Current Anthropology* 32: 391–428.

Kniffin, Kevin M., and David S. Wilson. 2005. "Utilities of Gossip Across Organizational Levels: Multilevel Selection, Free-Riders, and Teams." *Human Nature* 16: 278–292.

Kniffin, Kevin M., and Wilson, David S. 2010. "Evolutionary Perspectives on Workplace Gossip: Why and How Gossip Can Serve Groups." *Group and Organization Management* 35: 150–176.

Kurland, Nancy B., and Pelled, Lisa Hope. 2000. "Passing the Word: Toward a Model of Gossip and Power in the Workplace." *Academy of Management Review* 25: 428–438.

Levin, Jack, and Amluke, Arnold. 1985. "An Exploratory Analysis of Sex Differences in Gossip." *Sex Roles* 12: 281–286.

Machin, Barrie, and William, Lancaster. 1974. "Anthropology and Gossip," *Man* 9: 625–627.

March, James A. 1988. "Gossip, Information, and Decision-Making" in *Decisions and Organizations.* Oxford: Blackwell.

Martinez, Margarita. 2005. "Columbian Town Makes Gossip a Crime." Associated Press.

Machin, Barrie, and Lancaster, William. 1974. "Anthropology and Gossip," *Man* 9: 625–627.

McAndrew, Francis T., and Megan A. Milenkovic. 2002. "Of Tabloids and Family Secrets: The Evolutionary Psychology of Gossip." *Journal of Applied Social Psychology* 32: 1064.

McAndrew, Francis T., Bell, Emily K., and Garcia, Contitta Maria. 2007. "Who Do We Tell and Whom Do We Tell On? Gossip as a Strategy for Status Enhancement." *Journal of Applied Social Psychology* 37: 1562–1577.

McCall, Grant. 1979. "Teasing, Gossip, and Local Names on Rapanui." *Asian Perspectives* 22 (1): 41–60.

Merry, Sue Engle. 1984. "Rethinking Gossip and Scandal." In *Toward a General Theory of Social Control*, edited by Donald Black, 271–302. New York: Academic Press.

Michelson, Grant, Iterson, Ad van, and Waddington, Kathryn. 2010. "Gossip in Organizations: Contexts, Consequences, and Controversies." *Group and Organization Management* 35: 371–390.

Nachman, Steven R. 1986. "Discomfiting Laughter: 'Schadenfreude' among Melanesians." *Journal of Anthropological Research* 42: 53–67.

Nicholson, Nigel. 2001. "Evolved to Chat: The New Word on Gossip." *Psychology Today*, May/June, 41–45.

Noon, Mike and Delbridge, Rick. 1993. "News From Behind My Hand: Gossip in Organizations." *Organization Studies* 14: 23–36.

Paine, Robert. 1967. "What is Gossip About? An Alternative Hypothesis." *Man* 2: 278–285.

Pinker, Steven, Nowak, Martin A., and Lee, James J. 2008. "The Logic of Indirect Speech." *Proceedings of the National Academy of Sciences* 105: 833–838.

Rasmussen, Susan J. 1991. "Modes of Persuasion: Gossip, Song, and Divination in Tuareg Conflict Resolution." *Anthropological Quarterly* 64: 30–46.

Rosnow, Ralph L. 2001. "Rumor and Gossip in Interpersonal Interaction and Beyond: A Social Exchange Perspective." In *Behaving Badly: Aversive Behaviors in Interpersonal Relationships*, edited by Robin M. Kowalski, 203–32. Washington, DC: American Psychological Association.

Rosnow, Ralph L. and Fine, Gary A. 1976. *Rumor and Gossip: The Social Psychology of Hearsay.* Oxford: Elsevier.

Semmann, Dirk, Krambeck, Hans-Jürgen, and Milinski, Manfred 2004. "Strategic Investment in Reputation." *Behavioral Ecology and Sociobiology* 56: 248–252.

Semmann, Dirk, Krambeck, Hans-Jürgen, and Milinski, Manfred. 2005. "Reputation Is Valuable Within and Outside One's Own Social Group." *Behavioral Ecology and Sociobiology* 57: 611–616.

Shaw, Allison K., Tsvetkova, Milena, and Daneshvar, Roozbeh. 2011. "The Effect of Gossip on Social Networks." *Complexity* 16: 39–47.

Shea, John J. 2007. "Behavioral Differences between Middle and Upper Paleolithic Homo sapiens in the East Mediterranean Levant: The Roles of Intra-Specific Competition and Dispersal from Africa". *Journal of Anthropological Research* 63 (4): 449–488.

Shea, John J. 2011. "Homo Sapiens is as Homo Sapiens Was: Behavioral Variability Versus 'Behavioral Modernity' in Paleolithic Archaeology." *Current Anthropology*, 52, 1–35.

Shermer, Michael. 2004. *The Science of Good and Evil: Why People Cheat, Gossip, Care, Share, and Follow the Golden Rule.* New York: Henry Holt.

Solove, Daniel J. 2007. *The Future of Reputation, Gossip, Rumor, and Privacy on the Internet.* New Haven: Yale University Press.

Sommerfeld, Ralf D., et al. 2007. "Gossip as an Alternative for Direct Observation in Games of Indirect Reciprocity." *Proceedings of the National Academy of Sciences* 104: 17435–17440.

Spacks, Patricia Meyer. 1985. *Gossip.* Chicago: University of Chicago Press.

Suzuki, Shinsuke, and Akiyama, Eizo R. 2005. Reputation and the Evolution of Cooperation in Sizable Groups." *Proceedings of the Royal Society B: Biological Sciences* 272 (1570): 1373–1377.

Tasgin, Mursel, and Bingol, Haluk. 2012. "Gossip on Weighted Networks." *Advances in Complex Systems* 15: 1–8.

van Vleet, Krista. 2003. "Partial Theories: On Gossip, Envy and Ethnography in the Andes." *Ethnography* 13: 491–519.

Wiessner, Polly W. 2005. "Norm Enforcement among the Ju/'hoansi Bushmen: A Case of Strong Reciprocity?" *Human Nature* 16: 115–145.

Wiessner, Polly W. 2014. "Embers of Society: Firelight Talk among the Ju/'hoansi Bushmen." *Proceedings of the National Academy of Sciences USA* 111: 14027–14035.

Wilson, David S., and Wilson, Edward O. 2007. "Rethinking the Theoretical Foundation of Sociobiology." *Quarterly Review of Biology* 82: 327–348.

Wilson, David S., Wilczynski, C., and Wells, A. 2000. "Gossip and Other Aspects of Language as Group-Level Adaptations." In *The Evolution of Cognition*, edited by Cecilia M. Heyes. Cambridge, Mass: MIT Press.

Wilson, Peter J. 1974. "Filcher of Good Names: An Enquiry into Anthropology and Gossip." *Man* 9: 93–102.

Wilson, Peter J., Kolig, E., and Kapferer, Bruce. 1975. "Anthropology and Gossip," *Man* 10: 615–618.

Wittek, Rafael and Wielers, Rudi. 1998. Gossip in Organizations. *Computational & Mathematical Organization Theory* 4 (2): 189–204.

Yoeli, Erez, et al. 2013. "Powering up with Indirect Reciprocity in a Large-scale Field Experiment." *Proceedings of the National Academy of Sciences* 110: 10424–10429.

Young, Robert. 1987. "Egalitarianism and Envy." *Philosophical Studies: An International Journal for Philosophy in the Analytic Tradition* 2: 261–276.

Zinovieff, Sofka. 1987. "What Will the World Say?' The Fear and the Delight of Gossip in a Greek Town." *Cambridge Anthropology* 12: 1–15.

# CHAPTER 15

GOSSIP, REPUTATION,
AND FRIENDSHIP IN
WITHIN-GROUP
COMPETITION
*An Evolutionary Perspective*

NICOLE H. HESS AND EDWARD H. HAGEN

## INTRODUCTION

MEN and boys are substantially more aggressive than girls and women, according to early findings by aggression researchers. When developmental and social psychologists began to study nonphysical forms of aggression, however (e.g., those that did not involve hitting, pushing, or yelling), they discovered a very different pattern. These harmful nonphysical forms of aggression, such as gossip, ostracism, breaking confidences, and criticism (Owens, Shute, & Slee, 2000a, b), appeared to be more often used by females than males, at least in children and adolescents (e.g., Bjorkqvist & Niemela, 1992; Galen & Underwood, 1997; Lagerspetz, Bjorkqvist, & Peltonen, 1998.) In this chapter we review theories of human nonphysical aggression, where gossip and reputation play central roles. We then address aggression among non-human primates, where between-group physical defense of territories and within-group physical competition for resources like food and mates are key. Under certain social and ecological conditions, resource competition involves within-group coalitions and alliances. Whereas human between-group competition over territory mainly involves physical aggression among coalitions of men, we propose that within-group competition over material and social resources mainly involves nonphysical aggression among both men and women, sometimes in coalitions (cliques). Because access to resources often depends on having a good reputation, within-group aggression frequently utilizes gossip to harm the reputations of competitors. We propose that human friendships are analogous (and probably homologous) to within-group alliances in non-human primates, and similarly serve to increase successful competition for within-group resources by enhancing the effectiveness of gossip and reputational attacks, a strategy we term informational warfare. We conclude by offering testable hypotheses for this model.

# THREE TERMS FOR NON-PHYSICAL AGGRESSION: INDIRECT, RELATIONAL, AND SOCIAL AGGRESSION

Over the past few decades, developmental and social psychologists and other researchers have developed three theoretical constructs to characterize the suite of behaviors and psychological phenomena that are aggressive—that is, executed in order to harm another—but that do not involve the use of physical force, such as hitting or the use of weapons, to inflict bodily damage. These constructs include *indirect aggression*, *relational aggression*, and *social aggression*.

*Indirect aggression*, coined by Feshbach (1969), was adopted and elaborated by researchers in the late 1980s who sought to compare overt physical aggression, typical of boys, to forms of aggression that seemed to be more apparent in girls. The distinction between physical aggression and indirect aggression was confirmed by factor analysis. Items loading on the indirect aggression factor described various types of social manipulation in which aggressors would harm victims by, for example, lying about them behind their backs, calling them names, or attempting to exclude them from friendship groups (Lagerspetz, Bjorkqvist, & Peltonen, 1988). These researchers emphasized that the indirectness or covertness of the aggression is aimed at separating the perpetrator from the aggressive act, where the aggressor does not want the victim to know the aggressor's identity, perhaps with the intent of avoiding retaliation (Bjorkqvist, Lagerspetz, & Kaukianian, 1992; Lagerspetz, Bjorkqvist, & Peltonen, 1988; Bjorkqvist, 2001).

*Relational aggression*, introduced by Crick and colleagues in the 1990's, includes behaviors whose intent is to damage a peer's relationships and standing within the social group. As in indirect aggression, these behaviors could be covert, but they also include direct confrontations. Other examples of relational aggression include ostracism and ending a friendship. In their review, Voulgaridou & Kokkinos (2015) summarize relational aggression (p. 2):

> Relational aggression...includes behaviors that damage or threaten to harm relationships, acceptance and inclusion through manipulation of peer relationships (Crick, 1996; Crick, Ostrov, & Kawabata, 2007). Relationally aggressive behavior primarily involves the direct manipulation of peer relationships and does not include negative facial expressions or gestures (Crick and Grotpeter, 1995). These

behaviors may be confrontational (e.g., excluding a peer from the social group) or non-confrontational (e.g., character denigration) and may or may not involve members of the social community.    (Archer & Coyne, 2005)

*Social aggression* is a broad construct for nonphysical aggression that includes all the phenomena that fall under indirect aggression and relational aggression, such as the manipulation of group acceptance through alienation, ostracism, character defamation, and rejection. It also includes phenomena that are nonverbal, like negative facial expressions and gestures, which were explicitly excluded from relational aggression (Crick & Grotpeter, 1995), as well as direct social confrontations that would be excluded from indirect aggression (Cairns et al., 1989; Galen & Underwood, 1997; for reviews, see Heilbron & Prinstein, 2008; Card et al., 2008; Voulgaridou & Kokkinos, 2015).

# THREE TERMS, ONE PHENOMENON?

Reviews of the literature on indirect, relational, and social aggression (e.g., Archer, 2004; Card et al., 2008; Heilbron and Prinstein, 2008; and Voulgaridou and Kokkinos, 2015) concur that the three constructs overlap to a considerable degree, and that there is no consensus about which term should be used.

In his meta-analysis, Archer (2004) prefers the term *indirect aggression* to describe nonphysical aggression among humans, as historically it was the first construct that was explored. Card et al. (2008) argued that indirect aggression excludes nonphysical aggression: "The term *indirect aggression* is also limited in that it excludes more direct attacks on social well-being." (p. 1186). But like Archer (2004), Card et al. (2008) felt that historical precedence should be honored. In their 2008 meta-analysis on direct and indirect aggression, Card et al. use indirect aggression to include indirect aggression, relational aggression, social aggression, and covert aggression; direct aggression includes physical aggression and direct, overt, verbally aggressive behaviors like yelling, taunting, and threatening. Factor analysis studies cited by Card et al. support these categorizations (Card, 2008, p. 1186).

Heilbron and Prinstein's, 2008 review, which summarizes research on the development these nonphysical forms of aggression, favors the term *social aggression*, arguing that it is most all-encompassing of the behaviors that make up nonphysical aggression. Bjorkqvist (2001), however, pointed out that the term *social aggression* includes physical aggression, as any physically aggressive act involves at least two actors: a perpetrator and a victim.

In their recent review of relational aggression in adolescents, Voulgaridou and Kokkinos (2015) prefer the term *relational aggression* because it describes nonphysical forms of aggression that include behaviors and phenomena where the act is direct and where the victim can easily identify the perpetrator, like verbal confrontations, which would seem to be excluded by the indirect aggression construct.

Disagreements about precedent versus accuracy versus generality still exist. As all constructs intend to exclude physical aggression, these forms of aggression could also be described as nonphysical aggression. Here, we use these terms interchangeably to refer to all forms of nonphysical aggression.

# Major Findings about Nonphysical Aggression

We will now review the most important findings about nonphysical aggression with the aim of linking them to the ongoing debate about gossip.

## The Lack of an Important Sex Difference

In his meta-analysis of 124 studies of physical aggression, Archer (2004) found a very consistent, large male bias across cultures, a bias that appears at or before the age of 2, and that does not increase with age during childhood. He also found that the maximum sex differences in physical aggression occur well after puberty, between 18 and 30 years of age.

In his meta-analysis of sixty-one studies of nonphysical aggression, Archer (2004) found that a female bias increased with age from 6 to 17 years, reaching a peak between 11 and 17 years. He found little evidence of a sex bias in indirect among adults, however, and in the few cross-cultural studies of indirect aggression, there was either no sex bias, or a female bias. Archer also found that there were no sex differences in the experience of anger.

Card et al. (2008) conducted another meta-analysis of nonphysical aggression to clarify whether sex differences in aggression types were present, to see if physical and indirect were correlated, and to see what types of maladjustment were associated with each type of aggression (discussed under the next two subheadings). This meta-analysis included more studies than were available to Archer, focused on children and adolescents, included studies involving a wider range of aggression measurement methods, and used different statistical methods. They also explored variables that might be related to sex differences, but for which there were not necessarily any clear directional predictions, such as social norms, first author gender, the proportion of ethnic minorities included in the studies, and so on.

With regard to sex differences, Card et al.'s analysis corroborated Archer's (2004) conclusion: boys clearly use physical aggression more than girls, and girls use slightly more indirect aggression than boys, with the female bias in indirect aggression being statistically significant but trivial in effect size. The slight female bias was consistent across age, ethnicity, and country in which the data were collected. The authors conclude, "indirect aggression is *not* a 'female form' of aggression." (2008, p. 1209, emphasis in the original)

## Nonphysical and Physical Aggression are Strongly Correlated in Both Sexes

Card, et al. (2008) found that across ninety-eight studies, the average corrected correlation between the two aggression types was 0.76, meaning that about half (58%) of the variance in these two forms overlaps. The authors argue that the constructs are separate despite this considerable overlap. They also point out that accurately measuring indirectly aggressive behaviors is inherently more challenging because covert actions are more difficult to observe. Interestingly, Card et al. also report a somewhat greater overlap for boys than girls.

## No Strong or Consistent Association between Nonphysical Aggression and Maladjustment

High levels of physical aggression in childhood are associated with adult maladjustment, that is, with a high risk of being violent in adolescence and adulthood as well as a higher risk of substance abuse, accidents, depression, and suicide attempts; these associations are particularly clear for boys (Tremblay et al., 2004; Broidy et al., 2003).

Influential early studies of nonphysical aggression paralleled studies of physical aggression by investigating potential links between childhood nonphysical aggression and poor social and mental health outcomes in adolescence and adulthood; these studies are particularly associated with the term *relational aggression* (e.g., Crick and Grotpeter, 1995). Unlike physical aggression, however, nonphysical aggression in childhood is not consistently associated with poor outcomes at any age for either sex, possibly because successful nonphysical aggression against one person requires good social relationships with other people (Card et al., 2008).

# EVOLUTIONARY APPROACHES TO HUMAN PHYSICAL AGGRESSION AND DOMINANCE

Evolutionary theorists of human physical aggression unanimously view it as an evolved strategy to successfully compete for the social and material resources that increased biological fitness in our human and nonhuman ancestors (e.g., Archer, 2009; Burbank, 1987;

Buss and Shackelford, 1997; Campbell, 1999; Chagnon, 1988; Hawley, 1999; Manson and Wrangham, 1991, Sell et al., 2009; Van Vugt, 2009; Wilson and Daly, 1985; Wrangham and Glowacki, 2012; Wrangham and Peterson, 1996). They are also unanimous that it is physical injury, or the threat of it, that serves to deter or eliminate competitors.

High upper body strength appears to afford an advantage in physical fights (Sell et al., 2009). Most adult men have higher upper body strength than most adult women (Pheasant, 1983), and there is a large male bias in physical aggression that is present by about age 2 and persists throughout the lifespan, with male violence peaking during early adulthood (Archer, 2009). Evolutionary scholars largely agree that intrasexual selection resulted in the male-bias in physical formidability and physical aggression: due to their lower investment in offspring, males, more than females, benefit reproductively by competing with members of the same sex for access to members of the opposite sex (Trivers, 1972). In most mammals, including humans, this involves physical aggression directed toward male competitors. Males might also benefit by physically intimidating or coercing females (for review, see Archer, 2009).

Females, in contrast, due to their higher investment in offspring (e.g., pregnancy, lactation) are expected to compete with other females over access to resources. Unlike males in most other primate species, human males do provide resources to females. Hence, females might compete for access to males that are able to provide resources. Across cultures, physical fights among adult women are often over the means of subsistence (e.g., gardens, crops, money), and co-wives and other sexual competitors, as well as physical defense of their offspring (Burbank, 1987; Campbell, 1999).

The costs of physical fights (i.e., injuries) can be high for both winners and losers. Dominance hierarchies are thought to have evolved for the mutual benefit of avoiding the costs of a fight: when two animals are in competition over a resource, the one with higher rank in the hierarchy almost always obtains the resource without a fight (Maynard Smith & Parker, 1976; Drews, 1993). Dominance rank is often based on an individual's reputation for fighting ability, and it can also be inherited (e.g., Holekamp & Smale, 1991). In social species[1] that physically compete for material resources (e.g., food) and social resources (e.g., mates), dominance hierarchies are common (Schjelderup-Ebbe, 1922; Bernstein, 1981; Silk, 2007a,b).

In many primate species, dominance hierarchies are solidified, or challenged, via alliances with other group members (Harcourt & de Waal, 1992). For example, to maintain her rank, an alpha female might need to cooperate with a lower-ranking female in an alliance against the alpha's challengers. Thus, in species with complex social relationships, dominance hierarchies might involve intricate combinations of conflict and cooperation.

There is increasing evidence that humans, like many other social species, form dominance hierarchies, and that these are based on intricate combinations of agonism and prosociality (e.g., Hawley, 1999, 7). If so, this implies that human evolution was also characterized by potentially costly contests over material and social resources among within-group alliances, which in humans are termed "cliques." We return to this theme later.

# EVOLUTIONARY APPROACHES
# TO NONPHYSICAL AGGRESSION

Evolutionary theorists focusing on nonphysical aggression agree that it, too, is likely an evolved strategy to successfully compete for resources. (e.g., Campbell, 1999; Archer, 2009; Ingram, 2014; Hess, 1999, 2006, 2017; Hess and Hagen, 2002, 2003, 2006a,b; Hawley, 1999; Hawley, Little, and Card, 2008; Geary, 1998; and Buss and Dedden, 1990). These theorists have offered different accounts of why nonphysical aggression evolved as an alternative to physical aggression, and how, exactly, nonphysical aggression inflicts harm on competitors. Sex differences emerge as an important component in many of these accounts because there is a large sex difference in physical aggression (Archer, 2009) and early studies seemed to indicate that nonphysical aggression was more common in females than males (a view that is now known to be incorrect).

Campbell (1999) argued that indirect aggression evolved as an alternative to physical aggression because maternal care is more important to infant survival than paternal care is. Mothers with young children cannot risk the bodily harm that is associated with physical aggression, and engage in nonphysical aggression as a safer alternative. Further, indirectly aggressive strategies like gossip can separate the attacker from the victim, decreasing the likelihood of retaliation, and reducing the risk of physical harm, and idea endorsed by Archer (2004, 2009) and Ingram (2014), among others. (Presumably, males would also benefit from the reduced risk of physical harm afforded by indirect aggression.)

Geary (1998) and Buss & Dedden (1990) put forward theories to explain how indirect aggression harms competitors. Geary (1998, p. 250) argued that indirect aggression harms adversaries by "disrupt[ing]" the reciprocal relationships of unrelated female competitors, thereby inducing stress in female competitors. Disrupted relationships and stress indeed reduce fertility in other primates (Abbott, 1993; Smuts & Nicolson, 1989; cited in Geary, 1998). Geary suggested this might be a form of reproductive competition (1998, pp. 137–138,) where sex differences in hormonal responses to stress make indirect aggression an effective weapon against female reproductive competitors.

Buss & Dedden (1990, p. 398) suggested that, for example, using derogatory terms, makes "intrasexual competitors less attractive or appealing to members of the opposite sex," and explored sex differences in the content of the information. Schmitt & Buss (1996) further investigated the perceived effectiveness of these tactics in short-term and long-term mating competition.

Ingram (2014) argued that chimpanzee-like dominance hierarchies could not effectively regulate access to resources in the larger groups that characterize human societies. Instead, systems of indirect reciprocity (Alexander, 1987), in which a group member's cooperative and non-cooperative acts positively and negatively influence others' propensities to cooperate with her, lead to extended dominance hierarchies mediated by gossip and other nonphysical forms of aggression rather than physical aggression (Ingram, 2014).

# CRITIQUE OF CURRENT EVOLUTIONARY APPROACHES TO NONPHYSICAL AGGRESSION

Although each of these evolutionary theories offers important insights into indirect aggression and its relationship to physical aggression, each can be questioned on evolutionary grounds. Regarding Campbell and Archer's early arguments that sex differences in the costs of physical aggression explain the evolution of indirect aggression, we now know that males use indirect aggression as frequently as females. Thus, sex differences in the costs of physical fights might explain women's avoidance of physical aggression, but do not clearly explain the evolution of indirect aggression. Moreover, non-human female mammals all face the same high costs that human mothers face, and yet they still often engage in physical aggression, and consequently form female dominance hierarchies that help reduce the costs of physical fighting (Chapais & Schulman, 1980).

With regard to female physical aggression, it is important to distinguish intra- from inter-sexual conflict. Most anthropoid primate species, including humans, are sexually dimorphic, with a male advantage in body and canine size (Plavcan, 2001; Plavcan, 2012). Although human body dimorphism is modest—men weigh about 15% more than women—human upper body strength is highly sexually dimorphic, and in over 90% of chance encounters between an adult man and woman, the man would have higher upper body strength (Pheasant, 1983). Hence, in most anthropoid species, including humans, males would have the advantage over females in intersexual physical conflicts, which would select for female avoidance of physical conflicts with males.

Sexual body dimorphism says little, however, about the nature of *intra*sexual conflict. Females in many primate species have formidable canines, and it is increasingly recognized that there are many selection pressures on both male and female body sizes and fighting abilities. These can include male-male physical contests over mates and female-female physical contests over resources, but can also include, for example, benefits of higher or lower reproductive rates that select for smaller and larger female body size, respectively (Plavcan, 2001; Plavcan, 2012).

In summary, in species in which males have clear advantages in physical formidability over females, such as humans, females should avoid physical conflicts with males, but should not necessarily avoid physical conflicts with other females. In fact, physical fights among girls and women are not unknown, and when they do occur, fights are often over the means of subsistence and access to male resources (Burbank, 1987; Campbell, 1999). Campbell, Archer, and others have failed to explain why in human females the costs of female-female physical contests generally outweigh the benefits, but in other species the benefits often outweigh the costs.

Regarding the "indirectness" of indirect aggression, it is not clear how indirect it actually is, and the extent to which its putative indirectness protects attackers from retaliation. After all, retaliation could occur at a later time, which would be difficult for researchers to detect. A physically strong male victim of indirect aggression could inflict serious physical harm on his antagonist should he discover his or her identity (and in the small hunter-gatherer bands in which we evolved, would identifying the perpetrator be that difficult?). The putative ability of indirect aggression to avoid retaliation requires more investigation.

Regarding the ways in which nonphysical aggression inflicts harm, Geary's (1998) hypothesis that stress-induced endocrine disruption suppresses fertility provides a possible proximate mechanism by which indirect aggression could harm competitors. It does not provide an ultimate evolutionary explanation, however, because victims should have evolved endocrine systems that resisted disruption by verbal threats and harassment that did not actually reduce access to resources or cause injury. Why do victims remain vulnerable to stress-induced fertility reduction?

Buss & Dedden (1990) astutely pointed out that derogation of competitors might make them less attractive as mates (thus increasing one's own access to mates). But here, too, it is not clear why potential mates should avoid an individual simply because he or she was derogated by a competitor. If the derogations were baseless, the potential mates would erroneously pass up valuable mating opportunities, and should therefore have evolved to ignore derogations by competitors.

In our view, although there is widespread agreement that physical and nonphysical aggression are evolved strategies to gain access to contested material and social resources, several outstanding questions remain, including, (1) Why is physical aggression among women exceptionally infrequent? (2) Why did nonphysical forms of aggression evolve that are commonly used by both sexes? (3) Over human evolution, how did nonphysical forms of aggression harm competitors?

Drawing on the work of many others, we now sketch our evolutionary account of the evolution of physical and non-physical aggression in humans (Hess, 2006, 2017; Hess & Hagen, 2003, 2006a) that explains the rarity of physical aggression among women, the widespread use of non-physical forms of aggression by both sexes, and how the latter harms competitors.

# THE EVOLUTION OF AGGRESSION OVER RESOURCES IN HUMANS AND OTHER SPECIES

Physical and nonphysical aggression appear to be human universals (Archer, 2004; Card et al., 2008). We therefore sketch one scenario by which both forms of aggression could have evolved, drawing heavily on comparisons with our primate relatives and also with social carnivores, which probably occupied an ecological niche similar to our hunter-gatherer ancestors (e.g., Stiner, 2002; Smith et al., 2012).

Humans are one of about 400 primate species, which diverged from other mammals about 65 million years ago (MYA; Fleagle, 2013). Whereas most mammals are solitary as adults, most primates are gregarious, that is, they live permanently as members of social groups.

The human lineage split from that of our closest relative, the chimpanzee, sometime between 6 and 13 MYA (Langergraber et al., 2012). Until about 2 MYA, this lineage comprised species that were bipedal but had ape-sized brains and appear to have subsisted mostly on plant foods. The first notable increase in brain size occurred with the appearance of the genus *Homo* some 2–2.5 MYA, around the beginning of the Pleistocene (Antón et al., 2014). Although there is little agreement about the social organization and diet of early members of our genus, most anthropologists would agree that they probably lived in multi-female multi-male groups and that meat was a valuable and increasingly important component of the diet (e.g., Antón et al., 2014).

The role of aggression in human evolution is particularly contentious. Our theory relies heavily on distinguishing between-group aggression, which we discuss first, from within-group aggression, which we discuss second.

# BETWEEN-GROUP COMPETITION
# FOR TERRITORY

Most primate species are social. Many such species are territorial and vigorously defend their territories with physical aggression toward outsiders, but many others do not. Territorial defense among non-human primates (and other social animals) could be an analogy for human warfare (Crofoot & Wrangham, 2010).

Some anthropologists have argued that *lethal* competition between groups—warfare— was important throughout human evolution, basing their case on similar patterns of behavior in one of our sister species, the chimpanzee, on pervasive evidence of warfare in almost all modern human societies, and on clear evidence of warfare in the archaeological record of the last 10,000 years (e.g., Wrangham, 1999; Bowles, 2009).

Others vehemently deny any role for warfare in human evolution, basing their case on the putative rarity of warfare among contemporary band-level foragers, absence of archaeological evidence for warfare prior to about 10,000 years ago, on the apparent lack of warfare among our other sister species, the bonobo, and the rarity of lethal between-group conflict in other animals (Ferguson, 1997; Fry & Söderberg, 2013). For a recent overview of the ethnographic and archaeological evidence for warfare among hunter-gatherers, see Allen & Jones (2014). For a comparative analysis of lethal violence (not necessarily warfare) in humans and human ancestors relative to other primates and mammals, see Gómez et al. (2016).

We take a middle ground. There are solid theoretical and empirical grounds to suppose that human ancestors were territorial and were physically agonistic toward intruders, but physical defense of territories might or might not have involved lethal attacks.

According to some researchers, between-group agonism among non-human primates appears to depend on the presence or absence of collective action problems. Although territory is a valuable resource, defending it with physical aggression can be costly due to the risk of injury and death. If some members of a group pay the price of territorial defense but others do not, natural selection will favor the latter, and cooperative defense cannot evolve. In primates, the species that exhibit high levels of between-group agonism are those that appear to have solved the collective action problem by some combination of high degrees of relatedness among the dominant sex, small group size, and cooperative breeding, which all tend to align the interests of group members relative to outsiders (Willems & van Schaik, 2015). Modern humans often live in relatively small social groups with male philopatry (remaining as an adult in one's natal group) and cooperative breeding, and according to this model should therefore aggressively defend territories (Willems & van Schaik, 2015), which they do (Dyson & Smith, 1978).

If meat were an increasingly important part of the diet in Homo, as it appears it was, then early humans could also be compared to social carnivores like lions, hyenas, African wild dogs, and wolves. These species also vigorously defend territories (for brief review, see Hagen & Hammerstein, 2009).

Thus, as both philopatric, cooperatively breeding primates, and as social hunters, human ancestors were probably territorial and defended their territories with coalitional physical aggression toward outsiders. This does not necessarily mean that human evolution involved much, or any, warfare. Lethal between-group aggression is rare even in territorial primates (Crofoot & Wrangham, 2010), and in social carnivores, although lethal inter-group aggression is common in wolves, it is rare in lions (Hagen & Hammerstein, 2009). In addition, human groups commonly *cooperate* with other groups, often forming alliances by marriage that play important roles in defense of large regions (Rodseth et al., 1991).

Thus, in our model, the male bias in physical aggression is explained, at least in part, by an evolutionary history during which closely related male human ancestors (but not female ancestors) collectively defended hunting territories with physically agonistic behaviors toward outsiders; these behaviors might or might not have involved lethal aggression (warfare).

Women, we propose, mostly avoided direct participation in territorial defense because it would have brought them into physical fights with men, whose advantages in upper body strength would have posed severe threats to female fitness. Similar views about the evolutionary importance of human male intergroup aggression have been expressed by many others, including Tooby & Cosmides (1998), Sell et al. (2009), Wrangham & Glowacki, 2012, and Bowles (2009). Male-biased agonism between groups does not, however, explain why women rarely physically fight other women within groups.

# The Impact of Within-group Resource Competition on Social Behaviors in Non-human Primates

In the 1970s, biologists realized that social living would generally decrease biological fitness because it increased competition for resources and exposure to parasites (e.g., Alexander, 1974). Thus, gregariousness must have some valuable fitness benefit that compensated for these fitness costs. For primates, this benefit is thought to be either improved defense against predators (van Schaik, 1983) and/or a competitive advantage in competition over defensible resources (Wrangham, 1980).

Despite the benefits of group living, such as better protection from predators, within-group competition for resources still has a profound impact on primate social relationships. Primate social relationships can vary widely among different species, and even among the same species living in different ecologies. According to the *socioecological models* of primate sociality, the distribution and value of food resources plays a central role in determining the intensity of within-group competition, and thus patterns of social relationships.

# Frugivores Have Complex Social Relationships that Provide Advantages in Within-group Competition over Food

When resources are scarce, valuable, and clumped, and thus *monopolizable*, primates will compete aggressively or *contest* over them. These patterns characterize frugivores— primate species that rely mostly on fruit, which is a nutrient-rich food that is patchily distributed, and which is also only seasonably available. In frugivores and other primate species that rely on valuable, clumped food resources, within-group aggression is higher, and aggression tends to involve more complex aggressive strategies than just one-on-one physical fighting over monopolizable foods. Dominance is one such strategy.

Alliances and coalitions are also more common when food is monopolizable, because coalitions increase physical formidability in fights (e.g., Barrett and Henzi, 2002; Boinski, Sughrue, Selvaggi, Quatrone, Henry, & Cropp, 2002; Harcourt & de Waal, 1992; Isbell & Young, 2002; Kappeler & van Schaik, 2002; Koenig, 2002; Silk, 2002; Sterck, Watts, & van Schaik, 1997; Wrangham, 1980; cf. Janson, 2000). The term *coalition* refers to a temporary group of two or more individuals that forms to attack one or more individuals (Pandit & van Schaik, 2003). The term *alliance* refers to long-lasting relationships. Social relationships among frugivorous primates are characterized by dominance hierarchies, coalitions, and alliances.

# FOLIVORES HAVE SIMPLER SOCIAL RELATIONSHIPS REFLECTING REDUCED WITHIN-GROUP COMPETITION OVER FOOD

When resources are abundant, not valuable, and dispersed, on the other hand, and thus not monopolizable, primates will not engage in aggressive competition for them. These patterns characterize folivores—primate species that rely mostly on leaves, which are low in nutrients, high in toxins, abundant, and relatively evenly distributed. The benefits of winning physically competitive bouts over such resources are small. Relationships of dominance and subordinance are less apparent, aggression and displacement are lower, and aggression is less likely to involve complex strategies such as dominance hierarchies, coalitions, and alliances. When resources are nonmonopolizable, instead of engaging in high-stakes contest competition, primates engage in low-stakes *scramble* competition.

Socioecological models also include factors other than food monopolizability versus nonmonopolizability, such as protection from infanticide and the defense and acquisition of mates by males (van Schaik, Pandit, & Vogel, 2006).

# IMPORTANT CAVEATS

The tight causal links between food distribution, feeding competition, and social structure posited by the socioecological model are increasingly challenged by studies of species that do not conform to key predictions. Some primate species inhabiting similar feeding ecologies exhibit marked differences in social structure, for instance, whereas some species with similar social structures inhabit markedly different feeding ecologies (Clutton-Brock & Janson, 2012; Silk & Kappler, 2017). It is not yet clear whether these and other discrepancies will require only modest modifications to the theory, or abandonment of it altogether. Explanations for the discrepancies include the possibility that the feeding ecology of some species has been misclassified, or that some species entering a new feeding niche have not yet evolved the corresponding social structure (phylogenetic inertia).

According to one critical review (Clutton-Brock & Janson, 2012), certain tenets of the socioecological model are fairly well established in primates and other mammals.

Food value and distribution, for example, are related to the intensity of competition and group size. Social hierarchies and coalitions, on the other hand, might not always be related to feeding competition but instead to competition over other "resources," such as breeding opportunities. Inspired both by the socioecological model as well as this and other critiques, we therefore consider the role of competition over food and other resources in the evolution of human sociality.

## DID ANCESTRAL HUMANS CONTEST VALUABLE MONOPOLIZABLE RESOURCES?

Meat, like fruit, is a valuable but scarce and patchily distributed resource, and is thus monopolizable. Members of the genus *Homo* living during the late-middle Pleistocene and later clearly hunted large game animals, bringing kills to central processing sites like caves, where the meat was consumed by several individuals (Stiner, 2002; Stiner et al., 2009). If the principles of the socioecological model applied, then early humans, perhaps especially females, should have competed for meat with their fellow group members using aggression, alliances, coalitions, and dominance hierarchies that are associated with contest competition.

Among modern hunter-gatherers, an important part of the meat-sharing process involves distributions that are directed by the hunter and other individuals to kin, spouses, sex partners, and reciprocally sharing partners (for review, see Kaplan & Gurven, 2005). Although these distributions are regulated by rules whose function appears to be to reduce conflict, complaints over meat sharing abound (Peterson, 1993).

Items other than meat are shared in modern foragers and small-scale horticultural societies, and, importantly, these items are also scarce, valuable, and monopolizable. These items can include tools, weapons, medicines, scarce nutrients, status items, artifacts, and raw materials needed for manufacturing artifacts. Social resources like mates, hunting partners, and exchange partners can also be valuable, limited, and monopolizable. Tiger and Fox (1971) argued that in humans, social rank was equivalent, indeed homologous, to dominance hierarchies in our primate ancestors. They emphasize human male dominance hierarchies and access to females, similar to patterns seen among males in non-human primates. Because humans rely on monopolizable material and social resources, we should expect them to contest over access to them.

Evidence from the developmental literature supports the view that humans compete over both material and social resources. Hawley summarizes what children compete for (1999, p. 105; citations in the original omitted):

> In general, resources are anything outside the individual essential for survival, growth, and development...Although no one would deny that monkeys must compete for ecological resources in the environment (e.g., food, water), it is not

clear that children in peer groups must...But developmentalists are quick to recognize that optimal growth and development require much more than nutrients and hydration; important resources include social contacts..., play partners..., and cognitive stimulation...Thus, it should come as no surprise that developing humans are highly motivated to seek out others for interaction opportunities (e.g., peers and adults) and novelty for cognitive and physical stimulation (e.g., toys). Research in diverse domains such as motivation...and children's friendships...indicates that children, indeed primates in general..., are highly motivated to access social partners and novel stimuli. To the extent that novelty and peers are limited, individuals must compete for them in various ways...Therefore...resources can be social or material.

There is an important difference, however, between human and nonhuman contest competition: Humans have language.

# Reputation Mediates Access to Resources

Humans often obtain contested group resources via their reputations; in other words, they increase and defend access to resources, including food, mates, and care, by increasing and defending their reputations. Although Tiger & Fox (1971) acknowledged the importance of prestige in the evolution of human social rank, it was Barkow (1975, 1989) who emphasized that in humans, within-group hierarchies were usually established by striving for prestige within particular culture settings, rather than by physically fighting. As in other species, human reputations *can* involve fighting ability (Alexander, 1987; Chagnon, 1988; Hess, Helfrecht, Hagen, Sell, & Hewlett, 2010), but they are usually based on a much broader range of behaviors and capabilities such as being able to provide valuable group benefits (Gurven, Allen-Arave, Hill, & Hurtado, 2000; Sugiyama & Chacon, 2000), being able to take risks and come out winning (the "show-off" or "costly-signaling" models: Gintis, Smith, & Bowles, 2001; Hawkes, 1991; Smith & Bliege Bird, 2000), being a good reciprocator of benefits received (i.e., reciprocal altruism: Cox, Sluckin, & Steele, 1999; Enquist & Leimar, 1993; Pollock & Dugatkin, 1992), and having been observed to give benefits to others (i.e., indirect reciprocity: Alexander, 1987; Leimar & Hammerstein, 2001; Nowak & Sigmund, 1998). Experimental economists, whose research involves study participants sharing real money with other participants or keeping it for themselves, have shown that a sharing strategy can persist in an evolving population when players establish reputations as donors (e.g., Milinski, Semmann, Bakker, & Krambeck, 2001; Milinski, Semmann, & Krambeck, 2002; Wedekind & Milinski, 2000).

This empirical and theoretical research demonstrates that individuals must have reputation for being able to provide valuable benefits to others in order to receive benefits from others. A reputation is based on information about one's traits, behaviors, intentions, abilities, and culturally-specific competencies, and this information can be obtained via direct observation, or from other individuals. Reputations can be strongly impacted by the transfer of information about these various behaviors and capabilities, in other words, gossip.

## GOSSIP AS A STRATEGY TO MANIPULATE REPUTATION

Several theories have been put forward for the evolution of gossip, including "cultural learning" (e.g., Baumeister, Vohs, & Zhang, 2004), "social learning," such as learning norms or one's place in a group (e.g., Eckert, 1990; Fine, 1977; Fine & Rosnow, 1978; Gottman & Mettetal, 1986; Suls, 1977) or acquiring new and important knowledge (e.g., Watkins & Danzi, 1995), strategy learning (DeBacker, 2005), social comparison (e.g., Wert & Salovey, 2004), a mechanism for showing off one's social skill and connections, and therefore one's mate value (Miller, 2000), norm learning and enforcement, sanctioning, social control, or "policing" (e.g., Wilson, Wilczynski, Wells, & Weisner, 2000, Villatoro, Giardini, & Conte, 2011; Giardini & Conte, 2012), a means to maintain the good reputations of allies (e.g., Brenneis, 1984), and a means to maintain the unity, morals, and values of social groups (e.g., Gluckman, 1963). Dunbar (1996, 2004) proposed that gossip (and language more generally) evolved to facilitate social bonding and social cohesion in the very large groups that characterize human primates, but recent research by Grueter, Bissonnette, Isler, & van Schaik (2016) failed to find support for this hypothesis.

The importance of gossip for the evolution of human cooperation, especially via indirect reciprocity, has recently received considerable attention (e.g., Leimar & Hammerstein, 2001; Giardini & Vilone, 2016a, b; Wu, Baillet & van Lange, 2016a, b, c.). Gossip has been demonstrated to increase cooperation via indirect reciprocity in experimental economics games (e.g., Milinski, this volume; Sommerfeld et al., 2007), where reputational information impacts contributions to a shared pool of resources (e.g., Beersma & van Kleef, 2011), or where information about the past behaviors of cooperative partners impacts participants' inclinations to engage in future cooperation (e.g., Feinberg, Willer, & Schultz, 2014.) Recent research has also explored how varying the quantity and quality (i.e., noisiness) of gossip impacts cooperation in experimental economics games, such as the Public Goods Game (Giardini & Vilone, 2016a).

Despite numerous theories of the evolution of gossip, it is unclear how gossip differs from any other use of language (about gossip and language, see Mangardich and Fitneva, this volume). For reasons that are still obscure, human language evolved to permit one person to communicate detailed information about themselves and their environment, including their social and nonsocial environment, to another person. "Gossip" is the exchange of information about the doings of others. It is therefore probably fruitless to consider the evolution of gossip independently of the evolution of language. Indeed, Bloom (2004) opines, "[i]t is tempting to ask about the origins and functions of gossip, but this temptation should be resisted. From a psychological perspective, gossip is likely to be an arbitrary and unnatural category... it is a domain where the most interesting aspects of mental life are laid bare." We agree. Gossip, defined as the communication of information about others, is therefore *informative*, and not necessarily aggressive, competitive, cooperative, or pedagogical.

Nevertheless, we and many others have proposed that socially competitive strategies evolved that use gossip (language) as one tool. If one's reputation impacted his or her access to scarce, contested material and social resources in ancestral environments, as reputation does todays' small scale and large scale societies, selection should have favored psychological adaptations for the strategic manipulation of reputations in ways that benefitted oneself. Attack would involve transmitting negative information about the behaviors and traits of one's competitor(s) to resource providers, and withholding positive information about the behaviors and traits of competitors from resource providers. Strategies would also include transmitting positive information about oneself to resource providers (i.e., bragging), preventing the spread of negative information about oneself (e.g., punishing disseminators of such information), or challenging the veracity of negative information about oneself (e.g., providing alibis). In this process, the reputation of the attacker would improve relative to the reputation of the attacked, thereby increasing the attacker's access to contested group resources (Barkow, 1989, 1992; Buss & Dedden, 1990; Emler, 1990; Leimar & Hammerstein, 2001; McAndrew & Milenkovic, 2002; Paine, 1967; Radin, 1927; Hess, 2006, 2017; Hess & Hagen, 2006a). On this view, one way that indirect aggression harms adversaries is by harming their reputations.

# INDIRECT AGGRESSION IS BETTER THAN PHYSICAL AGGRESSION FOR WITHIN-GROUP COMPETITION

We argue that when it comes to *within-group* competition, indirect aggression is usually better than physical aggression. Members of one's local group provide valuable reproductive, kinship, political, economic, military, and other benefits to fellow group members. Within-group physical aggression involves injuring a fellow group member. Although this physical harm might increase the aggressor's access to a contested resource, it also reduces the victim's ability to provide benefits to other group members. Physical aggression within groups can also reduce the group's ability to compete with other groups. Within-group violence would therefore involve costs to the attacker well beyond the simple risk of injury associated with a physical attack. Knauft (1991) notes that in hunter-gatherers "interpersonal aggression and violence tend to be unrewarded if not actively devalued by men and women alike." Finally, winning a physical fight might gain a resource today, but unless it permanently alters dominance rank or seriously injures or kills the adversary, another fight with the same individual might be necessary to gain a resource tomorrow.

In contrast, gossip, whether it has a positive or negative impact on the reputation of the subject, can involve important information that fellow group members would want to know. Individuals *benefit* from knowing accurate information about other members of their community. Therefore, although many societies have norms against gossip, especially negative gossip, gossip should be discouraged less than physical aggression. Successful negative gossip against a competitor reduces the competitor's reputation, and thus access to material and social resources from potentially many group members and potentially for long periods of time, thus increasing the aggressor's access to resources, perhaps permanently.

Gossip and physical aggression also differ in the precision with which they can be used to strategically harm a competitor. Physically harming a competitor compromises the victim's ability to provide benefits to other community members in a sweeping manner. Injury or death damages or destroys a victim's ability to forage, to engage in intergroup conflict, to provide vital care to children or the ill, to accomplish multiple, valued tasks, and so on. Moreover, the relatives and allies of the victim might have to pay additional costs of caring for the victim while he or she heals. Gossip, in contrast, can be customized to benefit the attacker by strategically targeting a particular aspect of the victim's reputation. Negative gossip can target a competitor's reputation as a good mate, while sparing her reputation as a caretaker. Gossip can be used to decrease a competitor's access to specific contested resources, without preventing the competitor from providing resources to other community members; this makes gossip an excellent weapon for within-community competition.

Men do use physical aggression for within-group competition with other men, and to dominate and coerce women (Smuts, 1995). Pair bonding provides an additional possible explanation for women's avoidance of physical aggression: physical conflicts between women could draw in their husbands and other male relatives, who could use their advantages in physical formidability to either suppress female fighting, or to engage with each other in proxy fights. Nevertheless, a study that compared levels of physical violence in chimpanzees to that in humans found that whereas mortality from between-group violence was similar in the two species, humans had much lower levels of within-group physical aggression than chimpanzees (Wrangham et al., 2006).

According to our theory, then, there is little sex difference in nonphysical aggression because both men and women regularly compete with fellow group members for the good reputations that enhance access to the social and material resources that are important to both sexes (cf. Davis, Vaillancourt, Arnocky, Doyer, this volume). Within groups, nonphysical aggression simply outperforms physical aggression much of the time Hess (2006, 2017) argued that, under conditions where members of one sex consistently face more within-group competition, then members of that sex should use gossip competitively more than the other sex.

# FRIENDSHIPS, CLIQUES, AND INFORMATIONAL WARFARE: THE COALITIONAL MANIPULATION OF REPUTATIONS

Nonhuman primates form coalitions and alliances with other members of their groups to improve their ability to contest resources. Hess (2003, 2006, 2017) proposed that alliances, that is, friends and cliques, are valuable in human contests over monopolizable resources where the "weapon" could be physical aggression, a point emphasized by De Scioli & Kurzban (2009), but would more often be reputational manipulation via gossip. Cooperating individuals would be more powerful than individuals in using information to attack the reputations of their competitor(s) because of the improved abilities of coalitions to strategically collect, analyze, and disseminate reputation-relevant information. Allies provide more ears and eyes to collect negative information about competitors, more brains to analyze this information, and more mouths to disseminate it (see Hess, 2006 for a detailed discussion of "informational warfare theory"). In addition, information transmitted by multiple individuals may be more believable. For example, Hess & Hagen, 2006b ran a series of experiments and found that participants believe gossip more, not when it is simply reiterated, but when it is transmitted by multiple, independent sources without a clear conflict with the target of the gossip. Further, while coalitions might be able to better attack competitors' reputations with negative gossip, they would also be better able to defend coalition members' reputations by providing alibis, withholding negative gossip, and transmitting positive gossip about allies. Finally, coalitions might also be better able to deter negative gossip attacks by competitors against coalition members by threatening competitors with retaliatory negative gossip.

Based on the observation that "competing through competition" (i.e., competing coalitionally) is so widespread in primates, Chapais (1996, pp. 19–20) suggests that coalitional competition probably reflects a phylogenetically primitive process. Humans, Chapais argues, pool not just physical power but also goods, services, and information to enhance the acquisition and defense of resources. Along similar lines, Hess (1999, 2006, 2017) proposed that for humans, coalitional aggression relies not just on enhanced physical capabilities, but also informational capabilities, particularly those involving information relevant to reputation. Ostracizing others and disrupting their social relationships—key features of indirect aggression—harms competitors, in part, by depriving them of access to information and the allies that would help them make best use of it.

# Concluding Remarks

Nonphysical forms of aggression prominently feature the use of negative gossip to harm the reputations of competitors. They are commonly used by both sexes and are associated with the use of physical aggression, but unlike physical aggression, do not appear to be linked with adult adjustment problems. Evolutionary theorists of aggression concur that nonphysical forms of aggression probably evolved to increase access to material and social resources in competition with others, but disagree on (1) why an alternative to physical aggression evolved, (2) the role, if any, of sex differences, and (3) how, exactly, nonphysical aggression harms competitors.

Using evolutionary principles and comparisons of humans with non-human primate relatives, we propose a strategic account of the aggressive use of gossip that emphasizes within-group competition: when access to contested group material and social resources depends on having a good reputation, individuals and cliques collect, analyze, and disseminate information to improve their own reputations relative to competitors. Over human evolution, gossip could have been used by either sex to compete in multiple domains such as increasing access to food, mates, and valuable social partners. Between-group competition for territory, in contrast, relied more heavily on physical aggression by men because men have a substantial advantage in upper body strength, and because men probably benefitted more from acquiring and defending territories.

Several testable hypotheses can be derived from this model. Is gossip used more than physical aggression in the context of within-group aggression, whereas physical aggression is used more than gossip in between-group competition? Do contestable, valuable resources lead to more negative gossip about a competitor? Do participants allocate resources based on reputation, giving more resources to those with better reputations and fewer resources to those with poorer reputations? Are individual differences in indirect/relational/social aggression better explained by differences in the experience of within-group competition than by sex? Do allies allow better collection, analysis, and dissemination of gossip in reputational contests? Future research may explore these and other hypotheses.

## Note

1. Social species permanently reside in groups, in contrast to solitary species in which "groups" comprise brief dyads for mating, or mothers and infants only.

## References

Abbott, D. H. (1993). Social conflict and reproductive suppression in marmoset and tamarin monkeys. In W. A. Mason & S. P. Mendoza (Eds.), *Primate social conflict* (pp. 331–372). Albany: State University of New York Press.

Alexander, R. D. (1974). The evolution of social behavior. *Annual Review of Ecology, Evolution, and Systematics 5*, 325–383.

Alexander, R. D. (1987). *The biology of moral systems.* New York: de Gruyter.

Allen, M. W., & Jones, T. L. (2014). *Violence and warfare among hunter-gatherers.* Walnut Creek, CA: Left Coast Press.

Antón, S. C., Potts, R., & Aiello, L. C. (2014). Evolution of early Homo: An integrated biological perspective. *Science 345*(6192), 1236828.

Archer, J. (2004.) Sex differences in aggression in real-world settings: A meta-analytic review. *Review of General Psychology 8*(4), 291–322.

Archer, J., & Coyne, S. M. (2005). An integrated review of indirect, relational, and social aggression. *Personality and Social Psychology Review 9*, 212–230.

Archer, J. (2009). Does sexual selection explain human sex differences in aggression? *Behavioral and Brain Sciences 32*, 249–266.

Barkow, J. H. (1975). Prestige and culture: A biosocial interpretation. *Current Anthropology 16*(4), 553–572.

Barkow, J. H. (1992). Beneath new culture is old psychology: Gossip and social stratification. In J. H. Barkow, L. Cosmides, & J. Tooby (Eds.), *The adapted mind: Evolutionary psychology and the generation of culture* (pp. 627–637). New York: Oxford University Press.

Barkow, J. H. (1989). *Darwin, sex, and status: Biological perspectives on mind and culture.* Toronto: University of Toronto Press.

Barrett, L., & Henzi, S. P. (2002). Constraints on relationship formation among female primates. *Behaviour 139*, 263–289.

Baumeister, R. F., Vohs, K. D. & Zhang, L. (2004). Gossip as cultural learning. *Review of General Psychology 8*, 111–21.

Beersma, B., & Van Kleef, G. A. (2011). How the grapevine keeps you in line: Gossip increases contributions to the group. *Social Psychological and Personality Science 2*(6), 642–649.

Bernstein, I. S. (1981). Dominance: The baby and the bathwater. *Behavioral and Brain Sciences 4*, 419–429.

Björkqvist, K. (2001). Different names, same issue. Social Development *10*, 272–275.

Bjorkqvist, K., Lagerspetz, K. M. J., & Kaulkanian, A. (1992). Do girls manipulate and boys fight? *Aggressive Behavior 18*, 117–127.

Björkqvist, K., & Niemelä, P. (1992). Of mice and women: Aspects of female aggression, (pp. 3–16). San Diego, CA: Academic Press.

Bloom, P. (2004). Postscript to the special issue on gossip. *Review of General Psychology 8*, 138–140.

Boinski, S., Sughrue, K., Selvaggi, L., Quatrone, R., Henry, M., & Cropp, S. (2002). An expanded test of the ecological model of primate social evolution: Competitive regimes and female bonding in three species of squirrel monkeys (*Saimiri oerstedii, S. boliviensis, and S. sciureus*). *Behaviour 139*, 227–261.

Bowles, S., (2009). Did warfare among ancestral hunter-gatherers affect the evolution of human social behaviors? *Science 324*, 293–298.

Brenneis, D. (1984) Grog and gossip in Bhatgaon: Style and substance in Fiji Indian conversation. *American Ethnologist 11*, 487–506.

Broidy, L. M., Nagin, D. S., Tremblay, R. E., Bates, J. E., Brame, B., Dodge, K. A.,…Lynam, D. R. (2003). Developmental trajectories of childhood disruptive behaviors and adolescent delinquency: A six-site, cross-national study. *Developmental Psychology 39*(2), 222.

Burbank, V. K. (1987). Female aggression in cross-cultural perspective. *Cross-Cultural Research 21*(1–4), 70–100.

Buss, D. M., & Dedden, L. (1990). Derogation of competitors. *Journal of Social and Personal Relationships 7*, 395–422.

Buss, D. M., & Shackelford, T. K. (1997). Human aggression in evolutionary psychological perspective. *Clinical Psychology Review* 17(6), 605–619.

Cairns, R. B., Cairns, B. D., Neckerman, H. J., Ferguson, L. L., & Gariepy, J. L. (1989). Growth and aggression: 1. Childhood to early adolescence. Developmental Psychology 25, 320–330.

Campbell, A. (1999). Staying alive: Evolution, culture, and women's intra-sexual aggression. *Behavioral and Brain Sciences 22*, 203–252.

Card, N. A., Stucky, B. D., Sawalani, G. M., & Little, T. D. (2008). Direct and indirect aggression during childhood and adolescence: A meta-analytic review of gender differences, intercorrelations, and relations to maladjustment. *Child Development 79*(5), 1185–1229.

Chagnon, N. A. (1988). Life histories, blood revenge, and warfare in a tribal population. *Science 239*, 985–992.

Chapais, B. (1996). Competing through co-operation in nonhuman primates: Developmental aspects of matrilineal dominance. *International Journal of Behavioral Development 19*, 7–23.

Chapais, B., & Schulman, S. R. (1980). An evolutionary model of female dominance relations in primates. *Journal of Theoretical Biology 82*(1), 47–89.

Clutton-Brock, T., & Janson, C. (2012). Primate socioecology at the crossroads: Past, present, and future. *Evolutionary Anthropology: Issues, News, and Reviews 21*(4), 136–150.

Cox, S. J., Sluckin, T. J. & Steele, J. (1999). Group size, memory, and interaction rate in the evolution of cooperation. *Current Anthropology 40*, 369–377.

Crick, N. R., & Grotpeter, J. K. (1995). Relational aggression, gender, and social-psychological adjustment. *Child Development 66*, 710–722.

Crick, N. R. (1996). The role of overt aggression, relational aggression, and prosocial behavior in the prediction of children's future social adjustment. *Child Development 67*(5), 2317–2327.

Crick, N. R., Ostrov, J. M., & Kawabata, Y. (2007). Relational aggression and gender: An overview. In D. J. Flannery, A. T. Vazsonyi, & I. D. Waldman (Eds.), *The Cambridge handbook of violent behavior and aggression* (pp. 245–259). New York, NY: Cambridge University Press.

Crofoot, M. C., & Wrangham, R. W. (2010). Intergroup aggression in primates and humans: The case for a unified theory. In *Mind the Gap* (pp. 171–195). Berlin/ Heidelberg: Springer.

Davis, A., Vaillancourt, T., Arnocky, S., & Doyel, R. (2019). Women's gossip as an intrasexual competition strategy: An evolutionary approach to gender and discrimination. In F. Giardini & R. P. M. Wittek (Eds.), *Handbook of gossip and reputation*. New York, NY: Oxford University Press.

De Backer, C. (2005). Like Belgian chocolate for the universal mind: Interpersonal and media gossip from an evolutionary perspective (Doctoral Dissertation. Ghent University, Belgium).

De Scioli, P., & Kurzban, R. (2009). The alliance hypothesis for human friendship. *PLoS One 4*, e5802. doi:10.1371/journal.pone.0005802.

Drews, C. (1993). The concept and definition of dominance in animal behaviour. *Behaviour 125*, 283–313.

Dunbar, R. I. M. (1996). *Grooming, gossip, and the evolution of language*. Harvard: University Press.

Dunbar, R. I. M. (2004). Gossip in evolutionary perspective. *Review of General Psychology 8*, 100–110.

Dyson-Hudson, R., & Smith, E. A. (1978). Human territoriality: An ecological reassessment. *American Anthropologist 80* (1), 21–41.

Eckert, P. (1990). Cooperative competition in adolescent "girl talk." *Discourse Processes 13*, 91–122.

Emler, N. (1990). A social psychology of reputation. In W. Stroebe & M. Hewstone (Eds.), *European Review of Social Psychology* (vol. 1, pp. 171–93). Hoboken, NJ: Wiley and Sons.

Enquist, M., & Leimar, O. (1993). The evolution of cooperation in mobile organisms. *Animal Behaviour 45*, 747–757.

Feinberg, M., Willer, R., & Schultz, M. (2014). Gossip and ostracism promote cooperation in groups. *Psychological Science 25* (3), 656–664.

Ferguson, R. B. (1997). Violence and war in prehistory. In D. W. Marin & D. L. Frayer (Eds.), *Troubled times: Violence and warfare in the past*. Amsterdam: Gordon & Breach.

Feshbach, N. D. (1969). Sex differences in children's modes of aggressive responses toward outsiders. *Merrill-Palmer Quarterly of Behavior and Development 15*(3), 249–258.

Fine, G. A. (1977). Social components of children's gossip. *Journal of Communication 27*, 181–185.

Fine, G. A., & Rosnow, R. L. (1978). Gossip, gossipers, gossiping. *Personality and Social Psychology Bulletin 4*, 161–168.

Fleagle, John G. (2013). *Primate adaptation and evolution*, 3rd ed. Amsterdam, Netherlands: Academic Press/Elsevier.

Fry, D. P., & Söderberg, P. (2013). Lethal aggression in mobile forager bands and implications for the origins of war. *Science 341*(6143), 270–273.

Galen, B. R. & Underwood, M. K. (1997). A developmental investigation of social aggression among children. *Developmental Psychology 33*, 589–600.

Geary, D. C. (1998). *Male, female: The evolution of human sex differences*. Washington, DC: American Psychological Association.

Giardini, F., & Conte, R. (2012). Gossip for social control in natural and artificial societies. *Simulation 88*(1), 18–32.

Giardini, F., Paolucci, M., Villatoro, D., & Conte, R. (2014). "Punishment and gossip: sustaining cooperation in a public goods game." In Kamiński B., & Koloch G. (Eds.) *Advances in Social Simulation. Advances in Intelligent Systems and Computing* (vol. 229). Berlin, Heidelberg: Springer.

Giardini, F., & Vilone, D. (2016). Evolution of gossip-based indirect reciprocity on a bipartite network. *Scientific Reports 6*. doi:10.1038/srep37931

Gintis, H., Smith, E. A., & Bowles, S. (2001). Costly signaling and cooperation. *Journal of Theoretical Biology 213*, 103–119.

Gluckman, M. (1963). Gossip and Scandal. *Current Anthropology 4*, 307–316.

Gómez, J. M., Verdú, M., González-Megías, A., & Méndez, M. (2016). The phylogenetic roots of human lethal violence. *Nature 538*, 233–237.

Gottman, J. M., & Mettetal, G. (1986). Speculations about social and affective development: Friendship and acquaintance through adolescence. In J. M. Gottman & J. G. Parker (Eds.), *Conversations of Friends: Speculations on Affective Development* (pp. 192–237). Cambridge: Cambridge University Press.

Grueter, C. C., Bissonnette, A., Isler, K., & van Schaik, C. P. (2013). Grooming and group cohesion in primates: Implications for the evolution of language. *Evolution and Human Behavior 34*(1), 61–68.

Gurven, M, Allen-Arave, W., Hill, K. & Hurtado, M. (2000). "It's a Wonderful Life": Signaling generosity among the Ache of Paraguay. *Evolution and Human Behavior 21*, 263–282.

Hagen, E. H., & Hammerstein, P. (2009). Did Neanderthals and other early humans sing? Seeking the biological roots of music in the territorial advertisements of primates, lions, hyenas, and wolves. *Musicae Scientiae* 13(2_suppl.), 291–320.

Harcourt, A. H., & de Waal, F. (1992). *Coalitions and alliances in humans and other animals.* Oxford: Oxford University Press.

Hawkes, K. (1991). Showing off: Tests of an hypothesis about men's foraging goals. *Ethology and Sociobiology* 12, 29–54.

Hawley, P. H. (1999). The ontogenesis of social dominance: A strategy-based evolutionary perspective. *Developmental Review* 19, 97–132.

Hawley, P. H., Little, T. D., & Card, N. A. (2008). The myth of the alpha male: A new look at dominance-related beliefs and behaviors among adolescent males and females. *International Journal of Behavioral Development* 32, 76–88.

Hawley, P. H. (2007). Social dominance in childhood and adolescence: Why social competence and aggression may go hand in hand. In P. H. Hawley, T. D. Little, & P. C. Rodkin (Eds.), *Aggression and adaptation: The bright side to bad behavior.* New York: Psychology Press1-29.

Heilbron, N., & Prinstein, M. J. (2008). A review and reconceptualization of social aggression: Adaptive and maladaptive correlates. *Clinical Child and Family Psychology Review* 11(4), 176–217.

Hess, N. H. (1999). Female coalitions and gossip. Presented at Human Behavior and Evolution Society Conference, University of Utah, Salt Lake City.

Hess, N. H. (2006). Informational warfare: The evolution of female coalitional competition (Doctoral dissertation, University of California, Santa Barbara). *Dissertation Abstracts International* 67(1), 242.

Hess, N. H. (2017). Informational warfare: Coalitional gossiping as a strategy for within-group aggression. In M. L. Fisher (Ed.), The Oxford handbook of female competition. Oxford: Oxford University Press.

Hess, N. C., & Hagen, E. H. (2002). Informational warfare. Cogprints.

Hess, N. H., & Hagen, E. H. (2003). Applying the socioecological model of primate coalition formation to human females. Abstract in Program of the 4. Göttinger Freilandtage, Göttingen, Germany, December 9–12, 2003, Cooperation in primates and humans: Mechanisms and evolution, *The Primate Report* 66(1), 25.

Hess, N. H., & Hagen, E. H. (2006a). Sex differences in informational aggression: Psychological evidence from young adults. *Evolution and Human Behavior* 27, 231–245.

Hess, N. H., & Hagen, E. H. (2006b). Psychological adaptations for assessing gossip believability. *Human Nature* 17, 337–354.

Hess, N. H., Helfrecht, C., Hagen, E. H., Sell, A. and Hewlett, B. S. (2010). Interpersonal aggression among Aka hunter-gatherers of the Central African Republic: Assessing the effects of sex, strength, and anger. *Human Nature* 21, 330–354.

Holekamp, K. E. & Smale, L. (1991). Dominance acquisition during mammalian social development: The "inheritance" of maternal rank. *American Zoologist* 31(2), 306–317.

Ingram, G. P. (2014). From hitting to tattling to gossip: An evolutionary rationale for the development of indirect aggression. *Evolutionary Psychology* 12(2), 343–363.

Isbell, L. A., & Young, T. P. (2002). Ecological models of female social relationships in primates: Similarities, disparities, and some directions for future clarity. *Behaviour* 139, 177–202.

Janson, C. H. (2000). Primate socio-ecology: The end of a golden age. *Evolutionary Anthropology* 9, 73–86.

Kaplan, H., & Gurven, M. (2005). The natural history of human food sharing and cooperation: A review and a new multi-individual approach to the negotiation of norms. In
H. Gintis, S. Bowles, R. Boyd, & E. Fehr (Eds.), *Moral sentiments and material interests: The
foundations of cooperation in economic life* (pp. 75–113). Cambridge, MA: MIT Press.

Kappeler, P. M., & Van Schaik, C. P. (2002). Evolution of primate social systems. *International
Journal of Primatology 23*, 707–740.

Koenig, A. (2002). Competition for resources and its behavioral consequences among female
primates. *International Journal of Primatology 23*, 759–783.

Knauft, B. M. (1991). Violence and sociality in human evolution. *Current Anthropology 32*,
391–428.

Lagerspetz, K., Bjorkqvist, K., & Peltonen, T. (1988). Is indirect aggression typical of females?
Gender differences in aggressiveness in 11- to 12-year-old children. *Aggressive Behavior 14*,
403–414.

Langergraber, K. E., Prüfer, K., Rowney, C., Boesch, C., Crockford, C., Fawcett, K.,...&
Robbins, M. M. (2012). Generation times in wild chimpanzees and gorillas suggest earlier
divergence times in great ape and human evolution. *Proceedings of the National Academy of
Sciences USA 109*(39), 15716–15721.

Leimar, O. & Hammerstein. P. (2001). Evolution of cooperation through indirect reciprocity.
*Proceedings of the Royal Society of London B 268*, 745–753.

Mangardich, H., & Fitneva, S. A. (2018). Gossip, reputation, and the study of language, In
F. Giardini & R. P. M. Wittek (Eds). *Handbook of gossip and reputation*. New York: Oxford
University Press.

Manson, J. H., Wrangham, R. W., Boone, J. L., Chapais, B., Dunbar, R. I. M., Ember, C. R.,...&
Paterson, J. D. (1991). Intergroup aggression in chimpanzees and humans [and comments
and replies]. *Current Anthropology 32*(4), 369–390.

Maynard Smith, J., & Parker, G. R. (1976). The logic of asymmetric contests. *Animal Behavior
24*, 159–175.

McAndrew, F. T. & Milenkovic, M. A. (2002). Of tabloids and family secrets: The evolutionary
psychology of gossip. *Journal of Applied Social Psychology 32*, 1064–1082.

Milinski, M., Semmann, D. Bakker, T. C. M., & Krambeck, H.-J. (2001). Cooperation through
indirect reciprocity: Image scoring or standing strategy? *Proceedings of the Royal Society of
London B 268*, 2495–2501.

Milinski, M., Semmann, D., & Krambeck, H.-J. (2002). Reputation helps solve the "tragedy of
the commons." *Nature 415*, 424–426.

Milinski, M. (2018). Gossip and reputation in social dilemmas. In F. Giardini & R. P. M. Wittek
(Eds.), *Handbook of gossip and reputation*. New York: Oxford University Press.

Miller, G. (2000). *The mating mind: How sexual choice shaped the evolution of human nature*.
New York: Anchor Books.

Nowak, M. A. A. & Sigmund, K. (1998). Evolution of indirect reciprocity by image scoring.
*Nature 393*, 573–577.

Owens, L., Shute, R., & Slee, P. (2000a). "Guess what I just heard!": Indirect aggression among
teenage girls in Australia. *Aggressive Behavior 26*, 67–83.

Owens, L., Shute, R. & Slee, P. (2000b). "I'm in and you're out...": Explanations for teenage
girls' indirect aggression. *Psychology, Evolution, and Gender 2*, 19–46.

Paine, R. (1967). What is gossip about? An alternative hypothesis. *Man 2*, 278–285.

Pandit, S. A., & van Schaik, C. P. (2003). A model for leveling coalitions among primate males:
Toward a theory of egalitarianism. *Behavioral Ecology and Sociobiology 55*(2), 161–168.

Peterson, N. (1993). Demand sharing: Reciprocity and the pressure for generosity among for-agers. *American Anthropologist 95*(4), 860–874.

Pheasant, S. T. (1983). Sex differences in strength—some observations on their variability. *Applied Ergonomics 14*(3), 205–211.

Plavcan, J. M. (2001). Sexual dimorphism in primate evolution. *American Journal of Physical Anthropology 116*(S33), 25–53.

Plavcan, J. M. (2012). Sexual size dimorphism, canine dimorphism, and male-male competition in primates. *Human Nature 23*(1), 45–67.

Pollock, G., & Dugatkin, L. A. (1992). Reciprocity and the emergence of reputation. *Journal of Theoretical Biology 159*, 25–37.

Radin, P. (1927). *Primitive man as philosopher.* New York: Appleton.

Rodseth, L., Wrangham, R. W., Harrigan, A. M., & Smuts, B. B. (1991). The human community as a primate society. *Current Anthropology 32*, 221–254.

van Schaik C. P. (1983). Why are diurnal primates living in groups? *Behaviour 87*, 120–144.

van Schaik, C. P., Pandit, S. A., & Vogel, E. R. (2006). Toward a general model for male-male coalitions in primate groups. In P. M. Kappeler & C. P. van Schaik (Eds.), *Cooperation in primates and humans* (pp. 151–172). Berlin: Springer.

Schjelderup-Ebbe, T., 1922. Beitrage zur sozialpsychologie des haushuhns. Zeitschrift für Psychologie *88*, 225–252.

Schmitt, D. P., & Buss, D. M. (1996). Strategic self-promotion and competitor derogation: Sex and context effects on the perceived effectiveness of mate attraction tactics. *Journal of Personality and Social Psychology 70*(6), 1185–1204.

Sell, A., Cosmides, L., Tooby, J., Sznycer, D., von Rueden, C., & Gurven, M. (2009). Human adaptations for the visual assessment of strength and fighting ability from the body and face. *Proceedings of the Royal Society of London B: Biological Sciences 276*(1656), 575–584.

Silk, J. B. (2002). Females, food, family, and friendship. *Evolutionary Anthropology 11*, 85–7.

Silk, J. B. (2007a). Social components of fitness in primate groups. Science *317*, 1347–1351.

Silk, J. B. (2007b). The adaptive value of sociality in mammalian groups. *Philosophical Transactions of the Royal Society of London, B 362*, 539–559.

Silk, J. B., & Kappeler, P. M. (2017). Sociality in primates. In Rubenstein D. R., Abbot P. (Eds.), *Comparative Social Evolution* (ch. 9, p. 253). Cambridge: Cambridge University Press.

Smith, E. A., & Bliege Bird, R. L. (2000). Turtle hunting and tombstone opening: Public generosity as costly signaling. *Evolution and Human Behavior 21*, 245–261.

Smith, J. E., Swanson, E. M., Reed, D., & Holekamp, K. E. (2012). Evolution of cooperation among mammalian carnivores and its relevance to hominin evolution. *Current Anthropology 53*(S6), S436–S452.

Smuts, B. (1995). The evolutionary origins of patriarchy. *Human Nature 6*(1), 1–32.

Smuts, B. B., & Nicolson, N. (1989). Reproduction in wild female olive baboons. *American Journal of Primatology 19*, 229–246.

Sommerfeld, R. D., Krambeck, H. J., Semmann, D., & Milinski, M. (2007). Gossip as an alternative for direct observation in games of indirect reciprocity. *Proceedings of the National Academy of Sciences USA 104*(44), 17435–17440.

Sterck, E. H. M., Watts, D. P., & Van Schaik, C. P. (1997). The evolution of female social relationships in nonhuman primates. *Behavioral Ecology and Sociobiology 41*, 291–309.

Stiner, M. C. (2002). Carnivory, coevolution, and the geographic spread of the genus Homo. *Journal of Archaeological Research 10*, 1–63.

Stiner, M. C., Barkai, R., & Gopher, A. (2009). Cooperative hunting and meat sharing 400–200 kya at Qesem Cave, Israel. *Proceedings of the National Academy of Sciences USA 106*(32), 13207–13212.

Suls, J. M. (1977). Gossip as social comparison. *Journal of Communication 27,* 164–168.

Sugiyama, L. S., & Chacon, R. (2000). Effects of illness and injury among the Yora and Shiwiar. In L. Cronk, N. A. Chagnon, & W. Irons (Eds.), *Human behavior and adaptation: An anthropological perspective* (pp. 371–396). New York: Aldine de Gruyter.

Tiger, L. (1969). *Men in groups.* New York: Random House.

Tiger, L., & Fox, R. (1971). *The imperial animal.* New York: Holt, Rinehart, and Winston.

Tooby, J., & Cosmides, L. (1988). The evolution of war and its cognitive foundations. *Technical Report* 888–1. Palo Alto, CA: Institute for Evolutionary Studies.

Tremblay, R. E., Nagin, D. S., Séguin, J. R., Zoccolillo, M., Zelazo, P. D., Boivin, M.,...& Japel, C. (2004). Physical aggression during early childhood: Trajectories and predictors. *Pediatrics 114*(1), e43–e50.

Trivers, R. (1972). Parental investment and sexual selection. In B. Campbell (Ed.), *Sexual selection & the descent of man* (pp. 136–179). New York: Aldine de Gruyter.

Van Vugt, M. (2009). Sex differences in intergroup competition, aggression, and warfare. *Annals of the New York Academy of Sciences 1167*(1), 124–134.

Voulgaridou, I., & Kokkinos, C. M. (2015). Relational aggression in adolescents: A review of theoretical and empirical research. *Aggression and Violent Behavior 23,* 87–97.

Watkins, S. C. & Danzi, A. D. (1995). Women's gossip and social change: Childbirth and fertility control among Italian and Jewish women in the United States, 1920–1940. *Gender and Society 9,* 469–490.

Wedekind, C. & Milinski, M. (2000). Cooperation through image scoring in humans. *Science 288,* 850–852.

Wert, S. R. & Salovey, P. (2004). A social comparison account of gossip. *Review of General Psychology 8,* 122–137.

Willems, E. P., & van Schaik, C. P. (2015). "Collective action and the intensity of between-group competition in nonhuman primates." *Behavioral Ecology 26*(2), 625–631.

Wilson, D. S., Wilczynski, C., Wells, A., & Weiser, L. (2000). Gossip and other aspects of language as group-level adaptations. In C. Heyes & L. Huber (Eds.), *The evolution of cognition* (pp. 347–65). Cambridge, MA: MIT Press.

Wilson, D. S., Timmel, J. J., & Miller, R. R. (2004). Cognitive cooperation: When the going gets tough, think as a group. *Human Nature 15,* 1–15.

Wilson, M., & Daly, M. (1985). Competitiveness, risk taking, and violence: The young male syndrome. *Ethology and Sociobiology 6*(1), 59–73.

Wrangham, R. W. (1980). An ecological model of female-bonded primate groups. *Behaviour 75,* 262–300.

Wrangham, R. W. (1999). Evolution of coalitionary killing. *American Journal of Physical Anthropology 110*(S29), 1–30.

Wrangham, R. W., & Glowacki, L. (2012). Intergroup aggression in chimpanzees and war in nomadic hunter-gatherers. *Human Nature 23*(1), 5–29.

Wrangham, R. W., & Peterson, D. (1996). *Demonic males: Apes and the origins of human violence.* New York: Houghton Mifflin.

Wrangham, R. W., Wilson, M. L., & Muller, M. N. (2006). Comparative rates of violence in chimpanzees and humans. *Primates 47*(1), 14–26.

Wu, J., Balliet, D., & Van Lange, P. A. (2016a). Gossip versus punishment: The efficiency of reputation to promote and maintain cooperation. *Scientific Reports 6*. DOI: 10.1038/srep23919

Wu, J., Balliet, D., & Van Lange, P. A. (2016b). Reputation management: Why and how gossip enhances generosity. *Evolution and Human Behavior 37*(3), 193–201.

Wu, J., Balliet, D., & Van Lange, P. A. (2016c). Reputation, gossip, and human cooperation. *Social and Personality Psychology Compass 10*(6), 350–364.

CHAPTER 16

# WOMEN'S GOSSIP AS AN INTRASEXUAL COMPETITION STRATEGY

## *An Evolutionary Approach to Sex and Discrimination*

ADAM DAVIS, TRACY VAILLANCOURT,
STEVEN ARNOCKY, AND ROBERT DOYEL

## INTRODUCTION

GOSSIP, as a form of social information exchange, is core to human social relationships and perhaps even society itself (Barkow, 1992; Dunbar, 1996). It provides human beings with the ability to acquire specific knowledge about people embedded within vast social networks, and enables individuals to strategically manipulate information about themselves or others to produce desired negative or positive reputation outcomes (Hess and Hagen, 2006; Power, 1998). Gossip can also be an effective low-cost aggressive tactic, particularly within the realm of mate competition, when searching for and courting a mate, driving off rivals, and attempting to retain valued relationship partners (Arnocky and Vaillancourt, 2017; Vaillancourt, 2005, 2013). Within this context, gossip has been argued to be the weapon of choice among women to indirectly aggress against same-sex competitors (Campbell, 2004; McAndrew, 2014a,b). This may be the case because, over evolutionary time, women and men have encountered selective pressures that have differentially influenced their survival and reproduction, resulting in divergent adaptations to overcome these obstacles. As important as gossip and reputation are in modern society, they were also likely of great relevance to our human ancestors who evolved in small and highly social nomadic hunter-gatherer groups (Dunbar, 2004). As such, taking an evolutionary approach can yield unique insights into the origins, functions, and outcomes of gossip, as well as potential sex differences in gossiping.

Gossip is a complex and multifaceted psychological construct that has been defined differently from various disciplinary perspectives (De Backer et al. 2007). Holistically, *gossip* has been described as the transmitting or receiving of socially relevant information about the new, deviant, and/or prosocial behavior of other people (Amo, 1980). A further distinction can be made within this general definition between two subtypes of gossip termed *strategy learning gossip* and *reputation gossip* (De Backer et al. 2007; De Backer, Van den Bulck, Fisher, Ouvrein, this volume). With *strategy learning gossip*, there is little to no importance associated with the target of the gossip (i.e., the gossipee); rather, the focus of attention centers on the content of the communicated message and its relevance to genetic fitness. *Fitness*, in this evolutionary sense, refers to any information that may influence survival and reproduction (Buss, 2012). For instance, being told that "Jessica died after being stung by a blue insect" carries the same relevance to fitness if changed to "Rebecca died after being stung by a blue insect." Through strategy learning gossip, the receivers of the information learn vicariously about the successes and miscalculations of others, saving them from having to experience the same potentially dangerous events first hand (Bandura, 1977; De Backer et al. 2007). Strategy learning gossip may also be an effective cultural learning tool because it provides insight into how to effectively participate in a society governed by a complexity of rules, morals, scripts, norms, traditions, and structures (Baumeister et al. 2004).

In contrast, the identity of the individual associated with social information exchange is critical in regard to *reputation gossip*, because the content relates to a particular person's reputation of interest, meaning the collection of beliefs and opinions generally held about them by others. Those spreading this kind of information to others may manipulate the reputation of the subject of the gossip (e.g., "Emily has sex with a lot of different men") or even themselves indirectly (e.g., "I am a virgin") to achieve strategic outcomes (Dunbar, 1996). The receivers of reputation gossip benefit by efficiently learning reputation-relevant information about specific people of interest within their social network, and with whom they may be likely to interact again in the future (De Backer et al. 2007). In relation to heterosexual women's competition with members of the same sex, it is reputation gossip that is important. To appreciate why this is the case, it is necessary to assume an evolutionary perspective through which gossip is argued to be an adaptation that influences the capacity of human beings to survive and reproduce.

# GOSSIP AS AN ADAPTATION TO OVERCOME ADAPTIVE PROBLEMS

Gossip is conventionally understood to be a wicked, sneaky, and malicious form of information exchange between people. Within the evolutionary sciences, the proposed origins and functions of gossip extend well beyond a device whose sole purpose is to hurt the reputations of others. From an evolutionary perspective, gossip is argued to constitute an *adaptation*, defined as a heritable trait that evolved because it helped to solve a problem associated with survival and/or reproduction (Williams, 1966). The challenges that adaptations function to overcome are known as *adaptive problems*, which impact in some way an organism's ability to survive (e.g., learning about dangerous predators) and/or reproduce (e.g., gathering knowledge about available mates; Buss, 2012; Symons, 1979). McAndrew et al. (2007) further argued that a multilevel selection perspective, wherein traits evolve to fulfill both genetic and social group purposes, provides the best means of understanding the evolutionary origins and function of gossip.

For Dunbar (1996), the key adaptive problem gossip evolved to solve in humans was efficient information exchange in an ever expanding social network. From this perspective, gossip is understood to be a form of "social grooming" that first arose in nonhuman primates, such as one of our closest genetic relatives, the chimpanzee. According to Dunbar (1996, 2004), alliances are solidified through commitment and trust, which is achieved in nonhuman primates by physically grooming one's in-group allies. Because the amount of time spent grooming is proportional to a primate specie's group size, "there is an upper limit on the size of a group that can be bonded by this mechanism" (Dunbar, 2004, p. 102). As ancestral human groups grew in size, it became impossible to devote the necessary amount of time for physical grooming and, as a consequence, language may have evolved to promote bonding in large social groups through gossip. Dunbar (2004) argued that gossip in humans provided four key adaptive benefits: (1) keeping track of other individuals in an expansive social network, (2) advertising one's own advantages as a friend, ally, or mate, (3) seeking advice on personal problems, and (4) policing deceivers and free riders (i.e., social loafers).

An implication of Dunbar's (1996, 2004) argument, is that gossip extends to several distinct, yet interrelated, domains of psychological functioning. In regard to reputation gossip, this subsequently means that information could potentially come from a number of important sources. For Barkow (1992), potential mates, kin, social exchange partners, and high-ranking people should be the most important sources of social knowledge. Barkow (1992) further asserted that we should be most drawn to the information that can significantly impact our fitness and our *status* (i.e., our relative social standing), such as details regarding the sexual activity, alliances, and trustworthiness of people within our social network, as well as news concerning the allocation of valued resources (e.g., financial information) among group members. McAndrew et al. (2007) supported this view, arguing that gossip functions principally as a status-enhancing mechanism.

# Gossip as a Social Control Mechanism

Most of the evolutionary research on gossip has focused on its social control function within groups. This interest stems from the observation that gossip can be a very effective way of enforcing conformity by reminding group members which attitudes, values, and behavior are generally deemed appropriate or inappropriate amongst the group, as well as what happens to those who transgress against these group norms (Barkow, 1992; Giardini and Conte, 2011). Detecting rule-breakers has probably been a major impetus driving the evolution of our social behavior to encourage within-group cooperation (McAndrew et al. 2007). For a group to cooperate as a cohesive whole, cheaters who fail to meet group expectations (e.g., refusing to reciprocate prosocial behavior) must be identified and reprimanded or dispatched. Gossip has been shown to function effectively in this respect among modern hunter-gatherer societies (Lee, 1990; McPherson, 1991), cattle farmers in California (Ellickson, 1991), fishers in Maine (Acheson, 1988), and college rowing teams (Kniffin and Wilson, 2005). Thus, it is likely that two key adaptive problems that gossip evolved to solve is the detecting of cheaters and enforcing group norms to maintain cooperative groups.

Boehm (1999) also advanced the argument that gossip could function to prevent dominant individuals from compromising the integrity of the group. From this perspective, enforced egalitarianism can diminish within-group competitiveness and promote group cohesion. Again, keeping dominant individuals in check serves a social control function, consequently discouraging within-group aggression and encouraging cooperative behavior (McAndrew et al. 2007). Thus, gossip can be an effective way to manipulate public opinion and can be used to lampoon and shun dominant group members trying to undermine the group hierarchy.

## GOSSIP AS A FORM OF INTRASEXUAL COMPETITION

Although gossip can effectively promote conformity and cooperation, it can also be used competitively to elevate one's own reputation as a mate, ally, or friend, at the expense of others (Davis et al. 2018a; Farley, this volume; Massar et al. 2012; McAndrew, 2014a, 2014b; McAndrew et al. 2007). Gossip, either honest or deceptive, can be used to vie for valued resources (e.g., popularity, attractive mates, information about others in one's social network) by using information to damage an opponent's reputation to improve one's own status (Barkow, 1992; Dunbar, 1996; Emler, 1994; Hess and Hagen, 2006). From an evolutionary perspective, the primary competitors of heterosexual individuals, especially within the realm of courtship (i.e., the process of forming a romantic or sexual relationship) and mating, are members of the same sex who are contending for the same valued resources (Hess and Hagen, this volume; Wilson and Daly, 1996). When pursuing potential mates or attempting to retain a valued relationship partner, gossip is used strategically against same sex rivals to increase one's *reproductive success*, the ability to contribute genes to offspring that provide them with the best opportunity to carry one's genetic material onward. As an intrasexually competitive strategy, gossip is predicted to differ among the sexes (Davis et al. 2018b). This is because women and men have faced different adaptive challenges associated with selecting, attracting, and retaining a mate required for successful reproduction, as well as helping offspring survive and grow to sexual maturity (Buss, 2012). We define *sex* as normative differences in reproductive anatomy, physiology, and function that largely follows a biomodal distribution (i.e., female/male), but also includes a variety of expression (American Psychological Association, 2015).

**The theory of sexual selection.** Within the realm of courtship and mating, adaptations such as gossip arise as a consequence of successful reproduction. This is a core tenet of Darwin's (1871) theory of *sexual selection*, which involves two key components: intersexual selection and intrasexual competition. *Intersexual selection* involves an individual of one sex choosing a preferred opposite-sex partner (Buss, 2012). Those who possess desired traits will be preferentially chosen as mates and will thus pass along their heritable qualities to subsequent generations. Darwin (1871) referred to this kind of selection as "female choice" because he observed throughout the animal world that females tended to be the relatively more discerning sex in their mate selection decisions. In contrast, *intrasexual competition* refers to members of the same-sex competing with one another for access to sexually available members of the opposite-sex. When it comes to sexual selection, *differential parental investment* is a key driving force behind this mechanism of evolutionary change (Campbell, 2004; Vaillancourt, 2005, 2013; Williams, 1966). According to Trivers' (1972), the relative degree of parental investment dictates which sex has evolved to be more discriminatory in its mate selection and less likely to physically compete with intrasexual rivals. Across mammals, females in comparison to males, devote more obligatory parental investment in the form of gestation (due to the internal fertilization of the ovum and sperm), child bearing, and breastfeeding. In fact, among 95 percent of mammalian species, females provide all of the parental care, stressing the significance of maternal investment in the survival and development of offspring (Clutton-Brock, 1991). Consequently, males tend to be the larger and more physically dominant sex that engage in overt, direct competition with same-sex rivals. However, it is not "femaleness" or "maleness" that determines obligatory parental investment, as several male animals including the Mormon cricket and various species of poison arrow frog have higher initial investment and the females physically compete for access to available males (Buss, 2012; Trivers, 1985).

**Sex differences in aggression.** Intrasexual competition between males is well documented among humans and various other species (Archer, 2004, 2009; Daly and Wilson, 1988; Wilson and Daly, 1985). The pioneering work of Darwin (1871) focused principally on male antagonism when he first speculated about sexual selection, and he rarely considered female–female aggression. In the evolutionary sciences, women quickly became characterized as passive and submissive within the domain of courtship and mate selection (Arnocky et al. 2012; Campbell, 2006, 2013; Hrdy, 2013; Vaillancourt, 2005, 2013; Vaillancourt et al. 2010). It was reasoned that because men have relatively higher reproductive capacity (i.e., they can produce more lifetime offspring than women), lower obligatory parental investment, and are more directly combative in comparison to women, they evolved to be fierce warriors vying for the attention of yielding and coy female recipients. As a result, women's competition and aggression has been largely underrated, discounted, and/or at times ignored in comparison to men's, as androcentric theorizing has pervaded the evolutionary sciences in regard to these concepts (Nicolas and Welling, 2015; Vaillancourt and Krems, 2018).

It is true that across mammalian species, and most vertebrates, that males tend to engage in more conspicuous, risky, and lethal forms of intrasexual competition in comparison to females (Archer, 2004, 2009; Vaillancourt, 2005, 2013). In research on humans, few would contest that men are more *directly aggressive* than women, which concerns behavior like physically hitting or verbally threatening another person (Archer, 2004, 2009; Campbell, 2013; Vaillancourt, 2005, 2013; Vaillancourt et al. 2010). Cross-culturally and throughout the lifespan, men engage in more criminal behavior such as battery, rape, and murder in comparison to women (Daly and Wilson, 1988; Goetz et al. 2008). Importantly, however, ancestral women, relative to men, could less afford to be as physically combative. With relatively lower reproductive potential, the greater dependence of offspring on maternal care for survival, and the relative absence of overt armament designed for physical combat (Campbell, 1999, 2004), women needed to be more cautious and covert when aggressing against others. Direct aggression involves a much higher probability of injury and death and its benefits in regard to reproductive success are much greater for men than women (Campbell, 2013).

There exist a host of inconspicuous aggressive tactics that carry a much smaller risk of retaliation and harm in comparison to direct aggression. This kind of aggression has been termed *indirect aggression,* which "involves the use of socially conniving acts such as getting others to dislike a person, using derisive body language, befriending others as a form of revenge, deliberately divulging others' secrets, making negative remarks about a person to others, purposely excluding a person, etc." (Vaillancourt, 2005, p. 18). At times in the literature, this form of aggression has been termed either social (Galen and Underwood, 1997) or relational (Crick and Grotpeter, 1995) aggression; although, several authors have argued that each supposedly different type of aggression involves more stealthy and indirect strategies (e.g., Archer and Coyne, 2005; Vaillancourt, 2005, 2013).

The totality of evidence to date indicates that women engage proportionally in more indirect forms of aggression in comparison to men (see Vaillancourt, 2005, 2013). Across a variety of diverse cultures, ranging from Indonesia (French et al. 2002) to Israel (Österman et al. 1998), girls and women have shown a bias toward more hidden and socially manipulative aggressive tactics in favor of physical aggression. Curiously, in one meta-analysis conducted by Card et al. (2008), a reliable sex difference across studies was found but the authors reported that it was relatively small and "trivial." Missing from their analysis, however, was the recognition that women, throughout their lifetime, engage in proportionally more indirect aggression than their male counterparts, who prefer to physically or verbally aggress (Vaillancourt et al. 2010). This sex difference is also evident in several of our nonhuman primate relatives with whom we share a strong genetic relationship. Numerous reports of high-ranking females provoking and harassing lower-status females indirectly have been documented in the primate literature (Campbell, 1999). Furthermore, in at least 30 species of primates, females have been observed engaging in sexual interference, through harassment (e.g., approaching, touching, or slapping the recipient) and disrupting copulations (discussed in Vercaecke et al. 2003). Collectively, these findings demonstrate that human and nonhuman female primates, in comparison to males, are competing to influence their reproductive outcomes principally through indirect aggression (Arnocky and Vaillancourt, 2017).

Due to their penchant for indirect aggression, it has been argued that gossip is women's primary intrasexual competition strategy of choice and should thus vary predictably among the sexes (Davis et al. 2018b). Although the research is scant, investigators have generally found that women are more prone to gossip than men (Davis et al. 2018a; Levin and Arluke, 1985; Nevo et al. 1993; Watson, 2012) and that women are more likely to use gossip in an aggressive or socially destructive way (McAndrew, 2014a, 2014b). Whereas men are more likely to share gossip with their romantic partners than with anyone else, women report that they are just as likely to gossip with their same-sex friends as with their romantic partners (McAndrew et al. 2007). Women further demonstrate a stronger desire to hear gossip about a member of their own sex and are more likely to gossip about same-sex friends and relatives in comparison to men (Levin and Arluke, 1985; McAndrew and Milenkovic, 2002). Moreover, whether they agree with gossiped information or not, women tend to respond more positively to this information as opposed to objecting to it (Eder and Enke, 1991). Thus, despite the fact that women may be more bothered and damaged by gossip (Galen and Underwood, 1997), they may strategically suppress their disapproval in order to acquire the valuable socially transmitted information. Leaper and Holliday (1995) found that the amount of negative gossip shared between two people is highest among female friends; however, gossip frequency may not strongly predict the quality of women's friendships (Watson, 2012). Women have also been found to express favorable attitudes toward the social value of gossip (i.e., perceived enjoyment and value of sharing and learning gossip), which positively predicts intentions to share malicious gossip (Litman and Pezzo, 2005).

## GOSSIP AS WOMEN'S INTRASEXUAL COMPETITION STRATEGY OF CHOICE

Campbell (2004) argued that women primarily compete in two particular ways: (1) through advertising by enhancing their appearance (e.g., using make-up, wearing form-fitting clothing, having cosmetic surgery) and (2) by gossiping about other women to tarnish their reputation. Self-promotion through enhancing one's physical appearance is a competitive form of intersexual selection, which women use to attract the attention of men (Buss, 2012; Fisher and Cox, 2009; Symons, 1979; Vaillancourt and Sharma, 2011). In contrast, gossip is argued to be the key intrasexual tactic that women use to socially exclude other women, as well as to call their appearance and sexual reputation into question. Within this context, women's gossip is principally a form of *competitor derogation*, which refers to any act performed to reduce a same-sex rival's mate value, relative to one's own, by focusing specifically on the traits that are desired most by the opposite sex (Buss and Dedden, 1990; Massar et al. 2012). For women, this entails attacking a competitor's youthfulness, attractiveness, and her sexual reputation (Campbell, 2013; Vaillancourt, 2013).

# THE CONTENT OF WOMEN'S GOSSIP

**Youthfulness and reproductive value.** Over evolutionary time, ancestral boys and men have faced the primary adaptive problem of finding, courting, and securing reproductively viable girls and women (Buss, 1994, 2012). Thus, men have evolved to be particularly sensitive to cues of youth in women, because younger women have relatively higher reproductive value (i.e., they have a higher probability of conceiving and producing a healthy child; Shackelford and Larsen, 1999). Indeed, researchers have consistently shown that younger women have higher mate value and are rated as more desirable than older women (Buss, 1989; Kenrick and Keefe, 1992). Consequently, competition for male partners is more intense during the earlier reproductive years of a woman's life, meaning that younger women are most likely to gossip and compete with each other for mates in comparison to their older counterparts (Campbell, 2004; Vaillancourt, 2005, 2013). Massar et al. (2012) demonstrated that the age of women, regardless of relationship status, was inversely associated with a greater tendency to engage in gossip. However, these researchers also discovered that this association was mediated by women's self-perceived attractiveness and desirability as a potential partner, with women of higher mate value being far more likely to gossip than their less attractive peers.

Women's heightened intrasexual competitiveness also appears to be sensitive to another important component of fertility: her menstrual cycle phase position. Women at peak fertility within the periovulatory phase (i.e., around ovulation) of the menstrual cycle, rate other women's facial attractiveness more negatively in comparison to less fertile days of the cycle (Fisher, 2004). In fact, there are a range of relevant behavioral and psychological changes that occur around ovulation related to women's intrasexual competition, such as preferring to wear sexier clothing (Durante et al. 2008), applying more cosmetic products (Guéguen, 2012), and increasing self-grooming and ornamentation (Haselton et al. 2007). Furthermore, Maner and McNulty (2013) discovered that women exposed to the scent of another woman in the periovulatory phase subsequently had higher levels of testosterone, a key hormonal mediator of competitive and aggressive behavior, in comparison to women in a low fertile phase of the menstrual cycle (e.g., the mid-luteal phase).

**Attractiveness and mate value.** Along with youth, men are argued to have evolved to find a number of physical characteristics attractive in women, such as facial symmetry, a healthy complexion, large breasts, and a low waist-to-hip ratio (Buss, 2012; Shackelford and Larsen, 1999). Men place a premium on these traits because of their association with fertility, health, and genetic fitness, which can benefit prospective offspring. Consequently, women have probably evolved to direct their derogatory gossip toward the physical appearance of same-sex rivals in order to compete for desired opposite sex partners (Buss and Dedden, 1990). Indeed, women commonly insult the appearance of same-sex rivals by using words such as "ugly" and "fat" (see Campbell, 2004, 2013). Adolescent girls' indirect aggression, through gossip and social exclusion, has been observed to typically occur as a result of envy over the appearance of same-sex others and over preferred male partners (Owens et al. 2000). Furthermore, highly attractive teenage girls, likely due to their higher probability of spreading and being the subjects of gossip, are more often the targets of peer victimization through indirect aggression (see Vaillancourt, 2013). More attractive women, therefore, are argued to be more likely to initiate and be the targets of gossip (Campbell, 2013; Massar et al. 2012). Women with higher levels of attractiveness also appear more likely to "see" anger on neutral female faces, perhaps as an exaggerated threat detection bias (Krems et al. 2015). Women have also been found to report greater feelings of jealousy and competitiveness when exposed to images of attractive women (Arnocky et al. 2012; Fink et al. 2014). In fact, jealousy in response to the physical attractiveness of others is a commonly cited explanation for female indirect aggression (Owens et al. 2000).

In order for women's competitor derogation to have evolved, it would have had to produce a meaningful consequence in men's perceptions of women's mate value. In support of this logic, Fisher and Cox (2009) found that men rated women as significantly less attractive when derogatory remarks were made about their appearance by another woman. Interestingly, the impact of these disparaging remarks on men's judgments of attractiveness was greatest when it came from an attractive in comparison to an unattractive woman. Moreover, women appear to be more sensitive than men to the impact of indirect aggression and report being more damaged and devastated by it; frequently fearing that they are being "talked about" or excluded from a valued social group (Galen and Underwood, 1997). Fisher et al. (2010) also found that men's perception of women's attractiveness was unaffected by her tendency to gossip, which did correlate with lower ratings of her perceived friendliness, kindness, trustworthiness and overall appeal as a long-term mate. Arnocky and Vaillancourt (2012) showed in a longitudinal analysis of adolescent girls and boys, that the use of indirect aggression positively predicted being in a relationship one year later after controlling for a number of potential confounding variables (e.g., previous dating history). Similarly, Volk et al. (2015) showed that bullying for women was strongly associated with number of dating partners. These results support the argument that girls' and women's use of indirect aggression, such as malicious gossip, can be an effective mate competition strategy that influences reproductive outcomes.

**Fidelity and sexual reputation.** Another salient adaptive problem for ancestral men, due to the biological reality of internal fertilization, was not being able to be completely certain of their children's genetic relationship to them (i.e., paternity uncertainty). Further, men, unlike most mammalian males, invest significantly in their offspring and establish successive pair-bonds with preferred women (i.e., social monogamy; Fernandez-Duque et al. 2009). Consequently, men have evolved to be sensitive to cues of trustworthiness, commitment, and fidelity in women (Buss, 1994, 2012). However, men also demonstrate a relatively stronger proclivity toward uncommitted sexual relationships than women. Women appear to be aware of men's preference for fidelity and their desire for a sexually committed long-term partner, and, as such, benefit by maintaining a higher "market price" for sex (Campbell, 2013; Vaillancourt et al. 2010). In this way, women can effectively promote monogamy and fidelity in men by making sex somewhat contingent upon commitment. Consequently, those who provide sex too liberally reduce the "bargaining power" of other women. Thus, women gain by enforcing norms of sexual conservatism, ostracizing and punishing those who make sex too readily available (Baumeister and Twenge, 2002; Vaillancourt and Sharma, 2011).

Given men's preference for fidelity, it makes sense that the most common insults that women direct toward same-sex rivals concern questioning their faithfulness and drawing attention to, or exaggerating, their promiscuity (Buss and Dedden, 1990). Pejorative terms like "slut," "whore," and "ho" are common in the gossip and rumors of women's competitor derogation (Campbell, 2013). Moreover, as rare as physical violence is among women, the most commonly reported reason for an attack (accounting for 46 percent of fights) is a retaliation in response to allegations of being promiscuous (Campbell, 1986). The rise of the internet has also greatly facilitated the dissemination of material intended to damage women's sexual reputations. For instance, in one legal case, upon seeking an injunction (i.e., a legal warning or order) against his former wife for harassment after leaving her for another woman, a man and his new wife retaliated by circulating nude photographs of his former spouse to each person on her email list (Doyel, 2014). This kind of "revenge porn" is growing in popularity. Hosting websites, such as IsAnyoneUp, allow for anonymous user submissions of sexually explicit media, typically by spurned lovers, with information that openly identifies the victim online (Stroud, 2014). These websites also have online chat boards where submitters and users post lewd comments intended to harass and damage the sexual reputation of targets, who may consequently experience significant psychological distress (Kitchen, 2015; Power and Henry, 2017).

In one of the few experimental studies on women's intrasexual competition, Vaillancourt and Sharma (2011) examined how women responded to a conservatively dressed female confederate (condition 1) and the same woman wearing more provocative clothing (condition 2). Participants were audio and video recorded in each condition to capture their reactions and rated for how "bitchy" they reacted, which included extended eye gazing, eye rolling, derisive laughter, looking the woman up and down, and gossiping. It was demonstrated that women were significantly more "bitchy" toward the provocatively dressed, as opposed to the conservatively dressed, female confederate. One woman exclaimed that the "sexy" confederate's "boobs were about to pop out" and another implied that she was probably having sex with her professors. In a follow-up study, Vaillancourt and Sharma (2011) randomly assigned women to one of three conditions and had them rate photographs of the same female confederate dressed conservatively, provocatively, or a digitally altered image of the provocatively dressed confederate to make her appear significantly overweight. Despite the conservatively dressed confederate being rated as "cuter" than the other two women, participants were still significantly less likely to introduce their boyfriend and to allow him to spend time with the "sexy-thin" and "sexy-overweight" confederate. Female participants also reported being less likely to establish a friendship with either of the "sexy" confederates.

The results above show that women are competing against same-sex others and often maliciously manipulate the sexual reputation of their victims using gossip, among other tactics (Baumeister and Twenge, 2002; Leenaars et al. 2008). These results cast some doubt on the idea that women are innately highly promiscuous and that men have created a patriarchal system designed to stifle female sexuality due to insecurity, envy over women's greater sexual capacities, or to prevent social disorder (i.e., male control theory; see Baumeister and Twenge, 2002 for further discussion). Rather, women appear to be cooperating to suppress the sexuality of same-sex others in order to maintain a higher "market price" for sex due to their relatively lower sex drive in comparison to men and the larger cost associated with pregnancy for women (Baumeister and Tice, 2000). Gossip is an important means through which women may achieve this goal. In terms of competitively stifling each other's sexuality, women have also been shown to express more preventive courtship attitudes and are less likely to introduce their same-sex friends to available mates in comparison to men (i.e., lower facilitative courtship attitudes; Ackerman and Kenrick, 2009; Arnocky et al. 2014). This relation is particularly strong among women high in intrasexual competitiveness and among those with more conservative sexual attitudes and behavior (i.e., low sociosexuality). Even more telling was the finding by Arnocky et al. (2014) that altruism and reciprocity did not predict preventive courtship attitudes, implying that women were not impeding each other's sexuality to help or to be prosocial. Gossip is likely to factor into these negotiations, manifesting in women's discussions about absent third-party members as to why hindering courtship for same-sex friends is justified.

## THE DAMAGE WROUGHT BY COMPETITOR DEROGATION

Gossip has been viewed by some as trivial and minor form of aggression; however, this putative intrasexual competition strategy can produce physically and psychologically damaging outcomes, particularly for adolescent girls and women (Benenson et al. 2013; Crick, 1995, Galen and Underwood, 1997; Klomek et al. 2008). For instance, peer victimization, much of which involves derogatory gossip, among adolescent girls is associated with a greater risk of suicidal ideation (Kaltiala-Heino et al. 1999). Furthermore, Klomek et al. (2008) found that for adolescent girls, indirect peer victimization, regardless of frequency, positively predicted attempts to commit suicide. Lower self-esteem has also been associated with being the victim of indirect aggression among adolescent girls (Carbone-Lopez et al. 2010). News stories of cyberbullying on social media platforms (e.g., Facebook and Instagram) resulting in the suicide of the bullied are becoming increasingly prevalent and typically involve girls and women aggressing against same-sex victims (McAndrew, 2014a). These instances suggest that circuitous tactics, such as gossip, can produce devastating consequences for the target. Therefore, indirect aggression can be an effective way to remove competitors from the mating arena and that this mode of aggressive behavior may be particularly damaging to the mental health of girls and women. This perspective in no way justifies such insidious behavior; it merely provides Therefore, indirect aggression can be an evolutionary perspective through which to gather insight into why such acts may occur, to whom, and with what consequences.

Within a legal context, women's competitor derogation through gossip and direct aggression can also take on several destructive and violent forms. Retired Circuit Court Judge Robert Doyel (2014, in press), recounts that women who file restraining orders typically do so against other women with whom they have a romantic rivalry. Although gossip itself cannot be used as a legal basis for this kind of injunction, it is generally part of a larger pattern of aggressive behavior. Judge Doyel (2014, in press) reports that the single most common complaint one woman leverages against another has to do with making allegedly false reports of child abuse or neglect to authorities. For instance one woman told the court that

> Yesterday she called my job and told my supervisor that I was unfit and that I was stealing and writing prescriptions which has complicated my duties as a [medical professional]. . . . She called Children and Families on me.    (Doyel, in press)

Cyberstalking is another common means through which competitor derogation may be achieved among women. Stories of women impersonating one another online to post licentious and reputation-damaging information have been reported. One woman and her boyfriend, for example, posed as her "baby daddy's" (i.e., her ex male partner with whom she had a child out of wedlock) wife in ads soliciting clients for sex and posted them on Craig's List (a classified advertisements website; Doyel, in press). Judge Doyel (2014) also recounts a scenario wherein a "baby mama" (i.e., a woman with a child out of wedlock) created a Facebook page solely dedicated to taunting and antagonizing her ex partner's new girlfriend. Using fictitious names, the following is a description of one such post: "So u wrk @ JQWDT huh? Stupid ass bitch lets see how long u kp dat job. LMFAO @ ur dumb ass" (Doyel, in press). These aggressive acts may be intended to generate gossip about the material posted online and may cause a cascade of further reputation-damaging outcomes.

## AVENUES FOR FUTURE RESEARCH

Although researchers have argued that women use gossip to derogate competitors when vying for mates (e.g., McAndrew, 2014a; Vaillancourt, 2013), few have assessed the relation between gossip and an intrasexually competitive orientation. Davis et al. (2018a) found that gossip frequency and favorable attitudes toward gossiping were positively associated with intrasexual competitiveness. However, more research is needed to support the argument that gossip is an intrasexual competition strategy. Furthermore, limited research has been devoted to directly testing sex and gender differences in the frequency of gossip, both in a general sense and for socially destructive purposes. Moreover, the findings to date have been mixed (e.g., Davis et al. 2018a; Litman and Pezzo, 2005). Because of their greater engagement in competitor derogation, adolescent girls and young adult women have reasonably been the focus of research to date regarding gossip from an evolutionary perspective (Campbell, 2004; Davis et al. 2018b). As a result, little knowledge has been garnered about the foci of older women's gossip. For instance, not much is known about "cougars," a pejorative Western term for more mature women who assertively pursue short-term sexual relationships with younger men, and how they are perceived by other women (Montemurro and Siefken, 2014). More investigation is needed as well to determine how the frequency of social comparison to romantic rivals influences women's opinion of those competitors and their tendency to engage in gossip (Massar et al. 2012). Another branch of research in need of further attention concerns the extent to which women help or deter their same-sex friends and family members from pursuing short-term or long-term mates by using gossip (i.e., courtship attitudes; Arnocky et al. 2014). Due to their general tendency to prefer cultivating long-term romantic relationships, women may be relatively less likely than men to facilitate short-term sexual encounters. Also, little empirical knowledge of how menstrual cycle phase influences women's intrasexual competitive tendencies has been acquired (Maner and McNulty, 2013; Fisher, 2004). This is an important component of the argument that fertility status guides women's competition for mates via indirect aggression, which may be associated with a greater frequency of gossip during more fertile phases of the menstrual cycle. On this note, few researchers have examined how the use of hormonal contraceptives might alter women's same-sex aggression (Cobey et al. 2013) and how gossip may be implicated in this process.

# Conclusion

Language and the ability to share gossip may have enabled ancestral human beings to form large cooperative alliances and to exploit diverse and uncharted ecologies (Dunbar, 1996, 2004). Gossip also led the emergence of a new, efficient, and low-cost form of indirect aggression within the realm of courtship and mating: competitor derogation (Buss and Dedden, 1990; Hess and Hagen, this volume; Massar et al. 2012; McAndrew, 2017). An evolutionary perspective provides insight into why gossip may be the preferred weapon of choice for women when competing for desired mates and qualities tributary to reproductive success (e.g., popularity; Vaillancourt, 2013; Vaillancourt and Krems, 2018). Decades of androcentric theorizing in the evolutionary sciences has impeded, however, a well-rounded understanding of women's intrasexual competition and aggression (Campbell, 2013; Hrdy, 2013). This has contributed to a shortage of empirical research informed by an evolutionary perspective regarding girls' and women's aggressive behavior, such as malicious gossip, to compete against same-sex rivals. Nonetheless, it is evident that girls and women compete, at times producing insidious and damaging outcomes to the targets of their aggression (Arnocky and Vaillancourt, 2014; Campbell, 2004, 2013;

Vaillancourt, 2005, 2013). Further exploring how girls and women compete with same-sex rivals and in what circumstances will provide a richer understanding of the sex-differentiated aspects of human aggression, which may help inform interventions designed to prevent victimization.

## REFERENCES

Acheson, J. M. 1988. *The Lobster Gangs of Maine.* London: University Press of New England.

Ackerman, J. M., and Kenrick, D. T. 2009. "Cooperative Courtship: Helping Friends Raise and Raze Relationship Barriers." *Personality and Social Psychology Bulletin,* 35 (10): 1285–1300. doi:10.1177/0146167209335640 American Psychological Association. 2015. *APA Dictionary of Psychology* (2nd ed.). Washington, DC.

Amo, A. 1980. "Fijian Gossip as Adjudication: A Communicative Model of Informal Social Control." *Journal of Anthropological Research* 36 (3): 343–360. doi:10.1086/jar.36.3.3629529

Archer, J. 2004. "Sex Differences in Aggression in Real-World Settings: A Meta-Analytic Review." *Review of General Psychology* 8 (4): 291–322. doi:10.1037/1089-2680.8.4.291

Archer, J. 2009. "Does Sexual Selection Explain Human Sex Differences in Aggression?" *Behavioral and Brain Sciences* 32 (3–4): 249–311. doi:10.1017/S0140525X09990951

Archer, J., and Coyne, S. M. 2005. "An Integrated Review of Indirect, Relational, and Social Aggression." *Personality and Social Psychology Review* 9 (3): 212–230. doi:10.1207/s15327957pspr0903_2

Arnocky, S., Sunderani, S., Albert, G., and Norris, K. 2014. "Sex Differences and Individual Differences in Human Facilitative and Preventive Courtship." *Interpersona* 8 (2): 210–21. doi:10.5964/ijpr.v8i2.159

Arnocky, S., Sunderani, S., Miller, J. L., and Vaillancourt, T. 2012. "Jealousy Mediates the Relationship Between Attractiveness and Females' Indirect Aggression." *Personal Relationships* 19 (2): 290–303. doi:10.1111/j.1475-6811.2011.01362.x

Arnocky, S., and Vaillancourt, T. 2012. "A Multi-Informant Longitudinal Study on the Relationship Between Aggression, Peer Victimization, and Dating Status in Adolescence." *Evolutionary Psychology* 10 (2): 253–270. doi:10.1177/147470491201000207

Arnocky, S., and Vaillancourt, T. 2017. "Sexual Competition among Women: A Review of the Theory and Supporting Evidence." In *The Oxford Handbook of Women and Competition,* edited by Maryanne L. Fisher, 1–31. New York: Oxford University Press. doi:10.1093/oxfordhb/9780199376377.013.3

Bandura, A. 1977. *Social Learning Theory.* New York: General Learning Press.

Barkow, J. H. 1992. "Beneath New Culture is Old Psychology: Gossip and Social Stratification." In *The Adapted Mind: Evolutionary Psychology and the Generation of Culture,* edited by Jerome H. Barkow, L. Cosmides, and J. Tooby, 627–37. New York, NY: Oxford University Press.

Baumeister, R. F., and Tice, D. M. 2000. *The Social Dimension of Sex.* New York: Allyn & Bacon.

Baumeister, R. F., Twenge, J. M., and Nuss, C. K. 2002. "Effects of Social Exclusion on Cognitive Processes: Anticipated Aloneness Reduces Intelligent Thought." *Journal of Personality and Social Psychology* 83 (4): 817–27. doi:10.1037/0022-3514.83.4.817

Baumeister, R. F., Zhang, L., and Vohs, K. D., 2004. "Gossip as Cultural Learning." *Review of General Psychology* 8 (2): 111–21. doi:10.1037/1089-2680.8.2.111

Benenson, J. F., Markovits, H., Hultgren, B., Nguyen, T., Bullock, G., and Wrangham, R. 2013. "Social Exclusion: More Important to Human Females than Males." *PLoS One* 8 (2): e55851. doi:10.1371/journal.pone.0055851

Boehm, C. 1999. *Hierarchy in the Forest: The Evolution of Egalitarian Behavior.* Cambridge, MA: Harvard University Press.

Buss, D. M. 1989. "Sex Differences in Human Mate Preferences: Evolutionary Hypotheses Tested in 37 Cultures." *Behavioral and Brain Sciences* 12 (1): 1–14. doi:10.1017/S0140525X00023992

Buss, D. M. 1994. *The Evolution of Desire: Strategies of Human Mating.* New York: Basic Books.

Buss, D. M. 2012. *Evolutionary Psychology: The New Science of the Mind,* 4th ed. Boston, MA: Pearson.

Buss, D. M., and Dedden, L. A. 1990. "Derogation of Competitors." *Journal of Social and Personal Relationships* 7 (3): 395–422. doi:10.1177/0265407590073006

Campbell, A. 1986. "Self-report of fighting by females: A preliminary study". *British Journal of Criminology* 26: 28–46. doi:10.1093/oxfordjournals.bjc.a047581

Campbell, A. 1999. "Staying Alive: Evolution, Culture and Intra-Female Aggression." *Behavioral Brain Sciences* 22: 203–252. doi:10.1017/S014525X99001818

Campbell, A. 2004. "Female Competition: Causes, Constraints, Content, and Contexts." *Journal of Sex Research* 41 (1): 16–26. doi:10.1080/0022449049552210

Campbell, A. 2006. "Sex Differences in Direct Aggression: What Are the Psychological Mediators?" *Aggression and Violent Behavior* 11 (3): 237–264. doi:10.1016/j.avb.2005.09.002

Campbell, A. 2013. "The Evolutionary Psychology of Women's Aggression." *Philosophical Transactions of the Royal Society B* 368 (1631). doi:10.1098/rstb.2013.0078

Carbone-Lopez, K., Esbensen, F. A., and Brick, B. T. 2010. "Correlates and Consequences of Peer Victimization: Gender Differences in Direct and Indirect Forms of Bullying." *Youth Violence and Juvenile Justice* 8 (4): 332–350. doi:abs/10.1177/1541204010362954

Card, N. A., Stucky, B. D., Sawalani, G. M., and Little, T. D. 2008. "Direct and Indirect Aggression During Childhood and Adolescence: A Meta-Analytic Review of Gender Differences, Intercorrelations, and Relations to Maladjustments." *Child Development* 79 (5): 1185–1229. doi:10.1111/j.1467–8624.2008.01184.x

Cobey, K. D., Klipping, C., and Buunk, A. P. 2013. "Hormonal Contraceptive Use Lowers Female Intrasexual Competition in Pair-Bonded Women." *Evolution and Human Behavior* 34 (4): 294–298. doi:10.1016/j.evolhumbehav.2013.04.003

Clutton-Brock, T. H. 1991. *The Evolution of Parental Care.* Princeton, NJ: Princeton University Press.

Crick, N. R., and Grotpeter, J. K. 1995. "Relational Aggression, Gender, and Social-Psychological Adjustment." *Child Development* 66 (3): 710–722. doi:10.1111/j.1467-8624.1995.tb00900.x

Daly, M., and Wilson, M. 1988. *Homicide.* New Brunswick, NJ: Transaction Publishers.

Darwin, C. 1871. *The Descent of Man, and Selection in Relation to Sex.* New York, NY: D. Appleton.

Davis, A. C., Dufort, C., Desrochers, J., Vaillancourt, T., and Arnocky, S. 2018a. "Gossip as an Intrasexual Competition Strategy: Sex Differences in Gossip Frequency, Content, and Attitudes." *Evolutionary Psychological Science,* 4(2): 141–153. doi:10.1007/s40806017-0124-6

Davis, A., Vaillancourt, T., and Arnocky, S. 2018b. "Sex Differences in Initiating Gossip." In *Encyclopedia of Evolutionary Psychological Science,* edited by T. K. Shackelford and V. A. Weekes-Shackelford, 1–8. New York, NY: Springer. doi:10.1007/978-3-319-16999-6_190-1

De Backer, C. J., Nelissen, M., and Fisher, M. L. 2007. "Let's Talk about Sex: A Study on the Recall of Gossip about Potential Mates and Sexual Rivals." *Sex Roles* 56 (11–12): 781–791. doi:10.1007/s11199-007-9237-x

De Backer, Van den Bulck, H, M., Fisher, M. L., and Ouvrein, G. 2019. "Gossip and Reputation in the Media: How Celebrities Emerge and Evolve by Means of Mass-Mediated Gossip" In F. Giardini, R. P. M. Wittek (Eds.), *Handbook of Gossip and Reputation.* New York: Oxford University Press.

Doyel, R. 2014. *The Baby Mama Syndrome: Unwed Parents, Intimate Partners, Romantic Rivals, and the Rest of Us*. Winter Haven, FL: Lake Cannon Press.

Doyel, R. (in press). *The Baby Mama Syndrome: Stalking, Domestic Violence, and Murder*. Winter Haven, FL: Lake Cannon Press.

Dunbar, R. I. M. 1996. *Grooming, Gossip and the Evolution of Language*. Cambridge, MA: Harvard University Press.

Dunbar, R. I. M. 2004. "Gossip in Evolutionary Perspective." *Review of General Psychology* 8 (2): 100–110. doi:10.1037/1089-2680.8.2.100

Durante, K. M., Li, N. P., and Haselton, M. G. 2008. "Changes in Women's Choice of Dress Across the Ovulatory Cycle: Naturalistic and Laboratory Task-Based Evidence." *Personality and Social Psychology Bulletin* 34 (11): 1451–1460. doi:10.1177/0146167208323103

Eder, D., and Enke, J. L. 1991. "The Structure of Gossip: Opportunities and Constraints on Collective Expression among Adolescents." *American Sociological Review* 56 (4): 494–508. doi:10.2307/2096270

Ellickson, R. C. 1991. *Order without Law: How Neighbors Settle Disputes*. Cambridge, MA: Harvard University Press.

Emler, N. 1994. "Gossip, Reputation, and Social Adaptation." In *Good Gossip*, edited by Ralph F. Goodman, and A. Ben-Ze'ev, 117–38. Lawrence, KS: University of Kansas Press.

Farley, S. 2019. "On the Nature of Gossip, Reputation, and Power Inequality." In F. Giardini, R. P. M. Wittek (Eds.), *Handbook of Gossip and Reputation*. New York: Oxford University Press.

Fernandez-Duque, E., Valeggia, C. R., and Mendoza, S. P. 2009. "The Biology of Paternal Care in Human and Nonhuman Primates." *Annual Review of Anthropology* 38: 115–30. doi:10.1146/annurev-anthro-091908-164334

Fink, B., Klappauf, D., Brewer, G., and Shackelford, T. K. 2014. "Female Physical Characteristics and Intra-Sexual Competition in Women." *Personality and Individual Differences* 58: 138–141. doi:10.1016/j.paid.2013.10.015

Fisher, M. L. 2004. 'Female Intrasexual Competition Decreases Female Facial Attractiveness. *Proceedings of the Royal Society of London B: Biological Sciences* 271 (5). doi:10.1098/rsbl.2004.0160

Fisher, M., and Cox, A. 2009. "The Influence of Female Attractiveness on Competitor Derogation." *Journal of Evolutionary Psychology* 7 (2): 141–155. doi:10.1556/JEP.7.2009.2.3

Fisher, M., Shaw, S., Worth, K., Smith, L., and Reeve, C. 2010. "How We View Those Who Derogate: Perceptions of Female Competitor Derogators." *Journal of Social, Evolutionary, and Cultural Psychology* 4 (4): 265–276. doi:10.1037/h0099284

French, D. C., Jansen, E. A., and Pidada, S. 2002. "United States and Indonesian Children's and Adolescents' Reports of Relational Aggression by Disliked Peers." ' *Child Development* 73 (4): 1143–1150. doi:10.1111/1467-8624.00463

Galen, B. R., and Underwood, M. K. 1997. "A Developmental Investigation of Social Aggression among Children." *Developmental Psychology* 33 (4): 589–600. doi:10.1037/0012-1649. 33.4.589

Giardini, F., and Conte, R. 2011. "Gossip for Social Control in Natural and Artificial Societies." *Simulation*, 88(1): 18–32. doi:10.1177/0037549711406912

Goetz, A. T., Shackelford, T. K., Starratt, V. G., and McKibbin, W. F. 2008. "Intimate Partner Violence." In *Evolutionary Forensic Psychology*, edited by Joshua D. Duntley, and T. K Shackelford, 65–78. New York, NY: Oxford University Press.

Guéguen, N. 2012. "Makeup and Menstrual Cycle: Near Ovulation, Women Use More Cosmetics." *The Psychological Record* 62 (3): 541–548. doi:10.1007/BF03395819

Haselton, M. G., Mortezaie, M., Pillsworth, E. G., Bleske, A. E., and Frederick, D. A. 2007. "Ovulatory Shifts in Human Female Ornamentation: Near Ovulation, Women Dress to Impress." *Hormones and Behavior* 51 (1): 40–45. doi:10.1016/j.yhbeh.2006.07.007

Hess, N. H., and Hagen, E. H. 2006. "Sex Differences in Indirect Aggression: Psychological Evidence from Young Adults." *Evolution and Human Behavior* 27 (3): 231–245. doi:10.1016/j.evolhumbehav.2005.11.001

Hess, N., Hagen, E. 2019. "Gossip, Reputation and Friendship in within group Competition." In F. Giardini and R. P. M. Wittek (Eds.), *Handbook of Gossip and Reputation*. New York: Oxford University Press.

Hrdy, S. B. 2013. The "One Animal in All Creation about which Man Knows the Least." *Philosophical Transactions of the Royal Society of London B: Biological Sciences* 368 (1631). doi:10.1098/rstb.2013.0072

Kaltiala-Heino, R., Rimpelä, M., Marttunen, M., Rimpelä, A., and Rantanen, P. 1999. "Bullying, Depression, and Suicidal Ideation in Finnish Adolescents: School Survey." *British Medical Journal* 319 (7206): 348–51. doi:10.1136/bmj.319.7206.348

Kenrick, D. T., and Keefe, R. C. 1992. "Age Preferences in Mates Reflect Sex Differences in Human Reproductive Strategies." *Behavioral and Brain Sciences* 15 (1): 75–91. doi:10.1017/S0140525X00067595

Kitchen, A. N. 2015. "The Need to Criminalize Revenge Porn: How a Law Protecting Victims Can Avoid Running Afoul of the First Amendment." *Chicago-Kent Law Review* 90: 247–302. http://scholarship.kentlaw.iit.edu/cklawreview/vol90/iss1/11.

Klomek, A. B., Marrocco, F., Kleinman, M., Schonfeld, I. S., and Gould, M. S. 2008. 'Peer Victimization, Depression, and Suicidiality in Adolescents." *Suicide and Life-Threatening Behavior* 38 (2): 166–80. doi:10.1521/suli.2008.38.2.166

Kniffin, K. M., and Wilson, D. S. 2005. "Utilities of Gossip across Organizational Levels." *Human Nature* 16 (3): 278–292. doi:10.1007/s12110-005-1011-6

Krems, J. A., Neuberg, S. L., Filip-Crawford, G., and Kenrick, D. T. 2015. "Is She Angry? (Sexually Desirable) Women 'See' Anger on Female Faces." *Psychological Science* 26 (11): 1655–1663. doi:10.1177/0956797615603705

Leaper, C., and Holliday, H. 1995. "Gossip in Same-Gender and Cross-Gender Friends Conversations." *Personal Relationships* 2 (3): 237–246. doi:10.1111/j.1475–6811.1995.tb00089.x.

Lee, R. B. 1990. "Eating Christmas in the Kalahari." In *Conformity and Conflict: Readings in Cultural Anthropology*, edited by James B. Spradley and D. W. McCurdy, 30–37. 7th ed. Glenview, IL: Scott.

Leenaars, L. S., Dane, A. V., and Marini, Z. A. 2008. "Evolutionary Perspective on Indirect Victimization in Adolescence: The Role of Attractiveness, Dating and Sexual Behavior." *Aggressive Behavior* 34: 404–415. doi:10.1002/ab.20252

Levin, J., and Arluke, A. 1985. "An Exploratory Analysis of Sex Differences in Gossip." *Sex Roles* 12 (3–4), 281–286. doi:10.1007/BF00287594

Litman, J. A., and Pezzo, M. A. 2005. "Individual Differences in Attitudes towards Gossip." *Personality and Individual Differences* 38: 963–980. doi:10.1016/j.paid.2004.09.003

Maner, J. K., and McNulty, J. K. 2013. "Attunement to the Fertility Status of Same-Sex Rivals: Women's Testosterone Responses to Olfactory Ovulation Cues." *Evolution and Human Behavior* 34 (6): 412–418. doi:10.1016/j.evolhumbehav.2013.07.005

Massar, K., Buunk, A. P., and Rempt, S. 2012. "Age Differences in Women's Tendency to Gossip Are Mediated by Their Mate Value." *Personality and Individual Differences* 52 (1): 106–109. doi:10.1016/j.paid.2011.09.013

McAndrew, F. T. 2014a. "The 'Sword of a Woman': Gossip and Female Aggression." *Aggression and Violent Behavior* 19 (3): 196–199. doi:10.1016/j.avb.2014.04.006

McAndrew, F. T. 2014b. "How 'The Gossip' Became a Woman and How 'Gossip' Became Her Weapon of Choice." In *The Oxford Handbook of Women and Competition* edited by Maryanne L. Fisher, 191–205. New York: Oxford University Press.

McAndrew, F. T., Bell, E. K., and Garcia, C. M. 2007. "Who Do We Tell and Whom Do We Tell On? Gossip as a Strategy for Status Enhancement." *Journal of Applied Social Psychology* 37 (7): 1562–1577. doi:10.1111/j.1559–1816.2007.00227.x

McAndrew, F. T., and Milenkovic, M. A. 2002. "Of Tabloids and Family Secrets: The Evolutionary Psychology of Gossip." *Journal of Applied Social Psychology* 32 (5): 1064–1082. doi:10.1111/j.1559–1816.2002.tb00256.x

McPherson, N. M. 1991. "A Question of Morality: Sorcery and Concepts of Deviance Among the Kabana, West New Britain." *Anthropologica* 33 (1–2): 127–143. doi:10.2307/25605605

Montemurro, B., and Siefken, J. M. 2014. "Cougars on the Prowl? New Perceptions of Older Women's Sexuality." *Journal of Aging Studies* 28: 35–43. doi:10.1016/j.jaging.2013.11.004

Nevo, O., Nevo, B., and Derech-Zehavi, A. 1993. "The Development of the Tendency to Gossip Questionnaire: Construct and Concurrent Validity for a Sample of Israeli College Students." *Educational and Psychological Measurement* 53: 973–981. doi:abs/10.1177/0013164493053004010

Nicolas, S. C. A., and Welling, L. L. M. 2015. "The Darwinian Mystique? Synthesizing Evolutionary Psychology and Feminism." In *Evolutionary Perspectives on Social Psychology*, edited by V. Zeigler-Hill, L. L. M. Welling, and T. K. Shackelford, 203–212. New York, NY: Springer Publishing.

Österman, K., Björkqvist, K., Lagerspetz, K. M. J., Kaukiainen, A., Landau, S. F., Fraçzek, A., and Caprara G. V. 1998. "Cross-Cultural Evidence of Female Indirect Aggression." *Aggressive Behavior* 24 (1), 1–8. doi:10.1002/(SICI)1098-2337(1998)24:1<1:AID-AB1>3.0.CO;2-R.

Owens, L., Shute, R., and Slee, P. 2000. "Guess What I Just Heard! Indirect Aggression Among Teenage Girls in Australia." *Aggressive Behavior* 26 (1): 67–83. doi:10.1002(SICI)1098-2337 (2000)26:1<67::AID-AB6>3.0.CO;2-C

Powell, A., and Henry, N. 2017. "Not Just Revenge Porn: How Image-Based Abuse Is Harming Australians." Monash University, May 12. https://www.monash.edu/news/articles/not-just-revenge-porn-image-based-abuse-hits-1-in-5-australians

Power, C. 1998. "Old Wives Tales: The Gossip Hypothesis and the Reliability of Cheap Signals." In *Approaches to the Evolution of Language*, edited by James R. Hurford, M. Studdert-Kennedy, and C. Knight, 111–129. Cambridge: Cambridge University Press.

Shackelford, T. K., and Larsen, R. J. 1999. "Facial Attractiveness and Physical Health." *Evolution and Human Behavior* 20 (1): 71–76. doi:10.1016/S1090-5138(98)00036-1

Stroud, S. R. 2014. "The Dark Side of the Online Self: A Pragmatist Critique of the Growing Plague of Revenge Porn." *Journal of Mass Media Ethics* 29 (3): 168–183. doi:10.1080/0890052 3.2014.917976

Symons, D. 1979. *The Evolution of Human Sexuality*. Oxford: Oxford University Press.

Trivers, R. 1972. "Parental Investment and Sexual Selection." In *Sexual Selection and the Descent of Man*, edited by Bernard G. Campbell, 1871–1971. Chicago, IL: Aldine.

Trivers, R. 1985. *Social Evolution*. Menlo Park, CA: Benjamin/Cummings.

Vaillancourt, T. 2005. "Indirect Aggression Among Humans: Social Construct or Evolutionary Adaptation?" In *Developmental Origins of Aggression*, edited by Richard E. Tremblay, W. W. Hartup, and J. Archer, 158–177. New York, NY: Guilford.

Vaillancourt, T. 2013. "Do Human Females Use Indirect Aggression as an Intrasexual Competition Strategy?" *Philosophical Transactions of the Royal Society of London B: Biological Sciences* 368 (1631). doi:10.1098/rstb.2013.0080

Vaillancourt, T., and Krems, J. A. 2018., "An Evolutionary Psychological Perspective of Indirect Aggression in Girls and Women." In *The Development of Relational Aggression*, edited by S. Coyne, and J. Ostrov, 111–126. Oxford, UK: Oxford University Press.

Vaillancourt, T., Miller, J. L., and Sharma, A. 2010. "'Tripping the Prom Queen': Female Intrasexual Competition and Indirect Aggression." In *Indirect and Direct Aggression*, edited by Karin Österman, 17–31. New York, NY: Oxford University Press.

Vaillancourt, T., and Sharma, A. 2011. "Intolerance of Sexy Peers: Intrasexual Competition among Women." *Aggressive Behavior* 37 (6): 569–577. doi:10.1002/ab.20413

Vercaecke, H., Stevens, J., and van Elsacker, L. 2003. "Interfering with Others: Female–female Reproductive Competition in *Pan Paniscus*." In *Sexual Selection and Reproductive Competition in Primates*, edited by Clara B. Jones, 231–254. New York, NY: Alan R. Liss.

Volk, A., Dane, A. V., Marini, Z. A., and Vaillancourt, T. 2015. "Adolescent Bullying, Dating, and Mating: Testing an Evolutionary Hypothesis." *Evolutionary Psychology*, 13(4): 1–11. doi:10.1177/1474704915613909.

Watson, D. C. 2012. "Gender Differences in Gossip and Friendship." *Sex Roles* 67 (9–10), 494–502. doi:10.1007/s11199-012-0160-4

Williams, G. C. 1966. *Adaptation and Natural Selection*. Princeton, NJ: Princeton University Press.

Wilson, M., and Daly, M. 1985. "Competitiveness, Risk taking, and Violence: The Young Male Syndrome." *Ethology and Sociobiology* 6 (1): 59–73. doi:10.1016/0162-3095(85)90041-X

Wilson, M. I., and Daly, M. 1996. "Male Sexual Proprietariness and Violence Against Wives." Current Directions in Psychological Science 5 (1): 2–7. doi:10.1111/1467-8721. ep10772668?journalCode=cdpa

# PART V

## POWER AND STATUS

# CHAPTER 17

# GOSSIP AND REPUTATION IN THE MEDIA

## How Celebrities Emerge and Evolve by Means of Mass-Mediated Gossip

CHARLOTTE J. S. DE BACKER,
HILDE VAN DEN BULCK, MARYANNE L. FISHER,
AND GAËLLE OUVREIN

## INTRODUCTION

RECALL the last time you were standing in a cue at the grocery store, waiting to pay. In front of you was a display of magazines, showing the faces of familiar individuals that you recognize from television shows, movies, or music videos. Maybe you know their names, can anticipate what their voice sounds like, or have an impression of their personality. Some of these people you have known the majority of your life, just like an old friend. You grew up listening to their music, or watching the movies in which they starred. You are curious to see who they have married or divorced from, how they have aged, where they took their last vacation, what clothes they are wearing or car they are driving, or any other update on how life is going for them. Ironically, these people do not know who you are other than in the abstract as part of a statistic on music sales or cinema attendance, and certainly do not feel that you are an old friend. Furthermore, if you were to be in the same magazine without celebrity status, and were not well known in your local community, very few individuals would be interested in reading about your life, unless something spectacular happened to you. Why is it that we are interested in the big things happening to unknown people and the small things happening to stars we call "celebrities"? Who are these celebrities? How are they created? And why do certain people form some kind of relationship with them? In addressing these questions, we need to start from the beginning: what gossip is about, or the sorts of information gossip contains.

## FROM GOSSIP TO MASS MEDIA GOSSIP

### What is Gossip?

Listed as a human universal (Brown, 1991), gossip has been a prevalent part of all times and cultures. Gossip is about who is doing what to whom, dealing with social information (Dunbar, 1992, 1993, 2004; Rosnow & Fine, 1976). Above all, gossip is complex and this is reflected in the debates on how to define gossip (see Foster, 2004). Then again, "Whether or not experts have been able to concur on a definition of gossip, it is not very difficult to intuitively decide whether something is or isn't gossip" (Rosnow & Fine, 1976, p. 84). That is: everyone knows what gossip is, until one is asked to give a detailed, precise definition. Thomas (1994) once compared gossip with embroidery; both can be eye-catching and hard to ignore, and both can be covering a large space, but be almost unnoticeable. Therefore, we start this chapter section on definitions and theoretical constructs with a brief overview of some of the issues that give rise to debate about what can be included in the term "gossip" and what cannot, concluding with our own definitions relevant to study mass media and celebrity gossip.

Reviewing the most common disputable issues, Foster (2004, p. 83) summarized multiple definitions of gossip as follows: "in a context of congeniality, the exchange of personal information (positive or negative) in an evaluative way (positive or negative) about absent third parties." What strikes us, first of all, is that gossip includes both positive and negative talk. This is important, because "The traditional and prevailing view has regarded it [gossip] as an indirect form of aggression, akin to teasing. " (Baumeister, Zhang, & Vohs, 2004, p. 112). Interestingly, as we will discuss later, gossip magazines sometimes are seen as "slanderous" but, at a closer look, seem to cover more positive than negative talk (e.g., De Backer & Fisher, 2012). Moreover, most interpersonal gossip seems neutral or positive. Levin and Arluke (1985), who eavesdropped on the conversations of male and female college students, concluded that gossip could contain both clearly positive (27%) and negative (25%) references toward other people, but that most gossip did not even have a clear connotation. What is more, it is not so much the content but the intent of the gossiper that best reveals the goodness or badness of gossip (Almirol, 1981; de Soussa, 1994; Suls, 1977).

Next, what this definition also captures, and what is important for the definition of celebrity gossip, is that gossip is about absent human beings. Some restrict this group of potential people to gossip about persons from our own social network (Noon & Delbridge, 1993), which would exclude celebrities from any gossip conversation. Others, such as Hannerz (1967) are a little less strict and say that gossipers need some minimal awareness about the gossiped-about subject: the target must be identifiable to the gossipers. Consequently, "it is possible to gossip about movie stars and royalty, although one does not interact with them in face-to-face relationships. On the other hand, talking about an unknown man whom one passed in the street once is not gossip according to this view" (Hannerz, 1967, p. 39). Yet we do gossip about the unknown man passing us by on the street as well, for instance when he gets killed by a brick falling from the roof of a house. That is, unknown persons may become the topic of gossip when something "strange" has happened to them. Further, we agree with Ben-Ze'ev's (1994, p. 17) who claimed that "[t]he objects of gossip fall into three major groups: (a) people in our immediate surroundings, (b) famous people, and (c) people whose intimate and personal lives are unique." Mass media gossip deals with the former two forms of gossip: celebrity gossip about famous people; and, in a broader sense, mass media gossip about unknown people who experienced something extraordinary. Before we elaborate on this, however, it is useful to further classify all gossip about anyone in two general subsets based on the content of the gossip (i.e., what is gossiped about).

## Reputation Gossip and Strategy-learning Gossip

On the one hand, we discuss gossip that is solely focused on the behavior talked about, the event that happened; this will be called *strategy-learning gossip*. Acquiring information on how to deal with conflict, how to avoid disaster, as well as how to achieve success is transmitted via strategy-learning gossip. We gossip to transfer and acquire fitness-relevant information (see also De Backer & Gurven, 2006). We further exchange such gossip to learn how to behave to be culturally accepted according to the norms governing our social group (see also Baumeister, Zhang, & Vohs, 2004). On the other hand, gossip that is focused on the traits of a person or the actions that alter the way we perceive a person will be called *reputation gossip*. Reputation gossip is used to alter the reputations of self and other people, driven by a desire to gain personal prestige (Paine, 1967). To do so, we slander rivals and foes, and bask in the glorious gossip stories about family and friends (see McAndrew, this volume; McAndrew, Bell, & Garcia, 2007). Strategy-learning gossip can be about anyone, whereas reputation gossip is about people we know, directly or indirectly (see De Backer, Nelissen, Vyncke, Braeckman, & McAndrew, 2007).

With this in mind, consider following stories published on February 5, 2016, by People magazine: "Katy Perry and Orlando Bloom Heat Up Romance Rumors on Two Date Nights with Pals," "Solange Knowles Reportedly Loses Wedding Ring while on Mardi Gras Parade Route" and "Police Arrest Maryland Couple Who Allegedly Wrapped 7-Year-Old in Plastic Wrap and Restrained Him with Zip-Ties." The first story is a clear example of what we label reputation gossip, whereas the last story features strategy-learning gossip, and the in-between story can fit both types.

To start with the last story and strategy-learning gossip, what sets this story apart from most (if not all) other stories on People's website that day is not just the gruesome content of it, but also the fact that it features completely unknown people. A "Maryland couple" can be anyone from Maryland. Even if it would have been simply about "a couple" or just "someone" this story may have caught your attention. What is central here is the behavior; "what" has happened. This headline teaches us an important lesson: that some people can be very cruel toward others, including their own children. We do not expect this behavior, as most people treat their children with love and care, and would not harm them in this way. Yet via the stories about others we learn that not everyone behaves as we would expect. We vicariously learn that parenting can be about conflict and torture. It does not matter who these stories are about, it is what happened that teaches us a lesson. Beyond this example, research shows that the most popular topics of gossip revolve around "conflicts," "scandals," and "romantic behavior" (Levin & Kimmel, 1977), which all reflect adaptive problems crucial to the survival and reproduction of individuals living in the small, hunter-gatherer groups of our human ancestors (see Tooby & Devore, 1987).

This kind of gossip is remarkably different from what we label reputation gossip, which includes messages about traits/actions of third parties known to the gossipers, and where gossip alters the gossipers' opinion about the person gossiped about (i.e., the reputation of the gossipee). To come back to the first example: "Katy Perry and Orlando Bloom Heat Up Romance Rumors on Two Date Nights with Pals" changes their status from being single to being in a relationship. If this had been "Maryland couple heat up romance rumors on two date nights with pals," the message would have had little or no meaning. To those who do not know Katy Perry and Orlando Bloom or their history, this message is of little meaning. The key to reputation gossip is about knowing who is gossiped about, with the message changing the reputation information about the target(s). Reputation information is here broadly defined as "the beliefs that are held about the target by the gossipers." Therefore, reputation gossip can range from romantic and social reputations (who is befriended with whom, who are rivals, who is to be trusted, and so on) to scandals. Reputation gossip can uplift or ruin one's reputation. Given that reputations have always been of great importance, gossip thus becomes a crucial tool to navigate the social world. It has been shown that, among hunter-gatherers, individuals can gain access to important resources, such as food and mates, by having a good reputation. If they lose their good reputation, this often implies that they lose their access to resources, such as food and mates (Chagnon, 1988; Hawkes, 1991; Hawkes, 1993; Hawkes, O'Connell, & Blurton-Jones, 2001; Marlowe, 1999; Patton, 2000; Sugiyama & Chacon, 2000). In today's societies this is not different, or is it? Having a good reputation clearly gives access to many things, but does having a bad reputation necessarily take away these benefits? We will argue that slanderous gossip about scandals can sometimes uplift the reputation of celebrities, but for now it suffices to understand the difference between strategy-learning gossip and reputation gossip.

In most cases both types of gossip overlap. Such is the case with the story about Solange Knowles. Those not knowing her at all may still have an interest in learning that "Solange Knowles Reportedly Loses Wedding Ring While on Mardi Gras Parade Route" because it teaches us a lesson that one can lose items of financial and/or emotional value when out partying. Yet those knowing Solange Knowles and her very expensive wedding ring obtain additional information from this message; she lost a piece jewelry with great value, and she kept her reputation as "party girl" very much alive.

In outlining this difference between strategy-learning gossip and reputation gossip we automatically turned to celebrity gossip to render examples for reputation gossip. Yet we finish this section of the chapter with a more thorough discussion about what mass media gossip is about, and how celebrity gossip fits in to this conceptualization.

## Defining Mass Media Gossip

In 1883, Joseph Pulitzer started a tabloid journalism trend when he introduced cheap newspapers, printed on yellow paper. His "yellow penny paper" *World* was the first to mention detailed physical descriptions of the stories' subjects (Sloan, 2001). Others, such as Hearst, soon imitated his initiative and "by the 1930s, the tabloid form was established as a permanent feature of American journalism" (Bird, 1992, p. 23). In the 1960s, Generoso Pope changed the content of his tabloid from slanderous to a more "cleaned-up" version. With this strategy, Pope successfully managed to have his tabloid sold in supermarkets. Others, who did not follow this cleaner strategy, had to sell their tabloids through newsstands on the streets, which were becoming scarce (Sloan, 2001). So far, tabloids had mainly covered stories dealing with unexplained phenomena, rags to riches, people overcoming handicaps, medical breakthroughs, self-help articles, and so on. Pope decided to shift away from the everyday drama of unknown people toward the everyday chores of celebrities (Sloan, 2001). Thus, a shift away from the extraordinary scandalous strategy-learning gossip toward more everyday-life reputation gossip took place. This format became so successful that we almost forget that, even today, mass media gossip also covers the successes and misfortunes of "Average Joes" (Sloan, 2001).

As mentioned earlier, a major distinction between interpersonal and mass media gossip is that the people gossiped about in mass media stories are not physically part of our social network (Ben-Ze'ev, 1994; Bird, 1992; Davis & McLeod, 2003; Levin & Kimmel, 1977; Schely-Newman, 2004; Sloan, 2001). Then again, in terms of emotional connections, this exclusion is less straightforward, especially when it concerns gossip about celebrities. People develop so-called "parasocial" relations with celebrities, where reputation information flows from the celebrity to the audience, but not vice versa (Horton & Wohl, 1956; Rubin, Perse & Powel, 1985; Turner, 2004). Despite the predominant[1] unilateral information flow, audiences can become emotionally connected to a celebrity. This attachment becomes clear when major events happen to a celebrity, for instance in the outburst of grief following the death of Princess Diana (Brown, Basil, & Bocarnea, 2003), yet people also develop parasocial bonds with celebrities based on day-to-day events (Van den Bulck & Claessens, 2013a). Such close bonds with celebrities result in (the need for) even more gossip being spread.

Despite these differences in who is being gossiped about, media gossip and interpersonal gossip show great overlap with regards to what is being gossiped about. The range of topics that can be gossiped about is very broad, covering scandalous events as well as romantic news, and acts of cooperation and conflict (Divale & Seda, 1999). Similar topics appear in media gossip (Bird, 1992; Davis & McLeod, 2003; De Backer & Fisher, 2012; Levin & Kimmel, 1977; Schely-Newman, 2004; Sloan, 2001; Van den Bulck et al., 2016). Davis & McLeod (2003) analyzed sensational front cover news and concluded that the stories dealt with themes related to the reproductive fitness of our ancestors. In ancestral times, gossip was vital to the survival and reproduction of our ancestors (Barkow, 1989, 1992; Davis & McLeod, 2003; Dunbar, 1992, 1993, 2004; Hess & Hagen, 2006a,b; McAndrew & Milenkovic, 2002). Without having access to gossip, our ancestors could not learn vicariously about threats and opportunities by means of strategy-learning gossip, nor could they learn who was to be trusted and who allied with whom by means of reputation gossip. All of this information is crucial for navigating and surviving in the social world, and in the end, group living protected our ancestors from external environmental threats (see Dunbar, 2004). This evolved outcome may explain why, even today, we consider gossip fun and entertaining; it was and still is "good for us." Media gossip seems to cover such fitness-relevant information as well, spreading information about how to safeguard or improve one's life or social status. De Backer & Fisher (2012) reconfirmed this possibility in their analysis of tabloids covering celebrity gossip, and concluded that these magazines mainly cover the romance affairs, prestige, health and wealth status of celebrities, both in a positive and negative sense. Positive news even appears to outscore negative news in mass media gossip (De Backer & Fisher, 2012; Levin & Kimmel, 1977). Thus, the casual observation that gossip magazines are slanderous and badmouthing celebrities does not appear to be true. This finding was again confirmed by a more recent content analysis (Van den Bulck et al., 2016), that found a majority of celebrity gossip in newspapers and gossip magazines to be positive. Of course, though, we must not overlook the negative gossip. It exists and it may be a growing trend these days, with phenomena like "celebrity bashing" becoming a newly accepted norm among teenagers. Teenage girls tend to believe that celebrities should be able to deal with this bashing, because it is the price they pay for being famous (Ouvrein, Vandebosch, & De Backer, 2017. This most certainly is a trend that will need further follow-up and exploration, especially since (even a lower proportion of) negative news about celebrities may have considerable impact on our attitude toward mass media gossip, due to negativity bias. On average, negative information carries more weight than neutral or positive information, possibly due to both experiences and innate predispositions (Rozin & Royzman, 2001).

In sum, we conclude that mass media gossip is about the good news and the bad news concerning the amazing events happening to people like us, and the love life, health, wealth and downfall of celebrities. Mass media gossip deals with what miraculously happened to your unknown neighbor (Davis & McLeod, 2003) as well as with the everyday chores of (inter)national celebrities (De Backer & Fisher, 2012). Mass media gossip evolved from being mainly about strategy-learning gossip toward a mix of strategy-learning gossip and reputation gossip. In the next section we explain how this shift in focus actually overlaps with the transition from being an unknown person to becoming a celebrity.

# How Mass Media Reputation Gossip Creates Celebrities

In the previous sections, we focused on gossip and mass media gossip, but paid little attention to celebrity gossip itself which, in essence, is the product of reputation gossip as we explain in this section. Before we do so, however, a short synopsis of how we define celebrities is given. It immediately becomes apparent that we cannot separate the definition of gossip and the role mass media gossip plays in this process.

## Who is a Celebrity?

As with gossip, defining celebrities is complex (see Driessens, 2013, for an overview). We limit the debate to how reputation gossip is essential in the creation of celebrities. To start, celebrities are people that stand out because they have either achieved something or because they have their status attributed to them by inheritance or by media and audiences (Rojek, 2001). Being recognized or "known" is crucial in the definition of a celebrity, as is emphasized in the most paraphrased (and criticized!) definition that "the celebrity is a person who is well-known for their well-knownness" (Boorstin, 1961, p. 58). Boorstin's definition is often criticized because it is tautological, yet it captures the essence of what celebrities are about: recognition. In everyday interpersonal interactions, recognition leads to small-scale fame or "renown" (Rojek, 2001). The next step is recognition by those outside a personal network and media, who are key intermediating factors in this process (Braudy, 1997) to the extent that some (Driessens, 2013) see celebrity capital as accumulated media visibility through recurrent media representations. In other words, the more people are mentioned in the media, the more their celebrity grows, a view confirmed by recognition heuristic theory (Goldstein & Gigerenzer, 1999, p. 41). Media representations can involve personal stories self-disclosed in interviews, tweets or other forms of more direct communication with the audience as well as, indeed, mass media gossip. Such gossip can be both positive and negative, which nicely coincides with the fact that celebrities are people that stand out of the crowd, in a positive or negative sense, thus including those who are "celebrated" and the notorious (Rojek, 2001).

So far, we have established that celebrities are people well known outside the realm of their personal network because they became subject of positive or negative media representations. We add that this well-knownness needs to last for a certain amount of time. Celebrities are people who maintain their position in various media debates and thus maintain their (inter)national well-knownness beyond a single day, a year, a lifetime or even after death. Lady Diana passed away many years ago but is still talked about and, from our perspective, is still considered a "celebrity." In sum, we define celebrities as people well known outside the realm of their personal network for a substantial period of time as a result of positive or negative media representations. In contrast, individuals that are world-famous for just a day, we do not label "celebrities." Random individuals who win the lottery, kill their spouse or invent a miracle diet, may be hyped in the press and reach the status of being well known outside their personal network for a moment in time. Rojek (2001) terms those people "celetoids," emphasizing that their career is short-lived.

In what follows, we explain the important role of mass media gossip in going from being unknown to being a celetoid and/or a celebrity.

## From Unknown to Celetoid to Celebrity: The Role of Reputation Gossip

Maybe Chase Sherman once dreamed of becoming a celebrity, but he will never have dreamed to become famous the way he did: in a most negative fashion. Chase was on his way back from his brother's wedding when he reacted badly to some drugs he took. His behavior got so out of hand that his family called the police for help and he was stunned to death with Taser guns. In the days and months after his death, Chase and his family became well known far beyond their personal network. He became a celetoid, and time will tell if he will become a celebrity. However, when and how will we decide to label him a celebrity or not? Time is an essential but not sufficient criterion, as it leaves room for discussion. We argue that strategy-learning gossip made Chase a celetoid, and reputation gossip can turn him into a celebrity: focusing on what happened and why this happened (strategy-learning gossip) turned this unknown young man into someone people talked about. Some know him by name, others as "the guy that was stunned to death by Taser guns"—typical of celetoids and subjects of strategy-learning gossip.

If you search for Chase Sherman online, you find several articles about the gruesome day he became famous. Digging deeper, you learn he was a fairly well-known heavyweight fighter but you do not find any personal information, at least not reported by (inter)national media. On the same day that Chase Sherman died and became a celetoid, Kylie Jenner and Tyga ended their relationship. If Chase would have broken up with his girlfriend that day, no one outside of their personal network would have shown interest. Yet Kylie Jenner and Tyga at that point were big enough celebrities for reputation gossip to be spread about them.

From our point of view, strategy-learning gossip is the mechanism by which someone becomes well known outside of one's personal network, becoming a celetoid, while reputation gossip is what sets celebrities apart from celetoids. The day mass media start to share reputation gossip about a person, that person becomes a celebrity. The question remains, however, when this will happen and for what reason. Yet if it happens, this person's well-knownness is big enough for people to care about who they are and about behavior that is not teaching a valuable lesson on how to behave to avoid danger or seek success. For that reason reputation gossip is crucial in our understanding of what is a celebrity and when one becomes a celebrity. Without mass media, reputation gossip about celebrities simply would not exist.

One major factor in this entire process, that we have paid little attention to so far, is the audience. In the next and final section of this chapter we explain why people are so attracted to mass media gossip, and what happens when audience members become very involved with some celebrities.

# AUDIENCES OF MASS MEDIA GOSSIP

While media are the key vehicles through which information/gossip is passed on that helps to turn a person into a celebrity, the famous-person/audience axis is equally crucial, as celebrities need audiences to maintain their status. In turn, celebrities fulfil social roles for audiences (Dyer, 1998; Marshall, 2006; Rojek, 2001; Turner, 2004; Van den Bulck & Claessens, 2013a).

## Why People Love Mass Media Gossip

The reasons why individuals engage in mass media gossip are very similar to individuals' general interest in interpersonal gossip. Motivations to gossip can broadly be classified into reasons to share information, control social networks, manipulate reputations and entertain others and ourselves (see e.g., Foster, 2004). Similarly, celebrities' and celebrity gossip's function is to provide entertainment, relaxation, a pleasant pastime (De Backer et al., 2007; Van den Bulck & Claessens, 2013a; Claessens & Van den Bulck, 2015; Dyer, 1998). Beyond that, mass media gossip is informative and fosters social bonds. All these are motivations for audiences to pay close attention to mass media gossip. We explain why in the following section.

To start with the informative function, the fact that audiences can learn vicariously from the behavior of others explains why many are attracted to mass media gossip when strategy-learning gossip is present. That is, audiences can learn when information is given about how to achieve success, as well as how to prevent disasters (De Backer et al., 2007). This motivation explains why stories such as Chase Sheldon's case, as well as "Lessons on Love, Life and Heartbreak from Miranda Lambert" (featured on www.people.com, November 2, 2015), attract attention. Audiences learn how to avoid danger or how to achieve success. It also explains why people crave sensational news about the absurd events that happened to unknowns (Davis & McLeod, 2003). Yet the informative function of mass media gossip provides a further explanation for why people, and especially young adolescents, are attracted to random news about the behavior of celebrities (De Backer et al., 2007). Essentially, they are of the opinion that mimicking the celebrities' behavior may lead to similar success. Although this opinion may appear naïve, there are sound explanations for why some copy celebrities' actions. Henrich & Gil-White (2001) explained that mimicking higher-status individuals can lead to increased personal status, but that it is difficult to estimate what exactly contributed to the prestige of someone. According to Boyd & Richerson (1985), evolution did not favor individuals who carefully analyzed every strategy for success before mimicking this strategy, but favored a so-called general copying bias, with individuals mimicking behavior patterns of higher-status others. This includes strategies that lead to clear success or failure, but also traits and strategies with no clear consequences. This may explain why some people copy the overall behavior of their favorite celebrities.

A second reason for people to consume mass media gossip is to bond with real-life members in their social network to which mass media gossip can function as a "social glue." Putnam's (2000) work on the drastic decline of social activities in Western societies—only a few years after John Locke (1998a,b)  wrote about the de-voicing of societies—describes a general decline in individuals' number of and contacts with friends and neighbors. As a result people engage less in small talk with friends, neighbors and acquaintances. Locke's (1998a, b) social de-voicing refers to the fact that in most Western societies, people talk less due to urbanization, relocation, television, individualism, economic success and disappearance of social programs. He warns about the negative consequences hereof, as gossip may appear idle chitchat but has important functions. Indeed, it is known that gossip creates a sphere of intimacy for the gossipers. People who gossip feel connected (see e.g., Dunbar, 1992, 1993, 2004; Gluckman, 1963, 1968). Yet who should we gossip with if people do not know our family, friends and foes? Mass media gossip may be the answer to this problem, which explains why people love mass media gossip: it gives them a common ground to share with those in their environment (Fast, Heath, & Wu, 2009). Even amongst total strangers, sharing negative attitudes about others, heightens feelings of familiarity and social cohesion (Weaver & Bosson, 2011). Mass media gossip may just be about gratifying this need for connection.

Third, celebrity gossip can be of interest to people to strengthen the (parasocial) bonds with, and alter the reputation of public figures. This function explains why reputation gossip stories such as Kylie Jenner and Tyga's break-up make headlines. Moreover, prior and after such announcement, media and audiences dig for further news: Why did this happen? How did this happen? What is next? It could be argued that the "life lesson" from this message is that romantic relationships are not forever and people learn to understand why. However, it seems plausible that some people wanted to dig up dirt to recalibrate their opinion about Kylie and/or Tyga. Who was the "badass" in this story? Who was the wronged party? In everyday life, people gossip positively about family and friends and share negative news about rivals and foes (McAndrew, Bell, & Garcia, 2007). In doing so, individuals increase their personal status which, according to Paine (1967, 1968), is a major drive to gossip. It has been shown that people enjoy positive and negative gossip about celebrities and are amused by reading negative mass media gossip (Peng et al., 2015). Yet it is not clear whether this amusement is due to the fact that participants in this study disliked the celebrities gossiped about or if it was some kind of "schadenfreude." Schadenfreude here refers to taking delight in celebrity downfall (see Cross & Littler, 2010). More research is needed to investigate how audiences respond to good and bad news about their favorite and least-favorite celebrities. So far, we only know that pure reputation information about celebrities attracts large audiences, despite the fact that little can be "done" with this information, other than that it changes and maintains the reputations of those gossiped about. Perhaps, as Barkow (1989, 1992) explained, the fact that we perceive celebrities, or at least some celebrities, as part of our social network is sufficient to explain the success of these stories. "Mass media may activate the psychological mechanisms that evolved in response to selection for the acquisition of social information. [...] We see them in our bedrooms, we hear their voices when we dine: If this hypothesis is correct, how are we not to perceive them as our kin, our friends, perhaps even our rivals? As a result, we automatically seek information about their physical health, about changes in their relative standing, and above all about their sexual relationships" (Barkow, 1992, pp. 629–630). For some, this search for information becomes so important that they turn into active audience members, or what we call "prosumers," who actively contribute to the creation of celebrities by further sharing celebrity gossip. In the final section of this chapter we zoom in on this topic.

## How People's Involvement with Celebrities Reinforces the Creation of a Celebrity

Maybe you felt nothing, maybe you felt sad when hearing that Kylie and Tyga broke up and maybe you even felt angry with one or both of them for giving up on the relationship or for hurting your favorite celebrity. Here, we focus on celebrities as social companions with whom audience members can develop personal connections: parasocial interactions (PSI) or parasocial relationships (PSR). The PSI and PSR concepts are often used interchangeably, yet they point to distinct processes (Klimmt et al., 2006). PSI refers to short-term encounters in which audience members feel like they interact with celebrities, while PSR imply long-term connections developed over time and through various mediated encounters or PSI (Bocarnea & Brown, 2007; Giles, 2003; Hartmann et al., 2008; Klimmt et al., 2006). Indeed, audience members encounter celebrities in a range of performances, popular and quality media representations, and social conversations. In both PSI and PSR, though, there is the illusion of a face-to-face friendship between audience members and celebrities (Horton & Wohl, 1956; see Cohen, 2009; Giles, 2002, 2003). This relationship is decidedly one-sided, as a large audience group knows a lot about a celebrity, who hardly knows anything about them, and it almost exclusively takes place through mediated encounters, as people rarely meet celebrities in real life (Giles, 2002; see also Turner, 2004). However, while the information flow seems unilateral, audiences' involvement includes a considerable amount of gossip being spread; either in interpersonal or in a mediated form, for instance through reactions on websites (Van den Bulck & Claessens, 2013b). When reading celebrity gossip, you may want to further share that information with others. Reputation information shared via the media triggers emotional responses in, and active engagement of audiences. Audience members feel involved with celebrities, an involvement that can range from fandom (Sandvoss, 2005) and identification (Cohen, 2009) to PSI and PSR (Giles, 2002; Horton and Wohl, 1956; Claessens & Van den Bulck, 2015). The latter two are the most widespread forms of audience-celebrity involvement (Giles, 2002; Klimmt, Hartmann, & Schramm, 2006; Tian & Hoffner, 2010) and affect audiences' information processing, attitudes, and behavior (Boon & Lomore, 2001; Schiappa, Gregg, & Hewes, 2005).

Social media such as Facebook and Twitter in particular have become key players in these mediated, parasocial relationships as a means to bridge the real and symbolic "distance" between celebrities and media, fans and wider audiences. Social media allow celebrities to communicate (seemingly) directly, intimately and authentically with audiences and fans (McNamara, 2011; Muntean & Petersen, 2009; Marwick & Boyd, 2011) and, at the same time, hand audiences the tools to discuss celebrity news with the celebrity and with each other (Holiman, 2013), to strengthen parasocial relationships with the celebrity (Click et al., 2013), and to engage in fan activities (Van den Bulck et al., 2014). As such, audiences and their mediated celebrity gossip become vital parts in the ongoing process of celebrity construction.

Crucially, insight into a celebrity's public and private life does not just provide audiences with food for gossip but facilitates the articulation and discussion of moral, ethical, and social issues in contemporary society (Dyer, 1987, 1998; Marshall, 2006; Butler Breese, 2010). As Turner (2004, p. 24) states: "gossip [is] an important social process through which relationships, identity, and social and cultural norms are debated, evaluated, modified and shared." Gossip is often employed to crystallize and reinforce "community values, thereby furthering the coherence and unity of the social group" (Wilson, 1974, p. 93). Mediated celebrity gossip certainly contributes to this, as an analysis of a number of cases of online gossip about celebrity antics—from celebrity suicide to sex scandals—reveals the relevance of celebrity gossip in people's deliberations about good and bad, right and wrong in society. Gossip on online communities rooted in American, British, or Flemish (Belgian) culture, reveals how celebrity news readers reinforce their cultural values and coherence by being critical of celebrities' ideas and behaviors that fall outside of dominant norms.

When famous Flemish singer, television personality and gay icon Yasmine died by her own hand in June 2009, it created a frenzy with media and audiences that rivaled the attention for the death of pop icon Michael Jackson the same week, and that ignited discussions on social and ethical issues, norms, and values. Audience discussions ranged from pointing blame in relationship break-ups (seen as the cause of the suicide), appeals to break the taboo surrounding depression in general, the high levels of depression for lesbians and the plight of those left behind after a suicide, as well as the way celebrities get treated by media and audiences, the latter indicating a level of self-reflexivity of gossipers. Gossipers could be seen to disagree and to fight over the moral rights and wrongs involved in the suicide and various contributing factors in the celebrity's life (Van den Bulck & Claessens, 2013a). This and other studies into reactions to celebrity suicides confirm that, increasingly, celebrity deaths provide audiences with an occasion to unravel his/her private life, especially in the case of a sudden or unexpected death (Lumby, 2006, p. 544) and provides a moment for public discussion of shared ideals and identities, particularly when a celebrity's behavior, ideas, and/or values are at the fringe of social norms and values (Kitch, 2005, p. 69).

Audiences' fascination with celebrities' private lives finds its ultimate pleasure and creates food for gossip when provided with insight into celebrity's sexual behavior as it deals with the most intimate details, the "real" behind the celebrity construct. A celebrity's sex life is not just food for gossip but may facilitate the articulation of moral, ethical, and social views on sexual issues in contemporary society. Analysis of audience reactions to celebrity sex stories in a sample of three celebrity websites (Flemish *HLN*, British *Heat*, and American *People* reveal that audience gossip focuses mainly on the highly "scandalous" stories of married heterosexual men's adultery and that, while media refrain from explicit judgments, readers are eager to openly criticize celebrities' adulterous transgressions. However, while this suggest gossip's escapist function, further analysis also revealed that it created discussion regarding the moral rights and wrongs. Focusing on adultery, it became clear that people discuss the basis of adultery: is it a biological thing ("humans are not meant to be with one person")? Is it a sociological result of pressures we are all facing? Do celebrities represent proof of the moral decay following loss of religion? Or was Freud right all along? Even the sexual double standard ("women are responsible for a man's adultery") was implicitly or explicitly subject of discussion (Van den Bulck & Claessens, 2013b; Claessens & Van den Bulck, 2014).

Gossip about celebrity behavior thus helps audiences make sense of the social world and the changes that can be seen to take place in that regard (Gamson, 2001; Evans & Hesmondalgh, 2005). Gossip further functions as a means to protect individual self-interest and enhance one's moral status (Paine, 1967). This can be linked to Goffman's (1959) impression management theory which states that an individual represents oneself in the best possible way, for instance by discussing celebrities' transgressions to enhance their own status as morally "good" people. By vilifying Tiger Woods as a cheat, slamming the "cowardly act" of suicide or, reversely, discussing the need to understand the taboo that is depression, audience members can be seen to try and take the moral high ground, thus using celebrity gossip as a means to position themselves morally (Van den Bulck & Claessens, 2013b; Claessens & Van den Bulck, 2014; Claessens & Van den Bulck, 2015). Throughout these mediated celebrity debates, audiences help create new social norms which, in turn, become a new context for gossip to emerge.

# CONCLUSION

We started this chapter by reviewing some of the issues researchers have debated when trying to define gossip. We made reference to the distinction between strategy-learning gossip and reputation gossip to then explain what mass media gossip is about and how celebrities are created. Strategy-learning gossip, focusing on what happened to people, has the power to transform ordinary unknown people into extraordinary people known outside the realm of their personal network. Reputation gossip, which is information altering the reputation of the target and only relevant to gossipers who know the target, is what sets celebrities apart from the groups of ordinary and extraordinary people. As soon as mass media start to share reputation gossip about someone, that "someone" has become a celebrity, in our opinion. It would be interesting, for future research, to analyze mass media gossip about celebrities from the moment when they were first gossiped about and investigate if this transition from mere strategy-learning gossip toward increasing reputation gossip can be observed.

Of course, mass media also share strategy-learning gossip about celebrities. Audiences remain interested in that type of information as well, as they love to learn from the success and misfortunes, from the rags to riches and back. Strategy-learning gossip is best suited to fulfill this motive, whereas reputation gossip is more relevant to fulfill needs to share gossip about celebrities to maintain the (parasocial) bond with the target or to use celebrity gossip as means to bond with other people. These are avenues for future research as well. Although the fact that some people develop bonds with some celebrities, has been established, it has not been investigated if and how gossip mediates or moderates this bonding process. Similarly, it is known that people feel closer when sharing negative reputation information about third parties, but it has not yet been tested if gossip about celebrities leads to similar, or perhaps even stronger effects.

Finally, we have highlighted how this interpersonal gossip about celebrities again reinforces the creation and maintenance of celebrities. Becoming and remaining well known thrives on mass media gossip as well as on gossip by those who consume mass media gossip. This seems like a win-win situation, as audiences learn to make sense of the complexity of life while celebrities are guaranteed about their status of being well known well beyond their personal network.

## Note

1. One could argue that personal websites, blogs, and especially social media like Twitter and Facebook have enabled audiences to interact with celebrities, but most often these "social" media are being managed by a team surrounding the celebrity, and most information still flows unidirectional from the celebrities to the audience.

## References

Almirol, E. B. (1981). Chasing the elusive butterfly: Gossip and the pursuit of reputation. *Ethnicity 8*, 293–304.

Barkow, J. (1989). *Darwin sex and status. Biological approaches to mind and culture.* Toronto, Ontario, Canada: University of Toronto Press.

Barkow, J. H. (1992). Beneath new culture is old psychology: Gossip and social stratification. In J. H. Barkow, L. Cosmides, & J. Tooby (Eds.), *The Adapted Mind. Evolutionary Psychology and the Generation of Culture* (pp. 627–637). Oxford, England: Oxford University Press.

Baumeister, R. F., Zhang, L. Q., & Vohs, K. D. (2004). Gossip as cultural learning. *Review of General Psychology 8*, 111–121.

Ben-Ze-ev, A. (1994). The vindication of gossip. In R. F. Goodman & A. Ben-Ze-ev (Eds.), *Good gossip* (pp. 11–24). Lawrence, KS: The University Press of Kansas.

Bird, E. S. (1992). *For enquiring minds. A cultural study of supermarket tabloids*. Knoxville, TN: University of Tennessee Press.

Bocarnea, M. C., & Brown, W. J. (2007). Celebrity-persona parasocial interaction scale. In R. A. Reynolds, R. Woods, & J. D. Baker (Eds.), *Handbook of research on electronic surveys and measurements* (pp. 309–312). London, England: Idea Group.

Boon, S. D., & Lomore, C. D. (2001). Admirer-celebrity relationships among young adults: Explaining perceptions of celebrity influence on identity. *Human Communication Research 27*(3), 432–465.

Boorstin, D. (1961). *The image*. London: Weidenfeld and Nicolson.

Boyd, R., & Richerson, P. J. (1985). *Culture and the evolutionary process*. Chicago. IL: University of Chicago Press.

Braudy, L. (1997). *The frenzy of renown: Fame and its history*. New York, NY: Vintage Books.

Brown, D. (1991). *Human universals*. New York, NY: McGraw Hill.

Brown, W., Basil, M. D., & Bocarnea, M. C. (2003). Social influence of an international celebrity: Responses to the death of Princess Diana. *Journal of Communication 53*, 587–605.

Butler Breese, E. (2010). Meaning, celebrity and the underage pregnancy of Jamie Lynn Spears. *Cultural Sociology 4*, 337–355.

Chagnon, N. A. (1988). Life histories, blood revenge, and warfare in a tribal population. *Science 239*, 985–992.

Claessens, N., & Van den Bulck, H. (2014). A severe case of disliking bimbo Heidi, scumbag Jesse and bastard Tiger: Analysing celebrities' online anti-fans. In L. Duits, K. Zwaan & S. Reijnders (Eds.), *The Ashgate Research Companion to Fan Cultures* (pp. 63–75). London: Ashgate.

Claessens, N., & Van den Bulck, H. (2015). Parasocial relationships with audiences' favourite celebrities: The role of audience and celebrity characteristics in a representative Flemish sample. *Communications 40*(1), 43–56.

Click, M., Lee, H., & Wilson Holladay, H. (2013). Making monsters: Lady Gaga, fan identification, and social media. *Popular Music and Society 36*(3), 360–379. doi:10.1080/03007766.2013.79 8546

Cohen, J. (2009). Mediated relationships and media effects: Parasocial interaction and identification. In R. L. Nabi & M. B. Oliver (Eds.), *The SAGE handbook of media processes and effects* (pp. 223–236). London: Sage.

Cross, S., & Littler, J. (2010). Celebrity and schadenfreude: The cultural economy of fame in freefall. *Cultural Studies 24*(3), 395–417.

Davis, H., & Mcleod, S. L. (2003). Why humans value sensational news: An evolutionary perspective. *Evolution and Human Behavior 24*, 208–216.

De Backer, C. J. S., & Fisher, M. L. (2012). Tabloids as windows into our interpersonal relationships: A content analysis of mass media gossip from an evolutionary perspective. *Journal of Social, Evolutionary, and Cultural Psychology 6*, 404–424.

De Backer, C. J., & Gurven, M. (2006). Whispering down the lane: The economics of vicarious information transfer. *Adaptive Behavior 14*(3), 249–264.

De Backer, C. J. S., Nelissen, M., Vyncke, P., Braeckman, J., & McAndrew, F. T. (2007). Celebrities: From teachers to friends: A test of two hypotheses on the adaptiveness of celebrity gossip. *Human Nature: An Interdisciplinary Biosocial Perspective 18*, 334–354.

de Sousa, R. (1994). In praise of gossip: Indiscretion as a saintly virtue. In R. F. Goodman & A. Ben-Ze'ev (Eds.), *Good Gossip* (pp. 25–33). Lawrence, KS: The University Press of Kansas.

Divale, W., & Seda, A. (1999). Codes in gossip for societies in the standard sample. *World Cultures 10*, 7–22.

Driessens, O. (2013). Celebrity capital: redefining celebrity using field theory. *Theory and society 42*(5), 543–560.

Dunbar, R. (1992). Why gossip is good for you. *New Scientist 136*, 28–31.

Dunbar, R. I. M. (1993). Coevolution of neocortical size, group-size and language in humans. *Behavioral and Brain Sciences 16*, 681–694.

Dunbar, R. I. M. (2004). Gossip in evolutionary perspective. *Review of General Psychology 8*, 100–110.

Dyer, R. (1987). *Heavenly bodies: Film stars and society*. London: MacMillan.

Dyer, R. (1998). *Stars*. London: British Film Institute.

Evans, J., & Hesmondhalgh, D. (2005). *Understanding media: Inside celebrity*. Maidenhead: Open University Press.

Fast, N. J., Heath, C., & Wu, G. (2009). Common ground and cultural prominence how conversation reinforces culture. *Psychological Science 20*(7), 904–11.

Foster, E. K. (2004). Research on gossip: Taxonomy, methods, and future directions. *Review of General Psychology, 8*, 78–99.

Gamson, J., 2001. Normal sins: Sex scandal narratives as institutional morality tales. *Social Problems 48*(2), 185–205.

Giles, D. 2002. Parasocial interaction: a review of the literature and a model for future research. *Media Psychology 4*, 279–305. doi:10.1207/S1532785XMEP0403_04

Giles, D. (2003). *Media psychology*. London, England: Routledge.

Gluckman, M. (1963). Gossip and scandal. *Current Anthropology 4*, 307–316.

Gluckman, M. (1968). Psychological, sociological and anthropological explanations of witch-craft and gossip: Clarification. *Man 3*, 20–34.

Goffman, E. (1959). *The presentation of self in everyday life*. New York, NY: Anchor.

Goldstein, D. G., & Gigerenzer, G. (1999). The recognition heuristic: How ignorance makes us smart. In G. Gigerenzer, P. M. Todd, & The ABC Research Group (Eds.), *Simple heuristics that make us smart* (pp. 37–58). Oxford: Oxford University Press.

Hannerz, U. (1967). Gossip, networks and culture in a Black American ghetto. *Ethnos 32*, 35–60.

Hartmann, T., Stuke, D., & Daschmann, G. (2008). Positive parasocial relationships with drivers affect suspense in racing sports spectators. *Journal of Media Psychology 20*, 1, 24–34. doi:10.1027/1864-1105.20.1.24

Hawkes, K. (1991). Showing off: Tests of an hypothesis about men's foraging goals. *Ethology and Sociobiology 12*, 29–54.

Hawkes, K. (1993). Why hunter-gatherers work: An ancient version of the problem of public goods. *Current Anthropology 34*, 341–361.

Hawkes, K., O'Connell, J. F., & Blurton-Jones, N. G. (2001). Hadza meat sharing. *Evolution and Human Behavior 22*, 113–142.

Henrich, J., & F. J. Gil-White (2001). The evolution of prestige. *Evolution and Human Behavior 22*, 165–196.

Hess, N. H., & Hagen, E. H. (2006a). Psychological adaptations for assessing gossip veracity. *Human Nature: An Interdisciplinary Biosocial Perspective 17*, 337–354.

Hess, N. H., & Hagen, E. H. (2006b). Sex differences in indirect aggression: Psychological evidence from young adults. *Evolution and Human Behavior 27*, 231–245.

Holiman, J. M. 2013. iGrieve: *Social Media, Parasocial Mourning and the Death of Steve Jobs*. Unpublished manuscript, retrieved from http://www.suu.edu/hss/comm/masters/capstone/thesis/igrieve-holiman-j.pdf

Horton, D., & Wohl, R. R. (1956). Mass-communication and para-social interaction: Observations on intimacy at a distance. *Psychiatry 19, 215–229.*

Kitch, C. L. (2005). *Pages from the past: History and memory in American magazines.* Chapel Hill, NC: University of North Carolina Press.

Klimmt, C., Hartmann, T., & Schramm, H. (2006). Parasocial interactions and relationships. In J. Bryant & P. Vorderer (Eds.), *Psychology of entertainment* (pp. 291–313). London: Lawrence Erlbaum Associates.

Levin, J., & Arluke, A. (1985). An exploratory analysis of sex-differences in gossip. *Sex Roles 12,* 281–286.

Levin, J., & Kimmel, A. (1977). Gossip columns: Media small talk. *Journal of Communication 27,* 169–175.

Locke, J. (1998a). Where did all the gossip go? *ASHA, Summer 98, 40*(3): 26–31.

Locke, J. (1998b). *The DeVoicing of society: Why we don't talk to each other any more.* New York, NY: Simon & Schuster.

Lumby, C. (2006). Vanishing points. In P. D. Marshall (Ed.), *The celebrity culture reader* (pp. 530–546). London: Routledge.

Marlowe, F. (1999). Showoffs or providers: The parenting effort of Hadza men. *Evolution and Human Behavior 20,* 391–404.

Marshall, P. D. (2006). *The celebrity culture reader.* London: Routledge.

Marwick, A., & Boyd, D. (2011). To see and be seen: Celebrity practice on Twitter. *Convergence, the International Journal of Research into New Media Technologies 17*(2), 139–158. doi:10.1177/1354856510394539

McAndrew, F. T. (2019). Gossip as a social skill. In F. Giardini, R. P. M. Wittek (Eds.), Handbook of gossip and reputation. New York: Oxford University Press.

McAndrew, F. T., Bell, E. K., & Garcia, C. M. (2007). Who do we tell and whom do we tell on? Gossip as a strategy for status enhancement. *Journal of Applied Social Psychology 37,* 1562–1577.

McAndrew, F. T., & Milenkovic, M. A. (2002). Of tabloids and family secrets: The evolutionary psychology of gossip. *Journal of Applied Social Psychology 32,* 1064–82.

McNamara, K. (2011). The Paparazzi industry and new media: The evolving production and consumption of celebrity news and gossip websites. *International Journal of Cultural Studies 14*(5), 515–530. doi:10.1177/1367877910394567

Morreall, J. (1994). Gossip and humor. In R. F. Goodman & A. Ben-Ze-ev (Eds.), *Good Gossip* (pp. 56–64). Kansas: The University Press of Kansas.

Muntean, N., & Petersen, A. H. (2009). Celebrity twitter: Strategies of intrusion and disclosure in the age of technoculture. *M/C Journal, a Journal of Media and Culture* [online] 12, 5.

Noon, M., & Delbridge, R. (1993). News from behind my hand: Gossip in organizations. *Organization Studies 14,* 23–36.

Ouvrein, G., Vandebosch, H., & De Backer, C. J. S. (2017). Celebrity critiquing: Hot or not? Teenage girls' attitudes and responses to the practice of negative celebrity critiquing. *Celebrity Studies,* 1–16. doi:10.1080/19392397.2017.1307126

Paine, R. (1967). What is gossip about: Alternative hypothesis. *Man 2,* 278–285.

Paine, R. (1968). Gossip and transaction. *Man 3,* 305–308.

Patton, J. Q. (2000). Reciprocal altruism and warfare: A case from the Ecuadorian Amazon. In L. Cronk, N. A. Chagnon, & W. Irons (Eds.), *Adaptation and human behavior: An anthropological perspective* (pp. 417–436). New York: Aldine de Gruyter.

Peng, X., Li, Y., Wang, P., Mo, L., & Chen, Q. (2015). The ugly truth: Negative gossip about celebrities and positive gossip about self entertain people in different ways. *Social Neuroscience, 10(3)*, 320-36.1–17.

Putnam, R. D. (2000). *Bowling alone.* New York, NY: Touchstone, Simon & Schuster.

Rojek, C. (2001). *Celebrity.* London: Reaktion Books.

Rosnow, R. L., & Fine, G. A. (1976). *Rumor and gossip. The social psychology of hearsay.* New York, NY: Elsevier.

Rozin, P., & Royzman, E. B. (2001). Negativity bias, negativity dominance, and contagion. *Personality and Social Psychology Review, 5(4)*, 296–320.

Rubin, A. M., Perse, E. M., & Powell, R. A. (1985). Loneliness, parasocial interaction, and local television-news viewing. *Human Communication Research, 12*, 155–180.

Schely-Newman, E. (2004). Mock intimacy: Strategies of engagement in Israeli gossip columns. *Discourse Studies, 6(4)*, 471–488.

Sandvoss, C. (2005). *Fans.* Cambridge: Polity.

Schiappa, E., Gregg, P. B., & Hewes, D. E. (2005). The parasocial contact hypothesis. *Communication Monographs 72(1)*, 92–115. doi:10.1080/0363775052000342544

Sloan, B. (2001). *"I watched a wild hog eat my baby!" A colorful history of tabloids and their cultural impact.* New York, NY: Prometheus Books.

Sugiyama, L. S., & Chacon, R. (2000). Effects of illness and injury among the Yora and Shiwiar. In N. A. Chagnon, L. Cronk, & W. Irons (Eds.), *Human behavior and adaptation: An anthropological perspective* (pp. 371–395). New York, NY: Aldine de Gruyter.

Suls, J. M. (1977). Gossip and social comparison. *Journal of Communication 26*, 164–168.

Thomas, L. (1994). The logic of gossip. In R. F. Goodman & A. Ben-Ze-ev (Eds.), *Good gossip* (pp. 85–99). Lawrence, KS: University Press of Kansas.

Tian, Q., & Hoffner, C. A. (2010). Parasocial interaction with liked, neutral, and disliked characters on a popular TV series. *Mass Communication and Society 13(3)*, 250–69. doi:10.1080/15205430903296051

Tooby, J., & DeVore, L. (1987). The reconstruction of hominid behavioral evolution through strategic modelling. In W. G. Kinzey (Ed.), *Primate models of the origin of human behavior.* New York, NY: SUNY Press.

Turner, G. (2004). *Understanding Celebrity.* London: Sage Publications.

Van den Bulck, H., & Claessens, N. (2013a). Celebrity suicide and the search for the moral high ground: comparing frames in media and audience discussions of the death of a Flemish celebrity. *Critical Studies in Media Communication, 30(1)*, 69–74.

Van den Bulck, H., & Claessens, N. (2013b). Guess who Tiger is having sex with now? Celebrity sex and the framing of the moral high ground." *Celebrity Studies, 4(1)*, 46–57.

Van den Bulck, H., Claessens, N., & Bels, A. (2014). "By working she means tweeting": Online celebrity gossip media and audience readings of celebrity Twitter behaviour. *Celebrity Studies, 5(4)*, 514–517. doi:10.1080/19392397.2014.980655

Van den Bulck, H., Paulussen, S., & Bels, A. (2016). Celebrity news as hybrid journalism: An assessment of celebrity coverage in Flemish newspapers and magazines. *Journalism* (forthcoming).

Weaver, J. R., & Bosson, J. K. (2011). I feel like I know you: Sharing negative attitudes of others promotes feelings of familiarity. *Personality and Social Psychology Bulletin 37*, 481–491.

Wilson, P. J., 1974. Filcher of good names: An enquiry into anthropology and gossip. *Man 9(1)*, 93–102.

..............................................................................

# ON THE NATURE OF GOSSIP, REPUTATION, AND POWER INEQUALITY

..............................................................................

## SALLY FARLEY

> Fire and swords are slow engines of destruction, compared to the tongue of a Gossip.
>
> —Richard Steele

ANTHROPOLOGISTS, sociologists, and psychologists have learned a great deal about the nature of gossip since Gluckman's (1963) influential anthropological treatise on the subject, yet the empirical evidence is greatly supportive of his early thinking about why individuals gossip. Although Gluckman (1963) pointed out that gossip can be wielded as a weapon against others, he also asserted that gossip was a "privilege" and a "duty" of group membership, and was one of the first to highlight such virtuous functions of gossip as maintaining group cohesion, clarifying group boundaries, and communicating values.

The purpose of this chapter is to highlight the most recent theoretical and empirical insights into why people gossip, how gossip can be used to strategically alter reputation, and the consequences of gossip for power dynamics. In this chapter, I will argue that gossip is a highly efficient and impactful mechanism by which reputations are created, maintained, and altered. Furthermore, I will contend that the selective and strategic use of gossip increases a gossiper's power (i.e., ability to influence others), independent of his or her formal or informal status in a group (i.e., rank or position relative to others), but that engaging in gossip can be costly for both the initiator of the gossip and his/her target. I will also discuss the broader questions of gossip and power inequality, such as "Is power an *antecedent* or a *consequence* of gossip?" "Do individuals direct gossip to others of the same standing, higher standing, or lower standing?" and "Can gossiping damage one's reputation, thereby weakening one's power and social standing?"

The chapter begins by describing the way key terms will be defined. Next the chapter summarizes literature on four functions/motivations for gossip (group protection, social comparison, status enhancement/negative influence, and social bonding), and elaborates upon how these functions of gossip shape power and reputation. Following this discussion, I review recent empirical insights gleaned from the role of gossip in a broader group-level context. Next, the chapter clarifies the various ways gossip is enmeshed in the fabric of social hierarchies, serving as both an agent and outcome of power inequality. The final section of this chapter explores future directions to address gaps in the literature.

For the purposes of this chapter, gossip is defined as evaluative talk about others who are not present (Foster, 2004; Rosnow, 2001). Although many researchers primarily structure their operationalization of gossip as negative evaluative information about others (cf. Beersma & Van Kleef, 2012; Feinberg, Willer, & Schultz, 2014; Feinberg, Willer, Stellar, & Keltner, 2012), a broader definition offers increased flexibility and generalizability. In addition, the tendency for individuals to disseminate positive gossip much more readily when the actor is an ingroup as opposed to an outgroup member has important status implications which would be unexplored using a more restrictive definition of gossip (McAndrew, Bell, & Garcia, 2007). Reputation is defined as aggregated "social information about the value of people," according to Origgi (2019). Power is conceptualized in terms of informational power, power derived from possessing and disseminating important information (Raven, 1965), and in terms of influence, the ability to effect change in another person, either by altering their attitudes, perceptions, of behavior. Thus, power inequality pertains to a relative difference between individuals with regard to their ability to exert influence over others. "Social standing" and "status" will be used interchangeably to capture one's rank in the social hierarchy, relative to others (on the relationship between reputation and status, see also Grow & Flache, 2019).

# FUNCTIONS OF GOSSIP AND THEIR LINK TO POWER AND REPUTATION

## Group Protection

The motive for gossip that has perhaps received the most empirical attention is group protection. The group protection motive is designed to encourage cooperation in groups by punishing exploitative behavior (Feinberg, et al., 2012a). It is important to note that this motive captures a variety of seemingly related and/or overlapping group processes identified by other researchers: social control (Giardini & Conte, 2012), delineation of group boundaries (Gluckman, 1963; Foster, 2004), and communication of group norms and values (Baumeister, Zhang, & Vohs, 2004). From an evolutionary standpoint, it is critical to ferret out information about others as to their relative cooperative or egoistic nature, because free-riders threaten the benefits of social living (Boehm, 2019; Dunbar, 2004).

Gossip functions to increase cooperation in two ways. First, gossip facilitates partner selection—individuals use the information garnered via gossip to selectively interact with cooperative individuals (Feinberg et al., 2014; Giardini, Paolucci, Villatoro, &

## Table 18.1. Summary of the Functions of Gossip and Key Supportive Findings

|  | Function | Key Findings |
| --- | --- | --- |
| Group Protection | To increase group cooperation and solidarity | Group-serving gossip is not evaluated negatively (Beersma & Van Kleef, 2012) |
|  |  | Gossip is disproportionately about norm-violators and people who behave in self-serving ways (Beersma & Van Kleef, 2012) |
|  | Includes social control, delineation of group boundaries, and communication of group norms and values | Gossip effectively reduces self-serving behavior (Beersma & Van Kleef, 2011; Piazza & Bering, 2008), and increases cooperative behavior (Feinberg et al., 2014) |
|  |  | Gossip facilitates cooperative partner selection (Sommerfeld et al., 2007) |
| Social Comparison | To determine whether one's appraisal of others is normative and accurate | Most overheard gossip is related to social information gathering (Dunbar et al., 1997) |
|  |  | Of all motives for engaging in gossip, information-gathering was the most frequently observed (Beersma & Van Kleef, 2012) |
| Status Enhancement/ Negative Influence Gossip | To increase the status of oneself or one's group, often by tarnishing the reputation of others | Individuals selectively reveal positive information about in-group members and negative information about outgroup members (McAndrew et al., 2007) |
|  |  | Gossip can serve as a tool for sexual rivals to lower the reputation of competing mate partners (De Backer et al., 2007b) |
|  |  | Those with a high tendency to gossip are often quite powerful (Grosser et al., 2010; Jaeger et al, 1994;), although this is not always the case (Farley, 2011) |
| Social Bonding | To develop, maintain, and strengthen the bonds between members of a social group | Gossip is the antecedent of friendship (Ellwardt et al., 2012a) |
|  |  | Although positive gossip flows freely between those who are less close, negative gossip tends to be reserved for close friends (Grosser et al., 2010) |
|  |  | Coalition triads (involving shared dislike for a third party) are responsible for the highest proportion of gossip activity (Wittek & Wielers, 1998) |
|  |  | Experimental work identifying the causal direction of gossip and social bonding is scarce |

Conte, 2014; Sommerfeld, Krambeck, Semmann, & Milinski, 2007). Second, the deterrence hypothesis put forth by Feinberg et al. (2012a) maintains that gossip harnesses free-riding behavior because free-riders fear the consequences of their exploitative behavior being revealed. In support of this logic, evidence suggests that negative gossip is deemed to be more appropriate when it is group-serving (to communicate violations of group norms) rather than self-serving (Beersma & Van Kleef, 2012; Wilson, Wilczynski, Wells, & Weiser, 2000). Gossip is selectively revealed to ingroup members about norm violators (Beersma & Van Kleef, 2012), serving to effectively constrain self-serving behavior (Beersma & Van Kleef, 2011; Piazza & Bering, 2008). In a clever series of studies, Feinberg et al. (2012a) demonstrated that being exposed to self-serving behavior caused negative affect in observers (especially those with more prosocial orientations), which was assuaged by relaying negative gossip to the next interaction partner of the self-serving individuals. Feinberg et al. (2014) provided experimental evidence that threat of gossip (via notes directed to subsequent interaction partners) increased cooperative behavior, and interestingly, that punishing selfish players through ostracism was an effective strategy to increase prosocial norm compliance.

Research on the group protection motive reveals that gossip is also a powerful mechanism for altering reputation. Empirical results show that (1) prosocial gossip, i.e., negative gossip designed to protect recipients from exploitation (Feinberg et al., 2012b), is not evaluated unfavorably (Beersma & Van Kleef, 2012), (2) individuals eagerly share reputational-changing information about others via gossip (McAndrew, et al., 2007), (3) gossip is disproportionately about those who behave in self-serving ways, and (4) others are influenced by prosocial gossip, relying on it to selectively interact with cooperative partners. Thus, prosocial gossip serves to level the playing field, curbing the potential advantage people gain through free-riding. Clearly, targets of prosocial gossip suffer from reputational degradation, prompting them in some circumstances to increase cooperative behavior upon the threat of gossip, or worse, ostracism (Feinberg et al., 2014). The reputational consequences for prosocial gossip are positive for the gossiper as engaging in prosocial gossip may translate into being viewed as the group's benefactor, thus enhancing the gossiper's power and social standing in the group (on the link between gossip, reputation and cooperation see also Giardini & Wittek, 2019).

## Social Comparison

Social comparison gossip is seemingly "cold" and "cognitive," driven out of a desire to determine if one's appraisal of another person is accurate or normative (Foster, 2004). A number of researchers have emphasized the social comparison motive of gossip (Beersma & Van Kleef, 2012; De Backer, Nelisson, & Fisher, 2007b; Foster, 2004; Wert & Salovey, 2004). According to Wert & Salovey (2004), all gossip involves some degree of social comparison. For example, after meeting a woman who repeatedly stroked her hair during her professional presentation, one colleague might turn to another and say, "did you notice how nervous she looked? She could not keep her hands off her hair while she talked!" This bit of gossip serves to determine to what extent others share the same impression of the target of the gossip. In an observational study, Dunbar, Marriott, & Duncan (1997) noted that the bulk of overheard gossip pertained to social information gathering, and thus gossip represented an efficient mechanism to monitor one's social network. Research reveals that this sort of gossip, which Beersma & Van Kleef (2012) term information gathering/validation, emerged as the most important motivation for gossiping in two different studies.

Lateral social comparison, relying on similar others to gauge one's attitudes and behaviors, is more likely when individuals are motivated for accurate, objective evidence, yet often individuals engage in comparison processes for self-enhancement motives (Wert & Salovey, 2004). When people are motivated to protect and enhance their self-esteem, their social comparison processes may be more biased. For instance, after individuals experience failure, they are likely to compare themselves with those who are less competent in that particular domain (Wood, 1989). In these circumstances, negative gossip in the pursuit of increased self-esteem becomes more likely (Wert & Salovey, 2004).

Baumeister et al. (2004) argued that gossip may elevate the social status of the gossiper through inferred informational power. In addition, according to Guerin & Miyazaki (2006), the first person to relay gossip serves as a "gatekeeper," possessing the greatest conversational cash value, signaling their centrality in the communication network. However, informational power is only valuable to the extent to which it influences the perceptions, attitudes, and behaviors of the recipient (R. Wittek, personal communication, May, 2016). Furthermore, informational power is transient. After one relays a bit of gossip to another, the "power" ascribed to that gossip is transmitted from one to the other.

The bit of gossip just discussed is likely motivated from a lateral social comparison standpoint. The gossiper simply wants to determine if his/her audience shares the same impression of a target's behavior. Individuals use this sort of gossip in order to develop a more accurate and well-informed view of those in their social network. I would argue that lateral social comparison gossip has few reputation-altering consequences. However, downward social comparison appears to be motivated not by a desire to gain information about others, but as a means to tarnish others' reputations. Thus, it will be reviewed in the next section of the chapter.

## Status Enhancement/Negative Influence

Gossip derives its ruinous reputation because of the status-enhancement motive. In contrast to social comparison, status-enhancement gossip, which is designed to increase the status of oneself or one's group (McAndrew et al., 2007), and negative influence gossip (Beersma & Van Kleef, 2012), which is designed to tarnish the reputations of others, are clearly "hot" processes. Although several researchers have distinguished between status enhancement and negative influence, negative influence (speaking negatively about others) is often motivated by a desire to enhance status. The literature on social identity theory (Tajfel, 1982; Turner, 1987) offers some context into how disparaging outgroup members relates to self-esteem. Individuals derive self-esteem from both their personal successes and the successes of valued ingroup members (Crocker & Luhtanen, 1990), causing substantial ingroup bias. In addition, evidence suggests that collective self-esteem is increased after derogating outgroup members (Crocker & Luhtanen, 1990). Thus, gossip may represent a mechanism to elevate one's status through castigating others.

In support of the view that gossip serves status-enhancing motives, McAndrew & Milenkovic (2002) argued that individuals are especially interested in gossip about higher-status individuals, rivals (for potential exploitative value), and potential mates. Recipients of gossip selectively attune to and relay positive information about ingroup members and negative information about outgroup members (McAndrew et al., 2007; McAndrew & Milenkovic, 2002). These tendencies shield the group from negative reputational consequences. Although De Backer et al. (2007b) found that women were more likely to remember reputational details about romantic rivals than were men, this still provides evidence that gossip can serve as a tool for sexual rivals to lower the status/reputation level of competing mate partners.

As mentioned previously, prosocial gossip is evaluated more positively than egoistic/ selfish gossip, thus these two types of gossip likely have different status implications. Prosocial gossipers may experience a boost to their perceived status because they appear altruistic guards of group norms. However, egoistic gossip may be a costly strategy. Pilfering power through negative gossip may provide initial boosts to one's self-esteem and reputation (Turner, Mazur, Wendel, & Winslow, 2003), but if the motive to tarnish another person's reputation becomes transparent, then this could have unintentional reputational consequences for oneself (Ellwardt, 2019). These effects can be understood in relation to the transfer of attitudes reflectively framework, that negative attitudes by the sender about the target may have more negative implications for the *sender* than the target (Gawronski & Walther, 2008). It is not surprising, then, that gossipers are not uniformly liked (Farley, 2011; Farley, Timme, & Hart, 2010).

Yet despite the common conjecture that gossip is a "weapon of the weak," used by individuals in lower positions of power to control or influence those higher in power, research shows that individuals with a high propensity to gossip are often quite powerful individuals at the center of communication networks (Jaeger, Skleder, Rind, & Rosnow, 1994). In an organizational setting, individuals who self-reported the highest gossip behavior were rated as being the most influential by their coworkers (Grosser, Lopez-Kidwell, & Labianca, 2010).

## Social Bonding

Dunbar (1994) argued that the primary motivation for gossip was social bonding, that gossip supplanted grooming as the mechanism by which we keep well-informed of our social networks. In 2004, Dunbar wrote provocatively that gossip is "the core of human social relationships, indeed of society itself" (p. 100). Dunbar (2004) argued that gossip evolved as a strategy to keep abreast of one's social group, in part by identifying cooperators and free-riders, an essential skill for successful group living. Like grooming functions in our primate relatives to maintain and strengthen the bonds between members of social groups, so does gossip for our current social groups (Dunbar, 2004). Others have also speculated that "gossip is usually expressed in small trusted groups" (Michelson, van Iterson, & Waddington, 2010, p. 3), yet despite the profoundly social nature of gossip and the obvious relational ties that gossip has to friendship, few studies have been able to pinpoint the causal direction of gossip and friendship (but see Ellwardt, Steglich, & Wittek, 2012, for an important exception).

If gossip serves as "social glue" (Turner et al., 2003), then it would follow that gossip flows more frequently between those who report more emotional closeness, trust, and friendship. Indeed, gossip tends to occur between people who are friendly with one another (Grosser et al., 2010). Analysis of social network patterns in organizational settings revealed that individuals are likely to engage in positive gossip with both coworkers and friends, but that negative gossip is reserved only for close friends (Ellwardt et al., 2012a; Grosser et al., 2010), leading researchers to identify negative gossip as a marker of intimate friendships (Grosser et al., 2010; Thornborrow & Morris, 2004). Another finding by Grosser et al. (2010) which documented the centrality of negative gossip to friendship was that individuals who were highly structurally embedded in their networks (having multiple shared links with others) engaged in more negative gossip than those who were more peripheral.

A different way to frame the importance of negative gossip for social bonding processes relates to the coalition hypothesis posited by Wittek & Wielers (1998). According to this hypothesis, gossip is most likely to flourish between allies who are discussing a common enemy, an individual who is disliked by both parties. Wittek & Wielers (1998) wrote that "gossip requires potential allies and members of an outgroup as the objects of the gossip" (p. 201). Essentially, this hypothesis maintained that it is the shared dislike for a third party that drives negative gossip. Results from organizations and school settings were supportive of this hypothesis—the higher the proportion of coalition triads, the greater the gossip activity (Wittek & Wielers, 1998).

One question nagging this line of research pertains to whether gossip creates trusting bonds, increasing friendship ties, or whether gossip flows from pre-existing friendships. Experimental work attempting to determine temporal causality has been scarce. One exception, an experimental study conducted by Turner et al. (2003), enlisted the help of participant confederates to relay a bit of positive or negative gossip about the experimenter to a friend or a stranger. Contrary to the social bonding hypothesis, gossip of any kind hurt the gossipers' trust, liking, and expert power ratings (Turner et al., 2003). Furthermore, the deleterious consequences of gossiping were worse for friends than for strangers (Turner et al., 2003). Although these results are inconsistent with the social bonding hypothesis, they are likely to reflect an artifact of an unusual experimental manipulation. The experimenter was a stranger to the participants, and as a result, gossiping about this person may have represented a violation to the rules of appropriate gossip behavior (that we gossip to and about those in our social networks). Another experiment that involved utilizing a confederate to relay three items of positive, negative, or factual information to a stranger during a structured closeness induction task failed to find significant social bonding effects (Farley & Eyssell, 2014). These studies share some cautionary logic—that of failed mundane realism (failure to approximate a real-world gossip situation). It is extremely difficult to duplicate the conditions under which gossip occurs in laboratory settings because gossip does not typically occur between strangers. The alternative strategy of relying on pre-existing relationships presents another challenge—it becomes difficult to disentangle whether gossip is the bonding agent, or whether gossip emerges from pre-existing close relationships.

Some have argued that it is through gossip that trust is generated and alliances are created, maintained, and strengthened (Dunbar, 1996; Foster, 2004). Therefore, to be excluded from gossip signals a lack of trust (McAndrew, 2008). Evidence from a three-wave longitudinal study in an organizational setting provided convincing evidence that gossip *precipitates* friendship (Ellwardt et al., 2012a). In this study, researchers pitted two competing theories against one another, the social capital perspective (gossip flows from friendship) and the evolutionary perspective (gossip is the bonding agent that creates friendships), and found that early gossiping behavior predicted later friendship formation (Ellwardt et al., 2012a). Self-disclosure and gossip (or other-disclosure, as Turner et al., 2003 described it) likely operate in parallel, progressively becoming more intimate over time, thus deepening emotional closeness between members of a dyad. Individuals test the waters of friendship by self-disclosing relatively shallow inconsequential information about themselves in early stages, and only deepening the meaningfulness of self-disclosures if and when their partners reciprocate (Altman & Taylor, 1973). This serves to create trust and interpersonal intimacy. Gossipers signal an interest in forming friendships by revealing potentially sensitive information about others (Ellwardt et al., 2012a), and reciprocating gossip signals receptivity to friendship. The general pattern of research showing little gossip between strangers, positive gossip between acquaintances, and negative gossip between close friends offers indirect support for this notion. Nevertheless, it is likely that the direction between gossip and closeness is bi-directional (De Backer, Larson, & Cosmides, 2007a), as gossip and self-disclosure are natural outgrowths of intimate personal relationships.

Evidence suggests that gossip (especially negative gossip) is the hallmark of friendship, and that it is shared freely between allies and ingroup members, especially about disliked outgroup members. According to Wittek & Wielers (1998, p. 202) "gossip marks and enhances group boundaries by strengthening the relationship of (two friends) at the cost of an (enemy)," implying both a status motive and a social bonding motive. The most obvious point is that isolates in social networks, those who neither send nor receive gossip, are likely to be relatively low in status and power. People who are not included in gossip are clearly part of the outgroup. In organizational settings in which supervisors rely upon gossip to gauge a variety of information about workplace climate, supervisor effectiveness, and so on, those who are left out of gossip may be left behind in the organization (Baumeister et al., 2004). Furthermore, gossip clearly travels from person to person, and revealing where one learns information is diagnostic about relative status in a network. Individuals who are popular and more central to their social networks tend to gossip more than those who are less popular and more peripheral to their social networks (Jaeger et al., 1994; Lansford, Putallez, Grimes, Schiro-Osman, Kupersmidt, & Coie, 2006). If popularity is a proxy for social power, then certainly gossip is associated with high social power.

## GROUP-LEVEL INSIGHTS INTO GOSSIP AND REPUTATION

In an influential paper, Sommerfeld et al. (2007) revealed that individuals rely upon gossip even when they have direct experience that contradicts the gossip. Thus, in today's increasingly complex social environment, with both virtual and personal social networks, the ability to directly observe one's social acquaintances is diminished. In such a world, "gossip has a strong manipulative potential that could be used by cheaters to change the reputation of others or even change their own" (Sommerfeld et al., 2007, p. 17438). This study also revealed that individuals altered their behavior in accordance with gossip (Sommerfeld et al., 2007), showing that gossip served as an accurate reputational cue. As a result, individuals are sensitive to the reputational-consequences of their behavior. Individuals who thought they were interacting with others with a high tendency to gossip were significantly more generous to the group (Beersma & Van Kleef, 2011). Similarly, merely the threat of gossip increases generosity/prosociality to one's group, but only under conditions of personal identifiability (Piazza & Bering, 2008). Combined together, these findings suggest that at the group level, gossip is effective to increase cooperative/prosocial behavior which benefits the group.

In a series of experiments using trust games, Feinberg et al. (2012b) demonstrated that prosocial gossip is driven by a desire to protect the "system." Those with a greater prosocial orientation were particularly motivated to relay negative selfish-constraining gossip to others, even when doing so was costly (Feinberg et al., 2012b). Giardini, Paolucci, Villatoro, & Conte (2014) tested two different mechanisms by which gossip increased cooperation—punishment and reputation. They found that both punishment (decreasing free-riders' payoffs) and reputation via gossip were effective at constraining self-serving behavior, but that cooperation was highest when both methods were used. Primarily, gossip worked in this study by facilitating partner selection—refusing to interact with selfish others increased cooperation to 70%. In a similar study, Wu, Balliet, & Van Lange (2016a) found that gossip increased both cooperation and overall earnings, but found that gossip was a more effective strategy than was punishment. The authors wrote "Overall, our findings suggest that gossip can be relatively more efficient and effective than punishment to promote and maintain cooperation when gossip involves no cost whereas punishment is moderately costly" (Wu et al., 2016a, p. 4).

Feinberg et al. (2014) also provided experimental evidence that prosocial gossip influences partner selection, but further showed that the threat of ostracism increased cooperative behavior above and beyond that associated with gossip. In short, worry about being outed as a slacker or free-rider generally ramped up cooperative tendencies. Furthermore, individuals who experienced ostracism dramatically increased their contributions once they were allowed back into the game, showing that ostracism was a highly powerful mechanism of group-level social control (Feinberg et al., 2014).

## GOSSIP, POWER, AND POWER INEQUALITY

Given the theoretical speculation about the status-enhancing effects of gossip, one would expect gossip frequency to be associated with greater power and social standing. However, research findings have been inconsistent on this point. In one study, members of a service sorority who gossiped the most emerged as the most influential clique in the sorority (Jaeger et al., 1994). Similarly, in elementary school settings, higher-status popular girls were found to gossip more than lower-status girls (Eder & Enke, 1991; Lansford et al., 2006; McDonald, Putallaz, Grimes, Kupersmidt, & Coie, 2007). Eder & Enke (1991) also noted that the only people to challenge gossip were those of equal or higher status than the gossipers, prompting the authors to speculate that gossip was a privilege afforded to those higher in social standing. A more recent organizational study found that individuals who reported engaging in the most gossip were rated as the most influential by their coworkers (Grosser et al., 2010). These findings seem to converge on the notion that those of higher status gossip more than their lower status peers.

In contrast, two studies prompting participants to think of individuals who either frequently or rarely gossiped ("discussed information about others who were not present") found that high gossipers were perceived as more controlling and *less* influential than low frequency gossipers (Farley, 2011; Farley et al., 2010). These findings, coupled with other research showing that high-frequency gossipers are not especially well-liked (Jaeger et al., 1994) and have fewer friendships (Ellwardt, et al., 2012a) than those who gossip less highlights the complexity of the relationship between power and gossip.

One possible explanation for this pattern of results is that the relationship between gossip and social power is likely curvilinear. Although it remains unclear whether refraining from gossip prompts social exclusion or being a social isolate restricts one's access to gossip, what is clear is that individuals who are marginalized from the group are likely to suffer in terms of perceived social power. At the other end of the spectrum, individuals who gossip very frequently may be perceived as undiscriminating and untrustworthy (Foster, 2004; Kurland & Pelled, 2000; McAndrew, 2008) ultimately at the cost of status (Levin & Arluke, 1985). Successful status enhancement is likely to involve the selective and strategic use of gossip, thus engaging in gossip at a moderate level (Foster, 2004; McAndrew, 2008).

Another avenue shedding light on gossip and inequality pertains to the hierarchical distribution of gossip. To whom do we gossip? High status cliques tend to have high rates of gossip and often, members of these groups are directing the gossip to one another (Jaeger et al., 1994). Similarly, more recent empirical work suggests that we gossip to and about our ingroup members (Ellwardt et al., 2012a). One assumption derived from Eder & Enke's (1991) work is that gossip tends to flow between those of relatively equal status. Thus, gossip appears to be communicated laterally, rather than upward or downward.

Potentially more revealing of the informal status hierarchy is not the partners of gossip, but the targets of gossip. A number of studies have pointed to the tendency for low-status members of a group to be targets of gossip (Eder & Enke, 1994; Ellwardt, Labianca, & Wittek, 2012; McDonald et al., 2007), prompting Ellwardt et al. (2012b) to illustrate parallels between victimized by bullying and gossip. This tendency is particularly pronounced for negative gossip, which is selectively waged against low-status members of an organization (Ellwardt, et al., 2012b). Negative gossip utilized in this way may serve several functions. It may be initiated by members of a group to encourage norm compliance (Ellwardt, et al., 2012b) and constrain self-serving behavior (Beersma & Van Kleef, 2012). As some have posited, gossip may serve as an effective early stage signal that a group disapproves of someone's behavior, a warning that failure to conform will results in further punishment (Feinberg, Cheng, & Willer, 2012). Specifically, negative gossip signals to others that they are in danger of ostracism, the most devastating social consequence one can experience given our fundamental need to belong (Baumeister & Leary, 1995). Again, it is likely that there is a bi-directional relationship between social status and being targeted for negative gossip, one that would be difficult to disentangle empirically.

This logic points to the importance of the consequences of gossip for both the initiator and the target of gossip. Although gossip can be an efficient means to disseminate reputational information about others (Feinberg et al., 2012), "more socially connected people have greater potential to spread others' reputation, and so reputation resulting from behavior toward well-connected people can be more rewarding (and damaging) to one's reputation" (Wu, et al., 2016b, p. 355). Essentially, higher status individuals are afforded more power and deference because those of lesser status fear being targeted. For example, individuals are more generous toward more well-connected people (Wu, Balliet, & Van Lange, 2015), and increase their cooperative tendencies when engaging with those with a high tendency to gossip (Beersma & Van Kleef, 2011).

However, there are clearly some negative ramifications for engaging in frequent gossip. As was explicated earlier in the section "Status Enhancement/Negative Influence," some gossip is initiated with the intention of tarnishing others' reputations, and sometimes this has rebound effects (Gawronski & Walther, 2008). Gossiping about others can detract from one's own social standing because observers of gossip (accurately) infer that they may be similarly victimized. In addition to the deleterious interpersonal consequences of decreased liking (Farley, 2011), and in some cases, friendship nominations (Ellwardt et al., 2012a), gossip in organizational settings is associated with less peer cooperation (Wittek, Hangyi, Van Duijn, & Carroll, 2000). Furthermore, Wittek at al. (2000) demonstrated that gossip can actually escalate conflict rather than diminish it. Given that this research was conducted in a workplace setting, it is difficult to ascertain whether results would generalize to friend groups. Gossip is typically frowned upon in organizational settings, thus engaging in it might represent more of a norm violation than outside the workplace.

## CONCLUSIONS AND FUTURE DIRECTIONS

The last 15 years has seen a resurgence of interest in the study of gossip, and this has yielded rich insight into gossip's functions, virtues, and costs. Some of the functions that gossip serves are evaluatively neutral (such as social comparison), some positive (such as social bonding and group protection), and some more negative in nature (status enhancement). Partly due to the polysemous nature of gossip, gossip and power have a complicated relationship. Group benefactors who sanction the norm-violations of wayward ingroup members through gossip may accrue respect and status from their groups, while self-serving "chatty Kathys," who selfishly initiate gossip with the aim toward maligning others, may incur fear and loathing. There are few behaviors that can serve both as an agent of destruction and a way to test the waters of friendship, which is compelling from a scientific standpoint. It is our hope with this volume that other researchers will become similarly captivated by this complex and fascinating area of research.

Indeed, there are a number of fruitful avenues of future study. In sharp contrast to the importance of gossip in our everyday lives, experimental work in this area is relatively scarce. Research has responded to this challenge with creative approaches such as the use of vignettes (Beersma & Van Kleef, 2011, Wilson et al., 2000), trust games (cf. Feinberg, Miliniski, Giardini, Wu), and causal modeling based on sociometric field studies (Ellwardt, 2019), and many questions remain that can only be answered via experimental research. The longitudinal social network analysis methodology employed by Ellwardt et al. (2012a) was the most illuminating study conducted in the past decade with regard to the temporal ordering of friendship and gossip. It would be wise to employ this methodology to answer other pressing gossip questions, such as those relating to the temporal sequence of gossip and power inequality: Do social isolates evoke more negative gossip? Or is gossip the mechanism to cast out individuals, thus reducing their status and resulting in social isolation?

Some interesting remaining questions pertain to positive gossip, as there is very little theoretical speculation about its function. This is especially problematic given that recent prolific gossip scholars have designed experimental studies that lend themselves to operationalization of gossip as negative in nature (e.g., M. Feinberg and J. Wu). In other words, if gossip is operationalized as gossip designed to warn ingroup members about free-riders, it will always pertain to negative gossip. Greater empirical attention should be devoted to the functions of positive gossip. Furthermore, there is evidence to suggest that individuals gossip negatively about their close friends. This tendency is perplexing given the motivations of gossip described here. Why might we gossip negatively about our friends? Does this serve social comparison purposes? According to Dunbar (2004, p. 100), "gossip is what makes human society as we know it possible." It is our hope that fellow researchers will share Dunbar's view of the importance of gossip and will continue to pursue research questions in this fascinating research area.

## REFERENCES

Altman, I., & Taylor, D. (1973). *Social penetration: The development of interpersonal relationships.* New York: Holt.

Baumeister, R. F., & Leary, M. R. (1995). The need to belong: Desire for interpersonal attachments as a fundamental human motivation. *Psychological Bulletin 117,* 497–529.

Baumeister, R. F., Zhang, L., & Vohs, K. D. (2004). Gossip as cultural learning. *Review of General Psychology 8,* 111–121. doi:10.1037/1089-2680.8.2.111

Beersma, B., & Van Kleef, G. A. (2011). How the grapevine keeps you in line: Gossip increases contributions to the group. *Social Psychological & Personality Science 2,* 642–9. doi:10.1177/1948550611405073

Beersma, B., & Van Kleef, G. A. (2012). Why people gossip: An empirical analysis of social motives, antecedents, and consequences. *Journal of Applied Social Psychology 42,* 2640–2670. doi:10.1111/j.1559-1816.2012.00956.x

Boehm, C. (2019). Gossip and reputation in small scale societies: A view from evolutionary anthropology. In F. Giardini & R. P. M. Wittek (Eds.), *Handbook of gossip and reputation.* New York: Oxford University Press.

Crocker, J., & Luhtanen, R. (1990). Collective self-esteem and ingroup bias. *Journal of Personality and Social Psychology 58,* 60–67. doi:10.1037/0022-3514.58.1.60

De Backer, C., Larson, C., & Cosmides, L. (2007a). *Bonding through gossip? The effect of gossip on levels of cooperation in social dilemma games.* Paper Presented at 57th Annual ICA Conference, May 2007, San Francisco, California.

De Backer, C. S., Nelissen, M., & Fisher, M. L. (2007b). Let's talk about sex: A study on the recall of gossip about potential mates and sexual rivals. *Sex Roles 56,* 781–791. doi:10.1007/s11199-007-9237-x

Dunbar, R. I. M. (1996). *Grooming, gossip, and the evolution of language.* Cambridge, MA: Harvard University Press.

Dunbar, R. I. M. (2004). Gossip in evolutionary perspective. *Review of General Psychology 8,* 100–110. doi:10.1037/1089-2680.8.2.100

Dunbar, R. I. M., Marriott, A., & Duncan, N. C. (1997). Human conversational behavior. *Human Nature 8,* 231–246. doi:10.1007/BF02912493

Eder, D., & Enke, J. L. (1991). The structure of gossip: Opportunities and constraints on collective expression among adolescents. *American Sociological Review 56,* 494–508.

Ellwardt, L. (2019). Gossip and reputation in social networks. In F. Giardini & R. P. M. Wittek (Eds.), *Handbook of gossip and reputation.* New York: Oxford University Press.

Ellwardt, L., Steglich, C., & Wittek, R. (2012a). The co-evolution of gossip and friendship in workplace social networks. *Social Networks 34,* 623–33. doi:10.1016/j.socnet.2012.07.002

Ellwardt, L., Labianca, G., & Wittek, R. (2012b). Who are the objects of positive and negative gossip at work? *Social Networks 34,* 193–205. doi:10.1016/j.socnet.2011.11.003

Farley, S. D. (2011). Is gossip power? The inverse relationships between gossip, power, and likability. *European Journal of Social Psychology 41*, 574–579. doi:10.1002/ejsp.821

Farley, S. D., & Eyssell, K. (2014). *An experimental test of the social bonding hypothesis: Effect of gossip on trust and liking.* Unpublished manuscript, Division of Applied Behavioral Sciences, University of Baltimore, Baltimore, MD.

Farley, S. D., Timme, D. R., & Hart, J. W. (2010). On coffee talk and break-room chatter: Perceptions of women who gossip in the workplace. *Journal of Social Psychology 150*, 361–368. doi:10.1080/00224540903365430

Feinberg, M., Cheng, J., & Willer, R. (2012a and 2012b). Gossip as an effective and low-cost form of punishment. *Behavioral and Brain Sciences 35*(1), 25. doi: 10.1017/S0140525X11001233

Feinberg, M., Willer, R., & Schultz, M. (2014). Gossip and ostracism promote cooperation in groups. *Psychological Science 25*, 656–664. doi:10.1177/0956797613510184

Feinberg, M., Willer, R., Stellar, J., & Keltner, D. (2012). The virtues of gossip: Reputational information sharing as prosocial behavior. *Journal of Personality and Social Psychology 2012b*, 1015–1030. doi:10.1037/a0026650

Foster, E. K. (2004). Research on gossip: Taxonomy, methods, and future directions. *Review of General Psychology 8*, 78–99.

Gawronski, B., & Walther, E. (2008). The TAR effect: When the ones who dislike become the ones who are disliked. *Personality and Social Psychology Bulletin 34*, 1276–1289. doi: 10.1177/0146167208318952

Giardini, F., & Conte, R. (2012). Gossip for social control in natural and artificial societies. *Simulation: Transactions of the Society for Modeling and Simulation International 88*(1), 18–32. doi: 10.1177/0037549711406912

Giardini, F., Paolucci, M., Villatoro, D., & Conte, R. (2014). Punishment and gossip: Sustaining cooperation in a public goods game. In B. Kaminski & G. Koloch (Eds.), *Advances in Social Simulation*, (pp. 107–118). Springer Berlin Heidelberg.

Giardini, F., & Wittek, R. P. M. (2019). Gossip, Reputation, and Sustainable Cooperation: Sociological Foundations. In F. Giardini & R. P. M. Wittek (Eds.), *Handbook of gossip and reputation*. New York: Oxford University Press.

Gluckman, M. (1963). Gossip and scandal. *Current Anthropology 4*, 307–316.

Grosser, T. J., Lopez-Kidwell, V., & Labianca, G. (2010). A social network analysis of positive and negative gossip in organizational life. *Group & Organization Management 35*, 177–212. doi:10.1177/1059601109360391

Grow, A., & Flache, A. (2019). Agent-Based Computational Models of Reputation and Status Dynamics In F. Giardini & R. P. M. Wittek (Eds.), *Handbook of gossip and reputation*. New York: Oxford University Press.

Guerin, B., & Miyazaki, Y. (2006). Analyzing rumors, gossip, and urban legends through their conversational properties. *Psychological Record 56*, 23–34.

Jaeger, M., Skleder, A., Rind, B., & Rosnow, R. (1994). Gossip, gossipers, gossipees. In *Good gossip* (pp. 154–68). Lawrence, KS: University Press of Kansas.

Kurland, N. B., & Pelled, L. H. (2000). Passing the word: Toward a model of gossip and power in the workplace. *Academy of Management Review 25*, 428–38.

Lansford, J. E., Putallaz, M., Grimes, C. L., Schiro-Osman, K. A., Kupersmidt, J. B., & Coie, J. D. (2006). Perceptions of friendship quality and observed behaviors with friends: How do sociometrically rejected, average, and popular girls differ? *Merrill-Palmer Quarterly 52*, 694–719.

Levin, J., & Arluke, A. (1985). An exploratory analysis of sex differences in gossip. *Sex Roles 12*, 281–286.

McAndrew, F. T. (2008). Can gossip be good? *Scientific American Mind 19*, 26–33.

McAndrew, F., Bell, E., & Garcia, C. (2007). Who do we tell and whom do we tell on? Gossip as a strategy for status enhancement. *Journal of Applied Social Psychology 37*, 1562–1577.

McAndrew, F. T., & Milenkovic, M. A. (2002). Of tabloids and family secrets: The evolutionary psychology of gossip. *Journal of Applied Social Psychology 32*, 1064–1082. doi:10.1111/j.1559-1816.2002.tb00256.x

McDonald, K. L., Putallaz, M., Grimes, C. L., Kupersmidt, J. B., & Coie, J. D. (2007). Girl talk: Gossip, friendship, and sociometric status. *Merrill-Palmer Quarterly 53*, 381–411.

Michelson, G., van Iterson, A., & Waddington, K. (2010). Gossip in organizations: Contexts, consequences, and controversies. *Group & Organization Management 35*, 371–90. doi:10.1177/1059601109360389

Origgi, Gloria. G. (2019). Reputation in Moral Philosophy and Epistemology. In F. Giardini & R. P. M. Wittek (Eds.), *Handbook of gossip and reputation*, New York: Oxford University Press.

Piazza, J., & Bering, J. M. (2008). Concerns about reputation via gossip promote generous allocations in an economic game. *Evolution & Human Behavior 29*, 172–8. doi:10.1016/j.evolhumbehav.2007.12.002

Raven, B. H. (1965). Social influence and power. In I. D. Steiner & M. Fishbein (Eds.), *Current studies in social psychology* (pp. 371–82). New York: Holt, Rinehart, Winston.

Rosnow, R. L. (2001). Rumor and gossip in interpersonal interaction and beyond: A social exchange perspective. In R. M. Kowalski, R. M. Kowalski (Eds.), *Behaving badly: Aversive behaviors in interpersonal relationships* (pp. 203–232). Washington, DC: American Psychological Association. doi:10.1037/10365-008

Sommerfeld, R. D., Krambeck, H., Semmann, D., & Milinski, M. (2007). Gossip as an alternative for direct observation in games of indirect reciprocity. *Proceedings of the National Academy of Sciences, USA 104*, 17435–17440.

Steele, R. (n.d.). *BrainyQuote*. Retrieved March 14, 2016, from https://www.brainyquote.com/search_results?q=steele+gossip

Tajfel, H. (1982). Social psychology of intergroup relations. *Annual Review of Psychology 33*, 1–39. doi:10.1146/annurev.ps.33.020182.000245

Thornborrow, J., & Morris, D. (2004). Gossip as strategy: The management of talk about others on reality TV Show 'Big Brother.'" *Journal of Sociolinguistics 8*, 246–271.

Turner, M. M., Mazur, M. A., Wendel, N., & Winslow, R. (2003). Relational ruin or social glue? The joint effect of relationship type and gossip valence on liking, trust, and expertise. *Communication Monographs 70*, 129–141. doi: 10.1080/0363775032000133782

Turner, R. H. (1987). Articulating self and social structure. In K. Yardley, T. Honess, K. Yardley, T. Honess (Eds.), *Self and identity: Psychosocial perspectives* (pp. 119–32). Oxford, England: John Wiley & Sons.

Wert, S. R., & Salovey, P. (2004). A social comparison account of gossip. *Review of General Psychology 8*, 122–137. doi:10.1037/1089-2680.8.2.122

Wilson, D. S., Wilczynski, C., Wells, A., & Weiser, L. (2000). Gossip and other aspects of language as group-level adaptations. In C. Heyes & L. Huber (Eds.), *The evolution of cognition* (pp. 347–365), Vienna Series in Theoretical Biology. Cambridge, MA: MIT Press.

Wittek, R., Hangyi, H., Van Duijn, M., & Carroll, C. (2000). Social capital, third party gossip, and cooperation in organizations. In J. Weesie & W. Raub (Eds.), *The management of durable relations: Theoretical models and empirical studies of households and organizations* (pp. 1–26). Amsterdam, Thela Thesis.

Wittek, R., & Wielers, R. (1998). Gossip in organizations. *Computational & Mathematical Organization Theory 4*, 189–204.

Wood, J. V. (1989). Theory and research concerning social comparisons of personal attributes. *Psychological Bulletin 106*, 231–248. doi:10.1037/0033-2909.106.2.231

Wu, J., Balliet, D., & Van Lange, P. A. M. (2015). When does gossip promote generosity? Indirect reciprocity under the shadow of the future. *Social Psychological and Personality Science 6*, 923–930. doi:10.1177/1948550615595272

Wu, J., Balliet, D., & Van Lange, P. A. M. (2016a). Gossip versus punishment: The efficiency of reputation to promote and maintain cooperation. *Scientific Reports 6*, 1–8. doi:10.1038/srep23919

Wu, J., Balliet, D., & Van Lange, P. A. M. (2016b). Reputation, gossip, and human cooperation: Reputation and cooperation. *Social and Personality Psychology Compass 10*, 350–364. doi:10.1111/spc3.12255

# CHAPTER 19

# GOSSIP AND REPUTATION IN ADOLESCENT NETWORKS

DOROTTYA KISFALUSI, KÁROLY TAKÁCS,
AND JUDIT PÁL

## INTRODUCTION AND PROBLEM FORMULATION

INDIVIDUALS in any social context devote significant time to evaluate others and assign them positive and negative reputations. This is important for social orientation in the group and for the individual adjustment to normative expectations. Positive reputations can be turned to power, while negative reputations might imply negligence and social exclusion. It is not surprising, therefore, that individuals strive for receiving positive evaluations from others and try to avoid negative evaluations. Evaluations are made in comparison with others; hence reputation is a scarce resource and is subject to competition.

Reputations are not only formed in dyadic interactions, but are exchanged in informal communication. A typical and widespread form of communication that strongly affects individual reputations is *gossip*. Not only information about other individuals are exchanged, but more importantly, perceptions and impressions are shared and provide the basis of evaluations at least as importantly as direct observations and interactions (Rauwolf, Mitchell, & Bryson, 2015; Smith, 2014; Smith & Collins, 2009; Sommerfeld, Krambeck, Semmann, & Milinski, 2007).

In operationalized terms, we define interpersonal communication that includes negative evaluative information about—and in absence of—a third party as *negative (malicious) gossip*. The physical absence of the *object* (or target) of gossip is a necessary characteristic that prevents the object (or the target) to influence the information that is spread about him- or herself.

It is widely believed that gossip is channeling information that is *destructive* to the *reputation* of the object (Besnier, 2009). While sharing favorable information about a third party could increase the target's reputation, the impact of positive and negative gossip might indeed be *asymmetric:* the effect of positive gossip may be less severe than the effect of negative gossip on reputation. Moreover, the communication of positive and negative information could also be beneficial to a different extent for the production of collective goods. In line with the literature on altruistic punishment versus altruistic reward for cooperation (Bowles & Gintis, 2004; Fehr & Gächter, 2002), and also in line with the asymmetric impact of positive and negative gossip on cooperation (Giardini & Vilone, 2016), negative gossip might play a more important role for the collective than positive gossip. Being the object of malicious gossip might in fact effectively undermine somebody's chances to obtain good reputation.

Once gossip is effective, it could be used strategically to destroy the good standing of others and to improve the relative position of the sender of gossip (van de Bunt, Wittek, & de Klepper, 2005; Wittek & Wielers, 1998). In this perspective, malicious gossip is a political tool (Besnier, 2009) and intended to defame specific targets (Smith, 2014). The gossip action can only be instrumental, however, if it is effective (Faris & Felmlee, 2014).

Who becomes the object of *strategic* gossip is not independent of current reputations. Those who are looked down by others are likely to be the target of negative gossip. As a consequence of these self-reinforcing mechanisms, individuals with the lowest reputation could end up in a downward spiral by being subject of even more negative gossip over time.

In another view, the effectiveness of gossip is questionable. Gossip is often considered an unconscious activity that has the primary function of social bonding (Dunbar, 1996, 2004; Gluckman, 1963) and increasing trust between the discussants (Burt & Knez, 1995). Its prevalence might also have resulted in the emerging complexity of strategic social communication (Dunbar, 1996; Smith, 2010). Gossip reinforces interpersonal affection as it is a pleasure activity that parties enjoy (van de Bunt et al., 2005). If gossip is cheap talk, then everyone uses gossip without any reliable content. Consequently, senders of gossip are considered cautiously, which might underscore their reputation. This is in line with the frequent public condemnation of tell-tales.

All these concerns on gossip and reputation are also relevant in adolescence. Below, we review the explanations of the functions and origins of gossip and highlight the specific contextual features for adolescents in schools.

## GOSSIP AND ITS EXPLANATIONS AMONG ADOLESCENTS

Norms and behavior are under development at the age of pre-adolescence and adolescence (Veenstra, Dijkstra, & Kreager, 2018). Therefore adolescence is an important stage of human life, in which rules of the game are learnt, practiced, and sometimes enforced to exaggeration (Coleman, 1961, 1961). The fundamental processes that govern the formation and dynamics of norms and behavior among adolescents are studied across related disciplines (Coleman, 1960, 1961; Jessor, Donovan, & Costa, 1994; Lareau, 2011; Rutland, Nesdale, & Brown, 2017). Adolescents develop their identity and independence by trying to distance themselves from their parents and teachers and mimicking adult behavior at the same time. They experiment continuously by testing the limits of what is possible, allowed, tolerated, prohibited, and punished. Growing their independence liberates them from adult coercion, but the realization of liberty is only followed by the internalization of the need for the social regulation by norms only later.

Moreover, adolescents are constrained in their behavior as they spend most of their time in school. Schools and classroom units within them provide natural opportunities for the development of closed communities. Students are requested to obey to rules in school and to respect teacher's authority. Teachers sometimes implement policy methods aiming at integration or conflict prevention (Salmivalli, Kärnä, & Poskiparta, 2010). Otherwise, informal contacts, communication, and norms develop to a large extent in a self-organizing way among adolescents, since this is the life stage when peers' opinions become especially salient (Hartup, 1993). These dynamics are often centered on status competition. Status competition among pre-adolescents and adolescents is relatively intense and status orders change more rapidly than in adulthood (Coleman, 1961; Corsaro & Eder, 1990).

## Gossip and Social Bonding in Schools

Research on gossip in schools mostly follows the widely accepted definition that gossip is the exchange of evaluative information about someone who is not present (Eder & Enke, 1991; McDonald, 2011). Following the literature that attributes the primary function of social bonding to gossip (Dunbar, 1996, 2004; Gluckman, 1963), one could expect that gossip serves the enjoyment of the sender and the receiver, but does not have large consequences for the target. This is because communication partners do not take the juicy information content very seriously. There is no guarantee that the communication is honest and it is not rational to believe any word of it. Instead, gossip is expected to trigger laughter and ridicule behind the back of the third party (Billig, 2005; Eder, 1991; Morreall, 1983; Wooten, 2006). Present already among children, adolescents find joy in laughing at others (katagelasticism); and this is related to bullying others (Proyer, Meier, Platt, & Ruch, 2013).

First responses in a gossip conversation are therefore highly consequential for further development. Turn-taking, interruptions, the flow of conversation, and the point of consensus, therefore, describe well the power relations between the discussants rather than the factual evaluation of the target (Eder & Enke, 1991; Gibson, 2003). Idle chit-chat is observed among children, but the importance of these complex patterns of evaluative discussions and their relation to status enhancement has increasingly been realized at the age of adolescence (see Ingram, this volume).

The view that social bonding is a key function of gossip is reflected in research among adolescents who display a high need of expressing shared viewpoints (Eder & Enke, 1991; Gottman & Mettetal, 1986). This agreement, however, most often promotes *negative* evaluations (Eder & Enke, 1991), which might decrease with age (Gottman & Mettetal, 1986).

## Gossip as an Informal Sanction

In closed communities, such as the school, there are clear information benefits of gossip for the receiver. Information about individual skills and cooperation in academic and non-academic activities are particularly important. Gossip can therefore make an important contribution to the enhancement of cooperation and punishment of free-riders (Sommerfeld et al., 2007; Wu, Balliet, & Van Lange, 2016). In a positive reinforcement loop, free riding is punished with negative gossip and bad reputation (Bliege Bird & Smith, 2005; Gintis, Smith, & Bowles, 2001), which helps establish or even amplify reputation differences that are based on actual merits (Merton, 1968; Vaidyanathan, Khalsa, & Ecklund, 2016). Adolescent girls' talk have been found to be an important cooperative tool that is used for the construction and consolidation of social norms, for shepherding conformity, and for the survival of the group as a whole in competition with out-groups (Eckert, 1990). In a severe form, gossip can threaten to ostracize the target, which ensures cooperation within the group (Feinberg, Willer, & Schultz, 2014; Ouwerkerk, Kerr, Gallucci, & Van Lange, 2005).

## Gossip and Ostracism

One could become the target of gossip just because he or she has peculiar characteristics and is different from others. Adolescents find dissimilar others as easy targets of malicious talk, stigmatization, and ostracism (Smart Richman & Leary, 2009; Williams, 2002; Wooten, 2006). The characteristics, the targets, and the consequences of ostracism, however, change with age (Pharo, Gross, Richardson, & Hayne, 2011).

While being ostracized, the target could still have no objections or even appreciations toward those who ostracize them within the school (Cook, Hegtvedt, & Yamagishi, 1988; Fave, 1980; Stolte, 1983). Ostracizing gossip ties are expected to be asymmetric, because dissimilar targets are in a marginal social position that makes impossible for them to launch a "counter-attack" behind the back of their otherwise popular ostracizers (Salmivalli, Lagerspetz, Björkqvist, Österman, & Kaukialnen, 1996). Their chances to remain respected members of the group could better be achieved by remaining silent (Williams, 2002) and hoping for the empathy of peers (Wesselmann, Williams, & Hales, 2013).

Heterophobia could also be directed toward minority members and members of low-status groups. Negative gossip induced by heterophobia could in particular be intense in case of perceived out-group threat and scapegoating (Gemmill, 1989; Katz, Glass, & Cohen, 1973).

## Gossip as Relational Aggression

Spreading negative gossip about someone is one of the various forms of aggression. Besides gossiping (Ellwardt, Labianca, & Wittek, 2012), these include bullying (Espelage, Green, & Wasserman, 2007; Huitsing, Veenstra, Sainio, & Salmivalli, 2012; Salmivalli, Huttunen, & Lagerspetz, 1997; Veenstra, Huitsing, Dijkstra, & Lindenberg, 2010), mocking (Björkqvist, Lagerspetz, & Kaukiainen, 1992), and fighting (Arbona, Jackson, McCoy, & Blakely, 1999; Gest, Graham-Bermann, & Hartup, 2001; Mouttapa, Valente, Gallaher, Rohrbach, & Unger, 2004).

Students also display different types of relational aggression toward peers. Gossip is one possible type and can be also described as indirect non-physical bullying of the target. One needs to take it into account that other direct forms of aggression replace or supplement negative gossip acts (see Hess and Hagen in this volume). Macchiavellian social climbers might use gossip along with other forms of harassment and bullying (Faris & Felmlee, 2014).

While direct or overt aggression involves a face-to-face and visible verbal or physical act toward individuals with the intention to harm them, indirect or covert aggression, such as gossip or exclusion, does not involve direct confrontation with the victim (Björkqvist et al., 1992; Card, Stucky, Sawalani, & Little, 2008; Espelage & Swearer, 2003; Little, Henrich, Jones, & Hawley, 2003; Sijtsema et al., 2010). Hence gossip can be seen as a special form of indirect aggression, which refers to the manipulation of one's social relationships (Crick, 1995; Little et al., 2003).

## Gossip and Status Competition

Gossip could be the tool but also the consequence of competition. Competition for limited resources that are acquired in social processes such as popularity, social status, power, and better grades create strategic alliances and counter-alliances, and they could induce envy, anger, and frustration. All these forms go beyond the scope of dyadic rivalry, as it is witnessed, facilitated, and sometimes appreciated or mediated by relevant others. Hence, these processes are embedded in the network structure and the dynamics of evaluative information exchange about others is intertwined with competition.

The informal status dimension is particularly important in the pre-adolescent and adolescent age (Gest, Davidson, Rulison, Moody, & Welsh, 2007; Moody, Brynildsen, Osgood, Feinberg, & Gest, 2011), when the competition for status is particularly intense (Coleman, 1960, 1961). Adolescents increasingly realize the importance of forming and manipulating the informal hierarchy with the use of negative information spreading (Wargo Aikins, Collibee, & Cunningham, 2015) and other forms of relational aggression.

Competition for popularity and status is a major source of relational aggression (Faris & Ennett, 2012). Popular adolescents are more likely to harass their peers than less popular ones (de Bruyn, Cillessen, & Wissink, 2010; Faris & Felmlee, 2014; Juvonen, Graham, & Schuster, 2003; Rodkin & Berger, 2008; Sijtsema, Veenstra, Lindenberg, &

Salmivalli, 2009). This association is not only true for various forms of aggressions, but for gossip as well (Cillessen & Mayeux, 2004; Wargo Aikins et al., 2015).

Gossip might thus be used in a strategic way to establish norms and defend adolescents' reputations. Two reasons for its use can be distinguished: whereas unpopular students might be targeted to maintain the group norms, high status students might be targeted because of status competition among the students (Faris & Felmlee, 2014). As a result, gossiping about high status peers is an instrumental way of gaining status in the peer group.

It is not uncommon to see huge investments in strategic activities such as gossip, mediation, intervention, relational aggression, and sanctions on others for the sake of reputation and popularity (Adler & Adler, 1995; Eder, 1985; Faris & Ennett, 2012; Faris & Felmlee, 2014). If everyone does so, huge efforts are invested, a few individuals are severely chastised (Cillessen & Mayeux, 2004), but only marginal gains are achieved in the reputation order (Eder, 1985; Gould, 2002). This could contribute to the radicalization of relational aggression over time and its transformation from indirect means toward more overt or even demonstrative scenes (Houghton, Nathan, & Taylor, 2012).

## Gender and Gossip

According to a commonplace, gossip is a gendered activity. This perception might be attributed to prevalent gender differences in aggression (Eagly & Steffen, 1986; Lagerspetz, Björkqvist, & Peltonen, 1988). Girls are more likely the victims of bullying by girls; and boys bully girls more likely than the other way around (e.g., Faris & Felmlee, 2011, 2014; Veenstra, Lindenberg, Munniksma, & Dijkstra, 2010; Xie, Farmer, & Cairns, 2003). Moreover, girls and boys are likely to use different forms of aggression. Whereas boys are more likely than girls to use direct and overt physical or verbal forms of aggression (Card, Stucky, Sawalani, & Little, 2008), girls are more likely to use indirect and relational means such as exclusion and gossip (Olweus, 1993). Differences in girls' and boys' propensity to use indirect aggression, however, are not large in magnitude (Card et al., 2008), and mostly occur in specific age groups such as later childhood and adolescence (Archer, 2004). Indirect aggressive strategies are not yet fully developed in a younger age, but are already prominent among 11-year old girls (Björkqvist et al., 1992). Björkqvist et al. (1992) found that aggression assessed by the children themselves was highest in this age group. Except for 8-year olds, gossiping was found to be more frequent among girls than boys.

Different disciplines propose various theoretical explanations for these gender differences. From an evolutionary perspective, greater reproductive competition among males can explain more overt forms of aggression (Archer, 2004; see also Davis et al, and Hess and Hagen, this volume). Biological explanations emphasize that boys confront more often physically than girls due to their greater physical strength (Björkqvist, 1994; Xie, Cairns, & Cairns, 2005). In contrast, sociological explanations emphasize that the way how girls and boys are socialized may explain gender differences in aggression.

Girls face stricter normative constraints than boys not only in their romantic behavior (Kreager & Staff, 2009) but also in their socially acceptable retaliation methods (Faris & Felmlee, 2014), and in their direct confrontational behaviors (Xie et al., 2005).

Gender might also interact with social status asymmetries in determining who bullies whom and who is gossiping about whom. Rodkin and Berger (2008) found that popular students bully unpopular victims from their same gender, whereas unpopular boys are likely to bully popular girls.

# The Utility of a Social Network Perspective in Research on Gossip and Reputation among Adolescents

Gossip and reputation dynamics among adolescents are embedded in the social relationships of the group. In many countries, the primary group adolescents belong to is the classroom with its well defined memberships and boundary. Also because peer relations are especially important for adolescents, social network analysis has become an important tool in adolescence research. Social network methods take adequate care of the embeddedness and dependencies of dyadic peer relations in the classroom. In social network studies, usually all students from a class or school are asked to report their own opinion, attitudes, behavior, and relationships with their peers: students might be asked whom they like, whom they dislike, whom they consider popular or about whom they gossip.

Longitudinal models such as stochastic actor-based models (SABMs) (Snijders, van de Bunt, & Steglich, 2010) are used to analyze the co-evolution of two networks, or of one network and students' behavior, attitudes, and opinion (Veenstra, Dijkstra, Steglich, & Van Zalk, 2013). Several studies focus on the longitudinal analysis of adolescents' popularity, likeability, or peer status over time. Rambaran et al. (2015) for instance, investigated the co-evolution of positive and negative relations among adolescents. They found that students establish friendships if they dislike the same classmate; that friends agree on which classmates they dislike; and that students are likely to dislike those peers who are friends of classmates they dislike. Pál et al. (2016) showed that adolescents' disliking relations depend on their perceptions of the status of their peers. They found that individuals dislike those who they look down on, and conform to others by disliking those who they perceive as being looked down on by their peers. When individuals do not look up to those who they perceive to be admired by peers, it is more likely that disliking will occur.

In the past decade, a growing number of studies use social network methods to analyze different forms of aggression and school bullying and its associations with students' characteristics and other type of relations as well (e.g., Dijkstra, Berger, & Lindenberg, 2011; Huitsing, Snijders, Van Duijn, & Veenstra, 2014; Sentse, Dijkstra, Salmivalli, &

Cillessen, 2013; Sijtsema et al., 2010). We are not aware of any applications of stochastic actor-based models, however, focusing specifically on gossip among adolescents. In the next section, we illustrate the complex relation between gossip and reputation by analyzing adolescents' school networks with SABMs.

# ILLUSTRATION: AN EMPIRICAL STUDY AMONG ADOLESCENTS

To illustrate the bidirectional relationship between gossip and reputation, we present an exemplary analysis of longitudinal social network data from Hungarian secondary school classes. Following the path of earlier studies in organizations (Ellwardt, 2011; Ellwardt et al., 2012; Wittek & Wielers, 1998), we emphasize the embeddedness of gossip and reputations in adolescents' social network.

The data stem from the first three waves of a four-wave panel study conducted among Hungarian secondary school students (7 schools, 40 classes, $N_1 = 1313$). The research was conducted under the project *"Wired into Each Other: Network Dynamics of Adolescents in the Light of Status Competition, School Performance, Exclusion and Integration."* The main aim of the project was to examine the dynamics of students' social relations, and the associations between the individuals' characteristics and their actual or perceived position in the hierarchy of the class. The research started in the autumn of 2010 among all 9th-grade students enrolled in the selected schools (mean age = 15.1 years). Then, data were collected in the spring of 2011, 2012, and 2013.

We present descriptive statistics for gossip and reputation networks of the forty classes that participated in all of the first three waves of the study. The co-evolution of gossip and reputation among adolescents is illustrated by the longitudinal social network analysis of seven grammar school classes.

## Measures

*Malicious gossip.* The survey measured negative gossip by self-reports on the item *"Of whom do you say bad things to your friends?"* using a full network roster of the class. Students were thus able to nominate as many students they gossip about as they wanted. For descriptive purposes, both the incoming and outgoing nominations (known as indegree and outdegree in social network analysis) were calculated for each student. These measures show how often students are nominated by their classmates and how often they nominate their classmates.

For each class an adjacency matrix was created. In this matrix, dyads in which student $i$ (the sender) nominated student $j$ as the *target* of negative gossip were coded as 1 and dyads where there were no nominations from $i$ to $j$ were coded as 0. This matrix was used as a dependent variable.

*Reputational status.* Reputational status was measured as dyadic peer nominations on the full network roster items *"Who do you look up to?"* and *"Who do you disdain?"* Based on these questions, we created two networks for each class (the respect and the disdain network), and calculated the same measures as for the gossip network.

## Descriptive Statistics

Table 19.1 presents descriptive statistics on the gossip, disdain, and respect networks. On average, students were nominated by less than one classmate as targets of negative gossip. Only six percent of the nominations were reciprocated, and only a few nominations remained stable between the successive waves (represented by the low Jaccard-indices, which measure the proportion of stable nominations compared to existing nomina-tions). On average, the disdain and respect networks were denser and more frequently reciprocated than the gossip network.

Table 19.1. Descriptive Statistics about the Gossip, Disdain, and Respect Networks

| Network | Mean | Standard Deviation | Minimum | Maximum |
|---|---|---|---|---|
| **Gossip Networks** | | | | |
| Indegree w1 | 0.69 | 1.3 | 0 | 9 |
| Indegree w2 | 0.93 | 1.53 | 0 | 10 |
| Indegree w3 | 1.04 | 1.7 | 0 | 8 |
| Density | 0.03 | 0.02 | 0.01 | 0.09 |
| Reciprocity | 0.06 | 0.09 | 0 | 0.24 |
| Jaccard coefficient w1–w2 | 0.1 | 0.04 | 0.04 | 0.16 |
| Jaccard coefficient w2–w3 | 0.12 | 0.06 | 0.04 | 0.19 |
| **Disdain Networks** | | | | |
| Indegree w1 | 1.46 | 1.65 | 0 | 12 |
| Indegree w2 | 1.35 | 1.7 | 0 | 16 |
| Indegree w3 | 1.41 | 1.83 | 0 | 13 |
| Density | 0.05 | 0.03 | 0 | 0.15 |
| Reciprocity | 0.08 | 0.09 | 0 | 0.38 |
| Jaccard coefficient w1–w2 | 0.08 | 0.07 | 0 | 0.29 |
| Jaccard coefficient w2–w3 | 0.08 | 0.07 | 0 | 0.25 |
| **Respect Networks** | | | | |
| Indegree w1 | 1.58 | 1.67 | 0 | 15 |
| Indegree w2 | 1.52 | 1.87 | 0 | 16 |
| Indegree w3 | 1.6 | 1.89 | 0 | 14 |
| Density | 0.05 | 0.03 | 0.01 | 0.15 |
| Reciprocity | 0.14 | 0.1 | 0 | 0.52 |
| Jaccard coefficient w1–w2 | 0.15 | 0.08 | 0.01 | 0.34 |
| Jaccard coefficient w2–w3 | 0.12 | 0.09 | 0 | 0.3 |

Individual-level correlations between indegrees and outdegrees (the sum of incoming and outgoing nominations, respectively) in the gossip, disdain, and respect networks show a moderate positive correlation between being disdained and being the object of negative gossip (Wave 1: 0.42, Wave 2: 0.58, Wave 3: 0.59, $p$ <0.001). In contrast, there is a weak negative correlation between being respected and being the object of negative gossip (Wave 1: −0.07, $p$ <0.05, Wave 2: −0.13, $p$ <0.001, Wave 3: −0.11, $p$ <0.001). Whereas sending negative gossip is not significantly associated with being respected, there is a significant but weak positive correlation between sending gossip and being disdained (Wave 1: 0.06, $p$ <0.05, Wave 2: 0.09, $p$ <0.01, Wave 3: 0.06, $p$ <0.05).

Based on these associations low reputation is more strongly associated with being the object of negative gossip than high reputational status. We are, however, unable to differentiate between two mechanisms: whether students gossip about disdained classmates, or whether students disdain classmates who are targets of negative gossip. To disentangle these two mechanisms we estimated stochastic actor-based models.

## Results of the Empirical Analysis

We modelled the co-evolution of reputational status and self-reported gossip with stochastic actor-based models (Snijders et al., 2010). We estimated these models using RSiena (Ripley, Snijders, Boda, Vörös, & Preciado, 2015). We specified SABM's to estimate the effects of network processes and individual characteristics on the creation and maintenance of ties in each network. In our model, we simultaneously estimated gossip and disdain, and gossip and respect tie formation as dependent networks. We also included the cross-network effects between the two dependent networks. First, we analyzed each class separately, and then we undertook meta-analyses. We used the Fisher-tests for the meta-analysis to evaluate whether estimated parameter values were significantly different from zero across the classrooms.

We included several network effects in both the gossip and reputation models as controls to demonstrate the interplay between gossip and reputation networks. Mathematical formulas for the parameters and a detailed description of stochastic actor-based models can be found in Ripley et al. (2015). We did not find any significant cross-network effects in the co-evolution model of gossip and respect. Therefore, only the results for the co-evolution of gossip and disdain are presented in Table 19.2.

The models are reported for each class separately, and a Fisher-type combination of $p$-values is also presented. A significant right-sided $p$-value can be seen as evidence that some networks have a positive parameter value, whereas a significant left-sided $p$-value shows that some networks have a negative parameter value (Ripley et al., 2015).

The cross-network effects model how the gossip and reputation networks co-evolve. Based on the meta-analysis, two of these effects are statistically significant. On the one hand, the positive effect of gossip on reputation indicates that if a student is gossiping about a classmate, he or she is likely to disdain this classmate over time (combination of right one-sided $p$-values: $\chi^2 = 24.21$, d.f. = 8, $p = 0.002$). On the other hand, the positive

Table 19.2. Stochastic Actor-Based Models for the Co-evolution of Gossip and Disdain for Seven Classes

| | Class 1 | | Class 2 | | Class 3 | | Class 4 | | Class 5 | | Class 6 | | Class 7 | | Right-sided Fisher | Left-sided Fisher | classes |
|---|---|---|---|---|---|---|---|---|---|---|---|---|---|---|---|---|---|
| | Est | SE | Est. | SE | Est. | SE | Est. | SE | Est | SE | Est. | SE | Est. | SE | | | |
| **Gossip** | | | | | | | | | | | | | | | | | |
| Outdegree (density) | −3.64*** | 1.02 | −5.82*** | 1.01 | 1.73 | 2.51 | −0.97 | 1.23 | 2.06 | 1.86 | −3.41*** | 0.49 | −0.94 | 1.21 | 0.899 | <0.001 | 7 |
| reciprocity | 0.80† | 0.44 | 0.13 | 0.68 | N.A. | N.A. | −0.13 | 0.74 | 1.37** | 0.42 | 0.33 | 0.25 | −0.45 | 0.85 | 0.003 | 0.939 | 6 |
| Indegree popularity | 0.65* | 0.28 | 0.73* | 0.34 | 0.4 | 0.66 | 0.83*** | 0.19 | 0.28 | 0.47 | 0.67*** | 0.14 | 0.79*** | 0.19 | <0.001 | 1.000 | 7 |
| Outdegree activity | 0.32 | 0.21 | 0.74** | 0.27 | −1.88 | 1.23 | −0.56 | 0.44 | −1.60* | 0.8 | 0.33*** | 0.1 | −0.64 | 0.45 | 0.002 | 0.061 | 7 |
| Truncated outdegree | −2.71*** | 0.76 | N.A. | N.A. | −6.09*** | 1.76 | −4.87*** | 1.1 | −6.52*** | 1.46 | −2.26*** | 0.54 | −4.49*** | 1.11 | 1.000 | <0.001 | 6 |
| Boy alter | 0.17 | 0.28 | −0.49 | 0.51 | −0.55 | 0.39 | 0.12 | 0.2 | −0.06 | 0.23 | 0.02 | 0.18 | 0.38† | 0.2 | 0.363 | 0.535 | 7 |
| Boy ego | −0.04 | 0.27 | 0.92† | 0.53 | −0.17 | 0.48 | −0.47† | 0.23 | 0.03 | 0.21 | 0.23 | 0.18 | −0.13 | 0.19 | 0.360 | 0.337 | 7 |
| Same gender | 0.42 | 0.3 | 1.32* | 0.54 | 0.64† | 0.38 | 0.45* | 0.22 | 0.2 | 0.22 | 0.26 | 0.2 | 0.38† | 0.22 | <0.001 | 1.000 | 7 |
| Time dummy: ego | −0.76 | 1.21 | 0.02 | 1.68 | −1.2 | 2.3 | −1.07 | 1.05 | 2.5 | 1.84 | 0.12 | 0.75 | 1.26 | 1.13 | 0.478 | 0.622 | 7 |
| Time dummy: ego x indegree popularity | 0.62 | 0.61 | −0.11 | 0.69 | 0.77 | 1.35 | 0.08 | 0.37 | −0.56 | 0.94 | 0.13 | 0.29 | −0.32 | 0.39 | 0.568 | 0.744 | 7 |
| Tima dummy: ego x outdegree activity | −0.11 | 0.23 | 0.06 | 0.57 | −0.04 | 0.82 | 0.68† | 0.41 | −0.95 | 0.73 | −0.06 | 0.12 | −0.53 | 0.45 | 0.694 | 0.290 | 7 |
| **Disdain** | | | | | | | | | | | | | | | | | |
| Outdegree (density) | −1.99** | 0.75 | −4.37*** | 0.74 | −2.13** | 0.74 | −3.47*** | 0.95 | −2.59* | 1.25 | −3.02*** | 0.57 | −2.77*** | 0.77 | 1.000 | <0.001 | 7 |
| Reciprocity | 0.24 | 0.47 | 0.94* | 0.37 | 0.02 | 0.7 | 0.24 | 0.4 | 1.16** | 0.38 | 0.92*** | 0.22 | N.A. | N.A. | <0.001 | 0.997 | 6 |
| Indegree popularity | 0.59*** | 0.21 | 0.44 | 0.38 | 0.36 | 0.38 | 0.52* | 0.21 | 0.01 | 0.75 | 0.74*** | 0.12 | 0.2 | 0.44 | <0.001 | 0.999 | 7 |
| Outdegree activity | −0.01 | 0.22 | 0.64*** | 0.11 | 0.22† | 0.12 | 0.36† | 0.19 | 0.40*** | 0.11 | 0.27† | 0.14 | 0.35* | 0.16 | <0.001 | 1.000 | 7 |
| Truncated Outdegree | −3.27*** | 0.77 | N.A. | N.A. | −3.81*** | 0.68 | −3.08*** | 0.83 | −3.09*** | 0.67 | −2.61*** | 0.75 | −3.40*** | 0.68 | 1.000 | <0.001 | 6 |
| Boy alter | −0.29 | 0.19 | 0.29 | 0.3 | −0.26 | 0.21 | 0.23 | 0.21 | −0.04 | 0.22 | −0.43 | 0.27 | 0.93*** | 0.29 | 0.047 | 0.199 | 7 |
| Boy ego | −0.02 | 0.17 | 0.15 | 0.31 | −0.06 | 0.15 | 0.45 | 0.4 | 0.03 | 0.21 | −0.12 | 0.29 | 0.01 | 0.25 | 0.579 | 0.806 | 7 |
| Same gender | −0.12 | 0.2 | 0.54† | 0.31 | 0.08 | 0.2 | 0.15 | 0.22 | −0.29 | 0.21 | −0.3 | 0.27 | 0.37 | 0.29 | 0.259 | 0.522 | 7 |
| Time dummy: ego | 0.49 | 1.01 | 1.50 | 1.28 | 1.42 | 1.29 | −0.44 | 1.14 | −3.11 | 2.45 | 0.33 | 0.71 | −0.08 | 1.23 | 0.366 | 0.744 | 7 |

(continued)

# Table 19.2. Continued

| | Class 1 | | Class 2 | | Class 3 | | Class 4 | | Class 5 | | Class 6 | | Class 7 | | Right-sided Fisher | Left-sided Fisher | classes |
|---|---|---|---|---|---|---|---|---|---|---|---|---|---|---|---|---|---|
| | Est | SE | Est | SE | Est | SE | Est | SE | Est | SE | Est | SE | Est | SE | | | |
| Time dummy: ego × indegree popularity | -0.67 | 0.42 | -0.94 | 0.76 | -1.30† | 0.73 | -0.43 | 0.4 | 1.73 | 1.51 | 0.32 | 0.23 | 0.23 | 0.75 | 0.612 | 0.079 | 7 |
| Time dummy: ego × outdegree activity | 0.29 | 0.28 | -0.16 | 0.21 | 0.19 | 0.19 | 0.32 | 0.22 | 0.13 | 0.14 | -0.14 | 0.15 | -0.16 | 0.19 | 0.227 | 0.686 | 7 |
| **Cross-network effects** | | | | | | | | | | | | | | | | | |
| Gossip à disdain | N.A. | N.A. | N.A. | N.A. | N.A. | N.A. | 3.35* | -1.63 | 2.09 | -1.4 | 0.80† | -0.46 | 1.3 | -1.02 | 0.002 | 1.000 | 4 |
| Disdain à gossip | 2.08* | 1.03 | 2.03** | 0.65 | 2.38† | 1.4 | -0.51 | 1.02 | 0.47 | 0.5 | 0.27 | 0.28 | 0.47 | 0.89 | <0.001 | 0.996 | 7 |

Notes: †$p < 0.1$; *$p < 0.05$; **$p < 0.01$; ***$p < 0.001$. Rate functions were estimated but are not presented in the table.

effect of reputation on gossip suggests that if a student disdains a classmate, he or she is likely to gossip about this classmate over time (combination of right one-sided $p$-values: $\chi^2 = 38.15$, d.f. $= 14$, $p < 0.001$). We also examined whether higher number of incoming gossip nominations lead to higher number of incoming disdain nominations and vice versa, but this effects were not significant based on the meta-analysis and were therefore left out from the final model.

Besides these cross-network effects, we find several significant structural parameters in the meta-analysis of the gossip and disdain networks. The negative outdegree parameters in each network reflect the low density of the nominations. The positive reciprocity parameters show that students have a tendency to reciprocate gossip and disdain nominations. The positive indegree popularity parameters imply that students who have a high number of incoming nominations attract even more incoming nominations. The positive outdegree activity parameters in each network reflect that students who send many outgoing nominations will send even more nominations toward others. The negative truncated outdegree parameters in each network show the positive tendency of students to have zero outgoing nominations. Furthermore, the same gender effects show that students are likely to nominate same-gender peers in the gossip networks but not in the disdain networks. Moreover, boys are more likely to receive disdain nominations than girls.

## Implications of the Findings

The network of gossip target nominations is relatively sparse and it is only weakly correlated negatively with respect. This explains why we do not find significant (negative) effects in our co-evolution models of malicious gossip and respect. In line with Dunbar (1996, 2004) it could very well be that also among adolescents most informal communication can be characterized as gossip, but due to its sensitive character it is not reported in the questionnaire. Moreover, it could also be that underreporting is not random. Extrovert individuals may report more gossip activity, while strategic users might also be more strategic in withdrawing this information in a survey.

Correlations between indegrees in the gossip and disdain networks show a significant moderate positive association between being the object of negative gossip and being looked down by the classmates. In the longitudinal social network analysis we found support that malicious gossip significantly undermines the reputation of the target: if a student is gossiping about a classmate, he or she is likely to disdain this classmate over time. It was also found that looking down on somebody increases the chance of sending negative gossip about the person. We did not find, however, evidence that incoming nominations in gossip would increase incoming nominations in the disdain network beyond the above mentioned dyadic relations in the stochastic actor-based models.

Our results illustrate that endogenous network processes play a significant role in gossip and reputation. There was a significant dispersion in the distribution of incoming and outgoing nominations and most adolescents did not nominate any gossip targets.

Stochastic actor-based models showed that students were likely to reciprocate nominations, and were more likely to nominate same-gender peers in the gossip and respect networks than cross-gender peers.

# SUMMARY

Gossip is an important social activity already at a young age. In line with majority of the literature, we defined gossip as an evaluative talk between a sender and a receiver about a third person (target) who is not present. By reviewing the literature, we identified several functions, explanations, and consequences of negative gossip particularly that are relevant in the school context. Previous studies suggest that malicious gossip indeed can have multiple functions and explanations. It can serve to create social bonding between the sender and the receiver; it can constitute an informal sanction against the target; it can be used as a form of social exclusion or relational aggression; it can be a gendered activity; and it can be a tool of competition for informal status and reputation—or the consequence of status inequality. After this review, we speculated that for the question of who is gossiping about whom in negative terms probably the last dimension of status and reputation is the most important among adolescents. Hence, our empirical illustration aimed at the investigation of determinants of how negative gossip is interrelated with reputational concerns.

Our review highlighted that previous literature unequally considered these functions of gossip among adolescents. While the enjoyment of ridicule and laughter on others have been studied and there is a rich literature on relational aggression, bullying, ostracism, and their relationship to informal status, the group beneficial effects of malicious gossip are less investigated in the school context. Our empirical illustration was also the first we are aware of that utilized stochastic actor-based models for the analysis of the interrelation between gossip and reputation in adolescent classroom communities.

# FUTURE DIRECTIONS

Gossip is a pervasive social phenomenon among adolescents (McDonald, 2011). We illustrated with an empirical example that gossip has an impact on the reputational hierarchy among adolescence and at the same time disdain of a third person increases the likelihood that he or she is picked for malicious gossip. Relatively little is known, however, about the empirical relationship between gossip and the development and maintenance of group beneficial norms among adolescents. As the intimacy barrier is difficult to cross for any researcher, more observational studies are necessary to test which functions of gossip are prevalent at the age of adolescence. Observational and survey methods together could help us develop a deeper understanding of the complex interrelation and development of gossip, informal social status, and social norms; which together endow individuals with elementary competencies for later adult life.

## Acknowledgments

This project has received funding from the European Research Council (ERC) under the European Union's Horizon 2020 research and innovation programme (grant agreement no 648693). The data collection was supported by the Hungarian Scientific Research Fund under OTKA K81336 'Wired into Each Other: Network Dynamics of Adolescents in the Light of Status Competition, School Performance, Exclusion and Integration'; and the Hungarian Academy of Sciences under 'Competition and Negative Networks' Lendület program. The third author is currently working at the Organisation for Economic Co-operation and Development (OECD) on the Programme for International Student Assessment (PISA). The views expressed in the article belong to the authors and do not necessarily represent the views of the OECD or any of its member countries.

## References

Adler, P. A., & Adler, P. (1995). Dynamics of inclusion and exclusion in preadolescent cliques. *Social Psychology Quarterly 58*(3), 145. https://doi.org/10.2307/2787039

Arbona, C., Jackson, R. H., McCoy, A., & Blakely, C. (1999). Ethnic identity as a predictor of attitudes of adolescents toward fighting. *Journal of Early Adolescence 19*(3), 323–340. https://doi.org/10.1177/0272431699019003002

Archer, J. (2004). Sex differences in aggression in real-world settings: A meta-analytic review. *Review of General Psychology 8*(4), 291–322. https://doi.org/10.1037/1089-2680.8.4.291

Besnier, N. (2009). *Gossip and the everyday production of politics*. Honolulu: University of Hawai'i Press.

Billig, M. (2005). *Laughter and ridicule: Towards a social critique of humour* (1st ed.). London: Thousand Oaks, CA: Sage Publications Ltd.

Björkqvist, K. (1994). Sex differences in physical, verbal, and indirect aggression: A review of recent research. *Sex Roles 30*(3–4), 177–188. https://doi.org/10.1007/BF01420988

Björkqvist, K., Lagerspetz, K. M. J., & Kaukiainen, A. (1992). Do girls manipulate and boys fight? Developmental trends in regard to direct and indirect aggression. *Aggressive Behavior 18*(2), 117–127. https://doi.org/10.1002/1098-2337(1992)18:2<117::AID-AB2480180205>3.0.CO;2-3

Bliege Bird, R., & Smith, E. A. (2005). Signaling theory, strategic interaction, and symbolic capital. *Current Anthropology 46*(2), 221–248. https://doi.org/10.1086/427115

Bowles, S., & Gintis, H. (2004). The evolution of strong reciprocity: Cooperation in heterogeneous populations. *Theoretical Population Biology 65*(1), 17–28. https://doi.org/10.1016/j.tpb.2003.07.001

Burt, R. S., & Knez, M. (1995). Kinds of third-party effects on trust. *Rationality and Society 7*(3), 255–292. https://doi.org/10.1177/1043463195007003003

Card, N. A., Stucky, B. D., Sawalani, G. M., & Little, T. D. (2008). Direct and indirect aggression during childhood and adolescence: A meta-analytic review of gender differences, intercorrelations, and relations to maladjustment. *Child Development* 79(5), 1185–1229. https://doi.org/10.1111/j.1467-8624.2008.01184.x

Cillessen, A. H. N., & Mayeux, L. (2004). From censure to reinforcement: Developmental changes in the association between aggression and social status. *Child Development* 75(1), 147–163. https://doi.org/10.1111/j.1467-8624.2004.00660.x

Coleman, J. S. (1960). The adolescent subculture and academic achievement. *American Journal of Sociology* 65(4), 337–347.

Coleman, J. S. (1961). *The adolescent society. The social life of the teenager and its impact on education*. New York: Free Press.

Cook, K. S., Hegtvedt, K. A., & Yamagishi, T. (1988). Structural inequality, legitimation, and reactions to inequity in exchange networks. In M. Webster & M. Foschi (Eds.), *Status generalization: New theory and research*. Stanford, CA: Stanford University Press.

Corsaro, W. A., & Eder, D. (1990). Children's peer cultures. *Annual Review of Sociology* 16(1), 197–220. https://doi.org/10.1146/annurev.so.16.080190.001213

Crick, N. R. (1995). Relational aggression: The role of intent attributions, feelings of distress, and provocation type. *Development and Psychopathology* 7(02), 313–322. https://doi.org/10.1017/S0954579400006520

Davis, A., Vaillancourt, T., Arnocky, S., & Doyel, R. (2019). Women's gossip as an intrasexual competition strategy: An evolutionary approach to sex and discrimination. In F. Giardini & R. P. M. Wittek (Eds.), *Handbook of gossip and reputation*. New York, NY: Oxford University Press.

de Bruyn, E. H., Cillessen, A. H. N., & Wissink, I. B. (2010). Associations of peer acceptance and perceived popularity with bullying and victimization in early adolescence. *Journal of Early Adolescence* 30(4), 543–566. https://doi.org/10.1177/0272431609340517

Dijkstra, J. K., Berger, C., & Lindenberg, S. (2011). Do physical and relational aggression explain adolescents' friendship selection? The competing roles of network characteristics, gender, and social status. *Aggressive Behavior* 37(5), 417–429. https://doi.org/10.1002/ab.20402

Dunbar, R. (1996). *Grooming, gossip and the evolution of language*. Cambridge, MA: Harvard University Press.

Dunbar, R. (2004). Gossip in evolutionary perspective. *Review of General Psychology* 8(2), 100–110. https://doi.org/http://dx.doi.org/10.1037/1089-2680.8.2.100

Eagly, A. H., & Steffen, V. J. (1986). Gender and aggressive behavior: A meta-analytic review of the social psychological literature. *Psychological Bulletin* 100(3), 309–330. https://doi.org/10.1037/0033-2909.100.3.309

Eckert, P. (1990). Cooperative competition in adolescent "girl talk". *Discourse Processes* 13, 91–122. https://doi.org/10.1080/01638539009544748

Eder, D. (1985). The cycle of popularity: Interpersonal relations among female adolescents. *Sociology of Education* 58(3), 154. https://doi.org/10.2307/2112416

Eder, D. (1991). The role of teasing in adolescent peer group culture. *Sociological Studies of Child Development* 4, 181–197.

Eder, D., & Enke, J. L. (1991). The structure of gossip: Opportunities and constraints on collective expression among adolescents. *American Sociological Review* 56(4), 494. https://doi.org/10.2307/2096270

Ellwardt, L. (2011). *Gossip in organizations: A social network study*. Groningen: ICS Dissertation Series.

Ellwardt, L., Labianca, G. (Joe), & Wittek, R. (2012). Who are the objects of positive and negative gossip at work? *Social Networks* 34(2), 193–205. https://doi.org/10.1016/j.socnet.2011.11.003

Espelage, D. L., Green, H. D., & Wasserman, S. (2007). Statistical analysis of friendship patterns and bullying behaviors among youth. *New Directions for Child and Adolescent Development 2007*(118), 61–75. https://doi.org/10.1002/cd.201

Espelage, D. L., & Swearer, S. M. (2003). Research on school bullying and victimization: What have we learned and where do we go from here? *School Psychology Review 32*(3), 365–383.

Faris, R., & Ennett, S. (2012). Adolescent aggression: The role of peer group status motives, peer aggression, and group characteristics. *Social Networks 34*(4), 371–378. https://doi.org/10.1016/j.socnet.2010.06.003

Faris, R., & Felmlee, D. (2011). Status struggles: Network centrality and gender segregation in same- and cross-gender aggression. *American Sociological Review 76*(1), 48–73. https://doi.org/10.1177/0003122410396196

Faris, R., & Felmlee, D. (2014). Casualties of social combat school networks of peer victimization and their consequences. *American Sociological Review 79*(2), 228–257. https://doi.org/10.1177/0003122414524573

Fave, L. R. D. (1980). The meek shall not inherit the earth: Self-evaluation and the legitimacy of stratification. *American Sociological Review 45*(6), 955. https://doi.org/10.2307/2094912

Fehr, E., & Gächter, S. (2002). Altruistic punishment in humans. *Nature 415*(6868), 137–140. https://doi.org/10.1038/415137a

Feinberg, M., Willer, R., & Schultz, M. (2014). Gossip and ostracism promote cooperation in groups. *Psychological Science 25*(3), 656–664. https://doi.org/10.1177/0956797613510184

Gemmill, G. (1989). The dynamics of scapegoating in small groups. *Small Group Research 20*(4), 406–418. https://doi.org/10.1177/104649648902000402

Gest, S. D., Davidson, A. J., Rulison, K. L., Moody, J., & Welsh, J. A. (2007). Features of groups and status hierarchies in girls' and boys' early adolescent peer networks. *New Directions for Child and Adolescent Development 2007*(118), 43–60. https://doi.org/10.1002/cd.200

Gest, S. D., Graham-Bermann, S. A., & Hartup, W. W. (2001). Peer experience: Common and unique features of number of friendships, social network centrality, and sociometric status. *Social Development 10*(1), 23–40. https://doi.org/10.1111/1467-9507.00146

Giardini, F., & Vilone, D. (2016). Evolution of gossip-based indirect reciprocity on a bipartite network. *Scientific Reports, 6,* [37931]. https://doi.org/10.1038/srep37931

Gibson, D. R. (2003). Participation shifts: Order and differentiation in group conversation. *Social Forces 81*(4), 1335–1380. https://doi.org/10.1353/sof.2003.0055

Gintis, H., Smith, E. A., & Bowles, S. (2001). Costly signaling and cooperation. *Journal of Theoretical Biology 213*(1), 103–119. https://doi.org/10.1006/jtbi.2001.2406

Gluckman, M. (1963). Gossip and scandal. *Current Anthropology 4*, 307–315.

Gottman, J. M., & Mettetal, G. (1986). Speculations about social and affective development: Friendship and acquaintanceship through adolescence. In *Conversations of friends: Speculations on affective development* (Vol. 16, pp. 192–237). New York, NY: Cambridge University Press.

Gould, R. V. (2002). The origins of status hierarchies: A formal theory and empirical test. *American Journal of Sociology 107*(5), 1143–1178. https://doi.org/10.1086/341744

Hartup, W. W. (1993). Adolescents and their friends. *New Directions for Child and Adolescent Development 1993*(60), 3–22. https://doi.org/10.1002/cd.23219936003

Hess, N., Hagen, E. (2019). Gossip, Reputation, and Friendship in Within-group Competition: An Evolutionary Perspective. In F. Giardini & R. P. M. Wittek (Eds.), *Handbook of gossip and reputation.* New York: Oxford University Press.

Houghton, S. J., Nathan, E., & Taylor, M. (2012). To bully or not to bully, that is not the question: Western Australian early adolescents in search of a reputation. *Journal of Adolescent Research* 27(4), 498–522. https://doi.org/10.1177/0743558411432638

Huitsing, G., Snijders, T. A. B., Van Duijn, M. A. J., & Veenstra, R. (2014). Victims, bullies, and their defenders: A longitudinal study of the coevolution of positive and negative networks. *Development and Psychopathology* 26(3), 645–659. https://doi.org/10.1017/S0954579414000297

Huitsing, G., Veenstra, R., Sainio, M., & Salmivalli, C. (2012). "It must be me" or "It could be them?": The impact of the social network position of bullies and victims on victims' adjustment. *Social Networks* 34(4), 379–386. https://doi.org/10.1016/j.socnet.2010.07.002

Ingram, G. P. D. (2019). Gossip and reputation in childhood In F. Giardini & R. P. M. Wittek (Eds.), *Handbook of gossip and reputation*. New York: Oxford University Press.

Jessor, R., Donovan, J. E., & Costa, F. M. (1994). *Beyond adolescence: Problem behavior and young adult development* (rev. ed.). Cambridge: Cambridge University Press.

Juvonen, J., Graham, S., & Schuster, M. A. (2003). Bullying among young adolescents: The strong, the weak, and the troubled. *Pediatrics* 112(6), 1231–1237.

Katz, I., Glass, D. C., & Cohen, S. (1973). Ambivalence, guilt, and the scapegoating of minority group victims. *Journal of Experimental Social Psychology* 9(5), 423–436. https://doi.org/10.1016/S0022-1031(73)80006-X

Kreager, D. A., & Staff, J. (2009). The sexual double standard and adolescent peer acceptance. *Social Psychology Quarterly* 72(2), 143–164. https://doi.org/10.1177/019027250907200205

Lagerspetz, K. M. J., Björkqvist, K., & Peltonen, T. (1988). Is indirect aggression typical of females? Gender differences in aggressiveness in 11- to 12-year-old children. *Aggressive Behavior* 14(6), 403–414. https://doi.org/10.1002/1098-2337(1988)14:6<403::AID-AB2480140602>3.0.CO;2-D

Lareau, A. (2011). *Unequal childhoods: Class, race, and family life, 2nd edition with an update a decade later* (2nd ed.). Berkeley: University of California Press.

Little, T. D., Henrich, C. C., Jones, S. M., & Hawley, P. H. (2003). Disentangling the "whys" from the "whats" of aggressive behavior. *International Journal of Behavioral Development* 27(2), 122. https://doi.org/10.1080/01650250244000128

McDonald, K. L. (2011). Gossip. In R. J. R. Levesque (Ed.), *Encyclopedia of Adolescence* (pp. 1196–1200). New York: Springer. Retrieved from: http://www.springer.com/gp/book/9781441916945.

Merton, R. K. (1968). *Social theory and social structure*. New York, NY: Free Press.

Moody, J., Brynildsen, W. D., Osgood, D. W., Feinberg, M. E., & Gest, S. (2011). Popularity trajectories and substance use in early adolescence. *Social Networks* 33(2), 101–112. https://doi.org/10.1016/j.socnet.2010.10.001

Morreall, J. (1983). *Taking laughter seriously*. Albany, NY: State University of New York Press.

Mouttapa, M., Valente, T., Gallaher, P., Rohrbach, L. A., & Unger, J. B. (2004). Social network predictors of bullying and victimization. *Adolescence* 39(154), 315–335.

Olweus, D. (1993). *Bullying at school: What we know and what we can do*. Oxford: Wiley.

Ouwerkerk, J. W., Kerr, N. L., Gallucci, M., & Van Lange, P. A. M. (2005). Avoiding the social death penalty: Ostracism and cooperation in social dilemmas. In K. D. Williams, J. P. Forgas, & W. V. Hippel (Eds.), *The social outcast: Ostracism, social exclusion, rejection, and bullying* (1st ed., pp. 321–332). New York, NY: Psychology Press.

Pál, J., Stadtfeld, C., Grow, A., & Takács, K. (2016). Status perceptions matter: Understanding disliking among adolescents. *Journal of Research on Adolescence* 26(4), 805–818. https://doi.org/10.1111/jora.12231

Pharo, H., Gross, J., Richardson, R., & Hayne, H. (2011). Age-related changes in the effect of ostracism. *Social Influence 6*, 22–38. https://doi.org/10.1080/15534510.2010.525852

Proyer, R. T., Meier, L. E., Platt, T., & Ruch, W. (2013). Dealing with laughter and ridicule in adolescence: Relations with bullying and emotional responses. *Social Psychology of Education 16*(3), 399–420. https://doi.org/10.1007/s11218-013-9221-y

Rambaran, J. A., Dijkstra, J. K., Munniksma, A., & Cillessen, A. H. N. (2015). The development of adolescents' friendships and antipathies: A longitudinal multivariate network test of balance theory. *Social Networks 43*, 162–176. https://doi.org/10.1016/j.socnet.2015.05.003

Rauwolf, P., Mitchell, D., & Bryson, J. J. (2015). Value homophily benefits cooperation but motivates employing incorrect social information. *Journal of Theoretical Biology 367*, 246–261. https://doi.org/10.1016/j.jtbi.2014.11.023

Ripley, R. M., Snijders, T. A. B., Boda, Z., Vörös, A., & Preciado, P. (2015). *Manual for SIENA version 4.0.* Oxford: University of Oxford, Department of Statistics; Nuffield College.

Rodkin, P. C., & Berger, C. (2008). Who bullies whom? Social status asymmetries by victim gender. *International Journal of Behavioral Development 32*(6), 473–485. https://doi.org/10.1177/0165025408093667

Rutland, A., Nesdale, D., & Brown, C. S. (Eds.). (2017). *The Wiley handbook of group processes in children and adolescents* (1st ed.). Sothern Gate, Chichester, West Sussex: Wiley-Blackwell.

Salmivalli, C., Huttunen, A., & Lagerspetz, K. M. J. (1997). Peer networks and bullying in schools. *Scandinavian Journal of Psychology 38*(4), 305–312. https://doi.org/10.1111/1467-9450.00040

Salmivalli, C., Kärnä, A., & Poskiparta, E. (2010). From peer putdowns to peer support: A theoretical model and how it translated into a national anti-bullying program. In S. R. Jimerson, S. M. Swearer, & D. L. Espelage (Eds.), *Handbook of bullying in schools: An international perspective* (pp. 441–454). New York, NY: Routledge/Taylor & Francis Group.

Salmivalli, C., Lagerspetz, K., Björkqvist, K., Österman, K., & Kaukialnen, A. (1996). Bullying as a group process: Participant roles and their relations to social status within the group. *Aggressive Behavior22*(1),1–15.https://doi.org/10.1002/(SICI)1098-2337(1996)22:1<1::AID-AB1>3.0.CO;2-T

Sentse, M., Dijkstra, J. K., Salmivalli, C., & Cillessen, A. H. N. (2013). The dynamics of friendships and victimization in adolescence: A longitudinal social network perspective. *Aggressive Behavior 39*(3), 229–238. https://doi.org/10.1002/ab.21469

Sijtsema, J. J., Ojanen, T., Veenstra, R., Lindenberg, S., Hawley, P. H., & Little, T. D. (2010). Forms and functions of aggression in adolescent friendship selection and influence: A longitudinal social network analysis. *Social Development 19*(3), 515–534. https://doi.org/10.1111/j.1467-9507.2009.00566.x

Sijtsema, J. J., Veenstra, R., Lindenberg, S., & Salmivalli, C. (2009). Empirical test of bullies' status goals: Assessing direct goals, aggression, and prestige. *Aggressive Behavior 35*(1), 57–67. https://doi.org/10.1002/ab.20282

Smart Richman, L., & Leary, M. R. (2009). Reactions to discrimination, stigmatization, ostracism, and other forms of interpersonal rejection: A multimotive model. *Psychological Review 116*(2), 365–383. https://doi.org/10.1037/a0015250

Smith, E. A. (2010). Communication and collective action: Language and the evolution of human cooperation. *Evolution and Human Behavior 31*(4), 231–245. https://doi.org/10.1016/j.evolhumbehav.2010.03.001

Smith, E. R. (2014). Evil acts and malicious gossip: A multiagent model of the effects of gossip in socially distributed person perception. *Personality and Social Psychology Review 18*(4), 311–325. https://doi.org/10.1177/1088868314530515

Smith, E. R., & Collins, E. C. (2009). Contextualizing person perception: Distributed social cognition. *Psychological Review 116*(2), 343–364. https://doi.org/10.1037/a0015072

Snijders, T. A. B., van de Bunt, G. G., & Steglich, C. E. G. (2010). Introduction to stochastic actor-based models for network dynamics. *Social Networks 32*(1), 44–60. https://doi.org/10.1016/j.socnet.2009.02.004

Sommerfeld, R. D., Krambeck, H.-J., Semmann, D., & Milinski, M. (2007). Gossip as an alternative for direct observation in games of indirect reciprocity. *Proceedings of the National Academy of Sciences 104*(44), 17435–17440. https://doi.org/10.1073/pnas.0704598104

Stolte, J. F. (1983). The legitimation of structural inequality: Reformulation and test of the self-evaluation argument. *American Sociological Review 48*(3), 331. https://doi.org/10.2307/2095226

Vaidyanathan, B., Khalsa, S., & Ecklund, E. H. (2016). Gossip as social control: Informal sanctions on ethical violations in scientific workplaces. *Social Problems 63*(4), 554–572. https://doi.org/10.1093/socpro/spw022

van de Bunt, G. G., Wittek, R. P. M., & de Klepper, M. C. (2005). The evolution of intra-organizational trust networks: The case of a German paper factory—An empirical test of six trust mechanisms. *International Sociology 20*(3), 339–369. https://doi.org/10.1177/0268580905055480

Veenstra, R., Dijkstra, J. K., & Kreager, D. A. (2018). Pathways, networks, and norms: A sociological perspective on peer research. In W. M. Bukowski, B. Laursen, & K. H. Rubin (Eds.), *Handbook of Peer Interactions, Relationships, and Groups*. New York, NY: Guilford.

Veenstra, R., Dijkstra, J. K., Steglich, C., & Van Zalk, M. H. W. (2013). Network-behavior dynamics. *Journal of Research on Adolescence 23*(3), 399–412. https://doi.org/10.1111/jora.12070

Veenstra, R., Huitsing, G., Dijkstra, J. K., & Lindenberg, S. (2010). Friday on my mind: The relation of partying with antisocial behavior of early adolescents. The Trails Study: Partying, popularity, and antisocial behavior. *Journal of Research on Adolescence 20*(2), 420–431. https://doi.org/10.1111/j.1532-7795.2010.00647.x

Veenstra, R., Lindenberg, S., Munniksma, A., & Dijkstra, J. K. (2010). The complex relation between bullying, victimization, acceptance, and rejection: Giving special attention to status, affection, and sex differences. *Child Development 81*(2), 480–486. https://doi.org/10.1111/j.1467-8624.2009.01411.x

Wargo Aikins, J., Collibee, C., & Cunningham, J. (2015). Gossiping to the top: Observed differences in popular adolescents gossip. *Journal of Early Adolescence 37*(5), 642–661. https://doi.org/10.1177/0272431615617291

Wesselmann, E. D., Williams, K. D., & Hales, A. H. (2013). Vicarious ostracism. *Frontiers in Human Neuroscience 7*. https://doi.org/10.3389/fnhum.2013.00153

Williams, K. D. (2002). *Ostracism: The power of silence* (1st ed.). New York and London: The Guilford Press.

Wittek, R., & Wielers, R. (1998). Gossip in organizations. *Computational & Mathematical Organization Theory 4*(2), 189–204. https://doi.org/10.1023/A:1009636325582

Wooten, D. B. (2006). From labeling possessions to possessing labels: Ridicule and socialization among adolescents. *Journal of Consumer Research 33*(2), 188–198. https://doi.org/10.1086/506300

Wu, J., Balliet, D., & Van Lange, P. A. M. (2016). Gossip versus punishment: The efficiency of reputation to promote and maintain cooperation. *Scientific Reports 6*(1). https://doi.org/10.1038/srep23919

Xie, H., Cairns, B. D., & Cairns, R. B. (2005). The development of aggressive behaviors among girls: Measurement issues, social functions, and differential trajectories. In D. J. Pepler, K. C. Madsen, C. Webster, & K. S. Levene (Eds.), *The development and treatment of girlhood aggression* (pp. 105–136). Mahwah, NJ: Lawrence Erlbaum Associates.

Xie, H., Farmer, T. W., & Cairns, B. D. (2003). Different forms of aggression among inner-city African–American children: Gender, configurations, and school social networks. *Journal of School Psychology* 41(5), 355–375. https://doi.org/10.1016/S0022-4405(03)00086-4

PART VI

# MARKETS, ORGANIZATIONS, AND NETWORKS

# CHAPTER 20

..................................................................................................

# TRUST AND REPUTATION
# IN MARKETS

..................................................................................................

## ANDREAS DIEKMANN AND WOJTEK PRZEPIORKA

## INTRODUCTION

ASSUME you intend to buy a second-hand laptop from a seller on eBay. It has crossed
your mind that the laptop may have hidden defects and, even worse, that the seller may
keep your money without delivering the laptop. Would you be more likely to send your
money to the seller in advance if the laptop was much cheaper than other offers, if the
offer was from a registered computer-shop, and if the seller had a large number of
positive customer ratings? Or would you prefer to pay extra for your transaction to
be handled by an escrow service, which releases your payment to the seller once you
confirm receipt of the laptop? Problems of trust hamper mutually beneficial exchanges
not only in online markets.[1]

Heinrich Popitz (1980) formulated the trust problem in his work on the "normative
construction of reality" as follows:

> The condition for this reliance on the future behaviour of others is trust. Where
> trust is lacking, only limited and rudimentary forms of sociality are possible. In the
> extreme case of total distrust the interactions of the partners must be restricted to a
> strictly controllable simultaneity of the corresponding actions. The black market
> situation provides an example. I must hold my goods firmly in my right hand until
> I have grasped the goods of the other person with my left hand. We both pull at the
> same time and release the goods at the same time.
>
> (Popitz, 1980, p. 78; translated from German by the authors)

If an exchange between A and B is sequential, that is, if A moves first (e.g., sends
money) and B moves second (e.g., delivers merchandise), it becomes possible that B fails
to reciprocate A's advance. In what follows, we call A, the first moving party to the

exchange, *truster*, and we call B, the second moving party, *trustee*. A trust problem exists in as far as it is uncertain whether the trustee will return the advance the truster made in expectation of a benefit (Coleman, 1990).

A trust problem does not only arise if it is uncertain whether the trustee will deliver at all, but also if the agreed quality and/or quantity of the exchanged good or service is not directly observable. The trustee could deliver goods of inferior quality, whereas the truster might only recognize the quality after the conclusion of the transaction. If the trustee knows the quality of his goods whereas the truster does not until the exchange is completed, the exchange situation is one of *asymmetric information*. The degree of the information asymmetry can vary depending on the good. In the case of *inspection goods*, for example unpacked food, it is relatively easy for the truster to determine the quality before the exchange. In the case of *experience goods* the quality only becomes apparent in the course of use, often after a longer period of time. Second-hand cars, dental crowns or beauty creams are examples of experience goods.

We define the *trust problem* as the uncertainty regarding the trustworthiness and/or competence of the trustee that the truster faces. We define *trustworthiness* as the trustee's intention to meet the truster's advance, and distinguish it from *competence*, the trustee's ability (in terms of skill and knowledge) to meet the truster's advance. Finally, we define *trust* as the truster's belief regarding the trustee's trustworthiness and/or competence based on which the truster decides whether or not to make the advance. That is, by trusting, the truster acts upon the expectation that the trustee will abide by the agreement, for example, that a good will be delivered in a certain quality and quantity, although the trustee has the possibility to deviate from the agreement.

In what follows, we review the many ways trust problems inherent in economic exchanges have been tackled and studied in historic and contemporary as well as in offline and online markets. We thereby focus on solutions provided by opportunities for reputation formation and draw on evidence from various disciplines of the social and behavioral sciences. Our chapter contributes to a better understanding of the advantages and down sides of reputation formation as a mechanism for promoting cooperation in markets and points out some promising directions for future research.

## THE TRUST PROBLEM AND ITS SOLUTIONS

The trust problem arising in social and economic exchange is often described with the trust game known from game theory (Dasgupta, 1988; Kreps, 1990). In the trust game, if the truster does not trust the trustee, the exchange is refused and neither of the actors gains anything (i.e., the payoff for both actors is zero). But if the truster agrees to the exchange—thereby placing trust—the trustee then has two possibilities. The trustee can fulfil the agreement and both the truster and the trustee earn the gains from trade ($R$). However, the trustee can also abuse the truster's trust. The trustee then gains an exploitation profit ($T$) and the truster suffers a loss ($S$). In the latter case, the truster's position is even worse than it would have been without the exchange. In the trust game, the trustee's temptation to exploit the truster ($T$) is larger than the gains from trade ($R$), which is larger than no earnings at all, which, for the truster, is still larger than suffering a loss ($S$) from being exploited by the trustee (i.e., $T > R > 0 > S$). In a one-time-only trust game, a self-regarding trustee, who only maximizes his or her private benefit, will always abuse trust. As the truster can anticipate this move he or she will refuse to place trust. In the Nash equilibrium[2] of the trust game, both actors come away empty handed, although both could benefit from the trust-based exchange.

The social dilemma (Kollock, 1999; Milinski, this volume) inherent to social and economic exchanges (formally described as a trust game) can, in principle, be solved in three ways: first, by means of repeated exchanges; second, by institutional regulation of the exchanges; and third, by reputational incentives. Combinations of these solutions also exist. For example, institutions can intentionally or as a side product create opportunities for long-term exchange relations or reputation building.

It is known from game theory (Fudenberg and Maskin, 1986), simulation experiments (Axelrod, 1984) and behavioral experiments (Rapoport and Chammah, 1965; Dal Bó, 2005) that in repeated social dilemma situations as well as in repeated trust games cooperation can arise under certain conditions, even among self-regarding actors. A central condition is the "shadow of the future" (Axelrod, 1984), a figurative expression for the subjective probability that in a series of exchanges a further interaction will take place between the same actors. If this probability exceeds a critical level, cooperation can evolve; put differently, long-term exchange relations are more cooperative.[3]

The importance of repeated exchange relations was already observed by the anthropologist Bronisław Malinowski. In *Crime and Custom in Savage Society*, the classic study on the Trobriand peoples, Malinowski (1926, p. 22) describes how "the inland village supplies the fishermen with vegetables: the coastal community repays with fish." As Malinowski (1926, p. 25) further explains, exchange dyads emerge in this process: "every man has his permanent partner in the exchange." The same actors deal repeatedly with one another and can thus develop a lasting exchange relation. Long-term exchange relations can also provide a solution for the trust problem arising from asymmetric information. Siamwalla (1978) analyses markets for rice and rubber in Thailand. The quality of rice is immediately recognizable by the expert. But in the case of raw rubber, the production process plays a decisive part. The quality of raw rubber can only be ascertained after several months in use. Hence, rice can be characterized as an inspection good and rubber as an experience good. The different degrees of information asymmetry lead to different market relationships. In the case of rice, a producer deals with changing customers, whereas "rubber-growers generally prefer to trade continuously with one buyer" (Siamwalla, 1978; see also Geertz, 1979, who observes a similar mechanism in a Moroccan bazaar economy).

Simulating the situation on the rice and rubber markets described by Siamwalla (1978), Kollock (1994) shows in a behavioral experiment that different market relationships arise depending on the degree of information asymmetry. In his experiment Kollock varies the degree of uncertainty about the quality of the goods. In the control condition buyers and sellers are informed about the quality. In the experimental condition the seller alone is informed and the buyer learns the quality of the goods only after purchasing them. Four subjects in the role of buyers and four subjects in the role of sellers deal with each other over twenty rounds. The sellers can offer goods at the quality and price of their own choosing. In the experimental condition the sellers can advertise the quality of their goods but are not required to be honest. The results show that in the experimental condition, (1) buyers more frequently deal with the same seller, (2) the assessment of the trustworthiness of sellers by buyers diverges more strongly, (3) sellers make a greater effort to acquire a good reputation, and (4) the quality of the goods traded is on average lower than in the control condition (Kollock, 1994).

To the trust problem we have outlined, institutional solutions exist, such as contract law, which regulate economic exchanges in contemporary societies. But it is of course well known that taking legal action involves costs and uncertainties, so that problems arising between trading partners who are repeatedly engaged in business transactions are usually settled outside the courts (Macauley, 1963). It may be therefore useful to distinguish between two types of institutional regulations of markets: (1) exogenous institutions equipped with formal sanctioning powers, such as state authorities, and (2) endogenous, self-organized institutions (Ostrom, 1990). Self-organized solutions to the trust problem can, for example, be promoted by means of commitments, such as the payment of a deposit. An example is the rent deposit, which the landlord receives from the tenant and which the tenant receives back from the landlord at the end of the tenancy provided the property is left in good order. The interplay between exogenous and endogenous institutions for the regulation of markets in modern societies is moreover exemplified by the mortgaging process involved in the purchase of property. The property is mortgaged to the bank, but after the entry in the land register conflicts are settled by the legal institutions provided by the state. In the case of property acquisition, the mortgage interest issued by the bank would be substantially higher if (exogenous) trust-building institutions did not exist.

Whereas the expectation of repeated exchanges creates a "shadow of the future," reputation refers to the "shadow of the past." Reputation carries information about the perceived and rated activities of a person or organization (trustee) with third parties. If the transaction history of a trustee is known, cooperative exchanges can occur between self-regarding and rational actors in analogy to repeated exchange relations, provided that the trustee is interested in maintaining a good reputation. Game theoretic studies show formally that reputational incentives can create the basis for cooperative behavior even if it is unlikely that the same trading partners meet again in the future. Under certain conditions cooperative strategies of trusters and trustees can arise in a Nash equilibrium (Kreps, 1990; Milgrom et al. 1990; Roddie, this volume).

Social capital, social networks and, generally, the social "embeddedness" of market participants, are fundamental concepts in the social sciences in general and in economic sociology in particular (Beckert, 2009; Coleman, 1990; Diekmann, 2007; Granovetter, 1992; Nee, 2005; Przepiorka, 2014). In the light of these concepts, reputation can be described as a form of social embeddedness, and its causes and consequences can be more precisely grasped with the help of game theory and behavioral experiments. Buskens and Raub (2013) deal with various forms of social embeddedness and how it can promote cooperation by the two mechanisms of "learning" and "control." By learning actors consider information about the past. A trustor's decision to trust is based on information about past experiences with the trustee. By control actors consider their influence on the future course of action. A trustor's decision to trust is based on his or her power to inflict negative sanctions on the trustee in case his or her trust is abused. In dyadic embeddedness learning and control apply to the situation in which the same two interaction partners meet repeatedly; trust and cooperation are maintained via direct reciprocity (Axelrod, 1984; Gouldner, 1960; Trivers, 1971). In network embeddedness, learning and control apply indirectly and trust and cooperation are maintained via indirect reciprocity (Nowak and Sigmund, 2005; Milinski, 2016). That is, in network embeddedness, learning is based on the information transferred by third parties about a certain trustee, and control is based on the truster's possibility to induce third parties to inflict negative sanctions on a trustee (also see Buskens and Raub, 2002).

Long-term exchange relations, self-organized institutional rules and reputational incentives are three forms of organizational assurances which can promote the evolution of cooperation without state intervention and can thus be characterized as promoting "order without law" (Ellickson, 1991). Unsurprisingly, examples of the functioning of these mechanisms can also be found in prehistoric and historical societies, in which state authority is weak or entirely absent.

# REPUTATION AND MARKETS IN HISTORICAL AND MODERN SOCIETIES

In the evolution of mankind reputation has always played an important part in maintaining the cohesion of societies. In Dunbar's (2003) prehistoric communities, reputation was communicated through language, that is, spoken information about third parties or "gossip"—very much in the same way as in contemporary informal groups. Language makes it possible to pass on information on the deeds and misdeeds of others. In this way, individuals' reputations can be built or possibly even destroyed in large groups—Dunbar speaks of around 150 members of prehistoric communities (see also Milinski, 2016). In laboratory experiments, the spread of information about group members' reputations through gossip has been shown to promote cooperative exchanges (Sommerfeld et al. 2007; Feinberg et al. 2014), and does so in a more efficient way than other forms of peer-sanctioning (Grimalda et al. 2016; Guala, 2012; Wu et al. 2016).

Economic historians have described institutionalized forms of communicating information about reputation in social and economic exchanges from antiquity to modern times. Temin (2013) deals with the grain market in ancient Rome. A "peer-monitoring system" (Temin, 2013, p. 106) and the documentation of the quantities and prices of business deals reduced merchants' risks of being deceived by their agents in long-distance trade. The *annona*, a kind of authority responsible for the supply of grain, could punish fraudulent agents and exclude them from trade. Apart from the institutional regulations, agents were interested in maintaining their reputations. The unloading of the ships in the harbor of Ostia and the further transportation of the grain to Rome was the task of specialized guilds, which paid careful attention to the reputation of their members.

A mixed form of various institutional regulations involving enforceable contracts as well as reputation resulting from recommendations or the membership in guilds reduced the risk of agents deceiving their customers. In the late medieval Hanseatic city of Lübeck, Burkhardt (2010) finds among the "Bergen travelers" (i.e., merchants who traded with the Norwegian city of Bergen) a change in the structure of long-term relations. His analysis of commercial networks reveals the dominance of family relations in the fourteenth century. But already in the second half of the fifteenth century, the family networks were disappearing. According to Burkhardt the reason is that institutions such as clubs, guilds and brotherhoods had emerged, which provided alternative solutions to the trust problem by enabling merchants to build a good reputation.

Greif (1989) and Milgrom et al. (1990) analyze various forms of self-organized institutions which promote economic exchange based on reputational incentives. The economic historian Avner Greif has examined the reputation system created by Maghrebian merchants in the eleventh century, and Paul Milgrom, Douglas North, and Barry Weingast have analyzed the *Lex Mercatoria*, which regulated trade at the Champagne fairs in the twelfth and thirteenth centuries. These case studies make apparent the importance of reputation for economic exchange and are highly instructive for game theory argumentation. We will therefore take a closer look at these two studies.

Jewish merchants had settled in North Africa in the eleventh century, predominantly in Tunisia. These Maghrebian traders were active in long-distance trade, which was, however, burdened by great uncertainty. The sea voyage from Egypt to Sicily lasted from 13 to 50 days, and the price of goods fluctuated widely. The merchants had agents at the destination of the goods who looked after their sale. The agents had information which the merchants at first did not have. This was a situation involving both asymmetric information and exchanges with potentially large returns. Agents could, for example, inform the merchant of a price lower than the price that was actually realized in the sale of the goods and pocket the difference. But the agent had an incentive to act honestly in order to continue working for the merchant in the future, as for acting dishonestly, the merchant would no longer employ him. This mechanism only functioned, however, if the dishonest activities of the agent came to the merchant's knowledge. In fact the Maghrebian merchants formed a coalition, whose members observed the following rules: first, they informed each other about dishonest agents. Second, an agent who cheated not only lost his position with the merchant, but was never again offered employment by any other member of the coalition. The fact that agents and merchants did not belong to different social classes and often switched roles also played a part. A merchant could act as an agent for another merchant. Attempted fraud could not only cost him his wage as an agent but also the profits from his activities as a merchant, as a third rule stated that a fraudulent agent who operated as a merchant could be cheated with impunity by the other merchants of the coalition. An agent thus had a great interest in acting honestly as he would otherwise lose both his future wage as an agent and his profits as a merchant. The double incentive thus ensured honest actions to the benefit of all parties. Maghrebian Mediterranean trade only came to an end with the expansion of trade of the Italian city states and the conquests of the Bedouins in North Africa at the end of the eleventh century (Greif, 1989).

Traders in the Champagne fairs (Milgrom et al. 1990) also faced trust problems, as the traded goods were often delivered later and both the quality and the quantity could be subject to dispute. The Champagne fairs were of preeminent importance for trade in Europe of the twelfth and thirteenth centuries. In contrast to the reputation system maintained by the Maghrebian merchants, here the information about traders' reputations was communicated by specialized actors who kept a record of disputed transactions and at the same time administered justice. Merchants or local officials worked as private judges, who received information about disputed transactions and provided information on particular traders upon request and in return for a fee. These private judges could also pass judgment and impose penalties in case of dispute. But they were not able to impose penalties outside of the fairs. Why, then, should a trader accept the judge's verdict and pay a penalty on conviction after he had already returned to his home town? A good reason was the maintenance of his reputation and the prospect of good business, as traders with a bad reputation were excluded from trade or could only participate under worse conditions.

The Lex Mercatoria, which developed out of the merchant law of the Champagne and other trade centers of medieval Europe, was private law. Violations of the rules could not be punished under the sanctioning powers of state officials. Consequently all market participants had a personal interest in observing the rules. The interplay of various individual incentives has been analyzed by Milgrom et al. (1990) in an abstract model comprising the main features of the Lex Mercatoria. Their analysis reveals that a self-organized reputation system must fulfil four conditions to enable cooperation and hence an efficiently functioning market: (1) Norm violators must be punished. (2) Traders must be informed about the behavior of others in earlier transactions. (3) Traders must provide information on the behavior of their trading partners after a transaction. (4) Traders must comply with the judges' verdicts. Milgrom et al. (1990) apply game theory to examine the incentive problem in regard to the maintenance of a reputation system and hence of cooperative market transactions between traders. It turns out that observing the rules of the Lex Mercatoria is, under certain conditions, an equilibrium strategy. These conditions include the information costs and the profit from a single act of fraud. If these two factors do not exceed a certain level, the market participants will have a personal interest in playing by the rules.

These case studies show that the reputation mechanism can promote cooperative market transactions. Moreover, they show that self-organized reputation systems can be maintained without state intervention, as long as it is in all actors' own interest to observe certain rules.

As with the Roman professional guilds (Temin, 2013) or the Lübeck "Bergen travelers" (Burkhardt, 2010) reputation can be acquired through membership of a recognized social group or organization. The membership of a religious community can also confer reputation, particularly when admission to the religious community is accompanied by strict rules and tests and potential business partners know that the members of the community adhere to honest business conduct. The "Amish People" in North America can easily receive credit because the banks know that the credit agreements are virtually always kept. A banker with fifteen years of experience with the evangelical community said: "I never lost a dime lending to the Amish" (Kraybill, 2001, p. 257; Diekmann, 2007). In his study on "The Protestant Sects and the Spirit of Capitalism" Max Weber ([1920] 2002) reports on various observations which clearly show that membership of a religious group not only fulfils religious needs but also may have the important side effect of attributing business reputation. On a train journey, Weber meets a travelling salesman who assures him: "Sir, for my part everybody may believe or not believe as he pleases; but if I saw a farmer or a businessman not belonging to any church at all, I wouldn't trust him with 50 cents" (Weber [1920] 2002, p. 128). Weber's observations at the baptism of a new member of a Baptist community are also highly informative:

> "...once [he is] baptized he will get the patronage of the whole region and he will outcompete everybody." Further questions of "why" and "by what means" led to the following conclusion: Admission to the local Baptist congregation follows only upon the most careful "probation" and after closest inquiries into conduct going back to early childhood (Disorderly conduct? Frequenting taverns? Dance? Theatre? Card Playing? Untimely meeting of liability? Other Frivolities?) The congregation still adhered strictly to the religious tradition. Admission to the congregation is recognized as an absolute guarantee of the moral qualities of a gentleman, especially of those qualities required in business matters. Baptism secures to the individual the deposits of the whole region and unlimited credit without any competition. He is a "made man."    (Weber, [1920] 2002: pp. 129–130; also see Voss, 1998)

Three characteristics make a person's reputation in this case credible and effective. First, admission to the community only takes place after careful examination and with the agreement of the members of the community; second, membership cannot be faked and the reputation cannot therefore be falsely acquired, and third, the membership and hence the attestation of the ethical quality of all the business partners is known (see also Diekmann et al. 2009).

In secular societies we hardly any more rely on membership in a religious community when giving credit or choosing business partners. Specialized "reputation firms" such as credit bureaus, aka credit reference agencies (CRAs), collect and provide information on the credit history and business conduct of a customer or business partner (Djankov et al. 2007). Anyone who, for example, applies for a loan, buys a new mobile phone or car will come across a contract clause which permits the bank, mobile provider or car dealer, respectively, to do a "credit check" by obtaining information from a CRA. CRAs such as Experian operate globally and collect individual consumer information from different sources (e.g., credit payment histories, public records on bankruptcies and court judgements, etc.). Based on this information, CRAs calculate individual credit scores which are increasingly used by borrowers to assess lenders' creditworthiness (Einav et al. 2013). The parallel to the Lex Mercatoria with a system of notaries who keep a register of all known transactions is apparent. The same principles are applied; only the technology of communication has changed. Technological progress has drastically reduced the cost of acquiring and sharing information and has increased the speed at which information can be accessed.

## REPUTATION IN ONLINE MARKETS

In online trade trust problems arise due to the anonymity of market participants, who often interact with each other over large geographic distances and across national borders (also see Przepiorka, 2013). Most of their transactions are for one time only, that is, only a small proportion of business deals concluded on platforms such as eBay comprise repeated encounters between the same traders (e.g., Diekmann et al. 2014). According to the Nash equilibrium predictions of the standard trust game, one-time-only exchanges between online traders should not take place—online markets should not exist (Güth and Ockenfels, 2003). However, online markets are a growth sector.

To a large part, the popularity and success of online markets can be attributed to the implementation of decentralized reputation systems made possible by the development of internet technology (Kollock, 1999; Resnick et al. 2000). A person who buys something on eBay, for instance, is asked to rate the seller after the transaction. These ratings (positive and negative) make up the interaction history of a seller, which can be accessed online anywhere in the world, at no cost and within seconds. Because it is time consuming and cognitively demanding to read and interpret the entire interaction history of a seller, similar to a credit score calculated by CRAs (see previous section), a reputation index is calculated which informs potential buyers of the number and the percentage of a seller's positive ratings. The cost of acquiring this information, a central factor in the reputation model of the Lex Mercatoria (Milgrom et al. 1990), is virtually zero. Moreover, in contrast to the Lex Mercatoria and modern credit bureaus, online rating systems are decentralized, whereby the costs of providing information is also reduced (Dellarocas, 2003).

In anonymous online markets with a reputation system, buyers will trust and pay sellers with a good reputation more; in the case of sellers with a poor reputation buyers will demand a discount (i.e., they will bid lower amounts in auctions) to compensate for the risk they take when dealing with "unknown" sellers. Using econometric methods, Diekmann et al. (2014) have estimated the price increase in the case of positive ratings and the price reduction in the case of negative ratings based on more than 13,000 auctions of mobile phones and 180,000 auctions of DVDs. A significant effect on the selling price is revealed, whereby positive ratings have a smaller effect on price increases than negative ratings have on price reductions. This outcome is consistent with a large number of empirical studies (e.g., Kollock, 1999; Diekmann et al. 2009; Dellarocas, 2003; Resnick et al. 2006) and shows that sellers have a financial incentive to invest in a good reputation. They are, in particular, interested in avoiding negative ratings. Since this can mainly be achieved by means of honest transactions, fraudulent sellers have a reduced incentive to participate in online trade in the first place (Snijders, Matzat, this volume).

Todays' online market platforms offer great opportunities to study the functioning of reputation systems unobtrusively at a large scale. However, process data obtained from online markets only reflects traders' behavior and, as such, does not reveal much about these traders' motives and beliefs. The functioning of reputation systems is therefore also studied in laboratory experiments (e.g., Abraham et al. 2016; Bohnet et al. 2005; Kuwabara, 2015). Bolton et al. (2004), for example, compare three market structures: a market with one-off transactions and changing partners (stranger market), a market with repeated transactions with the same partner (partner market) and a stranger market in which transaction partners are informed about each other's decisions in previous trans-actions (rating market). Trust and cooperation were higher in the rating market than in the stranger market, but the highest level of cooperation was achieved in the partner market. A reason for the difference between the partner market and the rating market was that subjects are mistrustful when they interact with a partner who does not yet have an interaction history. This result also shows that for market entrants establishing a good reputation may pose a problem. However, building a good online reputation must be costly in order to deter fraudulent traders from entering the market or re-entering under a new pseudonym after a fraudulent transaction (Friedman and Resnick, 2001). Market entrants with honest intentions must thus accept lower prices to build their reputation; once they have built a good reputation they will be compensated for their initial investment by the higher prices they can charge for their goods (Shapiro, 1983).

Buyers can protect themselves against fraud by taking into account sellers' reputations and choose the sellers they want to buy from. Sellers, however, do not generally have the option to choose buyers. How, then, can sellers protect themselves against buyers with poor payment morale? The solution is simple. Sellers determine the mode of payment such that they make the "second move" and deliver the goods only after having received buyers' payment. Payment modalities can be ordered in regard to the degree to which they favor the seller. The rank order with decreasing seller power is: payment in advance > cash on mail delivery > cash on pick up > cash on delivery (in person) > mail delivery on account. In a study by Diekmann et al. (2009) on mobile phone auctions in the Swiss online market Ricardo.ch, 25 percent of the transactions were carried out by cash in advance and 70 percent by cash on delivery. It also turned out that the reputation of the seller correlated with seller power. The better a seller's reputation the more likely was the seller to determine a payment mode in his or her favor. This effect is also shown in (sec-ondary) online markets for game cards. Kollock (1999) reports an example of a market in which the norm developed that the exchange partner with the poorer reputation had to initiate the exchange by sending his or her card to the exchange partner first.

However, the functioning of decentralized reputation systems crucially depends on traders rating each other after finished transactions. Although the submission of a rating, for example by a buyer after receipt of the merchandise, costs very little effort, it is by no means a matter of course that ratings are made to a large extent. The sum of all ratings constitutes the collective good "reputation" that is subject to a free rider problem (Bolton et al. 2004). If traders spared themselves the trouble and provided no feedback, the rating system would deteriorate and with it the entire market. However, a little bit of reciprocity and altruism beyond the self-interest of the *homo oeconomicus* can get an anonymous online market with a reputation system up and running (Bolton et al. 2013; Diekmann et al. 2014). Reciprocity is one reason for giving positive feedback to a seller with whom one is highly satisfied because of the high quality of the goods or the rapid processing of the transaction. Correspondingly, many buyers are inclined to punish a seller who delivers poor quality goods with a negative rating (Resnick et al. 2000). In the case of two-sided rating systems, there are also strategic motives for leaving feedback (Dellarocas et al. 2004). If the seller and the buyer can rate each other, one gladly gives a positive rating in order to receive the same from the other. At the same time, traders will be more cautious with negative ratings as the trading partner has the possibility to retaliate. Hence, a side effect of the two-sided rating system is the inflation of positive ratings. In other words, although the reciprocal rating system of eBay may have helped to overcome the free rider problem in feedback provision, it boosted the amount of positive ratings possibly leading to biased evaluations (Dellarocas and Wood, 2008). However, it was possible to overcome this problem by means of a change in the rating system. In 2007, eBay essentially shifted to a one-sided system of buyer ratings, and even after the system change the proportion of rated transactions remained at a very high level (Bolton et al. 2013). This outcome supports the hypothesis that a majority of buyers are not only motivated by strategic considerations. "Strong reciprocity" (Gintis, 2000), that is, the tendency to respond to positive actions positively and to negative actions negatively, even when these responses involve a cost, seems to be common enough in online traders to guarantee a sufficient proportion of ratings.[4]

Note that in their analysis of the Lex Mercatoria, Milgrom et al. (1990) do not assume the existence of any altruism or norms of honorable traders. The rise of the "honorable merchant" could be a consequence of, but it is not a necessary precondition for the proper functioning of a market with a reputation system. In the analysis by Milgrom et al. (1990), the assumption of self-interest suffices, as all actors have an incentive to play by the rules. But this is not the case with online markets. There are no material incentives to provide ratings. If all online traders corresponded to the image of the *homo oeconomicus*, online markets would not emerge. Online markets can only function if a certain proportion of traders employ reciprocal behaviour. Only if a certain proportion of traders are motivated by *strong reciprocity*, and possibly other types of other-regarding preferences, can reputation systems function without additional incentives.

Thus far we have been primarily concerned with three elements which promote cooperation among anonymous traders in online markets: (1) the reputation system, (2) the payment mode, and (3) the notion of reciprocity. As a fourth element, institutional rules must be added to this list. Many online markets offer an escrow service, particularly when larger sums of money are involved. Whereas the power of the seller is strengthened by payment in advance, the availability of an escrow service shifts power back to the buyer. Finally, and as a fifth element, we should call to mind that all transactions are subject to contract law. It is possible to take a fraudulent trading partner to court, although this costs time, money and effort.

It is, however, remarkable that the four elements of *self-organized cooperation* alone are sufficient to enable economic transactions. This is demonstrated by the functioning of numerous cryptomarkets, markets for illegal goods in the so-called dark web (Bradbury, 2014). The dark web is only accessible by means of encryption software that obliterates all traces of the actors. In cryptomarkets such as Silk Road, AlphaBay, or Evolution, trade with hacked user accounts, forged passports, illegal drugs, weapons, and such is carried out in total anonymity (Barratt and Aldridge, 2016; Bartlett, 2014; Christin, 2012). As with eBay, finished transactions are rated by the customers and to this extent provide information on "honest" dealers.[5] Although none of the traders in cryptomarkets for illegal goods could ever take legal action to uphold their rights before a state court, trade in cryptomarkets nonetheless flourishes (Soska and Christin, 2015).

Recent findings corroborate that a good seller reputation is at least as important for business success in cryptomarkets as it is in surface web markets such as eBay. Using data of illegal drug transactions in the cryptomarket Silk Road 1.0 (Christin, 2012), Przepiorka et al. (2017) analyze the effect of buyer ratings on sellers' business success. They find that sellers with a better rating history charge higher prices and sell their merchandise faster than sellers with no or a bad rating history (see also Hardy and Norgaard, 2016). Anonymous traders in cryptomarkets do not, however, rely solely on ratings. There is also an escrow service which protects buyers by releasing the payment to the seller only upon confirmation of receipt of the merchandise by the buyer. The combination of reputational incentives and institutional precautions literally promotes "order without law" (Ellickson, 1991).

Reputation contributes decisively to the relatively smooth processing of millions of transactions in online markets, even in markets for illegal goods in the so-called dark web. Without a reputation system online markets in which anonymous actors do business over large geographic distances would fail on account of the problem of asymmetric information (Akerlof, 1970). Unsurprisingly, reputation systems have spread rapidly in the internet, in particular in online markets, but also in the form of review platforms of services, hotels, car sharing agencies, hospitals, universities, and so on.

# THE DOWN SIDE OF REPUTATION SYSTEMS

Reputation systems can promote cooperation in illegal activities as much as in (legal) online markets. In the same way as Mafia structures are strengthened by strict cooperation norms (e.g., the obligation to secrecy, the omerta), reputation systems also help markets for illegal goods to achieve a high degree of successful transactions (Hardy and Norgaard, 2016; Przepiorka et al. 2017).

Reputation is always based on perception and perception can be deceptive. This is true for gossip and title-tattle and equally so for online reputation indices. In particular, a good reputation can also be faked to a certain extent. This used to be called swindling but is nowadays termed reputation management. For example, companies or authors of books sold by Amazon may pay for services praising their products (Arthur, 2013; Flood, 2012). There is also the possibility to hire reviewers to give negative ratings to competing products. Examples of such services can be found on the online platform Fiverr.com. Recently, Amazon sued fake reviewers who were active on this platform (Kirchner and Beyer, 2016). By now, specially programmed algorithms or "bots" are able to generate "like" clicks on social media such as Facebook or YouTube (Clark, 2015). In certain domains it may be even simpler to fabricate favorable evaluations. Who knows whether hotel ratings really come from guests or whether they have been commissioned by the hotel owners. Rating agencies which decide on the quality of securities are paid by the issuers, with the result that questionable "collaterized debt obligations" are awarded a "Triple A," the highest possible rating. Finance experts put at least a part of the blame for the recent financial crisis on these agencies. Not only is fraudulently acquired reputation a problem, but also the destruction of honestly acquired reputation. This can take the shape of mobbing among schoolchildren or the destruction of the reputation of a competing product on the market. Thus, in general, for reputation systems the reliability of the information and the rating procedures are core issues.

However, in online markets the construction of a bogus reputation involves costs, as fees are charged for every transaction. A trader can pursue a policy of building up a reputation with a number of small business transactions ("whitewashing") and then act fraudulently in a big transaction. The strategy can pay off if the profit from the fraud exceeds the cost of building up the reputation. Counter measures are, however, available. In the case of big transactions, customers are well advised to make use of the escrow service. Moreover, a seller makes him- or herself suspicious if, to exaggerate a bit, he or she makes a hundred deals with the sale of chewing gum and then offers a Ferrari for sale with payment in advance. It is important that potential customers are not only informed about the evaluations of past transactions but also about the size of the concluded deals.

Apart from the question of fraudulent reputation building there is a further problem in connection with decentralized reputation systems. In the case of experience goods it can happen that deficiencies can, if at all, only be recognized by consumers after some time. If, for example, a toy bought in an online auction releases toxic chemicals which the buyer cannot notice, this serious deficiency will not of course be reflected in the buyer's rating of the seller. Deficiencies which can only be established by means of special tests and materials analysis require expert evaluation by institutions such as food inspection or consumer safety agencies. In these cases, decentralized ratings alone are, therefore, by no means sufficient and must be supplemented by the evaluations of experts.

In spite of all the reservations and the problems they give rise to, decentralized rating systems are evidently successful. They have spread rapidly in online markets and not only in the internet. The concept of a "reputation society" is perhaps rather exaggerated, but it makes clear that more and more corners of our society are being pervaded by quantifying reputation systems. Reputation is also being increasingly quantified in the field of science. A large number of digital archives exist alongside the Web of Science. Google Scholar, RePEc, Research Gate, and Academia.edu all publish indices and attribute reputations. Citations, the impact factor of journals, the h-index and other indices increasingly decide about the careers of researchers, who accordingly adapt their behaviour to the requirements of these indices. Reputation can create social order and promote cooperative behaviour but can also have negative (unintended) consequences. For example, public quality rankings of physicians, introduced to improve treatment quality, may induce these physicians to avoid sick patients, because sick patients are more likely to negatively affect their scores (Werner and Asch, 2005). Whether and to what degree reputation systems promote the welfare of society depends on the quality of the information measured with the individual indicators. More systematic research into the working of reputation systems, their interaction with individuals' preferences and constraints, as well as the consequences of reputation systems for society at large, is necessary. The analysis of reputation systems in past and present societies does show that in markets for goods and services, whether online or offline, reputation can help solve problems of asymmetric information and in this way promote cooperative and mutually beneficial trade.

## Notes

1. This chapter is a translated and extended version of Diekmann and Przepiorka (2016).
2. A Nash equilibrium is a combination of strategies such that no actor has an incentive to deviate (to switch to an alternative strategy) as long as all other actors stick to their strategies. In other words, a *unilateral* change of strategy does not pay off in a Nash equilibrium.
3. In terms of game theory, cooperative equilibrium strategies exist in a repeated game, if the probability of meeting one's interaction partner again is sufficiently high (see, e.g., Osborne 2009, ch. 15).
4. Based on a theory driven analysis of hundreds of thousands of rating events obtained from eBay, Diekmann et al. (2014) show that strong reciprocity, but also altruism (Becker, 1976) and strategic motives (Dellarocas et al., 2004), are important drivers of online traders' leaving feedback after finished transactions. Other motives such as "warm glow" altruism (Andreoni, 1990) or indirect reciprocity (Nowak and Sigmund, 2005) may also play a role in traders' leaving feedback but turned out to be difficult to identify with observational data (Diekmann et al., 2014).
5. However, the dark web also helps civil rights activists and journalists living in dictatorial regimes to communicate freely.

## References

Abraham, Martin, Veronika Grimm, Christina Neeß and Michael Seebauer. 2016. "Reputation Formation in Economic Transactions." *Journal of Economic Behavior & Organization* 121: 1–14.
Akerlof, George A. 1970. "The Market for 'Lemons': Quality Uncertainty and the Market Mechanism." *Quarterly Journal of Economics* 84(3): 488–500.

Andreoni, James. 1990. "Impure Altruism and Donations to Public Goods: A Theory of Warm-Glow Giving." *Economic Journal* 100(401): 464–477.

Arthur, Charles. 2013. "How Low-Paid Workers at 'Click Farms' Create Appearance of Online Popularity." *The Guardian*, Retrieved August 2, 2016 (https://www.theguardian.com/technology/2013/aug/02/click-farms-appearance-online-popularity).

Axelrod, Robert. 1984. *The Evolution of Cooperation*. New York: Basic Books.

Barratt, Monica J., and Judith Aldridge. 2016. "Everything You Always Wanted to Know About Drug Cryptomarkets* (*but Were Afraid to Ask)." *International Journal of Drug Policy* 35: 1–6.

Bartlett, Jamie. 2014. *The Dark Net: Inside the Digital Underworld*. London: Melville House.

Becker, Gary S. 1976. "Altruism, Egoism and Genetic Fitness: Economics and Sociobiology." *Journal of Economic Literature* 14(3): 817–826.

Beckert, Jens. 2009. "The Social Order of Markets." *Theory and Society* 38(3): 245–269.

Bohnet, Iris, Steffen Huck, Heike Harmgart and Jean-Robert Tyran. 2005. "Learning Trust." *Journal of the European Economic Association* 3(2–3): 322–329.

Bolton, Gary E., Ben Greiner, and Axel Ockenfels. 2013. "Engineering Trust: Reciprocity in the Production of Reputation Information." *Management Science* 59(2): 265–285.

Bolton, Gary E., Elena Katok, and Axel Ockenfels. 2004. "How Effective Are Electronic Reputation Mechanisms? An Experimental Investigation." *Management Science* 50(11): 1587–1602.

Bradbury, Danny. 2014. "Unveiling the Dark Web." *Network Security* 2014(4): 14–17.

Burkhardt, Mike. 2010. "The German Hanse and Bergen: New Perspectives on an Old Subject." *Scandinavian Economic History Review* 58(1): 60–79.

Buskens, Vincent, and Werner Raub. 2002. "Embedded Trust: Control and Learning." In *Group Cohesion, Trust and Solidarity*, Vol. 19, *Advances in Group Processes*, edited by E. J. Lawler and S. R. Thye, 167–202. Amsterdam: JAI.

Buskens, Vincent, and Werner Raub. 2013. "Rational Choice Research on Social Dilemmas: Embeddedness Effects on Trust." In *The Handbook of Rational Choice Social Research*, edited by R. Wittek, T. Snijders, and V. Nee, 113–150. Stanford, CA: Stanford University Press.

Christin, Nicolas. 2012. "Traveling the Silk Road: A Measurement Analysis of a Large Anonymous Online Marketplace." *arXiv*: 1207.7139.

Clark, Doug B. 2015. "The Bot Bubble: How Click Farms Have Inflated Social Media Currency." *New Republic*, Retrieved August 2, 2016. (https://newrepublic.com/article/121551/bot-bubble-click-farms-have-inflated-social-media-currency).

Coleman, James S. 1990. *Foundations of Social Theory*. Cambridge, MA: The Belknap Press of Harvard University Press.

Dal Bó, Pedro. 2005. "Cooperation under the Shadow of the Future: Experimental Evidence from Infinitely Repeated Games." *American Economic Review* 95(5): 1591–1604.

Dasgupta, Partha. 1988. "Trust as a Commodity." In *Trust: Making and Breaking Cooperative Relations*, edited by D. Gambetta, 49–72. Oxford: Basil Blackwell.

Dellarocas, Chrysanthos. 2003. "The Digitization of Word of Mouth: Promise and Challenges of Online Feedback Mechanisms." *Management Science* 49(10): 1407–1424.

Dellarocas, Chrysanthos, Ming Fan, and Charles A. Wood. 2004. "Self-Interest, Reciprocity, and Participation in Online Reputation Systems." Vol.: Working Paper 205, MIT Center for Digital Business.

Dellarocas, Chrysanthos, and Charles A. Wood. 2008. "The Sound of Silence in Online Feedback: Estimating Trading Risks in the Presence of Reporting Bias." *Management Science* 54(3): 460–476.

Diekmann, Andreas. 2007. "Dimensionen des Sozialkapitals." In *Sozialkapital. Grundlagen und Anwendungen, Sonderheft 47/2007 Der Kölner Zeitschrift für Soziologie und Sozialpsychologie*, edited by A. Franzen and M. Freitag, 47–65. Wiesbaden: VS Verlag für Sozialwissenschaften.

Diekmann, Andreas, Ben Jann, and David Wyder. 2009. "Trust and Reputation in Internet Auctions." In *eTrust: Forming Relationships in the Online World*, edited by K. S. Cook, C. Snijders, V. Buskens, and C. Cheshire, 139–165. New York: Russell Sage.

Diekmann, Andreas, Ben Jann, Wojtek Przepiorka, and Stefan Wehrli. 2014. "Reputation Formation and the Evolution of Cooperation in Anonymous Online Markets." *American Sociological Review* 79(1): 65–85.

Diekmann, Andreas, and Wojtek Przepiorka. 2016. "Reputation in Märkten." In *Handbuch Der Wirtschaftssoziologie*, edited by A. Maurer, 241–255. Wiesbaden: Springer VS.

Djankov, Simeon, Caralee McLiesh, and Andrei Shleifer. 2007. "Private Credit in 129 Countries." *Journal of Financial Economics* 84(2): 299–329.

Dunbar, R. I. M. 2003. "The Social Brain: Mind, Language, and Society in Evolutionary Perspective." *Annual Review of Anthropology* 32: 163–181.

Einav, Liran, Mark Jenkins, and Jonathan Levin. 2013. "The Impact of Credit Scoring on Consumer Lending." *RAND Journal of Economics* 44(2): 249–274.

Ellickson, Robert C. 1991. *Order without Law: How Neighbors Settle Disputes*. Cambridge, MA: Harvard University Press.

Feinberg, Matthew, Robb Willer, and Michael Schultz. 2014. "Gossip and Ostracism Promote Cooperation in Groups." *Psychological Science* 25(3): 656–664.

Flood, Alison. 2012. "Sock puppetry and Fake Reviews: Publish and Be Damned." *The Guardian*, Retrieved August 2, 2016 (https://www.theguardian.com/books/2012/sep/04/sock-puppetry-publish-be-damned).

Friedman, Eric J., and Paul Resnick. 2001. "The Social Cost of Cheap Pseudonyms." *Journal of Economics & Management Strategy* 10(2): 173–199.

Fudenberg, Drew, and Eric Maskin. 1986. "The Folk Theorem in Repeated Games with Discounting or with Incomplete Information." *Econometrica* 54(3): 533–554.

Geertz, Clifford. 1979. "Suq: The Bazaar Economy in Sefrou." In *Meaning and Order in Moroccan Society: Three Essays in Cultural Analysis*, edited by C. Geertz, H. Geertz, and L. Rosen, 123–225. Cambridge: Cambridge University Press.

Gintis, Herbert. 2000. "Strong Reciprocity and Human Sociality." *Journal of Theoretical Biology* 206(2): 169–179.

Gouldner, Alvin W. 1960. "The Norm of Reciprocity: A Preliminary Statement." *American Journal of Sociology* 25(2): 161–178.

Granovetter, Mark. 1992. "Problems of Explanation in Economic Sociology." In *Networks and Organizations: Structure, Form, and Action*, edited by N. Nohria and R. G. Eccles, 25–56. Boston: Harvard Business School Press.

Greif, Avner. 1989. "Reputation and Coalitions in Medieval Trade: Evidence on the Maghribi Traders." *Journal of Economic History* 49(4): 857–882.

Grimalda, Gianluca, Andreas Pondorfer, and David P. Tracer. 2016. "Social Image Concerns Promote Cooperation More than Altruistic Punishment." *Nature Communications* 7: 12288.

Guala, Francesco. 2012. "Reciprocity: Weak or Strong? What Punishment Experiments Do (and Do Not) Demonstrate." *Behavioral and Brain Sciences* 35(1): 1–15.

Güth, Werner, and Axel Ockenfels. 2003. "The Coevolution of Trust and Institutions in Anonymous and Non-Anonymous Communities." In *Jahrbuch Für Neue Politische Ökonomie*, edited by M. J. Holler, H. Kliemt, D. Schmidtchen, and M. Streit, 157–174. Tübingen: Mohr Siebeck.

Hardy, Robert Augustus, and Julia R. Norgaard. 2016. "Reputation in the Internet Black Market: An Empirical and Theoretical Analysis of the Deep Web." *Journal of Institutional Economics* 12(3): 515–539.

Kirchner, Stefan, and Jürgen Beyer. 2016. "Die Plattformlogik als digitale Marktordnung." *Zeitschrift für Soziologie* 45(5): 324–339.

Kollock, Peter. 1994. "The Emergence of Exchange Structures: An Experimental Study of Uncertainty, Commitment, and Trust." *American Journal of Sociology* 100(2): 313–345.

Kollock, Peter. 1999. "The Production of Trust in Online Markets." In *Advances in Group Processes, Volume 16*, edited by E. J. Lawler and M. W. Macy, 99–123. Amsterdam: JAI Press.

Kraybill, Donald B. 2001. *The Riddle of Amish Culture*. Baltimore: Johns Hopkins University Press.

Kreps, David. 1990. "Corporate Culture and Economic Theory." In *Perspectives on Positive Political Economy*, edited by J. E. Alt and K. A. Shepsle, 90–143. Cambridge, MA: Cambridge University Press.

Kuwabara, Ko. 2015. "Do Reputation Systems Undermine Trust? Divergent Effects of Enforcement Type on Generalized Trust and Trustworthiness." *American Journal of Sociology* 120(5): 1390–1428.

Macaulay, Stewart. 1963. "Non-Contractual Relations in Business: A Preliminary Study." *American Sociological Review* 28(1): 55–67.

Malinowski, Bronislaw. 1926. *Crime and Custom in Savage Society*. London: Routledge & Kegan Paul.

Milgrom, Paul R., Douglass C. North, and Barry R. Weingast. 1990. "The Role of Institutions in the Revival of Trade: The Law Merchant, Private Judges, and the Champagne Fairs." *Economics and Politics* 2(1): 1–23.

Milinski, Manfred. 2016. "Reputation, a Universal Currency for Human Social Interactions." *Philosophical Transactions of the Royal Society B* 371: 20150100.

Milinski, Manfred. 2019. "Gossip and Reputation in Social Dilemmas." In *Handbook of Gossip and Reputation*, edited by Francesca Giardini and Rafael Wittek, New York: Oxford University Press.

Nee, Victor. 2005. "The New Institutionalisms in Economics and Sociology." In *The Handbook of Economic Sociology*, edited by N. J. Smelser and R. Swedberg, 49–74. Princeton, NJ: Princeton University Press.

Nowak, Martin A., and Karl Sigmund. 2005. "Evolution of Indirect Reciprocity." *Nature* 437(7063): 1291–1298.

Osborne, Martin J. 2009. *An Introduction to Game Theory, International Edition*. Oxford: Oxford University Press.

Ostrom, Elinor. 1990. *Governing the Commons: The Evolution of Institutions for Collective Action*. Cambridge, UK: Cambridge University Press.

Popitz, Heinrich. 1980. *Die Normative Konstruktion Von Gesellschaft*. Tübingen: Mohr Siebeck.

Przepiorka, Wojtek. 2013. "Buyers Pay for and Sellers Invest in a Good Reputation: More Evidence from eBay." *Journal of Socio-Economics* 42(C): 31–42.

Przepiorka, Wojtek. 2014. "Reputation in Offline and Online Markets: Solutions to Trust Problems in Social and Economic Exchange." *Economic Sociology, the European Electronic Newsletter* 16(1): 4–10.

Przepiorka, Wojtek, Lukas Norbutas, and Rense Corten. 2017. "Order without Law: Reputation Promotes Cooperation in a Cryptomarket for Illegal Drugs." *European Sociological Review* 33(6): 752–764.

Rapoport, Anatol, and Albert M. Chammah. 1965. *Prisoner's Dilemma. A Study of Conflict and Cooperation*. Ann Arbor: University of Michigan Press.

Resnick, Paul, Richard Zeckhauser, Eric Friedman, and Ko Kuwabara. 2000. "Reputation Systems." *Communications of the ACM* 43(12): 45–48.

Resnick, Paul, Richard Zeckhauser, John Swanson, and Kate Lockwood. 2006. "The Value of Reputation on eBay: A Controlled Experiment." *Experimental Economics* 9: 79–101.

Roddie, Charles. 2018. "Reputation in Game Theory". In *Handbook of Gossip and Reputation*, edited by Francesca Giardini and Rafael Wittek, New York: Oxford University Press.

Shapiro, Carl. 1983. "Premiums for High Quality Products as Return to Reputation." *Quarterly Journal of Economics* 98(4): 659–680.

Siamwalla, Ammar. 1978. "Farmers and Middlemen: Aspects of Agricultural Marketing in Thailand." *Economic Bulletin for Asia and the Pacific* 29(1): 38–50.

Sommerfeld, Ralf D., Hans-Jürgen Krambeck, Dirk Semmann, and Manfred Milinski. 2007. "Gossip as an Alternative for Direct Observation in Games of Indirect Reciprocity." *Proceedings of the National Academy of Sciences of the USA* 104(44): 17435–17440.

Soska, Kyle, and Nicolas Christin. 2015. "Measuring the Longitudinal Evolution of the Online Anonymous Marketplace Ecosystem." In *24th Usenix Security Symposium (Usenix Security 15)*, 33–48. Washington, DC: USENIX Association.

Temin, Peter. 2013. *The Roman Market Economy*. Princeton, NJ: Princeton University Press.

Trivers, Robert L. 1971. "The Evolution of Reciprocal Altruism." *Quarterly Review of Biology* 46(1): 35–57.

Voss, Thomas. 1998. "Vertrauen in Modernen Gesellschaften. Eine Spieltheoretische Analyse." In *Der Transformationsprozess: Analysen Und Befunde Aus Dem Leipziger Institut Für Soziologie*, edited by R. Metze, K. Mühler, and K.-D. Opp, 91–129. Leipzig: Leipziger Universitätsverlag.

Weber, Max. [1920] 2002. *The Protestant Ethic and the Spirit of Capitalism*. Oxford: Blackwell.

Werner, Rachel M. and David A. Asch. 2005. "The Unintended Consequences of Publicly Reporting Quality Information." *Journal of the American Medical Association* 293(10): 1239–1244.

Wu, Junhui, Daniel Balliet, and Paul A. M. van Lange. 2016. "Gossip Versus Punishment: The Efficiency of Reputation to Promote and Maintain Cooperation." *Scientific Reports* 6: 23919.

CHAPTER 21

....................................................................................

# THE ECONOMICS OF GOSSIP AND COLLECTIVE REPUTATION

....................................................................................

## FEDERICO BOFFA AND STEFANO CASTRIOTA

## REPUTATION

....................................................................................

### Individual, Collective, and Institutional Reputation

REPUTATION develops in situations of asymmetric information where principals (buyers) cannot observe all the relevant attributes of the agent's (seller's) product, behavior, or skills before (in which case we talk about "adverse selection") or after (in which case we talk about "moral hazard") purchase/transaction. Through observations of past performance, experience with other sellers, gossips, and so on, agents form their expectation about the future. In this vein, Cabral (2005) defines *reputation* as the situation "when agents believe a particular agent to be something," while Bar Isaac and Tadelis (2008) define *reputation* as the beliefs about seller's skills and behavior. Therefore, it is important to emphasize that a seller's reputation—being related to the *expectation* of the quality of the goods or services they will provide—is certainly correlated with quality but often not coincident. Word-of-mouth phenomena and advertising campaigns can influence people's perceptions and opinions. This may produce a bias, especially when the number of interactions is limited or the level of buyers' expertise is low.

Economic theories of reputation show why rational buyers care about sellers' reputations. They broadly belong to two main groups, which regard reputation as a coordination device and as a Bayesian updating process, respectively. The first view is pioneered by the works of Klein and Leffler (1981) and Shapiro (1983). Here, buyers play an active role in 'punishing' sellers when there is a perception that sellers have not lived up to expectations. In the second view, pioneered by the works of Kreps and Wilson (1982), reputation is modelled as a Bayesian updating process: based on the observation of past transactions, buyers form a belief about the type of seller they interact with. Both approaches imply, from the buyers' perspective, a positive correlation between reputation and incentives to preserve a high reputation.

We may regard reputation as coming from three sources:

(i) *Individual reputation*—which is built and carried by single agents—is ubiquitous and can concern firms (Kreps, 1990), banks (Gorton, 1996), central banks (Barro and Gordon, 1983), minority shareholders (Gomes, 2000), managers (Yermack, 2004), public debt managers (Drudi and Prati, 2000), participants to auctions (Houser and Wooders, 2006), internal auditors (Sridhar, 1994), Supreme Courts (Caldeira, 1983), and even Countries with respect to military disputes (Orme, 1992; Crescenzi et al., 2007).

(ii) *Collective reputation* is built and especially carried by groups or coalitions of agents. When agents appear as a *group*, for example as producers of the same region or country, they usually provide goods of a certain quality or consistently display a certain pattern of behavior (e.g., effort and ethics at work). As pointed out by Fishman et al. (2008), geographical names have been used to identify high-quality products since ancient times, for example Corinthian wines and Sicilian honey. Here producers worked in *isolation*—without coordination or agreed rules—but within the same region, and they ended up with a common/shared reputation. Modern examples involve products associated with countries, such as Japanese and German cars, Italian fashion, and American internet companies, and to smaller regions, especially when they form industrial districts or clusters of firms, such as Bohemian crystals or Limoges porcelain vases.

When, instead, agents form a *coalition*, they share an official brand that cannot be exploited by non-members, define production disciplines (often in the form of minimum quality standards), and impose some forms of quality control. Coalitions of producers with shared rules and brand are very common in the agri-food (e.g., Parma ham or Parmigiano and Brie cheese) and wine (e.g., Barolo, Champagne, or Rioja) sectors.

A final case of collective reputation is that of franchise companies, where franchisors allow franchisees to use their brand and sell products according to some predefined quality standards and rules (e.g., McDonald's). Franchisors are allowed to make controls and eventually give fines or stop the collaboration with franchisees if the latter do not respect the agreements.

Collective reputations may be hard to preserve, due to the reputation externalities that each member of the group or coalition exerts on all the other members, under decentralized decision making. The severity of the problem is exacerbated when agents form a group rather than a coalition, in which case it is hard to sanction producers who do not adequately contribute to the public good of reputation.

Individual and collective reputation are not independent. In his paper on organized sets of producers, Tirole (1996) provides a seminal model on collective reputation persistence and on the way in which the incentives of group members are influenced by the group's reputation. He studies the joint dynamics of individual and collective reputation and shows a channel through which group behavior emerges. In his work, new members joining a group "inherit" the good or bad reputation of the coalition. Principals observe only imperfectly each agent's previous history. In the Social Sciences the principal–agent problem occurs when one person or entity (the "agent") can make decisions on behalf of, or that affect, another person or entity (the "principal"). Examples in economics include managers and company shareholders, sellers and buyers, and so on. Each agent trades off shirking and accumulating a good reputation. The value of reputation depends on the type of activity performed by the principal. Principals may choose either activities that potentially yield a high value (but that are more sensitive to reputation) or activities that provide a low value of the match (which are less sensitive to reputation). It turns out that, when group reputation is bad, principals have an incentive to choose activities yielding a lower reward but that are less sensitive to reputation, and agents, in turn, have an incentive not to accumulate reputation as if they correctly anticipated its low future value.

In Gergaud and Livat (2004), collective reputation is modelled as an aggregate of its most famous members and, as in Tirole (1996), individual and collective reputations influence each other.

Our background is economics, therefore the theories and the examples come from economics, especially from the agri-food sector. However, collective reputation can be relevant in social sciences, for example, with respect to the beliefs of people on the behavior and mentality of the citizens of different countries.

(iii) *Institutional reputation* is provided by international, national, regional and local institutions acting as institutional certifiers. It primarily applies, again, to the agri-food and wine sectors where, for instance, the European Union created a pyramidal classification system. The peak includes a minority of top products classified as Protected Designations of Origin (PDOs). They are followed by Protected Geographical Indications (PGIs), supposedly with a lower quality level, while products outside these two categories (including, for example, table wines) should be of the lowest quality.

This classification system represents an institutional response to the information asymmetry between producers and consumers aimed at guaranteeing a minimum expected level of quality. In this case, therefore, firms and coalitions invest to create an institutional reputation, which is, however, ultimately provided by public authorities in their role of certifiers. Thus, public authorities provide uninformed consumers with a possibly useful proxy for quality (Castriota and Delmastro, 2015): if a buyer has no time or resources to collect information, she can reduce the uncertainty by relying on an institutional signal.

Institutional reputation is related to collective reputation since the PDOs and the PGIs are awarded to coalitions; however, it differs because of the involvement of the public sector. Furthermore, even though collective and institutional reputation are correlated, they are not necessarily coincident. Public certifiers providing institutional reputation may, in some instances, have different perceptions of quality than the market, which determines collective reputation. Together, institutional and collective reputation may be termed as regional reputation (Schamel, 2009).

# Importance of Reputation

Why is reputation so crucial for firms? In his seminal paper, Akerlof (1970) demonstrates that markets can fail when there is asymmetric information and sellers cannot reliably signal product quality. This is true especially for "experience" goods and services, that is, whose quality is ascertained only after purchase upon consumption. However, the asymmetric information problem can be mitigated by the seller's reputation, which obviously comes at a cost. "Reputations are assets in which individuals and firms invest, requiring them to trade short-term pay-offs for long-term benefits" (Wilson, 1985).

Over the last three decades, a number of theoretical studies have predicted a positive effect of seller reputation on prices (see, among others, Klein and Leffler, 1981; Shapiro, 1983; Rogerson, 1983; Allen, 1984; Houser and Wooders, 2006). At the same time, a number of empirical (see, among others, Melnik and Alm, 2002; Cabral and Hortaçsu, 2010) and experimental (Keser, 2003; Resnick et al., 2006) papers confirm that the willingness to pay responds positively to the seller reputation. Reputation also affects the number of sales, as shown by Reinstein and Snyder (2005), who find that positive reviews by professional movie critics increase box office revenue and by Ye et al. (2009) with data from TaoBao.com, the largest online auction site in China. Not surprisingly, reputation also leads to superior financial performances (Roberts and Dowling, 2002) as measured by the Return on Assets. Price and sales premia are usually magnified in the agri-food sector since many attach value to regional traditions and are willing to pay a premium for them (Vogel, 1995).

A seller can strategically exploit its good reputation in a variety of ways. One of them is umbrella branding, that is the marketing practice to use a single brand name for the sale of two or more related products. An example can be the company Gillette which produces several different products under the same Gillette brand (men's safety razors and other personal care products such as shaving gels, foams, skin care, deodorants and shower gels). In a theoretical contribution Cabral (2000) shows that when a firm launches a new product, it uses the same name as its base product (reputation stretching) if and only if quality is sufficiently high. In this case stretching signals high quality and increases sales and/or price.

However, for non-experts it is often problematic to rely on individual reputation. When buying a bottle of wine, an unexperienced person would rely on the institutional signal; someone with a broader knowledge of the market would look for a famous collective brand; finally, the identification of the best firms and vintages requires a higher level of expertise (Fleckinger, 2007). Institutional and collective reputations are particularly relevant also when consumers want to economize on the costs of ascertaining quality (Andersson, 2002). When customers choose a product, they have to select the sources of information, as well as how deep to go in their search (Costanigro et al., 2010). Thus, the positive effect of collective and institutional reputation on price and sales has been shown by several empirical studies (see Oczkowski, 1994; Combris et al., 1997; Costanigro et al., 2007; San Martín et al., 2008; Cross et al., 2011 for the former and Combris et al., 1997; Corsi and Strøm, 2013 for the latter).

Another important advantage of a prestigious collective brand or an institutional certification involves economies of scale in building up reputation. Market concentration measures the extent to which sales in a market are dominated by one or more companies. The two most widely used indexes to capture market concentration are Concentration Ratios (CRn), given by the sum of the market shares of the $n$ largest companies, and the Herfindahl–Hirschman Index (HHI), given by the sum of the squared shares of all the companies in the market. When market concentration is low—like in agriculture—firm size tends to be so small that it often becomes too expensive to build an individual reputation. In such a context, collective brands and institutional signals become the only viable ways to reduce the information asymmetries. In fact, small producers reap the benefits from reputation without incurring all the costs that a company has to face when it seeks to establish it on an individual basis.

## Problems Connected with the Public Good Nature of Collective Reputation (and Possible Solutions)

An externality is a consequence caused by the activity of one agent to another agent and for which the former does not pay or receive a compensation. Externalities can be either positive or negative, the most relevant example being pollution, that is, negative consequences arising from consumption (e.g., transport) or production (i.e., factories). Collective branding may suffer from opportunistic behavior due to the reputational externalities it involves. Newcomers often end up taking advantage from the collective reputation accumulated by the existing members while not putting much effort, thereby free-riding on the accumulated asset.

As for firm reputation (see Rob and Fishman, 2005), size (in this case, of the coalition), at least in a certain range of values, is expected to have a positive impact on collective reputation, since a critical mass is required in order to be visible to the market. However, the effect of size on collective reputation may be non-linear: above a certain threshold, an increase in the number of coalition members likely generates coordination and free-riding problems. Albæk and Schultz (1998) point out that a too large group size can lead to overproduction as, under a decentralized decision making process, coalition members do not internalize the profit/loss incurred by other associates when the formers increase production.

In a similar vein, Fishman et al. (2008) claim that "If too many firms are admitted to the brand, the incentive to free ride necessarily overrides the reputation effect and reduces the incentive to invest, relative to stand-alone firms. This is because once the brand is sufficiently large, the marginal contribution of an individual member's investment to the brand's visibility and reputation becomes negligible, in comparison to the payoff from free riding." An additional rationalization of such non-linearity can be attributed to social norms, which become less effective as the number of community members increases (Kandori, 1992). In an empirical analysis of the determinants of the collective reputation of Italian wine appellations, Castriota and Delmastro (2015)—in line with the aforementioned studies—find a clear non-linear effect of number of coalition members: for a low enough number of firms, its increase makes the group more visible to the market; however, after a peak the collective reputation declines due to reputational externalities and the ensuing free-riding problems. Furthermore, a negative self-selection of newcomers might emerge and damage the leaders (see Becchetti et al., 2015 for a discussion of this problem in the Fair Trade sector).

While mitigation of the incentives to free-ride is difficult to achieve when agents are part of a group, it is easier to obtain when agents belong to a coalition. It may then be useful to move away from a decentralized decision-making process toward a centralized one. For instance, coalitions can establish an entry barrier when the number of members becomes excessive and/or when collective reputation increases. Free entry is not always optimal and should be allowed only in the early stages. A second possible solution is the introduction of minimum quality standards, that is, rules set by the public authorities or the firm associations aimed at guaranteeing that the quality of the goods or the services provided reaches a minimum expected level. Even though minimum quality standards are sometimes blamed for the lack of competition in professional sectors such as lawyers or notaries, their stated goal is to increase the average quality of the product or service.

In a theoretical contribution Rouvière and Soubeyran (2008) show that free entry is not optimal and advocate regulation through the introduction of minimum quality standards. The importance of minimum quality standards to create and preserve the group reputation is empirically tested by Castriota and Delmastro (2015). Minimum quality standards display a significant effect on the prestige of wine appellations both when they are compulsory and when they are achieved on a voluntary basis. In the first case all producers must respect the standards, otherwise they cannot use the collective brand. In the second, producers are not obliged to, but spontaneously decide to increase the quality to get an additional award on the label, like "Riserva" when they age the wine for some additional months in wooden barrels.

However, entry barriers and minimum quality standards are often useless unless supported by frequent and effective controls and high penalties. Lippert and Spagnolo (2011) theoretically analyze the optimal network structure under collective reputation. They study networks of relations, which are the links through which soft information, that is, information whose truthfulness of sent messages cannot be verified by partners or third parties, can flow. The value of a network lies in its ability to enforce agreements that could not be sustained without the information and sanctioning power provided by other network members.

With the development of internet and digital platforms as an expanding sales channel a relevant question arises: which measures do platforms undertake to preserve the collective reputation of their members and, simultaneously, its own reputation? In principle, the level of intervention could range from that of a laissez-faire platform, equivalent to decentralized decision making process within the group or the coalition, to that of an interventionist platform, equivalent to centralized decision making process within the group or the coalition. An interventionist platform accurately selects its members, either directly, by expelling those that do not conform to some standards, or indirectly, by sanctioning them. A laissez-faire platform does not tackle the reputational externalities, presumably considering them as a necessary bad.

As Nosko and Tadelis (2015) point out, as a platform shifts from a more intervention-ist to a more laissez-faire approach, it trades off quality in favor of variety. eBay's recently shifted toward a more interventionist approach by introducing a buyer protection pro-gram that imposes a monetary sanction on low-quality seller. The program increased efficiency and had a positive impact on welfare by an estimated 2.9 percent (Hui et al., 2016). The sanctioning approach meant to preserve collective reputation and support long-run relationships is not a novelty of the online feedback system. In fact, Greif (1989) documents the importance of coalitions as sanctioning mechanisms that have greatly contributed to sustaining long distance trade in the Mediterranean during the Middle Ages (see also Diekman and Przepiorka, this volume). Finally, Castriota and Delmastro (2015) show that the frequency of controls (measured as the percentage of wineries controlled each year) and the average amount of penalties per number of administrative notifications (measured in thousand euros per penalty each year) are positive drivers of collective reputation in the wine sector.

## Problems Connected with the Weakening Information Content of the Collective and Institutional Reputations (and Possible Solutions)

Establishing collective brands implies a number of advantages, especially to small pro-ducers who do not have the size and the resources to build their own reputation. However, an excessive variety of collective brands is confusing to consumers, especially to the usually majoritarian share of non-experts. In Italy, for example, over the last half century the number of wine appellations has grown to around 500, each with a different collective reputation. Some have received the PDO recognition by the Ministry of Agriculture because of the achieved prestige. Therefore, on average, PDO wines are better than PGI, which, in turn, are supposedly better than table wines. However, the legal procedure to obtain a PDO is long, complex, uncertain, and it requires a lot of lobbying activity. This sometimes makes the PDO a weak or inaccurate representation of quality and reputation.[1] Furthermore, once obtained, the award is currently like a title of nobility. It is permanent and cannot be withdrawn irrespectively of the future evolu-tion of the quality provided.

Finally, top producers may at times have an incentive to choose not to use the collective label—and consequently the PDO or PGI award—and rather produce a table wine, thus relying only on their individual reputation. This happens when they prefer to produce wine according to their own criteria (without following the rigid rules imposed by the legal requirements of the wine appellation), or when they believe that their own brand is more prestigious than the collective one (Yu et al., 2016). In this case, they renounce both the collective (e.g., Barolo or Amarone della Valpolicella) and the institutional (e.g., the PDO) reputation. As a result, the correlation between the PDO recognition and the collective reputation, along with the value of PDO as a signal of quality, have somewhat weakened over time, pushing many observers to invoke a reform.

The problem of the excessive number of collective brands can be solved only by the public authorities since coalitions will hardly suppress them, even when the level of reputation is at a minimum. As to the growing share of wine awarded with the institutional brand, a possible solution—presumably difficult to implement out of political economy considerations—could consist in allowing only a share (e.g., 10 or 20 percent) of the total production to receive the PDO award and perform evaluations on a regular (e.g., 3 years) basis. Such a system, similar to a sport championship, would allow some consortia to improve their ranking while others would worsen it, being downgraded to the PGI group (Castriota, 2015).

# Gossip and Reputation

## Social Learning and Word-of-Mouth

The way sellers' reputation is built up and preserved has a lot to do with how information spreads among buyers. It is therefore relevant to understand how individuals learn from each other. This is the object of study of social learning—a growing field in economic theory—which may occur in a variety of forms. This section focuses on the relation between one form of social learning, namely word-of-mouth, and reputation. In fact, the notion of word-of-mouth seems close, possibly even overlapping, with the generally accepted notions of gossip. Furthermore, the economics literature on gossip is scarce, one of the few existing economics definitions being provided by Fehr and Sutter (2016) as "in a context of congeniality, the exchange of personal information (positive or negative) in an evaluative way (positive or negative) about absent third parties." The concept of gossip is much more investigated by social scientists (for a review, see Foster, 2004).

Word-of-mouth has a long tradition in the literature of economics and marketing (see, e.g., Coleman et al., 1966). Banerjee and Fudenberg (2004) provide the following example of a word-of-mouth situation, within an academic context: "Someone in your department tells you that one of your colleagues is about to move to another university. She also tells you that she is sufficiently worried about it that she has started to make contingency plans. You decide that the rumor is probably not true and that contingency plans are unnecessary, but when you run into another colleague in the corridor, you pass on the story, adding that you do not think it's worth worrying about. Because you are rushing off to a meeting, you do not actually tell him how you came about the story. And so the story spreads. . . ."

Under word-of-mouth, the conveyor gives her opinion, but she typically does not provide hard evidence for the fact, nor she details her arguments. The report can thus be biased by personal feelings, such as hope or fear, or can be plagued with misperceptions. The receiver of the word-of-mouth is aware of these limitations and knows she should not believe everything she was being told. With word-of-mouth, then, each person receives the piece of information only from a subset of other people, often peers or people with similar preferences. We can conclude that word-of-mouth closely resembles gossip.

A natural and important question to ask is, then, how does word-of-mouth affect learning? As a result of word-of-mouth propagation, not always people come to agree. Applied to the context of reputation, not always buyers exposed to (both online and off-line) word-of-mouth end up sharing the same perceptions on sellers. This is reminiscent of a stylized fact in the political economics literature, that is, people persistently disagree on objective facts. Disagreement is structured mostly along partisan lines. A plausible explanation has to do with polarization, in particular to the fact that people tend to be exposed to like-minded people (a phenomenon known as homophily) and to like-minded news sources (see, for instance, Gentzkow and Shapiro, 2011; Bakshy, Messing, and Adamic, 2015).

## Word-of-Mouth and Individual Reputation

Word-of-mouth is a powerful determinant of reputation building. Moretti (2011) finds that the movies consumption decisions depend on information they receive from their peers, when quality is ex-ante uncertain. Duflo and Saez (2002) and Sorensen (2006) show that an employee's retirement and health plan choices affect the retirement and health plan choices of other employees in the same academic department. Cai, Chen and Fang (2009) show that customers that receive information about a restaurant's most popular dishes tend to order those dishes.

Word-of-mouth has gained additional prominence with the Internet. Given significant analogies between traditional offline word-of-mouth and online review systems (e.g., Tripadvisor, eBay, etc.), online feedback mechanism can be regarded as a "digitization of word-of-mouth" (Dellarocas, 2003). The information propagation mechanism is very similar in both cases. In the online review system, people do not usually provide hard evidence for their claims and reviews may be biased by personal feelings or by misperceptions. Also, since products or services usually have multiple characteristics, the summary judgement by the reviewer is affected by her own priorities over the various features of the product/services. Finally, while each user may look at a summary statistics (e.g., the average valuation of the product), she usually selects few comments to look deeper into. Differently than offline word-of-mouth, however, in the digital version the receiver may not know the identity of the sender and therefore may not make inference on the validity of the report based on that.

The empirical evidence on the relation between online word of mouth and reputation is expanding. Chevalier and Mayzlin (2006) finds that a book that has better reviews on Amazon.com than it does on bn.com tends to sell better on Amazon.com than it does on bn.com. A series of studies on eBay seller ratings consistently find that sellers with better ratings attract more bids or experience higher auction prices (Melnik and Alm, 2002; Jin and Kato, 2006; Resnick et al., 2006; Lucking-Reiley et al., 2007).

Cabral and Hortaçsu (2010) construct a panel of eBay seller histories for four representative products (an IBM ThinkPad notebook computer, two collectible coins, and the 1998 Holiday Teddy Beanie Babies—toys that soon became collectibles). In their analysis of eBay reputation mechanism, they find a strong effect of sellers' reputation on sales. This exhibits an interesting pattern. The effect of the first negative review for a seller who had none before is large and significant. On average, each seller's sales increase by a weekly 5 percent before the first negative review, then drop by 8 percent after it (amounting to a 13 percent difference). They also find that a seller is more likely to leave eBay the lower his reputation is. Before exiting, sellers tend to receive more negative feedbacks than their lifetime average. Overall, results in Cabral and Hortaçsu (2010) suggest a positive correlation between the level of reputation and the incentives to invest in reputation. Until the seller has a perfect record, his incentives to invest in reputation are high. After the first negative review, reputation drops significantly, and so do the incentives to invest in reputation. Considering the nature of the eBay market, and based on their own experience of interacting and talking to eBay traders, the authors believe that the aforementioned type of model à la Kreps and Wilson (1982) provides a more accurate description of their data (see also Snijders and Matzat, this volume).

Results by Cabral and Hortaçsu (2010) are rationalized in Rob and Fishman's (2005) subsequent paper, which proposes a model of incentives to invest in reputation. They consider informational frictions—such as search costs—that induce only a gradual diffusion of information about firms' past performance, consistently with a word of mouth propagation mechanism. A deterioration in the quality of the product of a large firm with a good reputation would immediately be known to a large audience. Such a firm has a lot to lose by not living up to the expectations of high quality and, as a result, has strong incentives to preserve its reputation. On the other hand, a deterioration in quality for a firm with a smaller customer base would be less well-known, as it would not be much propagated, so that its incentives to preserve its reputation are weaker. Rob and Fishman (2005) predict that companies start out small and invest little in reputation. Successful firms get larger, and so do their investment to build and preserve their reputation.

Word-of-mouth phenomena and repeated purchases request a long time span to generate valuable effects on the buyers' opinions. Furthermore, it takes time for a coalition to set proper quality standards and production techniques Therefore, age turns out being an important variable in collective reputation building (see Castriota and Delmastro, 2015 for empirical evidence from the collective reputation of wine appellations).

## Word-of-Mouth and Collective Reputation

A question is now in order: is offline and online word-of-mouth a determinant of collective reputation as well? The answer is: to some extent, yes. Nosko and Tadelis (2015) discuss some relevant and interesting features of the buyers' behavior on online platforms (in their example, eBay). One of them has to do with possible reputational externalities. A reputational externality emerges if, after a disappointing transaction, a buyer updates his beliefs about the quality of all sellers on the platform (rather than about the quality of that individual seller only) and, therefore, in some sense, on the quality of the platform itself. A reputational externality across sellers thus emerges in the market. With reputational externalities, reputation is no longer a feature of the individual seller, but it becomes a collective good of all the sellers in the platform. Nosko and Tadelis (2015), using eBay data recording reviews as well as buyers' retention, show that buyers respond to low-quality transactions by choosing to leave the platform. This is consistent with a mechanism based on a reputational externality, which implies collective reputation. An effective platform should actively take care of preserving its own reputation by sanctioning the members who contribute, with their misbehavior, to its deterioration. How can platforms overcome the reputational externalities? As previously discussed, by centralizing the decision process. Of course, this comes at a cost (Bresnahan and Greenstein, 2014).

## Problems with Fakery in Word-of-Mouth (and Possible Solutions)

The issue of online fakery is crucial. It has recently become even more salient in relation to Facebook's fake news that have apparently deeply affected the 2016 United States presidential elections. In the online reviews system, fakery has traditionally been associated to non-authentic reviews performed to manipulate sellers' reputation for strategic reasons. Anderson and Magruder (2012) study the restaurant reviews website Yelp.com and show that a rating increase by a half-star decreases significantly and substantially the restaurants reservation availability, implying that it increases the number of clients. An extra half-star rating causes restaurants to sell out 19 percent more frequently. This may raise incentives to non-authentic (fake) reviews. Evidence of them is searched for, but not detected, by Anderson and Magruder (2012).

It is, instead, detected by Mayzlin, Dover, and Chevalier (2014). They undertake an empirical analysis of promotional reviews and examine both the extent to which fakery occurs and the market conditions that encourage or discourage them. Specifically, they exploit the organizational differences between Expedia.com and TripAdvisor.com. While anyone can post a review on TripAdvisor, a consumer can only post a review of a hotel on Expedia if she actually booked at least one night at the hotel through the website. A fake review is less costly on Tripadvisor than it is on Expedia, which is expected to provide differential incentives to fakery across the two platforms. Mayzlin, Dover, and Chevalier (2014) show that hotels with a nearby neighbor have more one- and two-star (negative) reviews on TripAdvisor relative to Expedia. They then argue, out of differential reputation concerns, that the net gains from fake reviewing are likely to be highest for independent hotels that are owned by single-unit owner and lowest for branded chain hotels owned by multi-unit owners. They find that hotels that are neighbors of hotels with a high incentive to fake have more one- and two-star (negative) reviews on

TripAdvisor relative to Expedia than do hotels whose neighbors have a low incentive to fake. Also, hotels with a high incentive to fake have a greater share of five-star (positive) reviews on TripAdvisor relative to Expedia.

Luca and Zervas (2016) analyze the link between fake reviews and reputation in a recent paper. They use the fact that the Yelp platform has an algorithm that filters suspicious reviews and analyze the filtered reviews. Suspicious reviews occur often (roughly 16 percent of the time) and their frequency is increasing over time. They tend to be more extreme (favorable or unfavorable) than the average. The authors ask if reputation has an effect on the propensity of the restaurant to solicit fake reviews. The answer is yes. A restaurant is more likely to commit review fraud when its reputation is weak, that is, when it has few reviews or it has recently received bad reviews. Chain restaurants, whose reputation follows different channels than independently operated restaurants, are also less likely to commit review fraud. Luca and Zervas (2016) find that when restaurants face increased competition, they become more likely to receive unfavorable fake reviews.

Fake reviews undermine the reputational value of reviews, as do "reciprocal" reviews, that is, reviews done with the single purpose of reciprocating a good (or bad) review received. Bolton, Greiner, and Ockenfels (2013) suggest changes to the way feedback information flows through the system, to overcome the problem of reciprocal reviews. Again, eliminating fake reviews requires additional control on the coalition members, which probably calls for more centralized decision processes. Of course, one must reckon that centralized decision processes come at a cost, since it is clear that information is optimally used when it is decentralized.

In general, fakery is a very serious problem that can deeply affect political and economic outcomes. There are two issues at stake here: desirability and feasibility. As to desirability, many observers request a public control of the quality of the information released, especially over the internet. However, when a public agency verifies the reliability of the source and the validity of the news—especially on politically sensitive issues—the borderline between control and censorship becomes dangerously thin. As to feasibility, it has nowadays become much more difficult to prevent fakery since traditional media can be controlled but digital word-of-mouth cannot. Billions of people have access to the internet and can give their opinion without providing hard evidence for the facts nor the details of their arguments.

# CONCLUSIONS

The Internet has fundamentally changed the way reputation is built and preserved. Digital word-of-mouth has complemented traditional forms of collective and institutional reputations. Large private platforms, with their sophisticated online feedback systems, are gaining prominence as certifiers. Peer-to-peer is also emerging as a dominant channel through which reputation spreads. A somehow natural question—which future research will have to address—has to do with whether digital reputation will make collective and institutional reputation obsolete.

# NOTE

1. Without any reform, the share of products awarded the highest honor (PDO) has risen so much that the institutional signal is becoming useless ("todos caballeros," all knights [gentlemen]).

# REFERENCES

Akerlof, G. 1970. "The Market for 'Lemons': Quality Uncertainty and the Market Mechanism." *The Quarterly Journal of Economics* 84(3): 488–500.

Albæk, S. and Schultz, C. 1998. "On the Relative Advantage of Cooperatives." *Economics Letters* 59(3): 397–401.

Allen, F. 1984. "Reputation and Product Quality." *The RAND Journal of Economics* 15(3): 311–327.

Andersson, F. 2002. "Pooling Reputations." *International Journal of Industrial Organization* 20(5): 715–730.

Anderson, M. and Magruder, J. 2012. "Learning from the Crowd: Regression Discontinuity Estimates of the Effects of an Online Review Database." *The Economic Journal* 122 (563): 957–989.

Bakshy, E., Messing, S. and Adamic, L. 2015. "Exposure to Ideologically Diverse News and Opinions on Facebook." *Science* 348 (6239): 1130–1132.

Banerjee, A. and Fudenberg, D. 2004. "Word of Mouth Learning." *Games and Economic Behavior* 46(1): 1–22.

Bar-Isaac, H. and Tadelis, S. 2008. "Seller Reputation." *Foundations and Trends in Microeconomics* 4(4)273–351.

Barro, R. and Gordon, D. 1983. "Rules, Discretion, and Reputation in a Model of Monetary Policy." *Journal of Monetary Economics* 12(1): 101–121.

Becchetti, L., Castriota, S., and Conzo, P. 2015. "Quantitative Analysis of the Impacts of Fair Trade." In *Handbook of Research on Fair Trade*, edited by L. Raynolds and E. Bennett,. Cheltenam, UK: Edward Elgar.

Bolton, G., Greiner, B., and Ockenfels, A. 2013. "Engineering Trust: Reciprocity in the Production of Reputation Information." *Management Science* 59(2): 265–285.

Bresnahan, T. and Greenstein, S. 2014. "Mobile Computing: The Next Platform Rivalry." *American Economic Review* 104(5): 475–480.

Cabral, L. 2000. "Stretching Firm and Brand Reputation." *The RAND Journal of Economics* 31 (4): 658–673.

Cabral, L. 2005. "The Economics of Trust and Reputation: A Primer," New York University, Working Paper.

Cabral, L. and Hortaçsu, A. 2010. "The Dynamics of Seller Reputation: Evidence from eBay." *Journal of Industrial Economics* 58(1): 54–78.

Cai, H., Chen, Y., and Fang, H. 2009. "Observational Learning: Evidence from a Randomized Natural Field Experiment." *American Economic Review* 99(3): 864–882.

Caldeira, G. A. 1983. "On the Reputation of State Supreme Courts." *Political Behavior*, 5(1): 83–108.

Castriota, S. 2015. *Economia del Vino*. Milan Italy: EGEA-Bocconi University Press.

Castriota, S. and Delmastro, M. 2015. "The Economics of Collective Reputation: Evidence from the Wine Industry." *American Journal of Agricultural Economics*, 97(2): 469–489.

Chevalier, J. and Mayzlin, D. 2006. "The Effect of Word-of-Mouth on Sale: Online Book Reviews." *Journal of Marketing Research*, 43(3): 345–354.

Coleman, J. S., Katz, E. and Menzel, H. 1966. *Medical Innovation: A Diffusion Study*. Indianapolis, IN: Bobbs-Merrill.

Combris, P., Lecocq, S., and Visser, M. 1997. "Estimation of a Hedonic Price Equation for Bordeaux Wine: Does Quality Matter?" *Economic Journal*, 107(441): 390–402.

Corsi, A. and Strøm, S. 2013. "The Price Premium for Organic Wines: Estimating a Hedonic Farm-Gate Price Equation." *Journal of Wine Economics*, 8(1): 29–48.

Costanigro, M., McCluskey, J. J., and Goemans, C, 2010. "The Economics of Nested Names: Name Specificity, Reputation and Price Premia." *American Journal of Agriculture Economics*, 92(5): 1339–1350.

Costanigro, M., McCluskey, J. J., and Mittelhammer, R. C. 2007. "Segmenting the Wine Market Based on Price: Hedonic Regression When Different Prices Mean Different Products." *Journal of Agricultural Economics*, 58(3): 454–466.

Crescenzi, M. J. C., Kathman, J. D., and Long, S. B. 2007. "Reputation, History, and War." *Journal of Peace Research*, 44(6): 651–667.

Cross, R., Plantinga, A. J., and Stavins, R. N. 2011. "What Is the Value of Terroir?" *American Economic Review: Papers & Proceedings*, 101(3): 152–156.

Dellarocas, C. 2003. "The Digitization of Word-of-Mouth: Promise and Challenges of Online Feedback Mechanisms." *Management Science*, 49(10): 1407–1424.

Diekman, A., Przepiorka, W. 2019. "Trust and reputation in markets." In F. Giardini and R. P. M. Wittek (Eds.), *Handbook of gossip and reputation*. New York: Oxford University Press.

Drudi, F. and Prati, A. 2000. "Signaling Fiscal Regime Sustainability." *European Economic Review*, 44(10): 1897–1930.

Duflo, E. and Saez, E. 2002. "Participation and Investment Decisions in a Retirement Plan: The Influence of Colleagues' Choices." *Journal of Public Economics*, 85: 121–148.

Fehr, D. and Sutter, M. 2016. "Gossip and the Efficiency of Interactions." IZA Discussion Paper No. 9704.

Fishman, A., Finkelshtain, I., Simhon, A., and Yacouel, N. 2008. "The Economics of Collective Brands." Discussion Paper, 14.08, Hebrew University of Jerusalem.

Fleckinger, P. 2007. "Collective Reputation and Market Structure: Regulating the Quality vs. Quantity Trade-off." Discussion Paper, Ecole Polytechnique. Available at https://hal.archives-ouvertes.fr/hal-00243080

Foster, E. K. 2004. "Research on Gossip: Taxonomy, Methods, and Future Directions." *Review of General Psychology*, 8(2): 78–99.

Gentzkow, M. and Shapiro, J. M. 2011. "Ideological Segregation Online and Offline." *Quarterly Journal of Economics*, 126(4): 1799–1839.

Gergaud, O. and Livat, F. 2004. "Team Versus Individual Reputations: A Model of Interaction and Some Empirical Evidence." Université de Reims Champagne, Ardenne Working Paper.

Gomes, A. 2000. "Going Public without Governance: Managerial Reputation Effects." *The Journal of Finance*, 55(2): 615–646.

Gorton, G. 1996. "Reputation Formation in Early Bank Note Markets." *Journal of Political Economy*, 104(2): 346–397.

Greif, A. 1989. "Reputation and Coalitions in Medieval Trade: Evidence on the Maghribi Traders." *Journal of Economic History*, Vo. 49(4): 857–882.

Houser, D. and Wooders, J. 2006. "Reputation in Auctions: Theory and Evidence from eBay." *Journal of Economics and Management Strategy*, 15(2): 353–369.

Hui, X., Saeedi, M., Shen, Z., and Sundaresan, N. 2016. "Reputation and Regulations. Evidence from eBay." *Management Science*, 62(12): 3604–3616.

Jin, G. Z. and Kato, A. 2006. "Price, Quality and Reputation: Evidence from an Online Field Experiment." *RAND Journal of Economics*, 37(4): 983–1005.

Kandori, M. 1992. "Social Norms and Community Enforcement." *Review of Economic Studies*, 59(1): 63–80.

Keser, C. 2003. "Experimental Games for the Design of Reputation Management Systems." *IBM Systems Journal*, 42(3): 498–506.

Klein, B. and Leffler, K. B. 1981. "The Role of Market Forces in Assuring Contractual Performance." *Journal of Political Economy*, 89(4): 615–641.

Kreps, D. M. 1990. "Corporate Culture and Economic Theory." In J. Alt and K. Shepsle (Eds.), *Perspectives on Positive Political Economy*. Cambridge: Cambridge University Press.

Kreps, D. M. and Wilson, R. 1982. "Reputation and Imperfect Information." *Journal of Economic Theory*, 27(2): 253–279.

Lippert, S. and Spagnolo, G. 2011. "Networks of Relations and Word-of-Mouth Communication." *Games and Economic Behavior*, 72(1): 202–217.

Luca, M. and Zervas, G. 2016. "Fake It Till You Make It: Reputation, Competition, and Yelp Review Fraud." *Management Science*, 62(12): 3412–3427.

Lucking-Reiley, D., Bryan, D., Prasad, N., and Reeves, D. 2007. "Pennies from eBay: The Determinants of Price in Online Auctions." *Journal of Industrial Economics*, 55(12): 223–233.

Mayzlin, D., Dover, Y., and Chevalier, J. 2014. "Promotional Reviews: An Empirical Investigation of Online Review Manipulation." *American Economic Review*, 104(8): 2421–2455.

Melnik, M. and Alm, J. 2002. "Does a Seller's Ecommerce Reputation Matter? Evidence from eBay Auctions." *The Journal of Industrial Economics*, 50(3): 337–349.

Moretti, E. 2011. "Social Learning and Peer Effects in Consumption: Evidence from Movie Sales." *Review of Economic Studies*, 78(1): 356–393.

Nosko, C. and Tadelis, S. 2015. "The Limits of Reputation in Platform Markets." NBER Working Papers.

Oczkowski, E. 1994. "A Hedonic Price Function for Australian Premium Table Wine." *Australian Journal of Agricultural Economics*, 38(1): 93–110.

Orme, J. D. 1992. *Deterrence Reputation and Cold War Cycles*. New York: Palgrave Macmillan.

Reinstein, D. and Snyder, C. 2005. "The Influence of Expert Reviews on Consumer Demand for Experience Goods: A Case Study of Movie Critics." *The Journal of Industrial Economics*, 53(1): 27–51.

Resnick, P., Zeckhauser, R., Swanson, J. and Lockwood, K. 2006. "The Value of Reputation on eBay: A Controlled Experiment." *Experimental Economics*, 9(2): 79–101.

Rob, R. and Fishman, A. 2005. "Is Bigger Better? Customer Base Expansion through Word-of-Mouth Reputation." *Journal of Political Economy*, 113(5): 1146–1162.

Roberts, P. and Dowling, G. 2002. "Corporate Reputation and Sustained Superior Financial Performance." *Strategic Management Journal*, 23(12): 1077–1093.

Rogerson, W. 1983. "Reputation and Product Quality." *The Bell Journal of Economics*, 14(2): 508–516.

Rouvière, E. and Soubeyran, R. 2008. "Collective Reputation, Entry and Minimum Quality Standard." FEEM Working Paper No. 7. Available at SSRN: https://ssrn.com/abstract=1088296 or http://dx.doi.org/10.2139/ssrn.1088296

San Martín, G. J., Brümmer, B., and Troncoso, J. L. 2008. "Determinants of Argentinean Wine Prices in the U.S. Market." American Association of Wine Economists, AAWE Working Paper No. 15. (http://www.wine-economics.org/aawe/wp-content/uploads/2012/10/AAWE_WP15.pdf)

Schamel, G. 2009. "Dynamic Analysis of Brand and Regional Reputation: The Case of Wine." *Journal of Wine Economics*, 41: 62–80.

Shapiro, C. 1983. "Premiums for High Quality Products as Returns to Reputations," *The Quarterly Journal of Economics*, 98(4): 659–680.

Snijders, C., Matzat, U. 2019. "Online Reputation Systems," In F. Giardini and R. P. M. Wittek (Eds.), *Handbook of gossip and reputation*. New York: Oxford University Press.

Sorensen, A. T. 2006. "Social Learning and Health Plan Choice." *RAND Journal of Economics*, 37(4): 929–945.

Sridhar, S. 1994. "Managerial Reputation and Internal Reporting." *The Accounting Review*, 69(2): 343–363.

Tirole, J. 1996. "A Theory of Collective Reputations with Applications to the Persistence of Corruption and to Firm Quality," *Review of Economic Studies*, 63(1): 1–22.

Vogel, D. 1995. *Trading up. Consumer and Environmental Regulation in a Global Economy*. Cambridge, MA: Harvard University Press.

Wilson, R. 1985. "Reputations in Games and Markets." In A. E. Roth (Ed.), *Game-Theoretic Models of Bargaining*, : 65–84. New York: Cambridge University Press.

Ye, Q., Li, Y., Kiang, M., and Wu, W. 2009. "The Impact of Seller Reputation on the Performance of Online Sales: Evidence from TaoBao Buy-It-Now BIN Data." *ACM SIGMIS Database*, 40(1): 12–19.

Yermack, D. 2004. "Retention, and Reputation Incentives for Outside Directors," *Journal of Finance*, 59(5): 2281–2308.

Yu, J., Bouamra-Mechemache, Z., and Zago, A. 2016. "What's in a Name? Information, Heterogeneity, and Quality in a Theory of Nested Names." TSE Working Papers 17-866, Toulouse School of Economics (TSE).

CHAPTER 22

# ANTECEDENTS AND CONSEQUENCES OF GOSSIP IN WORK GROUPS

## BIANCA BEERSMA, GERBEN A. VAN KLEEF, AND MARIA T. M. DIJKSTRA

## INTRODUCTION

GROUPS are a breeding ground for gossip, and organizational work groups are no exception. Working in groups affords various benefits to group members, but it also poses serious challenges that may prompt group members to provide evaluative information about other group members who are not present—that is, to engage in gossip. In this chapter, we examine the relationship between gossip and work group functioning. In particular, we illuminate (1) how group dynamics give rise to gossip and (2) how gossip influences work group functioning. We use the terms "work group" and "team" interchangeably to refer to interdependent collections of individuals who share responsibility for specific organizational outcomes (Sundstrom, De Meuse, & Futrell, 1990).

Organizations increasingly structure work around teams (Garvey, 2002; Ilgen, 1999). From the perspective of the organization, group-based organizational structures are generally believed to facilitate adaptability, information exchange, learning, and control (e.g., Hollenbeck, Beersma, & Schouten, 2012; Hackman & Oldham, 1976). That is, groups tend to have more skills and have access to more knowledge than single individuals, and by pooling these skills and this knowledge, teamwork can provide performance gains that exceed the mere sum of individual members' performance (Hertel, 2011). In addition, the possibility of sharing ideas within the group is often believed to enhance creativity (Levine & Moreland, 1990), and this could in turn help organizations to come up with innovative solutions and as such adapt to a changing environment. Finally, working in teams reduces the cost of managerial control, as employees organized in teams are accountable to each other rather than to someone higher up in the organizational hierarchy (Crowley, Payne, & Kennedy, 2014). From the perspective of the individual worker, group work also offers several advantages. Through increased contact with co-workers, team-based structures enable higher levels of social-emotional and informational exchange, and these can benefit individual employees by facilitating interpersonal bonding, learning from one another, and the possibility to have a good time at work.

In spite of these advantages for organizations and individual workers, working in teams also has its difficulties. First, working with others in an interdependent setting makes social comparison salient (Beersma, Homan, Van Kleef, & De Dreu, 2013), and whereas comparing oneself to others may benefit self-assessment and self-verification (i.e. by enabling people to be known and understood by others according to their beliefs and feelings about themselves; Swann, 1983), individuals whose self-esteem is threatened by such comparisons may seek self-enhancement by for example downplaying others (Heatherton & Vohs, 2000).

Second, team-based work inherently means having to resolve tensions between cooperation and competition. Whereas in some situations, individual and collective interests are perfectly aligned, in many situations they are not, and in such social dilemma situations employees may be tempted to strive for their own rather than organizational goals (Beersma, Conlon, & Hollenbeck, 2007; Messick & Brewer 1983; Van Lange, Joireman, Parks, & Van Dijk, 2013). In order to achieve effective team performance, adaptability and organizational learning, it is essential that team members overcome the temptation to pursue their own goals and instead, cooperate with each other toward achieving the goals of the team (Beersma, Hollenbeck, Humphrey, Moon, Conlon, & Ilgen, 2003). An important question is therefore how to promote cooperation between individuals in the interest of the team.

In light of our previous discussion of the advantages and difficulties of group work, gossip within work groups is an interesting phenomenon. In line with Foster (2004), we define gossip as evaluative talk about an absent third party. Although it is difficult to give exact estimates about the prevalence of gossip, most authors who have studied work team gossip agree that it occurs frequently (e.g., Dunbar, 2004; Foster, 2004).

Gossip has been claimed to serve a number of different functions in groups, and many studies allude to the possible importance of gossip in affecting team cooperation and effectiveness. Interestingly, however, different lines of research lead to very different conclusions about what causes group members to gossip, and about the effects of gossip for work groups. On the one hand, several motives for, and effects of, gossip have been argued for that can be seen as furthering individual group members' as well as collective goals, such as bonding with group members (Rosnow, 2001), entertainment (Rosnow & Fine, 1976), venting emotions (Grosser, Lopez-Kidwell, Labianca, & Ellwardt, 2012; Waddington & Fletcher, 2005), information exchange (Dunbar, 2004), and maintaining social order (Beersma & Van Kleef, 2011; Feinberg, Willer, Stellar, & Keltner, 2012; Feinberg, Willer, & Schultz, 2014). On the other hand, gossip has been argued to be used by group members with the intention to aggress against others. Specifically, the motive to aggress against others can be seen as fueled by individual group members' self-interest exclusively. As such, gossip has been argued to "divide groups, disrupt group harmonies, and destroy loyalties" (Ribeiro & Blakely, 1995, p. 45), and has been related to workplace bullying (see Einarsen, 2002, see also Einarsen & Skogstad, 1996) and destructive power struggles (Wittek & Wielers, 1998). Thus, the overarching picture that emerges from research and theorizing on work group gossip points to the multiple possible functions and effects of gossip, and it remains unclear whether (or when) the effects of gossip for groups are primarily positive or negative.

Clarifying this picture warrants a proper overview of the field. To provide this overview, this chapter aims to answer two questions. The first question is: "What motivates work group members to engage in gossip?" Motivation represents the reasons for people's actions, desires, and needs, and we define gossip motives as the psychological reasons that prompt a person to engage in gossip (cf. Maehr & Mayer, 1997). Interestingly, many motives for gossip that have been discussed in the literature fit with the goals and advantages for group work discussed earlier, whereas others can be argued to be a response to the difficulties of group work. We will summarize the literature on the different motives for gossip that apply in a work group context, linking each of the motives to psychological goals that are relevant in a group-work setting. The second question we aim to answer is: "How does gossip in work groups affect group effectiveness?" Besides the many different reasons or motives that work group members may have for engaging in gossip, studies have examined different outcomes of gossip. In this chapter, we structure empirical findings in relation to three different operationalizations of group effectiveness (cf. Barrick, Stewart, Neubert, & Mount, 1998; Kozlowski & llgen, 2007): *task performance*, or the extent to which a group meets its task goals; *team member inclusion*, or the extent to which the team offers its members a sense of belonging and authenticity (Jansen, Otten, Van der Zee, & Jans, 2014); and *team viability*, or the extent to which teams are capable of functioning over time (Hackman, 1987).

We will structure our literature review by focusing on group members' motives to gossip first. After this, we review the consequences of gossip for team effectiveness (task performance, inclusion, and viability). After each of these two parts of the chapter, we reflect on our review and suggest avenues for future research.

# WHAT MOTIVATES WORK GROUP MEMBERS TO ENGAGE IN GOSSIP?

We structure this section by introducing six motives for gossip in work groups that have been discussed in the literature (i.e., bonding, seeking entertainment, emotional venting, information exchange, maintenance of group norms, and interpersonal aggression). We link each of the motives to relevant psychological theories and provide an overview of a number of representative studies pertaining to each motive. Not all of the studies we review here were conducted in the context of work groups. Rather, some of them were conducted in a lab setting or in a non-work group context (such as a group or friends or a sorority). We chose to include these studies nevertheless because we believe their findings are relevant to motives for, and consequences of, gossip in work groups, and we discuss this where applicable.

## Bonding

The need to form and maintain strong and stable interpersonal relationships, or, in short, the *need to belong*, has been argued to be a fundamental human need (Baumeister & Leary, 1995). Our brains seem to be "hard-wired" to seek connections with other individuals, and frustration of the need to belong (for instance by social exclusion from a valued group) results in activation of the same brain regions that are activated in case of physical pain (Eisenberger, Lieberman, & Williams, 2003). As people spend much of their time working, the workplace is not exempt of the need to belong. Work engagement—defined as the extent to which employees are involved with, committed to, and enthusiastic and passionate about their work (Attridge, 2009)—depends in large part on the extent to which one feels to be a member of a larger collective. Furthermore, Lips-Wiersema & Wright (2012) demonstrated that experiencing "unity with others" is an important determinant of experiencing work as meaningful. Therefore one's work team is a natural source of belongingness at work.

Many authors discuss how gossip could serve as a bonding mechanism (see, e.g., Dunbar 2004; Grosser et al., 2012, p. 56). The idea that gossiping could foster interpersonal bonds fits with social psychological research, which has since long demonstrated that both mutual friendship relations, but also mutual friendships (i.e. being the enemy of one's enemy) can foster closeness (e.g., Aronson & Cope, 1968). As such, gossiping about others can be a way to promote closeness with team members. Indeed, Grosser et al. (2010) found that both positive and negative gossip were related to more expressive friendship ties at work. Wittek & Wielers (1998) found that the percentage of coalition triads (in which two parties have a good relationship amongst themselves and both have a bad relationship with a third party) consistently predicts gossip behavior across various organizational settings, potentially pointing to the bonding motive as a reason to engage in gossip. Finally, in a qualitative study that examined the communicative practice of gossip among virtual employees, Blithe (2014) found that building relationships is one of the motives virtual employees report for engaging in gossip.

## Seeking Entertainment

Closely related to, yet different from the motivation to bond is the motivation to rewind and entertain oneself. Such motivation could easily emerge if job demands and job resources are not in balance (Bakker & Demerouti, 2007), resulting in employees experiencing either task overload (and in extreme cases burn-out symptoms), or, in contrast, a lack of challenge (and in extreme cases bore-out symptoms (Werder & Rothlin, 2007). In both situations, gossiping could be a way to temporarily detach from work and engage in a pleasurable experience with someone else.

Several authors indeed describe the motive to seek entertainment as a reason for gossip. For instance, Ben Ze'ev (1994) and Gilmore (1978) describe the pleasure individuals and groups derive from gossip activities (see also Melwani, 2012). Likewise, Roy (1958) provides a case description of a team seeking distraction and relief of boring, monotonous tasks by engaging in gossip. Furthermore, in a study aimed at distinguishing gossip from social curiosity, Hartung & Renner (2013) found that people predominantly conceptualize conversations about absent others as gossip when they serve the purpose of pleasure and amusement. Interestingly, Lyons & Hughes (2015) found that narcissism and psychopathy were correlated with social enjoyment as a motive for gossip, suggesting that people who score high on these traits hesitate less to engage in gossip when this is personally enjoyable to them than people who score low on these traits.

## Emotional Venting

Work can be emotionally taxing at times. Especially work that requires one to regulate one's emotions in relation to clients or customers (i.e., "emotional labor") can deplete employees' resources (Rafaeli & Sutton, 1989; Russell Hochschild, 1979). Moreover, working in groups is a notable source of emotions, and these emotions are clearly not all positive (Van Kleef & Fischer, 2016). Gossip has been argued to serve as a "pressure valve" for workers who experience negative emotions in the course of their jobs. For instance, Peters, Kashima, & Clark (2009) demonstrated that stories about others are more likely to be shared when they arouse emotions with an unspecified audience (see also the chapter on gossip and emotions by Martinescu, Janssen & Nijstad, this volume). A study by Waddington (2005), which combines diary analysis and in-depth interviews, demonstrates that among a group of nurses, gossip was used to express a range of emotions. Altuntas, Altun, & Akyil (2014), who also studied gossip among nurses, but in the context of four Turkish hospitals, found that anger, stress, and anxiety are related to gossip, and that approximately one third of the nurses in the sample indicated feeling a reduction in stress levels after having engaged in gossip. Among virtual workers as well, emotional venting was reported as an important reason to engage in gossip (Blithe, 2014).

## Information Exchange

Working with others is frequently characterized by uncertainty and ambiguity, and in order to make sense of their social surroundings, people often rely on others' judgments and opinions. The theory of informational social influence speaks to the importance of social influence as a source of information; we tend to see others as an important source of information about our environment (Aronson, Wilson, & Akert, 2010; Cialdini, 2001; Sherif, 1935). This perspective fits with Baumeister, Zhang, & Vohs' (2004) view on gossip as an extension of observational learning: by gossiping, senders can convey important information to the receiver about culture and society. As such, gossip conveys information about cultural and societal rules. Another underlying reason for why gossip can be motivated by information exchange is that information about others is needed for team members to make social comparisons. According to Festinger (1954) there is a drive within individuals to gain accurate self-evaluations. In order to be able to make these evaluations, they compare their own opinions and abilities to others. Because team members' opinions and abilities may be difficult to access directly at times, gossip can be motivated by deriving such information in order to allow for social comparison.

A study by Baxter, Dun, & Sahlstein (2001) demonstrated that gossip helps people to learn the rules of interaction in a group. That positive as well as negative gossip is conducive to this goal can be derived from the findings of Levin & Arluke (1985), who found that 30 percent of oral gossip was positive in valence. Altuntas, Altun, & Akyil (2014), in a survey on gossip among nurses in four Turkish hospitals, found that one of the purposes the nurses reported for gossip is obtaining work related information that cannot be obtained via formal ways. Likewise, Blithe (2014) found that exchanging gossip is seen by virtual workers as educating themselves regarding the politics of their organization and therefore as exchanging necessary work-related information. The need to gather information is also seen as a central element that facilitates cultural learning by Hartung & Renner (2013), but they distinguish this "social curiosity" from gossip, arguing that the need to gather social information and the need to disseminate social information "might represent the two sides of the cultural learning coin" (page 8).

Further demonstration of the importance of information exchange for gossip comes from a study by McAndrew & Milenkovic (2002), which showed that people were most interested in gossip if the gossip concerned information about others of the same age and gender. This points to the possibility that gossip is most useful as a source of information if it considers others that are comparable to oneself.

## Maintenance of Group Norms/Social Order

The motive for gossip that has perhaps drawn most research attention is the motive to maintain social order, or group norms. Some authors have argued that gossiping possibly operates as a mechanism to discourage people from deviating from group norms by taking a free ride (i.e., not investing effort in collective goals while still benefiting from others' investments) or otherwise failing to live up to these norms, and thus protects groups against those who violate group norms (Dunbar, 2004; Giardini & Wittek, this volume; Gluckman, 1963; Keltner, Van Kleef, Chen, & Kraus, 2008).

But what empirical evidence is there that supports these claims? Beersma & Van Kleef (2012) demonstrated that under circumstances where protecting one's group against norm violations becomes more important (that is, when one can gossip with an ingroup member rather than with an outsider, and when the gossip concerns a norm violation rather than harmless behavior), participants' tendencies to gossip increased, and this was related to the motive to protect the group against norm violators. Further support for the influence of the group protection motive on the tendency to gossip comes from a study by Feinberg, Willer, Stellar, & Keltner (2012, Study 2), in which they demonstrated that individuals possessing more prosocial orientations were the most motivated to engage in gossip when they observed a norm violation, even at a personal cost, and that these individuals exhibited the greatest reduction in negative affect as a result. In contrast to this, Lyons & Hughes (2015) found that secondary psychopathy, a form of psychopathy characterized by high levels of anxiety and more receptivity to environmental stressors than can be found in individuals with primary psychopathy, was positively correlated to the group protection motive for gossip. This suggests that group protection can be motivated by pro-self, as well as by prosocial motives.

## Interpersonal Aggression

The motive we describe last is the motive that has "earned" gossip its negative reputation: the motivation to enhance one's own reputation at the cost of others. There are several accounts in the literature that point to this motive for gossip. Under "information exchange," we discussed the findings by McAndrew & Milenkovic (2002), which showed that interest in gossip was highest when it concerned others of the same age and gender. These findings could point to the possibility that people are especially motivated to gossip when the information thus achieved gives them some advantage over others, especially because McAndrew & Milenkovic (2002) also found that their respondents were especially motivated to gossip when the gossip contained damaging, negative information about non-allies or positive information about allies. Richardson & Green (1997) also describe gossip as motivated by the willingness to indirectly aggress against others, and Crothers, Lipinski, & Minutolo (2009) point to gossip as an element of workplace bullying, especially among women. McAndrew (2014) argues that women are more likely to use gossip in an aggressive, competitive manner than men in order to damage the reputation and networking ability of potential rivals. Furthermore, Jeuken, Beersma, Ten Velden, & Dijkstra (2015) found, in a laboratory experiment, that interpersonal aggression as a motivation for gossip can be triggered by either one's internal motivation (i.e., a pro-self-motivation) or by features of the situation (i.e., a target demonstrating uncooperative behavior), and that power determines the influence of these two driving forces. Specifically, individuals with high power were most likely to be motivated to aggress through gossip when they had a pro-self rather than a prosocial motivation, whereas individuals with low power responded more to the behavior of the gossip target than to their own inclinations. As such, they were more likely to aggress through gossip when the gossip target behaved uncooperatively rather than cooperatively.

Possibly also pointing to the aggression motive for gossip, Ellwardt, Wittek, & Wielers (2012) found that among employees in a child care center, negative gossip about managers increased when employees had low-trust, non-friendly relationships, and infrequent contact with the managers.

# How Does Gossip in Work Groups Affect Group Effectiveness?

In the previous section of this chapter, we reviewed research that suggests that gossip can be motivated by many different psychological needs (bonding, seeking entertainment, emotional venting, information exchange, maintenance of group norms, and interpersonal aggression). We now turn to research on the outcomes that gossip entails for work groups. We structure the current section by reviewing theoretical accounts and research findings regarding the effects of gossip on task performance, inclusion, and team viability.

## Task Performance

Most studies directed at examining the effects of gossip on task performance have operationalized task performance as cooperation or conformity with the group's goals. Already in 1963, Gluckman proposed that the threat alone that one may be gossiped about by group members is enough to keep group members from behaving in a self-serving manner at the expense of the group. As such, gossip should foster cooperation. Research findings are generally in line with this perspective. Piazza & Bering (2008) demonstrated that the threat of gossip motivated prosocial allocations of scarce resources. Likewise, Beersma & Van Kleef (2011) found that study participants invested more personal resources in a collective goal when they believed their fellow team members scored high on the tendency to gossip than when they believed their group members were unlikely to engage in gossip. Milinski, Semmann, & Krambeck (2002), Feinberg et al. (2012), and Wu, Balliet, & Van Lange (2016a) also demonstrated that gossip fosters cooperation. Finally, research by Wu, Balliet, and Van Lange ((2016b) provides evidence that gossip may be more effective and efficient than direct punishment to promote and maintain cooperation.

## Inclusion

Compared to the generally favorable consequences of gossip for cooperation, the picture regarding the effects of gossip on inclusion looks a lot bleaker. Interestingly, whereas the possibility of exchanging reputational information can enhance team members' cooperation with team goals, it can at the same time reduce feelings of inclusion in the team.

What starts with gossip could eventually lead to exclusion from the group, something that is very negative for group members and that they thus want to avoid (Williams, Cheung, & Choi, 2000). Whereas the risk of being excluded may inhibit group members' tendency to behave in a self-serving manner (Baumeister et al., 2004; Dunbar, 2004), feeling a lack of inclusion in the team is related to reduced commitment to the team and this may in turn lead to deteriorated team performance in the long run (Jansen et al., 2014).

Studies paint a similarly mixed picture regarding the relationship between *engaging* in gossip and being accepted and included as a group member. Bosson, Johnson, Niederhoffer, & Swann (2006) demonstrated that sharing of negative (rather than positive) information about others increased interpersonal liking. Jaeger, Skelder, & Rosnow (1998) found that sorority members who engaged in "moderate" amounts of gossip had more friends than "low" or "high" gossipers. Farley (2011) also found that high-frequency negative gossipers were rated as less likeable than low-frequency gossipers and positive gossipers, perhaps suggesting that the relationship between gossip and belongingness is curvilinear.

In summary, the effects of gossip on group inclusion seem to be a lot less favorable than the effects on cooperative task performance. Both those who are the targets of gossip, or fear the risk of becoming targets, as well as those who engage in gossip risk suffering from being excluded from the group.

## Team Viability

Very few studies have examined the effects of gossip over time, which makes it difficult to provide a firm conclusion regarding the effects of gossip on team viability (i.e., the extent to which teams are capable of functioning over time). However, the few studies that have examined longitudinal effects seem to converge on the conclusion that, in contrast to the positive effects on team member cooperation, gossip mostly relates negatively to viability. Wittek & Wielers' (1998) findings speak to the flourishing of gossip in contexts where people build coalitions that include some, but exclude others. The emergence of such dynamics within groups poses a threat to group viability. Georganta, Panagopoulou, & Montgomery (2014) found that negative gossip in a hospital was positively related to burnout and negatively correlated with job engagement and patient safety. Likewise, Kuo, Chang, Quinton, Lu, & Lee (2015) found that gossip was related to employee cynicism (a negative attitude toward their organization, Dean, Brandes, & Dharwadkar, 1998). In the long run, these effects are likely to endanger group viability. Likewise, Wu, Kwan, Wu, & Ma (2015) found that negative gossip about employees was negatively related to proactive behavior, i.e., self-initiated and future-oriented actions aimed to change and improve the situation (Parker, Williams, & Turner, 2006) by these employees as rated by their supervisors two months later. Moreover, the relationship between gossip and proactive behavior was mediated by emotional exhaustion. In contrast to the studies we reviewed earlier, which showed positive effects of gossip on cooperation, these findings show that in the long run, gossip may deteriorate group viability by damaging psychological well-being.

# REFLECTIONS ON FINDINGS AND
# SUGGESTIONS FOR FUTURE RESEARCH

## Gossip Motives

Our review on gossip motives shows that gossip can be motivated by many different psychological needs (bonding, seeking entertainment, emotional venting, information exchange, maintenance of group norms, and interpersonal aggression). Several issues emerge from our review that merit further attention.

One important issue is that in a given situation, and therefore, in a given study, it can be difficult to pinpoint the exact motive that caused an individual to engage in gossip. As a case in point, Dijkstra, Beersma, & Van Leeuwen (2014 demonstrated that police officers reported to be more inclined to engage in negative gossip and less inclined to engage in positive gossip when their supervisor demonstrated unfair conflict management behavior. Motives for gossip were not measured in this study, and interestingly, gossip in this case could be motivated by multiple motives, including bonding, emotional venting, interpersonal aggression against the supervisor, and maintaining social order. As such, we do not know whether gossip in a specific situation such as this is driven by one motive or by multiple motives simultaneously, and if the latter is true, whether some motives are more likely to link to one another than others.

Our review shows that regarding motives to gossip, studies can be divided into three types: (1) studies that do not discuss gossip motives, but in which motives can be inferred (see e.g., Grosser et al., 2010; Wittek & Wielers, 1998); (2) studies or theoretical accounts that specifically include motivation in their theoretical analysis of gossip but do not explicitly measure motives for gossip (see e.g., Beersma & Van Kleef, 2011, Feinberg et al. 2012; McAndrew, 2014); and (3) studies that explicitly assessed gossip motives, for instance by having respondents fill in the "Motives to Gossip" questionnaire (Beersma & Van Kleef, 2012) or by alternative empirical assessments of underlying motives (see e.g., Hartung and Renner, 2013; Altunas et al., 2014; Lyons & Hughes, 2015; and Jeuken et al., 2015. Although we applaud the recent increase in studies that explicitly measure motives for gossip, we notice that even the studies that did explicitly measure gossip motives often focused on one specific motive, or on a subset of motives at most, ignoring the other motives identified in our review. In order for the field of gossip research to be able to answer the question of why group members gossip, it would be worthwhile for researchers to start taking a more comprehensive approach to assessing gossip motives by measuring multiple motives. This would enable conclusions regarding the situations that activate certain motives, about the co-occurrence or mutual exclusion of motives, and about the relative predictive value of the various motives for actual gossip behavior.

The relative predictive value of the various motives for actual gossip behavior is also important in light of the overarching focus of this book on gossip and reputation. Our review shows that whereas some research on motives for gossip in work groups specifically focused on reputational effects as a mediating, explanatory mechanism (i.e., the motivations to exchange information, maintain group norms, and to aggress interpersonally are each based on the possibility that gossip offers to exchange reputational information), other research on gossip (that examines it as a source for bonding, entertainment, or emotional venting) does not at all link gossip to reputation, but instead links gossip to other basic psychological drivers that are not related to reputation. The field of gossip research will only be able to answer questions about the motives that drive gossip in work groups if these motives are assessed explicitly and simultaneously. In the absence of such specific assessments, in a given situation, the centrality of reputational information in work group gossip may be a first clue regarding its motivational drivers. In other words, if gossip conversations in work groups contain a lot of reputational information about targets, this may be an indication that those engaging in these conversations are motivated by information exchange, maintenance of social norms, or interpersonal aggression). If, on the other hand, gossip conversations contain information that is peripheral to targets' reputation, this could indicate that gossipers are motivated by, for example, bonding, entertainment, or emotional venting. Indeed, research by Beersma and Van Kleef (2011) indicates that the tendency to gossip about a work group member's reputation-relevant behavior (i.e., free-riding behavior) or reputation-irrelevant behavior is related to different motives for gossip.

Finally, our overview points to the intriguing possibility that gossip could become more likely under circumstances where specific motives are not "fulfilled" at work. Reviewing the different motives, this leads to propositions about when gossip would be especially likely to occur. When the social structure at work provides few opportunities to bond, people could revert to gossip because of its role in interpersonal bonding. Workplaces in which work is particularly boring would also become a fertile breeding ground for gossip because of its role in enabling entertainment. Likewise, when organizations allow no structured possibilities to "blow off steam," gossiping could fill this gap. Teams that allow for little direct means to engage in social comparison would also be likely to be characterized by high levels of gossip. Furthermore, when failure to adhere to the norms of the group (for instance free-riding) is not punished by official means, gossip is likely to flourish and to be condoned (Van Kleef, Wanders, Stamkou, & Homan, 2015). And finally, high levels of intra-team competition could foster gossip because of the options it allows to aggress against rivaling team members. How design and cultural features of organizations stimulate gossip by increasing or decreasing gossip motives, and as a result, actual gossip behavior, is an interesting area for future research.

## Gossip Outcomes

Our review on gossip outcomes shows that gossip is related to different types of outcomes for work groups, as we discussed its relationships with task performance, inclusion, and, team viability. Reflecting on the findings brings to light a number of issues, and suggests a number of related areas for future research.

First, critically examining findings related to effects of gossip on task performance shows that the operationalization of performance that is typically used in these studies is very narrow. Team members are asked to contribute to their team, and the only aspect of their contribution that is assessed is the level of cooperation/conformity to collective norms, often assessed through investments study participants make in economic games (such as the dictator game or trust game, see for instance Beersma & Van Kleef, 2011; Feinberg et al., 2012; Wu et al., 2016a, b). Whereas cooperation is an important aspect of task performance in many real-life teams, and as such, these studies yield important insights in the gossip-team performance relationship, there is of course more to team performance than investing personal resources into a collective goal. Group performance can, for example, also be assessed as the quality, accuracy, or creativity of the team output, or as the efficiency with which a team invests its resources. Up to date, studies have not examined the extent to which these other performance criteria are affected by gossip processes. This is especially striking because previous studies have shown that trade-offs between these outcomes exist; fostering one often comes at the expense of other outcomes (Beersma et al., 2003; Beersma & De Dreu, 2005). The field of gossip research could gain from broadening the perspective on group performance by studying the consequences of gossip for these various outcome variables, and by examining possible trade-offs between them. For example, whereas gossip can on the one hand foster cooperation and norm-adherence in teams, it could at the same time reduce the originality of team member input, as when there is a high threat of being gossiped about, team members may want to keep a low profile in the group.

Second, besides moving toward a broader perspective on what constitutes task performance, gossip research would also benefit from looking beyond task performance when examining the effects of gossip in work teams. We noted two possible areas of interest in this chapter, team inclusion and viability. Although few studies have addressed these areas, our review showed that studies that did focus on these types of outcomes tend to point to the negative role that gossip may play in work teams (i.e., reducing feelings of inclusion and team viability). This highlights once again the importance of research that examines effects of gossip on multiple team effectiveness indicators simultaneously. Studies that do so are much needed to shed light on the trade-offs involved in effects of gossip; whereas gossip in teams may foster some aspects of teamwork, it may deteriorate others, and in order to design useful interventions for managing gossip in the workplace, practitioners need to have insight in these trade-offs.

## Integrating Gossip Motives and Outcomes

Reflecting on the two parts of our review pertaining to the antecedents and consequences of gossip, respectively, we note a discrepancy regarding levels of analysis between research on gossip motives on the one hand, and gossip effects on the other hand. Whereas studies about gossip motives tend to focus on the individual (group member) as the unit of analysis, studies about the latter (at least theoretically) center on the group as the unit of analysis. Given that our review demonstrated that gossip can be motivated by very different psychological motives, and that it can also have a diverse array of effects on work groups, an important question is whether these two aspects of gossip, its individual drivers and its group-level effects, relate to one another in any way. Does what motivated the gossip in a group matter for group-level effects? Does gossip that was instigated because group members want to bond or entertain themselves have different effects than gossip motivated by the maintenance of social norms or by aggression? In order to answer such questions, studies should examine how individual-level motives for gossip combine to result in group-level gossip behavior, and how group-level gossip behavior affects individual outcomes (such as feelings of inclusion in the team). In general, integrating units of analysis in theoretical accounts of gossip motives and effects is an important challenge for future research on gossip in work groups.

Another interesting issue is that although our overview does not allow us to systematically identify possible moderators of the gossip-team effectiveness relationship, several variables could be argued to play a moderating role. Gossip valence (whether gossip has a positive or a negative content), for instance, could be argued to moderate the relationship between gossip prevalence and team-level outcomes. Likewise, the legitimacy of gossip is also an interesting moderating variable to study. That is, cues that point to gossip being either justified or unjustified could moderate gossip's relationship with team performance, inclusion, and viability. Systematic study of these moderator variables could help further demarcate when and why gossip is functional or dysfunctional for work groups.

Finally, and related to the previous issues regarding levels of analysis and moderating variables, our overview of gossip motives and effects suggest that the antecedents and consequences of gossip in work groups have thus far been largely examined within separate lines of inquiry. A synthesis between our analysis of gossip motives and gossip effects would lead to the proposition that gossip effects could, in part, be moderated by motives underlying gossip. For instance, gossip motivated by maintenance of group norms could be argued to have different effects at the group level than gossip motivated by interpersonal aggression, or motivated by entertainment. This can be argued to only be the case, however, if gossip recipients are able to accurately distinguish between different motives. Research examining the path from individual motives to group level outcomes could help clarify how gossip instigated by one group member is understood by others (or what motive it is being attributed to), and whether and how these attributions in turn influence how gossip affects task performance, inclusion, and viability.

## CONCLUSION

At the beginning of the chapter, we argued that groups are a breeding ground for gossip, and organizational teams are no exception. We provided an overview of the different motives for gossip in work groups, linking each motive to psychological theory. We also provided an overview of the different types of influence gossip has been shown to have on various indicators of group effectiveness. Reflecting on both the motives underlying gossip in work groups as well as on its outcomes, we conclude that there is a lot of research evidence to back up our opening statement. The next step for research on gossip in groups, we feel, should be to start integrating the diverse insights provided here. Suggestions we provided for such integration are for example to simultaneously examine different motives to gossip within studies, to examine organizational context as a moderator of gossip motives, to integrate levels of analysis, and, perhaps most importantly, to examine how individual-level motives to gossip affect team-level outcomes. We hope these suggestions will stimulate gossip researchers to further increase our understanding of this phenomenon that is so prevalent and important for work groups.

# References

Altuntaş, S., Şahin Altun, Ö., & Çevik Akyil, R. (2014). The nurses' form of organizational communication: What is the role of gossip?. *Contemporary nurse 48*(1), 109–116.

Aronson, E., & Cope, V. (1968). My enemy is my friend. *Journal of Personality and Social Psychology 8*, 8–12.

Aronson, E., Wilson, T. D., & Akert, R. M. (2010). *Social Psychology*. Upper Saddle River, NJ: Prentice Hall 2010. Print.

Attridge, M. (2009). Measuring and managing employee work engagement: A review of research and business literature. *Journal of Workplace Behavioral Health 24*, 389–398.

Bakker, A. B., & Demerouti, E. (2007). The job demands–resources model: State of the art. *Journal of Managerial Psychology 22*, 309–328.

Barrick, M. R., Stewart, G. L., Neubert, M. J., & Mount, M. K. (1998). Relating member ability and personality to work-team processes and team effectiveness. *Journal of Applied Psychology 83*, 377–391.

Baxter, L. A., Dun, T., & Sahlstein, E. (2001), Rules for relating communicated among social network members. *Journal of Social and Personal Relationships 18*, 173–199.

Baumeister, R. F., & Leary, M. R. (1995). The need to belong: Desire for interpersonal attachments as a fundamental human motivation. *Psychological Bulletin 117*, 497–529.

Baumeister, R. F., Zhang, L., & Vohs, K. D. (2004). Gossip as cultural learning. *Review of General Psychology 8*, 111–121.

Beersma, B., Conlon, D. E., & Hollenbeck, J. R. (2007). Conflict and group decision-making: The role of social motivation. In C. K. W. De Dreu & M. Gelfand (Eds.), *The psychology of conflict and conflict management in organizations* (pp. 115–148). New Jersey: Lawrence Erlbaum.

Beersma, B., & De Dreu, C. K. W. (2005). Conflict's consequences: Effects of social motives on post-negotiation creative and convergent group functioning and performance. *Journal of Personality and Social Psychology 89*, 358–374.

Beersma, B., Hollenbeck, J. R., Humphrey, S. E., Moon, H., Conlon, D. E., & Ilgen, D. R. (2003). Cooperation, competition and team performance: Towards a contingency approach. *Academy of Management Journal 46*, 572–590.

Beersma, B., Homan, A. C., Van Kleef, G. A., & De Dreu, C. K. W. (2013). Outcome interdependence shapes the effects of prevention focus on team processes and performance. *Organizational Behavior and Human Decision Processes 121*, 194–203.

Beersma, B., & Van Kleef (2011). How the grapevine keeps you in line: Gossip increases contributions to the group. *Social Psychological and Personality Science 2*, 642–649.

Beersma, B., & Van Kleef, G. A. (2012). Why people gossip: An empirical analysis of social motives, antecedents, and consequences. *Journal of Applied Social Psychology 42*, 2640–2670.

Ben-Ze'ev, A. (1994). The vindication of gossip. In R. F. Goodman, & A. Ben-Ze'ev (Eds.), *Good gossip* (pp. 11–24). Lawrence, KS: University Press of Kansas.

Blithe, S. J. (2014). Creating the water cooler: Virtual workers' discursive practices of gossip. *Qualitative Research Reports in Communication 15*(1), 59–65.

Bosson, J. K., Johnson, A. B., Niederhoffer, K., & Swann, W. B. (2006). Interpersonal chemistry through negativity: Bonding by sharing negative attitudes about others. *Personal relationships 13*, 135–150.

Cialdini, R. B. (2001). The science of persuasion. *Scientific American 284*, 76–81.

Crothers, L. M., Lipinski, J., & Minutolo, M. C. (2009). Cliques, rumors, and gossip by the water cooler: Female bullying in the workplace. *The Psychologist-Manager Journal 12*, 97–110.

Crowley, M., Payne, J. C., & Kennedy, E. (2014). Working better together? Empowerment, panopticon and conflict approaches to teamwork. *Economic and Industrial Democracy 35*, 483–506.

Dean, J. W., Brandes, P., & Dharwadkar, R. (1998). Organisational cynicism. *Academy of Management Review 23*, 341–52.

Dijkstra, M. T. M., Beersma, B., & Van Leeuwen, J. (2014). Gossiping as a response to conflict with the boss: Alternative conflict management behavior? *International Journal of Conflict Management 25*, 431–454.

Dunbar, R. I. M. (2004). Gossip in an evolutionary perspective. *Review of General Psychology 8*, 100–110.

Einarsen, S. (2002). Bullying at work. *Magazine of the European Agency for Safety and Health at Work 5*, 25–26.

Einarsen, S., & Skogstad, A. (1996). Bullying at work: Epidemiological findings in public and private organizations. *European Journal of Work and Organizational Psychology 5*, 185–201.

Eisenberger, N. I., Lieberman, M. D., & Williams, K. D. (2003). Does rejection hurt? An fMRI study of social exclusion. *Science 302*, 290–292.

Ellwardt, L., Wittek, R., & Wielers, R. (2012). Talking about the boss: Effects of generalized and interpersonal trust on workplace gossip. *Group & organization management 37*(4), 521–549.

Farley, S. D. (2011). Is gossip power? The inverse relationships between gossip, power, and likability. *European Journal of Social Psychology 41*, 574–579.

Feinberg, M., Willer, R., Stellar, J., & Keltner, D. (2012). The virtues of gossip: Reputational information sharing as prosocial behavior. *Journal of Personality and Social Psychology 102*, 1015–1030.

Feinberg, M., Willer, R., & Schultz, M. (2014). Gossip and ostracism promote cooperation in groups. *Psychological Science 25*, 656–664.

Festinger, L. (1954). A theory of social comparison processes. *Human Relation, 7*, 117–140.

Foster, E. K. (2004). Research on gossip: Taxonomy, methods, and future directions. *Review of General Psychology 8*, 78–99.

Garvey, C. (2002). Steer teams with the right pay: Team-based pay is a success when it fits corporate goals and culture, and rewards the right behavior. *HR Magazine 34*, 33–36.

Giardini, F., Wittek, R. P. M. (2019). Gossip, Reputation, and Sustainable Cooperation: Sociological Foundations. In F. Giardini & R. P. M. Wittek (Eds.), *Handbook of gossip and reputation*. New York: Oxford University Press.

Gilmore, D. (1978). Varieties of gossip in a Spanish rural community. *Ethnology 1*, 89–99.

Gluckman, M. (1963). Gossip and scandal. *Current Anthropology 4*, 307–316.

Georganta, K., Panagopoulou, E., & Montgomery, A. (2014). Talking behind their backs: Negative gossip and burnout in hospitals. *Burnout Research 1*, 76–81.

Grosser, T. J., Lopez-Kidwell, V., & Labianca, G. (2010). A social network analysis of positive and negative gossip in organizational life. *Group & Organization Management 35*, 177–212.

Grosser, T. J., Lopez-Kidwell, V., & Labianca, G., & Ellwardt, L. (2012). Hearing it through the grapevine: Positive and negative workplace gossip. *Organizational Dynamics 41*, 52–61.

Hackman, J. R. (1987). The design of work teams. I. W. lorsch (ed.), Handbook of organizational behavior (pp. 315–342). Hackman, J. R., & Oldham, G. R. (1976). Motivation through design of work: Test of a theory. *Organizational Behavior and Human Performance 16*(2), 250–279.

Hartung, F. M., & Renner, B. (2013). Social curiosity and gossip: Related but different drives of social functioning. *PLoS ONE 8*,: e69996. doi:10.1371/journal.pone.0069996.

Heatherton, T. F., & Vohs, K. D. (2000). Interpersonal evaluations following threats to self: Role of self-esteem. *Journal of Personality and Social Psychology 78*, 725–736.

Hertel, G. (2011). Excellence in teams: How to achieve performance gains in working groups. *Journal of Managerial Psychology 26*, 176–258.

Hochschild, A. R. (1979). Emotion work, feeling rules, and social structure. *American Journal of Sociology 85*, 551–575.

Hollenbeck, J. R., Beersma, B., & Schouten, M. E. (2012). Beyond team types and taxonomies: A dimensional scaling conceptualization for team description. *Academy of Management Review 37*(1), 82–106.

Illgen, D. R. 1999. Teams embedded in organizations: Some implications. *American Psychologist 54*, 129–139.

Jaeger, M. E., Skelder, A. A., & Rosnow, R. L. (1998). Who's up on the low down: Gossip in interpersonal relations. In B. H. Spitzberg & W. R. Cupach (Eds.), *The dark side of close relationships* (pp. 103–117). Mahwah, NJ: Lawrence Erlbaum.

Jansen, W., Otten, S., van der Zee, K., & Jans, L. (2014). Inclusion: Conceptualization and measurement. *European Journal of Social Psychology 44*, 370–385.

Jeuken, E., Beersma, B., ten Velden, F. S., & Dijkstra, M. T. (2015). Aggression as a motive for gossip during conflict: The role of power, social value orientation, and counterpart's behavior. *Negotiation and Conflict Management Research 8*(3), 137–152.

Keltner, D., Van Kleef, G. A., Chen, S., & Kraus, M. W. (2008). A reciprocal influence model of social power: Emerging principles and lines of inquiry. *Advances in Experimental Social Psychology 40*, 151–192.

Kozlowski, S. W. J., & Ilgen, D. R. I. (2007). The science of team success. *Scientific American Mind, June/July* 54–61. Retrieved from http://blog.hrmexpertise.nl/downloads/ScAmteams.pdf.

Kuo, C. C., Chang, K., Quinton, S., Lu, C. Y., & Lee, I. (2015). Gossip in the workplace and the implications for HR management: A study of gossip and its relationship to employee cynicism. *The International Journal of Human Resource Management 26*(18), 2288–2307.

Levin, J., & Arluke, A. (1985). An exploratory analysis of sex differences in gossip. *Sex Roles 12*(3–4), 281–286.

Levine, J. M., & Moreland, R. L. (1990). Progress in small group research. *Annual Review of Psychology 41*, 585–634.

Lips-Wiersema, M., & Wright, S. (2012). Measuring the meaning of meaningful work: Development and validation of the comprehensive meaningful work scale (CMWS). *Group and Organizational Management 37*, 655–685.

Lyons, M. T., & Hughes, S. (2015). Malicious mouths? The Dark Triad and motivations for gossip. *Personality and Individual Differences 78*, 1–4.

Maehr, M. L., & Mayer, H. (1997). Understanding motivation and schooling: Where we've been, where we are, and where we need to go. *Educational Psychology Review 9*(4).

Martinescu, E., Janssen, O., & Nijstad, B. A. (2019). Gossip and emotion. In F. Giardini & R. P. M. Wittek (Eds.), *Handbook of gossip and reputation*. New York: Oxford University Press.

McAndrew, F. T., & Milenkovic, M. A. (2002). Of tabloids and family secrets: The evolutionary psychology of gossip. *Journal of Applied Social Psychology 32*, 1064–1082.

Melwani, S. (2012). *A little bird told me so...: The emotional, attributional, relational and team-level outcomes of engaging in gossip*. (Doctoral dissertation, University of Pennsylvania). Retrieved from http://repository.upenn.edu/dissertations/AAI3509335.

Messick, D. M., & Brewer, M. B. (1983). Solving social dilemmas: A review. In Wheeler, L. & Shaver, P. Review of personality and social psychology (Vol. 4, pp. 11–44). Beverly Hills, CA: Sage.

Milinski, M., Semmann, D., & Krambeck, H. (2002). Reputation helps solve the "tragedy of the commons." *Nature 415*, 424–426.

Parker, S. K., Williams, H. M., & Turner, N. (2006). Modeling the antecedents of proactive behavior at work. *Journal of Applied Psychology 91*, 636–652.

Peters, K., Kashima, Y., & Clark, A. (2009). Talking about others: Emotionality and the dissemination of social information. *European Journal of Social Psychology 39*, 207–222.

Piazza, J., & Bering, J. M. (2008). Concerns about reputation via gossip promote generous allocations in an economic game. *Evolution and Human Behavior 29*, 8–172.

Rafaeli, A., Sutton, R. I. (1989). The expression of emotion in organizational life. *Research in Organizational Behavior 11*, 1–42.

Ribeiro, V. E., & Blakely, J. A. (1995). The proactive management of rumour and gossip. *Journal of Nursing Administration 25*, 43–50.

Richardson, D. R., & Green, L. G. (1997). Circuitous harm: Determinants and consequences of nondirect aggression. In R. Kowalski (Ed.), *Aversive interpersonal behaviors* (pp. 171–188). New York: Plenum.

Rosnow, R. L. (2001). Rumor and gossip in interpersonal interaction and beyond: A social exchange perspective. In R. M. Kowalski (Ed.), *Behaving badly: Aversive behaviors in interpersonal relationships* (pp. 203–232). Washington, DC: American Psychological Association.

Rosnow, R. L., & Fine, G. L. (1976). *Rumor and gossip: The social psychology of hearsay*. New York: Elsevier.

Roy, F. R. (1958). Banana time: Job satisfaction and informal interaction. *Human Organisation 18*, 158–168.

Sherif, M. (1935). A study of some social factors in perception. *Archives of Psychology 27*, (187), 1–60.

Sundstrom, E., De Meuse, K. P., & Futrell, D. 1990. Work teams: Applications and effectiveness. *American Psychologist 45*, 120–133.

Swann, W. B., Jr. (1983). Self-verification: Bringing social reality into harmony with the self. In J. Suls & A. G. Greenwald (Eds.), *Psychological perspectives on the self* (Vol. 2, pp. 33–66), Hillsdale, NJ: Erlbaum.

Van Kleef, G. A., & Fischer, A. H. (2016). Emotional collectives: How groups shape emotions and emotions shape groups. *Cognition & Emotion 30*, 3–19.

Van Kleef, G. A., Wanders, F., Stamkou, E., & Homan, A. C. (2015). The social dynamics of breaking the rules: Antecedents and consequences of norm-violating behavior. *Current Opinion in Psychology 6*, 25–31.

Van Lange, P. A. M., Joireman, J., Parks, C. D., & Van Dijk, E. (2013). The psychology of social dilemmas: A review, *Organizational Behavior and Human Decision Processes, 120*(2), 125–141.

Waddington, K., & Fletcher, C. (2005). Gossip and emotion in nursing and healthcare organizations. *Journal of Health Organization and Management 19*, 378–394.

Waddington, K. (2005). Using diaries to explore the characteristics of work-related gossip: Methodological considerations from exploratory multimethod research. *Journal of occupational and Organizational Psychology 78*(2), 221–236.

Werder, P., & Rothlin, P. (2007). Diagnosis Boreout: How a lack of challenge at work can make you ill. Munich, Germany: *Redline* Wirtschaft.

Williams, K. D., Cheung, C. K. T., & Choi, W. (2000). Cyberostracism: Effects of being ignored over the internet. *Journal of Personality and Social Psychology 79*, 748–762.

Wittek, R., & Wielers, R. (1998). Gossip in organizations. *Computational and Mathematical Organization Theory 4*, 189–204.

Wu, X., Kwan, H. K., Wu, L. Z., & Ma, J. (2018). The effect of workplace negative gossip on employee proactive behavior in China: The moderating role of traditionality. *Journal of Business Ethics 148*(4), 801-815.

Wu, J., Balliet, D., & Van Lange, P. A. (2016b). Reputation management: Why and how gossip enhances generosity. *Evolution and Human Behavior 37*(3), 193–201.

Wu, J., Balliet, D., & Van Lange, P. A. (2016b). Gossip versus punishment: The efficiency of reputation to promote and maintain cooperation. *Scientific Reports 6*, 23919.

# CHAPTER 23

## GOSSIP AND REPUTATION IN SOCIAL NETWORKS

### LEA ELLWARDT

## INTRODUCTION AND MAIN PROPOSITIONS

COOPERATION between human beings, and thus the survival of social groups, largely bases on interpersonal trust. Trust in a group member is formed directly through repeated personal encounters and indirectly through others' disclosed evaluations of their encounters with that member. People recognized as trustworthy are perceived as attractive partners in business, teamwork and similar group settings of interdependency and social exchange. In other words, they have a favorable reputation. The perhaps most used channel through which humans convey and evaluate experiences with others is gossip (Dunbar, 2004): People praise and criticize the behaviors of absent third parties. However, information exchange neither takes place in an atomized social vacuum nor in an unlimited public space. It is typically context-bound, for example to trading platforms, financial systems, sports teams or organizational units. People embedded in these contexts are connected through a shared interest in cooperating with one another and thereby denote a social network. It is the properties of this network that ease or hamper interaction between network members, including gossip communication.

In this chapter, I propose that gossip and reputation are endogenous phenomena that are hard, if not impossible, to theoretically and empirically disentangle. This is because they influence one another during their emergence; in short: they coevolve. Reputation merely comes about without the involvement of appraisal and criticism. Likewise, it is evaluative statements that earmark gossip. Besides this entangled association, I propose that the coevolution of gossip and reputation is primarily driven by the opportunity and constraint structure of social networks. Structural characteristics are distinguished on the global, local and individual (i.e., ego-centric) level of networks.

PROPOSITION 1:    Gossip and reputation are coevolving phenomena.
PROPOSITION 2:    Both phenomena are driven by global, local and individual network structures.

Based on these propositions, I will review recent developments in theoretical and empirical research on gossip and reputation from a social network perspective, rather than describe antecedents and consequences from an individual or group-level perspective. Because much of the research using social network theorizing and data has relied on the organizational context, many presented examples stem from the organization and management literature addressing so-called workplace gossip. One reason is that organizations represent real-life environments of formalized social exchange between interdependent actors: The success of managerial decisions depends on the employees' cooperation and adherence to social norms. These conditions set the stage for information sharing about others' behavior. Another reason for the focus on organizational settings in previous studies is that particularly in empirical approaches the delineation of network boundaries is a prerequisite. Organizations—among others including firms, schools, and online communities—typically constitute a natural yet clearly distinguishable entity of formal and informal relationships. Because of this, members and non-members of the organizational network can be more easily defined than in other social environments.

I begin by introducing gossip and reputation as relational phenomena. After that, I present theoretical frameworks used for describing and explaining the emergence of gossip and reputation networks, with a brief description of relevant social network measures directed to readers less familiar with network analyses, as well as central empirical findings. This presentation is organized along the aforementioned three analytical levels. Finally, I close with suggestions for potentially interesting avenues for future research.

# GOSSIP AND REPUTATION AS COEVOLVING RELATIONAL PHENOMENA

This chapter focusses on the relational processes behind gossip and reputation. *Gossip* is broadly defined as informal evaluative talking about absent others (Dunbar, 2004; Foster, 2004; Kurland & Pelled, 2000). This at first glance simple description hints at several dimensions, turning gossip into a surprisingly multifaceted social phenomenon. A crucial implication for social network researchers is the so-called *gossip triad*: Two people, the sender and the receiver of gossip, talk about a third person, the object of gossip. As such, by definition, any incident of gossip involves three or more actors interconnected by three or more social ties, as illustrated in Figure 23.1. Actors may change forth and back between the roles of sender, receiver, and object, and multiple actors may exist per role. For instance, the sender shares information with several receivers, who become senders themselves through passing on the information to other receivers. By now, it becomes clear that researchers striving to fully capture and understand the mechanisms of gossip inevitably face thinking about it as a dynamic communication network. Note that the present description disregards what is sometimes called celebrity gossip, that is,

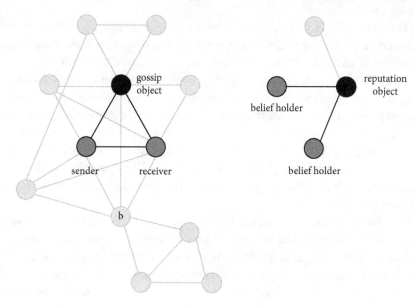

**FIGURE 23.1.** Gossip and reputation as relational phenomena.

taking about known but unconnected objects, and excludes rumor, a broader concept that also includes hearsay about events, not people.

*Reputation* is conceptualized as holding a belief or opinion about something or someone. Empirically, reputation is often measured as an average evaluation by others and must not be confused with status (Burt, 2005; Burt, 2014). Similar to gossip, reputation is a relational phenomenon that includes an object and several belief holders, and hence is at least *triadic* in nature. The focal person neither owns nor directly controls her reputation, but the people believing in and sharing it. This is also the case for gossip, where objects are excluded from the incident of information sharing and thus unable to exert an immediate influence on the information flow about themselves. Another joint feature is valence, meaning that contents of both reputation and gossip can be positive, negative or mixed. Finally, veracity is not a necessary condition as original contents may base on unsubstantiated hearsay, inaccurate or erroneous sources, and undergo modification as they spread throughout networks.

*Social networks* are social environments with interacting units, mostly actors (Wasserman & Faust, 1994, p. 3). Actors and their actions are interdependent rather than autonomous, with the relational ties between actors being channels for the transfer and flow of material and immaterial resources (Wasserman & Faust, 1994, p. 4). The network's structural environment thereby provides opportunities and constraints for individual action. When interactions between actors become regularities, they consolidate in lasting relationship patterns (i.e., network configurations), which can be quantified and formally described in structural variables. Examples are relationship density and reciprocity in a communication network. The network's structure greatly designs the emergence and evolution of relational phenomena like gossip and reputation

(Coleman, 1990; Eder & Enke, 1991): The gossip triad is characterized by high levels of interdependencies and coordination. A precondition of gossip is shared presence in social occasions and behavior settings. In a direct encounter, the sender is reliant on a cooperative receiver willing to listen. Likewise, reputation can only exist when a minimum number of belief holders agree on an opinion about a focal person or object. Besides the prescribed power of social networks, they are not static predictors of action but subject to dynamic changes. Social ties are created, modified and dropped based on outcomes of information sharing about others so that network structure is not only an antecedence but also a consequence of gossip and reputation. As I will outline, much of the theoretical literature perceives social networks as drivers rather than products of gossip and reputation formation.

Because gossip provides a medium for the informal gathering and coordinating of opinions about an object, it can initiate and steer reputation formation. However, once a reputation is established it may also influence gossip behavior: An agreed opinion about an object frames the way subsequent news is received and published. A neutral piece of information, for instance, may not be discussed at all, or through a negative or positive lens depending on the gossipers' predispositions. This reputation bias seems especially likely where people seek to confirm rather than balance their opinion on someone. This way, a negative reputation might further motivate to selectively collect and share additional information, which again reinforces the original reputation—leading to a self-fulfilling prophecy. Because of their intertwined dynamic association, gossip and reputation can be argued to evolve together.

In fact, boundaries between the two phenomena are blurry. People whose stories shape and control the collective memory about others have been described as *reputational entrepreneurs* (Fine, 1996). Furthermore, gossip behavior has been labeled as *reputational information sharing* (Feinberg, et al., 2012) and *reputational information flow* (Craik, 2008, p. 25). Not surprisingly, much conceptual overlap exists between the aforementioned definition of gossip as positive and negative talk about absent others and Craik's definition of reputation: "The network interpretation of reputation entails a finite number of other individuals who directly or indirectly know the person by face or name and who are more or less in communication with each other about the deeds and utterances of that person." (Craik, 2008, p. 25). I will refer to information sharing when subsuming acts of gossip and reputation formation in the following.

The latter network-oriented definition presents information sharing as collectively organized informal surveillance that may prevent selfish behaviors, also recognized as social control (Coleman, 1990). If after single encounters current partners are unable to directly reciprocate cooperative behaviors (or punish defective behavior), cooperation is likely rewarded via *indirect reciprocity* (Molleman, Van den Broek, & Egas, 2013; Sylwester & Roberts, 2013) from future partners who have been exchanging gossip. Through this mechanism, network embeddedness operates as a protective environment against exploitive behaviors in social exchanges that involve a leap of faith (e.g., in situations similar to a sequential prisoner's dilemma). Arguably, reputation is most effective in contexts of perfectly embedded social interactions (Raub & Weesie, 1990). Having said this, spreading gossip is not cheap as reporting on others comes at costs. The same principle applies: Sharing gossip is indirectly rewarded through the generalized exchange in networks where everyone is granted access to reputational information. Crucially, the effectiveness of promoting cooperation heavily depends on the coordinated communication with third parties, which in turns depends on the opportunities and constraints provided by the overall social network structure.

# GLOBAL NETWORK STRUCTURES AS DRIVERS OF INFORMATION SHARING

Besides the overall structure, the individual's scope of action is mainly influenced by its immediate network environment. It is thus useful to distinguish several analytical levels of network structure, as illustrated in Figure 23.2. First, networks may be described in global terms, such as the size of a network and the overall density of relationships therein. Second, networks consist of smaller local units, such as cliques and triads. Third, within this local environment individual network members are embedded, who differ in their quality and quantity of relationships with others. In the following, I review theory, measures, and findings separately for these levels.

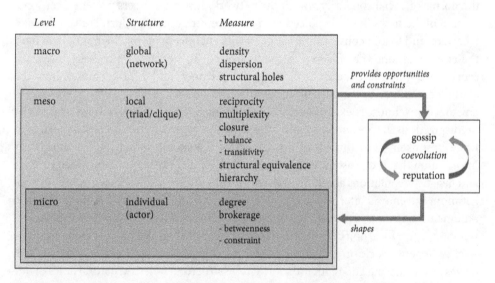

FIGURE 23.2. Schematic overview of different analytical levels associated with the emergence of information sharing.

## Theoretical Expectations

Because there is no need for past or future direct encounter between the focal object and the actors involved in information sharing, evaluations may travel through entire networks and produce sticky reputations without further verification or falsification. Picking up on that thought, Burt (2001) has asked how network closure drives the emergence of gossip and reputation. His answer yields two predictions.

The *Bandwidth Hypothesis* (Burt, 2001) presumes enhanced information flow in closed networks, where many well-connected social relationships exist that provide extensive opportunities for exchange and communication. More connections facilitate wider bandwidth for information flow. For example, in an online reputation system (e.g., trading network Amazon or eBay) a buyer can be more confident about the accuracy of a seller's average evaluation, the more reports of experience from previous buyers are included (Burt, 2014, Diekmann, Przepiorka, this volume). The key to this bandwidth effect is that the network does not operate as a distributive filter but displays the same information to every member accessing the evaluation platform. Following the bandwidth argument, as a result of closure, gossip flourishes and a collectively shared reputation on a focal object's behavior is created.

In opposition to that, social networks are often highly reactive to information flow. Because of this, the *Echo Hypothesis* (Burt, 2001) states less bandwidth in closed networks. People edit, filter and tailor information to conversations, be it strategically motivated or by the desire to establish and continue harmonic relationships with others. Specifically, when relationships are created and maintained through sharing information about others (i.e., there is reactivity to gossip), senders will be careful not to violate the norms of social solidarity within the network. Instead, senders present a censored version of the news that is balanced with the receiver's opinion (Burt, 2014). Likewise, receivers tend to join conversations aligned with their feelings, in which they hear back the emotional tone they favored in the first place. This echo promotes an unrealistic sense that opinions are shared by others, making senders and receivers more convinced about their opinion and eventually ignorant of the broader context. Through this mechanism, echo reinforces existing beliefs and blends out contradictory news that falsify predispositions. Importantly, opinion differences between sender and receiver can continue unspoken—and thus need no balance—because the sender will disclose only information that is consistent with what the receiver already knows. Moreover, positive and negative reputations about the same object not only co-exist across groups but even get more extreme as interpersonal evaluations travel the network. Following the echo argument, the result of closure is not a collectively shared but an amplified polarized reputation on a focal object's behavior (see also Giardini and Wittek, this volume).

Next to network closure, Burt (1992) discussed another structural characteristic that drives gossip sharing and reputation formation: structural holes. Structural holes divide networks into relatively disconnected cliques. There are many social ties within cliques (i.e., network closure is high) but few between (i.e., network closure is low). Actors connecting cliques by having social ties to two or more cliques are called *brokers* or gatekeepers. An example is the actor "b" positioned below sender and receiver in Figure 23.1. As much of the inter-clique communication can only operate indirectly via those bridging brokers, they have the unique power to disproportionally control the information flow between cliques, most importantly withhold true and spread false gossip without being caught.

The *Brokerage Hypothesis* states that brokers, who are weakly embedded in cliques, disseminate non-redundant news into an otherwise homogeneously informed clique environment (Burt, 2004). Bringing in innovative ideas is presumed to be a unique strength of weak ties (Granovetter, 1973) and part of so-called bridging social capital (Burt, 1992; Lin, 2001). Brokers can report on an actor to one clique about her behavior in another clique, thereby possibly shedding a different light on her. Crucially, due to the distance between cliques brokers have to worry less about a negative reactivity to their evaluation. Because of the brokers' special status within the network, others also tend to attribute much value to their opinions. According to this reasoning, a more balanced reputation of an object is created in the structural hole condition than under the closure condition. Yet as an entire clique may depend on the external reporting of a single broker, evaluations are still less accurate than in the bandwidth assumption. The broker may even propagate alternating gossip stories for her competitive advantage (e.g., exploit the echo effect), so that conflicting reputations of the same object co-exist among weakly connected cliques. Put differently; an actor has as many reputations as there are groups in which the actor is discussed because reputations are generated and maintained separately (Burt, 2014).

## Empirical Measures

Gossip and reputation triads are typically embedded in larger networks, such as formal organizations. Special research designs are needed to empirically inquire the role of network structure for the emergence of gossip and reputation. A suitable tool for the analysis of relational data in the social and behavioral sciences is social network analysis. However, there are only a few empirical studies on gossip and reputation using a social network perspective. One of the reasons is that gossip is still a rather novel topic in the field of (organizational) sociology. Another reason is that quantitative methods of collecting and analyzing social network data have only become broadly available and popular during the last two decades or so. A milestone in sociometric research on gossip was set by Burt and Knez' article on third-party effects on trust (Burt & Knez, 1995). This topic was further elaborated on and investigated in great detail in Burt's book 'Brokerage and Closure' (2005). A number of studies followed using experimental designs (Beersma & Van Kleef, 2012; Feinberg, Willer, & Schultz, 2014; Kniffin, Wilson, & Sloan Wilson, 2010), regression analysis (Rooks et al., 2011), and finally social network analysis (Ellwardt, Steglich, et al., 2012; Grosser et al., 2010; Wittek & Wielers, 1998). The latest questionnaire-based sociometric studies also included the statistical testing of global and local network structures: Essentially, an observed network graph is compared to a random graph expected by chance (Ellwardt, Labianca, et al., 2012; Ellwardt, Steglich, et al., 2012; Ellwardt, Wittek, et al., 2012; Grosser et al., 2010; van de Bunt et al., 2005). Statistical modeling of networks—such as exponential random graph models (ERGM) and stochastic actor-oriented models (SOAM)—was made possible through the development of computationally manageable programs like UNICET, Pajek and StOCNET—the forerunner of what is now known as RSiena.

Primary data on complete gossip networks have mostly been gathered with the so-called *roster method* or *round-robin design* (Burt, 2005; Ellwardt, Labianca, & Wittek, 2012; Grosser, Lopez-Kidwell, & Labianca, 2010; Rooks, Tazelaar, & Snijders, 2011). In this survey tool, network members (egos, e.g., employees) report on their relationships with every other network member (alters, e.g., co-workers). This can be simply ego selecting alters on a list with whom ego has been sharing gossip in the past, or ego rating the relationship quality with every alter on an ordinal scale (e.g., from trust to distrust). Since having to report on a large number of people can become a tedious task, social network studies are limited to settings with small sample sizes: for instance to organizational sites consisting of 30 and 36 employees (Ellwardt, Labianca, et al., 2012; Grosser et al., 2010; Jaeger, Skleder, Rind, & Rosnow, 1994). Ideally, all members take part in a social network survey, as only a nearly complete inventory permits measuring, drawing and testing whole networks.

Based on the collected relational data, structural characteristics may be quantified to describe the network in global terms. The two most popular variables include network density and reciprocity. *Density* is a simple measure of cohesion as it expresses the proportion of observed versus possible number of ties (e.g., an undirected network of five people has $5 \times 4/2 = 10$ possible ties, with four observed gossip ties density is $4/10 = 0.4$). *Reciprocity* is retrieved by dividing the number of reciprocated ties (e.g., ego nominates alter, and alter nominates ego) by the total number of ties. *Multiplexity* denotes the tendency to observe several ties between two actors (e.g., ego has a gossip tie and a trust tie with alter). Network *centralization* informs about the dispersion of ties, for example, whether gossip ties are evenly distributed throughout the network or cluster around few dominating actors. In a minimally centralized network, all actors have an equal number of ties (centralization = 0, e.g., in a ring-shaped network graph or a fully connected graph with density = 1), whereas in a maximally centralized network one central actor owns all ties (centralization = 1, in a star-shaped network graph).

## Empirical Findings

Because collecting panel data in real-life network settings is complicated and costly, cross-sectional designs dominate the field. Yet there seems no doubt that network closure is associated with vivid communication exchange. In their logistic regression study among 387 buyers and suppliers, Rooks and colleagues (2011) found gossip to be most likely in dense business networks, where cooperation partners were connected through many mutual partners. The likelihood of gossip further increased once a large problem occurred and future business exchange was expected.

An interesting question is how exactly gossip and reputation are shaped within dense, closed structures. In a log-linear model of 3,584 dyad relations between senior managers of a US American high-technology firm, the odds of trust were amplified from 41 percent to 61 percent when especially close relations were embedded in extensive indirect connections via third parties (Burt & Knez, 1996, p. 79). An explanation is that business partners call on reputational information about their partners' and that gossip exchange drives the motivation to cooperate in dense networks. Interestingly, also distrust in weak relations increased when surrounded by extensive indirect connections, namely from 16 percent to 44 percent (Burt & Knez, 1996, p. 80f). As negative effects on trust were more amplified than positive effects, Burt and Knez (1996, p. 82) conclude that the "dark side to network density" outweighs its familiar positive side.

This dark side was further accentuated in illustrative evidence supporting the *Echo Hypothesis* over the *Bandwidth Hypothesis* (Burt, 2001, 2005). The analysis included survey network data and logit models on 8,298 relations among 345 investment bankers. Strong connections enhanced gossip activity but not information flow. Because of this, positive and negative evaluations of bankers from their colleagues increased together, not in opposition. This finding clearly contradicts bandwidth's prediction of balance in adjacent relationships, but instead, underpins an echo pattern where actors are only open to confirmative stories. This way, social reinforcement of predispositions is given priority over accuracy, so that closed network structures eventually produce ignorant certainty. Burt (2001, p. 29) therefore concludes that dense networks are potent environments of (unintended) scapegoating, groupthink, polarized trust and distorted reputations. The tendency in clustered networks toward unverified, sometimes far-fetched rumor-driven consensus was later also verified in laboratory computer experiments (DiFonzo et al., 2013). An overview of the discussed studies is presented in Table 23.1

# LOCAL NETWORK STRUCTURES AS DRIVERS OF INFORMATION SHARING

The discussion until now focused on whole social networks as drivers of gossip and reputation formation. However, next to structural constraints and opportunities on the macro level, information sharing is also believed to depend on the meso level, that is the three social ties between the senders, receivers and objects of gossip in a triad. Specifically, several scholars have pointed to the strong interplay between trust and gossip (Burt & Knez, 1996; Ellwardt, Wittek, & Wielers, 2012; Van de Bunt, Wittek, & De Klepper, 2005). I will summarize three arguments relevant from a social network perspective here.

Table 23.1. Overview of Selected Studies on Gossip and Reputation Networks

| Study | Topic | Metric | Method | Association | Conclusion |
|---|---|---|---|---|---|
| Burt and Knez, 1995 | Gossip sending | Closure | Loglinear models of dyads | Positive (more for distrust than for trust) | Dark side of dense networks |
| Burt, 2001 | Gossip sending | Closure | Logit models of dyads | Positive (without balancing opinions) | Echo overpowers bandwidth effect |
| DiFonzo et al., 2013 | Gossip sending | Clustering | Mean comparisons of laboratory networks | Positive | Rumor clustering amplifies unverified belief polarization |
| Ebbers and Wijnberg, 2010 | Reputation | Transitivity (alliance) | SIENA | Positive | Reputation strength and closeness to past allies predict future alliance formation |
| Ellwardt, Labianca and Wittek, 2012 | Gossip object | Multiplexity Centrality (friendship eigenvector) | ERGM | Positive (for positive and negative gossip) Negative (for negative gossip) | People socially control team members and disliked others |
| Ellwardt, Steglich and Wittek, 2012 | Gossip sending Gossip receiving | Multiplex reciprocity Multiplex centrality | SIENA | Positive (dyads) Negative (popularity) | Gossip is reciprocated with friendship in dyads Extensive gossipers are unpopular in network |
| Erdogan et al., 2015 | Gossip sending | Centrality | Random coefficient regressions | None | Gossip may still act as moderator on advice centrality |
| Grosser et al., 2010 | Gossip sending Reputation | Structural equivalence Multiplexity Centrality | MRQAP and OLS regressions | Positive (for negative gossip) Positive Mixed | Central gossipers likely suffer reputation damage |
| Hu et al., 2012 | Reputation | In-degree (no. positive evaluations) Closure (mutual ties) Homophily | Conditional logistic regression Social network topology | Positive | Positive evaluations increase with past appraisal, sharing acquaintances and geographical location |

| Study | Variables | Network measure | Method | Result | Finding |
|---|---|---|---|---|---|
| Jaeger et al., 1994 | Gossip sending Gossip object Reputation | Centrality Multiplexity | Mean comparisons | Curvilinear Positive | People gossip about friends and disliked others |
| McDonald et al., 2007 | Gossip sending | Centrality | ANCOVA | Positive | Popular girls share (non-aggressive) information about peers and family |
| Mehra et al., 2006 | Reputation | Centrality (friendship eigenvector) Density (intragroup friendships) | OLS regressions | Positive Weakly positive | Popularity and density relate to positive reputation within group (but not beyond) |
| Rooks et al., 2011 | Gossip sending | Closure | Logistic regressions | Positive | Gossip likely in dense business networks with many common third-parties |
| Sommerfeld et al., 2007 | Gossip receiving | Direct versus indirect (= gossip) observation tie | Mean comparisons | Positive (positive gossip with cooperation) | Cooperation increases when gossip is positive |
| Sommerfeld et al., 2008 | Gossip sending Gossip receiving | Number of positive and negative gossip ties | Mean comparisons | Positive (positive gossip with cooperation) | Limited power of manipulative gossip where multiple sources of information exist |
| Van de Bunt et al., 2005 | Gossip sending | Centrality | SIENA models | Positive | Gossipers initiate trust ties with popular alters |
| Wittek and Wielers, 1998 | Gossip sending | Structural holes Closure Balance | OLS regressions | None None Positive | Coalition more important than closure or constraint |

## Theoretical Expectations

First, gossip is not cheap as the sender needs to consider that the receiver might disagree with the sender's negative or positive evaluation of the object. Disagreement, especially in reaction to negative evaluations, can imply severe repercussions for the sender: The receiver may break her tie with the sender and report the gossip incident to the object, who then also may break her tie with the sender. Because of this, the sender will likely share gossip with receivers trusted to approve the gossip and stay discrete about it. In many cases, this trust is established through the gradual social exchange of gossip from minor to major transactions (Blau, 1964)—the receiver reciprocates the sender's signal of trust and is willing to take the risk of sharing (negative) information with the sender herself. Based on this argument, *reciprocity* in sender-receiver dyads is a prerequisite of vivid gossip activity. Moreover, a pure gossip tie will be enriched with trust over time, and vice versa. The simultaneous evolution and existence of multiple relationships—for example, gossip and trust, formal and informal, frequent contact and friendship—within a tie is known as *multiplexity* (Ellwardt, Steglich, & Wittek, 2012; Grosser et al., 2010).

Second, to avoid disagreement, the sender will select the receiver based on the antici-pated trust tie between the receiver and the object. If the sender expects a positive, trust-ing tie, solely non-negative gossip will be shared about the object. Only when a negative tie is expected, negative gossip will be disclosed. This attempt at adapting to and balancing relationships with third parties has been posited in Heider's *Balance Theory* (Heider, 1958). Balanced triads are characterized by a trust tie between sender and receiver, and either presence or absence of trust ties with the object. In simple words, friends of friends are friends (closure), and enemies of enemies are friends (coalition). Imbalance is assumed to create cognitive dissonance in the triad that ultimately leads to the breaking of ties. Following this reasoning, another precondition of gossip is the *structural equivalence* of sender-object and receiver-object dyads, here meaning that sender and receiver have a similar relationship with the object.

Besides reciprocity and equivalence, scenarios of perfectly synchronized connected-ness yield the risk of information redundancy. In a specific gossip incident, the sender often will initially be more knowledgeable or opinionated about the object than the receiver. Otherwise, the transmitted message contains little news value. Because of this, some asymmetry of information will exist in most sender-receiver dyads.

Third, computer-mediated laboratory experiments suggested that gossip sharing in cliques as small as triads likely have direct implications for belief polarization, reputa-tion formation and the willingness to cooperate with third parties (DiFonzo et al., 2013; Sommerfeld, Krambeck, & Milinski, 2008; Sommerfeld, Krambeck, Semmann, & Milinski, 2007). There is a heightened interest in negative information, as exploitive behaviors are perceived to be disproportionally damaging as compared to the utility of compliant behaviors (Davis & McLeod, 2003; De Backer & Gurven, 2009). Nevertheless, a positive report of the sender increases the odds that the receiver will trust the object in future mixed-motives situations. Because of this, positive gossip is non-trivial and should not be underestimated in contexts of cooperation, such as buyer and supplier business networks (Diekmann, Jann, Przepiorka, & Wehrli, 2014; Rooks et al., 2011). Positive information from multiple sources is a valuable update that proofs useful for decision-making about adaptive matters (e.g., to whom to go for advice) and is freed from reliance upon one's personal observation.

## Empirical Measures

Descriptions of local structures firmly ground on the inspection and count of triads (Wasserman & Faust, 1994, p. 556). Thus, multiple means exist to describe the presence and absence of ties between three actors. Graphical examples of triadic configurations are shown in Figure 23.2.

A widely used measure is network closure. *Closure* describes the propensity to close triads through creating a third tie whenever two ties exist. Ties in open triads are believed to dissolve faster and be less stable than so-termed Simmelian ties that are structurally embedded in strong relations (Krackhardt, 1998). Triads may be closed in a transitive or a cyclic way, as explained in the following.

Closing triads in a balanced way does not necessarily imply the presence of three identical ties, for example, friends being connected through mutual friends. *Transitivity* also allows the presence of different ties in a triad. The focus lies on structurally balanced relationships between two actors, for example, the object is either a mutual friend or a mutual enemy. The latter case resembles a coalition between ego and alter, who oppose a third party. A way to assess global network transitivity is dividing the number of observed transitive triplets by the number of potentially transitive triplets in a network. Local conglomerations of closed triads hint to the existence of cliques, that is, there are areas with low versus high densities in the network.

A measure going beyond structural balance in triads is *structural equivalence*. In this metric, two network members are compared in their local connections. Actors who occupy the same role or position in a network are said to be role-equivalent and substitutable in their function. Typically, in organizations, two subordinates are more structurally similar than one subordinate and one manager. Brokers naturally feature low structural equivalence as their strength is avoiding mutual connections to establish a unique position. In contrast, members of a clique are highly equivalent in their connection patterns as they share many mutual contacts. Having a large number of common third-party ties—although not a precondition—goes along with greater structural equivalence. In a gossip triad, sender and receiver share a mutual contact as they both know the object, and their structural equivalence increases with the number of mutually discussed objects. In Figure 23.3, both the dark nodes are equivalent, and both the light nodes are equivalent.

Finally, ties may be undirected (e.g., two actors have a formal work relation) or directed pointing from ego to alter and back (e.g., ego trusts alter, and vice versa). Triads characterized by three ties pointing into the same direction, specifically all clock-wise or all counter clock-wise, have been called three-cycles. Their cyclic structure indicates

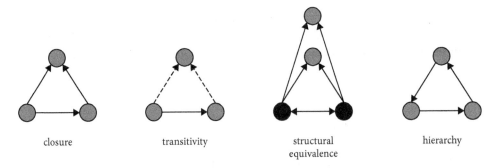

| closure | transitivity | structural equivalence | hierarchy |

**FIGURE 23.3.** Examples of local network structures based on triads.

*hierarchy*, implying that resources follow a path. Hierarchical information flow is found in formal organizations, but also in informal networks, where gossip diffuses through a chain of many actors.

## Empirical Findings

An influential approach to studying relationships with third parties stems from Wittek and Wielers (1998), who investigated network data from six German work organizations and six Dutch business school classes with OLS regression models. Three predictions were tested: The inclination toward gossip increases with (1) ego's number of structural holes and thus the potential to act as broker (*Constraint Hypothesis*), (2) the number of closed triads where ego, alter and tertius are connected through positive ties (*Closure Hypothesis*), and—in opposition to the previous prediction—(3) the number of balanced triads where ego and alter share a positive tie with one another but a negative tie with tertius (*Coalition Hypothesis*). Only the latter prediction was supported by the results, which was later termed Gossip Effect (Van de Bunt et al., 2005).

This shows that gossip ties do not exist in isolation but are typically accompanied and reinforced by other kinds of connections, for instance, instrumental and expressive exchanges in organizations. In a series of three studies in a Dutch childcare organization, Ellwardt and colleagues asked whether formal work ties and informal trust relations influence becoming sender and object of gossip (Ellwardt, Labianca, et al., 2012; Ellwardt, Steglich, et al., 2012; Ellwardt, Wittek, et al., 2012). Methods comprised of analyzing complete networks of up to 38 employees with exponential random graph models (ERGM) and Simulation Investigation for Empirical Network Analysis (SIENA) in StOCNET and RSiena. Gossip ties were highly reciprocal, and importantly, tended to be supplemented by trust ties over time, indicating multiplex reciprocity (Ellwardt, Steglich, et al., 2012). Furthermore, there was a strong disposition toward sharing positive and negative gossip with and about team members (Ellwardt, Labianca, et al., 2012). Gossip ties thus co-evolved along with pre-existing formal constraint and opportunity structures in local organizational networks.

Grosser and colleagues (2010) inquired the role of structural equivalence, multiplexity and centrality for the propensity to engage in positive and negative gossip at work. Their sociometric study included MRQAP (multiple regression quadratic assignment procedure) analysis and OLS regressions of the relations among 30 employees within a US American company. Friendship ties and sharing mutual third-party ties (i.e., structural equivalence) increased the likelihood of negative gossip, adding to the previous finding on coalitions. Positive gossip was most probable between friends and colleagues (i.e., multiplex ties). Interestingly, the study also assessed peer and supervisor evaluations, which can be seen as a proxy of reputation. Although employees engaging in much gossip activity (i.e., centrality in the gossip network) were perceived as influential by peers, supervisors rated their performance poor. The latter finding suggests that gossip not only shapes the reputation of the objects but also of the senders of gossip.

Despite these effects, preexisting reputations may influence the formation of local network structures, such as transitive triads: Ebbers and Wijnberg (2010) used SIENA models to show in a dynamic network of 226 Dutch film collaborators that the tendency to form collaborative alliances is driven by the actors' reputation and their close connections to previously reputable co-actors. Similarly, in their empirical study on an online evaluation network of open source software projects, Hu and colleagues (2012) found positive evaluations to be more probable when contributors had previously received appraisal from others and shared projects or acquainted contributors with their current evaluators.

# INDIVIDUAL NETWORK STRUCTURES AS DRIVERS OF INFORMATION SHARING

Even though global and local network structures frame opportunities and constraints for behavior in groups, individual decisions are greatly influenced by the individuals' myopic perceptions of their personal social environment. Specifically, individuals often rely on a cognitive map of the social network that is not perfectly aligned with the actual social network, with a bias toward their own direct relationships.

## Theoretical Expectations

Less network theorizing exists regarding the network structure surrounding individual actors. Individual network structure, better recognized as an ego-centric network, captures one ego and all her alters with their interconnections, but disregards alters not connected to ego (and any other egos in the network). This lack of focus on ego-centric structures seems hardly surprising given the commonly used global network perspective. In fact, a limited perspective on ego works against a strictly handled network interpretation of information sharing, where gossip and reputation are tackled as relational phenomena. Nevertheless, some expectations may be derived from ego's immediate network environment: The more ties ego has to alters, the more resources may be exchanged with different alters. The fewer ties occur between ego's alters, the more broker power ego has over the alters. The ego-centric structure thus provides opportunities and constraints for individual behavior in contexts of information sharing.

Consequently, multiple measures may be constructed to describe ego's positioning in the network. It should be noted, however, that ego's structural position is only meaningful in comparison to the structural positions of other egos in the same context. For example, high brokerage yields a competitive advantage as long as others in the overall network have a low brokerage.

## Empirical Measures

Besides global and local variables, structural characteristics can be quantified on the individual ego-centric level. *Degree centrality* is the count of an actor's ties. The higher an actor's degree, the more central the actor is located in the network. This centrality measure is further distinguished in directed networks into number of incoming nominations from alters to ego (indegree) and number of outgoing nominations from ego to alters (outdegree)—for instance, to describe popular sinks and sources of gossip.

Brokers often have a comparatively low degree centrality but score high on *betweenness* centrality (Burt, 2014; Freeman, 1979), also known as information centrality. This metric assesses the extent to that ego connects otherwise disconnected alters and thus ego's monopoly access to structural holes. For example, ego has been sharing information with alter A and alter B, while alter A and alter B did not share information with each other. Two disconnected alters facilitate one opportunity for ego to act as broker (betweenness = 1); four disconnected alters facilitate six opportunities to broker connections (betweenness = 6). However, if ego shares her advantageous position with another broker, her monopoly status is reduced, and the score is halved (betweenness = 3 for both brokers). Betweenness reaches its maximum value where one actor bridges the connections between all remaining actors (e.g., in a star network).

Another metric building on betweenness is network *constraint*. Egos are maximally constrained (constraint = 100) when they have no access to structural holes while all their alters are interconnected. In such a scenario, ego is surrounded by a highly closed network structure and hence exposed to much redundant information sharing together with an increased risk of echo.

Needless to say, there are many other metrics and modes used to inspect networks. This overview was limited to basic measures and to concepts addressed in the previous literature on gossip and reputation. It also focused on whole one-mode networks but disregarded egocentric networks, in which egos have no interconnections and are analyzed separately with regard to the structure of their personal alter networks.

The discussion further ignored important arguments pertaining to actor level attributes (e.g., formal status) as well as perceived similarities between actors (e.g., homophily). Comprehensive textbook introductions to the design and analysis of social network studies can be found in Robins (2015), Borgatti et al. (2013), Kadushin (2012) for complete networks, and Crossley et al. (2015) for ego-networks.

## Empirical Findings

Most social networks studies consider the individual's overall position in the network, called actor or degree centrality. Jaeger and colleagues (1994) were among the first to demonstrate the links between centrality, reputation, and gossip behavior. In a cross-sectional sociometric study among 36 US American sorority sisters, the authors assessed the relative popularity and likability of each sister within the sorority. Popularity here referred to degree centrality, whereas likability reflected the reputation of a sister. Mean comparisons revealed that moderate gossipers had significantly more friends than low and high gossipers, suggesting a curvilinear association between gossip activity and popularity. A similar effect was shown by Ellwardt, Steglich and Wittek(2012), who argue that people turn away from indiscrete others who excessively talk about colleagues. Yet empirical results are context-bound and vary across study populations and research designs. Erdogan and colleagues (2015) found no association between the tendency to gossip and centrality in advice networks in a Turkish survey on 250 retail employees. McDonald and colleagues (2007), who inspected videotape recordings in their observational study among 139 fourth-grade girls in US American schools, found sociometrically popular girls and their friends to gossip most. The researchers conclude that popular girls mainly shared informative and neutral contents, and thus were perceived as socially competent rather than aggressive by their peers.

Next to being the sender of gossip, also the roles of receiver and object have been related to network centrality. In a sociometric panel study of 17 employees in a German paper factory using SIENA modeling in StOCNET (Van de Bunt et al., 2005), frequent gossipers tended to engage in trust relationships with popular alters in the organizational network. Central actors are thus potential receivers of gossip. In contrast, peripheral actors with few supporters run the risk of becoming the objects of gossip (Ellwardt, Labianca, et al., 2012) and thereby being further ostracized from informal networks. Also, Jaeger and colleagues (1994) found that least likable people were frequent gossip objects, although having many friends did not protect from becoming a frequently discussed object—perhaps because friends tended to talk about each other. Finally, it should be noted that friendship centrality is correlated with positive performance evaluations, as has been shown within dense clusters of organizational networks (Mehra, Dixon, Brass, & Robertson, 2006), so that popularity and reputation are likely endogenous.

# CONCLUDING REMARKS AND FUTURE DIRECTIONS

This review demonstrated that gossip and reputation can be understood as coevolving relational phenomena, which partially overlap and strongly influence one another (*Proposition 1*), and which are largely driven by opportunities and constraints inherent to the structure of social networks (*Proposition 2*). The vast body of the empirical literature on information sharing networks has focused on gossip, using small cross-sectional samples of dyadic data to inspect individual and local structures in organizations. Fewer studies can be found on reputation networks, which often utilize data from large online collaborative platforms. As a result, future research employing social network analyses would benefit from designs that (1) are more tailored to and aligned with network theorizing, (2) based on a broader empirical scope to allow better inquiry of global structures, and (3) aimed at a stronger combination of gossip and reputation networks, preferably in an interdisciplinary framework. These three suggestions are outlined in the following.

## Alignment with Theory

Whereas scholars agree that gossip, in theory, involves three different social roles (sender, receiver, object), this view is hardly translated into empirical practice. Much of the research addresses either the senders or the objects of gossip but refrains from a rigorous implementation of a three-actor model. Future research may connect theory and empirical design more consistently by studying triads and network configurations beyond. Having said this, primary three-way data are nearly absent, as they are extremely tedious to collect and complex to analyze. Researchers will have to explore novel approaches, perhaps using computer-aided sociometric survey tools (Ellwardt, Labianca, et al., 2012) or computer-generated secondary data.

Another common mismatch between theoretical and empirical approaches is arguing from a dynamic viewpoint while employing cross-sectional methods. Similarly to triadic data, gathering first-hand panel network data yields particular challenges because it requires high response rates and extraordinary motivation from study participants. If researchers want to understand the diffusion of gossip and the emergence of reputation in networks, empirical designs need to integrate repeated measures. Crucially, longitudinal methods would better permit capturing—and possibly disentangling—the coevolution between gossip and reputation. Moreover, causal hypotheses on selection and influence could be tested (i.e., with SAOM) to answer questions like: How do polarized versus balanced reputations evolve in triads? Do gossip senders choose receivers who have comparable ex-ante opinions about an object (selection), or do senders and receivers become similar in their opinion during their course of social interaction (influence)?

## Extension of the Empirical Scope

Besides broadening the empirical range to longitudinal data, more large-scale socio-metric data would be desirable. To date, most research designs base on small intra-organizational samples so that findings are context-bound and incomparable across cases. Studying inter-organizational gossip and reputation networks (Chandler, Haunschild, Rhee, & Beckman, 2013; Rooks et al., 2011; Yu & Potoski, 1998) would allow inquiring the role of global structures and thereby generate insights on contextual macro variables. These variables may, for instance, assess structural holes in organizations where reputations matter for getting promoted and unique access to information offers a competitive advantage. Empirical multi-level designs would have to rely on measuring varying yet comparable organizational settings (i.e., a large organization with many subdivisions).

Alternatively, multiple networks could be gathered through the application of an ego-centric design, where egos are randomly chosen and next asked to extensively report on the relationships between their alters. Taking such an angle appears to be particularly useful where network boundaries are weakly defined, information sharing stretches across contexts (e.g., people gossip at the workplace and home), and researchers seek representative conclusions. A challenge, however, is informant accuracy (Marsden, 1990) because ego is likely incapable of completely overviewing her social landscape and reporting on the often hidden gossip activities between alters.

## Moving in an Interdisciplinary Direction

Lastly, research could more explicitly integrate the coevolving phenomena of gossip and reputation in a single framework. An integrated theory would further benefit from 'modernization': Much of the classical work has discussed face-to-face interactions between people. However, these days, processes of information sharing originate, unfold and evolve in computerized environments. Communication is exchanged via voice and text messaging and so-called social media, which come with different costs and benefits for senders, receivers and objects of gossip than unrecorded evaluative communication. On the one hand, electronic messaging is a cheap channel that potentially reaches a broadly networked audience. On the other hand, it leaves digital traces entailing destructive repercussions for gossip senders when forwarded or publicized. If costs and benefits vary across channels, the way gossip and reputation emerge within the different channels likely varies too.

Future research could hence opt for combining the different types of networked communication, ideally in a multidisciplinary effort. Classical data on information sharing could be supplemented with data from digital media. Examples are reputation scores generated in buyer-seller platforms like eBay (Diekmann et al., 2014; for a discussion on this methodology see also Snijders and Matzat, this volume) and programming forums like Ohloh (Hu et al., 2012). In fact, the field of social computing is on the rise, so that a growing community outside the social sciences is interested in network theorizing and makes statistical models for so-called big data available.

This review could show that gossip and reputation are established topics in the social networks literature. Both theoretical and empirical directions have already proven fruitful so that it will be interesting to see where future avenues lead. Either way, related research on trust and cooperation will likely benefit from approaches treating gossip and reputation as coevolving relational phenomena.

# REFERENCES

Beersma, B., & Van Kleef, G. A. (2012). Why people gossip: An empirical analysis of social motives, antecedents, and consequences. *Journal of Applied Social Psychology*, 42(11), 2640–2670. http://doi.org/10.1111/j.1559-1816.2012.00956.x

Blau, P. (1964). *Exchange and power in social life*. New York: John Wiley.

Borgatti, S. P., Everett, M. G., & Johnson, J. C. (2013). *Analyzing social networks*. London: Sage.

Burt, R. S. (1992). *The social structure of competition. structural holes*. Cambridge: Harvard University Press.

Burt, R. S. (2001). Bandwidth and echo: Trust, information, and gossip in social networks. In A. Casella & J. E. Rauch (Eds.), *Networks and Markets: Contributions from economics and sociology* (pp. 30–74). New York: Russel Sage Foundation.

Burt, R. S. (2004). Structural holes and good ideas. *American Journal of Sociology*, 110(2), 349–399. http://doi.org/10.1086/421787

Burt, R. S. (2005). *Brokerage and closure: An introduction to social capital*. Oxford: Oxford University Press.

Burt, R. S. (2014). Network structure of advantage, governance: closure, trust, status, and reputation. http://faculty.chicagobooth.edu/ronald.burt/research/files/NSAG.pdf (accessed 22-12-2016).

Burt, R. S., & Knez, M. (1995). Kinds of third-party effects on trust. *Rationality and Society*, 7(3), 255–292. http://doi.org/10.1177/1043463195007003003

Burt, R. S., & Knez, M. (1996). Trust and third-party gossip. In R. M. Kramer & T. R. Tyler (Eds.), *Trust in organizations: Frontiers of theory and research* (pp. 68–89). Thousand Oaks, CA: Sage Publications.

Chandler, D., Haunschild, P. R., Rhee, M., & Beckman, C. M. (2013). The effects of firm reputation and status on interorganizational network structure. *Strategic Organization*, 11(3), 217–244. http://doi.org/10.1177/1476127013478693

Coleman, J. S. (1990). *Foundations of social theory*. Cambridge, MA: Harvard University Press.

Craik, K. H. (2008). *Reputation: A network interpretation*. New York : Oxford University Press. http://doi.org/10.1093/acprof:oso/9780195330922.001.0001

Crossley, N., Belloti, E., Edwards, G., Everett, M. G., Koskinen, J., & Tranmer, M. (2015). *Social network analysis for ego-nets*. London: Sage.

Davis, H., & McLeod, S. L. (2003). Why humans value sensational news: An evolutionary perspective. *Evolution and Human Behavior*, 24(3), 208–216. http://dx.doi.org/10.1016/S1090-5138(03)00012-6

De Backer, C. J. S. J. S., & Gurven, M. (2009). Whispering down the lane: The economics of vicarious information transfer. *Adaptive Behavior*, 14(805), 249–264. http://doi.org/10.1177/105971230601400303

Diekmann, A., Jann, B., Przepiorka, W., & Wehrli, S. (2014). Reputation formation and the evolution of cooperation in anonymous online markets. *American Sociological Review*, 79(1), 65–85. http://doi.org/10.1177/0003122413512316

Diekmann, A., & Przepiorka, W. (2019). Trust and reputation in markets. In F. Giardini & R. P. M. Wittek (Eds.), *Handbook of gossip and reputation*. New York: Oxford University Press.

DiFonzo, N., Bourgeois, M. J., Suls, J., Homan, C., Stupak, N., Brooks, B. P.,…Bordia, P. (2013). Rumor clustering, consensus, and polarization: Dynamic social impact and self-organization of hearsay. *Journal of Experimental Social Psychology*, 49(3), 378–399. http://doi.org/10.1016/j.jesp.2012.12.010

Dunbar, R. I. M. (2004). Gossip in evolutionary perspective. *Review of General Psychology*, 8(2), 100–110. http://doi.org/10.1037/1089-2680.8.2.100

Ebbers, J. J., & Wijnberg, N. M. (2010). Disentangling the effects of reputation and network position on the evolution of alliance networks. *Strategic Organization*, 8(3), 255–275. http://doi.org/10.1177/1476127010381102

Eder, D., & Enke, J. L. (1991). The structure of gossip: Opportunities and constraints on collective expression among adolescents. *American Sociological Review*, 56(4), 494–508. http://doi.org/10.2307/2096270

Ellwardt, L., Labianca, G., & Wittek, R. (2012). Who are the objects of positive and negative gossip at work? A social network perspective on workplace gossip. *Social Networks*, 34(2), 193–205. http://doi.org/10.1016/j.socnet.2011.11.003

Ellwardt, L., Steglich, C., & Wittek, R. (2012). The co-evolution of gossip and friendship in workplace social networks. *Social Networks*, 34(4), 623–633. http://doi.org/10.1016/j.socnet.2012.07.002

Ellwardt, L., Wittek, R., & Wielers, R. (2012). Talking about the boss: Effects of generalized and interpersonal trust on workplace gossip. *Group & Organization Management*, 37(4), 521–549. http://doi.org/10.1177/1059601112450607

Erdogan, B., Bauer, T. N., & Walter, J. (2015). Deeds that help and words that hurt: Helping and gossip as moderators of the relationship between leader-member exchange and advice network centrality. *Personnel Psychology*, 68(1), 185–214. http://doi.org/10.1111/peps.12075

Feinberg, M., Willer, R., & Schultz, M. (2014). Gossip and ostracism promote cooperation in groups. *Psychological Science*, 25(3), 656–664. http://doi.org/10.1177/0956797613510184

Feinberg, M., Willer, R., Stellar, J., & Keltner, D. (2012). The virtues of gossip: Reputational information sharing as prosocial behavior. *Journal of Personality and Social Psychology*, 102(5), 1015–1030. http://doi.org/10.1037/a0026650

Fine, G. A. (1996). Reputational entrepreneurs and the memory of incompetence: Melting supporters, partisan warriors, and images of President Harding. *American Journal of Sociology*, 101(5), 1159. http://doi.org/10.1086/230820

Foster, E. K. (2004). Research on gossip: Taxonomy, methods, and future directions. *Review of General Psychology*, 8(2), 78–99. http://doi.org/10.1037/1089-2680.8.2.78

Freeman, L. C. (1979). Centrality in social networks conceptual clarification. *Social Networks*, 1(3), 215–239. http://doi.org/10.1016/0378-8733(78)90021-7

Giardini, F., Wittek, R. P. M. (2019). Gossip, Reputation, and Sustainable Cooperation: Sociological Foundations. In F. Giardini, R. P. M. Wittek (Eds.), *Handbook of gossip and reputation*. New York: Oxford University Press.

Granovetter, M. S. (1973). Strength of weak ties. *American Journal of Sociology*, 78(6), 1360–1380. https://*doi.org*/10.1086/225469

Grosser, T. J., Lopez-Kidwell, V., & Labianca, G. (2010). A social network analysis of positive and negative gossip in organizational life. *Group & Organization Management, 35*(2), 177–212. http://doi.org/10.1177/1059601109360391

Heider, F. (1958). *The psychology of interpersonal relations.* New York: John Wiley & Sons.

Hu, D., Zhao, J. L., & Cheng, J. (2012). Reputation management in an open source developer social network: An empirical study on determinants of positive evaluations. *Decision Support Systems, 53*(3), 526–533. http://doi.org/10.1016/j.dss.2012.02.005

Jaeger, M. E., Skleder, A. A., Rind, B., & Rosnow, R. L. (1994). Gossip, gossipers, gossipees. In R. F. Goodman & A. Ben-Ze'ev (Eds.), *Good gossip* (pp. 154–168). Lawrence: University of Kansas Press.

Kadushin, C. (2012). *Understanding social networks: Theories, concepts, and findings.* Oxford: Oxford University Press.

Kniffin, K. M., Wilson, D. S., & Sloan Wilson, D. (2010). Evolutionary perspectives on workplace gossip: Why and how gossip can serve groups. *Group & Organization Management, 35*(2), 150–176. http://doi.org/10.1177/1059601109360390

Krackhardt, D. (1998). Simmelian ties: Super strong and sticky. In R. Kramer & M. Neale (Eds.), *Power and Influence in Organizations* (pp. 21–38). Thousand Oaks, CA: Sage.

Kurland, N. B., & Pelled, L. H. (2000). Passing the word: Toward a model of gossip and power in the workplace. *Academy of Management Review, 25*(2), 428–438. http://doi.org/10.5465/AMR.2000.3312928

Lin, N. (2001). *Social capital: A theory of structure and action.* London and New York: Cambridge University Press.

Marsden, P. V. (1990). Network data and measurement. *Annual Review of Sociology, 16,* 435–463. https://doi.org/10.1146/annurev.so.16.080190.002251

McDonald, K. L., Putallaz, M., Grimes, C. L., Kupersmidt, J. B., & Coie, J. D. (2007). Girl talk: Gossip, friendship, and sociometric status. *Merrill-Palmer Quarterly, 53*(3), 381–411. http://doi.org/10.1353/mpq.2007.0017

Mehra, A., Dixon, A. L., Brass, D. J., & Robertson, B. (2006). The social network ties of group leaders: Implications for group performance and leader reputation. *Organization Science, 17*(1), 64–79. http://doi.org/10.1287/orsc.1050.0158

Molleman, L., van den Broek, E., & Egas, M. (2013). Personal experience and reputation interact in human decisions to help reciprocally. *Proceedings of the Royal Society B: Biological Sciences, 280.* http://doi.org/10.1098/rspb.2012.3044

Raub, W., & Weesie, J. (1990). Reputation and efficiency in social interactions: An example of network effects. *American Journal of Sociology, 96*(3), 626–654. https://doi.org/10.1086/229574

Robins, G. (2015). *Doing social network research: Network-based research design for social scientists.* London: Sage.

Rooks, G., Tazelaar, F., & Snijders, C. (2011). Gossip and reputation in business networks. *European Sociological Review, 27*(1), 90–106. http://doi.org/10.1093/esr/jcp062

Snijders, C., Matzat, U. (2019). Online reputation systems. In F. Giardini & R.P.M. Wittek (Eds.), *Handbook of gossip and reputation.* New York: Oxford University Press.

Sommerfeld, R. D., Krambeck, H. J., & Milinski, M. (2008). Multiple gossip statements and their effect on reputation and trustworthiness. *Proceedings of the Royal Society B-Biological Sciences, 275*(1650), 2529–2536. http://doi.org/10.1098/rspb.2008.0762

Sommerfeld, R. D., Krambeck, H. J., Semmann, D., & Milinski, M. (2007). Gossip as an alternative for direct observation in games of indirect reciprocity. *Proceedings of the National Academy of Sciences of the United States of America, 104*(44), 17435–17440. http://doi.org/10.1073/pnas.0704598104

Sylwester, K., & Roberts, G. (2013). Reputation-based partner choice is an effective alternative to indirect reciprocity in solving social dilemmas. *Evolution and Human Behavior, 34*(3). http://doi.org/10.1016/j.evolhumbehav.2012.11.009

Van de Bunt, G. G., Wittek, R. P. M., & De Klepper, M. C. (2005). The evolution of intra-organizational trust networks: The case of a German paper factory: An empirical test of six trust mechanisms. *International Sociology, 20*(3), 339–369. http://doi.org/10.1177/0268580905055480

Wasserman, S., & Faust, K. (1994). *Social network analysis.* Cambridge: Cambridge University Press.

Wittek, R., & Wielers, R. (1998). Gossip in organizations. *Computational & mathematical organization theory, 4*(2), 189–204. http://doi.org/10.1023/A:1009636325582

Yu, T., & Potoski, M. (1998). Moving beyond firm boundaries: A social network perspective on reputation spillover. *Corporate Reputation Review, 11*(1), 94–108. http://doi.org/10.1057/crr.2008.6.

# PART VII

## THE WEB, COMPUTERS, AND TECHNOLOGY

# CHAPTER 24

# GOSSIP AND REPUTATION IN COMPUTATIONAL SYSTEMS

JORDI SABATER-MIR

## GOSSIP AND REPUTATION IN COMPUTATIONAL SYSTEMS: AN OVERALL PERSPECTIVE

GOSSIP and reputation have been approached traditionally from the social sciences perspective. In other chapters of this handbook you will find plenty of examples of the different theories and models developed from the social sciences. The goal of the present chapter is to overview how gossip and reputation have been approached from a computational perspective.

As has happened with many other biological, psychological, and sociological concepts, computational systems have adopted gossip and reputation as useful mechanisms to solve specific engineering problems, such as the effective communication in decentralized and highly changeable environments (see "Gossip Algorithms" section for more details). This benefit, however, is not only going from the social sciences to the computational sciences.

Trying to use social mechanisms in a computational system requires a further effort in terms of specification and formalization. Therefore, apart from the intrinsic value of the computational model itself (that can be used to further study the social concept in the context of, for example, computational simulation), the process of building that kind of model contributes to better understanding of the target social theory or concept. Many times, this effort in terms of specification and formalization provides a new perspective that forces revisiting the original theories, thus creating a positive synergy between disciplines that traditionally do not work together. In other occasions, the original theories are modified and transformed thoroughly to adapt them to the challenges presented by new technologies. In other words, the simple exercise of building a computational model has been demonstrated to be highly beneficial from the social sciences perspective because it forces a level of detail and precision that reveals previously hidden problems and inconsistencies, thereby improving the original theories in a meaningful way. An example of this feedback process is the work on the computational reputation model RepAge. The development of the model (Sabater-Mir et al., 2006) and its formalization (Pinyol et al., 2012) helped improve the initial cognitive theory from which it had evolved (Conte and Paolucci, 2002). Among other things, it forced the researchers to identify and formalize the elements that form reputation and how these elements contribute to build it.

In computational systems, as in traditional human societies, it is maintained the use of gossip as an information spread mechanism and the use of reputation as a source for trust and a mechanism for social order. However, as we will see, many times computational systems use gossip and reputation as an inspiration source in order to design algorithms that do not necessarily try to model gossip and reputation as they appear in traditional human societies. The particularities that have some computational systems and the necessity to find optimized solutions (in contrast with the necessity to find "realistic" or human like solutions as it happens in a simulation context) cause that the computational models used for gossip and reputation not always fit with their human counterpart. Although the final function is the same, the internal mechanisms used to, for example, spread a rumor or calculate a reputation value, are specifically tailored to fit the target system, taking little care of mimicking how gossip and reputation really work in a human environment.

For example, gossip is taken as an inspiration for the design of lightweight communication protocols in electronic and online networks. These communication protocols are adapted to the particularities of network communication (many times only between artificial entities) that bear little resemblance to human communication in terms of content, speed, and frequency. Another example is the new forms of virtual attacks that can receive computational reputation mechanisms. This kind of attacks are a direct consequence of how online communities work so the solutions to them cannot be found in traditional human societies and "classical" reputation theories.

The chapter is divided into two main sections, one devoted to computational models of reputation ("Modelling Reputation: An Overview Existing Models" section) and the other to computational models of gossip ("Computational Models of Gossip" section). In the case of computational models of reputation, after an introduction to these models, we distinguish between models that are designed to be part of an agent architecture ("Models for Agents" section) and models that consider reputation as a service ("Reputation as a Service" section). In the case of gossip, first we talk about those models intended to provide to an artificial entity the capacity to "understand" gossip and use this understanding in its decision making ("Cognitive Models" section), then we present communication algorithms inspired in the mechanism that uses gossip to spread in social networks—what are called "Gossip algorithms"—("Gossip Algorithms" section), and finally we present an overview of different gossip detection mechanisms used to detect rumors and the sources of those rumors ("Gossip Detection Mechanisms" section). Then we present a discussion about the interplay between gossip and reputation ("The Interplay between Gossip and Reputation in Computational Systems" section), and we finish with some open questions and thoughts about future research ("Open Questions and Future Research" section).

## Modelling Reputation: An Overview Existing Models

If we talk about computational models (that is, models that finally are codified in a programming language and executed in a computer) we will see that many times reputation is considered just an element (although important) of the trust model. In these trust models, reputation is one of the sources to evaluate someone's trust, especially when there is a lack of direct experiences (Sabater, 2003).

The other use of reputation in computational systems is as a mechanism for social order. This is especially relevant in open multiagent systems[1] and online systems where if individuals follow the norms and have what is considered acceptable behavior, then they will increase their reputation. Having a good reputation increases the opportunities to interact with the other members of the society. But if they behave against the norms, their reputation will decrease and they will be ostracized (Sabater-Mir and Vercouter, 2013).

There is an extensive literature in the area of computational trust and reputation models. The amount of available reviews and surveys is a clear indicator of that (Pinyol and Sabater-Mir, 2013; Noorian and Ulieru, 2010; Jsang et al., 2007; Koutrouli and Tsalgatidou, 2006; Sabater and Sierra, 2005). Each review and survey establishes different dimensions to classify and characterize the large amount of models available. An analysis of these dimensions can be found in the work Pinyol and Sabater-Mir (Pinyol and Sabater-Mir, 2013) in which the authors perform a "survey of surveys" illustrating the different classifications that other authors have used in the past. Some of the surveys are based on online trust and reputation systems (Jsang et al., 2007), others on trust and reputation in peer-to-peer systems (Koutrouli and Tsalgatidou, 2006), and still others are more general (Sabater and Sierra, 2005). Given the amount of computational trust and reputation models available, it is out of the scope of this chapter to make an exhaustive description of all them. We refer the reader to these reviews and surveys for a detailed analysis.

Before going ahead we have to first understand what are the elements that are used in computational models to calculate a *reputation value*[2] and the relation among them (Sabater-Mir and Vercouter, 2013). These elements are depicted in Figure 24.1. The schema illustrated in the figure is based on the work of Conte and Paolucci (Conte and Paolucci, 2002) and the subsequent ideas presented in Sabater-Mir et al. (2006). Conte and Paolucci established the important difference between *image* and *reputation*, two concepts that many authors mistakenly mix. This distinction allows to characterize and

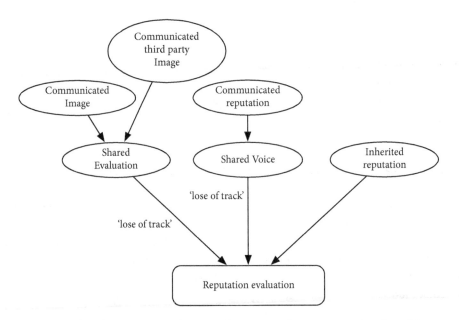

**FIGURE 24.1.** The schema presents the main elements used in a computational model to assess the value of reputation.

differentiate the individual's beliefs about a target (associated to the notion of *image*) and the information that is circulating (the main source of reputation). Without this distinction we consider that it is not possible to provide a correct description of the elements and the process that lead to a reputation evaluation from a cognitive perspective.

The most used elements to calculate a reputation value are the images that other members in the society communicate. An image is "an evaluative belief; it tells whether the target is good or bad with respect to a given behavior." Images are the result of an internal reasoning on different sources of information that leads the agent to create a belief about the behavior of another agent. These images can be either images that have been generated by the agent that is sending the communication (communicated image) or images that have been communicated to that agent also by third party agents (communicated third party images). All these images compound what is known as a shared evaluation. At a certain moment (usually when the number of received images is big enough), that shared evaluation is transformed into a reputation. This transformation implies less focus on the individual agents and a generalization to the *social entity*[3] as the source of the reputation. In other words, this step is moving from "agents A, B and C say that agent D has image X" to "people say that agent D has reputation X."

Instead of communicating images, the agents can decide to communicate reputation values directly (communicated reputation). Similar to the case of images, in this case the recipient builds what is known as a shared voice. Again at certain moment, that shared voice is transformed into a reputation, and again this implies to lose track of the individual communications. Instead of "agents A, B, and C say that the reputation of agent D is X" we move to "people say that the reputation of agent D is X."

Finally, a reputation can be inherited (inherited reputation). In this case, the reputation is not based directly on the target's behavior but on his/her role and social context. For example, because the target belongs to a certain social group, the target "inherits" the reputation associated to that social group. Notice that the reputation of the social group has been previously built using either shared evaluations and/or shared voices.

One important property of reputation is that it travels much faster than communicated images. In the transmission of reputation values (where the identity of the sources has been lost), the issuer assumes less responsibility than if it was transmitting personal opinions (images). This reduces the fear of retaliation and allows agents to transmit reputation values even if they are not really sure about their truthfulness. This property, however, makes reputation a less reliable source for trust evaluation and it is why many computational models use reputation only when images are scarce or not available.

As we have said, there are many characteristics that can be used to classify computational reputation models (see Pinyol and Sabater-Mir, 2013 for a comprehensive list). Among the dimensions that are used to classify computational reputation models we can find things like the information sources the models use to infer reputation (direct interaction, direct observation, witness information, etc.), if reputation is considered a global property or a private and subjective property, the assumptions the models make regarding the behavior of communicating agents (that is, if the model assumes the agents always tell the truth, if they can be biased or if they can lie, etc.). Here we will focus on a simple classification depending on what the models are intended for: models designed to be part of an agent architecture[4] and models to provide reputation values as a service in online communities.

The main differences between these categories rely, on the one hand, on the information that the models have available in order to calculate the reputation values and, on the other hand, on who is going to use those reputation values.

The models that are part of an agent architecture have access only to the information that the agent has available (therefore it is usually a very limited amount of information). Each agent has an independent mechanism to calculate the reputation values and therefore those values become something subjective and personal that reflect not only the limited perception that the agent has of the environment but also the agent individual biases. These are the models that usually approach the evaluation of reputation in a more human-like way.

However, the models for online communities have access to all the information that is provided by the members of those communities. This information is usually stored in a central repository that is used by the reputation model to calculate a reputation value for each target. The calculated reputation values are then made available as a service to all the community members. In this case, all the individuals in that community will share the same reputation values. Typical examples of these reputation models are those used in eBay or Tripadvisor. In eBay, both the buyers and the sellers can rate the mutual experiences after a sale. The aggregation of those rates is transformed into a reputation value that qualifies the seller and the buyer. This reputation value is calculated by the central system and made public so everybody in the community can have access to it when necessary. Specifically in the case of eBay it is represented by the "Feedback score." The Feedback score is calculated using the number of positive ratings minus the number of negative ratings. The resulting number is transformed into a color star (for example, with a Feedback score between 10 and 49 you earn a yellow star). eBay also provides other reputation measures based on different calculations like for example what they call "Positive Feedback" that is the *number of positives rates* divided by the *number of positive rates plus the number of negative ones* in the last 12 months.

## Models for Agents

This kind of model is intended to be part of an agent architecture. Usually these models are an integral part of the agent's trust model. A computational trust model is a computational model that gives an artificial entity the capability to evaluate the trustworthiness of a partner. With this capacity, an artificial entity improves its capability of taking decisions like, for example, if it is worth it to rely on the information provided by someone, if it is safe to do a commercial transaction or who is the best candidate to perform a specific task.

As we said, many times reputation is used in computational models as one of the main sources for trust evaluation. When there is not enough direct experience, many computational trust models rely on reputation to calculate a trust value.

These models are strongly based on gossip, therefore mimicking how reputation works in traditional worth-of-mouth networks. The agents usually only can access to the information that they have gathered directly or that has been communicated to them. There are no central repositories of evaluations so the amount of information that the model has available is quite limited. As a consequence the model has to be designed to squeeze till the last piece of information. Compared with the models that calculate reputation values using all the information in the system, these models are much more sophisticated from a cognitive perspective.

The internal structure is quite similar in all of them and the main differences rely on the sources of information taken into account, how the information from those sources and the reputation values are represented and how everything is aggregated to get a final reputation value. This aggregation usually reflects the biases of the agent and this, together with the differences in the information that each agent has available, makes reputation values something completely subjective.

One paradigmatic example of this kind of model is ReGreT (Sabater, 2003). In ReGreT, reputation is one of the sources used to evaluate the trust of an individual. ReGreT gives priority to direct experiences and only when the amount of direct experiences is not enough, it resorts to reputation. Reputation information is considered to be easier to obtain than direct experiences but at the same time less reliable.

ReGreT identifies different "types" of reputation (that in reality are just reputation values calculated using different information sources). Those types correspond to reputation values calculated using *communicated images* (in ReGreT terms what is called *witness reputation*) and inherited reputation (in ReGreT, *neighborhood reputation* and *system reputation*). Using a complex mechanism based on social network analysis to evaluate the reliability of the information sources, ReGreT uses this reliability to weight the aggregation of all the values into a single reputation value. Later this reputation value is aggregated to the trust that has been calculated using direct experiences to get a final trust value.

Extending this idea of considering the (subjective) reliability of the communicated images for their aggregation, the MORE model (Osman et al., 2015) and the RepAge model (Sabater-Mir et al., 2006), among others, take also into account the certainty of that information (as expressed by the agent providing the communicated image). RepAge goes a little bit further in the treatment of the information used to evaluate a reputation. The model is able to propose communicative actions to the decision making mechanisms of the agent that (1) can improve the accuracy of the elements that help to build a reputation value and (2) can help to solve cognitive dissonances[5] in order to reduce uncertainty.

This leads us to how computational models of reputation represent reputation values (see Sabater-Mir and Paolucci, 2007 for a further discussion). The simpler models use a single real value (usually between 0 to 1 or between –1 to 1) to represent a reputation value. ReGreT uses a tuple of real values, one element representing the reputation value and the other the reliability of that value. The MORE model uses probability distributions over a vector of qualitative values where the shape of the probability distribution represents the certainty over each possible value and a flat distribution means complete uncertainty. Other models such as AFRAS (Carbo et al., 2003) and RepAge use fuzzy sets in a similar way.

Having a measure of the reliability/certainty of a reputation value is crucial. Without this measure the agent does not know to which extend can base its decisions on the reputation information. Just to put an example, in ReGreT you can have a reputation value of 1 (fully trustworthy) for a given target that is based on a single opinion coming from a third party agent with very low credibility. Without the reliability value associated to the reputation value the agent could take a decision based on information that, indeed, is very dubious.

The aggregation mechanisms in these models go from simple weighted summations of the evaluations like in ReGreT (with different levels of sophistication, depending on the parameters associated to the evaluations like reliability or certainty) to complex aggregation mechanisms based on concepts like the "earth mover's distance"[6] in the case of the MORE model. As you can imagine, the complexity of the aggregation mechanism is strongly dependent on how expressive is the representation of reputation used by the model.

The main use currently of the models intended to be part of an agent architecture is as part of a trust model. Any autonomous entity that needs to evaluate the trustworthiness of another entity will benefit from the use of a reputation model. Entities with this necessity range from autonomous agents in e-commerce scenarios to autonomous robots in a cooperative environment.

There is no commonly accepted evaluation framework or benchmark to compare neither trust nor reputation models, although there have been a few initiatives in that direction. Probably the most well known is the ART Testbed (Fullam et al., 2005). The ART Testbed (quoting the authors), was a testbed designed to serve in two roles: as a competition forum in which researchers can compare their technologies against objective metrics (that is, metrics that are not biased to benefit specific models in front of others), and as an experimental tool, with flexible parameters, allowing researchers to perform customizable, easily repeatable experiments.

The testbed proposes a game based on art appraisal. In the art appraisal domain, the agents with the trust models that are being compared function as painting appraisers with varying levels of expertise in different artistic eras. Clients (controlled by the testbed) request appraisals for paintings from different eras to the appraisers. Appraisers receive more clients, and thus more profit, for producing more accurate appraisals. If an appraising agent does not have the expertise to complete the appraisal (something that happens very often), it can request opinions from other appraiser agents paying for those opinions a fixed amount of money. Then the requested appraiser can decide how much time spends in the requested appraisal. The amount of time spent has a direct effect in the quality but also in the profit it gets from the job. More time implies more accuracy but less profit. Also, the requested appraiser can lie and provide bad quality appraisals on purpose to decrease the number of clients that the requester will receive in the next turn, although at the cost of damaging its own reputation. Here is where the trust models enter into scene. The trust models being compared are used by agents to decide which appraisers are the best ones to ask for help when you don't have enough expertise for doing the appraisal yourself.

The ART testbed is no longer supported, but descriptions of other, more recent testbed proposals that try to overcome the limitations of the ART testbed (Gomez et al., 2007) are available (see Kerr and Cohen, 2009; Jelenc et al., 2013 and Chandrasekaran and Esfandiari, 2015, to name a few).

Surprisingly, although gossip is essential to this kind of models, literally none of them consider gossip and how it works as part of the model. This is linked with a second important missing aspect. All the models focus on how to calculate reputation values but at the same time ignore how to manage reputation spreading.

## Reputation as a Service

In the previous section, we talked about models that are intended to be part of an agent architecture. They are designed to be integrated in the architecture and provide information about reputation to the agent so it can improve its decision making. There is another group of models that are designed to provide reputation information as a service to all the members of a community. These models are usually part of the system and therefore have access to an important part of the information that the system manages.

The models that provide reputation as a service share some characteristics. First, the information about the subject is attached to the subject so every individual in the community can see it. Second, because the calculated reputation values are meant to be shared among all the individuals in the community, the models tend to be simple (many of them based on statistical aggregations) so any individual (usually humans) can understand how the reputation has been calculated and how can be adapted to its own personal bias. It is not strange that the model provides at the same time different reputation values based on different calculation mechanisms. Third, they rely on central repositories where the members of the community share their direct experiences or, if this repository does not exist like in the case of distributed systems, they have mechanisms to collect the information from the different individuals that belong to the community. This means that the models usually have a lot of data available, something that influences directly the mechanisms implemented to calculate the reputation values.

A paradigmatic example of this kind of models are the reputation systems for online communities. The main goal of these models is to attract the right individuals to the online community, motivate them to act in the right ways and empower them to know and trust others in the network. Although they have in common a lot of things with their worth-of-mouth counterpart, the particularities of Internet provide them with distinctive characteristics (Dellarocas, 2003).

First we have the change of scale. While traditional worth-of-mouth is restricted to small communities (or in case of big communities it takes a lot of time to evolve), Internet has made possible large scale worth-of-mouth networks that can evolve very quickly. This gives to online reputation mechanisms an increased power that "can influence on corporations and other powerful institutions of our society."

Second, while traditional worth-of-mouth evolves usually in an unpredictable way (or at least it is very difficult to control), online reputation mechanisms can be tailored to respond to certain desired properties.

Finally, in online reputation mechanisms new important challenges appear, most of them associated to the lack of personal and direct contact. Because in Internet it is relatively easy to falsify your identity, new forms of attack and strategic manipulation of the reputation mechanism are possible (Hoffman et al., 2009). For example, in a *Sybil* attack, the attacker creates many pseudonymous identities to gain a disproportionately large influence. These pseudonyms allow the attacker to issue many opinions (either positive or negative) on a target with the purpose of altering its reputation. One specific type of *Sybil* attack is what is known as *astroturfing* that consists on creating a false community of individuals (providing the illusion of a mass movement of distinct persons) that give support to a specific matter, whereas the reality is that a single entity fully controls the agenda. Another example is *whitewashing*. In this case the attacker abuses of her good reputation and changes to a different identity (with a "washed" reputation) once the reputation assigned to her old identity becomes too low to operate in the system. These are just two examples of attacks that are exclusive of the online reputation systems and have no equivalence in their worth-of-mouth counterpart. Identification of possible attacks and defense mechanisms are an important research topic among the scientific community that studies this kind of models.

Paradigmatic examples of reputation systems for online communities are those used in eBay (discussed earlier), Amazon, Tripadvisor, and YouTube, to name a few. All of them are strongly based on communicated images that are transformed by the system into shared evaluations and into reputations. The way how the system transforms the individual images to reputation is based on aggregated statistics (usually the number of positive and negative evaluations).

Another example of reputation mechanisms that provide reputation as a service are the reputation mechanisms used in Peer to Peer networks (P2P) and wireless sensor networks (WSN). Although in this case (on the contrary of what happens in the previously commented online communities case) usually there is no central repository, the reputation mechanisms have access to the information available to each node in the network by using for example a *gossip algorithm* (see "Reputation as a Service" section and "The Interplay between Gossip and Reputation in Computational Systems" section).

P2P networks are distributed networks in which interconnected nodes ("peers") share resources amongst each other without the use of a centralized administrative system. File sharing communities like Gnutella, Kazaa or BitTorrent are examples of P2P networks. In these networks, reputation mechanisms like EigenTrust (Kamvar et al., 2003) are used to detect and ostracize nodes that upload malicious or corrupted content.

EigenTrust is based on the transitivity of trust. If agent $i$ trusts agent $j$, then agent $i$ will trust the agents that agent $j$ trusts. In EigenTrust, each node in the network calculates an image for each agent with whom it has downloaded content as a simple aggregation of satisfactory vs unsatisfactory experiences. If an agent needs to know the reputation of an unknown agent (that is, an agent with whom there has not been a previous interaction) it asks to those agents that it knows about it and weights the answers according to the trust it has on each informer. The spreading of the query can go further several levels till it reaches someone who knows the target. EigenTrust can be implemented instead using a centralized entity that aggregates those values. In that case it is similar to the reputation mechanisms commented before that are used in online communities.

WSNs (Akyildiz et al., 2002) are networks of spatially distributed autonomous sensors that are deployed to monitor certain environment. A WSN is composed of a large number of usually low-cost and low-power sensors that are not necessarily reliable. In those networks, reputation is used as a measure of the accuracy/reliability of the sensor. A high reputation value means a highly accurate/reliable sensor that can be taken into account while a low reputation value means a sensor whose data cannot be trusted (and therefore that has to be "ostracized"). An example of reputation mechanism used in this context is that from Ganeriwal et al., 2008. In this work the authors use the beta reputation system (Jsang and Ismail, 2002), a reputation mechanism based on probability theory.

In summary, the models that are designed to provide reputation information as a service have become an important field of research due to its applicability in several areas like online communities, peer to peer networks and wireless sensor networks. The environments where these models are used determine a set of distinctive characteristics that detach them from the traditional reputation mechanisms found in human societies. In this sense, one important aspect to be taken into account is the new types of attacks that these environments make possible and that require new solutions in order to avoid them.

# Computational Models of Gossip

If we look at the presence of gossip in computational systems we will observe that, on the contrary of what happens with reputation where there exist a myriad of computational models, there are not many models of gossip as such.

Mainly we can identify three perspectives from which gossip is considered in computational systems.

- Gossip as a natural phenomenon in human societies that needs to be taken into account by an artificial entity so it can interact in an intelligent manner with those societies. This requires that the artificial entity has a model of how gossip works and incorporates this into its decision making mechanism. In this situation is where having cognitive computational gossip models would be useful. However, it requires that the artificial entities be ready to use such kind of models and also that these entities be able to evolve in an environment rich enough to make the gossip model relevant. Apart from simulation scenarios, current virtual environments lack this level of richness. This lack of environments where artificial entities would benefit from a gossip model is what probably makes them so scarce.
- Gossip as a source of inspiration for communication mechanisms (what are called *Gossip algorithms*).
- Gossip as wrong or false information that needs to be avoided. This implies having algorithms to detect gossip in order to avoid its spreading.

In the next three sections, we will briefly describe these three perspectives and the solutions available.

## Cognitive Models

In this section, we will describe the approaches that are intended to provide to an artificial entity the capacity to "understand" gossip and use this understanding in its decision making. On the contrary of what happens in the case of reputation, there are almost no computational models of gossip that are designed to be used in this way. In fact we have been able to find only one work in this direction.

In (Brusk, 2010) the author develops a model of gossip initiation that is used by an NPC (non-player character) to decide if it is worth it to engage in gossip conversations. The model is based on different sociological, ethnological and applied linguistics studies. From those studies the author extracts a set of elements that, according to her, determines when it is interesting to start the spreading of a gossip. These elements are then codified in a state chart that determines the NPC's behavior.

The main element taken into account to decide if it is worth it or not to gossip is the social distance between the potential receiver of the gossip and the target. According to the author, it is necessary (for the gossip spreading to be efficient and harmless for the initiator) that the recipient of the gossip does not be socially close to the target. On top of that, the other elements considered by the model are that the information provided by the gossip be new and relevant or the receiver, that the target of the gossip be known by the receiver and that the target cannot listen the conversation.

## Gossip Algorithms

A *gossip algorithm* or *gossip protocol* is a communication mechanism inspired in the mechanism that uses gossip to spread in social networks.[7] Although *gossip algorithms* are mainly used as communication protocols, they have been applied also to data aggregation, overlay maintenance, and resource allocation (Kermarrec and van Steen, 2007).

The popularity of these algorithms is mainly because they are very useful in domains where there is a network of arbitrarily connected nodes with (1) a topology that changes continuously as new nodes join and old nodes leave the network and (2) there is no centralized entity that knows and can reach all the network to facilitate communication. These characteristics are those that define, for instance, sensor networks, peer to peer networks and mobile networks of vehicles.

For example, in wireless sensor networks, a typical problem that is solved using gossip algorithms is that of *distributed averaging* (Boyd et al., 2006). The average consensus problem consists in computing the average of the measures taken by the different sensors in the network. In these networks it is not possible to have a centralized node that collects all the information and computes the average. The sensors are connected among them following a partially connected graph so the average has to be performed in an iterative and distributed way.

There are several elements that characterize these algorithms (Shah, 2009):

- Information spreads in an unreliable and asynchronous manner.
- Each node only communicates with a limited number of immediate neighbors.
- They have to be simple, distributed, robust against networks dynamics and efficient in resource utilization.

These algorithms are designed to be very efficient and use mathematical models that not necessarily resemble how gossip really works in traditional human societies.

The simplest kind of gossip algorithm is the *flooding algorithm* where a source node sends the message to all its neighbors that at the same time send the message to all its neighbors (except if they have already done it before) and so on. Taking that as a base, you can build several *random gossip algorithms* that instead of sending the message to all its neighbors, each node (1) sends the message to a fixed number of neighbors selected randomly, (2) sends the message to a neighbor (from all the neigh ours available) with a certain fixed probability or (3) sends the message to all its neighbors with certain probability.

Aspects that are taken into account to evaluate the performance of these algorithms are the mean number of messages received by each node (message complexity), the percentage of all nodes that delivered a message generated by a source in the end of the dissemination (fraction of total infected sites), the percentage of messages generated by a source that are delivered by all nodes (reliability) and the number of hops required to deliver a message to all recipients (latency). A good gossip algorithm should provide a large fraction of total infected sites, high reliability, and low message complexity and latency (Hu et al., 2012).

One element that is critical for these algorithms is the topology of the network. Many studies try to determine which algorithm is better for which topology. For example, in (Ganesh et al., 2005), the authors identify some topological properties of the network that determine the persistence of epidemics. In (Hu et al., 2012), three gossip random gossip algorithms (that correspond to those described at the beginning of this section) are tested and compared over three network topologies: Bernoulli graph, random geometric graph and scale-free graph. In (Villatoro et al., 2013), gossip algorithms are applied to convention emergence.[8] The authors identify what they call *self-reinforcing structures* that are topological configurations that promote the establishment and persistence of subconventions (and therefore, delay or even prevent the formation of the convention). After that, they propose two mechanisms for robust resolution of subconventions.

## Gossip Detection Mechanisms

Gossip activity is inherent to social networking services, with Twitter being probably the most paradigmatic example. In this services there is an important interest in detecting harmful gossip (or what the community call "rumor") as the first step to be able to stop the circulation of false or misleading information. Different authors propose mechanisms that allow to detect rumors and the sources of those rumors. The mechanisms are based on the analysis from different perspectives of the messages exchanged. All these algorithms assume there is a centralized entity that has access to all the exchanged messages as well as the structure of the social network.

In (Kwon et al., 2013) the authors use temporal, structural and linguistic properties to detect rumors in a social network (in this case Twitter). Specifically, they analyze time series of the number of tweets, diffusion networks showing how information has been spread and perform sentiment analysis on the tweets. From these set of properties, they extract a subset of significant features with high predictive power that improve the effectiveness of previous sets of features described in the literature (Castillo et al., 2011).

(Seo et al. 2012) present a mechanism to detect if a piece of information spread in a network is a rumor and what is the source of this rumor (where *rumor* is a synonym of false or wrong information). The mechanism relies on having individuals in the network that act as monitors and report if the analyzed rumor has reached them or not. Using the map of monitors that report that they have received or not a rumor and the distance of those monitors to the rest of the nodes in the network, the mechanism is able to identify the source of the rumor. In this approach, one important aspect is how to choose the nodes that will act as monitors. The authors explore different selection methods. To detect if a piece of information is a rumor, the information coming from the monitors is again used. The idea is to identify the sources of the rumor and use the heuristic that false information will come from a single individual or a small set of colluded individuals, while true information will have the origin in many unrelated individuals.

These are just two examples that illustrate how these mechanisms work. Basically all of them are based in two elements that can be used together: (1) analysis of the network topology and the origin of messages and (2) analysis of the content of the messages. With that information, different mechanisms use different heuristics. These heuristics many times are domain dependent.

# THE INTERPLAY BETWEEN GOSSIP AND REPUTATION IN COMPUTATIONAL SYSTEMS

As we have seen in the previous sections, the interplay between gossip and reputation in computational systems is almost non-existent. Although gossip is the origin of reputation, computational models of reputation do not take it explicitly into account. It is given for granted that information spreads but virtually no reputation model considers how, how fast and when this happens.

This connects directly with one important shortage of current reputation models: all of them focus on how to *calculate* the reputation value but do not provide the necessary tools to *manage* reputation spreading.

From the gossip's perspective, in computational systems reputation is not considered. In fact, there are almost no models of gossip as such and gossip is only either a source of inspiration for communication protocols (in a similar way as biological neural networks are an inspiration for artificial neural networks or ant colonies are an inspiration for ant algorithms) either something to be avoided. As we have pointed out before, one possible reason is the lack of scenarios rich enough to make this combination of reputation and gossip really worth it. However, we think it is a matter of time that this kind of scenarios be a reality.

An exception to this is the use of gossip algorithms to calculate reputation. In two examples of this kind of work, the authors use gossip algorithms to calculate aggregated global reputation values in distributed networks (Zhou and Hwang, 2007; Zhou et al., 2008; Bachrach et al., 2009). The problem is similar to the *distributed averaging problem* in wireless sensor networks, discussed earlier (Boyd et al., 2006). Each node in the network has had a small number of direct experiences with its neighbors and as a result has built images about them (using the terminology introduced in "Models for Agents" section). The reputation mechanism uses a gossip algorithm to spread efficiently the local images among the different nodes in the network so each node can calculate global reputation values based on those local images.

This is the only scenario where it is possible to find an interplay between gossip and reputation in computational systems and in fact is not a real integration between both but the use of one to calculate the other. Neither the gossip algorithm takes into account the fact that what is being aggregated are reputation values (as we said, similar algorithms are used in Wireless Sensor Networks), neither the reputation model considers gossip as such (the same reputation mechanism would work if there was a centralized repository, see for example EigenTrust (Kamvar et al., 2003)).

# Open Questions and Future Research

After this short overview on how gossip and reputation are considered from a computational, system design perspective, it should be clear that one of the missing elements is the interplay between gossip and reputation.

Computational reputation models have explored different mechanisms to calculate reputation values, taking into account several sources of information and using different mathematical tools to aggregate that information. What all of them are missing is a mechanism to manage reputation spreading. By reputation spreading management we mean what has to be done in order to efficiently change or favor a reputation value (usually in the positive sense, although it can be in the negative sense if what an individual wants is to harm someone) by controlling gossip. This is what reputation management companies do for significant people and companies both in traditional human communities and also in internet.

From the point of view of computational models, what would be interesting is to give artificial entities with this capacity of managing reputation spreading. This implies that those entities need first to have a model of how gossip works (probably focused to specific domains) and then they have to integrate this model with the reputation model and the rest of the decision-making mechanisms so the communication actions go in the right direction and become efficient. The entity should be able to answer questions such as, Who should be aware of my actions? Which actions will have greater impact? How will the topology of the network of my community affect reputation spreading? The first model described in "Cognitive Models" section leans precisely in that direction. However, that model is not designed to manage reputation spreading, and the integration with a reputation model is not considered.

Another aspect that would improve how reputation models work, related also to reputation-spreading management, is the capacity of an artificial entity to anticipate reputation values. Gossip detection mechanisms (see "Gossip Detection Mechanisms" section) are designed to identify a circulating gossip. This however is only part of the story. Anticipating how reputation will evolve given a circulating gossip so the affected individual can take measures before that reputation becomes established, requires mixing that information with a proper model of reputation spreading.

As a conclusion and considering what we have said up to now, an interesting addition to the field would be a complete and unified model of gossip and reputation that takes both into account and also their interplay: (1) reputation evaluation, or how to calculate reputation values; (2) gossip detection, or how to identify rumors that can affect reputation, and (3) reputation spreading, or how gossip can be actively used to influence reputation.

## NOTES

1. An open multiagent system consists of dynamically changing populations of self-interested agents whose internal design is not (completely) accessible to others (Rovatsos et al., 2003).
2. A *reputation value* is a measure of the reputation that, according to the reputation model, a target entity has (see "Models for Agents" section for a discussion about how reputation values are represented in different models). This measure is the main output of a computational reputation model and can be used as an input for a trust model or as a support for any decision making where reputation is relevant.
3. A social entity is a set of individuals plus a set of social relations among these individuals or properties that identify them as a group in front of its own members and the society at large.
4. An agent architecture defines a particular methodology for building an autonomous agent, how the construction of the agent can be decomposed into the construction of a set of component modules, and how these modules should be made to interact. A well-known example of agent architecture is the BDI architecture that is based on Bratman's practical reasoning theory (Bratman, 1987).
5. A cognitive dissonance is a contradiction between two pieces of information that are relevant for the individual and refer to the same target.
6. The 'earth mover's distance' (EMD) is a measure of the distance between two probability distributions. "Given two distributions, one can be seen as a mass of earth properly spread in space, the other as a collection of holes in that same space. Then, the EMD measures the least amount of work needed to fill the holes with earth. A unit of work corresponds to transporting a unit of earth by a unit of ground distance" (Rubner et al., 2000).
7. These algorithms are also named *epidemic algorithms* because the way gossip spreads in social networks is similar to how viruses spread in a biological community.
8. Conventions are a special type of norms that emerge to solve coordination problems, where what is desired is that everyone behaves in the same way without any major difference on which action agents are coordinated (Coleman, 1998).

## REFERENCES

Akyildiz, I. F., Su, W., Sankarasubramaniam, Y., and Cayirci, E. 2002. Wireless sensor networks: A survey. *Computer Networks* 38(4): 393–422.

Bachrach, Y., Parnes, A., Procaccia, A. D., and Rosenschein, J. S. 2009. Gossip-based aggregation of trust in decentralized reputation systems. *Autonomous Agents and Multi-Agent Systems* 19(2): 153–172.

Boyd, S. P., Ghosh, A., Prabhakar, B., and Shah, D. 2006. Randomized gossip algorithms. *IEEE Transactions on Information Theory* 52(6): 2508–2530.

Bratman, M. E. 1987. *Intentions, plans and practical reason.* Cambridge, MA: Harvard University Press.

Brusk, J. 2010. A computational model for gossip initiation. In *Aspects of semantics and pragmatics of dialogue: SemDial2010, 14th workshop on the semantics and pragmatics of dialogue,* 139–142, edited by P. Lupkowski, and M. Purver. Poznan: Polish Society for Cognitive Science.

Carbo, J., Molina, J., and Davila, J. 2003. Trust management through fuzzy reputation. *Int. Journal in Cooperative Information Systems* 12(1): 135–155.

Castillo, C., Mendoza, M., and Poblete, B. 2011. Information credibility on twitter. In *Proceedings of the 20th International Conference on World Wide Web*, 675–684, edited by S. Srinivasan, K. Ramamritham, A. Kumar, M. P. Ravindra, E. Bertino, and R. Kumar. New York: ACM Press.

Chandrasekaran, P., and Esfandiari, B. 2015. Toward a testbed for evaluating computational trust models: experiments and analysis. *Journal of Trust Management* 2(1): 1–27.

Coleman, J. 1998. *Foundations of social theory*. Cambridge, MA: Belknap Press of Harvard University Press.

Conte, R., and Paolucci, M. 2002. *Reputation in artificial societies: Social beliefs for social order*. Amsterdam: Kluwer Academic Publishers.

Dellarocas, C. 2003. The digitization of word of mouth: Promise and challenges of online feedback mechanisms. *Management Science* 49(10): 1407–1424.

Fullam, K. K., Klos, T. B., Muller, G., Sabater, J., Schlosser, A., Topol, Z., ... Voss, M. 2005. A specification of the agent reputation and trust (art) testbed: Experimentation and competition for trust in agent societies. In *Proceedings of the 4th International Joint Conference on Autonomous Agents and Multi-Agent Systems (AAMAS-2005)*, 512–518. New York: ACM Press.

Ganeriwal, S., Balzano, L. K., and Srivastava, M. B. 2008. Reputation-based framework for high integrity sensor networks. *ACM Transactions on Senor Networks* 4(3): 15:1–15:37.

Ganesh, A. J., Massouli, L., and Towsley, D. F. 2005. The effect of network topology on the spread of epidemics. In *Proceedings of the IEEE 24th Annual Joint Conference of the IEEE Computer and Communications Societies (INFOCOM 2005)*, 1455–1466. IEEE.

Gomez, M., Sabater-Mir, J., Carbo, J., and Muller, G. 2007. Improving the art-testbed, thoughts and reflections. Workshop on Competitive agents in Agent Reputation and Trust Testbed, Twelve Conference of the Spanish Association for Artificial Intelligence (CAEPIA), Salamanca, Spain, 1–15.

Hoffman, K. J., Zage, D., and Nita-Rotaru, C. 2009. A survey of attack and defense techniques for reputation systems. *ACM Computing Surveys* 42(1).

Hu, R., Sopena, J., Arantes, L., Sens, P., and Demeure, I. M. 2012. Fair comparison of gossip algorithms over large-scale random topologies. In *Proceedings of the IEEE 31st Symposium on Reliable Distributed Systems (SRDS 2012)*. IEEE, 331–340.

Jelenc, D., Hermoso, R., Sabater-Mir, J., and Trcek, D. 2013. Decision making matters: A better way to evaluate trust models. *Knowledge-Based Systems* 52: 147–164.

Jsang, A., and Ismail, R. 2002. The beta reputation system. In *Proceedings of the 15th BLED Conference on Electronic Commerce (BLED 2002)*.

Jsang, A., Ismail, R., and Boyd, C. 2007. A survey of trust and reputation systems for online service provision. *Decision Support Systems* 43(2): 618–644.

Kamvar, S. D., Schlosser, M. T., and Garcia-Molina, H. 2003. The eigentrust algorithm for reputation management in p2p networks. In *Proceedings of the 12th International Conference on World Wide Web (WWW 2003)*, 640–651. New York: ACM Press.

Kermarrec, A.-M., and Van Steen, M. 2007. Gossiping in distributed systems. *Operating Systems Review* 41(5), 2–7.

Kerr, R., and Cohen, R. 2009. Smart cheaters do prosper: Defeating trust and reputation systems. In *Proceedings of the First International Joint Conference on Autonomous Agents and Multiagent Systems (AAMAS 2002)*, 993–1000. New York: ACM Press.

Koutrouli, E., and Tsalgatidou, A. 2006. Reputation-based trust systems for p2p applications: Design issues and comparison framework. In *Trust and Privacy in Digital Business*, 152–161, edited by S. Fischer-Hbner, S. Furnell, and C. Lambrinoudakis, Lecture Notes in Computer Science, vol. 4083. Berlin/Heidelberg: Springer.

Kwon, S., Cha, M., Jung, K., Chen, W., and Wang, Y. 2013. Prominent features of rumor propagation in online social media. In *ICDM—2013 IEEE 13th International Conference on Data Mining*, 1103–1108, edited by H. Xiong, G. Karypis, B. M. Thuraisingham, D. J. Cook, and X. Wu. IEEE.

Noorian, Z., and Ulieru, M. 2010. The state of the art in trust and reputation systems: A framework for comparison. *Journal of Theoretical and Applied Electronic Commerce Research* 5(2), 97–117.

Osman, N., Provetti, A., Riggi, V., and Sierra, C. 2015. More: Merged opinions reputation model. In *Multi-Agent Systems*, edited by N. Bulling, 67–81. Lecture Notes in Computer Science, vol. 8953. Cham, Switzerland: Springer International Publishing.

Pinyol, I., Dellunde, P., Sabater-Mir, J., and Paolucci, M. 2012. Reputation-based decisions for logic-based cognitive agents. *Journal of Autonomous Agents and Multi-Agent Systems (JAAMAS)* 24(1): 175–216.

Pinyol, I., and Sabater-Mir, J. 2013. Computational trust and reputation models for open multi-agent systems: a review. *Artificial Intelligence Review* 40(1), 1–25.

Rovatsos, M., Nickles, M., and Weiss, G. 2003. Interaction is meaning: A new model for communication in open systems. In *Proceedings of the Second International Joint Conference on Autonomous Agents and Multiagent Systems*. AAMAS '03, 536–543. New York: ACM Press,

Rubner, Y., Tomasi, C., and Guibas, L. J. 2000. The earth mover's distance as a metric for image retrieval. *International Journal of Computer Vision* 40(2): 99–121.

Sabater, J. 2003. *Trust and Reputation for Agent Societies*. Number 20 in Monografies de l'institut d'investigacio´ en intelligència artificial. IIIA-CSIC.

Sabater, J., and Sierra, C. 2005. Review on computational trust and reputation models. *Artificial Intelligence Review* 24(1): 33–60.

Sabater-Mir, J., and Paolucci, M. 2007. On representation and aggregation of social evaluations in computational trust and reputation models. *International Journal of Approximate Reasoning* 46(3): 458–483.

Sabater-Mir, J., Paolucci, M., and Conte, R. 2006. Repage: REPutation and imAGE among limited autonomous partners. *Journal of Artificial Societies and Social Simulation* 9: 2.

Sabater-Mir, J., and Vercouter, L. 2013. Trust and reputation in multiagent systems. In *Multiagent systems* edited by G. Weiss, 2nd ed., ch. 9, 381–420. Cambridge, MA: MIT Press.

Seo, E., Mohapatra, P., and Abdelzaher, T. (2012). Identifying rumors and their sources in social networks. In *Proceedings of SPIE 8389, Ground/Air Multisensor Interoperability, Integration, and Networking for Persistent ISR III*, vol. 8389.

Shah, D. 2009. Gossip algorithms. *Foundations and Trends in Networking* 3(1): 1–125.

Villatoro, D., Sabater-Mir, J., and Sen, S. 2013. Robust convention emergence in social networks through self-reinforcing structures dissolution. *ACM Transactions on Autonomous and Adaptive Systems (TAAS)* 8(1): 2:1–2:21.

Zhou, R., and Hwang, K. 2007. Gossip-based reputation aggregation for unstructured peer-to-peer networks. In *Proceedings of 2007 IEEE International Parallel and Distributed Processing Symposium*, 1–10. IEEE.

Zhou, R., Hwang, K., and Cai, M. 2008. GossipTrust for fast reputation aggregation in peer-to-peer networks. *IEEE Transactions on Knowledge and Data Engineering* 20(9): 1282–1295.

CHAPTER 25

......................................................................................

# ONLINE REPUTATION
# SYSTEMS

......................................................................................

## CHRIS SNIJDERS AND UWE MATZAT

## INTRODUCTION

......................................................................................

THE potential benefits of having a good reputation are relatively clear and argued through in detail in the literature. Having a good reputation causes that others feel that whatever cooperation they want to set up will be more likely to end well with you than with others. All else equal, this makes you a more attractive partner, for instance because there is less need to invest in trying to safeguard the interaction. It could also imply that, because you know that others know that your reputation is good, you can ask and get a higher premium for cooperating with you. Research on (having a good) reputation can therefore be seen as part of the social exchange literature, where it fits in one basket with research on other mechanisms that increase mutual trust in mutual exchanges, such as the existence of reciprocal or other norms regarding appropriate conduct, network embeddedness, sanctioning systems, or exchanges embedded in longer-term relations.

Keeping track of reputations became more complicated as exchanges started taking place over larger distances and with lesser known partners. An extreme form of anonymous, long distance interaction is interaction on online platforms such as eBay. Buyers and sellers do not know each other, they probably will not meet again in the future (repeat business is relatively rare given the size of the market place), and there certainly are incentives, mainly for sellers, to not live up to their promise. Not delivering at all, not being careful with packaging, not being very precise in describing the item are some of the key problems that buyers may face. Online platforms have come up with ways to replace informal forms of reputation (which are not very likely to work effectively in an online market with these characteristics) with a more formal system of reputation that has in the meantime become well-established. After their transaction, buyers and sellers can leave feedback about the other party. This feedback is logged, summarized, and visible to future buyers and sellers. In this way, opportunistic behavior is made less attractive because it will be observable to potential future exchange partners. One could think about such a system as artificially establishing a network of connections between all online traders.

The potential benefits of reputation systems are therefore rather straightforward, and adequately summarized in for instance Diekmann et al. (2014):

> With their reputations at stake, rational and self-regarding sellers *who sufficiently care* about their future business have a strong incentive to behave cooperatively. Even in interactions with buyers whom they are unlikely to meet again, these sellers will forgo the short-term temptation to abuse a buyer's trust to avoid a negative rating that would hamper future business. Market entrants, however, have no reputation and are therefore likely to be distrusted by buyers. Consequently, to enter the market, sellers with no feedback record have to lower prices to compensate buyers for the risk they take buying from a new seller. *If new sellers sufficiently care about future business,* their good reputations will reimburse them for this initial investment in the future.    (Diekmann et al., 2014, p. 68; emphasis ours)

There are many issues that surround the reputation system that have been analyzed in the literature. For instance, why would anyone give any feedback, as doing this is a contribution to a collective good in which the benefits of a single feedback score may not outweigh the effort of giving it? However, the question that has been analyzed most often, is what it would mean for a seller *to care sufficiently* about reputation? To assess this, it is necessary to get an idea about how much a better reputation would help to get more likely and more beneficial sales and many studies have tried to estimate exactly this value of reputation. As we will see, the standard way of calculating this value is not without problems.

In this chapter, we focus on the reputation system as used on eBay, as this is the platform that has been analyzed the most by far (for an alternative account of trust and reputation in online markets see Diekmann and Przepiorka, this volume). Moreover, research on other platforms often concerns local variants (often previous competitors) of eBay. Most research on the effects of reputation has concluded that there indeed are benefits to having a positive reputation, although the benefits seem to be relatively small. We feel there are several reasons why it might be wise to rethink these findings. Not so much because we think they are wrong, but we do feel that possible arguments against these findings and the interpretation of these findings have gotten less attention than they deserve. The setup of this chapter is as follows. We first summarize some of the arguments in favor of using eBay field data and then introduce some known issues with these kinds of data. Then we present our two main arguments that we feel need more attention in future research. Some implications for future research conclude the chapter.

# The Missing Link between
# Experiments and Field Studies

Lab research gives the researcher control over all or almost all of the factors that subjects are confronted with. This is a key advantage, as in principle all measured behavior may be ascribed to these factors. There still are unmeasured matters that may play a role, but they are kept at a bare minimum. In our case, one could have subjects interact on a prepared auction system, for instance, expose them to various input and track their behavior. The disadvantage is that what subjects are confronted with in a lab setting does not need to really happen to them in reality. This puts them in a position in which they normally would not be and they might not react in the way they would do outside the lab. Or, subjects might in reality never interact on eBay, or if they do, they might do it quite differently. This low external validity is much less of a problem in, for instance, large-scale field studies that use surveys, where one measures actual behavior as it occurs or recently has occurred. One can imagine survey research, asking eBay users to report how often they provide feedback, how often they are online, and related matters. The obvious disadvantage of such a setup is that the conditions in these field studies are not under the control of the researcher, which makes it more complicated or even impossible to infer causal effects.

This difference between experimental research and survey field study research can of course be found in any methods handbook. However, research that measures actual online behavior can be argued to form a natural connection between these two kinds of studies. It is still true that when researchers use data downloaded from an online platform the factors that subjects are confronted with are not under the control of the researcher, but two arguments make online research potentially more attractive. The first one is that although the factors that subjects are confronted with are not under the control of the researcher, the researcher does measure a large part of the factors that must have played a role, because the researcher can reconstruct what the online trader must have seen. The second argument is that what is being measured is real behavior: people trade online and one measures the actual trails of it. What also must have played a role in sparking the interest of researchers, we suspect, is that it has meanwhile become relatively easy to collect online data. Whereas earlier studies have used "hand collected" data sets, virtually all later studies are based on automatically downloaded data, leading to data sets with (tens of) thousands of cases.

# Is There a Positive Effect of
# Reputation for Sellers?

After going through a substantial part of the literature, the picture that emerges when it comes to the potential positive effect of a high reputation for sellers remains somewhat

FIGURE 25.1.  Overview of an eBay reputation score.

muddy. Extensive reviews can be found in Bajari & Hortacsu (2005), Resnick, Zeckhauser, Swanson, & Lockwood (2006), and in the online supplement of Diekmann et al. (2014). Let us first consider the reputation score as it is displayed by eBay. In fact, this display has changed several times over the years, and may even be different for different users at a given point in time if eBay is experimenting with different kinds of layouts (as Netflix or Facebook typically do). However, the key information that has been used in online reputation research has stayed more or less constant.

Figure 25.1 shows a screenshot of the data for a random seller. The dots in the lower right part of the picture would allow potential buyers to click to get further feedback information. The percentage of positive feedback is based on the number of unique (that is, non-repeat business) ratings over the last 12 months. The number of positive, neutral, and negative ratings in the figure include the ratings based on repeat business, which is why $2566/(2566 + 17 + 16) = 98.7$ is not exactly equal to the mentioned 99.4% right above the "+ Follow" button. The feedback ratings in the lower left part concerning whether items were as described, communication, shipping time, and shipping charges, are most often not included in eBay research. They have also been a relatively recent addition to eBay. The number right behind the name of the seller is the total number of feedback ratings received, counting the unique ratings only (no repeat feedback from the same partner), and counting negative ratings as minus 1 and positive ratings as plus 1.

In any case, one can use the percentage of positive feedback as an indicator (this is done most often), or the number of completed transactions, the number of negative ratings in the past year (or the most recent shorter period), the number of non-positive ratings over a given period, or transformations and combinations of these variables. For instance, one could log-transform the reputation score to reflect that the added value of additional reputation decreases as reputation increases. Most research focuses on either the percentage of positive feedback or the total number of ratings, often controlling for negative reputation ratings.

The second question is then what kind of good a positive reputation will do. Here most research considers either the probability of a sale (higher reputation leads to a higher probability of sale), or the value of the sold good (higher reputation leads to a higher sales price when sold). Although some research considers both the effect of reputation on sale and on price, we know of no study that combines the two in a single estimate of the net benefit. Some research uses the probability that a potential buyer will bid on a given offer (e.g., Livingston, 2005), but this is rare.

The opinion on whether we should conclude that there is a positive effect of reputation for sellers has shifted somewhat during the last 15 years or so. Earlier review studies concluded that there might not be an effect at all, but also that the reason for not finding effects might be due to considerable heterogeneity in the offered goods that are being compared (Resnick et al., 2006; cf. Bajari & Hortacsu, 2005). This is the reason why some researchers have narrowed down the product that they analyze as much as possible (Snijders & Zijdeman, 2004; Diekmann, Jann, & Wyder, 2009). It indeed seems to be the case that positive effects of reputation are then more likely to surface. Also, Livingston (2005) argues that the effects of reputation are substantial only for lower values of reputation, and much less important, if at all, for higher ratings. Livingston suggests this could be the reason why the found effects are so small. If researchers do not separate the effects of initial positive ratings from later positive ratings, they basically average out the positive effect of initial positive ratings across a large range of ratings where reputation no longer has an influence, ending up with a close to zero positive result. Instead, Diekmann et al. (2014) summarize previous reviews in the online supplement of their paper, and instead conclude that "most of these studies find evidence of a positive relation between sellers" reputation and price or sales' (p. 70). Whether this suffices for a reputation system to allow for interactions to be self-enforcing if a reputation system is present, remains unclear though. The results by Livingston (2005) suggest they might not:

> The results are dramatic. If the seller has even a few positive reports, then the chance that the auction receives a bid, the chance that the auction results in a sale, and the amount of the winning bid all increase substantially. These early reports are apparently enough to largely convince bidders that the seller tends to perform, because the returns to additional positive reports are not nearly as strong.
>
> (Livingston, 2005; p. 464)

In fact, this would imply that sellers with a decent number of positive ratings need not invest in their reputation any more, which potentially undermines the viability of the system as a whole. One caveat of Livingston's research is that in the empirical part of his study, he obviously used the sales data as they appeared online at that point in time, and in all likelihood there weren't many sellers with a lot of ratings and a substantially lower positive feedback percentage, which makes a true comparison of this hypothesis unfeasible.

# PROBLEMS RELATED TO THE ESTIMATION
## OF THE EFFECT OF REPUTATION

There are several issues that we want to briefly address related to analyzing the effect of reputation, even though we will not get into these in much detail. The first one we have already mentioned, and relates to the product set that researchers choose to analyze. This has to be a rather homogenous set, as unobserved heterogeneity will otherwise cause estimated coefficients to be biased (Resnick et al., 2006). Even though what buyers see before reaching a decision is almost completely available, it is nevertheless still not possible to adequately control for differences across product offerings very well and different models may apply to different kinds of products. In addition, other factors might correlate with reputation, such as the clarity of the product description, or the look-and-feel of the offer. This is unfortunate, as it shows that the promise of having all the data available that is available to buyers at the moment that they reach a decision, is less easily realized than one would have hoped, and does not automatically lead to a single model that estimates reputation independent of the kind of product.

Another form of heterogeneity can stem from the fact that there are both professional and amateur sellers (and buyers) online. The strategies that professional sellers use are likely to be very different from amateur sellers. We know of no empirical papers that take this into account in any detail (though some control for eBay labels such as "Powerseller"), but professionals are likely to mind less about not getting a sale, and may instead keep offering items online automatically after an auction has not lead to a sale. This makes higher reservation prices possible for professional sellers, who might choose to simply wait for as long as it takes until they encounter someone who is willing to pay what they expect the good is worth—and they know this will happen eventually. For amateur sellers such strategies are much less feasible. Buyers who know this can anticipate lower prices from amateur sellers, but it is not straightforward to incorporate how buyers evaluate the type of seller they are dealing with.

Third, eBay is an (almost) second-price auction in that a potential buyer with the highest bid will need to pay only the second highest bid plus the minimum increment. That is, if a buyer bids 100 and it is the highest bid, the minimum increment is 1 and the second highest bid is 90, then the buyer who bid 100 only has to pay 91. Obviously, using just the winning bids as data points implies overestimating the actual selling prices. However, using the second highest bid (plus the increment) is not possible in cases where there were no other bids. As highlighted in some detail in Livingston (2005), this implies that a sample selection model should be used instead of standard OLS (and instead of less standard but also used tobit models), to correctly capture the effect of reputation. As Livingston shows, there have been several studies that have used standard OLS and tobit models, which he claims likely undervalues the effect of reputation.

Fourth, it is easy to forget that the actual eBay sales are the consequence of a process that is more complicated than can be represented in a relatively flat regression-type model. There are buyers and sellers, each with their own estimates about what the market's characteristics are, such as how many other buyers there are for the same item, what a reasonable selling price will be, and the extent to which others value reputation. Buyers might update this information based on the existence, timing, and height of bids by other buyers as the auction progresses, and may have beliefs about how others update their beliefs. Note that the fact that eBay uses a Vickrey-type auction (the second-price plus increment auction of the previous paragraph, cf. Vickrey 1961) does not imply that buyers should simply bid what they feel the product is worth to them. This is the prescribed equilibrium behavior in standard Vickrey auctions, but the possibility of sellers not living up to their promise crucially affects equilibrium behavior, in ways that depend strongly on the type of assumptions one makes about which kinds of information are common knowledge for whom. What equilibrium behavior might be also depends on whether, for a given kind of good at a given point in time, there are many buyers and a few sellers, the other way around, or whether there are many of both. If so many different kinds of factors play a role, one could wonder whether the estimated coefficient of reputation on sale or price is estimated well enough to measure what we would hope it to measure.

Whereas all these arguments are important, the first three are in principle solvable through a combination of a larger investment in coding online offers (for instance also coding the look-and-feel of an offer), in combination with the use of more sophisticated models. We want to focus however, on two other arguments. One is related to the fourth argument mentioned earlier, and one is completely different and instead focuses on other information about sellers that buyers can use instead of the reputation scores. We consider both arguments separately in the following two sections.

## What Do We Measure When Regressing Sales Price on Reputation Scores?

Most online reputation studies only consider the data from the goods that were sold and then regress the sales price on (some variant of a) reputation score, with several control variables included in the model. Whether this involves more sophisticated forms of regression such as tobit or selection models, or whether the probability of sale is analyzed instead, is not important at this point. Such a setup has all the problems mentioned previously, and one more. The general idea behind this additional problem has been introduced in Snijders & Weesie (2009), but we clarify and extend the argument here. The first thing to note is that it is not intuitively clear what a regression analysis with reputation score as a predictor and sales price as the target variable measures. Is it the extent to which the buyers value reputation in this market? Is it the value of reputation to the seller? Something else perhaps?

It might turn out to be less obvious than one would think. It is easiest to grasp the reasons for our concerns by considering the following highly simplified scenario of a market.

## Simulation 1: A mini "Buy-It-Now" eBay Market

Suppose that products have only two attributes, price and reputation. Price equals either 35 or 40, and reputation in this market equals 1, 2, 3, or 4. Higher reputation scores are better. There are therefore 8 different products that can arrive on this market.

Each day, 4 of these 8 products arrive on the market, randomly chosen (for ease of exposition we draw without replacement) from the available set of 8. Each day, one buyer arrives at the market, evaluates these 4 products, and buys the one that he prefers, using the value function:

V (price, rep) = 100 – price + 10*rep + noise

The 100 does not matter for comparison purposes, of course. Hence, in this example a single reputation point is equally valuable as 10 price units for the buyer. Actually, we could do away with the noise as well, but let us include it nevertheless (in this mini simulation we used N(0,2) noise). The remaining three products on the market remain unsold and disappear from the market. The next day, the process repeats itself.

Several complicating matters are disregarded in this model because they would only distract from the main point. For instance, there is no bidding (this is "Buy It Now" only), all products are assumed to be attractive enough to buy, and after a sale there is no feedback, so sellers do not get a higher reputation over time. Also, sellers do not set reservation prices based on what they think or know reputation is worth.

We have

V(35, 1) = 75 + noise
V(35, 2) = 85 + noise
V(35, 3) = 95 + noise
V(35, 4) = 105 + noise
V(40, 1) = 70 + noise
V(40, 2) = 80 + noise
V(40, 3) = 90 + noise
V(40, 4) = 100 + noise

We now simulate this market for 100,000 days. This gives us a data set that looks like this:

```
day price rep sold
================
1   35  1   0
1   40  3   0
1   40  2   0
1   35  4   1
------------------------
2   40  1   0
2   35  3   1
2   35  1   0
2   35  2   0
------------------------
```

```
3   40  4   1
3   35  2   0
...
------------------------
...
```

We now analyze the data in two ways. First, as a conditional logit model with "sold" as the dependent variable, conditioning on the fact that we know that exactly one product is sold per day. We therefore know that the sold product was preferred over the other three that were offered on that day.

Using this conditional logit model, we find that the coefficient of reputation equals 6.85 and that the coefficient of price equals −0.67. Comparing the coefficients of price and reputation, we can conclude that the value of reputation is estimated as 6.85/0.67 = 10.2, which is close to the (correct) value of 10. This should not come as a surprise. In essence we are (close to) estimating McFadden's choice model (McFadden, 1973).[1] Therefore, if we include the items that are not sold, our estimates are fine in the sense that we properly estimate what the value of reputation for the buyer is. This setup hence does give us the value of reputation for the buyer, but to do this it takes the non-chosen alternatives into account. The problem in most field studies is that we often do not know what the non-chosen alternatives have been.

Now consider what happens when we would only consider the products that have been sold. This is typically the kind of data that one would have, if these sales had occurred on an auction site from which only actual sales can be downloaded (NB on eBay one can download other data as well, but researchers do not do this often). Many papers follow this recipe. In the marketing literature, this kind of analysis is often called "hedonic regression" (Rosen, 1974).

It is tempting to think that because the equation V = 100 − price + 10 * rep is the only equation driving the decision making of the buyer, that the 1:10 ratio of price to reputation is likely to appear in this regression as well. It does not. Instead, we find

price = 32.2 + 0.71 reputation

The ratio of price to reputation is now estimated as 1:0.7, which is nowhere near the 1:10 ratio in the value function. To understand why this happens, let us sort the available products from most valuable to least valuable.

P1: V(35, 4) = 105 + noise
P2: V(40, 4) = 100 + noise
P3: V(35, 3) = 95 + noise
P4: V(40, 3) = 90 + noise
P5: V(35, 2) = 85 + noise
P6: V(40, 2) = 80 + noise
P7: V(35, 1) = 75 + noise
P8: V(40, 1) = 70 + noise

The hedonic regression data set with only the sales in it can obviously consist of these 8 products only; there are no other ones. So the results of the hedonic regression depend on how often one finds each product in the data set of sold products, and that depends on the probability with which a product is the highest ranking product on a random day. In our scenario, the P6, P7, and P8 product will hardly be sold at all (only when the noise gives them higher values coincidentally), given that we draw four products without replacement—there will often be a product in the set of four that is higher ranked. For the others, the frequency with which they will occur in the data set of sales is higher for the higher ranking products (and its expectation could in principle be calculated with some basic combinatorics). In essence, the hedonic regression estimates a regression model on the available products, with frequency weights per product that are larger for more attractive products.

This has several consequences for the comparative statics of this model:

1. As long as the value of reputation for the buyer does not have an effect on the rank order of the products, the hedonic regression model delivers the same results. For instance, an increase in the value of reputation from 10 to 11 has no impact on the hedonic regression results, because the extra value for reputation gives at best 4 extra value-points and the difference between the products is at least 5.

2. The hedonic regression model will produce a different price-to-reputation estimate, depending on:

   How many goods are on sale per day. A higher number of sales per day causes that the higher ranked products are more likely to be in the sample and hence win. This shifts the distribution in the frequency weights in the direction of the higher ranking products.

   The distribution of prices and of reputation scores. For instance, adding possible prices of 50 and reputation scores of 5, would change the estimated price-to-reputation estimate.

Note that the conditional logit model, which included the products that were on offer but not chosen, is not sensitive to such differences and would simply produce the correct ratio in all these cases.

These results should worry us, as the hedonic model is exactly what is being used to estimate the effect of reputation most often. Apparently, the hedonic regression model is not estimating the value of reputation for the buyers but instead something else, and that something else depends on market characteristics such as the number of products on sale and the distribution of price and reputation, and perhaps on other matters as well. So what is it that is being estimated with the hedonic regression model? Is it perhaps the value of reputation for the seller? In other words, is it perhaps what a seller could earn more if he would have had a higher reputation score? Our simulation suggests it does not.

To analyze this, we interpret the four different reputation scores as four different sellers, and increase the value of reputation for one seller while keeping the other reputation values constant.

**Table 25.1a. Effects of Increasing the Reputation Score for the Seller with Reputation Score Equal to 3**

| Reputation Score | Proportion of Sales (%) | Mean Sale Price | Increase in Price per Unit Increase |
|---|---|---|---|
| 1 | 0.40 | 35.45 | Base |
| 1.5 | 1.13 | 35.25 | <0 |
| 1.9 | 2.70 | 35.43 | <0 |
| 2.2 | 4.59 | 35.52 | 0.058 |
| 3.5 | 28.14 | 36.25 | 0.32 |
| 4.5 | 62.38 | 36.77 | 0.38 |

**Table 25.1b. Effects of Increasing the Reputation Score for the Seller with Reputation Score Equal to 3**

| Reputation Score | Proportion of Sales (%) | Mean Sale Price | Increase in Price per Unit Increase |
|---|---|---|---|
| 3 | 25.38 | 36.81 | Base |
| 3.5 | 31.22 | 36.56 | <0 |
| 4.1 | 50.64 | 36.48 | <0 |
| 5 | 67.49 | 37.00 | 0.095 |

First we do this for the seller with a reputation score equal to 1. Table 25.1a shows what happens to the proportion of times that the seller with reputation score 1 had the most attractive product offer (proportion of sales), the mean sale price, and the increase in price per unit increase. Table 25.1b shows the same, but then for the seller with reputation score equal to 3.

What we see in Tables 25.3a and 25.3b is, first, that the increase per extra unit of reputation is not constant both within and between the tables (see the last column of both tables). Apparently, the structure of the problem causes the reputation effect to be nonlinear. Note that this has nothing to do with whether buyers value reputation differently depending on how large the reputation value is. Perhaps more importantly, an increase in reputation score of 1, does not seem to give a price increase of 0.7 (as we found in the hedonic regression), although it is close. Redoing the analysis without the noise in the value function does not change this finding.

## Simulation 2: A Mini eBay Market with Buyers Who Value Reputation Differently

A potential way out would be to argue that the preceding example is all wrong, because normally people are bidding on these products and they are willing to pay in accordance with their value for a product with a given reputation, whereas in the example the buyers just pay the given price. So let us instead suppose that we have goods on offer with four different reputation values (1, 2, 3, 4) and two buyers, with the following value functions V1 and V2 for reputation:

$$V1 = 60 + 8 \text{ rep}$$
$$V2 = 57 + 10 \text{ rep}$$

If there is a single good on the market each day, and buyers are bidding exactly what the good is worth to them, then all goods with rep < 1.5 will be bought by the buyer with value function V1 and all goods with rep > 1.5 by V2, as V1 = 60+8 rep > 57+10 rep = V2 when rep < 1.5. A regression estimate of selling price on reputation then delivers:

selling price = 58.00 + 9.70 reputation

We see that the 9.7 value for reputation is not representing the average value of reputation across all buyers (that would be 9), again because the regression equation includes market characteristics: buyers with value function V2 get more of the sales, so they get a higher weight in the final estimate of reputation, shifting the estimate in the direction of the 10.

Again, we could try to see what would happen if the reputation score of a certain seller would change. This is easy to see here: if any of the sellers with a reputation score of 2 or higher would get a higher reputation still, then V2 buyers will buy all goods, albeit for a bit higher price. The value of reputation for the seller is dependent on who he is selling to. It is exactly 10 whenever a seller sells something to V2 and exactly 8 whenever he sells something to a V1. Given this, the 9.7 value could be seen as what an average seller would gain in the market from an increase in reputation of 1. Some would gain 8, others 10, but because more gain 10, the estimate of the average is closer to 10.

The example is of course highly stylized with only two value functions, but making the simulation more realistic would lead to similar insights. For instance, when we consider more (say, 100) buyers at the same time who compete over a given product, draw the buyer's constant term from [50,60] and the reputation value from [0,4], we end up with an estimated reputation coefficient of about 3.5, certainly not equal to the average of the reputation values (which would be 2). Because the ones who value reputation buy more goods (they beat the ones with lower reputation values in the market), the estimated reputation coefficient is in this case higher than the mean value for reputation. Note that this is different from the censoring problem. The censoring problem occurs because on eBay we cannot infer precisely from the selling price what somebody would have been willing to pay (what they paid is an underestimate). In these scenarios, arguments of this kind do not play a role.

There are at least two conclusions that can be derived from these small exercises. First, when one is interested in estimating the (average) value of reputation for the buyers in a given market, it is crucial (or at least way easier to interpret) to include the full choice set. The value of reputation to a buyer is obviously based on within buyer comparisons of different offers and excluding them will lead to results that are influenced by market characteristics in such dramatic ways that the estimated regression coefficient is potentially unrelated to the actual value of reputation for the buyers at all. Second, it is equally misleading to instead interpret the hedonic regression coefficient as the value of reputation for the sellers. Diekmann et al.'s (2014) statement that "For the sake of our argument, it is enough to show that buyers, on average, pay more for sellers with higher reputations and thus create financial incentives for sellers to behave cooperatively in the market" should be interpreted with some caution. As the simulations show, the estimated coefficient does not seem to be related to the benefits that sellers can achieve, these benefits are likely to depend on the distribution of reputations of others, and are not linear in terms of their added benefit.

# How Important is the Impact of the Numeric Reputation Scores Compared to Semantic Feedback?

Setting aside the issue whether the effect of the reputation scores is measured correctly, one could of course wonder whether there exist other matters that buyer (and sellers) consider instead. One such matter is the content of the semantic feedback that buyers and sellers can leave. Even though the reputation scores summarize a potentially very large set of previous interactions, it may be hard for buyers to attach value to these numbers. The basic argument is straightforward: buyers can rightfully argue that it may be easier to understand "what kind of seller they are dealing with" based on how the seller behaves in semantic interaction with his or her customers. Over the Internet this semantic interaction is comparatively limited, but it is there and collected in eBay's feedback forum.

There are certainly reasons to believe that written, qualitative feedback might have stronger effects than quantitative feedback. Text allows for more subtle messages than just numbers, and people in general are used to dealing with text rather than numbers and are therefore more likely to feel strongly about it, and we would expect that a single comment might lead traders to trust or distrust a particular seller (whereas we do not expect this to hold for numerical feedback, except in rare instances; Snijders, Bober, & Matzat, 2017).

Furthermore, it is known that the majority of eBay users reads at least one page of text feedback comments about a seller (Pavlou & Dimoka, 2006). Second, text comments that provide evidence for a seller's responsibility or credibility have been shown to increase the price premium for the seller's product, while comments that provide evidence for irresponsibility or poor credibility serve to diminish it. The extraordinary text comments explained an additional 20–30% of variance in price premiums (Pavlou & Dimoka, 2006; Utz, Snijders, & Matzat, 2009).

Although as far as we know there is not a lot of literature about the effect of (online) semantic feedback, some research starting from Kim et al. (2004) has considered its effects in some detail. In particular, Kim et al. (2004) distinguish between two kinds of mistakes a person can make: a competence-based violation and a morality-based violation. They further distinguish two standard rebuttal strategies: denial of the accusation, or accepting responsibility through apologizing. The study by Kim et al. (2004) considered offline behavior, and they argue and empirically establish that the rebuttal strategy should match the violation. A competence-based violation should be met with an apology, whereas a morality-based violation should be met with denial. Kim et al. base this claim on insights from research on causal inference and interpersonal perception by Reeder & Brewer (1979), who demonstrate that in the eyes of observers negative information about other parties in the *domain of morality* (or integrity) issues is considered more informative about the other parties' presumable traits than is positive information. At the same time, positive information about another individual is more diagnostic than negative information when it comes to inferring a party's traits in the *domain of skills and abilities* (Skowronski & Carlston, 1987). This asymmetry is argued to occur because humans use "hierarchically restrictive schema" for inferring dispositions from somebody's behavior (Reeder & Brewer, 1979). That is, humans believe that moral as well as immoral individuals can show moral behavior from time to time, whereas only an immoral person would show immoral behavior. Therefore, immoral behavior implies revealing oneself as being the immoral type (Skowronski & Carlston, 1987). The situation is reversed when observers make causal inferences about dispositions in the domain of skills and abilities. Individuals with little skill would be more restricted in their behavior than individuals with greater skill (Reeder & Brewer, 1979). A skilled individual may deliver a weak performance because of a lack of motivation or bad luck. Good performance, however, must necessarily be attributed to a strong skill level because individuals with few skills are simply unable to perform well (Skowronski & Carlston, 1987).

In our own research (Matzat & Snijders, 2012) we have not been able to replicate the match between mistakes and rebuttals in an online setting. Instead, our findings indicate that when an online user posts an accusation that a web shop seriously erred—intentionally or accidentally—the seller's optimal response is different from what was found in Kim et al. (2004). An apology restores trust successfully, whereas a denial does not, and may even reduce trust, consistent with the earlier findings in Utz et al. (2009). This seems to be because customers believe a denial much less than an apology. Contrary to our expectations, even though customers found the denials by a reputable web shop more believable than denials by a less reputable web shop, denials of morality-based accusation (i.e., an intentional error) by a highly reputable web shop restores trust no more than a denial by less reputable web shops. An apology by a web shop is always more successful in re-building trust than a denial, under both types of accusations and regardless of reputation.

The experiments that we ran (Utz et al., 2009; Matzat & Snijders, 2012; Snijders, Bober, & Matzat, 2017) are all scenario-based and hence no real eBay interactions. However, they do have one characteristics that is of special interest here: in these experiments both the reputation score of the sellers and the semantic feedback of buyer and seller have been varied, in a design where the effect size of the reputation score can be compared with the effect size of the semantic feedback.

As it turned out, buyers can strongly influence the sellers' perceived trustworthiness through textual feedback. Sellers can regain the loss that they suffer from after a mistake through the use of a specific and adequate semantic response (Snijders, Bober, & Matzat, 2017). However, the same seller would need to get an extra 2,300 reputation points to reduce the negative effect of, for instance, a buyer's accusation of incompetence. Obviously, the seller would need to know which semantic message to send, but if chosen appropriately, its value is as strong as 2,300 rating points.

Although clearly not conclusive evidence, this does show that the potential of semantic feedback is a force to be reckoned with when compared to the mere reputation score.

## DISCUSSION AND IMPLICATIONS

Reputation systems have found a massive following in the online world. Research on the effects of reputation scores has likewise proliferated. As we hope to have shown, there are reasons to rethink what the research that uses hedonic regression type approaches is actually measuring, and how (if at all) the results of these kinds of studies relate to the theoretical arguments regarding the positive effects of reputation. As our simulations show, it is not clear what is being measured in these models at all, and the estimated coefficient of reputation is the consequence of a complex interaction of characteristics of the market, buyers, suppliers, auctions, and products. Even if we disregard these methodological issues, then still the estimated effects of the reputation score are quite small. Investing in a good reputation, given the size of these effects, seems hardly worth the bother. Actually, the reverse argument, that misbehaving as a seller is a bad idea because it visibly influences the recent reputation score, might make more sense. If quite a few of the most recent sales would have ended in buyers giving negative feedback, which might damage sales and sales prices. Especially on eBay, where a large portion of the sellers have completed thousands of transactions and therefore have very high reputation scores, the benefit of an extra unit of positive feedback is negligible. An argument along a similar line has been made in Bolton, Katok, & Ockenfels (2004): they argued that perhaps what makes the reputation system work is just the fact that it is there. The positive effect of reputation might stem from having a reputation system versus not having one, rather than from benefiting from higher reputation scores in the given system. Moreover, experiment-based research suggests that other characteristics of the reputation system, namely the semantic feedback, might be factors that influence the perceived trustworthiness of sellers more than the mere numbers do.

Our line of argumentation has several implications for research on the value of reputation (scores) in online systems. The most apparent one is to be extremely careful in interpreting hedonic regression results, even when using more appropriate selection-type models. Using simulation studies that are an order of magnitude more extensive than the toy simulations that we used might be in order. Another concrete implication is, that whenever possible and whenever one is interested in the value of reputation to the buyer, to also measure the alternatives that were considered by the buyer but not chosen. This causes the measured comparisons to be within buyers, as they should be, instead of across buyers. Third, it makes sense to better evaluate what buyers actually compare when they are buying something online. One could think of lab studies using eye-tracking or mouse-tracking, or even field studies that use mouse- or click-tracking if the online provider would be willing to deliver such data. Field studies that include (coding of) the semantic feedback might be useful as well. We feel that, as it is, because the reputation scores are readily available and easy to work with, they have sparked a research domain that has delivered important initial steps, but it is time to move forward.

## NOTE

1. Distributional assumptions about the noise in McFadden's choice model are actually somewhat different.

## REFERENCES

Bajari, P., & Hortacsu, A. (2005). Are structural estimates of auction models reasonable? Evidence from experimental data. *Journal of Political Economy*, 113(4), 703–741.

Bolton, G. E., Katok, E., & Ockenfels, A. (2004). How effective are electronic reputation mechanisms? An experimental investigation. *Management Science*, 50(11), 1587–1602.

Diekmann, A., Jann, B., Przepiorka, W., & Wehrli, S. (2014). Reputation formation and the evolution of cooperation in anonymous online markets. *American Sociological Review*, 79(1), 65–85.

Diekmann, A., Jann, B., & Wyder, D. (2009). Trust and reputation in internet auctions. In Cook, K., Snijders, C. Buskens, V., & Cheshire, C (Eds.) *eTrust: Forming Relationships in the Online World* (pp. 139–165). New York: Russell Sage Foundation.

Kim, P. H., Ferrin, D. L., Cooper, C. D., & Dirks, K. T. (2004). Removing the shadow of suspicion: The effects of apology versus denial for repairing competence-versus integrity-based trust violations. *Journal of Applied Psychology*, 89(1), 104.

Livingston, J. A. (2005). How valuable is a good reputation? A sample selection model of internet auctions. *The Review of Economics and Statistics*, 87(3), 453–65.

Matzat, U., & Snijders, C. (2012). Rebuilding Trust in online shops on consumer review sites: Sellers' responses to user-generated complaints. *Journal of Computer-Mediated Communication*, 18(1), 62–79.

McFadden, D. (1973). Conditional logit analysis of qualitative choice behavior. In: *Frontiers in econometrics*, P. Zarembka (Ed.). New York: Wiley.

Pavlou, P. A., & Dimoka, A. (2006). The nature and role of feedback text comments in online marketplaces: Implications for trust building, price premiums, and seller differentiation. *Information Systems Research*, 17(4), 392–414.

Reeder, G. D., & Brewer, M. B. (1979). A schematic model of dispositional attribution in interpersonal perception. *Psychological Review*, 86(1), 61.

Resnick, P., Zeckhauser, R., Swanson, J., & Lockwood, K. (2006). The value of reputation on eBay: A controlled experiment. *Experimental economics*, 9(2), 79–101.

Rosen, S. (1974). Hedonic prices and implicit markets: Product differentiation in pure competition. *Journal of Political Economy*, 82(1), 34–55.

Snijders, C., & Weesie, J. (2009). Online programming markets. In Cook, K., Snijders, C. Buskens, V. & Cheshire, C. (Eds.) *eTrust: forming relationships in the online world* (pp. 166–185). New York: Russell Sage Foundation.

Snijders, C., & Zijdeman, R. (2004). Reputation and internet auctions: eBay and beyond. *Analyse & Kritik*, 26(1), 158–184.

Snijders, C., Bober, M. & Matzat, U. (2017). Online reputation in eBay auctions: Damaging and rebuilding trustworthiness through feedback comments from buyers and sellers. In Jann, B. & Przepiorka, W. Social dilemmas, institutions, and the evolution of cooperation (pp. 421–443). Walter de Gruyter GmbH.

Skowronski, J. J., & Carlston, D. E. (1987). Social judgment and social memory: The role of cue diagnosticity in negativity, positivity, and extremity biases. *Journal of Personality and Social Psychology*, 52(4), 689.

Utz, S., Matzat, U., & Snijders, C. (2009). On-line reputation systems: The effects of feedback comments and reactions on building and rebuilding trust in on-line auctions. *International Journal of Electronic Commerce*, 13(3), 95–118.

Vickrey, W. (1961). Counterspeculation, auctions, and competitive sealed tenders. *The Journal of Finance*, 16(1), 8–37.

........................................................

# CHAPTER 26

# GOSSIP, INTERNET-BASED REPUTATION SYSTEMS, AND GOVERNANCE

........................................................

## LUCIO PICCI

One of the greatest consolation of this world is friendship,
and one of the pleasure of friendship,
is to have some one to whom we may entrust a secret.

—Alessandro Manzoni, The Betrothed (1827)

## INTRODUCTION

........................................................

WE live in a world where the diffusion of information is incredibly easy. There are abundant recent examples of information dissemination that have captured global attention, such as WikiLeaks (Leigh and Harding, 2011), or the Snowden case (Greenwald, 2014) and, to add entertainment value because of its saucy implications, the breach of the on-line dating service Ashley Madison.[1,2] At first sight, these events may appear to be cases of good old gossip on steroids. However, we should not jump to such conclusion, because the current definitions of gossip are too generic to account for the novelties of Internet-mediated communication.

This chapter revolves around a conceptual framework which addresses such short-coming, while accommodating a vast variety of communication activities, gossip being one of them. The proposed characterization of concepts permits analytical clarity when considering forms of Internet-supported communications, and moreover organizes the analyses of a series of interesting questions. Among them, we are particularly concerned with forms of governance that are enabled by the Internet, and in particular by so-called "Internet-based reputation systems," which allow people to voice their assessments of products that they have acquired, or of services that they have experienced. Provided in the form of scores on a low dimensional scale, the assessments are aggregated to indicate, for example, the percentage of past customers of a given establishment who were satisfied of their choice. These systems are so ubiquitous that certainly all readers have experienced them, both to inform their choices among available alternatives, and possibly to contribute their assessments—of sellers or products on an e-commerce site, of hotels and restaurants, *et cetera*. The reason why they are called "reputation" systems, is because the aggregated scores are meant to summarize the overall quality of providers and, as such, to provide a measure of sort of their reputation. The information that they make available might refer to online markets (as in the case of eBay), or offline markets that are rated online (as in the case of Tripadvisor's ratings of restaurants).

Internet-based reputation systems are used mainly in the business sector to support the functioning of markets, and the reference to "governance" might sound strained. However, they also have attracted attention for use in the public sphere, where the concept of governance has instead an obvious salience. I shall focus upon such uses, also because I believe that they permit to obtain interesting insights on the nature of gossip and on its organizational implications.

To achieve these goals, I draw on different disciplines. The stage is set first by characterizing the concepts of reputation and of trust, which is done in the game theoretic tradition. Then, with a point of view borrowed from the management sciences, the essential characteristics of Internet-based reputation systems are considered. After having laid the ground, we ask to which extent these instruments might be seen as cases of gossip. The answer is negative, unless we choose to adopt a definition of gossip that is so broad as to be of little use. The same conclusion also applies to less structured types of Internet-based dissemination of information, such as those of the "leaks" mentioned earlier.

Traditional gossip is then compared with Internet-based reputation systems, with a focus on their organizational effects. Freely drawing on organizational theory, I present gossip as a tool in the daily struggle for resources, hence for power, which takes place within organizations. The same can be said of Internet-based reputation systems, which in a sense "democratize gossip," by leveling the playing field when it comes to the formulation, transmission, and processing of information which is relevant for the reputation of the organizational actors. The degree to which such democratization occurs depends on the context, and also on architectural choices: on this count, I refer extensively to the idea of reputation-based governance, as defined and discussed in Picci (2011).

A last concluding section muses about the future of gossip, in a world where Internet-based reputation systems become ubiquitous.

# Internet-Based Reputation
# Systems

The eBay electronic market provides one of the most interesting examples of Internet-based reputation systems. Founded in 1995, today it has over 170 million active users around the world, generating more than one billion yearly listings. One key of its success is the fact that both sellers and buyers might write an assessment, or "feedback," on each other, which can be positive, neutral, or negative. The percentage of positive feedbacks received in the previous 12 months forms an index of reputation of sort[3] (see Snijders and Matzat, this volume). In a situation where otherwise there would be ample room for cheating, this feature provides incentives to behave honestly, to be efficient, and to invest in quality. Similar mechanisms are in place in many electronic markets, and Internet-based reputation systems serve as tools to process reputationally relevant information in situations where traditional word-of-mouth would not work, because of the impersonal nature of the relationship among geographically scattered participants (Dellarocas, 2003, 2010).

The availability of the assessments is a problematic issue. In particular, if seen with the eyes of standard economics, the fact that people spend time to assess products or services constitutes a puzzle of sort. As Rockenbach and Sadrieh (2012) underline, "purely self-interested individuals would not engage in the voluntary provision of information public goods," where "providing [them] is even less attractive than providing other public goods, because the providers are already in possession of the information that they transmit to others and, thus, do not even participate in the benefits or provision." Overwhelming evidence shows instead that often assessments are abundantly provided, indicating the presence of other types of motivation, be them of other-regarding nature, or else. When these systems are applied to the public sphere, parallels with the paradox of voting might be drawn. In this respect, one advantage of Internet-based reputation systems as applied to public governance is the low cost of participation, a desirable property in today's "stealth democracies."[4]

The concept of reputation, which is central to the present discussion, has been the object of numerous characterizations in different strands of the literature. Unfortunately, this has created a degree of confusion, which is compounded by the fact that reputation has often been conflated with the cognate concept of *trust*. In the social and behavioral sciences, definitions of trust often revolve around the idea that a person trusts another when he thinks that she will do something that is "good or at least not detrimental" to him (Gambetta 1988: p. 277). In part because they are influenced by a vernacular understanding of the concept of trust, such definitions do not contribute to analytical clarity (Picci, 2011: pp. 34–35).

A useful characterization, both of trust and of reputation, might be grounded in the theory of incentives and in game theory (Picci, 2011: pp. 20–44). Under this light, reputation is usefully seen as the result of interactions among agents where observed behaviors provide clues about some of their key characteristics, which however are not directly observed. For example, when going to a restaurant for the first time, a client is uncertain about what to expect; however, being eventually satisfied with the meal amounts to a hint that the cook is highly skilled. In what game theorists call "Bayesian updating," agents update their beliefs about others by observing their actions (Bar-Isaac and Tadelis, 2008). Actions, in turn, are in part motivated precisely to influence beliefs: the cook in the example above knows that, by working hard, she'll hopefully make patrons believe that she is good.

Trust might be seen instead as arising in an abstract situation where actors have no uncertainty about their reciprocal characteristics, and when their best interest would be not to cooperate, if they interacted only once. Such relations could take the form of a prisoner's dilemma game, a well-known stylized interaction between players who, if the game is performed only once, have an interest in "cheating." However, if they play repeatedly in time, the calculus of convenience might change, because players expect that if they cheat now, they might forego the benefits of collaboration in the future. Under certain conditions, repeating in time the prisoners' dilemma game results in collaboration among completely selfish actors—that is, in the emergence of trust. In real-life situations, the two stylized types of strategic relationships, leading to the emergence of reputation and of trust, very often coexist and interact in complex ways. At least for the sake of analytical clarity, it is useful to distinguish between them.[5]

Internet-based reputation systems have been widely researched, and evidence has been found that reputation matters, in the following sense. Sellers with a better reputational measure were found to command a higher price for their goods (see Resnick et al. 2006, and the survey of results in Cabral, 2012; see also Diekmann and Przepiorka, this volume). Also, receiving a negative feedback entails a significant drop in sales (Cabral and Hortaçsu, 2010). Consequently, sellers care about their reputation: according to evidence presented in Cabral and Hortaçsu (2010), those with a good reputation are careful to maintain it, but if for some reasons it deteriorates, they might become less keen on pleasing buyers, thus damaging it further. Reputation might eventually be squandered before exiting the market (see, e.g., Jin and Kato, 2006) but, overall, much remains to be learned on the characterization and the determinants of its dynamics (Cabral, 2012).

Internet-based reputation systems are mostly been used in the private sector, but they have been proposed for application also in the public sphere, an issue which we shall consider in due time.

# GOSSIP IN THE INTERNET AGE

Internet-based reputation systems allow for a "digitalization of word of mouth," as Dellarocas (2003) aptly put it more than a decade ago. Then, there naturally arises the question of how this new type of word-of-mouth compares with the traditional gossip of yore. To what extent are they similar, in their character and functions? And, more generally, what are the mutual relationships between those traditional forms of dissemination of information that we call gossip, and the new forms enabled by the Internet?

To answers these questions, a clear definition of concepts is needed, the more so, considering that our discourse revolves around a word, gossip, amply used in everyday speech. In order to accommodate the specifics of Internet-enabled communication, the definition of gossip which is proposed here is more nuanced than the ones that are prevalent in the literature. According to Wittek and Wielers (1998), "gossip is the provision of information by one person (*ego*) to another one (*alter*) about an absent third person (*tertius*)." Similarly, workplace gossip has been defined as "informal and evaluative talk in an organization about another member of that organization who is not present" (Kurland and Peddel, 2000; see also Ellwardt et al. 2012). The present characterization of concepts moves from such familiar ones, but is more specific in describing the actors involved and their actions.

First, I consider the possibility that actors are not individuals, but organizations. For example, the provider of information (*ego*) could be a firm, and the target of the gossip (*tertius*) could be a public administration. I further distinguish depending on whether *ego*'s identity is known or unknown. In particular, Internet applications might be engineered to guarantee the anonymity of the source of information, or to permit anonymity as an option. Moreover, I contemplate the prospect that the information provided by *ego* refers to an *action* by an absent *tertius*, and not to *tertius* himself. This aspect is particularly relevant within Internet-based reputation systems, which most often allow to assess products or services, that is, the outcomes of actions. Similarly, in applications to the public sphere, as we will see what is assessed are the outcomes of public policies, that is, again, of actions. In market applications, assessments on actions easily reverberate on the actor who is responsible for them. For example, in eBay, buyers' assessments of the transactions of a given seller aggregate to form a "reputation score" for that seller. "Actions" and "actors" are often conflated also in traditional gossip: a rumor affirming that some person has done something bad might be taken as a signal that *that person* is bad. However, "action" and "actor" are distinct concepts. The difference is particularly important when *tertius* is an organization, because it raises the issue of how to assign responsibilities, or to distribute them among its members, a question which is particularly important in applications to the public sphere.

To be useful, a definition of gossip should not be too general, possibly to the point of encompassing all types of communication involving the assessments of absent parties or of their actions. Traditional communication contexts naturally provide limitations in this respect, but the unprecedented possibilities of unbridled communication that the Internet affords require more precision in defining concepts. I define gossip a situation where *ego* transmits information about *tertius* (or her actions) to *alter*, *ego* is not anonymous, and *alter* comprises at most a limited number of actors which do not include *tertius*. By this I mean that, in deciding to pass on a piece of information about *tertius*, *ego* implicitly intends such dissemination to be addressed to *some* (what we may call the "included" *alter*), but not to other possible recipients (the "excluded" *alter*). Ego, alter and *tertius* may indifferently be individuals, or organizations.

Table 26.1. Categories of Communication between *Ego* and *Alter*

| | | *Alter* (person or organization) | |
| --- | --- | --- | --- |
| | | Limited audience (excluding *tertius*) | General public |
| *Ego* (person or organization) | Anonymous with respect to *alter* | Not gossip<br>*Anonymous letter about alter sent to tertius* | Not gossip<br>*Ashley Madison case. WikiLeaks (some). Internet-based Reputation Systems (when ego is anonymous)* |
| | Identity known to *alter* | <u>Gossip</u> | Not gossip<br>*"Gossip" column in magazine WikiLeaks (some). Snowden's Global Surveillance Disclosures. Internet-based Reputation Systems (when ego's identity is known)* |

Table 26.1 illustrates such a definition of gossip, and it provides some concrete examples (in italic in the table). There is gossip only when *ego*'s identity is known to *alter*, and when *alter* is not the general public. As a consequence, and to exemplify, activities such as the gossip column of a magazine do not qualify as gossip, because *alter* is the general public. Nor is such the breach into the Ashley Madison database, cited in the introduction to this chapter, because the identity of the perpetrator remained anonymous, and also, because the information stolen was made available to anyone who cared to read it. WikiLeaks also is not an instance of gossip, and its precise classification in the scheme of Table 26.1 depends on whether the identity of the author of a given leak is disclosed or not. Neither is gossip, as it is here defined, the type of information sharing and processing occurring within Internet-based reputation systems, which in Table 26.1 are classified in two different boxes, depending on whether the identity of the persons providing the assessments is publicly revealed, or not. An example fitting into the top-left square of Table 26.1 would be an anonymous letter sent to a group of friends and containing damaging information about *alter*. What makes it *not* gossip is the anonymity of *ego*.

All examples involving the Internet have been classified in Table 26.1 as not being gossip, but certainly there can be gossip, as is defined here, on the Internet. First, the Internet supports traditional forms of gossiping by means of communication tools such as e-mail, chat programs, etc. Casual evidence, when not introspection, indicates that this type of "e-gossiping" is quite frequent. Also, it would be possible to create an Internet-based reputation system whose information generation and processing qualifies as gossip, as it will be discussed further in the concluding section of this chapter.

The present definition of gossip is more restrictive than the one implied, for example, in Giardini et al. (2013: 366), where, "transmission of reputation" is implicitly equated with gossip. All examples of informational activities cited above, and summarized in Table 26.1, would certainly contribute to the formation of the reputation of the *tertius* involved, but most of them would not constitute gossip according to the definition presented here. Such differences mostly derive from the fact that extant definition of gossip have been crafted with a traditional communication context in mind. Enter the Internet, and the need emerges for a more careful and nuanced characterization of concepts, unless we are prepared to accept a definition of gossip that, by being too wide, would deprive it of analytical traction.

# INTERNET-BASED REPUTATION
# SYSTEMS AND GOSSIP

We have concluded that communications enabled by Internet-based reputation systems should not be seen as gossip, but also that both perform a similar function: they affect the reputation of *tertius*. In particular, gossip has even been identified with such "transmission of reputation,"[6] while the processing and dissemination of reputationally relevant information is the raison d'être of Internet-based reputation systems. But the ways in which such function is executed differs greatly between the two, and these differences, being of great import, deserve a careful consideration.

We note first that, in both cases, reputation influences the allocation of various types of resources. These might be of the social type; for example, if *tertius* is the victim of negative gossip, she might be ostracized by her peers. Quite often, reputation affects economic outcomes, either directly or indirectly. A professional with a bad reputation encounters difficulties in finding a job, or in securing a high price for his services, regardless of whether such reputation is the result of traditional gossip, or the outcome of an Internet-based reputation system. Within organizations, reputation influences the chances of obtaining a promotion, and such incentives are particularly relevant in public administrations, where career-concerns incentives are particularly important (Picci, 2011: chapter 3).

Whereas both gossip and Internet-based reputation systems provide reputational incentives, they do so within a significantly different organizational context. In particular, Michelson and Waddington (2012: xv) note that gossip is "constituted through informal and unsanctioned interactions," in a situation where "key organizational stakeholders find this form of 'unofficial discourse' both disconcerting and threatening on the basis that it is almost impossible to meaningfully regulate and control." In this sense, gossip is but an episode of the well-researched conflict between the formal and the informal organization. It is an instrument used to sustain informal networks, which in turn allow for the distribution of organizational resources, and of power, possibly in contrast with the dictates of the formal organization. Certainly, gossip occurs also within cliques placed at the organizational top, and it is not necessarily a weapon in the hands of the lower echelons of an organization: the distinction between the formal and the informal organization should be seen as nuanced, and is not mechanically reflected in a top vs. bottom dialectic. Be as it may, the fact that gossip naturally belongs to the informal dimension of organizations might be one of the reasons why, as Michelson and Waddington (2012) remind us, it "gets such a bad press"—a theme on which I shall return.

While gossip is never sanctioned within organizations, Internet-based reputation systems often are. To clarify, consider the case of those Internet-based information systems allowing students to rate the courses that they take. Many educational institutions offer them, while regulating their use. Typically, the aggregated assessments are published under a set of conditions, so as to translate into scores for individual courses, which then reverberate to their instructors. An example is provided by the University of California at San Diego's "CAPE" service, which evolved from a traditional paper publication on sale at the campus' bookstore. It eventually became a full-fledged on-line system (see http://cape.ucsd.edu), where the ratings for all courses are made public.

Compare such case with the site "ratemyprofessors.com," which performs the same functions, but is unsanctioned by any educational institution,[7] so that students might rate their courses also in those institutions where such practice is not supported. In this case, the contrast between the formal and the informal organization is apparent. On the other hand, when such ratings are sanctioned from above, they might be seen simply as representing one of the routines of the formal organization.

Gossip is very often frowned upon not only by key organizational stakeholders, but also by society at large. Dunbar (2004) notes that gossip "is seen as malicious, destructive, and largely reprehensible," while Schein (1994: 145), mentions "Judeo-Christian writings against slander, and the association of gossip with transgressions such as sloth, malice, envy."[8] While gossip is seen as so reprehensible, many have underlined its positive effects. According to a point of view originating in Dunbar (1996), "gossip [is] a mechanism for bonding social groups, tracing these origins back to social grooming among primates" (Dunbar, 2004). Baumeister et al. (2004) affirms that gossip "can convey valuable information to the hearer about culture and society" and it spurs cultural learning, and several studies (for example, Gottman and Mettetal, 1986) sustain that gossip serves to promote group solidarity. In revealing "personal information about the gossiper," it "communicates to the listener that he or she is trusted" (Bosson et al. 2006) and helps "cement and maintain social bonds" (Baumeister et al, 2004). Also, (negative) gossip ties persons together by providing opportunities for downward social comparisons, considering that "by gossiping with a potential friend about her dislike of a third person, the gossiper signals to the gossipee that she considers him an in-group member, which should promote self-esteem and grease the wheels of their friendship" (Bosson et al. 2006, referring to Wert and Salovey, 2004).

In fact, gossip might facilitate human interactions also because it is perceived to be ethically wrong. *Ego* pays a cost in case *alter* exposes him as a gossiper, so that gossip might function as a bond of trust between *ego* and *alter*. *Alter* shares the moral blame with *ego*, to the extent that he approvingly accepts to hear the gossip, and even more so when, as it often happens, roles are interchanged in a "gossiping session." Willingly assuming the moral cost of gossiping, and the possibility of reciprocally exposing each other to the social stigma which accompanies such activity, facilitates cooperation by bonding *ego* and *alter*.[9] For all these reasons, even negative gossip, far from having the merely destructive role that it is often assumed, might actually positively affect organizational output, and encourage cooperation beyond the direct effects of the reputational information that it disseminates.

Internet-based reputation systems in general do not share this characteristic of gossip. Certainly, like gossip, they facilitate cooperation because negative assessments punish free riders and generally disincentivize poor performers. But, unlike gossip, Internet-based reputation systems are not stigmatized, and contributing to them is typically seen as a legitimate and even commendable activity. This might be so because most of the existing applications, such as eBay, have been in the field of business, where reputational scores act as a tool to punish the deserving "bad guys." Not being stigmatized, Internet-based reputation systems do not have the bonding effects of gossip that we have discussed. As to whether they might induce different types of bonding among participants, possibly of the more psychological types that have been described above, the answer depends to a great extent on implementation choices. In particular, some of these systems might provide ways for users to develop a virtual community of sort, while other systems might be more impersonal.[10]

# DEMOCRATIZING GOSSIP

Information on the reputation of the agents of governance is relevant for the allocation of organizational resources and for the distribution of power. Internet-based reputation systems and traditional gossip both contribute to the dissemination of such information, but the way in which they do so has differences of great import, which we now discuss.

As a weapon in the fight for the allocation of resources, gossip is not equally accessible to all, and its effectiveness varies. First of all, in order to be able to gossip within a network, it is necessary to have access to it. Moreover, the impact on the reputation of *tertius* of the gossip by a person who occupies a peripheral place will be modest, while centrality, and status, will command a higher effect.[11] The mere possibility of gossiping, and its effectiveness, may be seen as one of the perks accruing to network participants, and one of the reasons why they have an incentive to invest in "networking" activities.

Network membership, placement, and status, depend on many factors. Network membership might be shared within the family and may eventually be inherited. The effectiveness of any networking activity, moreover, certainly also depends on personal traits, while the benefits of traditional gossip, inasmuch as they represent a rent, spur rent-seeking investments. Also, there is mutual causation between participation in informal networks, and one's hierarchical position within formal organizations. Persons who are well-placed in networks find it easier to climb up the hierarchy of the organizations that they belong to; on the other hand, persons who are well-placed within the formal organization are more interesting targets for other people's networking efforts.[12] Overall, we expect the benefits that gossip might provide to be unequally distributed.

Internet-based reputation systems are significantly different in this respect, because access is typically open to all and on equal terms, so that every participant has an equal opportunity to generate reputationally relevant information. Actual participation has a cost, which might vary depending on the characteristics of the system, but in most cases it is negligible—once a referral activity is initiated, often its end is just a few clicks away. In general, investing resources in participation as a way to acquire rents is not a realistic option, at least while considering the average Internet-based reputation system available today. All participants are on the same foot in generating reputationally relevant information, since, unlike traditional gossip, Internet-based reputation systems provide equal opportunities both in producing and in accessing reputationally relevant information. In this sense, Internet-based reputation systems *democratize gossip*.

Certainly, in most cases the possibility of placing a referral is conditional on the verification that a given relevant transaction has occurred—for example, to rate a seller in eBay, one has to be a buyer in the first place. It is in the nature of markets that the number of transactions that a person might conclude strictly depends on the available resources, which in turn determine the reputationally relevant information that an individual might generate. Internet-based reputation systems do not change this fundamental reality, and the statement that they democratize gossip should not be taken as leading necessarily to a sort of "one person-one vote" principle. But when Internet-based reputation systems are applied to public governance, the question of how much reputationally relevant information a citizen is allowed to generate acquires greater salience. To this important issue we now turn our attention.

# Reputation-Based Public Governance

Internet-based reputation systems could be applied to the public sphere, and in Picci (2011) a full-fledged (public) governance model that is "reputation-based" is proposed. Using suitable Internet-based information systems, citizens would assess the outcomes of public policies, and the aggregate assessments would reverberate to the administrations and public officials which are responsible for them. In turn, these reputational information, appropriately summarized, would affect allocative decisions, for example by means of "career concerns" types of incentives—that is, by linking public officials' prospects of promotion to their reputational scores (see Picci, 2011, chapter 3; on the broader issue of reputation in public administrations, see Picci, 2014).

To fix ideas, consider the case of public works (Picci, 2011: pp. 129–134). The outcomes of such projects would be assessed by a variety of actors, by means of a suitable Internet-based information system. Public administrators in charge of a project would rate the quality of the work carried out by the contracting firms, which in turn would assess how the project is managed by the public administration in charge. Citizens would be allowed to judge the completed project. Such ratings would be highly structured, and would refer to well-defined characteristics, such as usefulness, aesthetic qualities, etc., and would allow for the computation of various types of statistics and of reputational indicators. These, in turn, would affect the allocation of resources: firms whose work receives mediocre assessments would find it more difficult to secure future public contracts, while public servants whose projects obtain poor ratings would imperil their chances of climbing the career ladder, and possibly would not be rewarded with monetary bonuses.

As it happens almost invariably when powerful information and communication technologies are involved, implementation choices might have very different practical implications. In particular, when applied to the public sphere, they raise important questions also of an ethical nature, because the powers of the technology could be harnessed to enhance state control on its people. For example, a recent document of the General Office of the Central Committee of the Chinese Communist Party, proposing what might be considered a variety of reputation-based governance, has been described as depicting "a world where an authoritarian government monitors everything you do, amasses huge amounts of data on almost every interaction you make, and awards you a single score that measures how "trustworthy" you are. In this world, anything from defaulting on a loan to criticizing the ruling party, from running a red light to failing to care for your parents properly, could cause you to lose points."[13]

Without engaging the merits of such journalistic interpretation of the Chinese initiative, it is clear that the concrete ways in which Internet-based reputation systems are applied to public governance could make a sea of difference in terms of their interpretation. Contrasting the risks that they might support a brave new world with a distinctly dystopian flavor to it, applying Internet-based reputation systems to public governance might appeal to the democratically minded, if it succeeds in enhancing control *of* the State *by* the people, and not the other way around. In this respect, two issues are of particular relevance.

First, that of equal access. We noted that in market applications, the amount of reputationally relevant information that a person might generate depends on the number of transactions and, ultimately, on the available economic resources. In a democratic context, the reputationally relevant information that each person might generate should be roughly equalized, together with the impact that it has on the allocation of resources, hence of power. Such goal might be seen as extending the democratic principle of "one person, one vote" to a new domain, that of Internet-based reputation systems, as they are applied to public governance. It is coherent with a principle of access in democracies (on which, see Philp, 2001), and the problem is explicitly addressed in Picci, 2011, chapter 8 (see in particular note n. 8, p. 131).

Second, there is a problem of the "legibility of the State" (Picci, 2011, 2012), which is the extent to which citizens may make sense of its overall action, in a context where they are willing to dedicate only limited energies to solve an often daunting cognitive effort (see, for the United States, Hibbing and Theiss-Morse, 2002). Concerns about legibility go beyond traditional issues of transparency, are particularly acute in a data abundant context, and need to be addressed appropriately (Picci, 2012). In market applications, reputationally relevant information usually refer to well-identified transactions and actors, regardless of whether they are generated by gossip, or by Internet-based reputation systems. For example, on eBay assessments refer to well-defined business transactions, whose parties are immediately identified, since both the buyer and the seller are registered users. Whether they are individuals or organizations is inconsequential, because the reputational score is attributed to the functional entity of buyer, or of seller.

The situation is quite different when Internet-based reputation systems are applied to public governance. The mere possibility of assessing public policies hinges on them being perceived as distinct "objects." However, public governance is very complex and invariably multilevel, so that the overall action of the state is balkanized into countless policies and programs that interact among themselves in complex ways (Picci, 2012). To limit confusion, the policy space should be structured appropriately; modularity of policies, it is argued in Picci (2011), would help in making the "policy objects" well-distinguishable, so that they could be assessed.

Moreover, for reputational measures to be computed, "the responsibilities of the actions that are assessed should be unambiguously attributed—to public administrations, to individual administrators, and possibly to politicians" (Picci, 2012; see also Philp, 2001, on the important distinction between formal vs. political accountability). The solution of such a legibility problem, which goes hand in hand with the possibility of holding the state accountable for its actions, is elusive when the focus is on the architecture of only a given Internet-based reputation system. To address the legibility problem architectural decisions are needed that, by framing the policy space appropriately, permit an attribution of responsibilities which is as clear as possible.

To summarize, the degree to which Internet-based reputation systems, as applied to public governance, "democratize gossip," depends on more than one factor. Equal access is a prerequisite. As for the indispensable legibility of the state, it might be enhanced by intervening both on architectural choices within the relevant Internet-based information systems, and by more difficult decisions to guarantee the legibility of the system of governance as a whole. In terms of the overall design of the governance system, the latter are positioned at a level which is hierarchically superior to the former.

## DISCUSSION AND CONCLUSIONS

This chapter has proposed a definition of gossip which is suited for the Internet age, and, adopting a framework where organizational preoccupations are at the forefront, has compared traditional gossip with the information processing enabled by Internet-based reputation systems. While being different, the two types of information transmission share a functional similarity: they both process reputationally relevant information, which in turn influence the distribution of resources, hence of power. This function however is performed rather differently in one and the other, and it is more "democratic" within Internet-based reputation systems. Such characteristic might be particularly evident when these systems are applied to the public sphere, where the questions of equal access and of the legibility of the state become particularly cogent.

These considerations have a normative appeal. In planning Internet-based reputation systems for public governance, traditional and unstructured gossip stands as a point of reference of what democratically minded policy makers should avoid. The goal to pursue should be equal access and opportunities to influence the political process, while navigating several constraints, prominent among them, the necessity that participation is not too costly. Hence the importance of the principle of "legibility" of the policy space.

An interesting question, to which only a tentative answer might be provided, regards the future of gossip in a world where Internet-based reputation systems are ubiquitous. When thinking about the functional similarity of the two, a crowding out of gossip might be expected: if reputationally relevant information were to be widely transmitted thanks to Internet-based reputation systems, then traditional gossip would be less needed. For example, there is less necessity of off-line gossip about restaurants today, since their reputational scores are widely available from many dedicated Web sites. Informal chat about the perceived quality of restaurants still takes place, but traditional gossip loses relevance, when it competes with the information generated by Internet-based information systems.

Also, the presence of competition from on-line information likely places a constraint on traditional gossip. In the example above, it might be argued that *ego* would feel free to express an oral opinion about a restaurant which is starkly in contrast with the general consensus, as expressed by a summary of on-line referrals: after all, *de gustibus non est disputandum*. However, in a less mundane context, going against the general consensus as it is expressed by Internet-based information systems might be frowned upon. For example, a negative gossip about some professional, whose reputation on-line is very good, might be seen as arising from a personal grudge, or envy, and backfire on *ego*.

Internet-based reputation systems could be engineered to resemble traditional gossip, by allowing only a limited number of persons to post assessments, while refusing access to the relevant *tertius*. For example, the information generated within an Internet-based system where a group of friends rate the restaurants that they visit, and where the ratings are not visible to outsiders, would qualify as gossip as I have defined it. Possibly, such practices could also be made to provide that type of "illicit bond" that the stigma of gossip confers to the participants of a gossiping party.

In closing, it should be admitted that the classification of gossip that has been proposed in this chapter has an inevitable degree of rigidity that does not do justice of certain real-life intricacies. For example, unlike in the definition here presented, sometimes *tertius* does hear the gossip of which she is the victim. Alessandro Manzoni, with his usual clarity, describes this possibility in the text that follows the citation which opened this chapter:

> When, then, a friend meets with an opportunity of deposing a secret in the breast of another, he, in his turn, seeks to share in the same pleasure. He is entreated, to be sure, to say nothing to anybody; and of such a condition, if taken in the strict sense

of the world, would immediately cut short the chain of these gratifications: but general practice has determined that it only forbids to entrust a secret to everybody but one equally confidential friend, imposing upon him, of course, the same conditions. Thus, from confidential friend to confidential friend, the secret threads its way along this immense chain, until, at last, it reaches the ear of him or the whom the first speaker exactly intended it should never reach.    (Manzoni, 1876: p. 204)

Such outcome could also be translated into Internet-based reputation systems by allowing for randomized "spilling of the beans." Unlike traditional gossip, which in its many variants is left unbridled, on-line gossip would be explicitly engineered in its nature, and corseted in the concrete possibilities of information sharing that it allows. Such forms of on-line gossip, to the best of my knowledge, have not been created yet, possibly because there is no need for them: good old traditional gossip—eventually, on a planetary scale, thanks to email, instant messaging and the social media—serves us well enough.

## NOTES

1. I would like to thank Francesca Giardini and Rafael Wittek for comments on a previous version of this chapter.
2. A breach of "an online service that facilitates extramarital affairs, [resulting] in the leak of personal information attached to more than 30 million accounts." Nicole Perloth, "Ashley Madison Chief Steps Down After Data Breach," *The New York Times*, August 28, 2015.
3. Information on eBay are from https://www.ebayinc.com/our-company/. For a more detailed description of eBay's referral system, see Cabral, 2012.
4. With reference to Hibbing and Theiss-Morse (2002); see also Picci (2011: 160–175). A separate question regards whether assessments honestly represent preferences, and are not attempts at gaming the system in one way or another. See Masum and Tovey (2012), where the possibility of "reputation gaming" is treated in several contexts.
5. A similar distinct treatment of the two concepts is in Cabral (2012), who notes that their "underlying mechanisms are quite different," but also adds that, regardless of that, "they are frequently treated as part of the same theory." A further complication arises when actors are not persons, but organizations. In this case, formulating expectations about their future behavior is contingent on a model of sort of how they function (Picci, 2011: 26–33).
6. On the issue of reputation formation in the context of gossip, see Giardini et al. (2013: 375 and following), and the discussion in Beersma and Van Kleef (2012).
7. The service is owned by Viacom, through its subsidiary mtvU. See http://www.ratemyprofessors.com/About.jsp.
8. See also the discussion in Beersma and Van Kleef (2012). For an anecdotal demonstration of how extreme opinions on gossip might be, consider the subtitle of a book by Mark D. Michael, "Overcoming gossip: How Satan, the Accuser of the Brethren, Uses Gossip to Fragment the Body of Christ" (Shippensberg, PA: Destiny Image Publishers), 2011.
9. In organized crime, cooperation also is often supported by different types of bonds of trust; see Von Lampe and Johansen (2004). Gambetta (1994) provides an interesting account of the role of gossip in the Italian mafia.
10. There is an ample literature on virtual communities, and on the extent to which they may surrogate, substitute, or even enhance traditional ones.

11. Some persons are more trustworthy than others, and their gossip might have a higher impact. As illustrated in Picci, 2011: pp.89–91, Internet-based reputation systems could be engineered so as to allow to weight *ego's* assessments according to a measure of her reputation. On the incentives for gossiping as they relate to social network structures, see Wittek and Wielers (1998).

12. This is but a simplification of a more complex reality. For example, being well-placed within networks which are perceived to be antagonist with respect to the formal organization (as it might be the case for a confrontational grassroots trade union) hardly provides an advantage in obtaining a promotion.

13. "China's plan to organize its society relies on 'big data' to rate everyone," by Simon Denyer, *The Washington Post*, October 22, 2016. The official document describing the project (available at http://tinyurl.com/ntoxhzz), however, indicates a focus on private behaviors, whereas what is described in Picci (2011) explicitly addresses the functioning of public administrations: the object of control is, simply, reversed. See the reference to the concept of "legibility" in "Reputation-Based Public Governance" section of this chapter.

## References

Bar-Isaac, Hesi, and Steven Tadelis. 2008. "Seller reputation." *Foundation and Trends in Microeconomics* 4(4): 185–205.

Baumeister, Roy F., Liqing Zhang, and Kathleen D. Vohs. 2004. "Gossip as cultural learning." *Review of General Psychology* 8(2): 111–21.

Beersma, Bianca, and Gerben A. Van Kleef. 2012. "Why people gossip: An empirical analysis of social motives, antecedents, and consequences." *Journal of Applied Social Psychology* 42(11): 2640–2670.

Bosson, Jennifer K., Amber B. Johnson, Kate Niederhoffer, and William B. Swann. 2006. "Interpersonal chemistry through negativity: Bonding by sharing negative attitudes about others." *Personal Relationships* 13(2): 135–150.

Cabral, Luis and Ali Hortaçsu. 2010. "The dynamics of seller reputation: Evidence from eBay." *The Journal of Industrial Economics* 58(1): 54–78.

Cabral, Luís. 2012. "Reputation on the Internet." In *The Oxford handbook of the digital economy*, edited by Peitz, Martin, and Joel Waldfogel, 343–354. Oxford: Oxford University Press.

Dellarocas, Chrysanthos. 2003. "The digitization of word of mouth: Promise and challenges of online feedback mechanisms." *Management Science* 49(10): 1407–1424.

Dellarocas, Chrysanthos. 2010. "Online reputation systems: How to design one that does what you need." *MIT Sloan Management Review* 51(3): 33–37.

Diekmann, Andreas, Przepiorka, Wojtek. (2019). Trust and reputation in markets. In *Handbook of gossip and reputation*, edited by Francesca Giardini and Rafael Wittek. New York: Oxford University Press.

Dunbar, Robin. 1996. *Grooming, gossip and the language*. London: Faber and Faber.

Dunbar, Robin. 2004. "Gossip in evolutionary perspective." *Review of General Psychology* 8(2): 100–110.

Ellwardt, Lea, Rafael Wittek, and Rudi Wielers. 2012. "Talking about the boss: Effects of generalized and interpersonal trust on workplace gossip." *Group & Organization Management* 20(10): 1–29.

Gambetta, Diego. 1988. "Can we trust trust?" In *Trust: Making and breaking cooperative relations*, edited by Diego Gambetta. New York: Basil Blackwell.

Gambetta, Diego. 1994. "Godfather's gossip." *European Journal of Sociology* 35(2): 199–223.

Giardini, Francesca, Rosaria Conte, and Mario Paolucci. 2013. "Reputation." In *Simulating social complexity: A handbook*, edited by Edmonds, Bruce and Ruth Meyer, 365–399. Berlin: Springer.

Gottman, John M., and Gwendolyn Mettetal. 1986. "Speculations about social and affective development: friendship and acquaintanceship through adolescence." In *Conversations of friends: Speculations on affective development*, edited by Gottman John M. and Jeffrey J. Parker, 192–237. Cambridge: Cambridge University Press.

Greenwald, Glenn. 2014. *No place to hide*. New York: Picador.

Hibbing, John R., and Elizabeth Theiss-Morse. 2002. *Stealth democracy: American's beliefs about how government should work*. Cambridge: Cambridge University Press.

Jin, Ginger Zhe, and Andrew Kato. 2006. "Price, quality, and reputation: Evidence from an online field experiment." *The Rand Journal of Economics* 37(4): 983–1005.

Kurland, Nancy B., and Lisa Hope Pelled. 2000. "Passing the word: Toward a model of gossip and power in the workplace." *Academy of Management Review* 25(2): 428–438.

Leigh, David, and Luke Harding. 2011. *WikiLeaks: Inside Julian Assange's war on secrecy*. New York: Public Affairs.

Manzoni, Alessandro. 2008. *The Betrothed* (I Promessi Sposi). London: George Bells and Sons (originally published in 1827).

Masum, Hassan, and Mark Tovey. 2012. *The reputation society: How online opinions are reshaping the offline world*. Cambridge: MIT Press.

Michelson, Grant, and Kathryn Waddington. 2012. *Gossip and organizations*. Abingdon-on-Thames: Routledge.

Philp, Mark. 2001. "Access, accountability and authority: Corruption and the democratic process." *Crime, Law & Social Change* 36: 357–377.

Picci, Lucio. 2011. *Reputation-based governance*. Stanford: Stanford University Press.

Picci, Lucio. 2012. "Reputation-based governance and making states 'legible' to their citizens." In *The reputation society: How online opinions are reshaping the offline world*, edited by Masum, Hassan, and Mark Tovey, 141–150. Cambridge, MA: The MIT Press.

Picci, Lucio. 2014. "Actors and strategies of the bureaucratic reputation game," in *Organizational reputation in the public sector*, edited by Wæraas, Arild, and Moshe Maor, 37–53. Abingdon-on-Thames: Routledge.

Resnick, Paul, Richard Zeckhauser, John Swanson, and Kate Lockwood. 2006. "The value of reputation on eBay: A controlled experiment." *Experimental Economics* 9(2): 79–101.

Rockenbach, Bettina, and Abdolkarim Sadrieh. 2012. "Sharing information." *Journal of Economic Behavior & Organization* 81(2): 689–698.

Schein, Sylvia. 1994. "Used and abused: Gossip in medieval society." In *Good gossip*, edited by Goodman, Robert F., and Aaron Ben-Ze'ev, 139–153. Lawrence: University Press of Kansas.

Snijders, Chris, Matzat, Uwe. 2019. Online reputation systems. In *Handbook of gossip and reputation*, edited by Francesca Giardini and Rafael Wittek. New York: Oxford University Press.

Von Lampe, Klaus, and Per Ole Johansen. 2004. "Organized crime and trust: On the conceptualization and empirical relevance of trust in the context of criminal networks." *Global Crime* 6(2): 159–184.

Wert, Sarah R., and Peter Salovey. P. 2004. "A social comparison account of gossip." *Review of General Psychology* 8: 122–137.

Wittek, Rafael and Rudi Wielers. 1998. "Gossip in Organizations." *Computational & Mathematical Organizational Theory* 4(2): 189–204.

# Index

Note: Tables and figures are indicated by an italic *t* or *f* following the page number.

reputation and status dynamics  231
social context of gossip  106
social media use  185
social skills  182–184
status differentiation models  239–244
territorial competition and  285
work group gossip  423
genetic competition  50
Georganta, K.  425
Gergaud, O.  403
Giardini, F.  9, 25, 30, 31, 38, 40, 54, 59, 108,
    110, 161, 200, 201, 202, 230, 245, 290,
    344, 345, 351, 360, 422, 501
Gilbert, N.  236
Gilmore, D. D.  264
Gilovich, T.  60
Gil-White, F. J.  334
Gintis, H.  224
global network structures  439–443
Gluckman, M.  5–6, 107, 245, 262, 343
goal-framing theory  41
Goffman, E.  61, 85, 337
Goodman, R. F.  3
Goodwin, M.  111
Goodwin, M. H.  140
gossip. See also *specific perspectives; specific
    types of gossip*
  definitions of  105, 153, 254–255, 326, 344,
      436, 499–502
  linguistic study of  84–85
  natural history of  258
  norm enforcement and  268–269
  in organizations  265–266
  origin of  174, 258–259
  personal uses of  263–264
  prosocial  35t, 37–38, 178, 346, 348, 352
  reputation  11, 304, 327–329, 332–333
  rumor versus  173–174
  in social dilemmas  200–202
  strategy learning  304, 327–329, 338
gossip algorithms  470, 471, 472–473, 474,
    476n7
gossip and reputation games  224–227
"Gossip and Scandal" (Gluckman)  107
gossip chains  260
gossip columns  105
gossip consumers  55, 60, 62

Gossip Effect  448
gossip episodes  91–94
gossiper's dilemma  202–203
gossip models, in computational
    systems  471–474
gossip triad  25, 436, 438, 447
  coalition models  32–35
  punishment models  37–38
  reputation models  26, 30–31
  social control models  35–37
governance, in online reputation systems
    12–13, 505–507
grain market in ancient Rome  387–388
Green, L. G.  423
Greif, A.  388–389, 407
Greiner, B.  412
Grice, H. P.  85
grim trigger equilibrium  222
*Grooming, Gossip, and the Evolution of
    Language* (Dunbar)  173
grooming, social  305
gross cheaters  177
Grosser, T. J.  349, 352, 420, 444t, 449
group benefits of gossip  5
group protection motive  344–346, 345t, 423
groups, effect of gossip in  14, 351–352
group selection  208
Grow, A.  233, 234, 238, 240
Guala, F.  40
Guerin, B.  347
guilt  155, 157, 161
Gumperz, J.  102

# H

Haddon, A. C.  101
Hagen, E. H.  2, 10, 59, 60, 184, 202, 281, 283,
    285, 289, 291, 293, 303, 306, 330
Hamlin, K.  134
Hannerz, U.  326–327
happiness  155, 160
Hardin, G.  193
Hartung, F. M.  421, 422
Hauert, C.  224
Haux, L.  138
Haviland, J.  103–104, 106, 112, 254, 262–263
Hawley, P. H.  288–289
hedonic regression  487–488, 493